Statistical Record of the Environment

GALE
ENVIRONMENTAL
LIBRARY

Statistical Record of the Environment

Compiled and Edited by
Arsen J. Darnay

Gale Research Inc. · DETROIT ·

Arsen J. Darnay, *Editor*

Editorial Code & Data Inc. Staff

Musadiq Shah and Marlita A. Reddy, *Associate Editors*
Nancy Ratliff, *Data Entry Associate*

Gale Research Inc. Staff

Mary Beth Trimper, *Production Manager*
Mary Winterhalter, *Production Assistant*

Arthur Chartow, *Art Director*
Bonnie Gornie, *Graphic Designer*

Cover photograph by Robert J. Huffman

Library of Congress Cataloging-in-Publication Data

Darnay, Arsen.
Statistical record of the environment / compiled and edited by Arsen J. Darnay.
  p. cm.
  Includes bibliographical references and index.
  ISBN 0-8103-8374-8
  1. Pollution—United States—Statistics. 2. Sanitation—United States—Statistics. 3. Pollution control industry—United States—Statistics. 4. Pollution—Law and legislation—United States—Statistics. 5. Environmental policy—United States—Statistics. 6. Man—Influence on nature—United States—Statistics. I. Title.
TD 180.D37 1991   363.73'00973'021—dc20   91-30214

A CIP catalogue record for this book is available from the British Library.

∞™ This book is printed on acid-free paper that meets the minimum requirements of American National Standard for Information Sciences—Permanence Paper for Printed Library Materials, ANSI Z39.48-1984.

♻ This book is printed on recycled paper that meets Environmental Protection Agency standards.

TABLE OF CONTENTS

Chapter 2 - Pollutants and Wastes continued:

Chapter 2 - Pollutants and Wastes continued:

Chapter 2 - Pollutants and Wastes continued:

Chapter 3 - Effects continued:

Chapter 5 - Tools, Methods, and Solutions continued:

Chapter 6 - Pollution Control Industry continued:

Chapter 7 - General Industry and Government Data continued:

Chapter 7 - General Industry and Government Data continued:

Chapter 7 - General Industry and Government Data continued:

Chapter 8 - Cities, States, Regions, and Nations continued:

Chapter 8 - Cities, States, Regions, and Nations continued:

INTRODUCTION

Statistical Record of the Environment (*SRE*) is a comprehensive presentation of statistical materials drawn from governmental and private sources. *SRE* features —

- More than 800 tables, many illustrated with graphics or maps.

- Broad coverage of environmental subjects in the United States.

- Selected presentations on environmental data worldwide.

- Easy-to-use arrangement into ten chapters and, within chapters, into topical categories.

- Detailed keyword index.

- Comprehensive source listings.

ORGANIZATION

Statistical Record of the Environment is divided into ten chapters which, in sequence, present environmental statistics beginning with a chapter on *The Media*, which gives a broad overview, followed by others that present information on specific aspects of environmental concern. Each chapter is subdivided into topics. Within each topic, tables are sorted alphabetically by title.

Organization by Chapter

Chapter 1 - The Media - Air, Water, Land. Tables and graphics show data on the Air, Water, and Land media which act as intermediate or final 'sinks' for manmade or natural pollutants. The chapter serves as an introduction to current conditions of the atmosphere, oceans, lakes, rivers, and land.

Chapter 2 - Pollutants and Wastes. The chapter holds detailed information on polluting gases, liquids, sludges, solids, and radiation as reported by government agencies and private sources. Tables are grouped by major types of pollutants (air pollutants, hazardous wastes, nuclear wastes, solid waste, toxic substances, etc.); within each topic, data are presented on a wide range of specific pollutants, measuring their quantitative occurrence, locus, composition, etc.

Chapter 3 - Effects. Tables in this chapter pinpoint the effects that pollutants cause, including accidents, deaths, deforestation, erosion, global warming, health effects, injuries, etc.

Chapter 4 - Costs, Budgets, and Expenditures. Data on the measurable costs of pollution and the costs of pollution control are shown arranged under topical headings such as air pollution control, construction and maintenance, consumer costs, cost/benefit, and the like. Public and private expenditures on pollution control and research & development will be found here. The chapter, in general, collects available statistics that present cost information, including also costs of specific control measures and of technological solutions.

Chapter 5 - Tools, Methods, and Solutions. The tables in this chapter provide statistics on methods of pollution abatement, technological solutions, recycling programs, source reduction, and other programs for waste elimination or pollution control.

Chapter 6 - Pollution Control Industry. This chapter presents data on companies engaged in controlling pollution. Various aspects of the subject are covered, including companies that participate in the environmental market, the size of that market for products and services, compensation of employees, etc.

Chapter 7 - General Industry and Government Data. This chapter is a collection of data on industrial production related to environmental pollution together with interesting facts and figures (about autos, for example, or water use) that do not easily fit elsewhere.

Chapter 8 - Cities, States, Regions, & Nations. Environmental facts and trends are often reported at the community level, by regions or states, or by countries in world regions. In this chapter are presented data with a specific geographical focus. Please note, however, that geographically organized tables may also be found elsewhere in *SRE*; some tables of states and countries were better placed elsewhere for context.

Chapter 9 - Laws and Regulations. The focus of this chapter is on statistics that deal with legislation, regulation, enforcement, and compliance, including also pending legislation at the state level related to such matters as packaging, resource recovery, and litter control.

Chapter 10 - Politics & Opinion. Public interest in the environment gives rise to public interest groups, opinion surveys, and media coverage. Statistical material on such aspects of the environment are brought together in this chapter under such topical headings as Compliance, Enforcement, Goals, Guidelines, and the like.

Organization of Tables

Each table is assigned to a broad topic. Topic headers are placed above groups of tables between bold rules. On succeeding pages, the name of the topic appears on the header of each page following the name of the current chapter.

Tables are numbered and may be located from the *Table of Contents,* the *Keyword Index*, or the three appendices of sources by table number. Page numbers are also provided in the *Table of Contents* and the *Keyword Index*.

The table title follows the table number. Thereafter, the table may display a graphical presentation as a map, a bar chart, or a pie chart. If the table has more than one column of data, the number of the column from which data were drawn for charting is identified on the graphic. In a few instances, only a map and its legend are shown. In most cases, tabular data follow whatever graphic is used.

If the table requires some explanation, a brief head note is presented. A note may not be necessary; in such cases, the data immediately follow in columns and rows.

At the bottom of the table, the source of the table is identified. If the source used identified another source, that source is identified following the word *from*. Footnotes or other explanatory notes are placed after the source information. Wherever possible, we have attempted to define abbreviations used in table itself. These may be explicitly footnoted or shown without footnotes.

SCOPE

SRE covers a wide range of environment conditions, facts, and issues from a statistical point of vantage. The major categories (air and water pollution, solid waste generation and management, hazardous wastes and toxic substances) are covered from various perspectives. *SRE* also assembles information on special problems and wastes (oil spills, global warming, soil erosion), provides profiles of the pollution control industry and legislation, and presents background information of the sort required to place environmental information into a broader context. Thus *SRE* shows a good deal of data on industrial production in sectors that are major polluters, presents cost and budgetary information, trends in consumption, public opinion, and the like.

Since *SRE* is drawn from today's report and periodicals literature, it tends to reflect current concerns, thrusts, and emphasis. There is now considerable interest in global warming, for instance, and much less public concern with storm sewer construction in cities. Hazardous wastes get much more emphasis than sanitary landfills, ozone depletion more coverage than noise pollution abatement. Although care was taken to present as balanced a view as possible, the depth of coverage is admittedly uneven; it mirrors the current preoccupations of agencies and the media and should not be interpreted as judgement, by the editors, of the importance of the subjects apparently slighted.

Most of the materials included deal with the environment in North America. Certain subjects, however, such as oil spills and global warming, have an international focus. Areas of significant concern, such as tropical forests, for example, are not covered thoroughly because of the intentional limitation of *SRE* to the North American sphere.

The majority of tables show data for the late 1980s and early 1990s. Unless an item of data was of very special interest and could not be found for a more recent date, 1986 data were included. In all other cases, data are for 1987 or later.

The method of presentation—multiple aspects of the same subject—would have made chapter and section notes tediously repetitive. For that reason, this *Introduction* is followed by another section, *Guide to the Subject Matter*, in which are presented capsule discussions of the major fields and topics covered in *SRE*.

SOURCES

Data for *SRE* were drawn from national and state government publications and data bases and from the periodical literature. More than 200 sources were consulted and approximately 150 sources were used in this edition. Sources are presented in three appendices with sufficient information to help the user contact primary and original sources directly. A statistical book, of course, invariably omits an important element of information—the knowledgable interpretation of the data, the extraction of significance. Almost invariably, tables were drawn from reports and articles which carried valuable commentary. If *SRE* serves as an introduction to the rich report and periodicals literature on the environment, one of its aims will have been realized.

APPENDED MATERIALS

Sources

Sources are listed in three separate appendices. *Appendix I - Report Literature Sources* lists reports consulted as primary sources and those cited in these reports or in the periodicals literature. Organization of the appendix is by U.S. Federal Agencies, Other Government Bodies, and Private Institutions and Companies. Within these segments, agencies and other institutions are shown in alphabetical order; if multiple reports are cited, they are arranged alphabetically by title. *Appendix II - Periodicals Literature Sources* lists periodicals consulted as well as periodicals cited by others as their original source of data. Arrangement of the appendix is alphabetically by periodical. Finally, *Appendix III - Organization Sources* lists companies, associations, and other institutions, including Federal agencies, which were cited by sources as the origin of data without further definition of the nature of the data.

In each appendix, the listing of a report or periodical is followed by one or more table numbers in which the source is cited. The table listing is arranged sequentially by appearance within *SRE*.

Abbreviations and Acronyms

Many abbreviations and acronyms are used in the environmental field, as in others. In this field, in addition, many chemical names are routinely used in abbreviated form. While efforts have been made to provide the user explanations of abbreviations within the source block of each table, a general listing of all abbreviations is also provided in *Appendix IV - Abbreviations and Acronyms*. Abbreviations appear in alphabetical order followed by an explanation.

Keyword Index

SRE features a *Keyword Index* (Appendix V) by means of which the user can locate all subjects, companies, institutions, agencies, and geographical entities. Items are followed by table and page numbers. Extensive cross-references are provided. Page references do not necessarily identify the page on which the table begins. In the case of tables that span two or more pages, items shown on the second or subsequent page of the table will point the user to the page on which the reference is used.

GUIDE TO THE SUBJECT MATTER

This section presents a brief introduction to the subject of *SRE*. The subject matter of the environment is as all-encompassing as the environment itself. The intent, therefore, is not to provide a comprehensive primer on such a vast subject; rather, we offer a minimal context for those users who can benefit from a thumbnail sketch. Of necessity, this summary leaves out much more than it shows; we hope that it will motivate the reader to delve further into the subject.

THE MEDIA

The term 'medium' is used in the environmental field to mean air, water and land—the 'media' to which pollutants are emitted or on which they are placed for disposal. Air, water, and land are also called 'sinks'; the word signifies a medium capable of absorbing wastes. None of the media is truly a permanent sink for pollutants. Airborne particles settle out; airborne chemicals interact with one another and with components of the air and come down again, e.g. as acid rain. Wastes placed on or under the land may come in contact with seeping precipitation and release pollutants to aquifers. Contaminants in water may evaporate, may be taken up by organisms and enter the human food chain, or can cause changes in water bodies with consequences for the other media. The interaction of media, their give-and-take of life-sustaining and endangering substances, the impossibility of isolating these great systems one from the other—the irreducible connectedness of everything to everything else—is at the very heart of environmental concern. There is no ultimate burial place for pollutants and wastes.

In what follows, each of the major media will be covered briefly. Interactions between them—and between pollution, technology, economics, and institutional/political factors—will be highlighted.

AIR POLLUTION

Among the chief sources of air pollution is transportation; the use of automobiles and trucks causes the emission of carbon monoxide, nitrogen oxides, hydrocarbons (in the form of gasoline and diesel fumes), and lead. Hydrocarbons and nitrogen oxides, in combination, produce smog and are responsible for respiratory ailments; and carbon monoxide is toxic. Another major source of pollution is power generation; it results in flyash, dust, and the emission of sulfur oxides—implicated in the formation of acid rain. A third major source is represented by the process industries (steel, petroleum, cement, chemicals, pulp and paper); they are responsible for large quantities of particulate emissions (ashes, dust) and chemicals of various kinds. But while these are the major source categories, virtually all other production activities emit some air pollutants from the combustion of fuels and the handling of raw materials, solvents, and other chemicals.

Control strategies are many and various and may be classified as technical, preventive, and social/institutional in mechanism.

Technical solutions include removal of *particulates* by—

- Filtering them out of effluent air streams or combustion gases in baghouses;

- Removing them by electrostatic precipitators; this process causes particles to be charged electrically; they are then collected on electrodes; the technology is particularly well suited for capturing very fine particulates; and

- Spinning or knocking them from air or combustion streams mechanically in cyclones and similar devices.

The management of *chemicals* takes many forms depending on the character of the pollutant. Methods include combustion of waste hydrocarbons, the distillation of pollutants in specialized towers, their transformation by catalytic conversion (as in automobiles), their capture in adsorption columns (a type of filtering), and their removal by similar processing methods usually built into refining and chemicals production plants. The removal of sulfur oxides from coal-burning power plant off-gases presents a special and difficult problem. Sulfur removal requires scrubbers in which the hot gases are contacted with lime in a water medium. Vast amounts of sludge occur.

All of these technical procedures, in fact, tend merely to *transform* air pollutants into solid wastes, sludges, or waterborne wastes which require further handling. If a polluting substance is extracted as a product—elemental sulfur, for example, from utility flue gases—the product must be sold on the open market. Air pollution control is rarely the last step in the process.

In recent decades, a great many so-called 'upstream' methods have been discovered, tried, and even mandated by legislation. The objective of these strategies is—

- To exchange potentially polluting with more suitable raw materials (low-sulfur coal in place of high-sulfur coal, unleaded gasoline in place of leaded).

- To introduce more efficient processing technology (more complete combustion of waste gases in after burners, for instance), and

- To promote recycling/reuse of what waste products remain.

Social/institutional strategies are also used or are in planning stages. These include (1) reducing the magnitude of a polluting activity (auto use by car pooling or by parking restrictions), (2) land use controls for locating factories, (3) regulating the content of fuels or type of fuel used, (4) mandating inspection of vehicles, (5) requiring more fuel-efficient vehicles, and so on.

The dominant issues in air pollution control have not changed significantly in the last twenty years—to pick a benchmark—but the public perception of the problem and the methods of remediation have. Auto use and electric power have the highest visibility. Methods for controlling automotive pollution have converged on fuel changes, fuel efficiency requirements, and technical controls. In electric generation, growing awareness of acid rain — in part a consequence of sulfur emissions — has galvanized political energy; the chief solution remains, as twenty years before, the installation of scrubbers that remove sulfur in a slurry of lime; scrubbers are costly and produce very large quantities of paste-like solid wastes; thus scrubbers are not an ideal or ultimate solution. Other alternatives have serious political or economic drawbacks: nuclear power is politically opposed in this post-Chernobyl age; natural gas is a costly if clean substitute for coal; and coal desulfurization appears to require massive federal investments in research and demonstration in an age of towering deficits.

Although an air pollution issue, *global warming* — thought to be due to an increase in carbon dioxide production by human activity — is discussed under a separate heading.

WATER POLLUTION

The water medium may be viewed as having distinct parts — the oceans, surface waters on land (rivers, streams, lakes), and deep-lying aquifers that hold groundwater. Pollution enters the 'water sink' as a consequence of human habitation, industry, and the pollutants carried by rain from cities and farms (runoff).

Municipal Sewage

The largest single impact on water is dense human population — cities. Organic human waste, if discharged untreated, can overwhelm the ability of bodies of water to absorb the waste. Microorganisms attempting to decompose the waste require oxygen for this 'combustion' process; they use the oxygen naturally dissolved in the water. At a high enough level of biological oxygen demand (usually abbreviated BOD), oxygen levels are exhausted; fish and other oxygen-consuming (aerobic) organisms die out; the waters become septic; only anaerobic organisms survive; the water is now putrid and dangerous for man and beast.

Industrial Waste Water

Industry uses large amounts of water for generating energy, cooling, processing, as a mechanism of transport, and in cleaning. Boiler feedwater must be very clean and free of minerals before use and remains pure during use. Cooling waters are generally recycled and are not polluted; in some applications, fungicides are injected into the water to keep cooling towers clean.

The other industrial uses of water — for processing, transport, and cleaning — invariably cause water to become contaminated with organic materials (functionally similar to human waste), with chemicals and hydrocarbons, suspended particles, dissolved minerals, and so on. Typical processing applications include water used in pulping wood, cooking food, tanning leather, etc. Water is used to transport many raw materials as slurries, suspensions, or emulsions in mining and manufacturing. And water has long been the universal cleanser in virtually all industrial activities. When the water is no longer useful for the process, transport, or cleaning step, it is said to be 'spent' and must be treated for recycling or disposal. In its spent state, water may be highly acidic or alkaline.

The most important sources of organic water pollutants are the pulp and paper, meat packing, food processing, textile, pharmaceutical, leather tanning and related industries that harvest and transform organic materials for human consumption. The petroleum refining, organic chemicals, and steel industries (steel by way of coking facilities) introduce hydrocarbons in various forms. The metals industries produce wastes with high acidity and alkalinity, oily waters, rusty waters. Inorganic chemicals, mining, and related operations emit water wastes heavy with suspended solids and dissolved minerals.

Urban and Agricultural Runoff

Pollutants also enter the water medium when rainfall runs off into lakes, rivers, and oceans carrying with it organics, solids, and chemicals occurring on land. Urban runoff is typically collected in storm sewers; in many cities, these sewers are permitted to bypass waste water treatment plants in whole or in part during storms. Storm sewer discharges introduce organics, debris, salt, and toxics. Agricultural runoff has similar characteristics but may include larger quantities of fertilizers and pesticides. Fertilizers in water can overstimulate the growth of aquatic plants and thus contribute to the eutrophication of bodies of water: they gradually turn into swamps. Diversion of urban runoff into longterm holding lagoons and careful grading of agricultural lands (fields, feedlots, etc.) are methods of minimizing the impact of runoff on water.

Treatment Technology

Waste water treatment is usually divided into three stages of advancing technical complexity—aptly named primary, secondary, and tertiary treatment.

- *Primary treatment* involves rough filtration to remove large solids; this may be followed by lagooning of the waste waters for whatever period is required for the natural oxidation of organics and for the settling out of fine solids.

- *Secondary treatment* calls for the introduction of oxygen into the waste at whatever rate is required to satisfy the waste stream's biological oxygen demand, meaning the extra oxygen required to help microorganisms to consume the waste rapidly. Since air is typically used as the source of oxygen, this process is also called aeration. Secondary treatment methods differ in the manner in which oxygen is introduced, the degree to which the waste is agitated mechanically during entrainment, and the capital/operating costs of the facility. Secondary treatment is applied to organic wastes.

- *Tertiary treatment* is a collective name for a host of different methods, each specific to a particular pollutant or a class of pollutants. Processes may be relatively simple, such as the adjustment of the waste stream's pH[1] — which, in addition to rendering the stream harmless, may also cause pollutants to be precipitated out; processes may be complex; an example is carbon black treatment to remove difficult-to-process organic chemicals in specialized adsorption towers.

A difficult waste stream may require primary and secondary treatment and one or more tertiary steps. Costs of treatment tend to go up with the level of technology. Control strategies, therefore, tend to be a compromise between the competing goals of pure water and its affordability.

Waste water treatment produces residues in the form of sludge or solids which must be handled again for disposal. Depending on the nature of the waste, sludges may have to be handled as toxic wastes or may be disposed of by landspreading, incineration, composting, and landfilling. The costs of sludge management may be as much as or more than the costs of the treatment processes that produced them.

Drinking Water

Our drinking water comes from wells or is pumped from surface waters and treated before distribution. The purification of drinking water is called *water* treatment; *waste* water treatment applies to sewage or industrial waste water streams. Water treatment always involves filtration (to remove silt) and chlorination (to kill bacteria); it may involve many other steps, including removal of iron and desalination of brackish waters; the water may also be treated to control odors.

Drinking water is threatened by pollution of rivers and lakes and the contamination of aquifers. Aquifers are permeable stone formations capable of retaining water; next to oceans and polar ice caps, they hold most of the earth's

---

1 pH is a symbol used to denote acidity and alkalinity on a scale of 0 to 14. Pure water has a pH of 7. Lower values indicate acidity, higher values alkalinity.

water. But the water in aquifers is not stationary. It is replenished by precipitation and depleted by use; and it moves, albeit slowly, under the impetus of gravity and pressure; this movement is measured in inches per year. The slow movement of water in aquifers can produce surprises. The burial of toxic wastes may produce well water contamination five, ten, thirty years later: the time required by the very slow-moving underground river to carry its poisons to a well. The burial of waste may have been forgotten, records of it lost, by the time its consequences surface.

Ocean Pollution

Oceans are threatened by massive accidental oil spills, illegal dumping of chemical and oily wastes at sea, ocean dumping of garbage, and the introduction of toxic substances and organics by polluted rivers and rain. Like the vegetative cover of the continents, so the ocean's phytoplankton are a major source of oxygen in the water and in the atmosphere. Any diminution of the organic life in the ocean by pollution invariably affects the ecosystems on land as well. Toxic metals dumped into the oceans will be taken up by small marine organisms and may eventually be ingested by us as harvested fish; the metals are cumulated and retained in tissue. Contaminated fish, of course, lead to fishing restrictions, harming those engaged in the fishing and processing industries.

The Regulatory Environment

A major part of waste water management is the responsibility of public bodies — cities, counties, independent sewerage districts, etc. These institutions, collectively, are a political force of significant dimensions. In the evolution of water pollution control, therefore, the public sector has been prominent; Federal funding for water treatment systems has long been a reality, and the Federal water programs represent the largest single Federal expenditure on environmental cleanup and maintenance. Since the Federal government both funds waste water treatment by cities and also regulates, it tends to balance regulatory fervor by budgetary realism. Industrial water pollution is regulated much as air pollution is regulated; however, the presence of a large public sector with water pollution facilities leads, in this field, to many joint ventures between industry and local government to process wastes in common facilities designed for that purpose.

SOLID WASTE

Solid and semi-solid wastes (sludges) are produced by all human activities — including, of course, air and water pollution control. The largest categories of solid wastes are mining wastes, municipal solid waste (which is further subdivided), and industrial wastes resulting from processing and distribution.

As a general rule, the larger the solid waste category (usually measured in tons), the more it is likely to be benign. Mining waste, in the form of overburden removed in strip mining or excavated rock, is essentially harmless — although careless treatment can cause the leaching out of metals and minerals into groundwater and, to be sure, surface mining represents a disturbance of established ecosystems. Most municipal waste is miscellaneous organics and paper. Many large industrial waste streams (utility ashes, metallurgical slags) are largely inert. At the same time, relatively small waste streams may be disproportionately dangerous; examples are certain hospital wastes and toxic sludges from industrial processes.

Terminology

Wastes are said to be generated, discarded, reused or salvaged, converted, recycled, reduced at the source, and avoided — giving rise to phrases like 'recyclables', 'source reduction', 'waste avoidance', etc. The mixture of discarded wastes is referred to as the waste stream, sometimes written as wastestream. Some terms, current in the past, are no longer widely used. 'Refuse', 'trash', and 'garbage' are becoming obsolete terms, although a well-known periodical has appropriated the last of these terms as its name.

The *generation* of waste is the act of producing a waste. The total waste generated may not be equivalent to the total waste *discarded*. Discarded waste is the generated waste less that portion of it which has been reused, converted, or recycled.

Wastes are *reused* when they are put back into use in much the same applications from which they were generated, e.g. bricks salvaged from construction rubble and placed into service in a wall. *Conversion* implies a transformation — yard waste into compost, waste into energy. *Recycling* means the return of a material to industry for reprocessing — aluminum cans back into aluminum ingot, old newspapers back into newsprint by way of a deinking plant. In many cases, material recycled reaches a lesser use. Bleached, white paper may be recycled as dark, grey board used in packaging or as backing for writing pads. It should be noted that reuse, conversion, and recycling invariably produce additional wastes; these may be solid, airborne, or in water. Recycling is often labelled more generically as *resource recovery* to include any and all methods of recovering values from the waste.

Source reduction means the elimination of waste at the source; *waste avoidance* has the same meaning and is used by some because source reduction has an inelegant sound. Examples are purchasing products known to have less packaging, using returnable rather than disposable containers, washable rather than disposable diapers, etc. Source reduction goes beyond personal acts by private individuals and may be mandated by government.

Municipal Solid Waste

Municipal Solid Waste, also called urban solid waste, is usually divided into residential, commercial and office, medical, and construction components, generated, respectively, by households, retail businesses and office buildings, hospitals/clinics, and demolition activities (construction rubble).

Within the residential waste category, distinctions have always been made between ordinary and 'bulky' wastes (old furniture, dead refrigerators, etc.). In recent years, residential waste has been further subdivided in many communities into household waste, recyclable materials, and yard waste — each of the three being collected and managed by separate systems.

Commercial waste is similar to household waste; it tends to have less organic content (food and yard waste) and more paper; much of the paper is in the form of corrugated board.

Industrial Solid Wastes

A portion of industrial solid waste is identical to commercial urban waste (packaging, miscellaneous paper, etc.). In some industries (food processing), solids are very similar to those that result from municipal waste water treatment. All other solid wastes tend to be specific to the industrial activity. Some of these wastes are homogeneous (sawdust, wood bark, rust) and occur in large quantities in one place. If they are recyclable physically, they tend to be recycled if the economics so warrant: wood wastes are burned to provide process heat, metal-rich sludges are reintroduced into furnaces, etc.

Major problems are presented by large quantities of essentially useless inerts — such as ash — and by small quantities of toxic or hazardous residues of processing, pollution control, or manufacturing. Flyash from electrical utilities has been shown to be an excellent paving additive; however, there is a disproportion between the quantities of flyash produced each year and the demand for paving materials. Therefore flyash is deposited on land. At the other end of the spectrum, industry generates highly contaminated and toxic wastes; these may be residuals of chemicals processing or spent solvents and lubricants in mechanical production facilities. The quantities generated at any one location may be relatively small — prohibiting economic resource recovery. And disposal requires special management because of the waste's toxicity or hazard. This subject is discussed more fully below.

Methods of Management

Solid wastes must be (1) collected, (2) optionally processed, and (3) disposed. Resource recovery may be accomplished as part of collection or processing.

Waste Collection. Waste collection is a labor-intensive and unpleasant activity. For that reason, technological effort has been devoted to improve the productivity of waste collection teams while, at the same time, reducing occupational exposure to waste. Residential collection systems have evolved over the past two decades that radically reduce labor requirements allowing, for instance, a single operator to drive a truck and to discharge waste from appropriately configured containers into the truck—without leaving the cab. Such techniques are not universally used, however. Reducing labor forces is politically difficult in some communities; new systems call for capital expenditures; and political pressure to increase recycling has caused communities to go in the other direction in recent years. Separate collection of household waste, recyclables, and yard wastes has called for more labor rather than less. Periodic 'bulky waste' collection, of course, has long been a routine aspect of municipal waste collection systems.

Commercial establishments normally place waste in large containers; these are mechanically emptied into collection trucks.

In communities where disposal sites are far away, wastes may be delivered to transfer stations and reloaded into larger trucks for long hauls. Transfer stations sometimes serve as processing sites for the removal of recyclable components.

Land Disposal. The most common method of solid waste disposal is to place it on land in a more or less disciplined manner. Open dumping is the least satisfactory of these approaches; wastes are simply discharged into a gully and left to lie—a breeding ground for rats, a haven for birds, and a source of polluted runoff. These dumps can catch on fire and produce air pollution.

Sanitary landfilling is the systematic placement of waste on land; waste deposited each day is covered by earth; the site is planned, engineered, and graded (to guide runoff away from the waste); after completion, it is converted to some public use (park, ballfield). Advanced sanitary landfills will, in addition, be equipped with liners—which may be of plastic or clay—designed to prevent rainwater from percolating through the waste and then into the groundwater. A lined fill requires, of course, that water accumulated at the bottom be pumped out and treated before release to bodies of water. Decomposing waste produces methane gas; a well-designed sanitary landfill will be equipped with appropriate vents to release gases to the atmosphere. Uncontrolled gases from landfills can seep into the basements of adjacent buildings and present a fire hazard.

The principal environmental impact of landfills is 'leachate'—water contaminated by waste that enters aquifers (see above) or flows on the surface. Over time, leachate will seep out of all landfills, lined or not. Liners deteriorate, clay liners shift . . . Thus even final resting places for waste are not—final.

Solid Waste Processing and Recycling. Solid wastes are also composted, incinerated, and co-fired with coal to generate electricity (see below). Modern versions of these technologies tend to have a recycling facility at the front end for the diversion of 'recyclables'—paper, metals, and glass. Waste is dumped on a moving belt from which people pick items for recycling (large pieces of cardboard, certain metals, glass). The waste is then shredded; more metals are removed by magnets. The residue is composted or burned. Technology for separating virtually every kind of material has been developed, including for instance, machinery capable of sorting glass particles by color. Such hi-tech solutions, however, are rarely justified by the system's overall economics. The desirable components—corrugated board, aluminum, steel—are removed; these have well-established markets. Composting, incineration, and co-firing are not widely practiced because substantial capital investments are required, high disposal fees ('dump fees') are necessary, and the institutional arrangements for selling the waste as compost or as fuel are often very difficult to realize; public opposition to such ventures is always certain; the economics are rarely attractive.

Separate collection of recyclable waste is gaining recognition as an alternative to capital-intensive solutions. In these programs, the public is asked to separate components of the waste so that they can be assembled for shipment to a recycler with minimal mechanical processing. Direct recycling depends for its economic success on the volatile market for secondary products, where demand and prices fluctuate sharply in response to economic conditions. Yard waste composting is less problematical. If these materials are separately collected, they are largely uncontaminated by the products of industrial civilization and are easy to compost; the resulting product can be used in urban landscaping by the city itself.

Waste-to-Energy. Municipal and commercial waste has a high energy content. When appropriately handled, refused-derived fuel (RDF) can be burned directly or in combination with another fuel such as coal. One method of turning waste into energy is in electric utilities. Shredded waste, with metals, glass, and other heavy objects removed, is injected into furnaces with powdered coal. The technology has been shown to work; institutional arrangements are more difficult to bring about. Large amounts of waste must be collected at predictable dump fees before electric utilities are willing to make furnace modifications and to build the required fuel delivery systems. 'Control of the waste stream' tends to become a political issue with municipal and commercial waste management agencies pulling in different direction, interest groups opposing any form of burning, and utilities, generally shy of adverse publicity, growing lukewarm as controversy escalates.

Other waste-to-energy projects involve generating steam in specially designed incinerators and selling the steam to utilities, an industrial complex, or for internal use (e.g., in waste water treatment). Solid waste may also be turned into a type of fuel oil by pyrolysis (combustion in an oxygen-poor atmosphere); the oil is then burned as fuel. Yet another method of combustion and energy recovery is in special fluid bed furnaces; the waste is introduced into a furnace filled with swirling hot sand held suspended by the incoming combustion air.

Medical Waste Management. Infectious medical wastes are normally incinerated in the hospital's own special incinerators; toxics are handled as hazardous wastes (see below); and normal housekeeping wastes are handled as commercial wastes.

Industrial Waste Management. With the exception of hazardous and toxic wastes, discussed below, industrial wastes are managed in the same way as urban wastes. Because waste streams are often homogeneous and large, much more recycling is often feasible.

Special Wastes

A number of wastes or obsolete products have special characteristics that require unusual management arrangements. A brief capsule of some of these wastes, and how they are handled, follows:

Municipal Sludges. Municipal waste water sludges are a special category of municipal solid wastes; they are usually managed within the institutional framework of municipal waste water treatment. Since waste water sludges are organic, they can be used as fertilizers. Intensive use of sludges to 'manure' farmland is restricted by economics on the one hand (synthetic fertilizers are relatively cheap) and by health concerns. Sludges contain trace metals that cumulate in tissue, most notably cadmium; people who eat vegetables grown on sludge-fertilized land are somewhat at risk; the risk is low—a lifetime of eating such vegetables exclusively, combined with heavy smoking, describe a person at risk; but while there is risk, health authorities are disinclined to promote the solution. There is also cultural bias in the United States against using human waste on food crops.

For these reasons, sludges are typically placed on land or burned The most effective land disposal method appears to be landfarming—a process whereby the sludge is plowed into the earth and the land is given time to process the waste (the method has also been used on oily sludges); sludges, however, are also landfilled with municipal waste. The most sophisticated sludge combustion methods involve the digestion of sludges, the combustion of the methane evolved, and the use of the heat to aid in the burning of digestor residues; and the residual heat is then used in the waste water treatment plant as steam.

Household waste is typically managed by the local government using either its own forces, one or more contractors, or a combination of both. Commercial waste is handled by private-sector waste management firms; many generators and waste management firms separate valuable paper components, especially corrugated board, for recycling before land disposal of the rest. Construction rubble is usually managed by the construction industry, using sites of its own, or by commercial waste haulers.

Tires. Old tires are difficult to bury. Unless cut into pieces, they have a tendency to rise to the top of a landfill after some period of months or years. For this reason, they are prohibited at some landfills or, if accepted, are placed into piles—where they represent a fire hazard. They burn very hot and may damage the refractory lining of incinerators. Management methods include tire shredding, combustion in special furnaces, pyrolysis, and remelting of the rubber portion of tires for use as an asphalt admixture. The technologies required for such hi-tech solutions are costly in relation to the value of the rubber. The aesthetic pollution of large accumulations of tires has led some to propose and to implement novel schemes, including disposal of tires under water to create fish habitats.

Waste Oil. Oil drained from the crankshaft by members of the public is normally taken to filling stations. From there, the oil is handled as hazardous waste or sent to waste oil rerefineries. The heavy residues of these operations are handled like other hazardous wastes.

White Goods. Obsolete refrigerators, freezers, and stoves hold some sheet metal and much else (insulation, wiring, electric motors, etc.). The metal is not much in demand by secondary metal dealers. Old white goods have mineral glazes and require extensive demolition and cleanup before they are suitable for remelting.

HAZARDOUS AND TOXIC WASTES

Hazardous wastes are highly acidic, alkaline, or explosive; contact with the waste causes burns or damages equipment and structures. Toxic wastes contain chemicals toxic to man, animals, and vegetation. Wastes labelled 'toxic' may also be hazardous and hazardous wastes may also be toxic. In what follows, the term 'hazardous waste' will be used to mean either or both. Radioactive wastes are discussed separately.

Although hazardous wastes occur in the household (paints, cleansers, pesticides, pharmaceuticals may contain hazardous chemicals), the bulk of such wastes are generated by the chemicals and petroleum industries. Careless disposal of these wastes in past decades has produced—and continues to produce — massive groundwater contamination. Since the early 1970s, the collection, transport, storage, and disposal of hazardous wastes has come under strict Federal regulation; a fund has been created to pay for the cleanup of old hazardous waste disposal sites ('Superfund'). And the generation and management of these wastes is closely monitored by the U.S. Environmental Protection Agency in its Toxic Release Inventory (TRI) data base.

Characteristics of Hazardous Waste Management

The most important aspect of hazardous waste management is the ultimate disposal of waste on land — which must be handled in such a manner that wastes will be isolated from the water and air media. Before strict regulation came into force, these wastes were typically dumped on land or buried in drums; the gradual deterioration of the containers resulted in the release of toxics into the soil and, by way of the soil, into ground- and surface waters. Wastes held in lagoons also found their way into groundwater and, eventually, into wells — producing poisonings, cancer, nervous disorders, learning disabilities, and other health problems in the populations thus exposed.

Ultimate containment of such wastes presents technically and socially formidable challenges similar to the problem presented by radioactive wastes. Containers used must last for long periods of time and must themselves be protected from damage by water, erosion, and the shifting of the earth. The burial site must be appropriately constructed and constantly monitored. As containers age, they must be replaced. And institutional structures must be maintained to manage the waste in perpetuity. Ideal disposal sites — deep salt caverns, for example — are few; their capacity is limited. The costs of long term care are high.

For these reasons, it is desirable to reduce the tonnage of waste requiring ultimate disposal to a minimum. This is accomplished by treatment processes as varied as the hazardous wastes themselves. Organic wastes can be rendered harmless by burning them in specially designed incinerators. Treatment processes include a variety of chemical processes in which harmful chemicals are recovered, combined into harmless substances by chemical reaction, neutralized, distilled from streams, etc.

Despite all of the above, many hazardous wastes are routinely disposed of by conventional means — discharge to sewers, surface waters, land disposal, injection into the ground, etc. This is permissible when the wastes have been treated, for instance, or they are diluted to such an extent that the concentration of toxic components in the waste stream is very low.

Clean-Up of Old Sites

Poor waste management in the past has left an unsavory legacy of abandoned hazardous waste sites — many of them forgotten, covered, and the land reused for housing and other activities. These sites are gradually being identified and eliminated.

Many offending hazardous waste disposal sites are on Federal facilities under the control of the Department of Defense or the Department of Energy. Federal actions to clean up its own house have always been sluggish at best; bureaucratic inertia, the sheer size and complexity of defense activities, and budgetary constraints are some of the reasons why. Groundwater contamination has spread from Federal sites as from others; in recent years, under Congressional prodding, the Department of Defense has begun to plan a massive, 30-year program to bring itself in compliance with national standards.

Clean-up of old sites is technically complex and invariably costs more than appropriate waste handling would have cost. Uncontrolled dumping of waste oil, to take a case, contaminates large quantities of soil, thus increasing the total tonnage of waste that must later be handled. Contaminated aquifers must be pumped, the dirty water treated, until the pool or pocket of pollution has been removed. Sinking wells for aquifer clean up is very costly. If wastes were dumped in barrels, new barrels must be acquired and the waste repackaged before they can be shipped to controlled disposal sites.

RADIOACTIVE WASTE

Radioactive/nuclear wastes occur in the mining of uranium, in nuclear power plants, in many industrial activities, in medical facilities, academic laboratories, and in defense establishments. Wastes are classified as high- and low-level nuclear wastes as measured by the emission of alpha, beta, and gamma particles released by radioactive substances. The radioactive waste stream is made up of low-level uranium mining and processing residues, low-level wastes from commercial and defense establishmnets, high-level wastes from the same sources, spent fuel, and other defense wastes. In form this waste ranges from mineral piles of low radioactivity all the way to highly toxic and 'hot' chemical solids and liquids.

Nuclear wastes must be handled like hazardous wastes — with the added proviso that radiation must be contained. Radioactive materials decay as they emit particles. The rate of decay is determined by the elemental composition of the waste and may be minutes, hours, years or many thousands of years; decay rate is usually expressed as a substance's half-life, the amount of time required for half of the substance to decay. Since the half-life of some waste components is longer than the age of the earth, ultimate solutions to the radioactive waste problem are not forseeable unless ways are found to export such wastes into some remote corner of the solar system.

The principal method of managing nuclear wastes is concentration followed by permanent storage deep underground or in closely guarded and monitored sites. High-level wastes produce heat and require that their containers be cooled; low-level wastes require relatively less intensive management; most are managed on-site by those who generate the waste.

GLOBAL ISSUES

Global Warming

A potentially significant consequence of fossil fuel use may be a gradual warming of the earth, referred to as 'global warming'. Once clearly established, this conjectured outcome of oil, gas, wood, and coal combustion could lead to dramatic changes in climate, hence in agricultural productivity, and even in the size and the shape of the continents: melting polar ice caps would cause a rise in the level of the oceans. There is no consensus that global warming is in fact taking place; long periods of warming and cooling appear to be a part of historical climate patterns; however, average temperatures have been rising since the late 19th century.

The mechanism thought to be responsible for global warming is the accumulation of carbon dioxide (CO_2) and other gases in the atmosphere. The amount of carbon in the atmosphere is regulated by the earth's carbon cycle. Plants and phytoplankton consume carbon dioxide in their cycles of growth; they 'exhale' oxygen into the air; oxygen-breathing life forms consume oxygen to create body heat and exhale carbon dioxide; and decaying plant matter also releases carbon dioxide into the air. Thus a cycle is established. The burning of fossil fuels—which, ultimately, are vegetable matter long buried underground—add carbon dioxide to the cycle. If the earth's plant life cannot use all of the carbon in the atmosphere, carbon dioxide will build up. Deforestation, road building, expansion of urban space, and climate changes are reducing the amount of land available for plants; and fossil fuel use increases the amount of carbon emitted. The circumstantial evidence is there.

Carbon dioxide—together with such other gases as methane (the chief component of natural gas), nitrous oxide, chlorofluorocarbons (used as refrigerants and aerosol propellants)—increases the atmosphere's ability to retain radiant heat while permitting sunlight to come in. For this reason, global warming is also known as the Greenhouse Effect.

If the earth is warming, the solution, ultimately, is to reestablish the balance between CO_2 emitted and carbon fixed by plants. This may be possible if other forms of energy are developed—solar power, nuclear power (which has environmental consequences of its own), and fuels derived from crops. The choices, however, will be between different kinds of disruptions of the status quo: global warming will affect sea levels, forests, agriculture, and wildlife; it may cause major migrations and displacements; kicking the fossil fuel habit, however, is likely to have similar consequences. If the processes of change are slow, i.e, if warming increases very slowly and new technologies and other measures have time to be adopted gradually, we may avoid the worst consequences of either route.

Ozone Depletion

In the highest levels of the atmosphere, the stratosphere, a band extending from 9 miles above the earth to 30 miles above, ozone acts as a filter to reduce the amount of harmful ultraviolet (UV) radiation that reaches the earth. UV splits normal oxygen molecules (O_2) into free oxygen atoms. These atoms then combine with other molecules to form ozone (O_3). UV also acts on ozone, breaking it into an oxygen atom and a molecule of O_2. The free oxygen again strives to combine with a molecule. The energy of UV radiation is consumed in this dance of oxygen atoms and molecules, shielding us from radiation that causes skin diseases, cancer, cataracts, retinal damage, corneal tumors, nutritional deficiencies, and infectious diseases.

When chlorine and other reactive gases are present in the stratosphere, they interfere with ozone creation and breakdown; harmful UV radiation increases. A number of chemicals used in modern life cause ozone depletion in the atmosphere. Among these are chlorofluorocarbons (CFCs) used as refrigerants, propellants (for aerosols), and as solvents; others include methyl chloroform (a solvent), carbon tetrachloride (used in CFC production), halons (fire extinguisher compounds), and nitrogen oxides. These products of modern industrial life have caused measurable reductions in the stratospheric ozone layer; an ozone 'hole' has been detected over Antarctica. Corresponding increases in UV radiation have also been detected.

Approaches to halt ozone depletion include a search for substitute refrigerants, propellants, and solvents combined with controlling the release of such reactive substances to the atmosphere.

A WORD ABOUT GALE AND THE ENVIRONMENT

We at Gale would like to take this opportunity to publicly affirm our commitment to preserving the environment. Our commitment encompasses not only a zeal to publish information helpful to a variety of people pursuing environmental goals, but also a rededication to creating a safe and healthy workplace for our employees.

In our effort to make responsible use of natural resources, we're publishing all books in the Gale Environmental Library on recycled paper. Our Production Department is continually researching ways to use new environmentally safe inks and manufacturing technologies for all Gale books.

In our quest to become better environmental citizens, we've organized a task force representing all operating functions within Gale. With the complete backing of Gale senior management, the task force reviews our current practices and using the Valdez Principles* as a starting point, makes recommendations that will help us to: reduce waste, make wise use of energy and sustainable use of natural resources, reduce health and safety risks to our employees, and finally, should we cause any damage or injury, take full responsibility.

We look forward to becoming the best environmental citizens we can be and hope that you, too, have joined in the cause of caring for our fragile planet.

The Employees of Gale Research, Inc.

---

* The Valdez Principles were set forth in 1989 by the Coalition for Environmentally Responsible Economies (CERES). The principles serves as guidelines for companies concerned with improving their environmental behavior. For a copy of the Valdez Principles, write to CERES at 711 Atlantic Avenue, 5th Floor, Boston, MA, 02111.

Statistical Record of the Environment

Chapter 1
THE MEDIA - AIR, WATER, LAND

Atmosphere

★ 1 ★

Air Quality Trends 1979-1988

Percent change in air quality trend statistics over ten years in the U.S.

	Total Suspended Particles	Lead	Sulfur Dioxide	Carbon Monoxide	Nitrogen Oxide	Ozone
National Average	-20	-89	-30	-28	-7	+1
Northeast						
Boston	-13	-	-10	-45	+12	+16
New York	-12	-	-14	-45	+2	0
Philadelphia	-21	-87	-3	-37	-15	+12
Midatlantic						
Baltimore	-12	-93	-4	-24	-	+17
Washington, DC	-10	-92	-	-21	-	+21
Midwest						
Detroit	-23	-	-25	-18	-	+17
Chicago	-28	-85	-46	-42	0	+15
St. Louis	-19	-	-20	-46	-17	+8
South						
Atlantic	+1	-	-	-30	-	+1
Houston	-35	-87	-17	-14	-39	-24
Rocky Mountain						
Denver	-29	-91	-45	-33	-17	-14
Phoenix	-21	-88	-	-25	-	+35
South Coast						
Los Angeles	-5	-92	-33	-14	-14	-22

[Continued]

1

★ 1 ★

Air Quality Trends 1979 -1988
[Continued]

	Total Suspended Particles	Lead	Sulfur Dioxide	Carbon Monoxide	Nitrogen Oxide	Ozone
Northwest						
Portland	-16	-80	-	-46	-	+19
Seattle	-25	-44	-43	-22	-	+10
Composite Average (weighted)	-19	-86	-23	-28	-13	+4

Source: National Air Quality & Emission Trend Reports, 1988, EPA, Research Triangle Park, N.C., March 1990, p. 136.

★ 2 ★

Carbon Dioxide Levels in the Atmosphere

Average concentrations of carbon dioxide in the atmosphere, shown in parts per million.

Year	Mauna Loa Hawaii	South Pole	American Samoa	Point Barrow Alaska
1979	336.5	334.8	336.3	337.9
1980	338.4	336.9	338.0	339.9
1981	339.5	338.1	338.3	341.7
1982	340.8	339.3	340.3	342.8
1983	342.8	341.0	341.6	344.1
1984	344.3	342.4	343.3	346.0
1985	345.7	343.7	344.4	347.0
1986	346.9	345.2	345.9	348.7
1987	348.6	346.8	347.6	349.8
1988	351.2	348.5	349.7	352.9

Source: Council on Environmental Quality, *20th Annual Report 1990*, Washington, D.C., p. 467, from Keeling, C.D., Scripps Institution of Oceanography, La Jolla, CA; and Thoning, K.W., Cooperative Institution for Research in Environmental Studies, University of Colorado, Boulder, CO. (Data provided by the Carbon Dioxide Information Analysis Center, Oak Ridge National Laboratory, Oak Ridge, TN).

★ 3 ★

Carbon in the Atmosphere

Carbon added to and removed from the atmosphere. The data show that carbon in the atmosphere is increasing by about 2.5 billion metric tons a year. The ultimate destination of 1 billion tons of carbon removed from the atmosphere is unknown.

	Billion metric tons per year
Carbon added to atmosphere	
Respiration	140.0
Burning fuel fossil	5.0
Deforestation	1.0
Total	146.0
Carbon removed from atmosphere	
Photosynthesis	140.0
Ocean uptake	2.50
Unaccounted for	1.0
Net increase in atmosphere	2.50

Source: U.S. News & World Report, October 31, 1988, p. 58.

★ 4 ★

Greenhouse Gas Emissions by Region

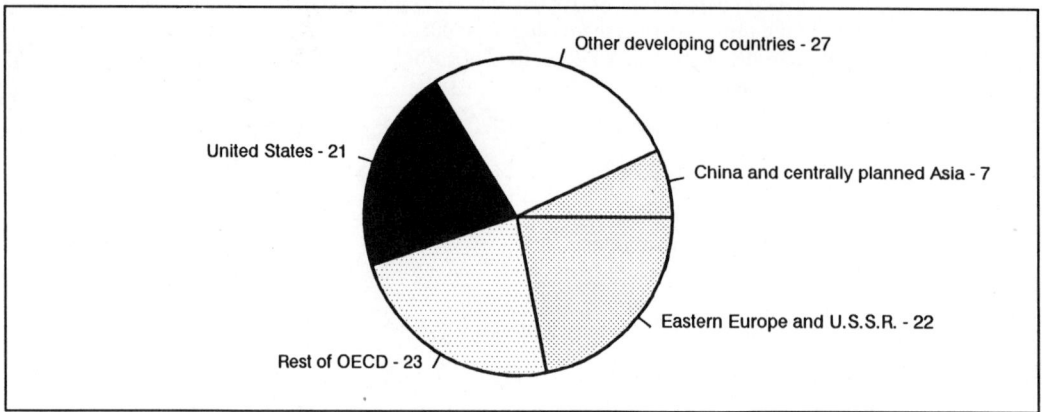

Region	Percent[1]
Eastern Europe and U.S.S.R.	22
United States	21
China and centrally planned Asia	7
Rest of OECD	23
Other developing countries	27

Source: Changing by Degrees: Steps to Reduce Greenhouse Gases, U.S. Congress, Office of Technology Assessment, OTA-O-482, Washington, D.C., February 1991, p. 5, from U.S. Environmental Protection Agency 1990. *Notes:* 1. Percentages are weighted according to their contribution to radiative forcing between 1980 and 1990.

★ 5 ★

Particulate Air Pollution in Eight Microenvironments

Estimates of annual particulate pollution. Numbers represent micrograms of pollutant per cubic meter of air.

Microenvironment	Outdoor	Indoor
Developed countries		
Urban[1]	75	100
Rural[2]	25	75
Developing countries		
Urban[3]	200	250
Rural[4]	50	300

Source: Environment, Volume 30, No. 10, December 1988, from the World Health Organization and the United Nations Environment Programme. *Notes:* 1. Based on World Health Organization (WHO) recommended outdoor levels. The estimate for indoor air is modified for environmental tobacco smoke. 2. Based on clean outdoor air, the figures are modified by wood stove emissions. The estimate for indoor air is also modified for environmental tobacco smoke. 3. The figures are based on data from WHO and the United Nations Environment Programme (UNEP), "Global Pollution and Health: Results of Health-related Environmental Monitoring" (London:WHO, 1987) and interpretations presented in WHO and UNEP, "Assessment of Urban Air Quality Worldwide," Draft, PEP/88.2 (Geneva: WHO, 1988), and modified by some solid-fuel cookstove emissions. The estimate for indoor air is also modified by environmental tobacco smoke. 4. The estimate for outdoor air is based on clean outdoor air modified by solid-fuel cookstove emissions. The estimate for indoor air based on typical daily averages determined from studies listed elsewhere in the source.

Biosphere

★ 6 ★

Worldwide Mobilization of Trace Metals in the Biosphere

```
┌──────────────────────────────────────────────────────────┐
│  ┌─────────────────────────────────────────────────────┐  │
│  │ Manganese - 1894                                    │  │
│  ┌───────────────────────────────────┐                   │
│  │ Zinc - 1427                       │                   │
│  ┌─────────────────────────┐                             │
│  │ Copper - 1048           │                             │
│  ┌─────────────────────────┐                             │
│  │ Chromium - 1010         │                             │
│  ┌──────────────┐                                        │
│  │ Lead - 565.0 │                                        │
│  ┌────────┐                                              │
│  │        │ Nickel - 356.0                               │
│  ┌──┐                                                    │
│  │  │ Arsenic - 105.0                                    │
│  ┌──┐                                                    │
│  │  │ Molybdenum - 98.0                                  │
│  ┌─┐                                                     │
│  │ │ Selenium - 76.0                                     │
│  ┌─┐                                                     │
│  │ │ Vanadium - 75.0                                     │
│  ┌┐                                                      │
│  ││ Antimony - 41.0                                      │
│  ┃ Cadmium - 24.0                                        │
│  ┃ Mercury - 11.0                                        │
│                        Chart shows data from column 2.   │
└──────────────────────────────────────────────────────────┘
```

Values are shown in thousands of metric tons per year. The values for chromium and manganese are approximations.

Element	Production from mines[1]	Total industrial discharges[2]
Antimony	55.0	41.0
Arsenic	45.0	105.0
Cadmium	19.0	24.0
Chromium	6800	1010
Cobalt	36.0	
Copper	8114	1048
Lead	3077	565.0
Manganese	16000	1894
Mercury	6.8	11.0
Molybdenum	98.0	98.0
Nickel	778.0	356.0
Selenium	1.6	76.0

[Continued]

★ 6 ★

Worldwide Mobilization of Trace Metals in the Biosphere
[Continued]

Element	Production from mines[1]	Total industrial discharges[2]
Vanadium	34.0	75.0
Zinc	6040	1427

Source: Environment, September 1990, p. 28, from J.O. Nriagu, "A Silent Epidemic of Environmental Metal Poisoning?" *Environmental Pollution 50* (1988): 139-161; J.O. Nriagu and J.M. Pacyna, "Quantitative Assessment of Worldwide Contamination of Air, Water and Soils with Trace Metals," *Nature* 333 (1988): 134-139; and D.C. Adriano, *Trace Elements in the Terrestrial Environment* (New York: Springer-Verlag, 1986). "Mobilization" means the movement of trace metals caused by industrial or natural activity. *Notes:* 1. Only a fraction of each metal mined each year is released into the environment in the same year. 2. Industrial discharges are calculated as discharges into soils and water minus the emissions to the atmosphere.

Estuaries

★ 7 ★

Impaired Estuary Square Miles - Part I

	Total Impaired Waters	Nutrients		Pathogens		Organic Enrichment		Oil & Grease		Metals		Siltation	
		Major	Mod/Min	Major	Mod/Min	Major	Mod/Min	Major	Mod/Min	Major	Mod/Min	Major	Mod/Min
Alabama[1]	3	3	-	-	-	3	-	-	-	-	-	-	-
Connecticut	234	6	215	23	54	25	182	-	-	-	26	-	-
District of Columbia	6	-	5	1	5	1	-	-	1	-	6	-	1
Florida[1]	1,106	222	-	1	-	203	-	-	-	550	-	398	-
Georgia	11	-	-	-	-	12	-	-	-	-	-	-	-
Hawaii	94	-	46	-	-	-	-	-	-	-	3	-	46
Louisiana	2,197	62	568	120	1,815	62	568	25	1,561	-	-	-	-
Maryland	1,981	1,981	-	13	396	700	8	-	-	-	-	-	1
Mississippi	7	-	2	-	4	-	2	-	-	-	-	-	1
North Carolina[1]	220	135	-	26	-	-	-	-	-	-	-	5	-
New Jersey	142	70	-	142	-	-	-	-	-	-	-	-	-
New York	413	-	100	251	120	14	99	-	24	-	-	-	-
Rhode Island	38	9	-	24	-	8	-	-	-	15	-	-	-
South Carolina[1]	80	-	-	59	-	21	-	-	-	-	-	-	-
Virginia	196	-	-	90	16	2	66	-	-	-	-	-	-
Washington	177	-	-	67	93	-	25	1	5	40	15	1	11
Totals	6,905	2,488	936	817	2,503	1,051	950	26	1,591	605	50	404	59
Combined Totals			3,424		3,320		2,001		1,617		655		463
Percent of Impaired Waters			49.6		48.1		29.0		23.4		9.5		6.7

Source: National Water Quality Inventory, 1988, Report to Congress, U.S. Environmental Protection Agency, Washington, D.C., April 1990, p. 52, from 1988 State Section 305(b) reports. *Notes:* - Zero or not reported. 1. These States did not specify the degree of impact (i.e., Major or Moderate/Minor); estuary square miles were placed in the "Major" column for national reporting purposes.

★8★

Impaired Estuary Square Miles - Part II

	Unknown Toxics		Priority Organics		Pesticides		pH		Other Inorganics		Ammonia	
	Major	Mod/Min	Major	Mod/Min	Major	Mod/Min	Major	Mod/Min	Major	Mod/Min	Major	Mod/Min
Alabama[1]	-	-	-	-	-	-	-	-	-	-	-	-
Connecticut	-	-	-	26	-	-	-	-	-	-	-	-
District of Columbia	-	-	-	1	-	-	-	5	-	-	-	6
Florida[1]	345	-	-	-	-	-	-	-	-	-	-	-
Georgia	-	-	-	-	-	-	-	-	-	-	-	-
Hawaii	-	-	-	-	-	-	-	-	-	-	-	-
Louisiana	-	-	-	2	-	-	-	-	25	-	-	-
Maryland	-	-	-	-	-	-	-	-	-	-	-	-
Mississippi	-	3	-	-	-	-	-	-	-	-	-	-
North Carolina[1]	-	-	-	-	-	-	-	-	-	-	-	-
New Jersey	-	-	70	-	70	-	-	-	-	-	-	-
New York	-	5	145	4	-	-	-	-	-	-	-	-
Rhode Island	-	-	-	-	-	-	-	-	-	-	-	-
South Carolina[1]	-	-	-	-	-	-	-	-	-	-	-	-
Virginia	-	-	-	-	-	-	2	21	-	-	-	-
Washington	-	-	21	14	-	2	-	-	-	-	-	5
Totals	345	8	236	47	70	2	2	26	25	-	-	11
Combined Totals		353		283		72		28		25		11
Percent of Impaired Waters		5.1		4.1		1.0		0.4		0.4		0.2

Source: National Water Quality Inventory, 1988, Report to Congress, U.S. Environmental Protection Agency, Washington, D.C., April 1990, p. 52, from 1988 State Section 305(b) reports. *Notes:* - Zero or not reported. 1. These States did not specify the degree of impact (i.e., Major or Moderate/Minor); estuary square miles were placed in the "Major" column for national reporting purposes.

Forests

★9★

National Forest System

Data, as of September 30, 1989, are shown in thousands of acres.

State or other area	Gross area within unit boundaries	National Forest System lands[1]	Other lands within unit boundaries[2]
Alabama	1,275	651	623
Alaska	24,233	22,437	1,796
Arizona	11,889	11,242	647
Arkansas	3,490	2,495	995
California	24,434	20,588	3,845
Colorado	16,027	14,444	1,582
Connecticut	[3]	[3]	-
Florida	1,246	1,122	124
Georgia	1,846	858	988
Hawaii	[3]	[3]	-

[Continued]

★ 9 ★

National Forest System
[Continued]

State or other area	Gross area within unit boundaries	National Forest System lands[1]	Other lands within unit boundaries[2]
Idaho	21,694	20,457	1,238
Illinois	840	264	576
Indiana	644	188	456
Kansas	116	108	8
Kentucky	2,102	667	1,435
Louisiana	1,023	601	422
Maine	93	53	40
Michigan	4,872	2,801	2,071
Minnesota	5,467	2,808	2,659
Mississippi	2,310	1,149	1,161
Missouri	3,082	1,474	1,608
Montana	19,101	16,796	2,305
Nebraska	442	352	90
Nevada	6,009	5,743	266
New Hampshire	825	720	105
New Mexico	10,367	9,320	1,046
New York	13	13	-
North Carolina	3,165	1,221	1,944
North Dakota	1,106	1,106	[3]
Ohio	833	191	642
Oklahoma	461	296	165
Oregon	17,496	15,634	1,862
Pennsylvania	743	512	231
South Carolina	1,376	605	770
South Dakota	2,342	1,997	345
Tennessee	1,212	626	586
Texas	1,994	753	1,241
Utah	9,128	8,041	1,086
Vermont	630	327	302
Virginia	3,226	1,642	1,584
Washington	10,045	9,147	898
West Virginia	1,861	1,021	840
Wisconsin	2,023	1,513	510
Wyoming	9,704	9,255	449
Puerto Rico	56	28	28

[Continued]

★ 9 ★

National Forest System
[Continued]

State or other area	Gross area within unit boundaries	National Forest System lands[1]	Other lands within unit boundaries[2]
Virgin Islands	3	3	-
Total	230,839	191,268	39,570

Source: Agricultural Conservation and Forestry Statistics, 1989, U.S. Government Printing Office, Washington, D.C., 1989, p. 458, from Forest Service. *National forests* - Units formally established and permanently set aside and reserved for national forest purposes. *Purchase units* - Units designated by the Secretary of Agriculture or previously approved by the National Forest Reservation Commission for purposes of Weeks Law Acquisition. *National grasslands* - Units designated "National grasslands" by the Secretary of Agriculture and permanently held by the Department of Agriculture under Title III of the Bankhead-Jones Farm Tenant Act. *Land utilization projects* - Units designated by the Secretary of Agriculture for conservation and utilization under Title III of the Bankhead-Jones Farm Tenant Act. *Research and experimental areas* - Units reserved and dedicated by the Secretary of Agriculture for forest or range research experimentation. *Other areas* - Units administered by the Forest Service that are not included in the above groups. *Notes:* 1. National Forest Systems lands. - A nationally significant system of Federally owned units of forest, range, and related land consisting of national forests, purchase units, national grasslands, land utilization, project areas, experimental forest areas, experimental range areas, designated experimental areas, other land areas, water areas and interests in lands that are administered by the Forest Service or designated for administration through the Forest Service. 2. Other lands within unit boundaries.- Lands within the unit boundaries in private, State, county, and municipal ownership and Federal lands over which the Forest Service has no jurisdiction. Areas of such lands which have been offered to the United States and have been approved for acquisition and subsequent Forest Service administration, but to which title had not been accepted by the United States. 3. Less than 500 acres.

★ 10 ★

Tree Planting in the U.S.

The data represents acres seeded and acres of windbarrier planting in the fiscal year 1989.

State or other area	Total	Federal lands			Non federal public[1] lands	Private[2] lands
		Total	National Forests	Other[3]		
Alabama	301,135	5,014	4,336	678	2,376	293,745
Alaska	1,728	672	672	-	396	360
Arizona	1,800	1,473	1,472	1	-	327
Arkansas	145,006	15,016	14,922	94	230	129,760
California	89,986	63,869	62,598	1,271	404	25,713
Colorado	6,821	1,716	1,422	294	144	4,961
Connecticut	929	6	-	6	65	858
Delaware	824	-	-	-	-	824
Florida	266,082	14,414	13,908	506	2,633	249,035
Georgia	484,791	5,606	4,020	1,586	569	478,616
Hawaii	217	-	-	-	80	137
Idaho	36,769	23,538	22,699	839	2,189	11,042
Illinois	6,299	50	50	-	600	5,649
Indiana	4,192	28	-	28	121	4,043

[Continued]

★ 10 ★

Tree Planting in the U.S.
[Continued]

State or other area	Total	Federal lands			Non federal public[1] lands	Private[2] lands
		Total	National Forests	Other[3]		
Iowa	7,286	110	-	110	102	7,074
Kansas	2,420	49	-	49	232	2,139
Kentucky	14,267	1,525	1,455	70	2	12,740
Louisiana	149,811	7,348	7,306	42	-	142,463
Maine	10,225	-	-	-	18	10,207
Maryland	7,854	151	-	151	225	7,478
Massachusetts	1	1	-	1	-	-
Michigan	18,595	3,269	3,249	20	4,865	10,461
Minnesota	43,266	3,367	2,908	459	19,866	20,033
Mississippi	256,967	12,666	11,317	1,349	14,030	230,271
Missouri	5,721	2,286	2,214	72	-	3,435
Montana	33,744	20,367	18,594	1,773	1,267	12,110
Nebraska	5,226	26	20	6	75	5,125
Nevada	255	-	-	-	145	110
New Hampshire	281	40	40	-	-	241
New Jersey	572	24	-	24	84	464
New Mexico	2,955	2,738	2,218	520	-	217
New York	6,338	-	-	-	298	6,040
North Carolina	142,051	3,085	2,664	421	549	138,417
North Dakota	408	51	-	51	12	345
Ohio	3,255	248	186	62	-	3,007
Oklahoma	19,969	2,024	1,716	308	-	17,945
Oregon	215,133	116,497	76,727	39,770	8,959	89,677
Pennsylvania	1,509	2	-	2	-	1,507
Rhode Island	101	-	-	-	-	101
South Carolina	218,453	9,187	6,292	2,895	582	208,684
South Dakota	6,084	621	404	217	323	5,140
Tennessee	26,829	2,537	2,180	357	860	23,432
Texas	163,281	6,159	6,110	49	35	157,087
Utah	1,351	977	977	-	105	269
Vermont	655	157	157	-	-	498
Virginia	117,297	1,614	1,301	313	1,288	114,395
Washington	177,941	35,448	30,276	5,172	12,493	130,000
West Virginia	3,500	25	20	5	9	3,466
Wisconsin	9,520	3,097	1,750	1,347	-	6,423
Wyoming	1,346	1,286	941	345	40	20
State totals	3,021,046	368,384	307,121	61,263	76,571	2,576,091
Puerto Rico	345	17	17	-	26	302
Other[4]	557	-	-	-	64	493
Total	3,021,948	368,401	307,138	61,263	76,661	2,576,886

Source: Agricultural Conservation and Forestry Statistics, 1989, U.S. Government Printing Office, Washington, D.C., 1989, p. 453, from Forest Service *Notes:* 1. State forest, other State, and other public agencies lands. 2. Forest industry, other industry, and nonindustrial lands. 3. U.S. Department of Interior and Indian Reservations, and other federal lands. 4. Guam and the Trust Territories of the Pacific Islands.

Global Conditions

★ 11 ★

Background Radiation

| Radon - 54 |
| Other natural radiation - 27 |
| Medical procedures - 14 |
| Other man-made radiation - 3 |
| Nuclear testing - 2 |

Radon dominates normal background radiation. Radon poses a threat of lung cancer.

Types of Radiation	Percentage
Radon	54
Other natural radiation	27
Medical procedures	14
Nuclear testing	2
Other man-made radiation	3

Source: C&EN, February 6, 1989, p. 7.

★ 12 ★

Nitrogen Sources in the Environment

Nitrogen for crop production may be derived from a variety of sources. However, commercial fertilizers comprise the main source of resupply of the soil nutrients.

	Percent
Nitrogen fertilizer	55-60
Manure	10-15
Legume	8-10
Rain	5-8
Soils	15-20

Source: Beneath the Bottom Line: Agricultural Approaches to Reduce Agricultural Contamination of Groundwater, U.S. Congress, Office of Technology Assessment, OTA-F-418, Washington, D.C., November 1990., p. 87, from Environmental Protection Commission, Iowa Department of Natural Resources, Iowa Groundwater Protection Strategy, 1987.

★ 13 ★

The Ten Warmest Years Since 1880

| 1990 - 59.81 |
| 1981, 1988 - 59.64 |
| 1987 - 59.56 |
| 1980, 1983 - 59.51 |
| 1989 - 59.45 |
| 1973 - 59.31 |
| 1977, 1986 - 59.30 |

Year	Temperature (Deg. F)
1990	59.81
1981, 1988	59.64
1987	59.56
1980, 1983	59.51
1989	59.45
1973	59.31
1977, 1986	59.30

Source: The New York Times, January 10, 1991, p. A1, from NASA/Goddard Institute for Space Studies.

Great Lakes

★ 14 ★

Impaired Great Lakes by Cause of Pollution - Part I

Data are in miles of shoreline.

State	Total Impaired Waters	Priority Organics		Metals		Nutrients		Organic Enrichment	
		Major	Mod/Min	Major	Mod/Min	Major	Mod/Min	Major	Mod/Min
Illinois	63	63	-	-	-	17	26	-	-
Indiana	43	-	43	-	-	-	-	-	-
New York	477	463	-	-	-	29	-	-	15
Ohio	236	4	188	86	129	-	4	-	46

[Continued]

★ 14 ★

Impaired Great Lakes by Cause of Pollution - Part I
[Continued]

State	Total Impaired Waters	Priority Organics		Metals		Nutrients		Organic Enrichment	
		Major	Mod/Min	Major	Mod/Min	Major	Mod/Min	Major	Mod/Min
Totals	819	530	231	86	129	46	30	0	61
Combined Totals			761		215		76		61

Source: National Water Quality Inventory, 1988, Report to Congress, U.S. Environmental Protection Agency, Washington, D.C., April 1990, p. 34.

★ 15 ★

Impaired Great Lakes by Cause of Pollution - Part II

Data are in miles of shoreline.

State	Pesticides		pH		Pathogens		Siltation	
	Major	Mod/Min	Major	Mod/Min	Major	Mod/Min	Major	Mod/Min
Illinois	-	-	-	-	-	-	-	-
Indiana	-	43	-	-	-	-	-	-
New York	-	-	-	-	-	15	-	14
Ohio	-	-	-	35	-	-	-	-
Totals	0	43	0	35	0	15	0	14
Combined Totals		43		35		15		14

Source: National Water Quality Inventory, 1988, Report to Congress, U.S. Environmental Protection Agency, Washington, D.C., April 1990, p. 34.

★ 16 ★

Impaired Great Lakes by Source of Pollution - Part I

Data are in miles of shoreline.

State	Total Impaired Waters	Land Disposal		Agriculture		Combined Sewers		Storm Sewers/Runoff	
		Major	Mod/Min	Major	Mod/Min	Major	Mod/Min	Major	Mod/Min
Illinois	63	-	-	-	-	-	6	45	-
Indiana	43	-	-	-	43	-	43	-	-
New York	477	-	477	14	15	-	14	-	14
Totals	583	0	477	14	58	0	63	45	14
Combined Totals			477		72		63		59

Source: National Water Quality Inventory, 1988, Report to Congress, U.S. Environmental Protection Agency, Washington, D.C., April 1990, p. 36, from 1988 State Section 305(b) reports. *Note:* - Zero or not reported.

★ 17 ★

Impaired Great Lakes by Source of Pollution - Part II

Data are in miles of shoreline.

State	Industrial		Municipal		Construction		Silviculture		Resource Extraction		Hydro/ Habitat Mod	
	Major	Mod/Min	Major	Mod/Min	Major	Mod/Min	Major	Mod/Min	Major	Mod/Min	Major	Mod/Min
Illinois	-	-	-	-	-	-	-	-	-	-	-	-
Indiana	-	43	-	43	-	-	-	-	-	-	-	-
New York	-	-	-	-	-	14	-	-	-	-	-	-
Totals	0	43	0	43	0	14	0	0	0	0	0	0
Combined Totals		43		43		14		0		0		0

Source: National Water Quality Inventory, 1988, Report to Congress, U.S. Environmental Protection Agency, Washington, D.C., April 1990, p. 36, from 1988 State Section 305(b) reports. - Stands for zero or not reported. .

Lakes

★ 18 ★

Impaired Lakes by Cause of Pollution - Part I

Data shown are in acres of lake surface.

State	Total Impaired Waters	Nutrients		Siltation		Organic Enrichment		Salinity		Habitat Modification		Pathogens	
		Major	Mod/Min	Major	Mod/Min	Major	Mod/Min	Major	Mod/Min	Major	Mod/Min	Major	Mod/Min
Alabama[1]	86,080	-	-	-	-	-	-	-	-	-	-	-	-
Colorado	1,672	-	500	-	-	-	650	-	-	-	-	-	-
Connecticut	12,389	9,612	2,777	812	7,914	1,462	8,930	-	-	-	-	-	-
District of Columbia	136	-	-	-	-	-	-	-	-	-	-	-	136
Florida[1]	637,440	75,520	-	171,520	-	175,360	-	272,000	-	-	-	640	-
Georgia	5,373	5,373	-	-	-	-	-	-	-	-	-	-	-
Illinois	160,641	44,552	108,699	69,364	90,500	56,645	90,484	-	-	-	-	2,437	4,837
Indiana	179	122	12	-	-	82	52	-	-	-	-	45	89
Iowa	53,448	19,048	34,278	46,112	2,268	44	16,815	-	-	222	-	15,300	-
Kansas	57,256	7	3,491	10	34,736	-	-	9,230	13,167	-	-	-	-
Kentucky[1]	35,148	6,707	-	4,517	-	-	-	-	-	-	-	-	-
Louisiana	141,141	-	121,262	-	986	-	42,548	-	46,394	-	-	-	100,352
Maryland	2,610	2,610	-	15	-	-	-	-	-	-	-	-	-
Minnesota[1]	236,845	236,845	-	-	-	-	-	-	-	-	-	-	-
Mississippi	18,260	-	18,260	724	17,060	-	-	-	1,200	-	-	-	-
Missouri	2,311	-	-	-	-	-	-	-	-	-	-	-	-
Montana	317,996	5,750	17,449	19,022	5,600	-	-	13,250	14,509	-	284,000	1,423	1,300
New Hampshire	19,146	95	4,281	-	-	-	-	-	-	-	-	-	-
New Mexico	47,308	2,338	40,346	1,178	8,665	-	-	-	-	10	200	-	-
New York	295,332	101,663	27,928	-	3,507	306	61,103	-	2,944	-	-	3,355	22,939
North Carolina[1]	11,897	2,015	-	707	-	1,900	-	-	-	-	-	-	-
North Dakota	48,125	37,467	10,555	6,288	12,800	11,984	30,663	5,000	1,750	67	-	-	-
Oregon[1]	130,625	115,965	-	15,594	-	69,147	-	-	-	-	-	13,248	-
Puerto Rico	7,345	1,448	447	135	-	891	581	348	-	300	16	354	137
Rhode Island	1,401	246	-	60	-	-	-	-	-	-	-	966	-
South Carolina[1]	1,165	-	-	-	-	50	-	-	-	-	-	865	-
South Dakota	94,720	75,190	13,574	55,629	5,287	130	28	-	-	-	-	-	-
Tennessee	86,648	35,383	35,647	21,123	30,445	34,655	43,575	-	-	16	-	-	25,130
Vermont	49,206	2,953	9,089	1,102	16,184	684	13,878	-	-	7,205	9,318	741	131
Virginia	13,737	-	12,518	-	2,698	-	8,001	-	-	-	-	-	129
Washington	33,684	-	33,104	-	-	-	580	-	580	-	-	580	33,104
West Virginia	19,171	1,236	2,933	2,047	9,136	-	642	-	-	-	-	-	-
Wyoming	30,404	-	17,749	-	12,919	-	53	-	459	-	-	-	-
Totals	2,658,839	782,145	514,899	415,959	260,705	353,340	318,583	299,828	81,003	7,820	293,534	39,954	188,292
Combined Totals			1,297,044		676,664		671,923		380,831		301,354		228,246
Percent of Impaired waters			48.8%		25.4%		25.3%		14.3%		11.3%		8.6%

Source: National Water Quality Inventory, 1988, Report to Congress, U.S. Environmental Protection Agency, Washington, D.C., April 1990, p. 20, from 1988 State Section 305(b) reports. *Notes:* 1. These States did not specify the degree of impact (i.e., Major or Moderate/Minor); lake acres were placed in the "Major" column for national reporting purposes. - Zero or not reported.

★ 19 ★

Impaired Lakes by Cause of Pollution - Part II

Data shown are in acres of lake surface.

State^	Priority Organics		Suspended Solids		Metals		Pesticides		pH		Flow Alteration	
	Major	Mod/Min	Major	Mod/Min	Major	Mod/Min	Major	Mod/Min	Major	Mod/Min	Major	Mod/Min
Alabama[1]	84,230	-	-	-	1,850	-	-	-	1,850	-	-	-
Colorado	105	-	-	-	102	410	160	-	-	-	-	-
Connecticut	-	-	-	-	-	-	-	-	-	-	-	-
District of Columbia	-	-	-	-	-	-	-	-	-	136	-	-

[Continued]

★ 19 ★

Impaired Lakes by Cause of Pollution - Part II
[Continued]

State	Priority Organics		Suspended Solids		Metals		Pesticides		pH		Flow Alteration	
	Major	Mod/Min	Major	Mod/Min	Major	Mod/Min	Major	Mod/Min	Major	Mod/Min	Major	Mod/Min
Florida[1]	-	-	-	-	41,600	-	-	-	11,520	-	-	-
Georgia	-	-	-	-	-	-	-	-	-	-	-	-
Illinois	2,937	2,228	74,401	83,665	5,196	17,355	13,395	1,070	-	-	-	-
Indiana	27	-	-	-	15	45	12	-	30	-	-	-
Iowa	-	-	-	-	-	-	-	49,400	1	-	10	-
Kansas	-	-	-	-	9,040	757	-	-	-	-	3	5,694
Kentucky[1]	-	-	-	-	23,584	-	-	-	-	-	-	-
Louisiana	-	-	-	22,490	-	-	-	1,229	-	-	-	-
Maryland	-	-	-	-	-	-	-	-	-	-	-	-
Minnesota[1]	-	-	-	-	-	-	-	-	-	-	-	-
Mississippi	-	-	-	-	-	-	-	17,060	-	-	-	-
Missouri	-	-	-	-	-	-	-	561	-	20	-	-
Montana	-	-	-	-	-	9,750	-	-	-	-	-	-
New Hampshire	-	-	-	-	-	-	-	-	269	5,135	-	-
New Mexico	-	-	-	-	-	-	-	-	-	-	-	-
New York	102,060	434	-	-	326	7,597	24,716	-	16,569	-	33,877	600
North Carolina[1]	-	-	-	-	9,680	-	-	-	-	-	40	-
North Dakota	-	-	220	-	-	-	-	-	-	-	-	5,469
Oregon[1]	-	-	-	-	-	-	-	-	81,365	-	-	-
Puerto Rico	-	-	836	251	47	-	-	350	141	10	-	-
Rhode Island	-	-	-	-	-	-	-	-	-	-	-	-
South Carolina[1]	-	-	-	-	-	-	-	-	-	-	-	-
South Dakota	-	-	359	593	-	-	-	-	-	-	-	79
Tennessee	18,508	6,149	383	17,041	69	29,257	-	-	69	11,924	-	24,905
Vermont	-	-	-	-	-	-	-	-	44	69	1,887	4,173
Virginia	-	-	-	-	-	1,034	-	79	-	2,810	-	-
Washington	580	-	-	-	580	33,104	-	33,104	-	-	580	-
West Virginia	-	-	-	-	2,930	3,475	-	-	2,973	1,761	-	-
Wyoming	-	-	-	-	-	-	-	-	-	-	-	9,420
Totals	208,447	8,811	76,199	124,040	95,019	102,784	38,283	102,853	114,858	21,865	36,397	50,340
Combined Totals	217,258		200,239		197,803		141,136		136,723		86,737	
Percent of Impaired waters	8.25		7.5%		7.4%		5.3%		5.1%		3.3%	

Source: National Water Quality Inventory, 1988, Report to Congress, U.S. Environmental Protection Agency, Washington, D.C., April 1990, p. 20, from 1988 State Section 305(b) reports. *Notes:* 1. These States did not specify the degree of impact (i.e., Major or Moderate/Minor); lake acres were placed in the "Major" column for national reporting purposes. - Zero or not reported.

★ 20 ★

Impaired Lakes by Source of Pollution - Part I

Data shown are in areas of lake surface.

State	Total Impaired Waters	Agriculture		Hydro/ Habitat Modification		Storm Sewers/ Runoff		Land Disposal	
		Major	Mod/Min	Major	Mod/Min	Major	Mod/Min	Major	Mod/Min
Alabama[1]	86,080	-	-	-	-	15,930	-	-	-
California	508,152	107,922	-	-	-	-	-	-	-
Colorado	1,672	-	148	-	-	-	1,000	325	-
District of Columbia	136	-	-	-	-	-	27	-	-
Florida[1]	637,440	616,320	-	437,760	-	631,680	-	582,400	-
Illinois	160,641	115,534	43,791	1,329	40,388	-	-	6,056	19,629
Indiana	179	12	85	40	-	35	67	-	-
Iowa	53,448	48,264	3,774	229	-	4,822	12,529	7	-
Kansas	57,256	10	34,769	3	5,734	-	16	-	-
Maryland	2,610	1,162	-	-	-	415	-	-	-
Mississippi	18,260	2,979	14,081	-	-	-	-	-	-

[Continued]

★ 20 ★

Impaired Lakes by Source of Pollution - Part I
[Continued]

State	Total Impaired Waters	Agriculture		Hydro/ Habitat Modification		Storm Sewers/ Runoff		Land Disposal	
		Major	Mod/Min	Major	Mod/Min	Major	Mod/Min	Major	Mod/Min
Missouri	2,311	-	-	-	1,730	-	561	-	-
Montana	317,996	12,600	18,322	-	284,000	-	-	150	5,420
New Hampshire	19,146	20	-	-	-	34	68	-	-
New Mexico	47,308	-	47,058	-	60	-	-	-	-
New York	295,332	28,205	93,991	33,877	-	1,314	3,720	2,844	48,829
North Carolina[1]	11,897	2,056	-	-	. -	2,055	-	1,900	-
North Dakota	48,125	37,729	6,677	665	6,453	22	5,951	-	-
Oregon[1]	130,625	98,145	-	-	-	10,866	-	13,129	-
Puerto Rico	7,345	948	870	-	-	1,505	782	25	378
Rhode Island	1,401	-	103	-	50	111	566	-	103
South Carolina[1]	1,165	-	-	-	-	25	-	-	-
South Dakota	94,720	83,628	1,516	1,209	7,868	99	-	12,731	9,272
Tennessee	86,648	15,520	45,813	9,221	31,559	33	41,481	-	7,800
Virginia	13,737	-	7,925	-	-	-	7,856	-	-
Washington	33,684	-	33,104	580	-	580	-	-	-
West Virginia	19,171	76	5,047	-	-	12	27	-	-
Wyoming	30,404	28,513	7,665	-	27,005	-	25	-	-
Totals	2,686,889	1,199,643	364,739	484,913	404,847	669,538	74,676	619,567	91,431
Combined Totals		1,564,382		889,760		744,214		710,998	
Percent of Impaired Waters		58.2		33.1		27.7		26.5	

Source: National Water Quality Inventory, 1988, Report to Congress, U.S. Environmental Protection Agency, Washington, D.C., April 1990, p. 24, from 1988 State Section 305(b) reports. *Notes:* 1. These States did not specify the degree of impact (i.e., Major or Moderate/Minor); lake acres were placed in the "Major" column for national reporting purposes.

★ 21 ★

Impaired Lakes by Source of Pollution - Part II
Data are shown in acres of lake surface.

State	Municipal		Industrial		Resource Extraction		Construction		Silviculture		Combined Sewers	
	Major	Mod/Min	Major	Mod/Min	Major	Mod/Min	Major	Mod/Min	Major	Mod/Min	Major	Mod/Min
Alabama[1]	-	-	68,300	-	1,850	-	-	-	-	-	-	-
California	160	-	-	-	31,082	-	-	-	-	-	-	-
Colorado	-	500	160	-	105	410	-	125	43	-	-	-
District of Columbia	-	-	-	-	-	-	-	-	-	-	-	-
Florida	252,160	-	62,720	-	32,000	-	42,240	-	-	-	-	-
Illinois	6,046	62,403	2,631	10,972	43	22,831	1,352	14,273	-	-	-	-
Indiana	99	-	15	-	30	-	-	-	-	-	45	12
Iowa	-	10,400	-	-	-	-	12	-	-	-	-	-
Kansas	-	-	-	-	190	-	-	-	-	-	-	-
Maryland	35	360	-	-	-	-	-	-	-	-	-	-
Mississippi	-	-	-	-	-	1,200	-	-	-	-	-	-
Missouri	-	-	-	-	-	20	-	-	-	-	-	-
Montana	-	-	-	-	-	2,100	-	-	-	3,200	-	-
New Hampshire	-	142	-	15	-	-	-	-	-	-	-	-
New Mexico	-	-	-	-	-	-	-	590	-	879	-	-
New York	15,468	8,203	-	7,800	-	-	-	35	-	3,180	2,944	-
North Carolina[1]	1,900	-	9,680	-	-	-	2,042	-	450	-	-	-
North Dakota	-	9,299	-	-	-	172	-	-	-	2,986	-	-
Oregon[1]	485	-	895	-	-	-	-	-	-	2,755	-	-
Puerto Rico	62	-	-	112	-	-	-	-	-	-	-	-
Rhode Island	-	-	-	-	-	-	-	-	-	-	-	-

[Continued]

★ 21 ★

Impaired Lakes by Source of Pollution - Part II
[Continued]

State	Municipal		Industrial		Resource Extraction		Construction		Silviculture		Combined Sewers	
	Major	Mod/Min	Major	Mod/Min	Major	Mod/Min	Major	Mod/Min	Major	Mod/Min	Major	Mod/Min
South Carolina[1]	-	-	250	-	-	-	-	-	-	-	-	-
South Dakota	1,870	-	-	-	-	-	-	-	162	463	-	-
Tennessee	14,600	9,556	-	40,391	1,993		49	15,500	-	4,550	-	4,400
Virginia	-	102	-	137	-	-	-	-	-	130	-	-
Washington	-	-	580	-	-	-	-	-	-	-	580	-
West Virginia	12	2,684	2,930	3	3,111	6,320	114	41	137	6,099	-	-
Wyoming	-	8,300	-	-	-	9,520	-	11,506	-	-	-	-
Totals	292,897	111,949	148,161	59,430	70,404	42,573	45,809	42,070	3,547	21,487	3,569	4,412
Combined Totals		404,846		207,591		112,977		87,879		25,034		7,981
Percent of Impaired Waters		15.1		7.7		4.2		3.3		0.9		0.3

Source: National Water Quality Inventory, 1988, Report to Congress, U.S. Environmental Protection Agency, Washington, D.C., April 1990, p. 24, from 1988 State Section 305(b) reports *Notes:* 1. These States did not specify the degree of impact (i.e., Major or Moderate/Minor); lake acres were placed in the "Major" column for national reporting purposes.

★ 22 ★

Nation's Lakes - Trophic Status

Data show number of lakes by trophic status. 'Oligotrophic' means deficient in plant nutrients; 'mesotrophic' means that a moderate amount of dissolved nutrients is present; 'eutrophic' indicates well-nourished and hypereutrophic excess of nutrients; 'dystrophic' indicates faulty nutritional status.

State	Lakes Assessed	Oligotrophic	Mesotrophic	Eutrophic	Hyper-eutrophic	Dystrophic	Unknown
Alabama	34	4	15	11	0	0	4
Arkansas	71	0	59	4	0	0	8
California	459	114	39	12	2	0	292
Colorado	82	9	35	38	0	0	0
Connecticut	160	34	78	17	0	0	31
Delaware	31	0	0	31	0	0	0
District of Columbia	2	0	1	0	0	0	1
Florida	91	57	19	13	0	0	2
Idaho	554	0	55	499	0	0	0
Illinois	412	2	25	239	146	0	0
Indiana	404	75	144	67	0	118	0
Iowa	114	0	0	114	0	0	0
Kansas	193	0	68	125	0	0	0
Kentucky	92	14	27	51	0	0	0
Louisiana	101	0	0	101	0	0	0
Maryland	59	2	13	44	0	0	0
Massachusetts	478	133	289	56	0	0	0
Michigan	682	98	367	217	0	0	0
Minnesota	1,409	167	439	536	267	0	0
Mississippi	127	0	0	33	0	0	94
Montana	1,880	452	428	371	0	127	502
Nebraska	23	0	1	12	10	0	0
Nevada	9	1	4	4	0	0	0

[Continued]

★ 22 ★

Nation's Lakes - Trophic Status
[Continued]

State	Lakes Assessed	Oligotrophic	Mesotrophic	Eutrophic	Hyper-eutrophic	Dystrophic	Unknown
New Hampshire	415	161	172	82	0	0	0
New York	3,340	85	132	84	0	0	3,039
North Carolina	144	11	21	25	9	8	70
North Dakota	216	0	0	216	0	0	0
Oklahoma	74	5	49	8	12	0	0
Oregon	204	46	78	69	11	0	0
Pennsylvania	37	1	29	7	0	0	0
Puerto Rico	17	0	3	14	0	0	0
Rhode Island	54	4	41	9	0	0	0
South Carolina	40	0	0	39	1	0	0
Tennessee	119	21	33	55	10	0	0
Utah	127	33	44	50	0	0	0
Vermont	719	19	72	28	0	11	589
Virginia	248	20	49	120	0	1	58
Washington	140	58	24	45	0	0	13
Wisconsin	2,153	605	746	802	0	0	0
Totals	15,514	2,231	3,599	4,248	468	265	4,703

Source: National Water Quality Inventory, 1988, Report to Congress, U.S. Environmental Protection Agency, Washington, D.C., April 1990, p. 29. *Notes:* 1. States not listed in the table either did not report the information or reported the information in a way that was inconsistent with the format.

Land

★ 23 ★

Areas of Irrigated Land in the United States

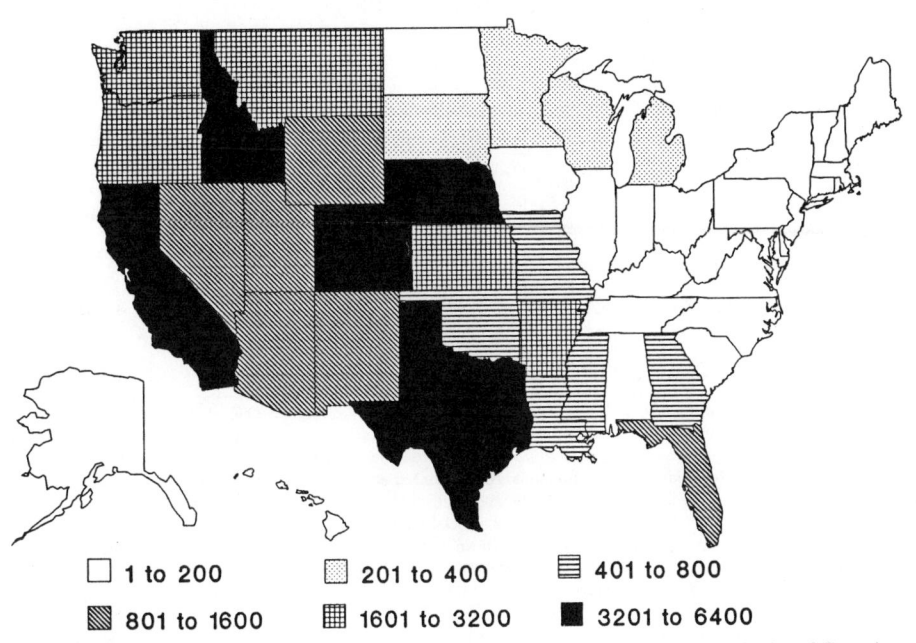

☐ 1 to 200	▦ 201 to 400	▤ 401 to 800
▩ 801 to 1600	▦ 1601 to 3200	■ 3201 to 6400

Source: Beneath the Bottom Line: Agricultural Approaches to Reduce Agricultural Contamination of Groundwater,
U.S. Congress, Office of Technology Assessment, OTA-F-418, Washington, D.C., November 1990., p. 130, from
U.S. Department of Agriculture, *Agricultural Statistics* (Washington, D.C.: U.S. Government Printing Office, 1986),
p. 374, *In*: Threadgill, E.D., 1989.

★ 24 ★

Forest Land and Area by Region

Data are in thousands of acres as of January 1, 1987.

Region	Total forest land[1]	Timberland[2]							
		All owner-ships	Federal			State, county and munici-pal[3]	Private		
			Total	National	Other		Total	Forest industry	Farmer and other private
Northeast	85,251	80,102	2,936	2,212	724	6,834	70,332	12,590	57,742
North Central	80,221	74,584	7,990	7,253	737	13,227	53,367	4,361	49,006
Great Plains	4,229	3,529	993	943	50	232	2,304	21	2,283
North	169,701	158,215	11,919	10,408	1,511	20,293	126,003	16,972	109,031
Southeast	87,744	84,594	6,983	4,871	2,112	1,789	75,822	16,793	59,029

[Continued]

★ 24 ★

Forest Land and Area by Region

[Continued]

Region	Total forest land[1]	Timberland[2]							
		All owner-ships	Federal			State, county and munici-pal[3]	Private		
			Total	National	Other		Total	Forest industry	Farmer and other private
South Central	115,741	110,790	8,917	6,896	2,021	1,994	99,879	21,438	78,441
South	203,485	195,384	15,900	11,767	4,133	3,783	175,701	38,231	137,470
Pacific Northwest[4]	178,958	54,697	22,424	19,487	2,937	9,534	22,739	9,702	13,037
Pacific Southwest[5]	41,129	17,412	9,051	8,742	309	544	7,817	2,757	5,060
Rocky Mountains	138,104	57,611	37,709	34,819	2,890	5,196	14,706	2,943	11,763
West	358,191	129,720	69,184	63,048	6,136	15,274	45,262	15,402	29,860
All regions	731,377	483,319	97,003	85,223	11,780	39,350	346,966	70,605	276,361

Source: Agricultural Conservation and Forestry Statistics, 1989, U.S. Government Printing Office, Washington, D.C., 1989, p. 454, from Forest Service Data may not add to totals because of rounding. *Notes:* 1. Forest land is land at least 10 percent stocked by forest trees of any size, including land that formerly had such tree cover and that will be naturally or artificially regenerated. Forest land includes transition zones, such as areas between heavily forested and nonforested lands that are at least 10 percent stocked with forest trees and forest areas adjacent to urban and built-up lands. Also included are pinyon-juniper and chaparral areas in the West and afforested areas. The minimum area for classification of forest land is 1 acre. Roadside, streamside, and shelterbelt strips of timber must have a crown width at least 120 feet wide to qualify as forest land. Unimproved roads and trails, streams, and clearings in forest areas are classified as forest if less than 120 feet in width. 2. Timberland is forest land which is producing or is capable of producing crops of industrial wood and not withdrawn from timber utilization by statute or administrative regulation. Areas qualifying as timberland have the capacity of producing in excess of 20 cubic feet per acre per year of industrial wood in natural stands. Currently inaccessible and inoperable areas are included. 3. Includes Indian lands. 4. Includes Alaska. 5. Includes Hawaii.

★ 25 ★

Land Utilization in the U.S.

Data for 1987 are shown in thousands of acres.

State	Cropland			Grassland pasture[2]	Forest land[3]	Special use areas[4]	Other land	Total land area
	Used for crops[1]	Idle	Used only for pasture					
Alabama	2,370	977	1,456	1,935	21,659	1,376	2,718	32,491
Alaska	31	40	6	1,209	88,643	142,520	132,884	365,333
Arizona	1,056	351	140	41,504	17,257	9,849	2,488	72,645
Arkansas	6,698	1,552	1,938	2,950	16,896	1,368	1,928	33,330
California	8,689	1,460	1,338	21,833	36,441	14,769	15,501	100,031
Colorado	8,684	2,058	1,170	27,898	18,837	4,795	2,859	66,301
Connecticut	152	15	40	47	1,776	311	777	3,118
Delaware	493	46	10	12	388	113	175	1,237
District of Columbia	0	0	0	0	0	0	40	40
Florida	2,300	560	1,004	5,792	16,260	4,505	4,237	34,658
Georgia	3,747	1,539	1,145	1,895	23,402	1,625	3,803	37,156
Hawaii	162	141	41	1,082	1,318	806	562	4,112
Idaho	5,102	1,045	816	19,943	17,767	5,278	2,793	52,744
Illinois	20,167	4,009	1,021	1,668	4,030	1,881	2,837	35,613

[Continued]

★ 25 ★

Land Utilization in the U.S.
[Continued]

State	Cropland			Grassland pasture[2]	Forest land[3]	Special use areas[4]	Other land	Total land area
	Used for crops[1]	Idle	Used only for pasture					
Indiana	10,711	2,183	747	1,326	4,296	966	2,767	22,996
Iowa	20,656	5,041	2,284	1,882	1,460	1,564	2,931	35,818
Kansas	26,780	4,078	3,485	13,255	1,207	1,703	1,830	52,338
Kentucky	4,751	1,472	3,402	1,653	11,909	1,006	1,195	25,388
Louisiana	3,934	1,145	829	2,070	13,873	1,318	5,325	28,494
Maine	390	100	87	72	17,437	429	1,322	19,837
Maryland	1,427	198	189	215	2,462	654	1,151	6,296
Massachusetts	196	22	53	45	3,010	557	1,125	5,008
Michigan	6,403	1,459	519	1,731	17,597	2,488	6,254	36,451
Minnesota	17,510	4,790	1,122	1,661	13,572	7,565	4,691	50,911
Mississippi	4,941	1,607	1,244	2,287	16,674	880	2,596	30,229
Missouri	12,323	2,725	5,396	6,465	12,192	1,743	3,281	44,125
Montana	15,321	1,651	1,292	47,139	18,709	6,145	2,791	93,048
Nebraska	18,000	3,660	2,565	20,435	699	1,514	2,179	49,052
Nevada	583	60	209	45,735	7,383	7,517	8,845	70,332
New Hampshire	107	9	31	50	4,803	263	493	5,756
New Jersey	499	80	73	35	1,914	712	1,466	4,779
New Mexico	1,217	665	557	51,818	17,127	3,647	2,623	77,654
New York	3,802	630	822	1,005	16,226	3,898	3,938	30,321
North Carolina	4,070	1,148	783	1,210	18,401	2,118	3,530	31,260
North Dakota	25,464	2,441	1,522	11,187	460	1,601	1,677	44,352
Ohio	9,689	1,742	942	1,502	7,141	1,184	4,043	26,243
Oklahoma	9,565	1,876	4,433	17,754	6,970	1,330	2,011	43,939
Oregon	3,695	831	858	22,913	26,278	3,568	3,415	61,558
Pennsylvania	4,240	509	803	1,093	16,189	2,409	3,485	28,728
Rhode Island	21	3	5	3	391	59	193	675
South Carolina	1,942	786	464	422	12,179	1,124	2,413	19,330
South Dakota	17,022	2,207	2,389	22,261	1,552	1,521	1,657	48,609
Tennessee	4,278	1,043	2,472	1,446	12,863	2,154	2,083	26,339
Texas	19,548	6,734	10,181	104,656	13,536	4,681	8,355	167,691
Utah	1,278	298	528	23,080	14,793	5,451	7,099	52,527
Vermont	438	29	188	200	4,424	422	234	5,935
Virginia	2,671	493	1,449	1,773	15,497	1,449	2,078	25,410
Washington	6,675	1,111	579	7,235	17,857	6,637	2,473	42,567
West Virginia	678	99	642	476	11,799	683	1,059	15,436
Wisconsin	8,251	1,177	1,162	2,079	15,058	2,150	4,956	34,833

[Continued]

★ 25 ★

Land Utilization in the U.S.
[Continued]

State	Cropland			Grassland pasture[2]	Forest land[3]	Special use areas[4]	Other land	Total land area
	Used for crops[1]	Idle	Used only for pasture					
Wyoming	2,150	248	550	45,146	5,552	6,293	2,134	62,073
United States	330,877	68,143	64,981	591,083	648,164	278,599	283,300	2,265,147

Source: Agricultural Conservation and Forestry Statistics, 1989, U.S. Government Printing Office, Washington, D.C., 1989, p. 359 Economic Research Service. Estimates based on reports and records of the U.S. Department of Agriculture and Commerce, and public land administering and conservation agencies. Estimates developed for years coinciding with a Census of Agriculture. *Notes:* 1. Cropland harvested, crop failure, and cultivated summer fallow. 2. Grassland and other nonforest pasture and range. 3. Excludes reserved and other forest land duplicated in parks and other special uses of land. Includes forested grazing land. 4. Includes rural transportation areas, Federal and State areas used primarily for recreation and wildlife purposes, military areas, farmsteads, and farm roads and lanes.

★ 26 ★

Organic Soil Annual Use
The values are estimated based on residential and commercial surveys conducted during July/August 1988.

Product	Market Segment (cu yd./yr.)				
	Resi-dential[1]	Nursery[2]	Landscape[3]	Public Agencies[2]	Total[3]
Yard debris compost	440,000-532,000	3,000- 4,000	31,000-38,000	8,200-10,000	482,000-584,000
Sewage sludge compost	Neg[4]	24,000-29,000	40,000-48,000	10,200-12,300	74,000-89,000
Manure/manure products	232,000-281,000	92,000-111,000	7,000-9,000	200	331,000-401,000
Bark/barkdust	881,000-1,066,000	642,000-777,000	240,000-290,000	4,700-5,700	1,768,000-2,139,000
Sawdust/shavings	23,000-28,000	299,000-362,000	35,000-43,000	100	357,000-433,000
Mushroom compost	45,000-55,000	26,000-32,000	5,000-7,000	200	76,000-94,000
Peat moss	22,000-26,000	48,000-58,000	5,000-6,000	Neg[4]	75,000-90,000
Other	27,000-33,000	15,000-18,000	5,000-6,000	4,800-5,900	52,000-63,000
Totals	1,670,000-2,021,000	1,149,000-1,391,000	368,000-447,000	28,400-34,400	3,215,000-3,893,000

Source: BioCycle, May 1989, p. 32. Ranges reflect + or - 10% of estimated values. *Notes:* 1. Estimated for three counties in Metropolitan Service District: Clackamas, Multnomah, and Washington (Oregon) and includes homemade and commercially produced yard debris compost and yard debris mulch. 2. Estimated for seven-county study area: Clackamas, Multnomah, Washington, Marion, Yamhill and Columbia (Oregon) and Clark (Washington). 3. Rounded to nearest 1,000 cu yd./yr. 4. Neg. Negligible quantities reported.

★ 27 ★

Pollution Levels in Selected National Parks

Park	Shenandoah - 11.1
Great Smoky Mountains - 10.4	
Acadia - 4.9	

Shenandoah - 11.1
Great Smoky Mountains - 10.4
Acadia - 4.9
Mount Rainier - 2.8
Yellowstone - 1.7
Grand Canyon (rim) - 1.4
Mesa Verde - 1.4
Yosemite - 0.9
Crater Lake - 0.8
U.S. Health Standard - 0.2

Chart shows data from column 1.

Sulfate and ozone concentrations. In micrograms per cubic meter.

Park	Sulfates[1]	Ozone[2]
Grand Canyon (rim)	1.4	NA
Shenandoah	11.1	291
Acadia	4.9	345
Yellowstone	1.7	245
Yosemite	0.9	149
Mesa Verde	1.4	NA
Crater Lake	0.8	NA
Great Smoky Mountains	10.4	228
Mount Rainier	2.8	97
U.S. Health Standard	0.2[3]	235[4]

Source: The Wall Street Journal, March 8, 1991, p. B1, from the National Park Service *Notes:* 1. 1989 summer average concentration. 2. 1988 highest hourly concentration. 3. Natural background level established for Eastern U.S. 4. National ambient air quality standard. NA = Not available.

★ 28 ★

Soil Conservation Districts

The total area and number of farms are cumulative through September 30, 1990.

State or Territory	Date district law became effective	Districts organized[1] (number)	Approximate area and number of farms within organized districts	
			Total area (1,000 acres)	Farms and ranches (thousands)
Alabama	Mar. 18, 1939	67	32,454	115,917
Alaska	Mar. 25, 1947	10	375,304	1,469
Arizona	June 16, 1941	38	75,989	2,496
Arkansas	July 1, 1937	76	33,176	51,871
California	June 26, 1938	118	75,202	83,000
Colorado	May 6, 1937	80	61,257	30,693
Connecticut	July 18, 1945	8	3,135	3,605
Delaware	Apr. 2, 1943	3	1,309	2,966
District of Columbia	July 12, 1982	1	44	0
Florida	June 10, 1937	63	32,686	60,193
Georgia	Mar. 23, 1937	40	37,665	78,353
Hawaii	May 19,1947	15	4,035	4,944
Idaho	Mar. 9, 1939	51	52,416	32,103
Illinois	July 9, 1937	98	28,502	89,070
Indiana	Mar. 11, 1937	92	23,168	70,506
Iowa	July 4, 1939	100	36,016	107,000
Kansas	Apr. 10, 1937	105	51,873	133,197
Kentucky	June 11, 1940	121	25,377	102,000
Louisiana	July 27, 1938	43	26,414	27,766
Maine	Mar. 25, 1941	16	18,735	17,421
Maryland	June 1, 1937	24	6,636	14,776
Massachusetts	June 28, 1945	16	5,065	6,558
Michigan	July 23, 1937	83	36,034	58,742
Minnesota	Apr. 26, 1937	90	50,921	123,306
Mississippi	Apr. 4, 1938	82	30,236	126,481
Missouri	July 23, 1943	112	41,755	145,918
Montana	Feb. 28, 1939	59	88,703	26,285
Nebraska	May 18, 1937	23	47,795	59,504
Nevada	Mar. 30, 1937	29	50,339	3,217
New Hampshire	May 10, 1945	10	5,955	2,515
New Jersey	July 1, 1937	16	4,779	8,277
New Mexico	Mar. 17, 1937	47	75,295	27,135
New York	July 20, 1940	57	30,488	40,180
North Carolina	Mar. 22, 1937	100	33,709	73,857
North Dakota	Mar. 16, 1937	60	42,958	42,512
Ohio	June 5, 1941	88	26,260	87,134
Oklahoma	Apr. 15, 1937	89	44,000	128,209
Oregon	Apr. 7, 1939	45	58,730	31,362
Pennsylvania	July 2, 1937	66	28,503	52,374
Rhode Island	Apr. 26, 1943	3	675	614
South Carolina	Apr. 17, 1937	47	19,912	26,000

[Continued]

★ 28 ★

Soil Conservation Districts
[Continued]

State or Territory	Date district law became effective	Districts organized[1] (number)	Approximate area and number of farms within organized districts	
			Total area (1,000 acres)	Farms and ranches (thousands)
South Dakota	July 1, 1937	69	49,355	36,376
Tennessee	Mar. 10, 1939	95	25,353	163,477
Texas	Apr. 24, 1939	210	147,379	239,816
Utah	Mar. 23, 1937	38	49,857	15,644
Vermont	Apr. 18, 1939	14	6,186	5,877
Virginia	Apr. 1, 1938	45	25,346	52,195
Washington	Mar. 17, 1939	48	38,350	42,111
West Virginia	June 12, 1939	14	14,439	17,237
Wisconsin	July 1, 1937	72	35,938	82,199
Wyoming	May 22, 1941	34	62,094	10,462
United States	-	2,930	2,177,803	2,764,920
Virgin Islands	June 1946	18	2,311	31,004
PAC[2]	May 31, 1984	6	271	1,000
Puerto Rico	July 1, 1946	1	85	1

Source: Agricultural Conservation and Forestry Statistics, 1989, U.S. Government Printing Office, Washington, D.C., 1989, p. 448, from Soil Conservation Service *Notes:* 1. For specific procedure on organization of soil conservation districts, reference should be made to each of the respective State soil conservation district's laws. 2. Guam and Northern Marianas.

★ 29 ★

Soil Conservation Districts by Year

The numbers represent approximate total area and land in farms in the United States and its territories, 1975-90.

Year	Number districts organized[2]		Total area in districts	
	Net increase for the year	Cumulative total	New districts and additions (1,000 acres)	Cumulative total (1,000 acres)
1975	-5	2,942	1,968	2,213,735
1976	-2	2,940	2,450	2,216,185
1977	-3	2,937	1,578	2,217,763
1978	-	2,937	-2,735	2,215,028
1979	-	2,937	-	2,215,028
1980	-5	2,932	-3,602	2,211,426
1981	5	2,932	7,649	2,219,075
1982	1	2,938	44	2,219,119

[Continued]

★ 29 ★

Soil Conservation Districts by Year
[Continued]

Year	Number districts organized[2]		Total area in districts	
	Net increase for the year	Cumulative total	New districts and additions (1,000 acres)	Cumulative total (1,000 acres)
1983	-	2,939	-	2,219,119
1984	2	2,941	135	2,219,254
1985	1	2,940	100	2,219,154
1986	7	2,947	-24,839	2,194,315
1987	-6	2,941	3,219	2,197,534
1988	15	2,956	-13,837	2,183,697
1989	-	2,956	-	2,183,697
1990	-1	2,955	-3,227	2,180,470

Source: Agricultural Conservation and Forestry Statistics, 1989, U.S. Government Printing Office, Washington, D.C., 1989, p. 447, from Soil Conservation Service. *Notes:* 1. Fiscal years July 1 to June 30 to 1976; Oct. 1 through September 30 through 1990. 2. Totals at the end of each year are net, including corrections and adjustments made during the year.

★ 30 ★

Soil Conservation Districts in the U.S.
Data are cumulative through September 30, 1988.

State or territory	Date district law became effective	Districts organized[1] (number)	Approximate area and number of farms within organized districts	
			Total area (1,000 acres)	Farms[2] (thousands)
Alabama	Mar. 18, 1939	67	32,454	116
Alaska	Mar. 25, 1947	10	375,304	1
Arizona	June 16, 1941	38	75,989	2
Arkansas	July 1, 1937	76	33,176	82
California	June 26,1938	118	75,202	83
Colorado	May 6, 1937	80	61,257	31
Connecticut	July 18, 1945	8	3,135	4
Delaware	Apr. 2, 1943	3	1,309	3
District of Columbia	July 12, 1982	1	44	0
Florida	June 10, 1937	63	31,864	61
Georgia	Mar. 23, 1937	40	37,665	78
Hawaii	May 19, 1947	15	4,035	5
Idaho	Mar. 9, 1939	51	51,178	26
Illinois	July 9, 1937	98	28,502	89
Indiana	Mar. 11, 1937	92	23,168	71
Iowa	July 4, 1939	99	35,106	106
Kansas	Apr. 10, 1937	105	51,873	133
Kentucky	June 11, 1940	121	25,377	102

[Continued]

★ 30 ★

Soil Conservation Districts in the U.S.
[Continued]

State or territory	Date district law became effective	Districts organized[1] (number)	Approximate area and number of farms within organized districts	
			Total area (1,000 acres)	Farms[2] (thousands)
Louisiana	July 27, 1938	43	26,414	28
Maine	Mar. 25, 1941	16	15,071	17
Maryland	June 1, 1937	24	6,636	15
Massachusetts	June 28, 1945	16	5,065	5
Michigan	July 23, 1937	83	36,034	59
Minnesota	Apr. 26, 1937	90	50,745	121
Mississippi	Apr. 4, 1938	82	30,521	54
Missouri	July 23, 1943	112	41,755	146
Montana	Feb. 28, 1939	63	88,703	26
Nebraska	May 18, 1937	23	47,795	60
Nevada	Mar. 30, 1937	29	50,339	3
New Hampshire	May 10, 1945	10	5,955	3
New Jersey	July 1, 1937	16	4,779	8
New Mexico	Mar. 17, 1937	47	72,604	27
New York	July 20,1940	57	30,488	40
North Carolina	Mar. 22, 1937	100	33,709	74
North Dakota	Mar. 16, 1937	61	43,322	43
Ohio	June 5, 1941	88	26,260	87
Oklahoma	Apr. 15, 1937	89	44,000	128
Oregon	Apr. 7, 1939	45	60,603	31
Pennsylvania	July 2, 1937	66	28,503	52
Rhode Island	Apr. 26, 1943	3	675	1
South Carolina	Apr. 17, 1937	46	19,912	26
South Dakota	July 1, 1937	69	45,026	42
Tennessee	Mar. 10, 1939	95	25,353	165
Texas	Apr. 24, 1939	208	169,890	174
Utah	Mar. 23, 1937	38	43,409	10
Vermont	Apr. 18, 1939	14	6,150	6
Virginia	Apr. 1, 1938	45	25,410	52
Washington	Mar. 17, 1939	48	37,073	34
West Virginia	June 12, 1939	14	14,439	17
Wisconsin	July 1, 1937	72	35,938	82
Wyoming	May 22, 1941	35	62,094	10
U.S.	-	2,932	2,181,308	2,639
Puerto Rico	July 1, 1946	17	2,033	34
Virgin Islands	June 1946	1	85	1

[Continued]

★ 30 ★

Soil Conservation Districts in the U.S.
[Continued]

State or territory	Date district law became effective	Districts organized[1] (number)	Approximate area and number of farms within organized districts	
			Total area (1,000 acres)	Farms[2] (thousands)
Guam and Northern Marianas	May 31, 1984	6	271	1
Total		2,956	2,183,697	2,675

Source: Agricultural Conservation and Forestry Statistics, 1989, U.S. Government Printing Office, Washington, D.C., 1989, U.S. Government Printing Office, Washington, D.C., 1989, p. 471, from the Soil Conservation Service. *Notes:* 1. For specific procedure on organization of soil conservation districts, reference should be made to each of the respective State soil conservation district's laws. 2. Includes ranches.

★ 31 ★

Soil Conservation - Area Mapping

Total area mapped for conservation planning and other uses under all programs, by states and territories, year ending September 30, 1989, and cumulative through September 30, 1989.

State or Territory	Progressive Soil Survey Program[1]		
	Acres mapped	Work during year ending Sept. 30, 1989 (acres updated)	Total acres to date
Alabama	666,741	44,145	26,764,671
Alaska	64,644	442,900	38,027,049
Arizona	1,517,028	0	42,469,298
Arkansas	166,998	278,290	32,393,404
California	888,795	345,644	71,274,352
Colorado	1,226,612	221,683	58,580,009
Connecticut	0	0	3,211,700
Delaware	0	135,000	1,308,500
Florida	1,069,000	131,000	30,093,905
Georgia	325,101	202,117	33,347,022
Hawaii	0	0	4,582,436
Idaho	537,800	0	32,291,095
Illinois	1,943,658	32,148	33,861,905
Indiana	0	70,505	23,158,600
Iowa	118,889	297,707	36,016,200
Kansas	0	231,575	52,657,500
Kentucky	590,990	128,502	23,187,832
Louisiana	1,131,908	196,862	26,426,658
Maine	295,583	94,035	14,545,336

[Continued]

★ 31 ★

Soil Conservation - Area Mapping
[Continued]

State or Territory	Progressive Soil Survey Program[1]		
	Acres mapped	Work during year ending Sept. 30, 1989 (acres updated)	Total acres to date
Maryland	0	109,800	6,694,500
Massachusetts	31,665	27,183	5,301,800
Michigan	1,076,566	240	28,303,038
Minnesota	1,589,292	474,725	38,316,844
Mississippi	309,465	280,569	27,007,553
Missouri	2,218,409	81,507	32,718,344
Montana	5,440,458	3,350	68,812,479
Nebraska	492,170	117,920	46,577,475
Nevada	1,519,091	139,960	51,183,864
New Hampshire	33,000	43,000	5,063,039
New Jersey	0	0	4,703,100
New Mexico	303,166	176,856	67,495,212
New York	979,984	243,446	26,455,838
North Carolina	1,033,299	41,346	26,991,917
North Dakota	2,937,466	183,736	40,131,667
Ohio	423,000	252,130	26,166,905
Oklahoma	0	208,520	44,771,700
Oregon	1,193,843	15,000	31,961,261
Pennsylvania	0	409,416	28,997,200
Rhode Island	0	0	775,900
South Carolina	126,492	109,346	19,895,730
South Dakota	740,000	0	47,422,074
Tennessee	419,496	226,067	23,562,189
Texas	1,124,131	1,258,805	155,332,078
Utah	812,025	45,000	44,842,793
Vermont	161,352	3,611	4,462,482
Virginia	1,010,000	0	18,436,181
Washington	516,142	263,175	34,071,818
West Virginia	362,615	73,300	13,008,205
Wisconsin	477,668	112,380	30,343,836
Wyoming	379,107	185,414	37,570,537
Caribbean[2]	0	0	2,333,800
Total	36,253,649	8,046,915	1,623,908,831

Source: Agricultural Conservation and Forestry Statistics, 1989, U.S. Government Printing Office, Washington, D.C., 1989, p. 449, from Soil Conservation Service. *Notes:* 1. The National Cooperative Soil Survey of the Soil Conservation Service and cooperating agencies is designed to locate, classify, describe, and show on maps the different kinds of soil and make multiple-use interpretations of each kind of soil for town-and-country planning and for other purposes. 2. Puerto Rico and Virgin Islands.

Oceans

★ 32 ★

Impaired Ocean Coastal Miles by Cause of Pollution - Part I

State	Total Impaired Waters	Pathogens		Priority Organics		Nutrients		Siltation		Unknown Toxicity	
		Major	Mod/Min	Major	Mod/Min	Major	Mod/Min	Major	Mod/Min	Major	Mod/Min
Mississippi	41	-	41	-	-	-	-	-	-	-	-
New York	70	12	-	-	70	-	-	-	.-	-	-
Puerto Rico	184	10	14	-	-	10	27	12	22	7	25
Totals	295	22	55	0	70	10	27	12	22	7	25
Combined Totals			77		70		37		34		32

Source: National Water Quality Inventory, 1988, Report to Congress, U.S. Environmental Protection Agency, Washington, D.C., April 1990, p. 72, from 1988 State Section 305(b) reports. The state of Washington reports no impaired miles. *Note:* - Zero or not reported.

★ 33 ★

Impaired Ocean Coastal Miles by Cause of Pollution - Part II

State	Total Impaired Waters	Other Habitat Mod		Metals		Oil & Grease		Organic Enrichment		pH		Thermal Mod	
		Major	Mod/Min	Major	Mod/Min	Major	Mod/Min	Major	Mod/Min	Major	Mod/Min	Major	Mod/Min
Mississippi	41	-	-	-	-	-	-	-	-	-	-	-	-
New York	70	-	-	-	-	-	-	-	-	-	-	-	-
Puerto Rico	184	17	11	2	8	6	1	3	3	1	2	-	1
Totals	295	17	11	2	8	6	1	3	3	1	2	0	1
Combined Totals			28		10		7		6		3		1

Source: National Water Quality Inventory, 1988, Report to Congress, U.S. Environmental Protection Agency, Washington, D.C., April 1990, p. 72, from 1988 State Section 305(b) reports. The state of Washington reports no impaired miles. *Note:* - Zero or not reported.

★ 34 ★

Impaired Ocean Coastal Miles by Source of Pollution - Part I

State	Total Impaired Waters	Land Disposal		Storm Sewers/Runoff		Municipal		Industrial	
		Major	Mod/Min	Major	Mod/Min	Major	Mod/Min	Major	Mod/Min
Mississippi	41	-	41	-	41	-	-	-	-
New York	70	-	-	-		-	12	-	-
Puerto Rico	184	2	43	5	14	12	10	16	2
Totals	295	2	84	5	55	12	22	16	2
Combined Totals			86		60		34		18

Source: National Water Quality Inventory, 1988, Report to Congress, U.S. Environmental Protection Agency, Washington, D.C., April 1990, p. 72, from 1988 State Section 305(b) reports. The state of Washington reports no impaired miles. *Note:* - Zero or not reported.

★ 35 ★

Impaired Ocean Coastal Miles by Source of Pollution - Part II

State	Total Impaired Waters	Combined Sewers		Hydro/Habitat Modification		Silviculture		Construction		Resource Extract	
		Major	Mod/Min	Major	Mod/Min	Major	Mod/Min	Major	Mod/Min	Major	Mod/Min
Mississippi	41	-	-	-	-	-	-	-	-	-	-
New York	70	12	-	-	-	-	-	-	-	-	-
Puerto Rico	184	-	-	-	6	-	-	-	-	-	-
Totals	295	12	-	0	6	0	0	0	0	0	0
Combined Totals			12		6		0		0		0

Source: National Water Quality Inventory, 1988, Report to Congress, U.S. Environmental Protection Agency, Washington, D.C., April 1990, p. 72, from 1988 State Section 305(b) reports. The state of Washington reports no impaired miles. *Note:* - Zero or not reported.

Outer Space

★ 36 ★

Debris in Space

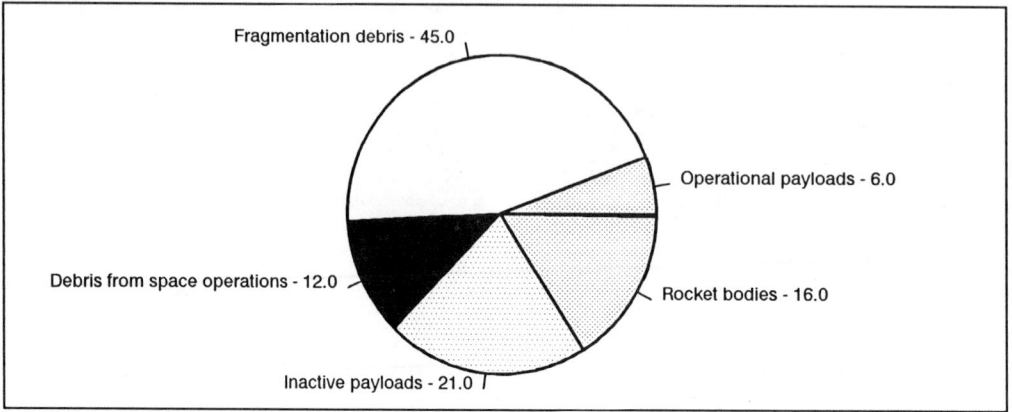

The figures refer to on-orbit population as of December 8, 1989.

Type	Percent
Fragmentation debris	45.0
Inactive payloads	21.0
Rocket bodies	16.0
Debris from space operations	12.0
Operational payloads	6.0

Source: Orbiting Space Debris: A Space Environmental Problem - Background Paper, U.S. Congress, Office of Technology Assessment, OTA-BP-ISC-72, September 1990, p. 2, from Nicholas L. Johnson and David J. Nauer, *History of On-Orbit Satellite Fragmentations, 4th ed.* (Colorado Springs: Teledyne Brown Engineering, January 1990), NASA 9-18209.

★ 37 ★

Objects in Space by Nationality of Origin

Distribution by country of origination of orbiting objects catalogued by the Space Surveillance Network.

Source	Percent
U.S.S.R.	48.0
U.S.	45.0
Other	7.0

Source: Orbiting Space Debris: A Space Environmental Problem - Background Paper, U.S. Congress, Office of Technology Assessment, OTA-BP-ISC-72, September 1990, p. 39, from Darren S. McKnight, 1990.

Radiation

★ 38 ★

Radiation Levels in Air and Milk

Annual mean exposure in picocuries per liter. Data for 1989 are for the first six months of the calendar year.

Year	Krypton-85 in air	Strontium-90 in pasteur- ized milk	Cesium-137 in pasteur- ized milk
1960	[1]	8.6	18.0
1961	[1]	8.0	11.0
1962	7.5	13.4	44.0
1963	9.0	23.5	108.0
1964	9.5	23.8	109.0
1965	10.0	17.6	58.0
1966	11.0	13.3	29.0
1967	11.5	10.2	16.0
1968	12.5	8.9	11.0
1969	13.5	7.5	9.0
1970	15.4	7.3	8.0
1971	14.8	6.8	9.0
1972	14.9	5.6	6.0
1973	16.7	4.4	5.0
1974	17.0	4.7	8.0
1975	17.5	3.9	9.0
1976	16.5	3.5	7.0
1977	17.1	3.6	6.0
1978	[1]	3.8	7.3
1979	21.8	3.5	4.0
1980	[1]	2.8	6.8
1981	[1]	2.8	2.5
1982	26.4	2.8	4.1
1983	38.6	2.3	1.6
1984	[1]	2.1	2.1
1985	[1]	2.0	2.7
1986	[1]	1.9	5.5
1987	[1]	1.9	6.6
1988	[1]	1.6	4.0
1989	[1]	1.5	2.8

Source: Council on Environmental Quality, *20th Annual Report 1990*, Washington, D.C., p. 449, from U.S. Environmental Protection Agency, Office of Radiation Programs, EPA-520/5, Montgomery, AL. *Note:* 1. Not available.

Rivers

★ 39 ★

Flows of Largest U.S. Rivers

River	Location of of mouth	Length (miles)[1]	Average discharge at mouth (1,000 cubic ft. per second)	Drainage area (1,000 square miles)
Mississippi	Louisiana	2,340[2]	593[3]	1,150[4,5]
St. Lawrence	Canada	1,900	348	396[5]
Ohio	Illinois-Kentucky	1,310	281	203
Columbia	Oregon-Washington	1,240	265	258[5]
Yukon	Alaska	1,980	225	328[5]
Missouri	Missouri	2,540	76.2	529[5]
Tennessee	Kentucky	886	68	40.9
Mobile	Alabama	774	67.2	44.6
Kuskokwim	Alaska	724	67	48
Copper	Alaska	286	59	24.4
Atchafalaya[6]	Louisiana	1,420	58	95.1
Snake	Washington	1,040	56.9	108
Red	Louisiana	1,290	56	93.2
Stikine	Alaska	379	56	20[5]
Susitna	Alaska	313	51	20
Tanana	Alaska	659	41	44.5
Arkansas	Arkansas	1,460	41	161
Susquehanna	Maryland	447	38.2	27.2
Willamette	Oregon	309	37.4	11.4
Nushagak	Alaska	285	36	13.4
Alabama	Alabama	729	34.6	22.8
Wabash	Indiana-Illinois	512	31	32.9
White	Arkansas	722	30.5	27.8
Pend Oreille	Canada	531	30.4	26.3[5]
Alsek	Alaska	290	30	10.7[5]

Source: U.S. Department of Commerce, Bureau of the Census, *Statistical Abstract of the United States 1990 (110th ed.),* Superintendent of Documents, Washington, D.C., p. 200, from U.S. Geological Survey, Largest Rivers in the United States, in Discharge, Drainage Area, or Length, August 1987. *Notes:* 1. From source to mouth. 2. The length from the source of the Missouri River to the Mississippi River and thence to the Gulf of Mexico is about 3,710 miles. 3. Includes about 167,000 cubic ft. diverted from the Mississippi into the Atchafalaya River but excludes the flow of the Red River. 4. Excludes the drainage areas of the Red and Atchafalaya Rivers. 5. Drainage area includes both the U.S. and Canada. 6. In east-central Louisiana, the Red River flows into the Atchafalaya River, a distributary of the Mississippi River. Data on average discharge length and drainage area include the Red River, but excludes all water diverted into Atchafalaya from the Mississippi River.

★ 40 ★

Impaired River Miles by Cause of Pollution - Part I

State	Total Impaired Waters	Siltation Major	Siltation Min/Mod	Nutrients Major	Nutrients Min/Mod	Pathogens Major	Pathogens Min/Mod	Organic Enrichment Major	Organic Enrichment Min/Mod	Metals Major	Metals Min/Mod	Pesticides Major	Pesticides Min/Mod
Alabama[1]	1056	57	-	879	-	-	-	931	-	51	-	-	-
Arkansas	2393	-	-	-	-	1759	199	56	-	-	-	-	-
Colorado	1395	-	-	-	-	176	505	21	-	527	767	-	-
Connecticut	298	-	12	119	44	112	64	85	71	69	29	-	-
Delaware[1]	187	-	-	126	-	144	-	76	-	24	-	19	-
District of Columbia	26	-	-	-	-	7	18	-	-	24	3	-	-
Florida[1]	2656	376	-	992	-	376	-	990	-	280	-	-	-
Georgia	557	-	-	-	-	9	183	163	192	-	8	-	-
Illinois	7187	129	6660	375	7095	147	241	155	1270	23	908	-	-
Indiana	1662	14	167	82	173	413	375	192	320	66	194	68	232
Iowa	8166	6751	1408	42	8107	1190	141	25	1431	2358	213	545	7603
Kansas	2894	-	35	-	49	1238	741	81	406	114	-	-	-
Kentucky	2477	724	126	100	4	969	-	300	114	370	125	28	-
Louisiana	2753	-	22	513	808	405	1451	514	1086	26	5	-	103
Maryland	665	157	16	259	93	102	144	43	42	-	-	-	13
Minnesota[1]	2890	1870	-	1567	-	2196	-	1999	-	-	-	-	-
Mississippi	1773	415	181	595	911	-	28	78	423	284	606	-	-
Missouri	9483	6	8299	-	-	-	-	1	58	-	-	-	-
Montana	7244	394	6441	310	2895	79	410	22	92	82	35	-	-
New Hampshire	381	-	-	-	-	136	232	69	62	11	88	5	47
New Mexico	576	108	313	31	193	11	71	-	-	246	-	-	-
New York	16594	126	44	8	151	15	144	66	122	255	321	31	-
North Carolina[1]	10900	6299	-	-	-	77	-	115	-	-	-	-	-
North Dakota	3016	1396	748	1286	1725	289	1110	210	156	255	321	31	-
Ohio River Valley	981	-	981	-	-	162	26	-	250	981	-	-	981
Oklahoma[1]	5942	2804	-	2582	-	1180	-	518	-	684	-	2381	-
Oregon[1]	15192	1260	-	745	-	885	-	603	-	-	-	52	-
Pennsylvania[1]	3600	-	-	368	-	194	-	278	-	834	-	175	-
Puerto Rico	2914	224	151	91	368	383	228	34	283	12	33	14	86
Rhode Island	92	-	-	16	4	20	33	17	18	70	4	-	-
South Carolina[1]	971	-	-	-	-	618	-	321	-	-	-	-	-
South Dakota	2363	110	275	-	232	150	1003	-	161	11	-	-	-
Tennessee	3452	1426	952	245	969	546	831	504	1224	87	548	60	205
Vermont	628	342	123	205	122	64	174	132	256	10	17	-	-
Virginia	2322	-	-	-	-	820	1016	20	90	-	-	-	-
Washington	2326	425	376	238	251	805	865	184	364	187	632	120	43
West Virginia	11439	846	4405	383	1602	57	363	627	2948	1308	1544	-	2
Wyoming	3357	-	2623	-	-	-	273	-	-	7	-	-	130
Totals	142808	26259	34358	12157	25796	15734	10869	9430	11439	9084	6410	3660	11087
Combined Totals			60617		37953		26603		20869		15494		14747
Percent of Impaired Waters			42.4		26.6		18.6		14.6		10.8		10.3

Source: National Water Quality Inventory, 1988 Report to Congress, U.S. EPA, Washington, DC, April 1990, pp. 4-5. *Notes:* 1. These States did not specify the degree of impact (i.e., Major or Moderate/Minor); river miles were placed in the "Major" column for national reporting purposes. - Zero or not reported.

★ 41 ★

Impaired River Miles by Cause of Pollution - Part II

State	Suspended Solids		Salinity		Flow Alteration		Habitat Modification		pH		Thermal Modification	
	Major	Min/Mod	Major	Min/Mod	Major	Min/Mod	Major	Min/Mod	Major	Min/Mod	Major	Min/Mod
Alabama[1]	-	-	-	-	155	-	-	-	21	-	-	-
Arkansas	-	-	-	15	-	-	-	-	56	62	-	-
Colorado	-	-	-	-	-	-	-	-	-	-	-	-
Connecticut	-	11	-	-	-	-	10	101	-	-	-	-
Delaware[1]	-	-	-	-	-	-	-	-	16	-	-	-
District of Columbia	-	-	-	-	-	-	-	-	-	7	-	-
Florida[1]	-	-	259	-	-	-	-	-	-	-	-	-
Georgia	-	-	-	-	-	-	-	-	-	-	-	-
Illinois	-	-	-	18	-	701	371	1242	14	141	-	-
Indiana	-	-	-	-	4	13	14	-	44	113	-	6
Iowa	-	-	-	-	-	-	3	86	92	-	-	-
Kansas	-	-	800	141	89	294	-	-	22	30	-	-
Kentucky	-	-	158	50	-	-	111	20	185	-	-	-
Louisiana	339	646	18	323	-	22	-	-	-	-	-	20
Maryland	-	-	-	-	-	7	-	-	49	67	-	-
Minnesota[1]	-	-	-	-	-	-	-	-	354	-	-	-
Mississippi	-	-	11	5	-	-	-	-	-	172	-	-
Missouri	-	-	-	-	-	-	-	180	15	40	-	-
Montana	-	-	140	2981	231	2312	-	1510	614	97	213	1441
New Hampshire	-	-	-	-	-	-	-	-	-	-	-	-
New Mexico	-	-	56	-	72	30	275	108	27	60	-	-
New York	-	-	9	13	56	95	-	-	60	-	103	10
North Carolina[1]	-	-	-	-	-	-	-	-	48	-	-	-
North Dakota	1041	363	426	459	234	100	-	-	-	-	-	-
Ohio River Valley	-	-	-	-	-	-	-	-	-	-	-	-
Oklahoma[1]	1969	-	1154	-	22	-	-	-	22	-	-	-
Oregon[1]	-	-	-	-	1355	-	1480	-	455	-	1320	-
Pennsylvania[1]	544	-	-	-	-	-	-	-	730	-	16	-
Puerto Rico	-	-	1	-	300	-	43	-	-	-	-	-
Rhode Island	-	-	-	-	-	-	-	-	-	-	-	-
South Carolina[1]	-	-	-	-	-	-	-	-	2	-	-	-
South Dakota	772	964	-	-	-	-	-	-	-	656	5	4
Tennessee	848	706	8	11	144	250	113	172	150	336	14	39
Vermont	-	-	-	-	168	89	259	150	16	3	116	358
Virginia	-	-	-	-	-	-	-	-	81	256	-	39
Washington	224	469	-	58	201	65	289	26	135	136	248	874
West Virginia	-	-	80	648	356	538	135	724	1031	866	94	665
Wyoming	-	-	-	811	-	347	-	741	-	-	-	-
Totals	5737	3159	3120	5533	3387	4864	3103	5060	4239	3042	2129	3456
Combined Totals		8896		8653		8251		8163		7281		5585
Percent of Impaired Waters		6.2		6.1		5.8		5.7		5.1		3.9

Source: National Water Quality Inventory, 1988 Report to Congress, U.S. EPA, Washington, DC, April 1990, pp. 4-5. *Notes:* 1. These States did not specify the degree of impact (i.e., Major or Moderate/Minor); river miles were placed in the "Major" column for national reporting purposes. - Zero or not reported.

★ 42 ★

Impaired River Miles by Source of Pollution - Part I

State	Total Impaired Waters	Agriculture		Municipal		Resource Extraction		Hydrologic/ Habitat Modification		Storm Sewers/ Runoff	
		Major	Mod/Min	Major	Mod/Min	Major	Mod/Min	Major	Mod/Min	Major	Mod/Min
Alabama[1]	1,056	35	-	694	-	76	-	160	-	69	-
Arkansas	2,393	1,722	174	294	-	117	85	-	-	-	-
California[1]	3,307	395	-	51	-	301	-	-	--	-	-
Connecticut	298	-	102	212	52	-	44	10	69	-	148
Delaware[1]	187	146	-	35	-	-	-	-	-	99	-
District of Columbia	26	-	-	4	-	-	-	-	3	-	26
Florida[1]	2,656	1,711	-	785	-	464	-	880	-	1,786	-
Georgia	557	-	-	140	189	-	-	-	-	9	183
Illinois	7,187	144	6,964	371	2,405	14	1,211	223	3,526	38	112
Indiana	1,662	47	934	285	217	49	121	-	-	145	112
Iowa	8,166	7,395	753	524	828	-	103	-	86	680	1,234
Kansas	2,894	918	677	512	546	229	12	89	280	37	13
Maryland	665	172	133	33	94	49	84	-	5	15	108
Mississippi	1,773	933	288	135	345	-	-	19	-	46	97
Missouri	9,483	-	8,267	16	58	22	88	-	189	-	154
Montana	7,244	420	5,603	43	118	319	1,385	171	1,299	27	61
Nebraska[1]	2,446	1,394	-	441	-	-	-	196	-	24	-
New Hampshire	381	-	-	92	190	-	-	-	-	-	-
New Mexico	576	36	374	34	-	37	21	87	13	-	-
New York	16,594	33	22	153	130	1	16	97	41	1	98
North Carolina[1]	10,900	5,559	-	635	-	19	-	-	-	274	-
North Dakota	3,016	1,539	1,472	12	1,339	-	255	1,228	589	12	31
Ohio	4,789	917	1,724	2,831	929	649	328	931	1,203	503	883
Ohio River Valley	981	350	280	-	-	350	280	-	-	150	-
Oklahoma[1]	5,942	3,986	-	-	-	2,302	-	1,103	-	853	-
Oregon[1]	15,192	7,605	-	1,062	-	2,280	-	-	-	-	-
Pennsylvania[1]	3,600	464	-	378	-	1,775	-	31	-	49	-
Puerto Rico	2,914	294	684	79	34	-	-	49	-	302	223
Rhode Island	92	16	2	18	32	-	-	-	-	62	9
South Carolina[1]	971	364	-	170	-	-	-	2	-	157	-
South Dakota	2,363	1,187	1,022	11	43	-	62	-	-	47	215
Tennessee	3,452	1,289	1,269	628	924	360	700	847	1,102	252	796
Vermont	628	510	-	86	-	42	-	326	-	55	-
Virginia	2,322	453	801	229	145	-	-	--	-	87	69
Washington	2,326	1,049	564	143	694	27	54	522	581	354	103
West Virginia	11,439	517	2,748	535	2,281	645	2,953	220	1,501	489	1,133
Wyoming	3,357	2,192	734	6	110	54	770	569	378	10	282
Totals	143,835	43,792	35,591	11,677	11,703	10,181	8,572	7,760	10,865	6,632	6,090
Combined Totals			79,383		23,380		18,753		18,625		12,722
Percent of Impaired waters			55.2%		16.3%		13.0%		12.9%		8.8%

Source: National Water Quality Inventory, 1988, Report to Congress, U.S. Environmental Protection Agency, Washington, D.C., April 1990, p. 8, from 1988 State Section 305(b) reports. *Notes:* 1. These States did not specify the degree of impact (i.e., Major or Moderate/Minor); river miles were placed in the "Major" column for national reporting purposes. - Zero or not reported.

★ 43 ★

Impaired River Miles by Source of Pollution - Part II

	Silviculture		Industrial		Construction		Land Disposal		Combined Sewers	
	Major	Mod/Min	Major	Mod/Min	Major	Mod/Min	Major	Mod/Min	Major	Mod/Min
Alabama[1]	-	-	406	-	6	-	-	-	-	-
Arkansas	-	-	115	39	-	-	-	-	-	-
California[1]	-	-	8	-	-	-	-	-	-	-
Connecticut	-	-	69	48	-	16	13	111	126	11
Delaware[1]	-	-	37	-	4	-	-	-	69	-
District of Columbia	-	-	1	-	-	1	-	13	-	26
Florida[1]	63	-	578	-	792	-	947	-	-	-
Georgia	-	-	24	11	-	-	-	-	-	-
Illinois	-	-	14	1,201	-	470	14	16	113	692
Indiana	-	-	165	225	26	56	12	1	386	130
Iowa	-	-	219	221	-	16	3	165	-	-
Kansas	-	-	124	92	-	-	-	-	-	-
Maryland	-	-	2	-	-	-	22	-	-	12
Mississippi	-	-	103	214	-	-	-	-	-	-
Missouri	-	-	-	10	-	-	-	1	-	-
Montana	44	806	-	233	5	762	22	154	-	-
Nebraska[1]	-	-	49	-	-	-	-	-	-	-
New Hampshire	-	-	38	36	-	-	-	92	10	78
New Mexico	3	76	-	-	3	87	3	15	-	-
New York	-	32	28	90	-	32	62	133	36	70
North Carolina[1]	48	-	159	-	79	-	59	-	-	-
North Dakota	-	-	-	91	-	-	-	-	-	-
Ohio	9	29	1,061	629	9	85	243	977	10	26
Ohio River Valley	-	-	-	-	-	-	-	-	-	-
Oklahoma[1]	20	-	-	-	271	-	666	-	-	-
Oregon[1]	7,580	-	368	-	1,420	-	-	-	1,675	-
Pennsylvania[1]	-	-	201	-	-	-	169	-	39	-
Puerto Rico	-	-	58	126	-	-	208	466	-	1
Rhode Island	-	-	1	69	16	-	16	2	15	3
South Carolina[1]	4	-	55	-	4	-	-	-	-	-
South Dakota	-	-	11	-	-	26	-	26	-	-
Tennessee	76	64	191	386	110	822	14	155	78	22
Vermont	23	-	16	-	142	-	32	-	-	-
Virginia	-	-	48	13	-	-	-	-	-	4
Washington	100	13	113	246	239	89	201	228	12	31
West Virginia	426	2,	856	2,674	446	1,769	224	878	428	1,233
Wyoming	58	65	334	169	362	858	-	-	-	-
Totals	8,454	3,938	5,452	6,823	3,934	5,089	2,930	3,433	2,997	2,339
Combined Totals		12,39		12,275		9,023		6,363		5,336
Percent of Impaired waters		8.6%		8.5%		6.3%		4.4%		3.7%

Source: National Water Quality Inventory, 1988, Report to Congress, U.S. Environmental Protection Agency, Washington, D.C., April 1990, p. 8, from 1988 State Section 305(b) reports. *Notes:* 1. These States did not specify the degree of impact (i.e.,Major or Moderate/Minor); river miles were placed in the "Major" column for national reporting purposes. - Zero or not reported.

★ 44 ★

River Flows in Great Britain

River flows in March 1991, shown as percent of normal.

River	Percent of Normal
Eden	183
Dee	160
Severn	148
Exe	124
Clyde	120
Trent	86
Itchen	78
Thames	77
Medway	52
Ouse	35

Source: The Economist, April 13,1991, p. 54, from the Meteorological Office; the Institute of Hydrology.

Shorelines

★ 45 ★

Shore Debris in the U.S.

State	Volume
Georgia - 4,000	
Texas - 3,550	
Mississippi - 3,000	
Louisiana - 2,350	
New York - 1,100	
Hawaii - 950	
Virginia - 650	
New Jersey - 650	
North Carolina - 650	
Florida - 400	
Massachusetts - 350	
Pennsylvania - 350	
Oregon - 250	
California - 200	
Alabama - 200	
Maryland - 200	
South Carolina - 150	
Maine - 150	
Rhode Island - 150	
Connecticut - 100	
Delaware - 100	

Debris collected by volunteers who cleaned up 3,500 miles of beaches and shorelines in September and October of 1988. Volumes are shown in pounds of debris per mile.

States	Volume
Maine	150
Massachusetts	350
Rhode Island	150
New York	1,100
Pennsylvania	350
Connecticut	100
New Jersey	650
Delaware	100
Maryland	200
Virginia	650

[Continued]

★ 45 ★

Shore Debris in the U.S.
[Continued]

States	Volume
North Carolina	650
South Carolina	150
Georgia	4,000
Florida	400
Alabama	200
Mississippi	3,000
Louisiana	2,350
Texas	3,550
California	200
Hawaii	950
Oregon	250

Source: U.S. News & World Report, January 15, 1990, p. 67, from the Center for Marine Conservation. In Alaska, a total of 10,300 pounds was collected; in Washington, the total was 64,000 pounds. Information on the number of miles cleaned up there was not available. Other states with shorelines were not included because they did not participate in the organized cleanup.

Water

★ 46 ★

Pesticides in Groundwater

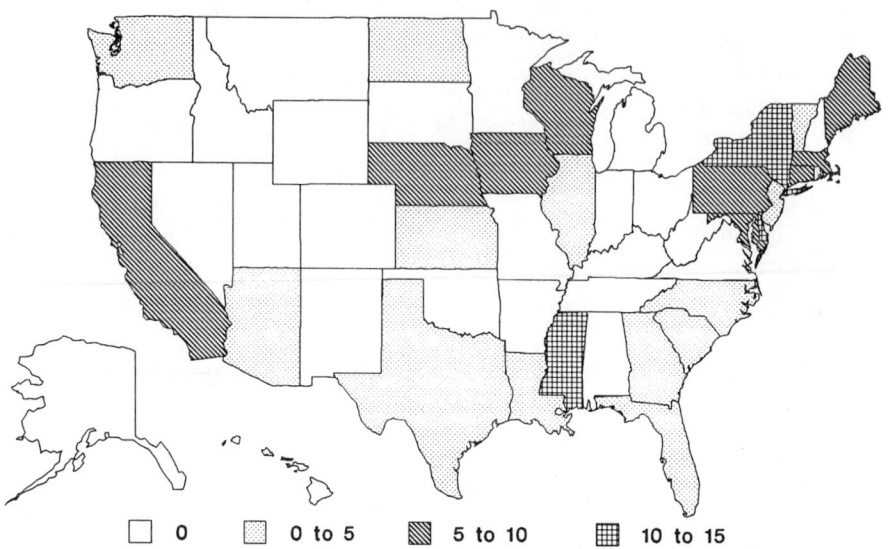

| ☐ 0 | ▦ 0 to 5 | ▨ 5 to 10 | ▦ 10 to 15 |

Source: Beneath the Bottom Line: Agricultural Approaches to Reduce Agricultural Contamination of Groundwater, U.S. Congress, Office of Technology Assessment, OTA-F-418, Washington, D.C., November 1990., p. 30, from U.S. Environmental Protection Agency, "Pesticides in Ground Water Data Base 1988 Interim Report," December 1988. *Note*: Values refer to number of pesticides found in the groundwater of each state.

★ 47 ★

Population Served by Groundwater for Domestic Supply

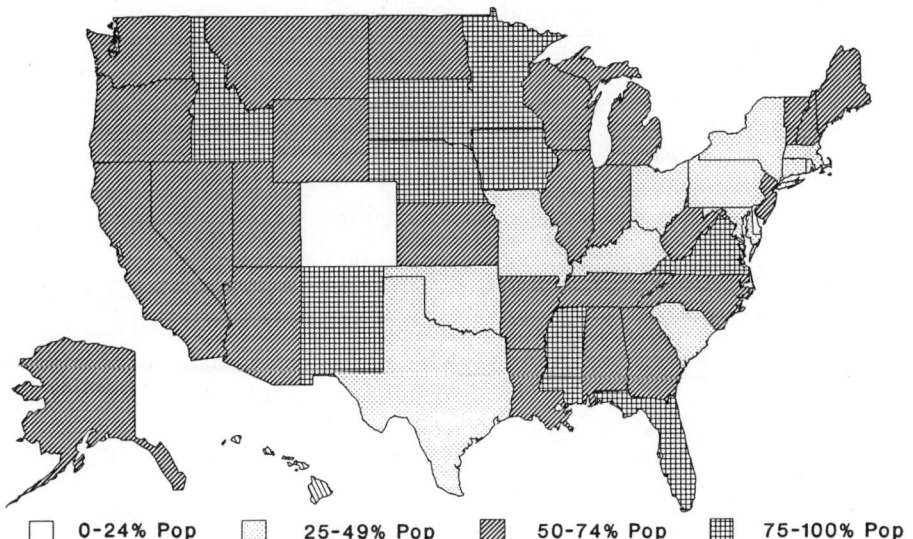

| | 0-24% Pop | | 25-49% Pop | ▨ | 50-74% Pop | ▦ | 75-100% Pop |

Source: The Quality of Our Nation's Water: A Summary of the 1988 National Water Quality Inventory, U.S. Environmental Protection Agency, EPA 440/4-90-005, May 1990, p. 19, from 1988 State Section 305(b) Reports or 1988 U.S.G.S. National Water Summary. *Note*: Data show percent of the population serviced in each state.

★ 48 ★

River Runoff by Continent

Global river runoff is 44,500 cubic kilometers (excluding polar glaciers and ice); of this total, 43,500 cubic kilometers flow to the oceans and the rest into endorheic area (Caspian and Aral seas, Lake Tchad, Andean altiplano, etc.).

Territory	Annual stream flow		Percent of total runoff	Area (000 square kilometers)
	(mm)	(cubic kilometers)		
Europe	306	3,210	7	10,500
Asia	332	14,410	31	43,475
Africa	151	4,570	10	30,120
North and Central America	339	8,200	17	24,200
South America	661	11,760	25	17,800
Australia and Tasmania	45	348	1	7,683
Oceania	1,610	2,040	4	1,267
Antarctica	160	2,230	5	13,977
Total land area	314	46,768	-	149,022

Source: Nature and Resources, vol. 26, no. 3, 1990, p. 35.

★ 49 ★

U.S. Water Withdrawals

Values shown are in millions of gallons per day, except as noted. Figures may not add due to rounding. Withdrawal signifies water physically withdrawn from a source. Includes fresh and saline water.

State or Other Area	Water Withdrawn								Consumptive use,[4] fresh water
	Source		Use				Per capita (gal. per day fresh)	Total[1]	
	Ground water	Surface water	Irrigation	Public supply[2]	Industrial[3]	Thermoelectric			
Total	74,000	325,000	137,000	39,900	29,300	187,000	1,400	399,000	92,300
Alabama	347	8,250	69	654	851	6,920	2,140	8,600	541
Alaska	72	334	-	86	133	30	727	406	27
Arizona	3,100	3,330	5,520	645	133	58	1,960	6,430	3,700
Arkansas	3,810	2,100	3,870	317	175	1,090	2,500	5,910	3,210
California	15,100	34,600	30,600	5,450	1,159	12,180	1,420	49,700	21,100
Colorado	2,340	11,200	12,400	754	211	110	4,190	13,600	4,850
Connecticut	144	3,640	3	401	147	3,210	375	3,780	106
Delaware	79	1,580	27	87	410	1,121	222	1,650	39
District of Columbia	-	348	-	218	-	130	556	348	24
Florida	4,050	13,000	2,910	1,939	679	11,351	554	17,000	2,730
Georgia	1,000	4,440	453	935	656	3,326	899	5,450	838
Hawaii	655	1,490	906	215	20	970	1,100	2,150	132
Idaho	4,800	17,500	20,600	301	334	-	22,200	22,300	5,290
Illinois	968	13,500	71	1,910	639	11,700	1,250	14,500	686
Indiana	635	7,400	47	714	2,751	4,480	1,470	8,030	454
Iowa	671	2,090	67	415	260	1,810	960	2,770	473
Kansas	4,800	866	4,730	358	95	415	2,310	5,670	4,710
Kentucky	205	3,990	8	451	266	3,410	1,130	4,200	260
Louisiana	1,440	8,980	1,480	675	2,100	5,964	2,210	10,400	2,090
Maine	66	1,460	2	127	250	1,074	733	1,520	203
Maryland	219	6,490	34	834	371	5,429	321	6,710	423
Massachusetts	315	9,340	16	802	153	8,450	1,070	9,660	316
Michigan	600	10,800	210	1,373	1,385	8,390	1,270	11,400	611
Minnesota	685	2,150	209	604	457	1,470	676	2,830	768
Mississippi	1,580	933	886	328	236	670	885	2,510	661
Missouri	640	5,470	306	699	116	4,930	1,210	6,110	504
Montana	203	8,450	8,300	174	60	67	10,500	8,650	1,900
Nebraska	5,590	4,450	7,270	272	167	2,210	6,250	10,000	4,910
Nevada	908	2,830	3,350	300	35	23	3,860	3,740	1,890
New Hampshire	84	810	1	111	239	543	688	894	76
New Jersey	668	6,270	132	1,114	1,137	4,546	307	6,940	279
New Mexico	1,510	1,780	2,820	264	83	59	2,320	3,280	1,530
New York	1,100	14,100	38	3,051	1,080	10,870	508	15,200	1,400
North Carolina	435	8,320	132	764	539	7,266	1,260	8,760	439
North Dakota	127	1,040	154	84	13	892	1,690	1,160	201
Ohio	730	12,000	17	1,559	540	10,500	1,180	12,700	396
Oklahoma	568	707	445	547	113	134	386	1,270	576
Oregon	660	5,880	5,710	496	301	12	2,450	6,540	2,600
Pennsylvania	799	13,500	11	1,784	2,208	10,200	1,210	14,300	589
Rhode Island	27	381	3	122	20	261	152	409	23

[Continued]

★ 49 ★

U.S. Water Withdrawals

[Continued]

| State or Other Area | Water Withdrawn | | | | | | | | Consumptive use,[4] fresh water |
| | Source | | Use | | | | Per capita (gal. per day fresh) | Total[1] | |
	Ground water	Surface water	Irrigation	Public supply[2]	Industrial[3]	Thermoelectric			
South Carolina	214	6,610	34	421	1,130	5,186	2,040	6,820	340
South Dakota	249	425	460	96	46	4	956	675	361
Tennessee	444	8,010	9	697	1,613	6,060	1,770	8,450	275
Texas	7,410	17,900	8,120	3,095	2,763	11,010	1,230	25,300	8,650
Utah	815	3,500	3,590	453	213	28	2,540	4,320	2,130
Vermont	37	89	1	65	55	1	235	126	26
Virginia	341	6,910	52	691	673	5,760	853	7,250	269
Washington	1,220	5,810	4,940	1,053	559	427	1,600	7,030	4,700
West Virginia	227	5,210	4	172	1,028	4,210	2,810	5,440	877
Wisconsin	570	6,170	84	659	461	5,440	1,400	6,740	321
Wyoming	526	5,700	5,660	111	184	236	12,200	6,220	2,670
Puerto Rico	175	2,430	157	409	18	2,005	176	2,600	163
Virgin Islands	2	123	-	6	14	103	68	124	1

Source: U.S. Department of Commerce, Bureau of the Census, *Statistical Abstract of the United States 1990 (110th ed.)*, Superintendent of Documents, Washington, D.C., p. 201, from U.S. Geological Survey, *Estimated Use of Water in the United States in 1985*, circular 1004. *Notes:* - Represents zero. 1. Includes self-supplied withdrawals for commercial use not shown separately under "use." 2. Includes domestic withdrawals for normal household purposes. 3. Includes water used in mining. 4. Water that has been evaporated, transpired, or incorporated into products, plant, or animal tissue; and therefore, is not available for immediate reuse.

★ 50 ★

Water Area

Water area includes portion of water body under the jurisdiction of the U.S., excluding Alaska, Hawaii, and inland waters.

| Body of Water | Area | |
	Sq. mi.	Sq. km.
Total	74,364	192,603
Atlantic coastal water	2298	5952
Florida	37	96
Georgia	48	124
Maine	1102	2854
Massachusetts	959	2484
Rhode Island	14	36
South Carolina	138	357
Chesapeake Bay	3237	8384
Maryland	1726	4470
Virginia	1511	3913
Delaware Bay	665	1722
Delaware	350	907
New Jersey	315	816

[Continued]

★ 50 ★

Water Area
[Continued]

Body of Water	Area	
	Sq. mi.	Sq. km.
Lake Erie	5002	12,955
Michigan	216	559
New York	594	1538
Ohio	3457	8954
Pennsylvania	735	1904
Straits of Georgia and		
Juan de Fuca: Washington	1610	4170
Lake Huron: Michigan	8975	23,245
Long Island Sound	1298	3364
Connecticut	573	1484
New York	726	1880
Gulf of Mexico coastal water	3837	9938
Alabama	560	1450
Florida	1698	4398
Louisiana	1016	2631
Mississippi	556	1440
Texas	7	18
Lake Michigan	22,178	57,441
Illinois	1526	3952
Indiana	228	591
Michigan	13,037	33,766
Wisconsin	7387	19,132
New York Harbor	92	238
New Jersey	69	179
New York	23	60
Lake Ontario: New York	3033	7855
Pacific coastal water	343	888
California	69	179
Oregon	48	124
Washington	226	585
Puget Sound: Washington	561	1453
Lake St. Clair: Michigan	116	300
Lake Superior	21,118	54,696
Michigan	16,231	42,038
Minnesota	2212	5729
Wisconsin	2675	6928

Source: U.S. Department of Commerce, Bureau of the Census, *Statistical Abstract of the United States 1990 (110th ed.),* Superintendent of Documents, Washington, D.C., p. 200, from U.S. Bureau of the Census, *Areas of the United States: 1940.*

★ 51 ★

World Water Storage

```
┌─────────────────────────────────────────────┐
│  ┌─────────────────────────────────────────┐ │
│  │ Oceans - 97.60                          │ │
│  └─────────────────────────────────────────┘ │
│  ▯ Icecaps, glaciers - 1.90                   │
│  ▮ Ground water - 0.50                        │
│  │ Rivers, lakes, inland seas - 0.02          │
│  │ Soil moisture - 0.01                       │
│  │ Atmosphere - 0.0001                        │
└─────────────────────────────────────────────┘
```

Relative amounts of free water stored on the earth, by location. Data are shown as percentage of all water.

Water Source	Percent of Total
Oceans	97.60
Icecaps, glaciers	1.90
Ground water	0.50
Rivers, lakes, inland seas	0.02
Soil moisture	0.01
Atmosphere	0.0001

Source: National Water Quality Inventory, 1988, Report to Congress, U.S. Environmental Protection Agency, Washington, D.C., April 1990, p. 3.

★ 52 ★

World Water Storage by Type

The total volume of fresh water on earth is about 35 million cubic kilometers, which is only 2.5% of the water in the hydrosphere. Most of the fresh water (69%) occurs in the form of ice and snow in the polar regions.

Type of water	Reference area (000 square kilometers)	Volume (000 cubic kilometers)	Equivalent depth (m)	Total water storage (%)	Freshwater storage (%)
Sea	361,300	1,338,000	3,700	96.5	-
Total groundwater	134,800	23,400	174	1.7	-
Fresh groundwater	134,800	10,530	78	0.76	30.1
Soil moisture	82,000	17.5	0.2	0.001	0.05
Glaciers and permanent snow pack	16,232	24,064	1,482	1.74	68.7
Antarctica	13,980	21,600	1,545	1.55	61.7
Greenland	1,802	2,340	1,299	0.17	6.68
Arctic islands	226	83	367	0.006	0.24
Mountain regions	224	41	183	0.003	0.12
Underground ice in the permafrost zone	21,000	300	14	0.022	0.86
Lakes	2,258	176	85.5	0.013	-

[Continued]

★ 52 ★

World Water Storage by Type
[Continued]

Type of water	Reference area (000 square kilometers)	Volume (000 cubic kilometers)	Equivalent depth (m)	Total water storage (%)	Freshwater storage (%)
Freshwater	1,236	91	74	0.007	0.26
Salt-water	822	85	103	0.006	-
Swamps	2,683	11.5	4.3	0.0008	0.03
Rivers	148,800	2.1	0.014	0.0002	0.006
Water in the biosphere	510,000	1.1	0.002	0.00007	0.003
Water in the atmosphere	510,000	12.9	0.025	0.0009	0.04
Total	510,000	1,385,984	2,718	-	-
Freshwater	148,800	35,029	235	2.53	-

Source: Nature & Resources, vol. 26, N. 3, 1990, p. 34.

Wetlands

★ 53 ★

U.S. Constructed Wetlands

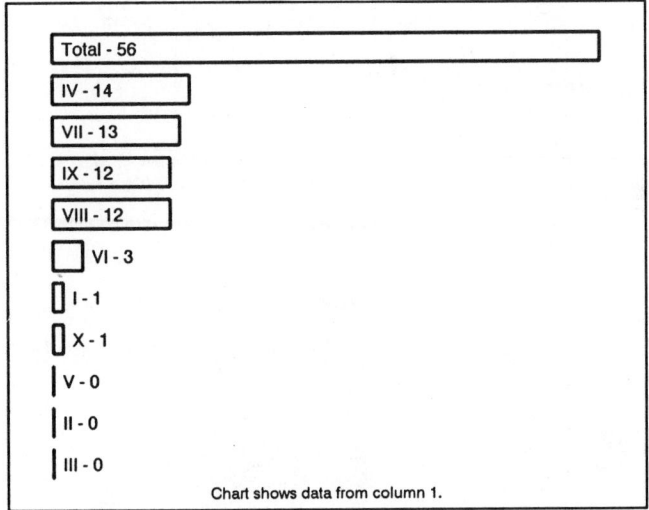

Total - 56
IV - 14
VII - 13
IX - 12
VIII - 12
VI - 3
I - 1
X - 1
V - 0
II - 0
III - 0

Chart shows data from column 1.

U.S. EPA Region	Free water surface type	Subsurface flow type
I	1	2
II	0	2
III	0	6
IV	14	34
V	0	3
VI	3	46
VII	13	2
VIII	12	1
IX	12	1
X	1	1
Total	56	98

Source: BioCycle, January 1991, p. 45.

★ 54 ★

Wetland Types

Extent of wetlands in the lower 48 states.

Wetland Types	Millions of Acres
Coastal Wetlands	5.2
Inland Marshes and Wet Meadows	28.4
Inland Shrub Swamps	10.6
Inland Forested Wetlands	49.7
Other Inland Wetlands	5.0

Source: National Water Quality Inventory, 1988, Report to Congress, U.S. Environmental Protection Agency, Washington, D.C., April 1990, p. 80, from OPA-87-016.

★ 55 ★

Wetlands Acerage Distribution Nationwide

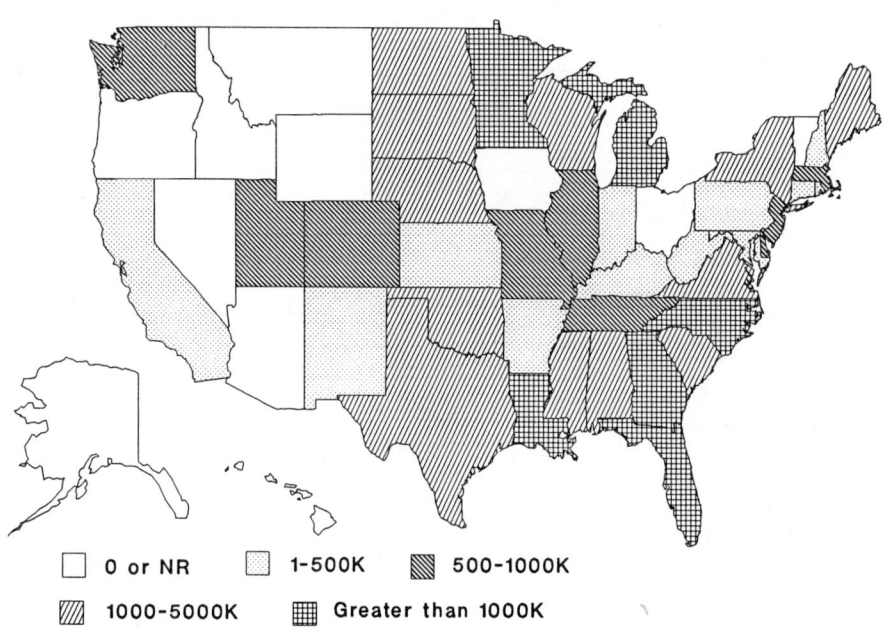

Source: The Quality of Our Nation's Water: A Summary of the 1988 National Water Quality Inventory, U.S. Environmental Protection Agency, EPA 440/4-90-005, May 1990, p. 17, from National Wetlands Inventory.

★ 56 ★

Wetlands Acreage

Original and remaining acreages of wetlands in the lower 48 states. Remaining area was 99 million acres.

	Percent
Remaining in the mid-1970's	46.0
Lost	54.0

Source: National Water Quality Inventory, 1988, Report to Congress, U.S. Environmental Protection Agency, Washington, D.C., April 1990, p. 83, from OPA-87-016.

Chapter 2

POLLUTANTS AND WASTES

Agrichemicals

★ 57 ★

Cropland Nitrogen Sources in the U.S.

Sources	Million tons/year
Fertilizers	11.0
Wastes (manure), crop residues	9.7
Soil nitrogen	9.0
Biological fixation (legumes)	8.0
Atmosphere	3.2
Irrigation	0.4
Total	41.3

Source: Farm Journal, September 1990, p. A-6, from Resource Washington, Inc.

★ 58 ★

Fertilizer Use in the U.S.

Fertilizer application rates shown in pounds per acre.

Year	Corn			Wheat			Soybeans			Cotton		
	Nitrogen	Phosphorous Pentoxide	Potassium Oxide	Nitrogen	Phosphorous Pentoxide	Potassium oxide	Nitrogen	Phosphorous Pentoxide	Potassium Oxide	Nitrogen	Phosphorous Pentoxide	Potassium Oxide
1965	75	50	48	31	30	35	10	32	39	81	55	57
1970	112	71	72	39	30	36	14	37	51	75	55	57
1975	105	58	67	46	35	35	15	40	53	78	50	55
1980	130	66	86	58	39	40	17	46	70	72	46	46
1985	140	60	84	60	35	36	15	43	72	80	46	52
1988	137	63	85	64	37	52	22	48	79	78	42	39

Source: Beneath the Bottom Line: Agricultural Approaches to Reduce Agrichemical Contamination of Groundwater, Office of Technology Assessment, November 1990, p. 83, from U.S. Department of Agriculture, Economic Research Service, *Agricultural Resources: Inputs, Situation and Outlook*, AR-15 (Washington, DC: U.S. Government Printing Office, August 1989.

★ 59 ★

Fertilizer Use on Rice in Selected Asian Countries

	Paddy/fertilizer ratio		Location	Fertilizer applied per hectare (kg/ha)		Paddy yields (ka/ha)	
	1976	1981		1976	1981	1976	1981
India	0.17	0.37	Coimbatore	32	34	1,637	1,962
South Korea	0.65	0.84	Hwaseong-gun	311	351	5,966	5,841
Taiwan	1.25	0.75	Taichung	205	287	4,539	4,953
Indonesia	0.40	0.62	Central Java	57	74	2,784	3,493
Malaysia	0.49	0.56	Selangor	97	92	2,733	3,225
Philippines	0.28	0.27	Central Luzon	29	32	1,821	2,362
Thailand	0.24	0.30	Suphan Buri	11	18	1,780	1,952
Bangladesh	0.51	0.57	Joydebpur	11	44	1,784	1,955
Myanmar	0.55	0.55	Rangoon	9	17	1,799	2,942
Nepal	0.33	0.45	Kathmandu	8	9	1,891	2,000
Pakistan	0.27	0.28	Punjab	46	53	2,347	2,604
Sri Lanka	0.60	0.93	Kurunegala	65	77	1,971	2,646

Source: The Economist, May 4, 1991, p. 13, from *Asian Development*, by William James, Seiji Naya and Gerald Meier. kg/ha stands for kilograms per hectare.

★ 60 ★

Nitrous Oxide Emissions by Fertilizer Type

Fertilizer Type	Percent of Nitrogenous Fertilizer Evolved as Nitrous Oxide
Anhydrous ammonia	0.500-6.84
Ammonium nitrate	0.040-1.71
Ammonium type	0.025-0.10
Urea	0.067-0.50
Nitrate	0.001-0.50

Source: Eichner, M.J., 1988: "Current Knowledge of Fertilizer-Derived Nitrous Oxide Emissions." Paper prepared for U.S. Environmental Protection Agency, Washington, DC.

★ 61 ★

Nutrient Concentrations in Waste Materials

Total concentration of nitrogen, potassium and phosphorus in selected waste materials.

Waste material	Nitrogen	Phosphorus	Potassium
Solid or semisolid:[1]			
Composted/shredded refuse	0.57-1.30	0.08-0.26	0.27-0.98
Waste food fiber	2.00	0.01	0.36
Paper mill sludge	0.15-2.33	0.16-0.50	0.44-0.85
Citric acid production wastes	0.51-4.13	0.06-0.29	0.01-0.19
Tomato processing wastes	2.33	0.29	0.28
Municipal sewage sludge	<0.10-17.60	<0.10-14.30	0.02-2.64
Liquids:[2]			
Municipal wastewater	16-37	7-13	14-22
Whey	1500	500	1820
Vegetable and fruit processing wastes	19-318	4-91	-

Source: Office of Technological Assessment, *Beneath the Bottom Line: Agricultural Approaches to Reduce Agrichemical Contamination to Ground Water*, November 1990, p. 95, from L.F. Sommers and P.M. Giordano, "Use of Nitrogen From Agricultural, Industrial, and Municipal Wastes," *Nitrogen in Crop Production* (Madison, WI: ASA-CSSA-SSSA, 1984), pp. 207-220. - Not available *Notes:* 1. Expressed on a dry-weight basis. 2. Expressed on a wet-weight basis (commonly called suspended solids). .

★ 62 ★

Pesticide Contamination of Groundwater

Pesticide and nitrate contamination of groundwater by pesticide mixing and loading areas.

	Maximum concentrations detected		
	In pools and soils in loading and rinse areas	Groundwater in affected wells and seeps	Local background groundwater
	micrograms/liter		
Atrazine	70,000	65.0	No-0.65
Alachlor	270,000	145.0	No-1.30
Cyanizine	225,000	36.0	No-0.26
Metolachlor	270,000	50.0	No-0.80
Metribuzin	52,000	8.0	No
Trifluralin	(1,000+)	0.20	No
Insecticides:			
Carbofuran	(1,000+)	No	No
Fonofos	(1,000+)	1.30	No-0.30
Fumigants:			
EDB	10-100	1.00	No

[Continued]

★ 62 ★

Groundwater Contamination from Pesticides
[Continued]

	Maximum concentrations detected		
	In pools and soils in loading and rinse areas	Groundwater in affected wells and seeps	Local background groundwater
1,2, dce	10-100	2.00	No
Carbon Tet	10-100	66.00	No
Chloroform	10-100	4.00	<1.0
	miligrams/liter		
Nitrate	137-480	18-41	
Nitrate-Nitrogen	30-105	4-9	

Source: Beneath the Bottom Line: Agricultural Approaches to Reduce Agrichemical Contamination of Groundwater, Office of Technological Assessment, November 1990, p. 133, from G. Hallberg, "Pesticide and Nitrate Concentrations From 8 Case Studies Where Groundwater Has Been Contaminated in the vicinity of Farm-Chemical Supply Dealerships," In: Hall, F., 1989.

★ 63 ★

Pesticide Use in the U.S.

Projected use of pesticide on major field crops in 1989.

Crop	June 1 Acres (million)	Million pounds		
		Herbicides	Insecticides	Fungicides
Row:				
Corn	72.8	219	27.1	0.06
Cotton	10.5	16	15.6	0.16
Grain/sorghum	11.9	11	1.90	0.00
Peanuts	1.70	6	1.30	6.19
Soybeans	61.30	108	9.50	0.06
Tobacco	0.70	1	2.70	0.35
Subtotal	158.9	361	58.1	6.82
Small grains:				
Barely & oats	21.4	5	0.20	0.00
Rice	76.7	12	0.50	0.07
Wheat	76.7	16	2.20	0.88
Subtotal	100.9	33	2.90	0.95

[Continued]

★ 63 ★

Pesticide Use in the U.S.

[Continued]

Crop	June 1 Acres (million)	Million pounds		
		Herbicides	Insecticides	Fungicides
Total	259.8	394	61.0	7.77
1988 total	243.4	372	59.7	7.56

Source: Beneath the Bottom Line Agricultural Approaches to Reduce Agrichemical Contamination of Groundwater, Office of Technical Assessment, November 1990, p. 83, from U.S. Department of Agriculture, Economic Research Service, *Agricultural Resources: Inputs, Situation and Outlook,* AR-15 (Washington, DC: U.S. Government Printing Office , August 1989). June 1 planted acreage for the 10 major field crops increased from 243 million acres in 1988 to 260 million. The area planted to corn, grain sorghum, soybeans, tobacco, and wheat went up while cotton, barley, oats, and rice declined. Peanuts remained constant.

★ 64 ★

Pesticides in Food

Vegetables - 5.6

Grains/grain products - 2.5

Fruits - 1.9

Milk/dairy products - 0.9

Chart shows data from column 4.

No violative pesticide residues were found in more than 96% of foods sampled by the Food and Drug Administration in 1988 and no residues at all were found in 61% of the samples. The samples included both domestic and imported.

Samples	Number of samples	No pesticides residue found percent	Not violative pesticide residue amount (percent)	Violative amount of pesticide (percent)
Grains/grain products	648	61.1	36.4	2.5
Milk/dairy products	1,222	81.1	18.0	0.9
Fruits	5,256	54.8	43.3	1.9
Vegetables	9,080	61.7	32.7	5.6

Source: Farm Journal, April 1990, p. AC 1, from Food and Drug Administration.

Air Pollution

★ 65 ★

Air Pollution Emissions by Source, 1970 to 1987.

In millions of metric tons, except lead, which is in thousands of metric tons.

Year and Pollutant	Total emissions	Controllable Emissions						Misc. uncon-trollable	Percent of total		
		Transportation		Fuel combustion[1]		Industrial processes	Solid waste disposal		Transpor-tation	Fuel com-bustion[1]	Industrial
		Total	Road vehicle	Total	Electric						
1970: Carbon monoxide	100.2	73.2	64.2	4.4	.2	9.0	6.4	7.2	73.1	4.4	9.0
Sulfur oxides	28.4	.6	.3	21.3	15.8	6.4	-	.1	2.1	75.0	22.5
Volatile organic compounds	26.2	11.1	9.8	1.1	-	8.9	1.8	3.8	42.4	4.2	34.0
Particulates	18.5	1.2	.9	4.6	2.3	10.5	1.1	1.1	6.5	24.9	56.8
Nitrogen oxides	18.3	7.7	6.1	9.1	4.4	.7	.4	.3	42.1	49.7	3.8
Lead	203.8	163.6	156.0	9.6	.3	23.9	6.7	-	80.3	4.7	11.7
1980: Carbon monoxide	77.0	53.5	46.2	7.3	.3	6.3	2.2	7.6	69.5	9.5	8.2
Sulfur oxides	23.4	.9	.4	18.7	15.5	3.8	-	-	3.8	79.9	16.2
Volatile organic compounds	22.3	7.4	6.2	2.2	-	9.2	.6	2.9	33.2	9.9	41.3
Particulates	8.5	1.3	1.1	2.4	.8	3.3	.4	1.1	15.3	28.2	38.8
Nitrogen oxides	20.4	9.3	7.4	10.1	6.4	.7	.1	.2	45.6	49.5	3.4
Lead	70.6	59.4	56.4	3.9	.1	3.6	3.7	-	84.1	5.5	5.1
1987: Carbon monoxide	61.4	40.7	33.4	7.2	.3	4.7	1.7	7.1	66.3	11.7	7.7
Sulfur oxide	20.4	.9	.5	16.4	13.5	3.1	-	-	4.4	80.4	15.2
Violatile organic compounds	19.6	6.0	4.7	2.3	-	8.3	.6	2.4	30.6	11.7	42.3
Particulates	7.0	1.4	1.1	1.8	.5	2.5	.3	1.0	20.0	25.7	35.7
Nitrogen oxides	19.5	8.4	6.6	10.3	6.9	.6	.1	.1	43.1	52.8	3.1
Lead	8.1	3.0	2.8	.5	.1	2.0	2.6	-	37.0	6.2	24.7

Source: U.S. Department of Commerce, Bureau of the Census, *Statistical Abstract of the United States 1990 (110th ed.)*, Superintendent of Documents, Washington, D.C., p. 203, from U.S. Environmental Protection Agency, *National Air Pollutant Emission Estimates*, 1940-1987. *Notes:* - Represents zero. 1. Stationary plants.

★ 66 ★

Air Pollution Emissions, 1940-1987

In millions of metric tons, except lead in thousands of metric tons. A metric ton is 1.1023 short tons. PM stands for Particulate matter, SO_x - Sulfur oxides, NO_x - Nitrogen oxide, VOC - Volatile organic compound, CO - Carbon monoxide, Pb - Lead.

Year	Emissions						Percent Change[1]					
	PM	SOx	NOx	VOC	CO	Pb	PM	SOx	NOx	VOC	CO	Pb
1940	23.1	17.6	6.8	18.1	81.5	(NA)	(NA)	(NA)	(NA)	(NA)	(NA)	(NA)
1950	24.9	19.8	9.3	20.2	86.1	(NA)	7.8	12.5	36.8	11.6	5.6	(NA)
1960	21.6	19.7	12.8	22.6	88.1	(NA)	-13.3	-.5	37.6	11.9	2.3	(NA)
1970	18.5	28.3	18.3	26.2	100.2	203.8	-14.4	43.7	43.0	15.9	13.7	(NA)
1975	10.6	25.8	19.2	22.1	82.2	147.0	-42.7	-8.8	4.9	-15.6	-18.0	-27.9
1980	8.5	23.4	20.4	22.3	77.0	70.6	-19.8	-9.3	6.3	.9	-6.3	-52.0
1981	8.0	22.6	20.4	21.0	74.4	55.9	-5.9	-3.4	-	-5.8	-3.4	-20.8
1982	7.1	21.4	19.6	19.7	69.4	54.4	-11.2	-5.3	-3.9	-6.2	-6.7	-2.7
1983	7.1	20.7	19.0	20.4	71.3	46.3	-	-3.3	-3.1	3.6	2.7	-14.9
1984	7.4	21.5	19.7	21.5	68.7	40.1	4.2	3.9	3.7	5.4	-3.6	-13.4
1985	7.0	21.1	19.8	20.1	64.6	21.1	-5.4	-1.9	.5	-6.5	-6.0	-47.4

[Continued]

★ 66 ★

Air Pollution Emissions, 1940-1987
[Continued]

Year	Emissions						Percent Change[1]					
	PM	SOx	NOx	VOC	CO	Pb	PM	SOx	NOx	VOC	CO	Pb
1986	6.8	20.7	19.3	19.3	61.1	8.6	-2.9	-1.9	-2.5	-4.0	-5.4	-59.2
1987	7.0	20.4	19.5	19.6	61.4	8.1	2.9	-1.4	1.0	1.6	.5	-5.8

Source: U.S. Department of Commerce, Bureau of the Census, *Statistical Abstract of the United States 1990 (110th ed.),* Superintendent of Documents, Washington, D.C., p. 203, from U.S. Enviromental Protection Agency, *National Pollutant Emission Estimates,* 1940-1987. - Represents zero. NA means not available. *Note:* 1. Percent change from prior year shown.

★ 67 ★

Air Pollution From Different Fuels
Number values represent kilograms of pollutant per billion joules delivered.

Fuel	Percent Efficiency	Fuel Equivalent to billion Joules Delivered	Total Particulates	Sulfur Oxides	Nitrogen Oxides	Hydrocarbons	Carbon Monoxide
Industrial boilers							
Wood	70	89 mt[2]	500	53	400	400	450
Bituminous coal	80	43 mt[2]	2800	820	320	22	45
Residual oil	80	33000 l	94	1310	240	4	20
Distillate oil	90	31400 l	8	1120	83	4	19
Natural gas	90	28200 cu.m	7	1	99	2	8
Residential heating stoves							
Wood	50	130 mt[2]	2700	30	100	6800	17000
Anthracite	65	49 mt[2]	46	200	250	100	1000
Bituminous coal	65	53 mt[2]	550	1100	270	530	5300
Distillate oil	85	32900 l	11	1170	71	4	20
Natural gas	85	30000 cu.m	7	1	38	4	10
Residential cooking stoves							
Tropical wood	15	420 mt[2]	3800	250	300	3200	34000
Hawaiian cowdung	15	530 mt[2]	10000	3200			44000
Indian coal	20	220 mt[2]	280	2200	460	2200	27000
Coconut husks	15	480 mt[2]	17000				54000
Natural gas	80	3200 cu.m	0.5	1	10	5	250

Source: Environment, December 1988, p. 28, modified from K.R. Smith, *Biofuels, Air Pollution, and Health: A Global Review* (New York: Plenum Publishing Corp., 1987). Actual efficiencies and emissions vary greatly according to fuel quality and combustion conditions. Combustion-derived particulates and hydrocarbons contain complex mixtures of hundreds or thousands of organic chemicals, many of which are mutagenic or toxic. Residential heating stoves were measured under U.S. conditions. Biomass and coal cooking stoves were measured under Indian rural conditions. Blank spaces indicate that no measurement was taken. *Notes:* 1. Negligible. 2. Represents metric tons.

★ 68 ★

Ambient Air Pollutant Concentrations

Data represent annual composite averages of pollutant based on daily 24-hour averages of monitoring stations; carbon monoxide is based on the second-highest, non-overlapping, 8-hour average; ozone, average of the second-highest maximum one hour value; and lead, quarterly average of ambient levels. Based on data from the National Aerometric Data Bank.

Pollutant	Unit	Monitoring stations number	Air quality standard[1]	1978	1979	1980	1981	1982	1983	1984	1985	1986	1987
Carbon monoxide	ppm	198	9[2]	9.9	9.6	8.9	8.6	8.1	7.9	7.9	7.1	7.1	6.7
Ozone	ppm	274	.122[3]	.15	.14	.14	.13	.13	.14	.13	.13	.12	.13
Sulfur dioxide	ppm	347	.03	.013	.012	.011	.010	.010	.009	.009	.009	.009	.008
Total suspended particulates	microgram/m^3	1,726	75	62.3	63.0	64.2	60.0	49.8	49.4	51.0	48.6	48.5	49.5
Nitrogen dioxide	ppm	84	.053	.026	.026	.026	.024	.023	.022	.023	.023	.023	.023
Lead	Micrograms/m^3	97	1.5	1.01	.86	.63	.47	.49	.41	.37	.25	.14	.12
Index	1987=100												
Carbon monoxide		198	9[2]	100	97	90	87	82	80	80	72	72	68
Ozone		274	.122[3]	100	93	93	87	87	93	87	87	80	87
Sulfur dioxide		347	.03	100	92	85	77	77	69	69	69	69	62
Total suspended particulates		1,726	75	100	101	103	96	80	79	82	78	78	79
Nitrogen dioxide		84	.053	100	100	92	88	88	85	88	88	88	88
Lead		97	1.5[4]	100	85	62	47	49	41	37	25	14	12

Source: U.S. Department of Commerce, Bureau of the Census, *Statistical Abstract of the United States 1990 (110th ed.)*, Superintendent of Documents, Washington, D.C., p. 203, from U.S. Environmental Protection Agency, National Air Quality and Emissions Trends Report, 1987, February 1989. PPM stands for parts per million. *Notes:* 1. Refers to the primary National ambient Air Quality Standard that protects the public health. 2. Based on 8-hour standard of 9 ppm. 3. Based on 1-hour standard of .12 ppm. 4. Based on 3-month standard of 1.5 micrograms per square meter.

★ 69 ★

Auto Emissions in the U.S.

Amount of chloroflourocarbon (CFC) and carbon dioxide released by automobile use. Approximately 90 to 95 million auto air conditioners are in use in the U.S.

Installed auto air conditioner	2.5 lb. of CFC's
Annual recharge of air conditioner	1 lb. of CFC's
Drive for one year	5 tons of Carbon dioxide

Source: U.S. News & World Report, October 31, 1988, from World Resources Institute, Alliance for CFC Policy, Rainforest Action Network, U.S. Department of Agriculture, Worldwatch Institute.

★ 70 ★

Carbon Content of Selected Fuels

Fuel	Pounds of carbon[1]	Per	Kg Carbon per gigajoules	Mg carbon per Btu
Wood (dry poplar)	1,032	Cord	24.9	26
Bituminous coal (dry)	1,300	Short ton	24.4	26
Heating oil	6.4	Gallon	120.0	21
Diesel fuel	6.0	Gallon	19.7	21
Crude oil	255	Barrel	18.9	20
Gasoline	5.5	Gallon	18.9	20
No. 2 Diesel	6.0	Gallon	18.8	20
Gasohol	5.3	Gallon	18.8	20
Ethanol	3.5	Gallon	17.6	19
Methanol	2.5	Gallon	16.6	18
Propane	9.5	100 cu ft	16.3	17
Natural gas	3.3	100 cu ft	13.6	14
Natural gas	3.3	Therm	13.6	14
Electricity (U.S. avg.)	0.4	Kwh	50.5	53

Source: Changing by Degrees: Steps to Reduce Greenhouse Gases, U.S. Congress, Office of Technology Assessment, OTA-O-482, Washington, D.C., February 1991, p. 333 *Notes:* 1. To convert carbon to carbon dioxide, multiply by 3.667; from CO_2 to carbon, multiply by 0.27.

★ 71 ★

Carbon Dioxide Emissions by Autos

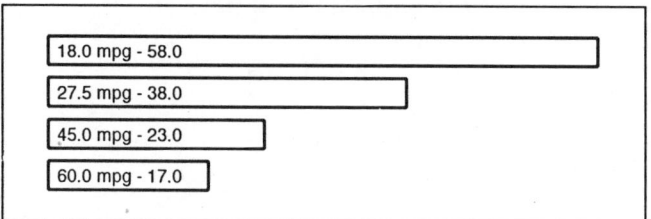

Tons of carbon dioxide discharged over a car's lifetime based on average mileage performance of the car.

Auto with gas mileage of-	Tons of carbon dioxide
18.0 mpg	58.0
27.5 mpg	38.0
45.0 mpg	23.0
60.0 mpg	17.0

Source: Sierra, July/August 1990, p. 23, from Environmental Action Foundation.

★ 72 ★

Carbon Dioxide Emissions by Industry by Source

Source	Percent
Machine drive and electrolytic	32
Steam	27
Process heat	19
Off-highway oil	7
HVAC and light	6
Feedstocks	6
Lease and plant	3

Source: *Changing by Degrees: Steps to Reduce Greenhouse Gases*, U.S. Congress, Office of Technology Assessment, OTA-O-482, Washington, D.C., February 1991, p. 8, from Office of Technology Assessment.

★ 73 ★

Carbon Dioxide Emissions by Transportation by Sectors

Source	Percent
Automobiles	43
Light trucks	20
Heavy trucks	14
Aircraft	14
Rail, marine	7
Nonoil-based	2

Source: *Changing by Degrees: Steps to Reduce Greenhouse Gases*, U.S. Congress, Office of Technology Assessment, OTA-O-482, Washington, D.C., February 1991, p. 8, from Office of Technology Assessment.

★ 74 ★

Carbon Dioxide Emissions by U.S. Industry

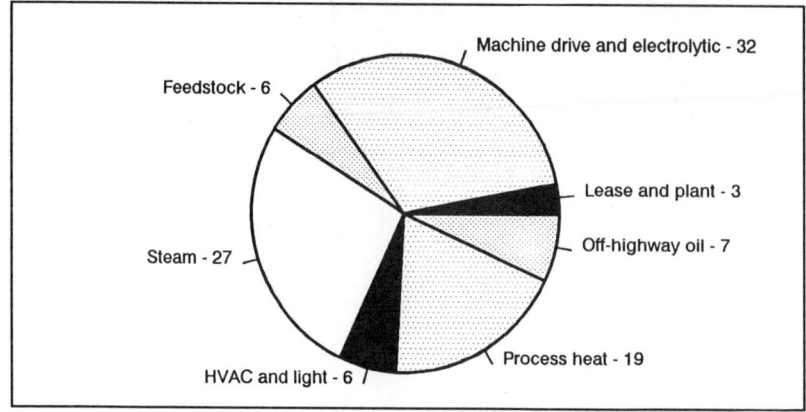

Values shown are percent of emissions from industry (0.42 billion metric tons per year) in 1987.

Source	Percent
Machine drive and electrolytic	32
Steam	27
Process heat	19
Off-highway oil	7
HVAC and light[1]	6
Feedstock	6
Lease and plant	3

Source: Changing by Degrees: Steps to Reduce Greenhouse Gases, U.S. Congress, Office of Technology Assessment, OTA-O-482, Washington, D.C., February 1991, p. 178, from Office of Technology Assessment, 1991. *Note:* 1. Heating, Ventilation and Air-Conditioning.

★ 75 ★

Carbon Dioxide Emissions From Fossil Fuel in the U.S.

Values shown by sector are percentages of a total output of 1.3 billion metric tons per year.

Source	% Carbon Dioxide Emissions
Buildings	36
Space heat	43
Appliances	20
Cooling	14
Lights	14
Water heat	9

[Continued]

★ 75 ★

Carbon Dioxide Emissions from Fossil Fuel in the U. S.
[Continued]

Source	% Carbon Dioxide Emissions
Industry	32
Transportation	32

Source: *Changing by Degrees: Steps to Reduce Greenhouse Gases*, U.S. Congress, Office of Technology Assessment, OTA-O-482, Washington, D.C., February 1991, p. 116, from Office of Technology Assessment, 1991.

★ 76 ★

Carbon Dioxide Emissions in Buildings by Source

Source	Percent
Space heat	43
Appliances	20
Cooling	14
Lights	14
Water heat	9

Source: *Changing by Degrees: Steps to Reduce Greenhouse Gases*, U.S. Congress, Office of Technology Assessment, OTA-O-482, Washington, D.C., February 1991, p. 8, from Office of Technology Assessment.

★ 77 ★

Carbon Dioxide Emissions, U.S. Transportation Sector
Percentages shown are based on carbon dioxide output related to transportation, a total emission of 0.42 billion metric tons per year.

Transportation Sector	Annual Percentage
Automobiles	43
Buildings	36
Industry	32
Light trucks	20
Heavy trucks	14
Aircraft	14
Rail, marine	7

[Continued]

★ 77 ★

Carbon Dioxide Emissions, U.S. Transportation Sector
[Continued]

Transportation Sector	Annual Percentage
Non-oil based	2
Total transportation	32

Source: *Changing by Degrees: Steps to Reduce Greenhouse Gases*, U.S. Congress, Office of Technology Assessment, OTA-O-482, Washington, D.C., February 1991, p. 149, from Office of Technology Assessment, 1991.

★ 78 ★

Carbon Emissions by Source
Figures shown are percent of 1987 emissions.

	Percent
Residential buildings	
Heating	9
Appliances	5
Hot water	3
Cooling	2
Electric lighting	1
Subtotal	20
Commercial buildings	
Heating	6
Electric lighting	4
Cooling	4
Appliances, hot water	2
Subtotal	16
Transportation	
Cars	14
Light trucks	6
Medium, heavy trucks	4
Air	4
Rail & marine	2
Subtotal	32
Industry	
Motors	9
Steam power	9
Processing	6
Off-highway oil	2
Heating, cooling, electric lighting	2
Feedstocks	2
Electrolytic	1

[Continued]

★ 78 ★

Carbon Emissions by Source

[Continued]

	Percent
Lease and plant	1
Subtotal	32

Source: Changing by Degrees: Steps to Reduce Greenhouse Gases, U.S. Congress, Office of Technology Assessment, OTA-O-482, Washington, D.C., February 1991, p. 314, from Office of Technology Assessment, 1991, based on data from Gas Research Institute, *Baseline Projection Data Book, 1988 GRI Baseline Projection of U.S. Energy Supply and Demand to 2010* (Washington, DC, 1988).

★ 79 ★

Carbon Emissions From Goods and Services

	Carbon emissions (percent)[1]	Intensity (Pounds Carbon per dollar)
Energy		
Petroleum refining and related industries	22.5	NA[2]
Electricutilities	18.2	NA[2]
Natural gas utilities	7.4	NA[2]
Total	48.0	NA[2]
Manufacturing		
Food and kindred products	7.1	0.8
Motor vehicles and equipment	3.1	0.8
Apparel	1.9	0.7
Drugs, cleaning and toilet preparations	1.1	0.8
Paper and allied products, except containers	0.8	1.8
Rubber and miscellaneous plastic products	0.6	1.2
Printing and publishing	0.5	0.7
Household appliances	0.5	0.9
Household furniture	0.5	0.8
Radio, TV, and communication equipment	0.5	0.6
Other manufacturing	4.0	-
Total	20.0	0.8
Transportation		
Air transportation	1.7	1.8
Motor freight transport	0.7	1.1
Water transportation	0.4	2.6
Local transport	0.4	0.9
Railroad	0.3	1.0
Total	3.0	1.4

[Continued]

★ 79 ★

Carbon Emissions from Goods and Services
[Continued]

	Carbon emissions (percent)[1]	Intensity (Pounds Carbon per dollar)
Services		
Wholesale and retail trade	12.0	0.5
Health, educational & social services and nonprofit organizations	6.8	0.5
Finance and insurance	1.6	0.3
Hotels: personal and repair services (except auto)	1.5	0.5
Real estate and rental	1.5	0.1
Automobile repair and services	1.1	0.6
Water and sanitary services	0.7	1.6
Amusements	0.6	0.4
Other services	1.0	-
Total	27.0	0.4

Source: Changing by Degrees: Steps to Reduce Greenhouse Gases, U.S. Congress, Office of Technology Assessment, OTA-O-482, Washington, D.C., February 1991, p. 315, from Office of Technology Assessment, 1991. *Notes:* 1. Emissions expressed as percent of carbon from household purchases (about 1 billion tons per year). 2. Not applicable.

★ 80 ★

Carbon Monoxide Emissions in the U.S.

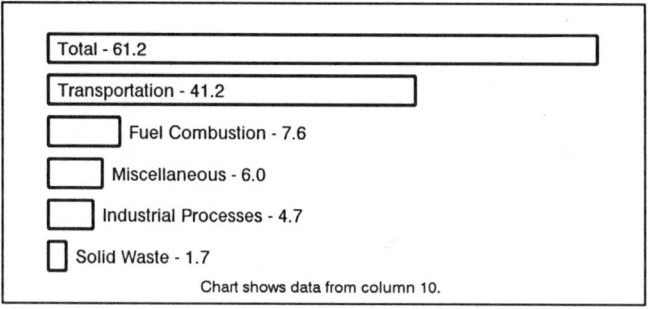

Total - 61.2

Transportation - 41.2

Fuel Combustion - 7.6

Miscellaneous - 6.0

Industrial Processes - 4.7

Solid Waste - 1.7

Chart shows data from column 10.

Carbon monoxide emissions, by source, shown in millions of metric tons.

Source Category	1979	1980	1981	1982	1983	1984	1985	1986	1987	1988
Transportation	59.1	56.1	55.4	52.9	52.4	50.6	47.9	44.6	43.2	41.2
Fuel Combustion	6.7	7.4	7.7	8.2	8.2	8.3	7.4	7.5	7.6	7.6
Industrial Processes	7.1	6.3	5.9	4.3	4.3	4.7	4.4	4.3	4.5	4.7
Solid Waste	2.3	2.2	2.1	2.0	1.9	1.9	2.0	1.7	1.7	1.7
Miscellaneous	6.5	7.6	6.4	4.9	7.7	6.3	5.3	5.0	7.1	6.0
Total	81.7	79.6	77.4	72.4	74.5	71.8	67.0	63.1	64.1	61.2

Source: U.S. Environmental Protection Agency, Office of Air Quality Planning and Standards, 1989. *National Air Quality and Emissions Trends Report, 1988*. EPA-450/4-90-002. Research Triangle Park, NC, p. 57. The sums of sub-categories may not equal total due to rounding.

★ 81 ★

Chlorofluorocarbon Releases Worldwide

Releases shown in millions of kilograms.

Year	CFC-11	CFC-12
1931	0.0	0.1
1932	0.0	0.1
1933	0.0	0.1
1934	0.0	0.2
1935	0.0	0.3
1936	0.0	0.5
1937	0.0	0.8
1938	0.1	1.2
1939	0.1	1.7
1940	0.1	2.3
1941	0.1	3.0
1942	0.1	3.7
1943	0.2	4.5
1944	0.2	6.1
1945	0.3	8.0
1946	0.6	13.9
1947	1.3	21.3
1948	2.3	24.8
1949	3.8	26.6
1950	5.5	29.5
1951	7.6	32.4
1952	11.0	33.7
1953	15.0	37.9
1954	18.6	42.9
1955	23.0	48.2
1956	28.7	56.1
1957	32.2	63.8
1958	30.2	66.9
1959	30.9	74.8
1960	40.5	89.1
1961	52.1	99.7
1962	65.4	114.5
1963	80.0	133.9
1964	95.0	155.5
1965	108.3	175.4
1966	121.3	195.0
1967	137.6	219.9
1968	156.8	246.5
1969	181.9	274.3
1970	206.6	299.9
1971	226.9	321.8
1972	255.8	349.9
1973	292.4	387.3
1974	321.4	418.6
1975	310.9	404.1
1976	316.7	390.4

[Continued]

★ 81 ★

Annual Chlorofluorocarbon Releases Worldwide
[Continued]

Year	CFC-11	CFC-12
1977	303.9	371.2
1978	283.6	341.3
1979	263.7	337.5
1980	250.8	332.5
1981	248.2	340.7
1982	239.5	337.4
1983	252.8	343.3
1984	271.1	359.4
1985	280.8	368.4
1986	295.1	376.5
1987	310.6	386.5
1988	314.5	392.8

Source: Council on Environmental Quality, *20th Annual Report 1990*, Washington, D.C., p. 468, from the Chemical Manufacturers Association, 1989, "Production, sales, and calculated release of CFC-11 and CFC-12 through 1988," Table 3. Washington, DC. Data are supplied by reporting companies participating in the Chemical Manufacturers Association's chlorofluorocarbon research program.

★ 82 ★

Emissions From Household Appliances
Pounds of carbon dioxide added to the atmosphere by household appliances using electricity.

Appliance	Pounds of Carbon Dioxide per hour or day
Toaster oven	12.80/hour
Air conditioner, room	4.00/hour
Vacuum cleaner	1.70/hour
Steam iron	.85/hour
Color television	.64/hour
Waterbed heater	24.00/day
with thermostat	12.80/day
Refrigerator, frostless	12.80/day
Ceiling fan	4.00/day

Source: U.S. News & World Report, April 23, 1990, from National Wildlife Federation.

★ 83 ★

Emissions From Steam-Electric Plants

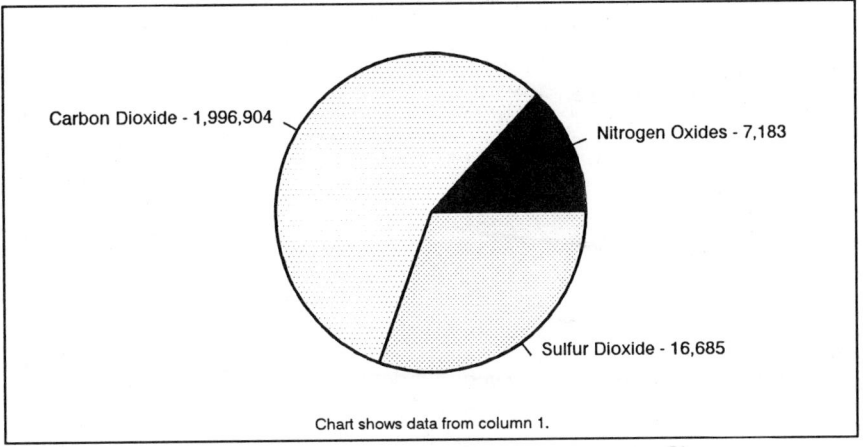

Carbon Dioxide - 1,996,904

Nitrogen Oxides - 7,183

Sulfur Dioxide - 16,685

Chart shows data from column 1.

Air emissions from fossil-fueled steam-electric plants, shown in thousands of short tons.

Emission	1989[1]	1988	1987	1986	1985
Sulfur Dioxide	16,685	16,636	16,170	16,191	16,171
Nitrogen Oxides	7,183	7,091	6,796	6,571	6,626
Carbon Dioxide	1,996,904	1,969,272	1,876,325	1,809,186	1,798,370

Source: Energy Information Administration, *Electric Power Annual*, January 1991, p. 74, from Energy Information Administration, Form EIA-767, "Steam-Electric Plant Operation and Design Report." Data include petroleum coke. These data are estimates derived from Form EIA-767, "Steam-Electric Plant Operation and Design Report." Data for 1985 through 1988 are revised. *Note:* 1. Data for 1989 are preliminary.

★ 84 ★

Emissions From Steam-Electric Plants by Fuel and by State

Emissions from fossil-fueled steam-electric plants in 1989, shown in thousands of short tons.

Census Division and State	Coal			Petroleum			Gas		
	Sulfur Dioxide	Nitrogen Oxides	Carbon Dioxide	Sulfur Dioxide	Nitrogen Oxides	Carbon Dioxide	Sulfur Dioxide	Nitrogen Oxides	Carbon Dioxide
New England	163	74	17,787	267	71	33,412	0	11	3,059
Connecticut	10	7	2,438	56	19	10,693	0	0	204
Maine	0	0	0	15	5	2,854	0	0	0
Massachusetts	106	46	12,119	161	41	16,487	0	10	2,726
New Hampshire	47	21	3,230	33	5	2,964	0	0	0
Rhode Island	0	0	0	2	1	407	0	1	125
Vermont	0	0	0	0	0	7	0	0	4
Middle Atlantic	1,597	497	148,107	185	91	48,417	0	40	13,026
New Jersey	76	47	9,379	14	12	5,265	0	10	2,483
New York	267	71	26,949	159	68	36,466	0	30	10,449
Pennsylvania	1,254	379	111,779	12	11	6,686	0	0	94

[Continued]

★ 84 ★

Emissions from Steam-Electric Plants by Fuel and by State
[Continued]

Census Division and State	Coal			Petroleum			Gas		
	Sulfur Dioxide	Nitrogen Oxides	Carbon Dioxide	Sulfur Dioxide	Nitrogen Oxides	Carbon Dioxide	Sulfur Dioxide	Nitrogen Oxides	Carbon Dioxide
East North Central	5,505	1,725	391,266	12	7	3,342	0	21	4,445
Illinois	886	317	58,007	3	2	1,085	0	1	395
Indiana	1,564	456	100,581	0	1	185	0	18	3,536
Michigan	397	273	71,444	7	3	1,541	0	2	380
Ohio	2,368	535	124,287	2	1	489	0	0	37
Wisconsin	290	144	36,947	0	0	42	0	0	97
West North Central	1,632	770	189,715	1	0	308	0	5	1,562
Iowa	189	97	28,399	0	0	31	0	1	142
Kansas	169	104	27,982	0	0	68	0	3	996
Minnesota	152	106	33,270	0	0	32	0	1	245
Missouri	885	272	54,060	1	0	92	0	0	39
Nebraska	47	70	13,857	0	0	42	0	0	132
North Dakota	160	102	28,962	0	0	35	0	0	0
South Dakota	30	19	3,185	0	0	8	0	0	8
South Atlantic	3,401	1,214	342,290	250	83	36,330	0	41	11,600
Delaware	70	20	6,548	15	8	2,266	0	3	680
District of Columbia	0	0	0	4	1	716	0	0	0
Florida	544	235	62,127	168	52	23,243	0	35	9,464
Georgia	835	216	64,751	0	0	88	0	0	31
Maryland	252	84	23,845	46	15	6,051	0	3	1,085
North Carolina	351	172	51,156	0	0	156	0	0	0
South Carolina	170	83	25,013	0	0	63	0	0	114
Virginia	172	80	25,340	17	6	3,536	0	0	219
West Virginia	1,007	324	83,510	0	1	211	0	0	7
East South Central	2,182	709	182,069	12	3	1,087	0	9	2,398
Alabama	564	193	55,106	0	0	88	0	0	106
Kentucky	751	306	70,809	0	0	125	0	0	20
Mississippi	105	33	9,405	12	3	772	0	9	2,272
Tennessee	762	177	46,749	0	0	102	0	0	0
West South Central	840	615	206,678	9	8	2,556	0	314	86,830
Arkansas	66	68	21,289	1	0	135	0	5	1,808
Louisiana	90	71	22,247	1	1	276	0	51	14,711
Oklahoma	96	85	27,683	0	0	27	0	39	9,440
Texas	588	391	135,459	7	7	2,118	0	219	60,871
Mountain	520	650	208,691	2	1	696	0	17	5,196
Arizona	133	117	35,582	0	0	154	0	6	1,769
Colorado	98	109	32,718	0	0	26	0	2	440
Idaho	0	0	0	0	0	0	0	0	0
Montana	29	61	19,002	0	0	23	0	0	26
Nevada	59	56	18,590	2	1	348	0	5	1,300
New Mexico	72	85	30,158	0	0	43	0	4	1,652
Utah	44	85	30,820	0	0	40	0	0	4
Wyoming	85	137	41,821	0	0	62	0	0	5

[Continued]

★ 84 ★

Emissions from Steam-Electric Plants by Fuel and by State
[Continued]

Census Division and State	Coal			Petroleum			Gas		
	Sulfur Dioxide	Nitrogen Oxides	Carbon Dioxide	Sulfur Dioxide	Nitrogen Oxides	Carbon Dioxide	Sulfur Dioxide	Nitrogen Oxides	Carbon Dioxide
Pacific Contiguous	64	43	10,291	16	28	8,518	0	121	29,856
California	0	0	0	15	28	8,422	0	121	29,856
Oregon	2	2	534	0	0	5	0	0	0
Washington	62	41	9,757	1	0	91	0	0	0
Pacific Noncontiguous	1	1	479	26	14	6,893	0	0	0
Alaska	1	1	479	0	0	1	0	0	0
Hawaii	0	0	0	26	14	6,892	0	0	0
U.S. Total	15,905	6,298	1,697,373	780	306	141,559	0	579	157,972

Source: Energy Information Administration, *Electric Power Annual 1989*, January 1991. p. 76, from Energy Information Administration, Form EIA-767, "Steam - Electric Plant Operation and Design Report" Totals may not equal sum of components because of independent rounding. Data for 1989 are preliminary. Data include petroleum coke. These data are estimates derived from Form EIA-767, "Steam-Electric Plant Operation and Design Report."

★ 85 ★

Environmental Effects Due to Energy Demand
The values reflect percent change from 1970 to 1988.

	Canada	United States	France	Western Germany	Italy	United Kingdom	Japan	OECD
Total primary Energy requirements	62	22	35	16	32	0	49	30
Air pollutant emissions								
Sulfur oxides	-43	-27	-55	-65	-27	-42	-83	-38
Nitrogen oxides	42	8	34	21	11	5	-29	13
Carbon dioxide	32	19	-18	-5	17	-13	25	15

Source: The OCED Observer, No. 168, February/March 1991, p. 11, from OECD.

★ 86 ★

Lead Emissions in the U.S.

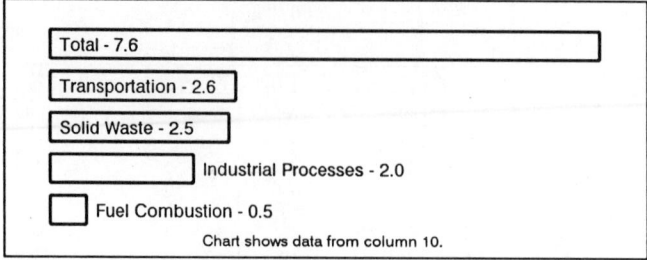

Chart shows data from column 10.

Lead emissions, by source, shown in thousands of metric tons.

Source Category	1979	1980	1981	1982	1983	1984	1985	1986	1987	1988
Transportation	94.6	59.4	46.9	46.9	40.8	34.7	15.5	3.5	3.0	2.6
Fuel Combustion	4.9	3.9	2.8	1.7	0.6	0.5	0.5	0.5	0.5	0.5
Industrial Processes	5.2	3.6	3.0	2.7	2.4	2.3	2.3	1.9	1.9	2.0
Solid Waste	4.0	3.7	3.7	3.1	2.6	2.6	2.8	2.7	2.6	2.5
Total	108.7	70.6	56.4	54.4	46.4	40.1	21.1	8.6	8.0	7.6

Source: U.S. Environmental Protection Agency, Office of Air Quality Planning and Standards, 1989. *National Air Quality and Emissions Trends Report, 1988.* EPA-450/4-90-002. Research Triangle Park, NC, p. 79. The sums of sub-categories may not equal total due to rounding.

★ 87 ★

Methane Emissions by Source

Source	Teragrams (trillions of grams)
Natural sources	115-345
Rice production	60-170
Fossil fuel production	50-95
Domestic animals	65-100
Biomass burning	50-100
Landfills	30-70

Source: Cicerone and Oremland, 1988; Crutzen et al., 1986; Lerner et al., 1988; United Nations, 1987; IRRI, 1986.

★ 88 ★

Methane Release Rates by Source

Values are shown in trillions of grams.

Identity	Annual Release	Range
Enteric fermentation (animals)	80	65-100
Natural wetlands (forested and nonforested bogs, forested and nonforested swamps, tundra, and alluvial formations)	115	100-200
Rice fields	110	60-170
Biomass burning	55	50-100
Termites	40	10-100
Landfills	40	30-70
Oceans	10	5-20
Freshwaters	5	1-25
Methane hydrate destablization	5?	0-100 (future)
Coal mining	35	25-45
Gas drilling, venting, transmission	45	400-640
Total	540	400-640

Source: "Climate Surprises," Hearing before the Congress, 101st Congress, May 8, 1989, p. 105.

★ 89 ★

Nitrogen Oxide Emissions by Source

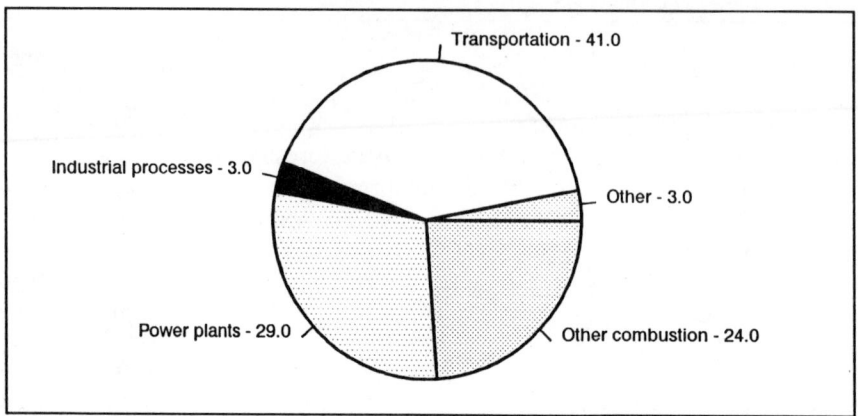

Source	Percent emitted
Power plants	29.0
Transportation	41.0
Industrial processes	3.0
Other combustion	24.0
Other	3.0

Source: American Forests, May/June 1989, p. 37, from "Breathing Easier: Taking Action on Climate Change, Air Pollution, and Energy Insecurity," by James J. MacKenzie, World Resources Institute.

★ 90 ★

Nitrogen Oxide Emissions in the U.S.

```
┌──────────────────────────────────────────────────┐
│  ┌──────────────────────────────────────────┐     │
│  │ Total - 19.8                             │     │
│  └──────────────────────────────────────────┘     │
│  ┌──────────────────────────────┐                 │
│  │ Fuel Combustion - 10.8       │                 │
│  └──────────────────────────────┘                 │
│  ┌──────────────────────┐                         │
│  │ Transportation - 8.1 │                         │
│  └──────────────────────┘                         │
│  ▯ Industrial Processes - 0.6                      │
│  ▮ Miscellaneous - 0.2                             │
│  ▮ Solid Waste - 0.1                               │
│                    Chart shows data from column 10.│
└──────────────────────────────────────────────────┘
```

Nitrogen oxide emissions, by source, shown in millions of metric tons.

Source Category	1979	1980	1981	1982	1983	1984	1985	1986	1987	1988
Transportation	10.1	9.8	10.0	9.4	8.9	8.8	8.9	8.3	8.0	8.1
Fuel Combustion	10.5	10.1	10.0	9.8	9.6	10.2	10.2	10.0	10.5	10.8
Industrial Processes	0.7	0.7	0.6	0.5	0.5	0.6	0.6	0.6	0.6	0.6
Solid Waste	0.1	0.1	0.1	0.1	0.1	0.1	0.1	0.1	0.1	0.1
Miscellaneous	0.2	0.2	0.2	0.1	0.2	0.2	0.1	0.1	0.1	0.2
Total	21.6	20.9	20.9	20.0	19.3	19.8	19.8	19.0	19.3	19.8

Source: U.S. Environmental Protection Agency, Office of Air Quality Planning and Standards, 1989. *National Air Quality and Emissions Trends Report, 1988.* EPA-450/4-90-002. Research Triangle Park, NC, p. 63. The sums of sub-categories may not equal total due to rounding.

★ 91 ★

Nitrogen Oxide Emissions Nationwide

Estimated nitrogen oxide emissions by source category for 1985, 1994, 1999, and 2004. Data are in millions of tons per year and assume no new laws or regulations.

Source category	1985	1994	1999	2004
Utility boilers	6.8	8.0	8.6	9.3
Highway vehicles	6.8	6.0	6.2	6.8
Other large stationary	1.8	2.3	2.6	3.1
Small stationary	1.3	2.1	2.5	2.9
Other mobile sources	2.0	2.2	2.3	2.5

Source: Office of Technology Assessment, U.S. Congress, based on work by E.H. Pechan and Associates.

★ 92 ★

Organic Compounds by Source

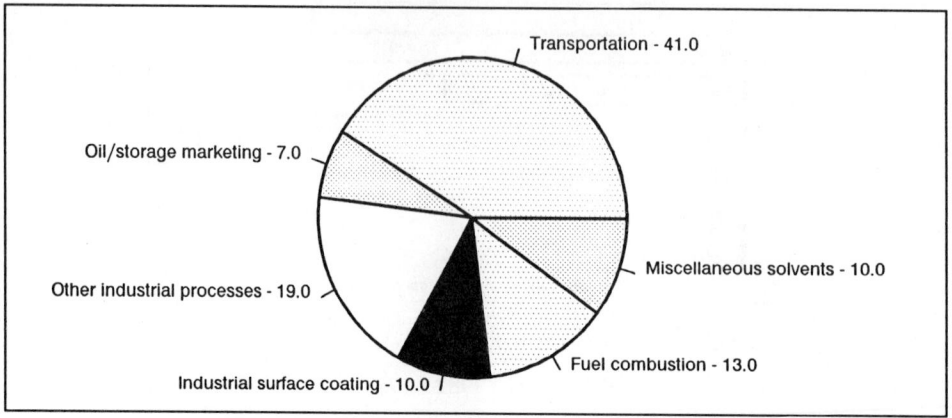

Source	Percent
Transportation	41.0
Oil/storage marketing	7.0
Fuel combustion	13.0
Industrial surface coating	10.0
Other industrial processes	19.0
Miscellaneous solvents	10.0

Source: American Forests, May/June 1989, p. 37, from "Breathing Easier: Taking Action on Climate Change, Air Pollution, and Energy Insecurity," by James J. MacKenzie, World Resources Institute.

★ 93 ★

Origin of Toxic Chemical Releases to the Air

Data, for 1987, show that 68% of toxic chemicals released to the atmosphere came from point sources (facilities of some kind) while the rest came from fugitive emissions (in transit, during use, etc.). Total emissions were 2.7 billion pounds.

Type of emission	% of total
Point source	68.0
Fugitive	32.0

Source: The Toxic Release Inventory, A National Perspective, U.S. Environmental Protection Agency, Washington, D.C., June 1989, p. 109.

★ 94 ★

Particulate Emissions in the U.S.

Total - 6.9
Industrial Processes - 2.6
Fuel Combustion - 1.7
Transportation - 1.4
Miscellaneous - 0.9
Solid Waste - 0.3

Chart shows data from column 10.

Total suspended particulate emissions, by source, shown in millions of metric tons.

Source Category	1979	1980	1981	1982	1983	1984	1985	1986	1987	1988
Transportation	1.4	1.3	1.3	1.3	1.3	1.3	1.4	1.4	1.4	1.4
Fuel Combustion	2.5	2.4	2.3	2.2	2.0	2.1	1.8	1.8	1.8	1.7
Industrial Processes	3.8	3.3	3.0	2.6	2.4	2.8	2.8	2.5	2.5	2.6
Solid Waste	0.4	0.4	0.4	0.3	0.3	0.3	0.3	0.3	0.3	0.3
Miscellaneous	0.9	1.1	0.9	0.7	1.1	0.9	0.8	0.8	1.0	0.9
Total	8.9	8.5	8.0	7.1	7.1	7.4	7.1	6.8	7.0	6.9

Source: U.S. Environmental Protection Agency, Office of Air Quality Planning and Standards, 1989. *National Air Quality and Emissions Trends Report, 1988.* EPA-450/4-90-002. Research Triangle Park, NC, p. 36. The sums of sub-categories may not equal total due to rounding.

★ 95 ★

Pollution From Urban Transport

Toxic emissions from typical urban transport, based on national average vehicle occupancy rates. Data in grams per 100 passenger miles.

Mode	Hydro-carbons	Carbon Monoxide	Nitrogen Oxides
Rapid rail	0.3	2	49.0
Light rail	0.4	3	69.0
Transit bus	20.0	305	154.0
Van pool	36.0	242	38.0
Car pool	70.0	52	69.0
Single occupant auto	209.0	1,506	206.0

Source: World Watch, November/December 1990, p. 22, from American Public Transit Association, "Mass Transit: The Clean Air Alternative," Washington, DC, 1989.

★ 96 ★

Sulfur Dioxide Emissions by Source

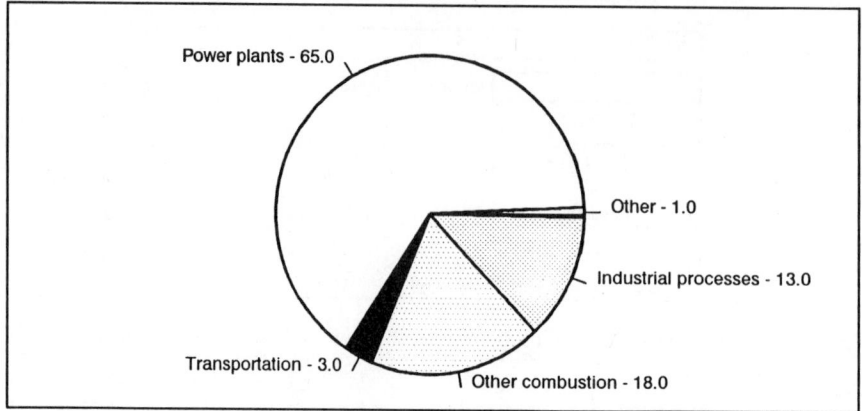

Source	Percent emitted
Power plants	65.0
Transportation	3.0
Industrial processes	13.0
Other combustion	18.0
Other	1.0

Source: American Forests, May/June 1989, p. 37, from "Breathing Easier: Taking Action on Climate Change, Air Pollution, and Energy Insecurity," by James J. MacKenzie, World Resources Institute.

★ 97 ★

Sulfur Dioxide Emissions in the U.S.

Total - 20.7

Fuel Combustion - 16.4

Industrial Processes - 3.4

Transportation - 0.9

Solid Waste - 0.0

Miscellaneous - 0.0

Chart shows data from column 10.

Sulfur dioxide emissions, by source, shown in millions of metric tons.

Source Category	1979	1980	1981	1982	1983	1984	1985	1986	1987	1988
Transportation	0.9	0.9	0.9	0.8	0.8	0.8	0.9	0.9	0.9	0.9
Fuel Combustion	19.5	18.7	17.8	17.3	16.7	17.4	17.0	16.9	16.6	16.4
Industrial Processes	4.4	3.8	3.9	3.3	3.3	3.3	3.2	3.1	3.2	3.4
Solid Waste	0.0	0.0	0.0	0.0	0.0	0.0	0.0	0.0	0.0	0.0
Miscellaneous	0.0	0.0	0.0	0.0	0.0	0.0	0.0	0.0	0.0	0.0
Total	24.8	23.4	22.6	21.4	20.7	21.5	21.1	20.9	20.6	20.7

Source: U.S. Environmental Protection Agency, Office of Air Quality Planning and Standards, 1989. *National Air Quality and Emissions Trends Report, 1988.* EPA-450/4-90-002. Research Triangle Park, NC, p. 49. The sums of sub-categories may not equal total due to rounding.

★ 98 ★

Suspended Particulate Emissions by Source

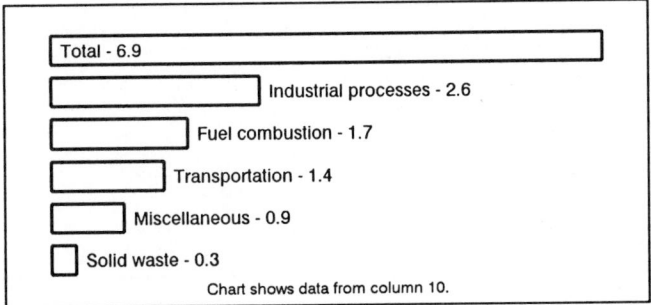

Total - 6.9

Industrial processes - 2.6

Fuel combustion - 1.7

Transportation - 1.4

Miscellaneous - 0.9

Solid waste - 0.3

Chart shows data from column 10.

Total emission estimates for the U.S. shown in millions of metric tons per year.

Source Category	1979	1980	1981	1982	1983	1984	1985	1986	1987	1988
Transportation	1.4	1.3	1.3	1.3	1.3	1.3	1.4	1.4	1.4	1.4
Fuel combustion	2.5	2.4	2.3	2.2	2.0	2.1	1.8	1.8	1.8	1.7
Industrial processes	3.8	3.3	3.0	2.6	2.4	2.8	2.8	2.5	2.5	2.6
Solid waste	0.4	0.4	0.4	0.3	0.3	0.3	0.3	0.3	0.3	0.3

[Continued]

★ 98 ★

Suspended Particulate Emissions by Source
[Continued]

Source Category	1979	1980	1981	1982	1983	1984	1985	1986	1987	1988
Miscellaneous	0.9	1.1	0.9	0.7	1.1	0.9	0.8	0.8	1.0	0.9
Total	8.9	8.5	8.0	7.1	7.1	7.4	7.1	6.8	7.0	6.9

Source: *National Air Quality and Emission Trend Report, 1988*, EPA, Research Triangle Park, N.C., March 1990, p. 36. The sums of sub-categories may not equal total due to rounding.

★ 99 ★

Volatile Organic Compound Emissions
The emissions are in millions of tons per year, by vehicle.

Source Category	1985	1994	1999	2004
Air, Rail, Marine	1.4	1.6	1.6	1.8
Large Stationary	2.1	2.5	2.5	2.5
Highway Vehicles	11.0	8.1	7.8	8.0
Small Stationary	10.6	11.4	12.2	13.1

Source: *Catching Our Breath: Next Steps for Reducing Urban Ozone*, U.S. Congress, Office of Technology Assessment, OTA-F-412, Washington, D.C., July 1989, p. 12, from Office of Technology Assessment, 1989.

★ 100 ★

Volatile Organic Compound Emissions in the U.S.

Total - 18.6

Industrial Processes - 8.5

Transportation - 6.1

Miscellaneous - 2.4

Fuel Combustion - 0.9

Solid Waste - 0.6

Chart shows data from column 10.

Volatile organic compound emissions, by source, shown in millions of metric tons.

Source Category	1979	1980	1981	1982	1983	1984	1985	1986	1987	1988
Transportation	8.0	7.5	7.4	7.2	7.1	7.2	6.9	6.5	6.4	6.1
Fuel Combustion	0.9	0.9	0.9	1.0	1.0	1.0	0.9	0.9	0.9	0.9
Industrial Processes	9.9	9.2	8.3	7.5	7.9	8.8	8.5	8.1	8.3	8.5
Solid Waste	0.7	0.6	0.6	0.6	0.6	0.6	0.6	0.6	0.6	0.6

[Continued]

★ 100 ★

Volatile Organic Compound Emissions in the U.S.
[Continued]

Source Category	1979	1980	1981	1982	1983	1984	1985	1986	1987	1988
Miscellaneous	2.9	2.9	2.5	2.2	2.7	2.7	2.2	2.2	2.4	2.4
Total	22.4	21.1	19.8	18.4	19.3	20.3	19.1	18.3	18.6	18.6

Source: U.S. Environmental Protection Agency, Office of Air Quality Planning and Standards, 1989. *National Air Quality and Emissions Trends Report, 1988*. EPA-450/4-90-002. Research Triangle Park, NC, p. 69. The sums of sub-categories may not equal total due to rounding.

Global Warming

★ 101 ★

Appliance Use Contribution to Global Warming

Appliance	Carbon Dioxide Added to Atmosphere[1]	
	Time Measurement	Pounds
Color television	per hour	.64
Steam iron	per hour	.85
Vacuum cleaner	per hour	1.70
Air conditioner, room	per hour	4.00
Toaster oven	per hour	12.80
Ceiling fan	per day	4.00
Refrigerator, frostless	per day	12.80
Waterbed heater	per day	24.00
Waterbed heater with thermostat	per day	12.80
Clothes dryer	per load	10.00
Dishwasher	per load	2.60
Toaster	per use	.12
Microwave oven	per 5-min use	.25
Coffeemaker	per brew	.50

Source: National Wildlife, Feb-March 1990, p. 53. *Notes:* 1. At room temperature and sea level, every pound of carbon dioxide occupies 8.75 cubic feet, about half the size of a refrigerator.

★ 102 ★

Contribution of Gas Guzzlers to Global Warming

BMW 750il - 58.6	
Jaguar XJ-S Convertible - 57.6	
Mercedes 560SEC - 55.6	
Mercedes 500SL - 54.1	
Audi V8 - 53.0	
Mercedes 420SEL - 51.6	
Cadillac Brougham - 50.3	
Mercedes 300SE, 300SEL - 48.8	
BMW 735il; BMW 535i - 47.6	
Cadillac Allante - 47.4	
Volvo 760, Volvo 780 - 45.8	
Infiniti Q45 - 45.4	

Data show cars with fuel economy below 22.5 miles per gallon, based on a 100,000-mile life. These cars emit the most carbon dioxide, which may contribute to global warming. Figures for emissions in tons.

Make/model	Carbon dioxide emissions per 100,000 miles
BMW 750il	58.6
Jaguar XJ-S Convertible	57.6
Mercedes 560SEC	55.6
Mercedes 500SL	54.1
Audi V8	53.0
Mercedes 420SEL	51.6
Cadillac Brougham	50.3
Mercedes 300SE, 300SEL	48.8
BMW 735il; BMW 535i	47.6
Cadillac Allante	47.4
Volvo 760, Volvo 780	45.8
Infiniti Q45	45.4

Source: U.S. News & World Report, July 2, 1990. *Notes:* Basic data: Public Citizen; Environmental Protection Agency. Figures apply to the highest-mileage version for each model. Sports and specialty cars are excluded.

★ 103 ★

Contribution of Greenhouse Gases to Global Warming

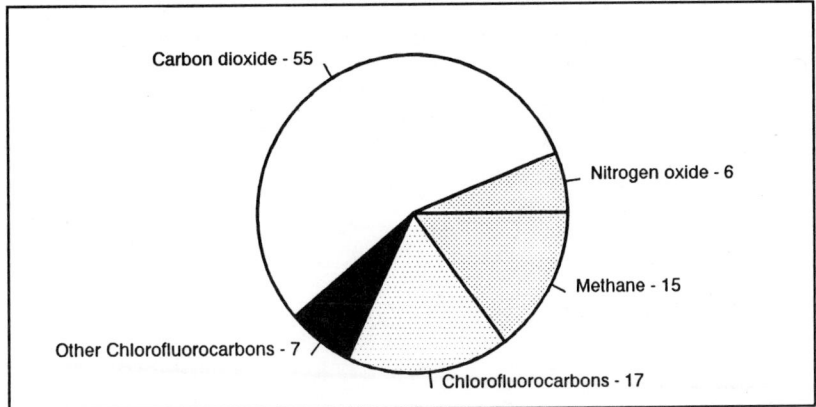

The values are contribution of manmade greenhouse gases to the change in radiative forcing from 1980 to 1990. The contribution from urban ozone may also be significant, but cannot be qualified at present.

Source	Percent
Carbon dioxide	55
Chlorofluorocarbons	17
Methane	15
Nitrogen oxide	6
Other Chlorofluorocarbons	7

Source: Changing by Degrees: Steps to Reduce Greenhouse Gases, U.S. Congress, Office of Technology Assessment, OTA-O-482, Washington, D.C., February 1991, p. 5, from Intergovernmental Panel on Climate Change, *Scientific Assessment of Climate Change*, Summary and Report, World Meteorological Organization/U.N. Environment Program (Cambridge, MA: Cambridge University Press, 1990).

★ 104 ★

Global Warming Causes

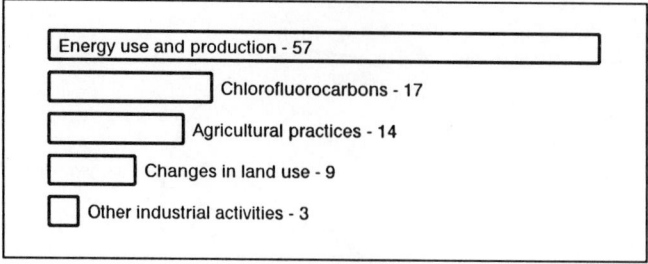

Energy use and production - 57

Chlorofluorocarbons - 17

Agricultural practices - 14

Changes in land use - 9

Other industrial activities - 3

Activity	Percent of contribution
Energy use and production	57
Chlorofluorocarbons	17
Agricultural practices[1]	14
Changes in land use[2]	9
Other industrial activities	3

Source: C&EN, March 27, 1989, p. 22, from Environmental Protection Agency. Each activity's contribution to greenhouse warming for the 1980's is estimated based on it share of greenhouse-gas emissions. *Notes:* 1. Includes methane emissions from animals, rice cultivation, and use of nitrogenous fertilizer. 2. Includes deforestation and biomass burning.

★ 105 ★

Greenhouse Gas Contributions to Global Warming (1980s)

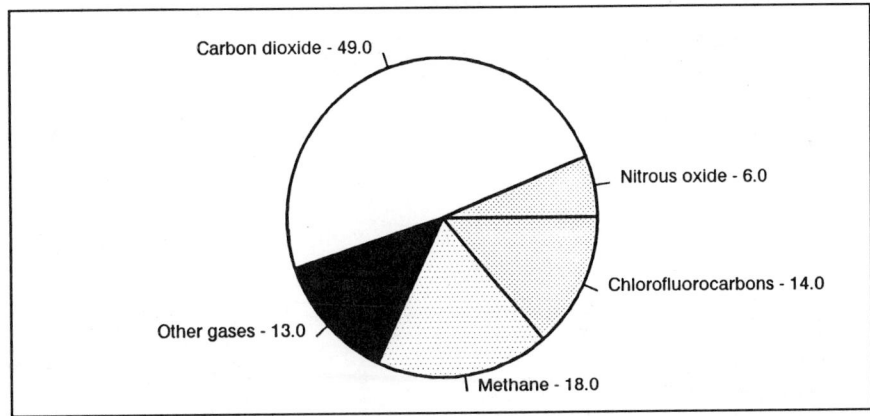

Gases contributing to the global warming effect. Contribution of each gas is shown in percent.

Gas	% Contributed
Nitrous oxide	6.0
Carbon dioxide	49.0
Methane	18.0
Chlorofluorocarbons	14.0
Other gases	13.0

Source: EPA Journal, March/April 1990, p. 10 from J. Hansen et al.

★ 106 ★

Projected Decline in Greenhouse Gas Emissions

Estimated decline in greenhouse index scores from 1988 to 2005 based on planned stabilization, decreases, or increases in greenhouse emissions and total recycling of chlorofluorocarbon-11 (CFC-11) and CFC-12 in 2005.

Country	Percentage decline
Australia	34.9
Austria	46.5
Belgium	34.7
Canada	19.8
Denmark	43.4
Finland	28.2
France	44.5
Greece	42.4
Iceland	20.1
Ireland	33.2
Italy	43.5
Japan	26.0

[Continued]

★ 106 ★

Projected Decline in Greenhouse Gas Emissions
[Continued]

Country	Percentage decline
Luxembourg	19.6
Netherlands	37.6
New Zealand	26.8
Norway	8.5
Portugal	57.4
Spain	48.3
Sweden	25.6
Switzerland	43.6
United Kingdom	33.2
United States	5.1
West Germany	45.8

Source: Environment, January/February 1991, p. 15.

★ 107 ★

Regional Contributions to Global Warming

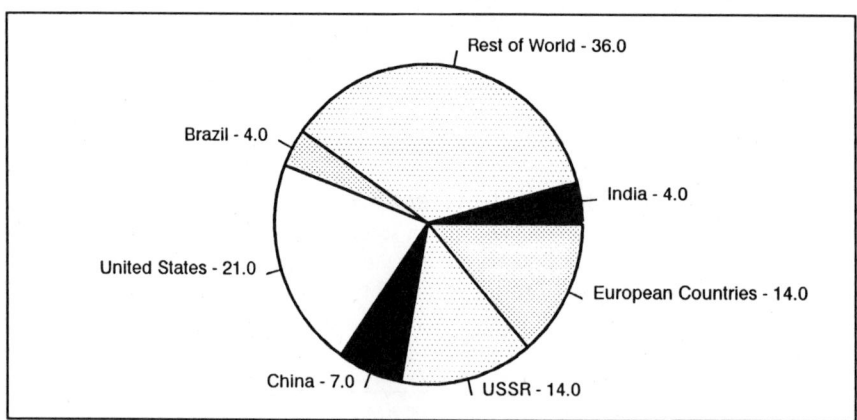

Source of greenhouse gases by regions of the world.

Country	% Contributed
China	7.0
Brazil	4.0
India	4.0
United States	21.0
USSR	14.0
European Countries	14.0
Rest of World	36.0

Source: EPA Journal, March/April 1990, p. 10, from J. Hansen et al.

Hazardous Waste

★ 108 ★

Facts About Hazardous Waste

	Amount	Measure
Hazardous waste generated in the average home each year[1]	15	pounds
Waste per participant brought to household hazardous waste collection days[2]	116	pounds
New pest-control chemicals registered with the EPA annually[3]	10	chemicals
New pesticide products introduced annually[3]	2,200	number
Indoor pest control expenditures a year[4]	$1.5	billion

Source: Garbage, March/April 1990, p. 16. *Notes:* 1. Dana Duxbury and Associates. 2. Dana Duxbury and Associates. Data include first-time collections, to which people bring years of accumulated wastes. One participant may represent more than one household. 3. EPA. 4. American Pest Control Association.

★ 109 ★

Hazardous Household Waste

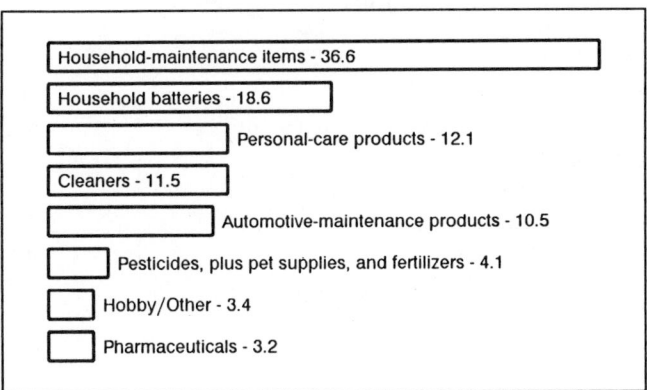

Household-maintenance items - 36.6

Household batteries - 18.6

Personal-care products - 12.1

Cleaners - 11.5

Automotive-maintenance products - 10.5

Pesticides, plus pet supplies, and fertilizers - 4.1

Hobby/Other - 3.4

Pharmaceuticals - 3.2

Hazardous household waste by type, shown as percent of total.

Type of waste	Percent of all waste
Household-maintenance items[1]	36.6
Household batteries	18.6
Personal-care products[2]	12.1
Cleaners	11.5
Automotive-maintenance products[3]	10.5
Pesticides, plus pet supplies, and fertilizers	4.1

[Continued]

★ 109 ★

Hazardous Household Waste
[Continued]

Type of waste	Percent of all waste
Hobby/Other[4]	3.4
Pharmaceuticals	3.2

Source: Garbage, March/April, 1990, p. 16, from The Garbage Project, University of Arizona. *Notes:* 1. Mostly paint, plus thinners, adhesives 2. Includes nail polish and remover, hair spray, deodorant 3. Mostly oil 4. Includes pool chemicals, lighter fluid, art supplies.

★ 110 ★

Hazardous Waste Generation

Data show quantities of hazardous waste generated by major industry groups in millions of metric tons per year.

Industry	Hazardous waste volume
Industrial organic chemicals	60-80
General chemical manufacturing	40-50
Petroleum refining	20-30
Explosives	10-15
Plastic materials/resins	6-10
Refuse systems (commercial TSDR facility)[1]	5-8
Agricultural chemicals	5-8
Cyclic crudes/intermediates	5-8
Inorganic pigments	3.5-5
Alkalies/chlorine	2.5-4.5

Source: C&EN, February 6, 1989, p. 19. *Note:* 1. Transportation, storage, disposal, or recycling.

★ 111 ★

Hazardous Waste Generation by Industry

Total - 761
Chemicals & allied products - 373
Primary metals - 119
Petroleum & coal - 88
Other - 71
Fabricated metal - 68
Rubber & plastic - 42

Chart shows data from column 1.

According to a forecast by Leading Edge Reports, the hazardous waste treatment and disposal industry handled 761 billion pounds in 1990, a $73 billion market. The market is expected to grow to 959 billion pounds and nearly $174 billion by 1995.

Types of waste	Billions of Pounds	
	1990	1995
Chemicals & allied products	373	470
Primary metals	119	143
Petroleum & coal	88	110
Fabricated metal	68	86
Rubber & plastic	42	60
Other	71	90
Total	761	959

Source: C&EN, February 25, 1991, p. 12, from Leading Edge Reports.

★ 112 ★

Household Hazardous Waste for Collection

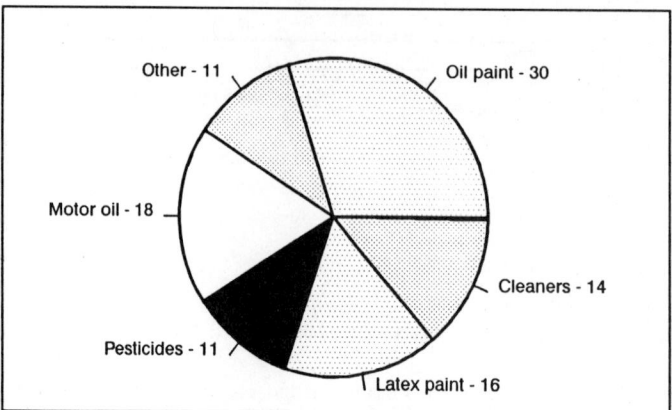

Based on waste collected in seven randomly chosen events, which varied in size.

Types	Percent
Oil paint	30
Motor oil	18
Latex paint[1]	16
Cleaners	14
Pesticides	11
Other[2]	11

Source: Garbage, March/April 1990, p. 16, from Dana Duxbury and Associates. *Notes:* 1. Designated as hazardous waste in California. 2. Adhesives, antifreeze, asbestos, batteries, gasoline, hobby chemicals, home maintenance products, household batteries, paint thinners, pool cleaners, radioactives.

★ 113 ★

Solid & Hazardous Waste in the U.S.

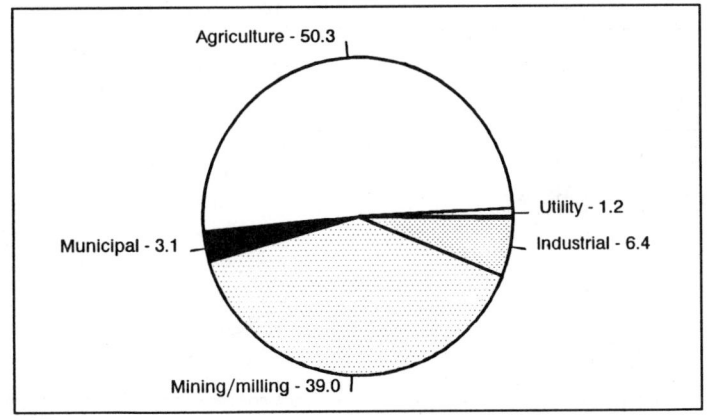

Type of waste	Percent of Total
Industrial	6.4
Municipal	3.1
Utility	1.2
Agriculture	50.3
Mining/milling[1]	39.0

Source: EPA Journal, January/February 1987, p. 15, from EPA's Office of Solid Waste *Note:* 1. Includes uranium mill tailings.

★ 114 ★

Superfund Sites Containing Radioactive Contaminants

Site name	City/county	State/EPA region	Acres	Cu. yds.
Shpack/ALI	Norton/ Attleboro	MA/I	31.00	-
Maywood Chemical Co./Sears Property	Maywood/ Bergen Co.	NJ/II	42.00	270,000
U.S. Radium Corp.	Orange, Essex Co.	NJ/II	1.00	10,000
W.R. Grace & Co.	Wayne/Passaic Co.	NJ/II	6.50	120,000
Montclair, West Orange	Essex Co.	NJ/II	-	-
Glen Ridge Radium Site	Essex Co.	NJ/II	127.00	350,000
Lodi Municipal Well	Lodi, Bergen Co.	NJ/II	Wells	-
Lansdowne Property	Lansdowne	PA/III	1.90	2,000

[Continued]

★ 114 ★

Superfund Sites Containing Radioactive Contaminants
[Continued]

Site name	City/county	State/EPA region	Acres	Cu. yds.
Maxey Flats Nuclear Disposal Site	Fleming City/ Hillsboro	KY/IV	25.00	178,000
West Chicago Sewage Treatment Plant	West Chicago	IL/V	25.00	40,000
Reed-Keppler Park	West Chicago	IL/V	0.25	20,000
Kerr-McGee Off-Site Properties	West Chicago	IL/V	-	61,000
Kerr-McGee Kress Creek/West Branch of Dupage River	West Chicago	IL/V	-	-
The Homestake Mining Co.	Cibola Co.	NM/VI	245.00	16,500,000
United Nuclear Corp.	Church Rock	NM/VI	170.00	4,700,000
Weldon Spring Quarry	St. Charles City	MO/VII	220.00	780,000
Monticello Radioactivity-Contaminated Properties	Monticello/ San Juan, Co.	UT/VIII	-	182,000
Denver Radium Superfund Sites	Denver	CO/VIII	40.00	106,000
Lincoln Park	Conon City	CO/VIII	900.00	1,900,000
U.S. DOE Rocky Flats Plant	Golden	CO/VIII	6,550.00	-
Uravan Uranium Project	Montrose City/Uravan	CO/VIII	900.00	10,000,000
Teledyne Wah Chang	Albany	OR/X	-	-
Hanford 200-area (USDOE)	Benton, CO	WA/X	-	1,000,000,000
Hanford 300-area (USDOE)	Benton, CO	WA/X	-	27,000,000
Hanford 100-area (USDOE)	Benton, CO	WA/X	-	4,300,000,000

Source: Third International Conference on New Frontiers for Hazardous Waste Management Proceedings, Sept. 10-13, EPA/600/9-89/072, Aug. 1989, p. 60.

★ 115 ★

Top Ten Industrial Waste Generators

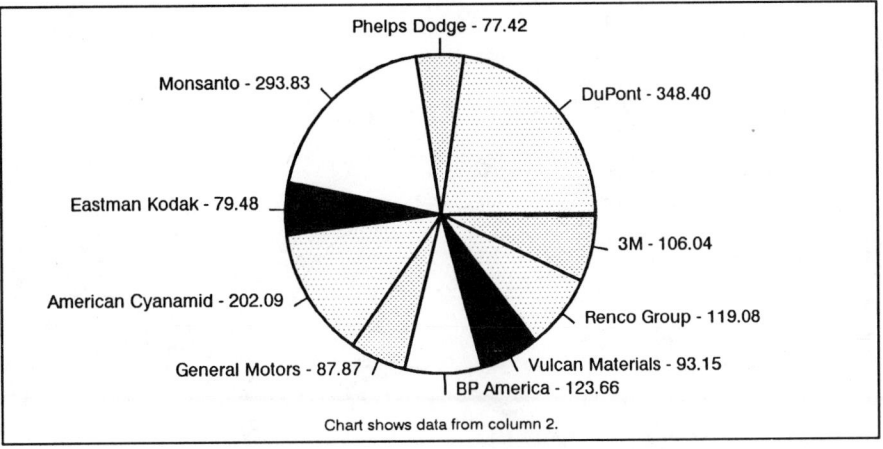

Chart shows data from column 2.

Data reflect amount of toxic waste produced by each company in 1989 (using latest figures available).

Company	Number of Facilities	Toxic Waste (millions of pounds)
DuPont	85	348.40
Monsanto	33	293.83
American Cyanamid	29	202.09
BP America	18	123.66
Renco Group	2	119.08
3M	51	106.04
Vulcan Materials	2	93.15
General Motors	133	87.87
Eastman Kodak	23	79.48
Phelps Dodge	19	77.42

Source: The Wall Street Journal, June 11, 1991 from U.S. Environmental Protection Agency.

Nuclear Waste

★ 116 ★

Generation of Nuclear Waste

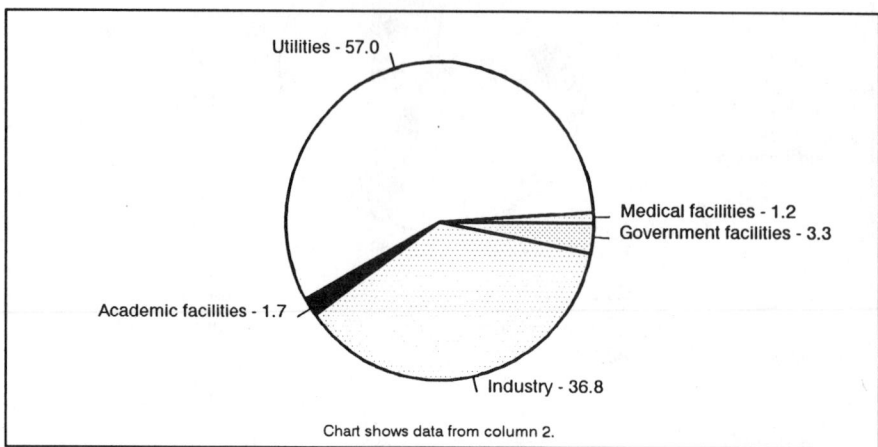

Chart shows data from column 2.

Generation of nuclear waste shown by the sectors producing it. Data show percent generated by each sector based (1) on total radioactivity generated and (2) total volume generated.

	Percent by source	
	Radio-activity	Volume
Utilities	77.8	57.0
Industry	21.1	36.8
Government facilities	1.0	3.3
Academic facilities	0.1	1.7
Medical facilities	-	1.2

Source: Sierra, September/October 1987, p. 17, from EG&G Idaho, for the Department of Energy.

★ 117 ★

High-Level Nuclear Waste Radioactivity

The values are total waste radioactivity through 1988.

Site	Curies	Percent
Hanford	446,000,000	37.1
Savannah River	661,000,000	54.9
Idaho Chemical Processing Plant (ICPP)	67,000,000	5.6
West Valley Demonstration Project (WVDP-commercial)	29,300,000	2.4
Total	1,200,000,000	

Source: Complex Cleanup: The Environmental Legacy of Nuclear Weapons Production, U.S. Congress, Office of Technology Assessment, OTA-O-484, Washington, D.C., February 1991, p. 47, from U.S. Department of Energy, *Integrated Data Base for 1989*, DOE/RW-0006, November 1989.

★ 118 ★

High-Level Nuclear Waste Volume

The values are total waste through 1988.

Site	Volume	Percent
Hanford	244,000	63.3
Savannah River	128,000	33.2
Idaho Chemical Processing Plant (ICPP)	11,000	2.9
West Valley Demonstration Project (WVDP-commercial)	2,130	0.6
Total	385,000	

Source: Complex Cleanup: The Environmental Legacy of Nuclear Weapons Production, U.S. Congress, Office of Technology Assessment, OTA-O-484, Washington, D.C., February 1991, p. 46, from U.S. Department of Energy, *Integrated Data Base for 1989*, DOE/RW-0006, November 1989. Volumes are in cubic meters. These percentages will change after treatment.

★ 119 ★

Nuclear Weapons Site Contaminants

Examples of nuclear weapons site contaminats and mixtures.

Inorganic contaminants:
Radionuclides:
Americium-241
Cesium-134, 137
Cobalt-60
Plutonium-238, 239
Radium-224, 226
Strontium-90
Technetium-99
Thorium-228,232
Uranium-234, 238

Metals:
Chromium
Copper
Lead
Mercury
Nickel

Other:
Cyanide

Organic contaminants:
Benzene
Chlorinated hydrocarbons
Methylethyl ketone, cyclohexanone, acetone
acetonc
Polychlorinated biphenyls, select poly-
select polycyclie aromatic
hydrocarbons
Tetraphenylboron
Toulene

Tributylphosphate

Organic facilitators:
Aliphatic acids
Aromatic acids
Chelating agents
Solvents, diluents, and chelate
radiolysis fragments

Mixtures of contaminants:
Radionuclides and metal ions
Radionuclides, metals, and
organic acids
Radionuclides, metals, and
natural organic substances
Radionuclides and synthetic
chelating agents
Radionuclides and solvents
Radionuclides, metal ions, and
organophosphates
Radionuclides, metal ions, and
petroleum hydrocarbons
Radionuclides, chlorinated
solvents, and petroleum
hydrocarbons
Petroleum hydrocarbons and
polychlorinated biphenyls
Complex solvent mixtures
Complex solvent and petroleum
hydrocarbon mixtures

Source: Complex Cleanup: The Environmental Legacy of Nuclear Weapons Production, U.S. Congress, Office of Technology Assessment, OTA-O-484, Washington, D.C., February 1991, p. 24, from U.S. Department of Energy/Office of Health and Environmental Research, Subsurface Science Program, Co-Contaminant Chemistry Subprogram, *"Draft Strategy Document,"* March 1990. *Notes:* The contaminant list is being upgraded as new information becomes available. *Facilitators* are organic compounds that interact with and modify metal or radionuclide geochemical behavior. *Mixtures:* information on mixture types is sparse, and concentration data are limited.

★ 120 ★

Radioactive Waste Generation

Cumulative amounts of radioactive waste generated through 1988. Amounts do not include mill tailings or waste from remedial action projects.

Waste Type	Volumes (in 000 cubic feet)	Percent	Activity (in millions of Curies)	Percent
Low-level waste				
Commercial	46,000	29.30	5	0.02
Defense	87,000	55.50	14	0.06
High-level waste				
Commercial[1]	80	0.05	30	0.20
Defense	13,500	8.60	1,175	5.40
Commercial spent fuel	270	0.17	20,400	94.30
Defense waste	10,000	6.40	4	0.02
Total	156,850	100.02	21,628	100.00

Source: Office of Technical Assessment, *Partnership Under Pressure: Managing Commercial Low-level Radioactive Waste*, November 1989, p. 88, from U.S. Department of Energy, DRAFT *Intergrated Data Base for 1989: Spent Fuel and Radioactive Waste Inventories, Projections, and Characterstics*, DOE/RW-0006, Rev. 5, August 1988, p. 22. *Notes:* 1. Commercial waste now located at West Valley, N.Y. Also assumes no commercial reprocessing of spent fuel.

★ 121 ★

Radionuclides in Commercial Low-Level Waste

Principal radionuclides found in commercial low-level radioactive wastes.

Radionuclide	Approximate half-life		Type of radiation emitted
	Number	Duration	
Technecium-99	6	hours	Gamma
Xenon-133	5	days	Beta,Gamma
Phosphorus-32	14	days	Beta
Cobalt-58	2	months	X-rays,beta, gamma
Iodine-125	2	months	Gamma
Sulfur-35	3	months	Beta
Magnesium-54	10	months	X-rays,gamma
Cesium-134	2	years	Beta,gamma
Cobalt-60	5	years	Beta,gamma
Tritium	12	years	Beta
Cesium-137	30	years	Beta,gamma
Strontium-90	30	years	Beta
Nickel-61	90	years	Beta
Carbon-14	5,700	years	Beta
Nickel-59	80,000	years	X-rays

[Continued]

★ 121 ★

Radionuclides In Commercial Low-Level Waste
[Continued]

Radionuclide	Approximate half-life		Type of radiation emitted
	Number	Duration	
Iodine-129	15,700,000	years	Beta
Uranium-235	700,000,000	years	Alpha,gamma
Uranium-238	4,470,000,000	years	Alpha,gamma

Source: Office of Technological Assessment, *Partnership Under Pressure: Changing Commercial Low-Level Radioactive Waste*, November 1989, p. 83.

★ 122 ★

Uranium Mill Tailings

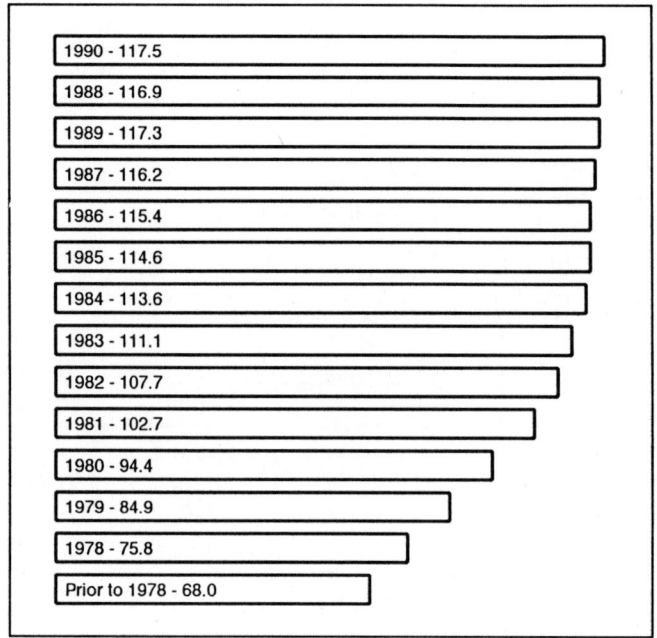

1990 - 117.5
1988 - 116.9
1989 - 117.3
1987 - 116.2
1986 - 115.4
1985 - 114.6
1984 - 113.6
1983 - 111.1
1982 - 107.7
1981 - 102.7
1980 - 94.4
1979 - 84.9
1978 - 75.8
Prior to 1978 - 68.0

Annual accumulated volumes shown in millions of cubic meters.

Year	Accumulation
Prior to 1978	68.0
1978	75.8
1979	84.9
1980	94.4
1981	102.7
1982	107.7
1983	111.1
1984	113.6
1985	114.6

[Continued]

★ 122 ★

Uranium Mill Tailings
[Continued]

Year	Accumulation
1986	115.4
1987	116.2
1988	116.9
1989	117.3[1]
1990	117.5[1]

Source: Council on Environmental Quality, *20th Annual Report 1990*, Washington, D.C., p. 447, from U.S. Department of Energy, 1989. "Integrated data base for 1990: Spent fuel and radioactive waste inventories, projections, and characteristics," Table 5-1, p. 133. Washington, DC. *Note:* 1. Projected.

★ 123 ★

Waste Comparisons for 1988

These comparisons do not illustrate the relative risks associated with each waste type, only the volume and weight of each.

Waste type	Volume (1,000 cubic feet)	Weight (tons)
Hazardous waste[1]	13,000,000	270,000,000
LLW[2]	1,440	36,000
Spent fuel	1.8	620

Source: Partnerships Under Pressure: Managing Commercial Low-Level Radioactive Waste, U.S. Congress, Office of Technology Assessment, OTA-F-426, Washington, D.C. November 1989, p. 8, from Office of Technology Assessment, 1989. LLW stands for low-level radioactive waste. *Notes:* 1. About 96 percent of this waste is managed onsite, with 4 percent shipped to commercial landfills. 2. Commercial, nonmixed LLW. As with hazardous waste, a very high percentage of utility LLW is treated onsite, greatly reducing that shipped for disposal.

Solid Waste

★ 124 ★

Annual Material Generation Rate in Municipal Wastes

```
Plastics - 7.8
All Other Materials - 5.5
Metals - 3.1
Total MSW - 3.1
                          Paper and Paperboard - 3.0
                  Yard Wastes - 1.9
Glass - 1.6
        Population - 1.0
Food Wastes - 0.0
              Chart shows data from column 5.
```

The generation rates are averages and in annual percent by weight.

	1960-1970	1970-1980	1980-1988	1986-1988	1987-1988
Paper and Paperboard	4.0	2.2	3.5	4.6	3.0
Glass	7.0	1.7	-2.2	-1.9	1.6
Metals	3.1	0.2	0.7	2.6	3.1
Plastics	22.8	9.8	7.9	8.6	7.8
All Other Materials[1]	3.5	3.4	2.6	5.9	5.5
Food Wastes	0.5	0.3	0.0	0.0	0.0
Yard Wastes	1.5	1.7	1.8	2.3	1.9
Total MSW	3.3	2.1	2.3	3.5	3.1
Population	1.2	1.1	1.0	1.0	1.0

Source: Characterization of Municipal Solid Waste in the United States: 1990 Update, U.S. Environmental Protection Agency, EPA/530-SW-90-042, Washington, D.C., June 1990, p. 52. *Notes:* 1. Rubber and leather, textiles, wood, batteries (partial), disposable diapers (partial), miscellaneous inorganics.

★ 125 ★

Beach Waste by Type

Plastic - 541.80	
Glass - 94.60	
Metal - 91.16	
Paper - 84.28	
Wood - 20.64	
Rubber - 17.20	
Cloth - 11.18	

Chart shows data from column 2.

Beach waste collected in 1989 in the U.S., Canada, and Mexico along a total of 2,946 miles of shoreline. Volumes for each type of waste are shown as percentages of all beach waste collected.

Type of Litter	Volume (Percentage)	Weight (in tons)
Plastic	63.0	541.80
Glass	11.0	94.60
Metal	10.6	91.16
Paper	9.8	84.28
Wood	2.4	20.64
Rubber	2.0	17.20
Cloth	1.3	11.18

Source: Garbage, September/October 1990, p. 26, from the Center for Marine Conservation.

★ 126 ★

Chlorine in Municipal Solid Waste

Amount of chlorine generated by components of municipal solid waste. Generated amounts for each type are shown as mass percentage on a dry basis.

Component	Baltimore, MD	Brooklyn, NY
Paper	0.251	0.224
Plastics, soft	0.055	0.123
Plastics, hard	0.083	0.332
Wood/vegetable	0.005	0.056
Textiles	0.019	0.020
Metal	-	-
Glass/ceramics	-	-
Fines	0.042	0.131
Total	0.455	0.886

Source: Plastics World, September 1990, p. 39 from the National Bureau of Standards.

★ 127 ★

Christmas Waste

Number of gifts wrapped by average household	30
Christmas gift wrap market	$500 million
Rolls/sheets of wrapping paper sold 1989	28,497,464
Package tags and bows sold 1989	16,826,362
Greeting cards (boxed and single) sold 1989	372,430,684
Number of Christmas trees cut, 1989	35,200,000
Success rate of tree-recycling programs	38%

Source: Garbage, November/December 1990, p. 63, from Hallmark Cards, Inc., A.C. Neilsen, from supermarkets with over $4 million in annual sales; National Christmas Association; and *Resource Recycling* survey of tree recycling practices.

★ 128 ★

Comparisons of Waste Compositions

Comparison of solid waste components for the United Kingdom, an Asian city, and a Middle Eastern city illustrate how different cultural and economic patterns produce different waste profiles. In percent or as noted.

Component	United Kingdom	Asian city	Middle East city (OPEC)
Vegetables	28	75	50
Paper	37	2	16
Textiles	3	3	3
Plastics	2	1	1
Glass	9	0.2	2
Metals	9	0.1	5
Other	12	18.7	23
Total	100	100	100
Density (kg/m)^3	132.000	570.000	211.000
Weight per person per day (kg)	0.845	0.415	1.060
Weight per household per day (kg)	1.900	2.490	5.300

Source: Resources, Conservation and Recycling, August 1990, p. 80.

★ 129 ★

Containers and Packaging Generated in the Municipal Wastestream
Generation before materials recovery or combustion.

Products	Percent of Total Generation						
	1960	1965	1970	1975	1980	1985	1988
Glass Packaging							
Beer and Soft Drink Bottles	1.6	2.5	4.6	4.9	4.5	3.5	3.0
Wine and Liquor Bottles	1.3	1.4	1.6	1.6	1.7	1.4	1.1
Food and Other Bottles and Jars	4.2	4.0	3.6	3.4	3.2	2.6	2.2
Total Glass Pkg.	7.1	7.8	9.8	9.9	9.4	7.5	6.3
Steel Packaging							
Beer and Soft Drink Cans	0.7	0.9	1.3	1.0	0.3	0.1	0.1
Food and Other Cans	4.3	3.5	2.9	2.7	1.9	1.6	1.4
Other Steel Packaging	0.2	0.3	0.2	0.2	0.1	0.1	0.1
Total Steel Pkg.	5.2	4.6	4.4	3.8	2.4	1.8	1.6
Aluminum Packaging							
Beer and Soft Drink Cans	0.1	0.1	0.2	0.4	0.6	0.8	0.8
Other Cans	0.0	0.0	0.1	0.0	0.0	0.0	0.0
Foil and Closures	0.1	0.2	0.2	0.2	0.2	0.2	0.2
Total Aluminum Pkg.	0.2	0.3	0.5	0.6	0.8	1.0	1.0
Paper & Paperboard Pkg.							
Corrugated Boxes	8.3	9.7	10.4	10.5	11.4	11.8	12.9
Milk Cartons	0.0	0.0	0.0	0.0	0.4	0.3	0.3
Folding Cartons	0.0	0.0	0.0	0.0	2.5	2.5	2.4
Other Paperboard Packaging	4.3	4.4	3.9	3.4	0.2	0.2	0.2
Bags and Sacks	0.0	0.0	0.0	0.0	2.3	1.9	1.6
Wrapping Papers	0.0	0.0	0.0	0.0	0.1	0.1	0.1
Other Paper Packaging	3.3	3.2	3.1	2.6	0.5	0.8	0.9
Total Paper & Board Pkg.	15.9	17.2	17.5	16.5	17.4	17.6	18.3
Plastics Packaging							
Soft Drink Bottles	0.0	0.0	0.0	0.0	0.2	0.2	0.2
Milk Bottles	0.0	0.0	0.0	0.0	0.1	0.2	0.2
Other Containers	0.1	0.3	0.7	1.0	0.6	0.7	1.0
Bags and Sacks	0.0	0.0	0.0	0.0	0.3	0.4	0.4
Wraps	0.0	0.0	0.0	0.0	0.5	0.6	0.6
Other Plastics Packaging	0.1	0.7	1.0	1.1	0.5	0.6	0.7
Total Plastics Pkg.	0.2	1.0	1.7	2.1	2.3	2.8	3.1

[Continued]

★ 129 ★

Containers and Packaging Generated in the Municipal Waste Stream

[Continued]

Products	Percent of Total Generation						
	1960	1965	1970	1975	1980	1985	1988
Wood Packaging	2.3	2.0	1.7	1.6	1.4	1.3	1.2
Other Misc. Packaging	0.1	0.1	0.1	0.1	0.1	0.1	0.1
Total Containers & Pkg.	31.1	33.1	35.7	34.7	33.8	32.1	31.6
Other Nonfood, Food and Yard Wastes	68.9	66.9	64.3	65.3	66.2	67.9	68.4
Total MSW Generated-Percent	100.0	100.0	100.0	100.0	100.0	100.0	100.0

Source: Characterization of Municipal Solid Waste in the United States: 1990 Update, U.S. Environmental Protection Agency, EPA/530-SW-90-042, Washington, D.C., June 1990, p. 43, from Franklin Associates, Ltd. Details may not add to totals due to rounding.

★ 130 ★

Containers and Packaging in the Municipal Wastestream

The values are in millions of tons. Packaging listed is generated before materials recovery or combustion.

	1960	1965	1970	1975	1980	1985	1988
Glass Packaging							
Beer and Soft Drink Bottles	1.4	2.6	5.6	6.3	6.7	5.7	5.4
Wine and Liquor Bottles	1.1	1.4	1.9	2.0	2.5	2.2	2.0
Food and Other Bottles & Jars	3.7	4.1	4.4	4.4	4.8	4.2	3.9
Total Glass Packaging	6.2	8.1	11.9	12.7	14.0	12.1	11.4
Steel Packaging							
Beer and Soft Drink Cans	0.6	0.9	1.6	1.3	0.5	0.1	0.1
Food and Other Cans	3.8	3.6	3.5	3.4	2.9	2.6	2.5
Other Steel Packaging	0.2	0.3	0.3	0.2	0.2	0.2	0.2
Total Steel Packaging	4.6	4.8	5.4	4.9	3.6	2.9	2.8
Aluminum Packaging							
Beer and Soft Drink Cans	0.1	0.1	0.3	0.5	0.9	1.3	1.4
Other Cans	0.0	0.0	0.1	0.0	0.0	0.0	0.1
Foil and Closures	0.1	0.2	0.2	0.3	0.3	0.3	0.3
Total Aluminum Packaging	0.2	0.3	0.6	0.8	1.2	1.6	1.8
Paper and Paperboard Packaging							
Corrugated Boxes	7.3	10.0	12.7	13.5	17.0	19.0	23.1
Milk Cartons	0.0	0.0	0.0	0.0	0.6	0.5	0.5
Folding Cartons	0.0	0.0	0.0	0.0	3.7	4.0	4.4
Other Paperboard Packaging	3.8	4.5	4.8	4.4	0.3	0.4	0.3
Bags and Sacks	0.0	0.0	0.0	0.0	3.4	3.1	2.9
Wrapping Papers	0.0	0.0	0.0	0.0	0.2	0.1	0.1
Other Paper Packaging	2.9	3.3	3.8	3.3	0.8	1.3	1.6

[Continued]

★ 130 ★

Containers and Packaging in the Municipal Waste Stream
[Continued]

	1960	1965	1970	1975	1980	1985	1988
Total Paper & Board Packaging	14.0	17.8	21.3	21.2	26.0	28.4	32.9
Plastics Packaging							
Soft Drink Bottles	0.0	0.0	0.0	0.0	0.3	0.4	0.4
Milk Bottles	0.0	0.0	0.0	0.0	0.2	0.3	0.4
Other Containers	0.1	0.3	0.9	1.3	0.9	1.2	1.7
Bags and Sacks	0.0	0.0	0.0	0.0	0.4	0.6	0.8
Wraps	0.0	0.0	0.0	0.0	0.8	1.0	1.1
Other Plastics Packaging	0.1	0.7	1.2	1.4	0.8	1.0	1.2
Total Plastics Packaging	0.2	1.0	2.1	2.7	3.4	4.5	5.6
Wood Packaging	2.0	2.1	2.1	2.0	2.1	2.1	2.1
Other Misc. Packaging	0.1	0.1	0.1	0.1	0.2	0.2	0.2
Total Containers and Packaging	27.3	34.2	43.5	44.4	50.5	51.8	56.8

Source: Characterization of Municipal Solid Waste in the United States: 1990 Update, U.S. Environmental Protection Agency, EPA/530-SW-90-042, Washington, D.C., June 1990, p. 42, from Franklin Associates, Ltd. Details may not add to totals due to rounding.

★ 131 ★

Containers and Packaging Percent of Total in the Municipal Wastestream

The values are percent of total products generated in the waste stream. Packaging listed is generated before materials recovery or combustion.

	1960	1965	1970	1975	1980	1985	1988
Glass Packaging							
Beer and Soft Drink Bottles	1.4	2.6	5.6	6.3	6.7	5.7	5.4
Wine and Liquor Bottles	1.1	1.4	1.9	2.0	2.5	2.2	2.0
Food and Other Bottles & Jars	3.7	4.1	4.4	4.4	4.8	4.2	3.9
Total Glass Packaging	6.2	8.1	11.9	12.7	14.0	12.1	11.4
Steel Packaging							
Beer and Soft Drink Cans	0.6	0.9	1.6	1.3	0.5	0.1	0.1
Food and Other Cans	3.8	3.6	3.5	3.4	2.9	2.6	2.5
Other Steel Packaging	0.2	0.3	0.3	0.2	0.2	0.2	0.2
Total Steel Packaging	4.6	4.8	5.4	4.9	3.6	2.9	2.8
Aluminum Packaging							
Beer and Soft Drink Cans	0.1	0.1	0.3	0.5	0.9	1.3	1.4
Other Cans	0.0	0.0	0.1	0.0	0.0	0.0	0.1
Foil and Closures	0.1	0.2	0.2	0.3	0.3	0.3	0.3
Total Aluminum Packaging	0.2	0.3	0.6	0.8	1.2	1.6	1.8
Paper and Paperboard Packaging							
Corrugated Boxes	7.3	10.0	12.7	13.5	17.0	19.0	23.1
Milk Cartons	0.0	0.0	0.0	0.0	0.6	0.5	0.5

[Continued]

★ 131 ★

Containers and Packaging Percent of Total in the Municipal Waste Stream
[Continued]

	1960	1965	1970	1975	1980	1985	1988
Folding Cartons	0.0	0.0	0.0	0.0	3.7	4.0	4.4
Other Paperboard Packaging	3.8	4.5	4.8	4.4	0.3	0.4	0.3
Bags and Sacks	0.0	0.0	0.0	0.0	3.4	3.1	2.9
Wrapping Papers	0.0	0.0	0.0	0.0	0.2	0.1	0.1
Other Paper Packaging	2.9	3.3	3.8	3.3	0.8	1.3	1.6
Total Paper & Board Packaging	14.0	17.8	21.3	21.2	26.0	28.4	32.9
Plastics Packaging							
Soft Drink Bottles	0.0	0.0	0.0	0.0	0.3	0.4	0.4
Milk Bottles	0.0	0.0	0.0	0.0	0.2	0.3	0.4
Other Containers	0.1	0.3	0.9	1.3	0.9	1.2	1.7
Bags and Sacks	0.0	0.0	0.0	0.0	0.4	0.6	0.8
Wraps	0.0	0.0	0.0	0.0	0.8	1.0	1.1
Other Plastics Packaging	0.1	0.7	1.2	1.4	0.8	1.0	1.2
Total Plastics Packaging	0.2	1.0	2.1	2.7	3.4	4.5	5.6
Wood Packaging	2.0	2.1	2.1	2.0	2.1	2.1	2.1
Other Misc. Packaging	0.1	0.1	0.1	0.1	0.2	0.2	0.2
Total Containers and Packaging	27.3	34.2	43.5	44.4	50.5	51.8	56.8
Total Durable, Nondurable, and Other Waste	60.0	69.2	78.9	84.0	99.1	109.8	122.8

Source: Characterization of Municipal Solid Waste in the United States: 1990 Update, U.S. Environmental Protection Agency, EPA/530-SW-90-042, Washington, D.C., June 1990, p. 42, from Franklin Associates, Ltd. Details may not add to totals due to rounding.

★ 132 ★

Containers/Packaging in the Municipal Wastestream - Percent

Discards after materials and compost recovery. The values are percent of total discards in the waste stream.

Products	Percent of total discards						
	1960	1965	1970	1975	1980	1985	1988
Glass Packaging							
Beer and Soft Drink Bottles	1.6	2.6	4.8	5.0	4.4	3.2	2.8
Wine and Liquor Bottles	1.3	1.4	1.7	1.7	1.9	1.4	1.2
Food and Other Bottles and Jars	4.5	4.2	3.9	3.7	3.6	2.9	2.3
Total Glass Pkg.	7.4	8.3	10.3	10.4	9.8	7.6	6.3
Steel Packaging							
Beer and Soft Drink Cans	0.7	0.9	1.4	1.1	0.3	0.1	0.1
Food and Other Cans	4.6	3.6	3.0	2.8	2.1	1.7	1.4
Other Steel Packaging	0.2	0.3	0.3	0.2	0.1	0.1	0.1
Total Steel Pkg.	5.6	4.9	4.7	4.1	2.5	1.9	1.6
Aluminum Packaging							
Beer and Soft Drink Cans	0.1	0.1	0.3	0.3	0.4	0.5	0.4

[Continued]

★ 132 ★

Containers/Packaging in the Municipal Wastestream - Percent
[Continued]

Products	Percent of total discards						
	1960	1965	1970	1975	1980	1985	1988
Other Cans	0.0	0.0	0.1	0.0	0.0	0.0	0.0
Foil and Closures	0.1	0.2	0.2	0.3	0.2	0.2	0.2
Total Aluminum Pkg.	0.2	0.3	0.5	0.6	0.7	0.7	0.7
Paper and Paperboard Pkg.							
Corrugated Boxes	5.9	8.1	8.8	8.4	7.9	8.1	8.1
Milk Cartons	0.0	0.0	0.0	0.0	0.4	0.3	0.3
Folding Cartons	0.0	0.0	0.0	0.0	2.4	2.6	2.6
Other Paperboard Packaging	4.3	4.2	3.8	3.3	0.2	0.3	0.2
Bags and Sacks	0.0	0.0	0.0	0.0	2.3	2.1	1.7
Wrapping Papers	0.0	0.0	0.0	0.0	0.1	0.1	0.1
Other Paper Packaging	3.3	3.1	3.0	2.5	0.6	0.9	1.0
Total Paper & Board Pkg.	13.4	15.4	15.6	14.1	14.0	14.4	14.0
Plastics Packaging							
Soft Drink Bottles	0.0	0.0	0.0	0.0	0.2	0.2	0.2
Milk Bottles	0.0	0.0	0.0	0.0	0.1	0.2	0.2
Other Containers	0.1	0.3	0.8	1.1	0.7	0.8	1.1
Bags and Sacks	0.0	0.0	0.0	0.0	0.3	0.4	0.5
Wraps	0.0	0.0	0.0	0.0	0.6	0.7	0.7
Other Plastics Packaging	0.1	0.7	1.1	1.2	0.6	0.7	0.8
Total Plastics Pkg.	0.2	1.0	1.9	2.3	2.5	3.0	3.5
Wood Packaging	2.4	2.2	1.9	1.7	1.6	1.4	1.3
Other Misc. Packaging	0.1	0.1	0.1	0.1	0.1	0.1	0.1
Total Containers & Pkg	29.5	32.2	35.0	33.2	31.2	29.2	27.6
Other Nonfood and Yard Wastes	70.5	67.8	65.0	66.8	68.8	70.8	72.4
Total MSW Discarded-Percent	100.0	100.0	100.0	100.0	100.0	100.0	100.0

Source: Characterization of Municipal Solid Waste in the United States: 1990 Update, U.S. Environmental Protection Agency, EPA/530-SW-90-042, Washington, D.C., June 1990, p. 47, from Franklin Associates, Ltd. Details may not add to totals due to rounding.

★ 133 ★

Containers/Packaging in the Municipal Wastestream - Weight

	Millions of Tons						
	1960	1965	1970	1975	1980	1985	1988
Glass Packaging							
Beer and Soft Drink Bottles	1.3	2.5	5.5	5.9	5.9	4.7	4.3
Wine and Liquor Bottles	1.1	1.4	1.9	2.0	2.5	2.1	1.9
Food and Other Bottles and Jars	3.7	4.1	4.4	4.4	4.8	4.2	3.6

[Continued]

★ 133 ★

Containers/Packaging in the Minicipal Wastestream - Weight
[Continued]

	Millions of Tons						
	1960	1965	1970	1975	1980	1985	1988
Total Glass Packaging	6.1	8.0	11.7	12.3	13.2	11.0	9.9
Steel Packaging							
Beer and Soft Drink Cans	0.6	0.9	1.6	1.3	0.4	0.1	0.1
Food and Other Cans	3.8	3.5	3.4	3.3	2.8	2.5	2.1
Other Steel Packaging	0.2	0.3	0.3	0.2	0.2	0.2	0.2
Total Steel Packaging	4.6	4.7	5.3	4.8	3.4	2.8	2.4
Aluminum Packaging							
Beer and Soft Drink Cans	0.1	0.1	0.3	0.4	0.6	0.7	0.6
Other Cans	0.0	0.0	0.1	0.0	0.0	0.0	0.1
Foil and Closures	0.1	0.2	0.2	0.3	0.3	0.3	0.3
Total Aluminum Packaging	0.2	0.3	0.6	0.7	0.9	1.0	1.0
Paper & Paperboard Packaging							
Corrugated Boxes	4.8	7.8	10.0	9.9	10.7	11.8	12.6
Milk Cartons	0.0	0.0	0.0	0.0	0.6	0.5	0.5
Folding Cartons	0.0	0.0	0.0	0.0	3.2	3.8	4.1
Other Paperboard Packaging	3.5	4.1	4.3	3.9	0.3	0.4	0.3
Bags and Sacks	0.0	0.0	0.0	0.0	3.1	3.0	2.7
Wrapping Papers	0.0	0.0	0.0	0.0	0.2	0.1	0.1
Other Paper Packaging	2.7	3.0	3.4	2.9	0.8	1.3	1.6
Total Paper & Board Packaging	11.0	14.9	17.7	16.7	18.9	20.9	21.9
Plastics Packaging							
Soft Drink Bottles	0.0	0.0	0.0	0.0	0.3	0.3	0.3
Milk Bottles	0.0	0.0	0.0	0.0	0.2	0.3	0.4
Other Containers	0.1	0.3	0.9	1.3	0.9	1.2	1.7
Bags and Sacks	0.0	0.0	0.0	0.0	0.4	0.6	0.8
Wraps	0.0	0.0	0.0	0.0	0.8	1.0	1.1
Other Plastics Packaging	0.1	0.7	1.2	1.4	0.8	1.0	1.2
Total Plastics Packaging	0.2	1.0	2.1	2.7	3.4	4.4	5.5
Wood Packaging	2.0	2.1	2.1	2.0	2.1	2.1	2.1
Other Misc. Packaging	0.1	0.1	0.1	0.1	0.2	0.2	0.2
Total Containers and Packaging	24.2	31.1	39.6	39.3	42.1	42.4	43.0
Other Durable, Nondurable Food and Yard Wastes	57.7	65.5	73.7	78.9	93.0	102.8	113.0
Total MSW Discarded-Weight	81.9	96.6	113.3	118.2	135.1	145.2	156.0

Source: Characterization of Municipal Solid Waste in the United States: 1990 Update, U.S. Environmental Protection Agency, EPA/530-SW-90-042, Washington, D.C., June 1990, p. 46, from Franklin Associates, Ltd. Details may not add to totals due to rounding.

★ 134 ★

Disposable Diaper Composition

Composition of single-use diapers, by material, shown as percent of total weight.

Component	Percent of total weight
Polypropylene cover	16.0
Tape	1.1
Pulp fluff	65.0
Acrylic absorber	2.0
Rayon liner	8.0
Packaging	7.9

Source: *Recycling Today*, August 1989, from *Diapers in the Waste Stream*, 1988.

★ 135 ★

Durable Goods Discarded in the Municipal Wastestream - I

```
┌─────────────────────────────────────────────────────┐
│ ┌───────────────────────────────────────────────┐   │
│ │ Total MSW Discard-Weight - 156.0              │   │
│ └───────────────────────────────────────────────┘   │
│ ┌──────────────────────────────────────────┐        │
│ │ Total Nonfood products - 133.0           │        │
│ └──────────────────────────────────────────┘        │
│ ┌──────┐ Total Durable Goods - 23.0                 │
│ └──────┘                                             │
│ ┌────┐ Miscellaneous Durables - 10.5                │
│ └────┘                                               │
│ ┌───┐ Furniture and Furnishings - 7.5               │
│ └───┘                                                │
│ ▐ Major Appliances - 2.8                             │
│ ▐ Rubber Tires - 2.1                                 │
│ │ Batteries, lead acid - 0.2                         │
│           Chart shows data from column 7.            │
└─────────────────────────────────────────────────────┘
```

Products listed are discarded after materials and compost recovery.

Products	Millions of Tons						
	1960	1965	1970	1975	1980	1985	1988
Major Appliances	1.5	1.0	2.7	2.6	2.7	2.5	2.8
Furniture and Furnishings	2.1	2.7	3.4	4.1	5.1	5.8	7.5
Rubber Tires	0.7	1.1	1.6	2.3	2.5	1.8	2.1
Batteries, lead acid	0.0	0.1	0.2	0.4	0.5	0.5	0.2
Miscellaneous Durables	4.7	5.4	6.3	7.1	7.6	9.5	10.5
Total Durable Goods	9.0	10.2	14.2	16.5	18.4	20.1	23.0
Total Nonfood products	72.9	86.4	99.1	101.7	116.7	125.1	133.0
Total MSW Discard-Weight	81.9	96.6	113.3	118.2	135.1	145.2	156.0

Source: *Characterization of Municipal Solid Waste in the United States: 1990 Update*, U.S. Environmental Protection Agency, EPA/530-SW-90-042, Washington, D.C., June 1990, p. 34, from Franklin Associates, Ltd. Details may not add to totals due to rounding.

★ 136 ★

Durable Goods Discarded in the Municipal Wastestream - II

```
┌─────────────────────────────────────────────────────────────┐
│  ┌──────────────────────────────────────────────┐           │
│  │ Total MSW Discard-Percent - 100.0            │           │
│  └──────────────────────────────────────────────┘           │
│  ┌────────────────────────────────────────────┐             │
│  │ Other nonfood Products, Food and Yard Wastes - 85.3 │    │
│  └────────────────────────────────────────────┘             │
│  ┌──────┐ Total Durable Goods - 14.7                        │
│  └──────┘                                                    │
│  ┌────┐ Miscellaneous Durables - 5.7                        │
│  └────┘                                                      │
│  ┌──┐ Furniture and Furnishings - 4.8                       │
│  └──┘                                                        │
│  ▯ Major Appliances - 1.8                                   │
│  ▯ Rubber Tires - 1.3                                       │
│  │ Batteries, lead acid - 0.1                               │
│              Chart shows data from column 7.                 │
└─────────────────────────────────────────────────────────────┘
```

Products listed are discarded after materials and compost recovery.

Products	Percent of Total Discards						
	1960	1965	1970	1975	1980	1985	1988
Major Appliances	1.8	1.0	2.4	2.2	2.0	1.7	1.8
Furniture and Furnishings	2.6	2.8	3.0	3.5	3.8	4.0	4.8
Rubber Tires	0.9	1.1	1.4	1.9	1.9	1.2	1.3
Batteries, lead acid	0.0	0.1	0.2	0.3	0.4	0.3	0.1
Miscellaneous Durables	5.7	5.6	5.6	6.0	5.6	6.5	5.7
Total Durable Goods	11.0	10.6	12.5	14.0	13.6	13.8	14.7
Other nonfood Products, Food and Yard Wastes	89.0	89.4	87.5	86.0	86.4	86.2	85.3
Total MSW Discard-Percent	100.0	100.0	100.0	100.0	100.0	100.0	100.0

Source: Characterization of Municipal Solid Waste in the United States: 1990 Update, U.S. Environmental Protection Agency, EPA/530-SW-90-042, Washington, D.C., June 1990, p. 34, from Franklin Associates, Ltd. Details may not add to totals due to rounding.

★ 137 ★

Durable Goods in the Municipal Wastestream - I

Products listed are generated before materials recovery or combustion.

Products	Millions of Tons						
	1960	1965	1970	1975	1980	1985	1988
Major Appliances	1.5	1.0	2.7	2.6	2.8	2.7	3.0
Furniture and Furnishings	2.1	2.7	3.4	4.1	5.1	5.8	7.5
Rubber Tires	1.1	1.4	1.9	2.5	2.6	1.9	2.2
Batteries, lead acid	0.0	0.7	0.8	1.2	1.5	1.5	1.6
Miscellaneous Durables	4.7	5.4	6.3	7.1	7.7	9.6	10.6
Total Goods	9.4	11.1	15.1	17.5	19.7	21.5	24.9
Total Nondurable, containers and packages and other waste	78.4	92.3	106.8	110.6	129.5	140.1	154.7
Total MSW Generated-Weight	87.8	103.4	121.9	128.1	149.6	161.6	179.6

Source: Characterization of Municipal Solid Waste in the United States: 1990 Update, U.S. Environmental Protection Agency, EPA/530-SW-90-042, Washington, D.C., June 1990, p. 32, from Franklin Associates, Ltd. Details may not add to totals due to rounding.

★ 138 ★

Durable Goods in the Municipal Wastestream - II

Products listed generated before materials recovery or combustion.

Products	Percent of Total Generation						
	1960	1965	1970	1975	1980	1985	1988
Major Appliances	1.7	1.0	2.2	2.0	1.9	1.7	1.7
Furniture and Furnishings	2.4	2.6	2.8	3.2	3.4	3.6	4.2
Rubber Tires	1.3	1.3	1.6	2.0	1.7	1.2	1.2
Batteries, lead acid	0.0	0.6	0.7	0.9	1.0	0.9	0.9
Miscellaneous Durables	5.4	5.2	5.2	5.5	5.1	5.9	5.9
Total Goods	10.7	10.7	12.4	13.7	13.2	13.3	13.9
Total Nondurable and other wastes	89.7	89.7	87.6	86.3	86.8	86.7	8.61
Total MSW Generated - Percent	100.0	100.0	100.0	100.0	100.0	100.0	100.0

Source: Characterization of Municipal Solid Waste in the United States: 1990 Update, U.S. Environmental Protection Agency, EPA/530-SW-90-042, Washington, D.C., June 1990, p. 32, from Franklin Associates Ltd. Details may not add to totals due to rounding.

★ 139 ★

Glass Products in Municipal Solid Waste

The values are for 1988.

Product Category	Generation (Million tons)	Recovery (Million tons)	Recovery (Percent of generation)	Discards (Million tons)
Durable Goods[1]	1.2	Neg.	Neg.	1.2
Containers and Packaging				
Beer and Soft Drink Bottles	5.4	1.1	20.0	4.3
Wine and Liquor Bottles	2.0	0.1	5.0	1.9
Food and Other Bottles and Jars	3.9	0.3	8.1	3.6
Total Glass Containers	11.4	1.5	13.3	9.9
Total Glass	12.5	1.5	12.0	11.0

Source: Characterization of Municipal Solid Waste in the United States: 1990 Update, U.S. Environmental Protection Agency, EPA/530-SW-90-042, Washington, D.C., June 1990, p. 15, from Franklin Associates, Ltd. Neg. stands for Negligible. Details may not add to totals due to rounding. *Notes:* 1. Glass as a component of appliances, furniture, consumer electronics, etc.

★ 140 ★

Household Waste by Type

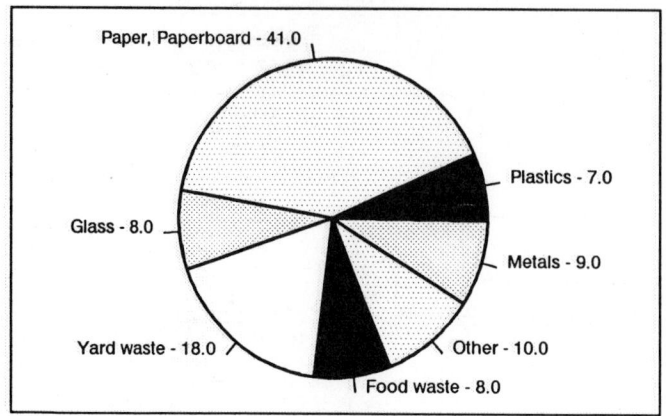

Type	Percent
Plastics	7.0
Food waste	8.0
Glass	8.0
Metals	9.0
Other	10.0
Yard waste	18.0
Paper, Paperboard	41.0

Source: EPA Journal, September/October 1990, p. 23.

★ 141 ★

Litter in the U.S.

Percent of convenience-item packages littered	**2-5**
Pieces per mile visible to person standing	**1,457**
Pieces per mile visible to person kneeling	**5,828**
Cost to remove and dispose of one piece of litter	**9 cents**
Cost to remove 5,828 pieces	**$524.52**
Average decrease in city litter after three years in the Keep America Beautiful program	**49%**

Source: Garbage, September/October 1990, p. 26, from litter expert Daniel Syrek and Keep America Beautiful.

★ 142 ★

Material Discarded in Municipal Solid Waste

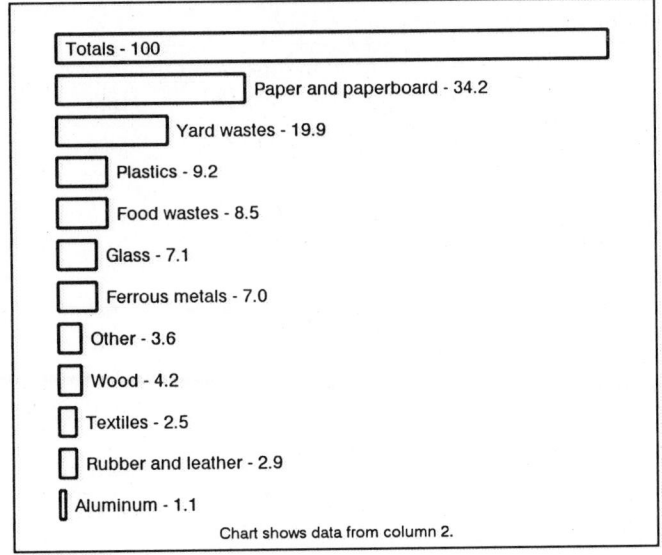

Totals - 100

Paper and paperboard - 34.2

Yard wastes - 19.9

Plastics - 9.2

Food wastes - 8.5

Glass - 7.1

Ferrous metals - 7.0

Other - 3.6

Wood - 4.2

Textiles - 2.5

Rubber and leather - 2.9

Aluminum - 1.1

Chart shows data from column 2.

Values shown are for 1988.

	1988 Discards (mil tons)	Weight (% of MSW total)	Volume (% of MSW total)	Ratio (Vol %/ wt %)
Paper and paperboard	53.4	34.2	34.1	1.0
Plastics	14.3	9.2	19.9	2.2
Yard wastes	31.0	19.9	10.3	0.5
Ferrous metals	10.9	7.0	9.8	1.4
Rubber and leather	4.4	2.9	6.4	2.3
Textiles	3.8	2.5	5.3	2.1
Wood	6.5	4.2	4.1	1.0
Food wastes	13.2	8.5	3.3	0.4
Other	5.6	3.6	2.5	0.7
Aluminum	1.7	1.1	2.3	2.1
Glass	11.1	7.1	2.0	0.3
Totals	156	100	100	1.0

Source: Characterization of Municipal Solid Waste in the United States: 1990 Update, U.S. Environmental Protection Agency, EPA/530-SW-90-042, Washington, D.C., June 1990, p. ES-11.

★ 143 ★

Material Discards in 1995

The estimated values are in millions of tons and percent of total discards. Discards after materials and compost recovery.

Materials	Million tons		% of discards	
	High	Low	High	Low
Paper and paperboard	59.2	52.9	36.6	37.0
Glass	9.0	8.0	5.5	5.6
Metals				
Ferrous	10.2	9.3	6.4	6.4
Aluminum	2.0	1.7	1.2	1.3
Other nonferrous	0.6	0.5	0.3	0.4
Total metals	12.8	11.5	8.0	8.0
Plastics	18.1	17.3	12.0	11.3
Rubber and leather	4.8	4.6	3.2	3.0
Food wastes	13.2	12.2	8.4	8.3
Yard wastes	26.4	22.0	15.2	16.5
Other materials[1]	16.1	15.9	11.0	10.1
Totals	159.8	144.5	100.0	100.0

Source: Characterization of Municipal Solid Waste in the United States: 1990 Update, U.S. Environmental Protection Agency, EPA/530-SW-90-042, Washington, D.C., June 1990, p. 73, from Franklin Associates, Ltd. High estimates of discards correspond to low estimates of recovery. Details may not add to totals due to rounding. *Note:* 1. Textiles, wood, other.

★ 144 ★

Materials as Percent of Total Municipal Wastestream

Values shown reflect percent of total materials generated in the waste stream.

Materials	Percent of Total Generation						
	1960	1965	1970	1975	1980	1985	1988
Paper and Paperboard	34.1	36.8	36.3	33.6	36.6	38.1	40.0
Glass	7.6	8.4	10.4	10.5	10.0	8.2	7.0
Metals							
Ferrous	11.3	9.8	10.3	9.6	7.8	6.7	6.5
Aluminum	0.5	0.5	0.7	0.9	1.2	1.4	1.4
Other Nonferrous	0.2	0.5	0.6	0.7	0.7	0.6	0.6
Total Metals	12.0	10.7	11.6	11.2	9.7	8.8	8.5
Plastics	0.5	1.4	2.5	3.5	5.2	7.2	8.0

[Continued]

★ 144 ★

Materials as Percent of Total Municipal Waste Stream
[Continued]

Materials	Percent of Total Generation						
	1960	1965	1970	1975	1980	1985	1988
Rubber and Leather	2.3	2.5	2.6	3.0	2.9	2.4	2.5
Textiles	1.9	1.8	1.6	1.7	1.7	1.7	2.1
Wood	3.4	3.4	3.3	3.4	3.3	3.3	3.6
Other	0.1	0.3	0.7	1.3	1.9	2.1	1.7
Total Nonfood Product Wastes	61.8	65.3	69.0	68.3	71.3	71.7	73.5
Other Wastes							
Food Wastes	13.9	12.3	10.5	10.5	8.8	8.2	7.4
Yard Wastes	22.8	20.9	19.0	19.7	18.4	18.6	17.6
Miscellaneous Inorganic Wastes	1.5	1.5	1.5	1.6	1.5	1.5	1.5
Total Other Wastes	38.2	34.7	31.0	31.7	28.7	28.3	26.5
Total MSW Generated-Percent	100.0	100.0	100.0	100.0	100.0	100.0	100.0

Source: Characterization of Municipal Solid Waste in the United States: 1990 Update, U.S. Environmental Protection Agency, EPA/530-SW-90-042, Washington, D.C., June 1990, p. 10, from Franklin Associates, Ltd. Details may not add to totals due to rounding.

★ 145 ★

Materials Discarded as Percent of Total Discards
The values are percent of total discards.

Materials	Percent of Total Discards						
	1960	1965	1970	1975	1980	1985	1988
Paper and Paperboard	29.9	33.4	32.5	29.4	31.7	33.3	34.2
Glass	8.1	8.9	11.0	11.1	10.5	8.4	7.1
Metals							
Ferrous	12.0	10.4	11.0	10.2	8.3	7.2	7.0
Aluminum	0.5	0.5	0.7	0.8	1.1	1.2	1.1
Other Nonferrous	0.2	0.2	0.4	0.4	0.4	0.3	0.3
Total Metals	12.7	11.1	12.1	11.5	9.8	8.7	8.4
Plastics	0.5	1.4	2.7	3.8	5.8	7.9	9.1
Rubber and Leather	2.1	2.4	2.6	3.1	3.1	2.5	2.9
Textiles	2.1	2.0	1.8	1.9	1.9	1.9	2.5
Wood	3.7	3.6	3.5	3.7	3.6	3.7	4.2
Other	0.1	0.0	0.4	1.1	1.8	2.0	1.6
Total Nonfood Product Wastes	59.1	62.8	66.6	65.7	68.2	68.5	69.9
Other Wastes							
Food Wastes	14.9	13.1	11.3	11.3	9.8	9.1	8.5
Yard Wastes	24.4	22.4	20.5	21.3	20.4	20.7	20.0
Miscellaneous Inorganic Wastes	1.6	1.7	1.6	1.7	1.6	1.7	1.7

[Continued]

★ 145 ★

Materials Discarded as Percent of Total Discards
[Continued]

Materials	Percent of Total Discards						
	1960	1965	1970	1975	1980	1985	1988
Total Other Wastes	40.9	37.2	33.4	34.3	31.8	31.5	30.1
Total MSW Discarded-Percent	100.0	100.0	100.0	100.0	100.0	100.0	100.0

Source: Characterization of Municipal Solid Waste in the United States: 1990 Update, U.S. Environmental Protection Agency, EPA/530-SW-90-042, Washington, D.C., June 1990, p. 12, from Franklin Associates, Ltd. Details may not add to totals due to rounding.

★ 146 ★

Materials Discarded in the Municipal Wastestream

The values are in millions of tons. Materials are discarded after materials and compost recovery.

Materials	Millions of Tons						
	1960	1965	1970	1975	1980	1985	1988
Paper and Paperboard	24.5	32.3	36.8	34.8	42.8	48.4	53.4
Glass	6.6	8.6	12.5	13.1	14.2	12.2	11.0
Metals							
Ferrous	9.8	10.0	12.5	12.1	11.2	10.5	10.9
Aluminum	0.4	0.5	0.8	1.0	1.5	1.7	1.7
Other Nonferrous	0.2	0.2	0.4	0.5	0.6	0.5	0.4
Total Metals	10.4	10.7	13.7	13.6	13.3	12.7	13.1
Plastics	0.4	1.4	3.1	4.5	7.8	11.5	14.3
Rubber and Leather	1.7	2.3	2.9	3.7	4.2	3.6	4.4
Textiles	1.7	1.9	2.0	2.2	2.6	2.8	3.8
Wood	3.0	3.5	4.0	4.4	4.9	5.4	6.5
Other	0.1	0.0	0.5	1.3	2.4	2.9	2.4
Total Nonfood Product Wastes	48.4	60.7	75.5	77.6	92.2	99.5	109.0
Other Wastes							
Food Wastes	12.2	12.7	12.8	13.4	13.2	13.2	13.2
Yard Wastes	20.0	21.6	23.2	25.2	27.5	30.0	31.1
Miscellaneous Inorganic Wastes	1.3	1.6	1.8	2.0	2.2	2.5	2.7
Total Other Wastes	33.5	35.9	37.8	40.6	42.9	45.7	47.0
Total MSW Discarded-Weight	81.9	96.6	113.3	118.2	135.1	145.2	156.0

Source: Characterization of Municipal Solid Waste in the United States. 1990 Update, U.S. Environmental Protection Agency, EPA/530-SW-90-042, Washington, D.C., June 1990, p. 12, from Franklin Associates, Ltd. Details may not add to totals due to rounding.

★ 147 ★

Materials Generated in the Municipal Wastestream

Values shown reflect generation before materials recovery.

Materials	Millions of tons						
	1960	1965	1970	1975	1980	1985	1988
Paper and Paperboard	29.9	38.0	44.2	43.0	54.7	61.5	71.8
Glass	6.7	8.7	12.7	13.5	15.0	13.2	12.5
Metals							
Ferrous	9.9	10.1	12.6	12.3	11.6	10.9	11.6
Aluminum	0.4	0.5	0.8	1.1	1.8	2.3	2.5
Other Nonferrous	0.2	0.5	0.7	0.9	1.1	1.0	1.1
Total Metals	10.5	11.1	14.1	14.3	14.5	14.2	15.3
Plastics	0.4	1.4	3.1	4.5	7.8	11.6	14.4
Rubber and Leather	2.0	2.6	3.2	3.9	4.3	3.8	4.6
Textiles	1.7	1.9	2.0	2.2	2.6	2.8	3.9
Wood	3.0	3.5	4.0	4.4	4.9	5.4	6.5
Other	0.1	0.3	0.8	1.7	2.9	3.4	3.1
Total Nonfood Product Wastes	54.3	67.5	84.1	87.5	106.7	115.9	132.1
Other Wastes							
Food Wastes	12.2	12.7	12.8	13.4	13.2	13.2	13.2
Yard Wastes	20.0	21.6	23.2	25.2	27.5	30.0	31.6
Miscellaneous Inorganic Wastes	1.3	1.6	1.8	2.0	2.2	2.5	2.7
Total Other Wastes	33.5	35.9	37.8	40.6	42.9	45.7	47.5
Total MSW Generated-Weight	87.8	103.4	121.9	128.1	149.6	161.6	179.6

Source: Characterization of Municipal Solid Waste in the United States: 1990 Update, U.S. Environmental Protection Agency, EPA/530-SW-90-042, Washington, D.C., June 1990, p. 10, from Franklin Associates, Ltd. Details may not add to totals due to rounding.

★ 148 ★

Metal Products in Municipal Solid Waste

The values are for 1988.

Product Category	Generation (Million tons)	Recovery (Million tons)	Recovery (Percent of generation)	Discards (Million tons)
Durable Goods				
Ferrous Metals[1]	8.8	0.3	3.4	8.5
Aluminum[2]	0.5	Neg.	Neg.	0.5
Batteries (Lead)	0.8	0.7	89.9	0.1
Other Nonferrous Metals[3]	0.3	Neg.	Neg.	0.3
Total Metals in Durable Goods	10.4	1.0	9.9	9.4

[Continued]

★ 148 ★

Metal Products in Municipal Solid Waste
[Continued]

Product Category	Generation (Million tons)	Recovery (Million tons)	Recovery (Percent of generation)	Discards (Million tons)
Nondurable Goods				
Aluminum	0.2	Neg.	Neg.	0.2
Containers and Packaging				
Steel				
Beer and Soft Drink Cans	0.1	Neg.	Neg.	0.1
Food and Other Cans	2.5	0.4	15.0	2.1
Other Steel Packaging	0.2	Neg.	Neg.	0.2
Total Steel Packaging	2.8	0.4	13.8	2.4
Aluminum				
Beer and Soft Drink Cans	1.4	0.8	55.0	0.6
Other Cans	0.1	Neg.	Neg.	0.1
Foil and Closures	0.3	Neg.	Neg.	0.3
Total Aluminum Packaging	1.8	0.8	44.1	1.0
Total Metals in Containers and Packaging	4.7	1.2	25.7	3.5
Total Metals	15.3	2.2	14.6	13.1

Source: Characterization of Municipal Solid Waste in the United States: 1990 Update, U.S. Environmental Protection Agency, EPA/530-SW-90-042, Washington, D.C., June 1990, p. 17, from Franklin Associates Ltd. Neg. stands for Negligible. Details may not add to totals due to rounding. *Notes:* 1. Ferrous metals in appliances, furniture, tires, and miscellaneous durables. 2. Aluminum in appliances, furniture, and miscellaneous durables. 3. Other nonferrous metals in appliances, lead-acid batteries, and miscellaneous durables.

★ 149 ★

Mine Ore and Waste Production in the U.S.

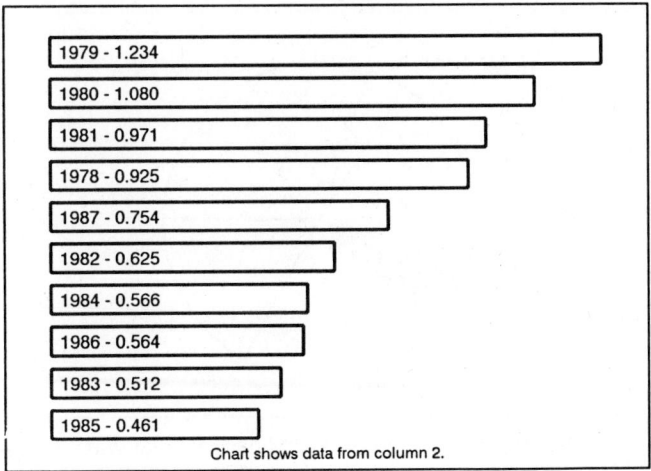

1979 - 1.234
1980 - 1.080
1981 - 0.971
1978 - 0.925
1987 - 0.754
1982 - 0.625
1984 - 0.566
1986 - 0.564
1983 - 0.512
1985 - 0.461

Chart shows data from column 2.

Figures are shown in billions of metric tons.

Year	Metal crude ore	Metal waste	Nonmetal crude ore	Nonmetal waste
1978	0.570	0.925	2.186	0.519
1979	0.611	1.234	2.214	0.535
1980	0.542	1.080	1.941	0.562
1981	0.611	0.971	1.107	0.535
1982	0.391	0.625	0.816	0.334
1983	0.387	0.512	1.025	0.141
1984	0.432	0.566	0.998	0.260
1985	0.416	0.461	1.198	0.410
1986	0.426	0.564	1.052	0.345
1987[1]	0.483	0.754	1.370	1.161

Source: Council on Environmental Quality, *20th Annual Report 1990*, Washington, D.C., p. 440, from U.S. Department of the Interior, Bureau of Mines, Minerals Yearbook, annual. Washington, DC. *Note:* 1. Preliminary data.

★ 150 ★

Municipal Solid Waste Composition by Type

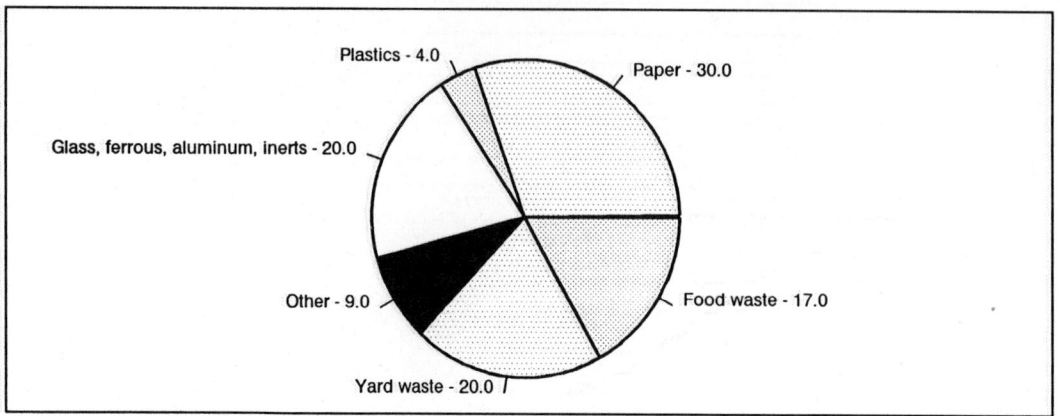

Figures represent average composition of Municipal Solid Waste (MSW).

Composition	Percent
Paper	30.0
Glass, ferrous, aluminum, inerts	20.0
Yard waste	20.0
Food waste	17.0
Plastics	4.0
Other	9.0

Source: Rivard, Christopher J., Vinzant, Todd B., Adney, William S., and Grohmann, Karel, "Waste to Energy: Nutrient Requirements for Aerobic and Anaerobic Digestion," *Journal of Environmental Health*, September/October 1989, Volume 52, Number 2, p. 96. Primary source: Christopher J. Rivard, Ph.D., Fermentation Technology Section, Applied Biological Sciences Section, Solar Energy Research Institute. .

★ 151 ★

Municipal Solid Waste Generation in 1988

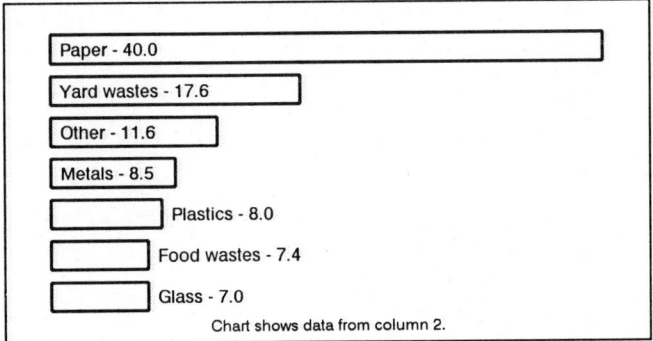

Paper - 40.0

Yard wastes - 17.6

Other - 11.6

Metals - 8.5

Plastics - 8.0

Food wastes - 7.4

Glass - 7.0

Chart shows data from column 2.

Materials generated in municipal solid waste (MSW) in 1988. Materials are shown by weight in millions of tons and as percent of a total generation of 179.6 million tons.

Material	Weight (Million Tons)	Percent of total MSW
Paper	71.8	40.0
Yard wastes	31.6	17.6
Metals	15.3	8.5
Plastics	14.4	8.0
Food wastes	13.2	7.4
Glass	12.5	7.0
Other	20.8	11.6

Source: Characterization of Municipal Solid Waste in the United States: 1990 Update, U.S. Environmental Protection Agency, EPA/530-SW-90-042, Washington, D.C., June 1990, p. ES-5.

★ 152 ★

Municipal Solid Waste in Landfills by Type

Other paper - 40.4	
Yard waste - 31.0	
All Other - 20.4	
Plastics - 14.3	
	Corrugated boxes - 13.0
Food waste - 13.2	
Metals - 12.6	
Glass - 11.1	

Landfill volumes of discards in 1988, shown in millions of tons.

Type of Waste	Volumes
Corrugated boxes	13.0
Other paper	40.4
Plastics	14.3
Yard waste	31.0
Food waste	13.2
Metals	12.6
Glass	11.1
All Other	20.4

Source: Pulp & Paper, December 1990, p. 122, from the American Paper Institute.

★ 153 ★

Municipal Solid Waste Products

Estimates products and materials in MSW, after recovery, for years 1960-2000 by decade and including values for 1986. Data are shown in percent by weight.

Category	1960	1970	1980	1986	1990	2000
Durables[1]	11.1	12.4	13.8	13.6	13.6	13.6
Nondurables[2]	18.5	19.0	22.1	25.1	25.8	28.1
Containers & packaging	29.4	34.9	32.6	30.3	30.5	30.3
Food wastes	14.9	11.4	9.2	8.9	8.4	8.9
Yard wastes	24.5	20.6	20.5	20.1	19.8	20.1
Miscellaneous inorganics	1.6	1.7	1.7	1.8	1.9	1.8

Source: Facing America's Trash: What's Next for Municipal Solid Waste?, p. 110, from Franklin Associates, Ltd., *Characterization of Municipal Solid Waste in the United States, 1960 to 2000 (Update 1988)*, report prepared for the U.S. Environmental Protection Agency, Office of Solid Waste and Emergency Response (Prairie Village, KS: Mar. 30, 1988). *Notes:* 1. Includes major appliances, furniture, tires, and miscellaneous items such as sporting equipment, hobby supplies, toys, jewelry, consumer electronics, and watches. 2. Includes paper products such as newspapers, books and magazines, office paper and commercial printing, tissue, towels, plates and cups, plus clothing and footwear.

★ 154 ★

Municipal Waste Generation & Recovery

Year	Gross discards		Materials recovery		Energy recovery (million tons)	Net discards (million tons)
	Per capita (pounds per day)	Total (pounds per day)	Per capita (pounds per day)	Total (million tons)		
1960	2.65	87.5	0.18	5.8	0	81.7
1965	2.88	102.3	0.17	6.2	0.2	95.9
1970	3.22	120.5	0.21	8.0	0.4	112.1
1975	3.18	125.3	0.23	9.1	0.7	115.5
1980	3.43	142.6	0.32	13.4	2.7	126.5
1985	3.49	152.5	0.35	15.3	7.6	129.7
1990	3.67	167.4	0.40	18.4	13.3	135.7

Source: Council on Environmental Quality, *20th Annual Report 1990*, Washington, D.C., p. 492, from U.S. Environmental Protection Agency, Office of Solid Waste and Emergency Response. "Characterization of municipal solid waste in the United States, 1960 to 2000." Prepared by Franklin Associates, Ltd., Prairie Village, KS. Data for 1990 are projections.

★ 155 ★

Nondurable Goods Discarded in the Municipal Wastestream - I

Goods Listed are discarded after materials and compost recovery.

Nondurable Goods	Percent of Total Discards						
	1960	1965	1970	1975	1980	1985	1988
Newspapers	5.3	6.3	7.2	6.4	8.0	9.0	8.9
Books and Magazines	1.8	2.1	2.2	2.1	3.0	4.2	4.6
Office Papers	1.2	1.8	2.0	1.9	3.0	4.6	5.7
Commercial Printing	1.2	1.6	1.8	1.8	2.7	2.7	3.5
Tissue Paper and Towels	1.1	1.5	2.1	2.1	2.3	2.7	3.0
Paper Plates and Cups	0.3	0.3	0.4	0.4	0.6	0.6	0.7
Plastic Plates and Cups	0.0	0.0	0.0	0.0	0.2	0.3	0.4
Disposable Diapers	0.0	0.0	0.3	1.2	2.3	2.9	2.7
Other Nonpackaging Paper	2.6	3.8	3.4	3.3	4.2	3.5	5.2
Clothing and Footwear	1.3	1.5	1.5	1.7	2.3	2.7	3.9
Other Miscellaneous Nondurables	0.4	0.5	0.8	0.9	3.1	3.8	4.6
Total Nondurable Goods	15.2	19.4	21.7	21.8	31.7	37.0	43.0
Other nonfood, products, Food and Yard Wastes	66.7	77.2	91.6	96.4	103.4	108.2	113.0
Total MSW Discarded-Weight	81.9	96.6	113.3	118.2	135.1	145.2	156.0

Source: Characterization of Municipal Solid Waste in the United States: 1990 Update, U.S. Environmental Protection Agency, EPA/530-SW-90-042, Washington, D.C., June 1990, p. 38, from Franklin Associates, Ltd. Details may not add to totals due to rounding.

★ 156 ★

Nondurable Goods Discarded in the Municipal Wastestream - II

Goods listed are discarded into the municipal waste stream after materials and compost recovery.

Nondurable Goods	Percent of Total Discards						
	1960	1965	1970	1975	1980	1985	1988
Newspapers	6.5	6.5	6.4	5.4	5.9	6.2	5.7
Books and Magazines	2.2	2.2	1.9	1.8	2.2	2.9	2.9
Office Papers	1.5	1.9	1.8	1.6	2.2	3.2	3.6
Commercial Printing	1.5	1.7	1.6	1.5	2.0	1.9	2.2
Tissue Paper and Towels	1.3	1.6	1.9	1.8	1.7	1.9	1.9
Paper Plates and Cups	0.4	0.3	0.4	0.3	0.4	0.4	0.4
Plastic Plates and Cups	0.0	0.0	0.0	0.0	0.1	0.2	0.2
Disposable Diapers	0.0	0.0	0.3	1.0	1.7	2.0	1.7
Other Nonpackaging Paper	3.2	3.9	3.0	2.8	3.1	2.4	3.3
Clothing and Footwear	1.6	1.6	1.3	1.4	1.7	1.9	2.5
Other Miscellaneous Nondurables	0.5	0.5	0.7	0.8	2.3	2.6	2.9
Total Nondurable Goods	18.6	20.1	19.2	18.4	23.5	25.5	27.6
Other Nonfood products, Food and Yard Waste	81.4	79.9	80.8	81.6	76.5	74.5	72.4
Total MSW Discarded-Percent	100.0	100.0	100.0	100.0	100.0	100.0	100.0

Source: Characterization of Municipal Solid Waste in the United States: 1990 Update, U.S. Environmental Protection Agency, EPA/530-SW-90-042, Washington, D.C., June 1990, p. 38, from Franklin Associates, Ltd. Details may not add to totals due to rounding.

★ 157 ★

Nondurable Goods in the Municipal Wastestream - I

The values are in millions of tons. Products listed are generated before material recovery or combustion.

Products	1960	1965	1970	1975	1980	1985	1988
Newspapers	7.1	8.3	9.5	8.8	11.0	12.5	13.3
Books and Magazines	1.9	2.2	2.5	2.3	3.4	4.7	5.3
Office Papers	1.5	2.2	2.7	2.6	4.0	5.7	7.3
Commercial Printing	1.3	1.8	2.1	2.1	3.1	3.2	4.1
Tissue Paper and Towels	1.1	1.5	2.1	2.1	2.3	2.7	3.0
Paper Plates and Cups	0.3	0.3	0.4	0.4	0.6	0.6	0.7
Plastic Plates and Cups	0.0	0.0	0.0	0.0	0.2	0.3	0.4
Disposable Diapers	0.0	0.0	0.3	1.2	2.3	2.9	2.7
Other Nonpackaging Paper	2.7	3.9	3.6	3.5	4.2	3.5	5.2
Clothing and Footwear	1.3	1.5	1.5	1.7	2.3	2.7	4.0
Other Miscellaneous Nondurables	0.4	0.5	0.8	0.9	3.1	3.8	4.6
Total Goods	17.6	22.2	25.5	25.6	36.5	42.6	50.4

[Continued]

★ 157 ★

Nondurable Goods in the Municipal Waste Stream - I
[Continued]

Products	1960	1965	1970	1975	1980	1985	1988
Total Durable Goods and Other Wastes	70.2	81.52	96.4	102.5	113.1	119.0	129.2
Total MSW Generated-Weight	87.8	103.4	121.9	128.1	149.6	161.6	179.6

Source: Characterization of Municipal Solid Waste in the United States: 1990 Update, U.S. Environmental Protection Agency, EPA/530-SW-90-042, Washington, D.C., June 1990, p. 36, from Franklin Associates, Ltd. Details may not add to totals due to rounding.

★ 158 ★

Nondurable Goods in the Municipal Wastestream - II

The values are percent of total nondurable goods generated. Products listed are generated before materials recovery or combustion.

Products	1960	1965	1970	1975	1980	1985	1988
Newspapers	8.1	8.0	7.8	6.9	7.4	7.7	7.4
Books and Magazines	2.2	2.1	2.1	1.8	2.3	2.9	3.0
Office Papers	1.7	2.1	2.2	2.0	2.7	3.5	4.1
Commercial Printing	1.5	1.7	1.7	1.6	2.1	2.0	2.3
Tissue Paper and Towels	1.3	1.5	1.7	1.6	1.5	1.7	1.7
Paper Plates and Cups	0.3	0.3	0.3	0.3	0.4	0.4	0.4
Plastic Plates and Cups	0.0	0.0	0.0	0.0	0.1	0.2	0.2
Disposable Diapers	0.0	0.0	0.2	0.9	1.5	1.8	1.5
Other Nonpackaging Paper	3.1	3.8	3.0	2.7	2.8	2.2	2.9
Clothing and Footwear	1.5	1.5	1.2	1.3	1.5	1.7	2.2
Other Miscellaneous Nondurables	0.5	0.5	0.7	0.7	2.1	2.4	2.5
Total Goods	20.0	21.5	20.9	20.0	24.4	26.4	28.1
Total Durable and Other Wastes	80.0	78.5	79.1	80.0	75.6	73.6	71.9
Total MSW Generated-Percent	100.0	100.0	100.0	100.0			

Source: Characterization of Municipal Solid Waste in the United States: 1990 Update, U.S. Environmental Protection Agency, EPA/530-SW-90-042, Washington, D.C., June 1990, p. 36, from Franklin Associates, Ltd. Details may not add to totals due to rounding.

★ 159 ★

Packaging in the Municipal Wastestream

| 2000 - 50.7 |
| 1990 - 45.4 |
| 1980 - 42.1 |
| 1970 - 39.3 |
| 1960 - 24.0 |

Year	Million Tons
1960	24.0
1970	39.3
1980	42.1
1990	45.4[1]
2000	50.7[1]

Source: Garbage, May/June 1990, p. 68, from Franklin Associates, Ltd. *Note:* 1. Projected.

★ 160 ★

Paper and Paperboard in Municipal Solid Waste

Generation, recovery, and discards of paper and paperboard products in municipal solid waste in 1988.

Product category	Generation (million tons)	Recovery (million tons)	Recovery (percent of generation)	Discards (million tons)
Nondurable goods				
Newspapers	13.3	4.4	33.3	8.9
Books and magazines	5.3	0.7	13.2	4.6
Office papers	7.3	1.6	22.5	5.7
Commercial printing	4.1	0.6	14.6	3.5
Tissue paper and towels	3.0	Neg.	Neg.	3.0
Paper plates and cups	0.7	Neg.	Neg.	5.2
Other nonpackaging paper[1]	5.2	Neg.	Neg.	5.2
Total paper and paperboard nondurable goods	38.9	7.4	18.9	31.5
Containers and packaging				
Corrugated boxes	23.1	10.5	45.4	12.6
Milk cartons	0.5	Neg.	Neg.	0.5
Folding cartons	4.4	0.3	7.7	4.1
Other paperboard packaging	0.3	Neg.	Neg.	0.3
Bags and sacks	2.9	0.2	7.0	2.7

[Continued]

★ 160 ★

Paper and Paperboard in Municipal Solid Waste
[Continued]

Product category	Generation (million tons)	Recovery (million tons)	Recovery (percent of generation)	Discards (million tons)
Wrapping papers	0.1	Neg.	Neg.	0.1
Total paper and paperboard containers and packaging	32.9	11.0	33.5	21.9
Total paper and paperboard	71.8	18.4	25.6	53.4

Source: Characterization of Municipal Solid Waste in the United States: 1990 Update, U.S. Environmental Protection Agency, EPA/530-SW-90-042, Washington, D.C., June 1990, p. 13, from Franklin Associates, Ltd. Neg. stands for negligible. Details may not add due to rounding. *Notes:* 1. Includes tissue in disposable diapers, paper in games and novelties, posters, tags, cards, ect.

★ 161 ★

Paper Products Generated in Solid Waste

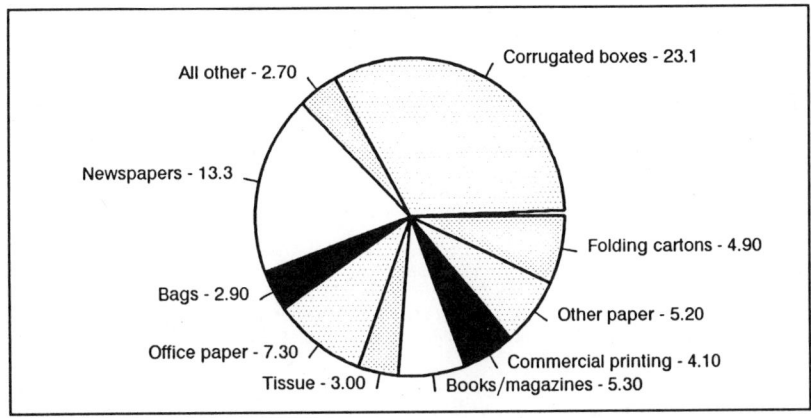

Paper and paperboard products generated in municipal solid waste in 1988, shown in millions of tons.

Product	Volume
Corrugated boxes	23.1
Newspapers	13.3
Office paper	7.30
Books/magazines	5.30
Other paper	5.20
Folding cartons	4.90
Commercial printing	4.10
Tissue	3.00
Bags	2.90
All other	2.70

Source: Pulp & Paper, December 1990, p. 121, from EPA.

★ 162 ★

Plastic Products in Municipal Solid Waste

The values are for 1988.

Product Category	Generation (Million tons)	Recovery (Million tons)	Recovery (Percent of generation)	Discards (Million tons)
Durable Goods[1]	4.1	<0.1	1.5	4.1
Nondurable Goods				
Plastic Plates and Cups	0.4	Neg.	Neg.	0.4
Clothing and Footwear	0.2	Neg.	Neg.	0.2
Disposable Diapers[2]	0.3	Neg.	Neg.	0.3
Other Miscellaneous Nondurables[3]	3.8	Neg.	Neg.	3.8
Total Plastics Nondurable Goods	4.6	Neg.	Neg.	4.6
Containers and Packaging				
Soft Drink Bottles[4]	0.4	0.1	21.0	0.3
Milk Bottles	0.4	Neg.	<0.1	0.4
Other Containers	1.7	Neg.	Neg.	1.7
Bags and Sacks	0.8	Neg.	Neg.	0.8
Wraps	1.1	Neg.	Neg.	1.1
Other Plastic Packaging	1.2	Neg.	Neg.	1.2
Total Plastics Containers and Packaging	5.6	0.1	1.6	5.5
Total Plastics	14.4	0.2	1.1	14.3

Source: Characterization of Municipal Solid Waste in the United States: 1990 Update, U.S. Environmental Protection Agency, EPA/530-SW-90-042, Washington, D.C., June 1990, p. 20, from Franklin Associates Ltd. Neg. stands for Negligible. Details may not add up to totals due to rounding. *Notes:* 1. Plastics as a component of appliances, furniture, lead-acid batteries and miscellaneous durables. 2. Does not include other materials in diapers. 3. Trash bags, eating utensils and straws, shower curtains, etc. 4. Includes bottles and base cups.

★ 163 ★

Plastics in the Solid Waste Stream

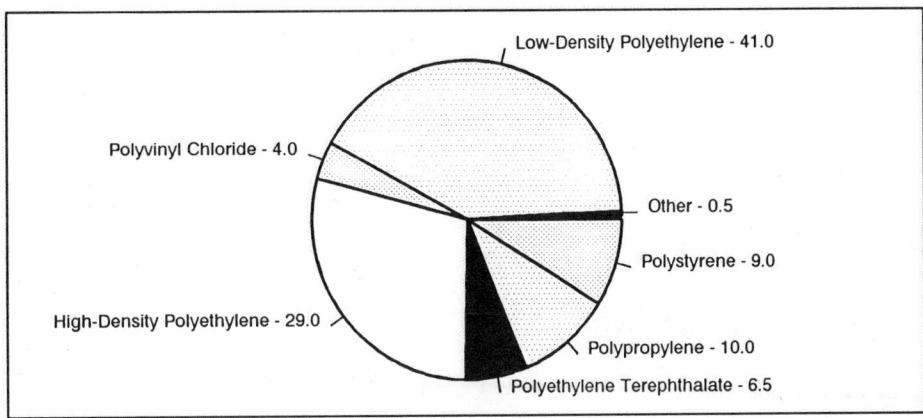

Data are shown as percent of total plastic, by type of resin.

Type	Percent of Total
Low-Density Polyethylene	41.0
High-Density Polyethylene	29.0
Polypropylene	10.0
Polystyrene	9.0
Polyethylene Terephthalate	6.5
Polyvinyl Chloride	4.0
Other	0.5

Source: Plastics World, September 1989, p. 13, from the Society of the Plastics Industry.

★ 164 ★

Products Discarded in 1988

	1988 Discards[1] (mil tons)	Weight (% of total)	Landfill Density[2] (lb/cu yd)	Landfill Volume[3] (mil cu yd)	Volume (% of total)
DURABLE GOODS	23.0	14.7	520	88.5	22.2
NONDURABLE GOODS					
Newspapers	8.9	5.7	800	22.1	5.5
Books and magazines	4.6	2.9	800	11.5	2.9
Office papers	5.7	3.6	800	14.2	3.5
Commercial printing	3.5	2.2	800	8.8	2.2
Tissue paper and towels	3.0	1.9	800	7.6	1.9
Paper plates and cups	0.7	0.4	800	1.6	0.4
Plastic plates and cups	0.4	0.2	355	2.1	0.5
Disposable diapers	2.7	1.7	400	13.3	3.3

[Continued]

★ 164 ★

Products Discarded in 1988
[Continued]

	1988 Discards[1] (mil tons)	Weight (% of total)	Landfill Density[2] (lb/cu yd)	Landfill Volume[3] (mil cu yd)	Volume (% of total)
Other nonpackaging paper	5.2	3.3	800	12.9	3.2
Clothing and footwear	3.9	2.5	435	18.1	4.5
Other misc. nondurables	4.6	2.9	390	23.4	5.9
Total Nondurable Goods	43.0	27.6	634	135.6	34.0
CONTAINERS AND PACKAGING					
Glass Packaging					
Beer and soft drink	4.3	2.8	2,800	3.1	0.8
Wine and liquor	1.9	1.2	2,800	1.4	0.3
Food and other bottles & jars	3.6	2.3	2,800	2.6	0.6
Total Glass Packaging	9.8	6.3	2,800	7.0	1.8
Steel Packaging					
Beer and soft drink cans	0.1	0.1	560	0.3	0.1
Food and other cans	2.1	1.4	560	7.6	1.9
Other steel packaging	0.2	0.1	560	0.8	0.2
Total Steel Packaging	2.4	1.6	560	8.7	2.2
Aluminum Packaging					
Beer and soft drink cans	0.6	0.4	250	4.8	1.2
Other cans	0.1	<0.1	250	0.8	0.2
Foil and closures	0.3	0.2	550	1.1	0.3
Total Aluminum Packaging	1.0	0.7	299	6.7	1.7
Paper and Paperboard Packaging					
Corrugated boxes	12.6	8.1	750	33.6	8.4
Milk cartons	0.5	0.3	820	1.2	0.3
Folding cartons	4.1	2.6	820	10.0	2.5
Other paperboard packaging	0.3	0.2	820	0.8	0.2
Bags and sacks	2.7	1.7	740	7.3	1.8
Wrapping paper	0.1	0.1	800	0.3	0.1
Other paper packaging	1.6	1.0	740	4.3	1.1
Total Paper & Board Packaging	21.9	14.0	763	57.5	14.4
Plastics Packaging					
Soft drink bottles	0.3	0.2	355	1.7	0.4
Milk bottles	0.4	0.3	355	2.3	0.6
Other containers	1.7	1.1	355	9.7	2.4
Bags and sacks	0.8	0.5	670	2.4	0.6
Wraps	1.1	0.7	670	3.3	0.8
Other plastic packaging	1.2	0.8	185	13.2	3.3
Total Plastic Packaging	5.5	3.5	341	32.4	8.1
Wood packaging	2.1	1.3	800	5.3	1.3
Other misc. packaging	0.2	0.1	1,015	0.4	0.1
Total Containers & Packaging	43.0	27.6	729	118.0	29.6
Total Nonfood Product Waste	109	69.9	637	342.0	85.8

[Continued]

★ 164 ★

Products Discarded in 1988
[Continued]

	1988 Discards[1] (mil tons)	Weight (% of total)	Landfill Density[2] (lb/cu yd)	Landfill Volume[3] (mil cu yd)	Volume (% of total)
Other Waste					
Food	13.2	8.5	2,000	13.2	3.3
Yard	31.1	20.0	1,500	41.3	10.4
Misc. inorganics	2.7	1.7	2,500	2.2	0.5
Total Other Wastes	47.0	30.1	1,659	56.7	14.2
Total MSW Discarded	156	100.0	783	399	100.0

Source: Characterization of Municipal Solid Waste in the United States: 1990 Update, U.S. Environmental Protection Agency, EPA/530-SW-90-042, Washington, D.C., June 1990, p. 87, from Franklin Associates, Ltd. *Notes:* 1. Discards after materials recovery and composting, before combustion and landfilling. 2. From table 43. 3. This assumes that all waste is landfilled, but some is combusted and otherwise disposed.

★ 165 ★

Products Discarded in Municipal Solid Waste by Volume

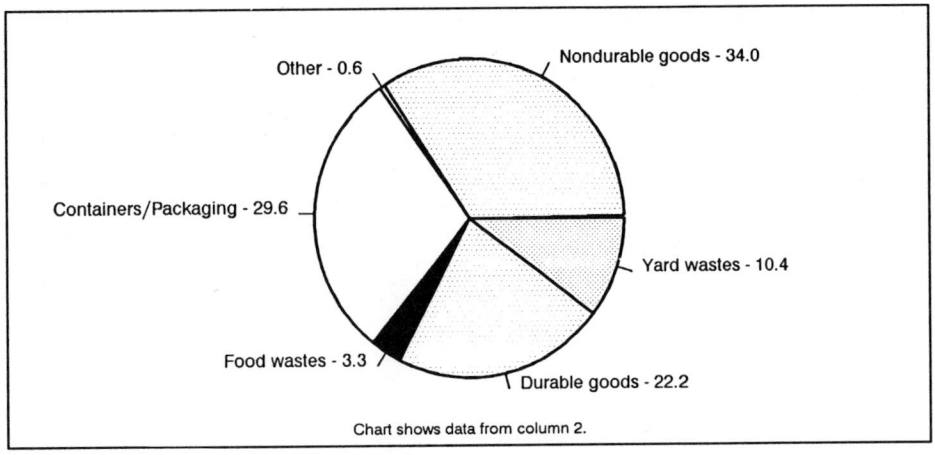

Chart shows data from column 2.

The total product volume discarded in 1988 was 400 million cubic yards.

Product	Volume Discarded (cubic yards)	Percent
Nondurable goods	135.6	34.0
Containers/Packaging	118.1	29.6
Durable goods	88.5	22.2
Yard wastes	41.3	10.4

[Continued]

★ 165 ★

Products Discarded in Municipal Solid Waste by Volume
[Continued]

Product	Volume Discarded (cubic yards)	Percent
Food wastes	13.2	3.3
Other	2.2	0.6

Source: Characterization of Municipal Solid Waste in the United States: 1990 Update, U.S. Environmental Protection Agency, EPA/530-SW-90-042, Washington, D.C., June 1990, p. ES-12.

★ 166 ★

Products Discarded in the Municipal Wastestream - I
Products listed are discarded after materials and compost recovery.

Products	Millions of Tons						
	1960	1965	1970	1975	1980	1985	1988
Durable Goods	9.0	10.2	14.2	16.5	18.4	20.1	23.0
Nondurable Goods	15.2	19.4	21.7	21.8	31.7	37.0	43.0
Containers and Packaging	24.2	31.1	39.6	39.3	42.1	42.4	43.0
Total Nonfood Product Wastes	48.4	60.7	75.5	77.6	92.2	99.5	109.0
Other Wastes							
Food Wastes	12.2	12.7	12.8	13.4	13.2	13.2	13.2
Yard Wastes	20.0	21.6	23.2	25.2	27.5	30.0	31.1
Miscellaneous Inorganic Wastes	1.3	1.6	1.8	2.0	2.2	2.5	2.7
Total Other Wastes	33.5	35.9	37.8	40.6	42.9	45.7	47.0
Total MSW Discarded-Weight	81.9	96.6	113.3	118.2	135.1	145.2	156.0

Source: Characterization of Municipal Solid Waste in the United States: 1990 Update, U.S. Environmental Protection Agency, EPA/530-SW-90-042, Washington, D.C., June 1990, p. 30, from Franklin Associates, Ltd. Details may not add to totals due to rounding.

★ 167 ★

Products Discarded in the Municipal Wastestream - II
Products listed are discarded after materials and compost recovery.

Products	Percent of Total Discards						
	1960	1965	1970	1975	1980	1985	1988
Durable Goods	11.0	10.6	12.5	14.0	13.6	13.8	14.7
Nondurable Goods	18.6	20.1	19.2	18.4	23.5	25.5	27.6
Containers and Packaging	29.5	32.2	35.0	33.2	31.2	29.2	27.6
Total Nonfood Product Wastes	59.1	62.8	66.6	65.7	68.2	68.5	69.9
Other Wastes							
Food Wastes	14.9	13.1	11.3	11.3	9.8	9.1	8.5
Yard Wastes	24.4	22.4	20.5	21.3	20.4	20.7	20.0
Miscellaneous Inorganic Wastes	1.6	1.7	1.6	1.7	1.6	1.7	1.7
Total Other Wastes	40.9	37.2	33.4	34.3	31.8	31.5	30.1
Total MSW Discarded-Percent	100.0	100.0	100.0	100.0	100.0	100.0	100.0

Source: Characterization of Municipal Solid Waste in the United States: 1990 Update, U.S. Environmental Protection Agency, EPA/530-SW-90-042, Washington, D.C., June 1990, p. 30, from Franklin Associates, Ltd. Details may not add to totals due to rounding.

★ 168 ★

Products in Municipal Solid Waste by Weight

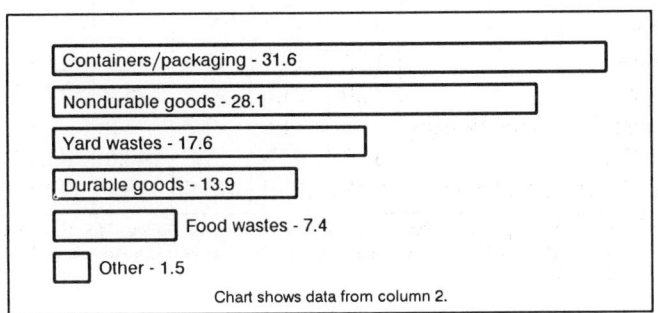

Containers/packaging - 31.6
Nondurable goods - 28.1
Yard wastes - 17.6
Durable goods - 13.9
Food wastes - 7.4
Other - 1.5
Chart shows data from column 2.

The total municipal solid waste generated in 1988 was 179.6 million tons.

Product	Weight (million tons)	Percent
Containers/packaging	56.8	31.6
Nondurable goods	50.4	28.1
Yard wastes	31.6	17.6
Durable goods	24.9	13.9

[Continued]

★ 168 ★

Products in Municipal Solid Waste by Weight
[Continued]

Product	Weight (million tons)	Percent
Food wastes	13.2	7.4
Other	2.7	1.5

Source: Characterization of Municipal Solid Waste in the United States: 1990 Update, U.S. Environmental Protection Agency, EPA/530-SW-90-042, Washington, D.C., June 1990, p. ES-8.

★ 169 ★

Products in Municipal Waste - I
Products listed are generated before materials recovery or combustion.

Products	Millions of Tons						
	1960	1965	1970	1975	1980	1985	1988
Durable Goods	9.4	11.1	15.1	17.5	19.7	21.5	24.9
Nondurable Goods	17.6	22.2	25.5	25.6	36.5	42.6	50.4
Containers and Packaging	27.3	34.2	43.5	44.4	50.5	51.8	56.8
Total Nonfood Product Wastes	54.3	67.5	84.1	87.5	106.7	115.9	132.1
Other Wastes							
Food Wastes	12.2	12.7	12.8	13.4	13.2	13.2	13.2
Yard Wastes	20.0	21.6	23.2	25.2	27.5	30.0	31.6
Miscellaneous Inorganic Wastes	1.3	1.6	1.8	2.0	2.2	2.5	2.7
Total Other Wastes	33.5	35.9	37.8	40.6	42.9	45.7	47.5
Total MSW Generated-Weight	87.8	103.4	121.9	128.1	149.6	161.6	179.6

Source: Characterization of Municipal Solid Waste in the United States: 1990 Update, U.S. Environmental Protection Agency, EPA/530-SW-90-042, Washington, D.C., June 1990, p. 28, from Franklin Associates, Ltd. Details may not add to totals due to rounding.

★ 170 ★

Products in Municipal Waste - II
Products listed are generated before materials recovery or combustion.

Products	Percent of Total Generation						
	1960	1965	1970	1975	1980	1985	1988
Durable Goods	10.7	10.7	12.4	13.7	13.2	13.3	13.9
Nondurable Goods	20.0	21.5	20.9	20.0	24.4	26.4	28.1
Containers and Packaging	31.1	33.1	35.7	34.7	33.8	32.1	31.6
Total Nonfood Product Wastes	61.8	65.3	69.0	68.3	71.3	17.7	73.5
Other Wastes							
Food Wastes	13.9	12.3	10.5	10.5	8.8	8.2	7.4
Yard Wastes	22.8	20.9	19.0	19.7	18.4	18.6	17.6
Miscellaneous Inorganic Wastes	1.5	1.5	1.5	1.6	1.5	1.5	1.5
Total Other Wastes	38.2	34.7	31.0	31.7	28.7	28.3	26.5
Total MSW Generated-Percent	100.0	100.0	100.0	100.0	100.0	100.0	100.0

Source: Characterization of Municipal Solid Waste in the United States: 1990 Update, U.S. Environmental Protection Agency, EPA/530-SW-90-042, Washington, D.C., June 1990, p. 28, from Franklin Associates, Ltd. Details may not add to totals due to rounding.

★ 171 ★

Projected Containers and Packaging in Municipal Solid Waste
Generation before materials recovery or combustion. The estimated values are in millions of tons and percent of total generation.

Products	Millions of tons			% of total generation		
	1995	2000	2010	1995	2000	2010
Durable goods	28.6	31.3	35.7	14.3	14.5	14.3
Nondurable goods	60.5	68.3	86.3	30.3	31.6	34.4
Containers and packaging						
Glass packaging						
Beer and soft drink bottles	3.8	2.8	2.0	1.9	1.3	0.8
Wine and liquor bottles	2.0	2.0	2.0	1.0	0.9	0.8
Food and other bottles and jars	4.0	4.1	4.0	2.0	1.9	1.6
Total glass packaging	9.8	8.9	8.0	4.9	4.1	3.2
Steel packaging						
Beer and soft drink cans	0.1	0.1	0.2	0.1	0.1	0.1
Food and other cans	2.2	2.0	1.6	1.1	0.9	0.6
Other steel packaging	0.2	0.2	0.3	0.1	0.1	0.1
Total steel packaging	2.5	2.3	2.0	1.3	1.1	0.8
Aluminum packaging						
Beer and soft drink cans	1.8	2.1	2.2	0.9	0.9	0.9
Other cans	0.1	0.1	0.1	0.0	0.0	0.0

[Continued]

★ 171 ★

Projected Containers and Packaging in Municipal Solid Waste
[Continued]

Products	Millions of tons			% of total generation		
	1995	2000	2010	1995	2000	2010
Foil and closures	0.3	0.4	0.4	0.2	0.2	0.2
Total Aluminum packaging	2.2	2.5	2.7	1.1	1.2	1.1
Paper and paperboard packaging						
Corrugated boxes	27.6	31.2	39.9	13.8	14.5	15.9
Milk cartons	0.5	0.4	0.4	0.2	0.2	0.2
Folding cartons	5.0	5.1	5.1	2.5	2.3	2.0
Other paperboard packaging	0.3	0.3	0.3	0.2	0.1	0.1
Bags and sacks	2.5	2.2	2.0	1.2	1.0	0.8
Wrapping papers	0.1	0.1	0.1	0.0	0.0	0.0
Other paper packaging	2.0	2.3	2.9	1.0	1.0	1.2
Total paper and board packaging	38.0	41.6	50.7	19.0	19.3	20.2
Plastics packaging						
Soft drink bottles	0.6	0.7	0.9	0.3	0.3	0.3
Milk bottles	0.5	0.5	0.6	0.2	0.2	0.2
Other containers	2.4	2.7	3.5	1.2	1.3	1.4
Bags and sacks	1.0	1.2	1.6	0.5	0.6	0.6
Wraps	1.3	1.4	1.6	0.7	0.6	0.6
Other plastics packaging	1.4	1.6	1.9	0.7	0.7	0.8
Total plastics packaging	7.1	8.1	10.1	3.6	3.8	4.0
Wood packaging	2.1	2.1	2.1	1.0	1.0	0.8
Other misc. packaging	0.2	0.2	0.3	0.1	0.1	0.1
Total containers & packaging	61.9	65.7	75.8	31.0	30.4	30.2
Total nonfood product wastes	150.9	165.4	197.8	75.5	76.6	78.9
Other wastes						
Food wastes	13.2	13.3	13.7	6.6	6.2	5.5
Yard wastes	33.0	34.4	36.0	16.5	15.9	14.4
Miscellaneous inorganic wastes	2.7	2.9	3.1	1.4	1.3	1.2
Total other wastes	48.9	50.6	52.8	24.5	23.4	21.1
Total MSW generated	199.8	216.0	250.6	100.0	100.0	100.0

Source: Characterization of Municipal Solid Waste in the United States: 1990 Update, U.S. Environmental Protection Agency, EPA/530-SW-90-042, Washington, D.C., June 1990, p. 66, from Franklin Associates, Ltd. Details may not add to totals due to rounding.

★ 172 ★

Projected Durable Goods in Municipal Solid Waste

The estimated values are in millions of tons and percent of total generation.

Products	Millions of Tons			% of Total Generation		
	1995	2000	2010	1995	2000	2010
Durable Goods						
Major Appliances	3.2	3.3	3.1	1.6	1.5	1.2
Furniture and Furnishings	8.8	10.0	12.3	4.4	4.6	4.9
Rubber Tires	2.0	2.1	2.2	1.0	1.0	0.9
Batteries, Lead-Acid	2.0	2.2	2.6	1.0	1.0	1.0
Miscellaneous Durables	12.6	13.8	15.6	6.3	6.4	6.2
Total Durable Goods	28.6	31.3	35.7	14.3	14.5	14.3
Nondurable Goods	60.5	68.3	86.3	30.3	31.6	34.4
Containers and Packaging	61.9	65.7	75.8	31.0	30.4	30.2
Total Nonfood Product Wastes	150.9	165.4	197.8	75.5	76.6	78.9
Other Wastes						
Food Wastes	13.2	13.3	13.7	6.6	6.2	5.5
Yard Wastes	33.0	34.4	36.0	16.5	15.9	14.4
Miscellaneous Inorganic Wastes	2.7	2.9	3.1	1.4	1.3	1.2
Total Other Wastes	48.9	50.6	52.8	24.5	23.4	21.1
Total MSW Generated	199.8	216.0	250.6	100.0	100.0	100.0

Source: Characterization of Municipal Solid Waste in the United States: 1990 Update, U.S. Environmental Protection Agency, EPA/530-SW-90-042, Washington, D.C., June 1990, p. 64, from Franklin Associates, Ltd. Details may not add to totals due to rounding.

★ 173 ★

Projected Material Generation in the Municipal Waste Stream

Values are in millions of tons and percent of total generation. Generation before materials recovery or combustion.

Materials	Millions of Tons			% of Total Generation		
	1995	2000	2010	1995	2000	2010
Paper and Paperboard	85.5	96.1	121.2	42.8	44.5	48.4
Glass	11.1	10.3	9.5	5.6	4.8	3.8
Metals						
Ferrous	11.7	12.0	12.0	5.9	5.5	4.8
Aluminum	3.1	3.5	3.8	1.6	1.6	1.5
Other Nonferrous	1.4	1.5	1.7	0.7	0.7	0.7
Total Metals	16.2	16.9	17.5	8.1	7.8	7.0
Plastics	18.6	21.1	25.7	9.3	9.8	10.3
Rubber and Leather	4.9	5.3	5.8	2.4	2.5	2.3

[Continued]

★ 173 ★

Projected Material Generation in the Municipal Waste Stream
[Continued]

Materials	Millions of Tons			% of Total Generation		
	1995	2000	2010	1995	2000	2010
Textiles	4.1	4.3	4.6	2.0	2.0	1.8
Wood	7.4	8.4	10.2	3.7	3.9	4.1
Other	3.0	3.0	3.3	1.5	1.4	1.3
Total Nonfood Product Wastes	150.9	165.4	197.8	75.5	76.6	78.9
Other Wastes						
Food Wastes	13.2	13.3	13.7	6.6	6.2	5.5
Yard Wastes	33.0	34.4	36.0	16.5	15.9	14.4
Miscellaneous Inorganic Wastes	2.7	2.9	3.1	1.4	1.3	1.2
Total Other Wastes	48.9	50.6	52.8	24.5	23.4	21.1
Total MSW Generated	199.8	216.0	250.6	100.0	100.0	100.0

Source: Characterization of Municipal Solid Waste in the United States: 1990 Update, U.S. Environmental Protection Agency, EPA/530-SW-90-042, Washington, D.C., June 1990, p. 59, from Franklin Associates, Ltd. Details may not add to totals due to rounding.

★ 174 ★

Projected Municipal Solid Waste Generation Rate
The generation rates are average and in annual percent by weight.

	1980-1988	1988-2000	2000-2010
Paper and paperboard	3.5	2.5	2.4
Glass	-2.2	-1.6	-0.8
Metals	0.7	0.8	0.3
Plastics	7.9	3.2	2.0
All other materials[1]	2.6	0.7	0.7
Food wastes	0.0	0.1	0.3
Yard wastes	1.8	0.7	0.5
Total MSW	2.3	1.6	1.5
Population	1.0	0.7	0.5

Source: Characterization of Municipal Solid Waste in the United States: 1990 Update, U.S. Environmental Protection Agency, EPA/530-SW-90-042, Washington, D.C., June 1990, p. 61. *Notes:* 1. Rubber and leather, textiles, wood, batteries (partial), disposable diapers (partial), miscellaneous inorganics.

★ 175 ★

Projected Nondurable Goods in Municipal Solid Waste

The estimated values are in millions of tons and percent of total generation. Generation before materials recovery or combustion.

Products	Millions of tons			% of total generation		
	1995	2000	2010	1995	2000	2010
Durable goods	28.6	31.3	35.7	14.3	14.5	14.3
Nondurable goods						
Newspapers	15.0	16.4	19.4	7.5	7.6	7.7
Books and magazines	6.8	8.1	12.0	3.4	3.8	4.8
Office papers	9.8	11.8	16.0	4.9	5.5	6.4
Commercial printing	5.7	6.8	9.0	2.8	3.1	3.6
Tissue paper and towels	3.6	4.1	5.1	1.8	1.9	2.0
Paper plates and cups	0.7	0.7	0.7	0.3	0.3	0.3
Plastic plates and cups	0.5	0.6	0.7	0.3	0.3	0.3
Disposable diapers	2.4	2.3	2.4	1.2	1.1	1.0
Other nonpackaging paper	5.9	6.6	8.2	2.9	3.0	3.3
Clothing and footwear	4.5	4.9	5.3	2.3	2.3	2.1
Other miscellaneous nondurables	5.5	6.1	7.3	2.8	2.8	2.9
Total nondurable goods	60.5	68.3	86.3	30.3	31.6	34.4
Containers and packaging	61.9	65.7	75.8	31.0	30.4	30.2
Total nonfood product waste	150.9	165.4	197.8	75.5	76.6	78.9
Other wastes						
Food wastes	13.2	13.3	13.7	6.6	6.2	5.5
Yard wastes	33.0	34.4	36.0	16.5	15.9	14.4
Miscellaneous Inorganic wastes	2.7	2.9	3.1	1.4	1.3	1.2
Total other wastes	48.9	50.6	52.8	24.5	23.4	21.1
Total MSW generated	199.8	216.0	250.6	100.0	100.0	100.0

Source: Characterization of Municipal Solid Waste in the United States: 1990 Update, U.S. Environmental Protection Agency, EPA/530-SW-90-042, Washington, D.C., June 1990, p. 34, from Franklin Associates, Ltd. Details may not add to totals due to rounding.

★ 176 ★

Projected Per Capita Generation of Municipal Wastes

The estimated values are in pounds per person per day. Generation before materials or energy recovery.

Materials	1988	1995	2000	2010
Paper and Paperboard	1.60	1.80	1.96	2.35
Glass	0.28	0.23	0.21	0.18
Metals	0.34	0.34	0.35	0.34
Plastics	0.32	0.39	0.43	0.50
Rubber and Leather	0.10	0.10	0.11	0.11
Textiles	0.09	0.09	0.09	0.09
Wood	0.14	0.16	0.17	0.20
Other	0.07	0.06	0.06	0.06
Total Nonfood Products	2.94	3.18	3.38	3.84
Food Wastes	0.29	0.28	0.27	0.27
Yard Wastes	0.70	0.70	0.70	0.70
Miscellaneous Inorganic Wastes	0.06	0.06	0.06	0.06
Total MSW Generated	4.00	4.21	4.41	4.86

Source: Characterization of Municipal Solid Waste in the United States: 1990 Update, U.S. Environmental Protection Agency, EPA/530-SW-90-042, Washington, D.C., June 1990, p.61. Details may not add to totals due to rounding.

★ 177 ★

Projected Products Generation in Municipal Solid Waste

The estimated values are in millions of tons and percent of total generation. Generation before materials recovery or combustion.

Products	Millions of tons			% of total generation		
	1995	2000	2010	1995	2000	2010
Durable goods	28.6	31.3	35.7	14.3	14.5	14.3
Nondurable goods	60.5	68.3	86.3	30.3	31.6	34.4
Containers and packaging	61.9	65.7	75.8	31.0	30.4	30.2
Total nonfood products waste	150.9	165.4	197.8	75.5	76.6	78.9
Other wastes						
Food wastes	13.2	13.3	13.7	6.6	6.2	5.5
Yard wastes	33.0	34.4	36.0	16.5	15.9	14.4
Miscellaneous inorganic wastes	2.7	2.9	3.1	1.4	1.3	1.2

[Continued]

★ 177 ★

Projected Products Generation in Municipal Solid Waste
[Continued]

Products	Millions of tons			% of total generation		
	1995	2000	2010	1995	2000	2010
Total other wastes	48.9	50.6	52.8	24.5	23.4	21.1
Total MSW generated	199.8	216.0	250.6	100.0	100.0	100.0

Source: Characterization of Municipal Solid Waste in the United States: 1990 Update, U.S. Environmental Protection Agency, EPA/530-SW-90-042, Washington, D.C., June 1990, p. 63, from Franklin Associates, Ltd. Details may not add to totals due to rounding.

★ 178 ★

Pulp and Paper Mill Sludge Composition

Characteristics of wastewater sludges, expressed on a dry-weight basis. Means and ranges are shown as miligrams of the given element per kilogram of sludge.

Parameter	Primary sludge		Secondary sludge		Combined sludge	
	Mean	Range	Mean	Range	Mean	Range
Total Solids (%)	22	17 to 32	15	12 to 19	29	15 to 48
Macronutrients						
Primary						
Nitrogen	2,157	700 to 6,900	31,925	13,000 to 59,400	14,056	1,100 to 45,200
Phosphorous	743	300 to 1,000	8,075	3,100 to 13,100	3,322	300 to 8,600
Potassium	1,119	156 to 2,620	2,905	1,530 to 5,070	1,048	132 to 3,310
Secondary						
Calcium	20,176	460 to 80,800	16,762	4,870 to 45,600	38,118	1,360 to 189,000
Magnesium	1,794	192 to 3,550	1,980	1,240 to 3,420	1,502	203 to 3,430
Sulfur	2,027	<0.01 to 3,49	04,187	49.8 to 9,820	1,323	66 to 2,220
Micronutrients						
Iron	2,397	550 to 4,550	2,842	1,390-4,030	4,910 24	2 to 14,500
Manganese	716	56.6 to 1,380	483	112 to 1,400	684	16 to 3,380
(Copper)						
(Zinc)						
Other elements						
Aluminum	17,807	1,670 to 73,900	17,667	4,570 to 33,300	38,244	20,900 to 60,000
Sodium	5,723	325 to 5,000	4,586	469 to 15,700	2,418	332 to 14,900
Tin	2.6	<0.02 to 13	15.0	<0.02 to 50	7.9	4.8 to 12
Arsenic	0.24	0.03 to 0.44	0.17	<0.01 to 0.46	0.31	<0.01 to 1.4

[Continued]

★ 178 ★

Pulp and Paper Mill Sludge Composition
[Continued]

Parameter	Primary sludge		Secondary sludge		Combined sludge	
	Mean	Range	Mean	Range	Mean	Range
Regulated metals						
Cadmium	0.35	0.003 to 1.6	4.5	0.39 to 12	0.91	<0.003 to 2.1
Chromium	13.8	6.0 to 33.8	20.8	9.89 to 29.7	38.9	12.7 to 168
Copper	21.9	7.5 to 55.8	206	63.8 to 519	85.8	7.6 to 277
Lead	28.1	4.0 to 83	42.0	17 to 95	69.0	3.0 to 294
Nickel	21.3	4.9 to 57.8	35.0	6.3 to 92.5	20.0	6.4 to 33.8
Mercury	0.15	<.0001 to .079	0.30	0.01 to 1.0	0.42	0.02 to 1.9
Zinc	93.2	30.1 to 228	513	144 to 932	176	43 to 460

Source: Pulp & Paper, September 1989, p. 212.

★ 179 ★

Restaurant Waste Sources at a Typical McDonald's

Breakdown of waste by type, shown as percent of total weight. A typical McDonald's restaurant serves approximately 2,000 customers and produces 238 pounds of waste per day.

Type of waste	Percent of Total Weight
Behind the counter	
Food waste, egg shells, coffee grounds	34
Corrugated shipping boxes	34
Liquids, office paper, other	8
Plastic wraps, syrup jugs	3
Over the counter	
Uncoated paper (napkins)	4
Coated paper (sandwich wraps)	7
Polystyrene (hot cups, lids, cutlery)	4
Non-McDonald's waste (diapers, other)	6

Source: The Wall Street Journal, April 17, 1991, p. B1, from McDonald's and the Environmental Defense Fund. Based on a week-long waste audit of two restaurants in Sycamore, Ill., and Denver, CO. in November 1990. Adjusted to reflect conversion to quilted paper wraps from polystyrene foam clamshells.

★ 180 ★

Rubber and Leather in Municipal Solid Waste

Generation, recovery, and discard of rubber and leather products in municipal solid waste in 1988.

Product category	Generation (millions tons)	Recovery (millions tons)	Recovery (percent of generation)	Discards (millions tons)
Durable goods				
Rubber tires[1]	1.9	0.1	5.6	1.8
Other durables	1.2	Neg.	Neg.	1.2
Total rubber & leather durable goods	3.0	0.1	3.4	2.9
Nondurable goods				
Clothing and footwear	1.1	Neg.	Neg.	1.1
Other nondurables	0.4	Neg.	Neg.	0.4
Total rubber and leather nondurable goods	1.5	Neg.	Neg.	1.5
Total rubber and leather	4.6	0.1	2.3	4.4

Source: Characterization of Municipal Solid Waste in the United States: 1990 Update, U.S. Environmental Protection Agency, EPA/530-SW-90-042, Washington, D.C., June 1990, p. 24, from Franklin Associates, Ltd. Neg. stands for negligible. Details may not add to totals due to rounding. *Note:* 1. Does not include other materials in tires.

★ 181 ★

Solid Waste Composition by Volume

Composition of solid waste in landfills shown by material as percentage of total volume.

Material	Percent of Total
Plastic	16.3
Paper packaging	16.2
Newspaper	14.1
Other paper	11.0
Yard waste	5.1
Cardboard	4.5
Magazines	1.6
Diapers	1.0
Fast-food packaging	0.3
Glass	0.9
Other[1]	29.0

Source: Plastics World, September 1989, p. 12, from the Garbage Project, University of Arizona.
Note: 1. Includes food waste, metal, rubber, wood, textiles, etc.

★ 182 ★

Solid Waste Composition by Weight

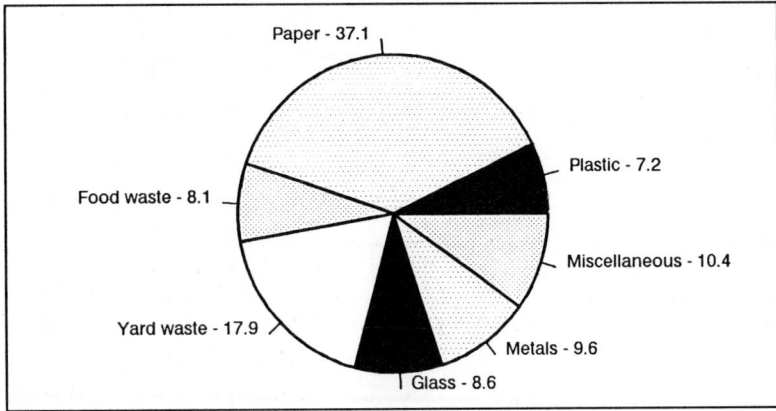

Composition of solid waste in landfills shown by material as percentage of total weight.

Material	Percent of Total
Paper	37.1
Yard waste	17.9
Metals	9.6
Glass	8.6
Food waste	8.1
Plastic	7.2
Miscellaneous	10.4

Source: Plastics World, September 1989, p. 12, from Franklin Associates and the Environmental Protection Agency.

★ 183 ★

Solid Waste Composition - 40 Studies

Comparison of estimated percentages of different components of municipal solid waste (MSW), by weight.

Material	9 studies[1]		40 studies[2]	
	Mean	Range	Mean	Range
Total paper	38.8	29.9-45.9	46.7	36.5-54.7
Newspaper	6.3	4.3-8.1	-	-
Corrugated board	7.9	4.7-13.1	-	-
Mixed paper	21.9	19.6-25.2	-	-
Magazines	0.7	0.7	-	-
Total metal	4.9	1.5-9.4	8.5	4.0-14.7
Aluminum cans	0.9	0.8-1.0	-	-
Miscellaneous aluminum	0.7	0.2-1.6	-	-
Other non-ferrous	1.0	.0-3.4	-	-

[Continued]

★ 183 ★

Solid Waste Composition - 40 Studies
[Continued]

Material	9 studies[1]		40 studies[2]	
	Mean	Range	Mean	Range
Total glass	7.8	3.6-12.9	8.4	6.0-13.7
Glass containers	6.4	6.1-6.6	-	-
Total plastic	8.8	5.3-12.6	5.3[3]	2.0-9.0[3]
Plastic film	3.1	3.1	-	-
Plastic containers	0.9	0.7-1.0	-	-
Yard debris	18.2	0.0-39.7	9.5	0.4-25.0
Food waste	14.7	1.3-28.8	7.8	0.9-18.2
Wood	2.6	0.7-8.2	2.6	0.5-7.0
Textiles	3.4	1.1-6.2	3.3	0.7-5.0
Rubber	0.4	0.0-1.0	-[3]	-[3]
Diapers	-	-	1.5	0.5-2.9
"Not elsewhere classified"	9.2	3.8-16.6	-	0.5-10.0

Source: Facing America's Trash: What Next for Municipal Solid Waste, U.S. Congress, Office of Technology Assessment, OTA-O-412, Washington, D.C., July 1989., p. 80, from Office of Technology Assessment, 1989, after K. Cox, *Background on Municipal Solid Waste: Generation, Composition, Costs, Management Facilities, State Activities* (Takoma Park, MD: 1989); R.N. Kinman and D.K. Nutini, "Household Hazardous Waste in the Sanitary Landfill," *Chemical Times & Trends 11:23-29 and 39-40*, 1988. *Notes:* 1. Compiled from 9 local studies that did not have more than 10 percent (on average) of MSW in the "Not elsewhere classified" category. 2. Compiled from 40 local studies: whether these studies were selected on the basis of the same criteria (i.e., less than 10 percent in the "Not elsewhere classified" category as the 9 local studies is unknown. 3. Plastic, rubber, and leather were compiled together.

★ 184 ★

Solid Waste Miscellaneous Facts

Solid waste	Units
Daily waste per hotel room[1]	.5-28 pounds
Number of 2-liter plastic soda-bottles recycled to stuff one men's ski vest	5
Number of 2-liter bottles made each year[2]	4.7 billion
Garbage generated in South Windsor, Conn. (pop. 23,000) daily[3]	66 tons
Garbage generated in the twin towers of New York's World Trade Center	65 tons
Number of horse carcasses collected in 1880 in New York[4]	15,000

Source: Garbage, September/October 1990, p. 26 *Notes:* 1. Central Florida Hotel and Motel Association. 2. NAPCOR, Johnson Controls, Inc. 3. South Windsor Public Works Dept.; World Trade Center. 4. *Garbage in the Cities*, Texas A&M University.

★ 185 ★

Waste Generation and Material Recovery

Values are for 1988. Food and yard waste figures reflect composting.

	Weight Generated (in millions of tons)	Weight Recovered (in millions of tons)	Percent of Generation of Each Material
Paper and paperboard	71.8	18.4	25.6
Glass	12.5	1.5	12.0
Metals			
Ferrous	11.6	0.7	5.8
Aluminum	2.5	0.8	31.7
Other Nonferrous	1.1	0.7	65.1
Total metals	15.3	2.2	14.6
Plastics	14.4	0.2	1.1
Rubber and leather	4.6	0.1	2.3
Textiles	3.9	0.0	0.6
Wood	6.5	0.0	0.0
Other	3.1	0.7	21.7
Total nonfood product waste	132.1	23.1	17.5
Other wastes			
Food wastes	13.2	0.0	0.0
Yard wastes	31.6	0.5	1.6
Miscellaneous inorganic wastes	2.7	0.0	0.0
Total other wastes	47.5	0.5	1.1
Total MSW	179.6	23.5	13.1

Source: Characterization of Municipal Solid Waste in the United States: 1990 Update, U.S. Environmental Protection Agency, EPA/530-SW-90-042, Washington, D.C., June 1990, p. ES-7.

Toxic Substances

★ 186 ★

Amount of TRI Releases & Transfers - I

Toxic Release Inventory (TRI) releases and transfers by type of transfer or release in pounds and percent for 1987.

Industry	TRI Facilities Number	Total Air Releases		Surface Water		Transfers To Public Sewage	
		(1,000) Pounds	Percent	(1,000) Pounds	Percent	(1,000) Pounds	Percent
Food products	1,576	17,338	6.04	30,561	10.65	205,827	71.71
Tobacco manufacturers	24	7,567	72.32	132,545	1.27	2,293,820	21.93
Textile mill products	469	38,306	10.95	182,364	52.12	119,540	34.16
Apparel	37	2,295	48.11	42,810	0.90	2,337	48.99
Lumber and wood products	644	26,880	74.75	1,001,064	2.78	1,545	4.30
Furniture and fixtures	332	50,928	85.28	47,984	0.08	853,889	1.43
Paper products	663	232,640	8.29	2,183,494	77.78	184,880	6.59
Printing, publishing	287	54,122	85.99	3,521	0.01	3,444	5.47
Chemical products	3,849	946,396	7.83	5,835,404	48.27	784,203	6.49
Petroleum refining	343	79,138	10.38	366,052	48.02	50,531	6.63
Rubber and plastic products	1,125	143,761	51.88	54,078	19.52	48,225	17.40
Leather products	117	14,098	27.07	1,959,66	3.76	31,985	61.41
Stone, clay, glass products	629	27,035	23.11	1,322,017	1.13	7,147	6.11
Primary metals	1,305	234,284	9.03	105,944	4.09	180,432	6.96
Fabricated metals	2,393	109,922	35.89	9,079,26	2.96	76,586	25.00
Machinery, except electrical	787	49,699	50.15	4,439,271	4.48	10,529	10.63
Electric and electronic equipment	1,426	110,350	37.14	13,080,342	4.40	85,642	28.82
Transportation equipment	908	213,564	64.25	3,878,314	1.17	18,199	5.48
Measuring, photographic goods	306	46,331	57.10	3,153,101	3.89	9,767	12.04
Misc. manufacturing	337	24,865	68.45	264,802	0.73	2,103	5.79
Combination of above	1,317	211,290	12.36	799,136	46.73	100,432	5.87
Other industry	404	14,736	9.96	20,237	13.68	9,016	6.09
Grand total	19,278	2,655,543	11.79	9,615,674	42.70	1,935,517	8.60

Source: The Toxic Release Inventory, A National Perspective, U.S. Environmental Protection Agency, Washington, D.C., June 1989, p. 14.

★ 187 ★

Amount of TRI Releases & Transfers - II

Toxic Release Inventory (TRI) releases and transfers by type of transfer or release in pounds and percent for 1987.

Industry	Total On-Site Land		Underground Injection		Transfers Off-Site		Total TRI Releases/ Transfers	Total Releases/ Transfer Rank
	(1,000) Pounds	Percent	(1,000) Pounds	Percent	(1,000) Pounds	Percent	(1,000) Pounds	
Food products	23,018	8.02	190,566	0.07	10,078	3.51	287,012	10
Tobacco manufacturers	10,810	0.10	0	0.00	458,196	4.38	10,462	21
Textile mill products	642,327	0.18	0	0.00	9,059	2.59	349,911	6
Apparel	1,500	0.03	0	0.00	94,221	1.98	4,770	22
Lumber and wood products	2,625	7.30	0	0.00	3,909	10.87	35,961	20
Furniture and fixtures	28,105	0.05	0	0.00	7,857	13.16	59,716	17
Paper products	77,351	2.76	30,894	0.00	129,014	4.60	2,807	2
Printing, publishing	2,597	0.00	0	0.00	5,364	8.52	62,936	16
Chemical products	900,323	7.45	2,902,167	24.01	720,337	5.96	12,089	1
Petroleum refining	39,702	5.21	21,175	2.78	205,765	26.99	762,361	5
Rubber and plastic products	806,162	0.29	49,800	0.02	30,177	10.89	277,097	11
Leather products	166,320	0.32	0	0.00	3,878	7.45	52,087	18
Stone, clay, glass products	25,057	21.42	6,326	5.41	50,081	42.82	116,969	13
Primary metals	1,022	39.39	90,419	3.49	960,608	37.04	2,593	3
Fabricated metals	4,971	1.62	1,454	0.47	104,278	34.05	306,289	8
Machinery, except electrical	660,719	0.67	0	0.00	33,764	34.07	99,091	14
Electric and electronic equipment	7,316	2.46	2,437	0.82	78,292	26.35	297,117	9
Transportation equipment	5,398	1.62	47,339	0.01	91,310	27.47	332,397	7
Measuring, photographic good	164,116	0.20	0	0.00	21,726	26.78	81,141	15
Misc. manufacturing	248,233	0.68	250	0.00	8,843	24.34	36,324	19
Combination of above	249,505	14.59	217,854	12.74	131,768	7.71	1,709,985	4
Other industry	92,343	62.42	312,352	0.21	11,296	7.64	147,940	12
Grand total	2,451,890	10.89	3,242,463	14.40	2,617,957	11.63	22,519,044	

Source: The Toxic Release Inventory, A National Perspective, U.S. Environmental Protection Agency, Washington, D.C., June 1989, p. 15.

★ 188 ★

Asbestos in the Environment

Source	Asbestos fibers
	Millions per liter
Water	
Potable water	
Drinking water standard, lifetime[1]	0.3

[Continued]

★ 188 ★

Asbestos in the Environment
[Continued]

Source	Asbestos fibers
Duluth, MN	12.0
Niagara Falls, ON	2.6
Toronto, ON	1.9
Chicago, IL	1.8
St. Catharines, ON	1.0
London, ON	0.5
Sudbury, ON	0.3
Surface water	
Creek water, Castro Valley, California	116.3
Detroit River	18.2
Thunder Bay, Canada	0.8
	Millions per gram
Particulates	
Rooftop asphalt shingles more than 1 yr. old	1900.0
Rooftop asphalt shingles less than 1 yr. old	1200.0
Paved school playground	830.0
School turf	730.0
Sludge, Los Angeles	550.0
Street dust, Alameda County, CA	300.0
Urban vacant lot	110.0
Rural vacant lot	77.0
Unpaved parking lot	54.0
Street dust, Washington, DC	0.05
	Millions per cubic meter
Air	
Standard, for 8-hour period[2]	0.1

Source: BioCycle, January 1989, p. 53. Data in the original table were taken from 17 separate primary sources. *Notes:* 1. At 2 liters/day (15), ingestion is 600,000 fibers/day; for increased cancer risk of 1 per 100,000. 2. At 12.1 cubic meters per 8 hour day, inhalation of 1.2 million fibers/working day.

★ 189 ★

Most Common Toxic Chemicals

The 25 chemicals reported on the most Toxic Release Inventory (TRI) forms to EPA, 1987.

Chemical name	Number of TRI Forms Reporting	Percent of TRI Forms Reporting	Facilities Reporting Only One Chemical	
			Number	Percent of all Forms for the Chemical
Sodium Hydroxide (solution)	6815	9.19	822	12.06
Sulfuric Acid	4944	6.67	270	5.46
Toluene	3174	4.28	305	9.61
1,1,1-Trichloroethane	3084	4.16	1	0.03
Hydrochloric Acid	2905	3.92	113	3.89
Xylene (mixed isomers)	2761	3.72	274	9.92
Ammonia	2421	3.26	364	15.04
Methyl Ethyl Ketone	2102	2.83	157	7.47
Acetone	2089	2.82	166	7.95
Phosphoric Acid	2048	2.76	94	4.59
Methanol	2043	2.76	116	5.68
Chlorine	1738	2.34	123	7.08
Nitric Acid	1688	2.28	52	3.08
Dichloromethane	1413	1.91	139	9.84
Sodium Sulfate (solution)	1401	1.89	23	1.64
Copper	1320	1.78	184	13.94
Aluminum Oxide	1303	1.76	243	18.65
Ethylene Glycol	1192	1.61	120	10.07
Zinc compounds	1103	1.49	89	8.07
Glycol Ethers	1035	1.40	64	6.18
Freon 113	1033	1.39	244	23.62
N-Butyl Alcohol	899	1.21	15	1.67
Trichloroethylene	868	1.17	195	22.47
Chromium compounds	847	1.14	42	4.96
Styrene	847	1.14	104	12.28
Subtotal	51,073	68.88	4319	8.46
Total for all others	23,079	31.12	2177	9.43
Grand total	74,152	100.0	6496	8.76

Source: The Toxic Release Inventory, A National Perspective, U.S. Environmental Protection Agency, Washington, D.C., June 1989, p. 55.

★ 190 ★

Off-Site Toxic Releases

About 51% of the total toxic substances are released by 25 counties.

County	State	TRI Off-site Transfers (pounds)	Percent of Tri Off-Site Transfers in the State
Wayne	MI	483,567,083	89.63
Harris	TX	135,307,397	48.03
Los Angeles	CA	48,082,390	49.24
Bucks	PA	47,994,138	27.06
Jefferson	TX	43,138,979	15.31
Colbert	AL	42,331,820	67.64
Cuyahoga	OH	39,918,584	17.19
St. Bernard	LA	37,605,062	36.94
Lamar	MS	35,898,000	66.35
Warren	NY	34,711,800	35.54
Sedgwick	KS	33,244,227	63.56
Cook	IL	31,251,237	28.01
Wood	WI	30,428,826	46.18
Lake	IN	28,679,825	26.78
Middlesex	NJ	27,803,452	33.57
Charleston	SC	26,422,827	49.96
Union	NJ	25,730,567	31.07
Boyd	KY	23,583,046	29.58
Nueces	TX	22,688,764	8.05
Grays Harbor	WA	22,566,000	67.18
Ashtabula	OH	22,532,559	9.70
Morehouse	LA	22,409,500	22.01
Madison	IL	20,252,479	18.15
Haywood	NC	19,640,926	43.66
Stark	OH	19,092,475	8.22
Subtotal		1,324,881,963	
Percent of Grand total		50.61	
Total for all others		1,293,075,402	
Grand total		2,617,957,365	

Source: The Toxic Release Inventory, A National Perspective, U.S. Environmental Protection Agency, Washington, D.C., June 1989, p. 221.

★ 191 ★

On-Site Toxic Releases to Land

Approximately 82% of the total toxic substances were released by 25 counties in 1987.

County	State	Total On-Site Land Releases (pounds)	Percent of Total On-Site Land Releases in the State
Calhoun	TX	453,791,380	54.34
Milam	TX	320,737,000	38.41
Salt Lake	UT	158,463,912	95.77
St. James	LA	149,131,694	96.28
Lake	IN	108,389,629	43.97
Saline	AR	103,001,630	94.90
Warrick	IN	92,500,000	37.52
Hamilton	FL	91,000,000	47.69
Polk	FL	90,219,449	47.28
Colbert	AL	53,030,500	54.06
Pinal	AZ	50,371,323	51.87
Gila	AZ	44,232,100	45.55
Butler	PA	44,149,899	62.22
Jefferson	MO	38,552,438	68.31
Lewis and Clark	MT	31,202,530	96.83
Wabash	IN	30,078,163	12.20
Sweetwater	WY	23,454,457	96.99
Inyo	CA	23,120,000	48.48
Cowlitz	WA	18,800,750	74.89
Trumbull	OH	15,336,584	32.18
Jefferson	AL	13,622,371	13.89
Harris	TX	13,443,758	1.61
Defiance	OH	12,643,375	26.53
Bucks	PA	12,059,550	17.00
Lawrence	AL	12,037,600	12.27
Subtotal		2,003,370,092	
Percent of grand total		81.71	
Total for all others		448,519,872	
Grand total		2,451,889,964	

Source: The Toxic Release Inventory, A National Perspective, U.S. Environmental Protection Agency, Washington, D.C., June 1989, p. 179.

★ 192 ★

Radon Emission Sources

Groundwater (potential) - 500.00	
Soil releases - 2400.00	
Oceans - 34.00	
Phosphate residues - 3.00	
Uranium mill tailings - 2.00	
Coal residues - 0.02	
Human exhalations - 0.00001	

The radon emissions are in millions of curies.

Sources	Annual radon emissions
Soil releases	2400.00
Groundwater (potential)	500.00
Oceans	34.00
Phosphate residues	3.00
Uranium mill tailings	2.00
Coal residues	0.02
Human exhalations	0.00001

Source: C&EN, February 6, 1989, p. 9, from National Council on Radiation Protection & Measurements.

★ 193 ★

Releases From National Priority List Landfills

Releases may occur from leachate, run off to surface water, emissions of volatile gases, or through explosive gas build-up (e.g. methane).

Observed Releases from NPL Landfills to Water and Air	Percent
Ground water only	37
Ground water and surface water	23
None observed	15
Surface water only	9
Ground water, surface water, air	9
Ground water and air	3
Surface water and air	3
Air only	2

Source: Facing America's Trash: What Next for Municipal Solid Waste, U.S. Congress, Office of Technology Assessment, OTA-O-412, Washington, D.C., July 1989., p. 285, from U.S. Environmental Protection Agency, *Report to Congress: Solid Waste Disposal in the United States, Vol. II*, EPA/530-SW-88-011B (Washington, D.C.: Oct. 1988). NPL stands for National Priorities List.

★ 194 ★

Selected Materials Containing Asbestos

Cement Pipes	Elevator Brake Shoes
Cement Wallboard	HVAC Duct Insulation
Cement Siding	Boiler Insulation
Asphalt Floor Tile	Breeching Insulation
Vinyl Floor Tile	Ductwork Flexible Fabric
Vinyl Sheet Flooring	Connectors
Flooring Backing	Cooling Towers
Construction Mastics	Pipe Insulation (corrugated
(floor tile, carpet, ceiling tile, etc.)	air-cell, block, etc.)
Acoustical Plaster	Heating and Electrical Ducts
Decorative Plaster	Electrical Panel Partitions
Textured Paints/Coatings	Electrical Cloth
Ceiling Tiles and Lay-in Panels	Electric Wiring Insulation
Spray-Applied Insulation	Chalkboards
Blown-in Insulation	Roofing Shingles
Fireproofing Materials	Roofing Felt
Taping Compounds (thermal)	Base Flashing
Packing Materials (for wall/floor	Thermal Paper Products
preparations)	Fire Doors
High Temperature Gaskets	Caulking/Putties
Laboratory Hoods/Table Tops	Adhesives
Laboratory Gloves	Wallboard
Fire Blankets	Joint Compounds
Fire Curtains	Vinyl Wall Coverings
Elevator Equipment Panels	Spackling Compounds

Source: Managing Asbestos in Place : A Building Owner's Guide to Operations and Maintenance Programs for Asbestos Containing Materials, U.S. Environmental Protection Agency, 20T-2003, July 1990, p. 40.

★ 195 ★

Top Toxic Chemicals by Volume

The 25 toxic chemicals with the largest total releases and transfers in 1987.

Chemical name	Total Air Emissions (pounds)	Total Discharges To Surface Waters (pounds)	Total Transfers to Public Sewage (pounds)	Total On-Site Releases to Land (pounds)	Total Underground Injection (pounds)	Total Off-Site Transfers (pounds)	Total Releases/ Transfers (pounds)	Percent
Sodium Sulfate (Solution)	0	9,061,039,211	1,052,044,58	8 91,199,023	1,738,973,178	130,606,774 1	2,079,565,192	53.64
Aluminum Oxide	83,845,554	36,101,026	2,976,516	1,393,735,259	56,724,250	861,591,039	2,434,973,644	10.81
Ammonium Sulfate (Solution)	6,381,186	90,169,835	189,392,111	7,249,407	611,231,000	13,419,977	917,843,516	4.08
Hydrochloric Acid	52,512,848	13,674,536	57,602,155	12,144,031	413,453,666	107,387,120	656,744,356	2.92
Sulfuric Acid	19,406,368	77,533,817	100,123,426	79,173,009	135,999,729	230,515,099	642,751,448	2.85
Sodium Hydroxide (Solution)	7,880,603	78,730,126	239,349,220	131,481,032	34,336,640	135,071,893	626,849,514	2.78
Ammonia	318,028,225	31,641,355	36,650,299	4,967,305	47,783,820	5,413,883	444,484,887	1.97
Methanol	196,038,365	24,909,084	92,511,680	14,702,600	19,582,087	71,802,772	419,546,588	1.86
Toluene	258,279,298	339,959	3,418,364	1,747,264	1,520,943	79,259,364	344,565,192	1.53
Phosphoric Acid	1,615,570	128,832,077	15,425,906	187,196,716	73,704	10,778,338	343,922,311	1.53
Acetone	178,348,341	2,032,678	14,057,015	258,979	2,280,943	37,614,073	234,592,029	1.04
Xylene (mixed Isomers)	137,243,778	473,529	4,102,755	644,953	586,751	74,612,447	217,664,213	0.97
Methyl Ethyl Ketone	145,810,523	75,691	612,678	88,763	75,250	46,085,612	192,748,517	0.86
1,1,1-Trichlorethane	151,233,854	40,700	418,380	199,061	28,325	29,998,240	181,918,560	0.81
Copper	2,370,791	276,053	537,980	138,313,940	452,890	35,926,437	177,878,091	0.79

[Continued]

★ 195 ★

Top Toxic Chemicals by Volume
[Continued]

Chemical name	Total Air Emissions (pounds)	Total Discharges To Surface Waters (pounds)	Total Transfers to Public Sewage (pounds)	Total On-Site Releases to Land (pounds)	Total Underground Injection (pounds)	Total Off-Site Transfers (pounds)	Total Releases/ Transfers (pounds)	Percent
Zinc Compounds	5,753,287	1,630,598	1,734,423	106,238,413	707,666	60,512,500	176,576,887	0.78
Dichloromethane	118,439,343	369,150	1,627,208	67,621	560,000	31,225,718	152,289,040	0.68
Carbon Disulfide	136,167,830	22,791	180,511	3,480	89,500	251,400	136,715,512	0.61
Chlorine	110,349,352	10,975,651	6,552,692	1,529,801	84,439	1,743,642	131,235,577	0.58
Ammonium Nitrate (Solution)	7,545,171	11,716,298	9,804,639	15,076,212	58,565,000	12,140,708	114,848,028	0.51
Manganese Compounds	2,043,072	669,597	599,083	33,932,193	10,800,800	66,692,040	114,736,785	0.51
Nitric Acid	7,204,493	16,642,456	30,900,534	8,914,511	9,187,612	25,287,175	98,136,781	0.44
Zinc (Fume or dust)	4,270,474	454,434	1,777,237	44,081,364	189,574	40,574,726	91,347,809	0.41
Ethylene	60,792,720	12,686	250	7,436	0	8,658,936	69,472,028	0.31
Freon 113	53,105,656	36,587	105,101	22,562	617	9,090,684	62,361,207	0.28
Subtotal	2,064,666,702	9,588,399,925	1,862,504,751	2,272,944,935	3,143,288,384	2,126,260,597	21,063,767,71	293.54
Total for all others	590,876,008	27,274,000	73,012,619	178,945,029	99,174,373	491,696,768	1,455,276,379	6.46
Grand Total	2,655,542,710	9,615,673,925	1,935,517,370	2,451,889,964	3,242,462,757	2,617,957,365	22,519,044,09	1100.00

Source: The Toxic Release Inventory, A National Perspective, U.S. Environmental Protection Agency, Washington, D.C., June 1989, p. 18.

★ 196 ★

Total TRI Releases & Transfers - 1987

Total Toxic Release Inventory (TRI) releases and transfers by industry segment for four industry groups.

Industry	SIC Codes	Total Releases/ Transfers	
		1,000 Pounds	Percent
Paper & Allied Products - General	26-	14,350	0.51
Pulp Mills	261	644,522	22.96
Paper Mills, except Building Paper	262	372,890	13.28
Paperboard Mills	263	316,980	11.29
Paper Products & Coatings	264	106,354	3.79
Paperboard Boxes	265	10,531	0.38
Building Paper & Building Board Mills	266	4,694	0.17
Multiple SIC codes in 26		1,337,089	47.63
Total		2,807,409	100.00
Chemicals & Allied Products - General	28-	17,176	0.14
Industrial Inorganic Chemicals	281	1,722,789	14.25
Plastics & Synthetic Organics	282	533,078	4.41
Pharmaceutical & Biological Products	283	563,752	4.66
Soaps, Cleansers, Cosmetics	284	20,246	0.17
Paints	285	70,359	0.58

[Continued]

★ 196 ★

Total TRI Releases & Transfers - 1987
[Continued]

Industry	SIC Codes	Total Releases/ Transfers	
		1,000 Pounds	Percent
Industrial Organic Chemicals	286	938,659	7.76
Pesticides & Agricultural Chemicals	287	453,221	3.75
Printing Inks, Explosives & Other	289	5,317,647	43.99
Multiple SIC codes in 28		2,451,903	20.28
Total		12,088,830	100.00
Petroleum Refining & Allied Industries - General	29-	29,407	3.86
Petroleum Refining	291	709,395	93.05
Paving Mixtures, Asphalt Coatings	295	1,740	0.23
Lubricating Oils & Other	299	15,334	2.01
Multiple SIC codes in 29		6,486	0.85
Total		762,361	100.00
Primary Metals - General	33-	44,866	1.73
Blast Furnaces & Basic Steel Products	331	886,118	34.17
Iron & Steel Foundries	332	61,182	2.36
Primary Nonferrous Metals	333	879,236	33.90
Secondary Nonferrous Metals	334	457,018	17.62
Rolling & Drawing of Nonferrous Metals	335	89,629	3.46
Nonferrous Foundries (Casting)	336	17,269	0.67
Primary Metal Products & Other	339	51,518	1.99
Multiple SIC codes in 33		106,402	4.10
Total		2,593,238	100.00

Source: The Toxic Release Inventory, A National Perspective, U.S. Environmental Protection Agency, Washington, D.C., June 1989, p. 97.

★ 197 ★

Toxic Chemical Emissions by Industry

Air emissions shown in millions of pounds per year.

Source	SIC code	Total air emissions
Chemicals	28	886.6
Primary metals	33	215.1
Paper	26	207.9
Transportation equipment	37	192.0
Rubber and plastics	30	132.0
Fabricated metals	34	110.2

[Continued]

★ 197 ★

Toxic Chemical Emissions by Industry
[Continued]

Source	SIC code	Total air emissions
Electrical and electronics equipment	36	89.7
Petroleum and coal	29	75.5
Machinery	35	46.2
Furniture and fixtures	25	45.3
Instruments	38	41.6
Textiles	22	34.9
Stone, clay, and glass	32	25.7
Lumber and wood	24	25.0
Miscellaneous manufacturing	39	21.7
Food	20	15.7
Leather	31	7.5
Apparel	23	2.1

Source: C&EN, April 3, 1989, p. 23, from Environmental Protection Agency.

★ 198 ★

Toxic Chemical Releases to the Environment - 1987

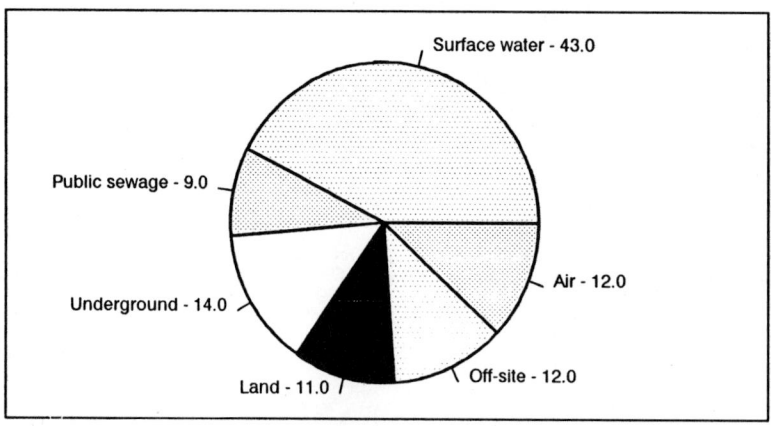

Toxic chemical releases and transfers into the environment in 1987. Total volume released was 22.5 billion pounds.

Emission source	Percent
Surface water	43.0
Underground	14.0
Off-site	12.0
Air	12.0

[Continued]

★ 198 ★

Toxic Chemical Releases to the Environment - 1987
[Continued]

Emission source	Percent
Land	11.0
Public sewage	9.0

Source: Toxic Release Inventory, A National Perspective, U.S. EPA, Washington, DC, June 1989, p. 109.

★ 199 ★

Toxic Chemical Releases, Excluding Sodium Sulfate

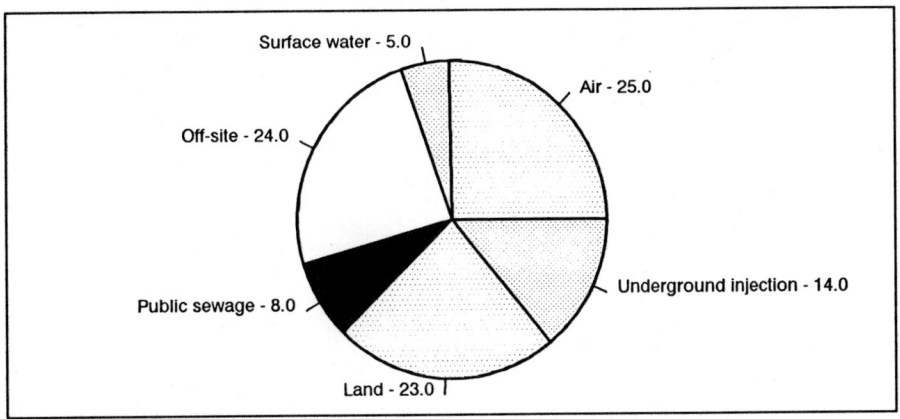

Data, for 1987, show disposition of 10.4 billion pounds of toxic chemicals, excluding sodium sulfate.

Destination	Percent of total
Surface water	5.0
Public sewage	8.0
Underground injection	14.0
Air	25.0
Land	23.0
Off-site	24.0

Source: The Toxic Release Inventory, A National Perspective, U.S. Environmental Protection Agency, Washington, D.C., June 1989, p. 1. This report is based on data retrieved from the March 15, 1989 version of EPA's TRI database. Numbers reported may differ slightly from those available now.

★ 200 ★

Toxic Chemical Releases, Including Sodium Sulfate

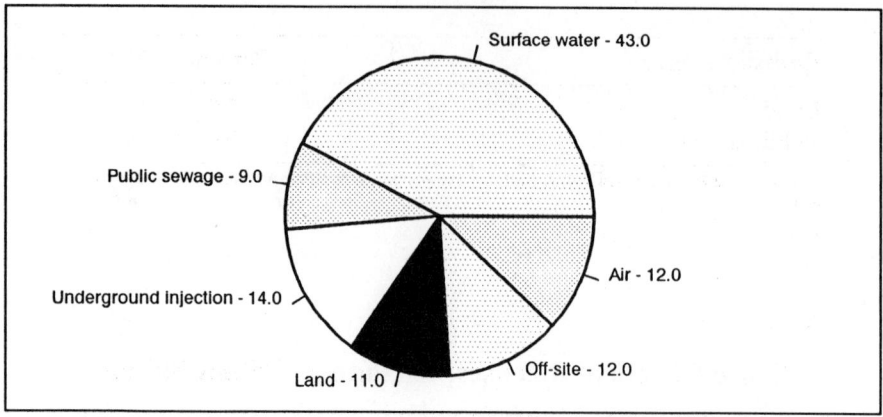

Data, for 1987, include a total of 22.5 billion pounds of chemicals, shown as percent by destination after release.

Destination	Percent of total
Surface water	43.0
Public sewage	9.0
Underground injection	14.0
Air	12.0
Land	11.0
Off-site	12.0

Source: The Toxic Release Inventory, A National Perspective, U.S. Environmental Protection Agency, Washington, D.C., June 1989, p. 1. This report is based on data retrieved from the March 15, 1989 version of EPA's TRI database. Numbers reported may differ slightly from those available now.

★ 201 ★

Toxic Chemical Waste Generation

Toxic chemical waste generation in 1986 and 1987 based on data from the EPA Toxic Release Inventory reporting system. Amounts shown are in pounds.

Chemical	Waste Generation		Amount of Wastes Reduced
	1986	1987	
Sodium Sulfate	8,095,022	1,492,642	6,602,380
Sodium Hydroxide	11,793,130	7,004,418	4,788,712
Propylene	4,328,300	800,340	3,527,960
2,4,-Dichlorophenoxyacetic Acid	3,282,896	28,216	3,254,680
Acetaldehyde	3,100,000	0	3,100,000
Chlorobenzene	4,690,000	2,115,000	2,575,000

[Continued]

★ 201 ★

Toxic Chemical Waste Generation
[Continued]

Chemical	Waste Generation		Amount of Wastes Reduced
	1986	1987	
Aluminum Oxide	4,797,518	2,415,000	2,382,021
Ammonia	6,956,332	4,996,079	1,960,253
Asbestos	4,072,338	2,170,727	1,901,611
Xylene	3,573,112	1,776,758	1,796,354
Dichloromethane	4,143,209	2,393,536	1,749,673
1,1,1-Trichloroethane	3,885,577	2,219,008	1,666,569
Methyl Ethyl Ketone	7,714,626	6,136,780	1,577,846
Toluene	3,597,209	2,060,325	1,536,884
Sulfuric Acid	3,300,775	1,973,951	1,326,824

Source: Toxic Release Inventory, A National Perspective, U.S. EPA, Washington, DC, June 1989, p. 275.

★ 202 ★

Toxic Emissions From Alternative Fuels
Values represent percent change from gasoline.

Fuel (and Feedstock)	Greenhouse Gas Emissions
Electric Vehicles (Solar)	-100.0
Hydrogen (Solar)	-99.0
Doubling Fleet Efficiency	-50.0
Hydrogen (Nuclear)	-47.0
Compressed Natural Gas	-9.0
Electric Vehicles (Current U.S. Electric Mix)	-9.0
Methanol (Natural Gas)	0.0
Methanol (Coal)	+80.0
Ethanol (Corn-CRS)	-63.0
Ethanol (Corn-DeLuchi)	+12.0

Source: World Watch, May/June 1990, p. 22, from Mark A. DeLuchi, "Emissions of Greenhouse Gases from the Use of Gasoline, Methanol, and Other Alternative Transportation Fuels," University of California-Davis; Migdon Segal, "Ethanol Fuel and Global Warming," U.S. Congressional Research Service.

★ 203 ★

Toxic Waste in the Balance

Data represent millions of pounds of toxic industrial waste hauled to another state totaling 750,000,000 pounds. Numbers are rounded and refer to 1987.

State	Net imported	Exported	Imported
Louisiana	46.2	21.2	67.4
Alabama	27.3	8.0	35.3
Tennessee	14.6	10.5	25.1
Michigan	12.3	29.4	41.7
Indiana	9.3	43.5	52.8
Ohio	8.9	82.7	91.6
South Carolina	6.4	6.2	12.6
Utah	6.2	0.4	6.6
Kansas	5.9	4.4	10.3
Minnesota	5.0	3.6	8.6
Oregon	3.2	1.0	4.2
Alaska	3.2	[1]	3.2
Nebraska	3.1	0.8	3.9
Oklahoma	2.7	4.0	6.7
Idaho	2.7	0.2	2.9
Nevada	0.6	0.1	0.7
Montana	0.1	0.1	0.2
Hawaii	[1]	[1]	0.0
	Net exported	Exported	Imported
Wyoming	0.1	0.1	0
North Dakota	0.2	0.2	0
New Mexico	0.4	0.4	[1]
South Dakota	0.4	0.4	0
Connecticut	0.6	12.4	11.8
Arizona	0.7	1.5	0.8
Maryland	0.9	6.1	5.2
Kentucky	1.1	32.8	31.7
Maine	1.1	1.1	[1]
Rhode Island	1.3	1.7	0.4
Vermont	1.6	1.6	[1]
Colorado	1.7	2.6	0.9
Florida	2.6	4.2	1.6
Delaware	2.7	2.7	[1]
Iowa	2.7	2.8	0.1
Arkansas	3.3	13.1	9.8
Washington	3.6	4.6	1.0
West Virginia	3.7	16.8	13.1
New Hampshire	3.9	4.1	0.2
Texas	6.0	20.5	14.5
Illinois	6.9	34.5	27.6
Virginia	7.0	11.2	4.2
Wisconsin	7.1	15.8	8.7

[Continued]

★ 203 ★

Toxic Waste in the Balance
[Continued]

State	Net imported	Exported	Imported
North Carolina	9.8	12.0	2.2
Georgia	11.1	13.7	2.6
California	13.9	15.8	1.9
Montana	14.8	16.7	1.9
Massachussets	15.3	22.1	6.8
New York	16.1	31.3	15.2
New Jersey	20.5	53.4	32.9
Pennsylvania	30.0	71.6	41.6
Mississippi	50.2	50.7	0.5

Source: U.S. News & World Report, June 11, 1990, p. 74, from INFORM Inc. *Note:* 1. Indicates less than 100,000 pounds.

★ 204 ★

Treatment & Release of Toxic Chemicals

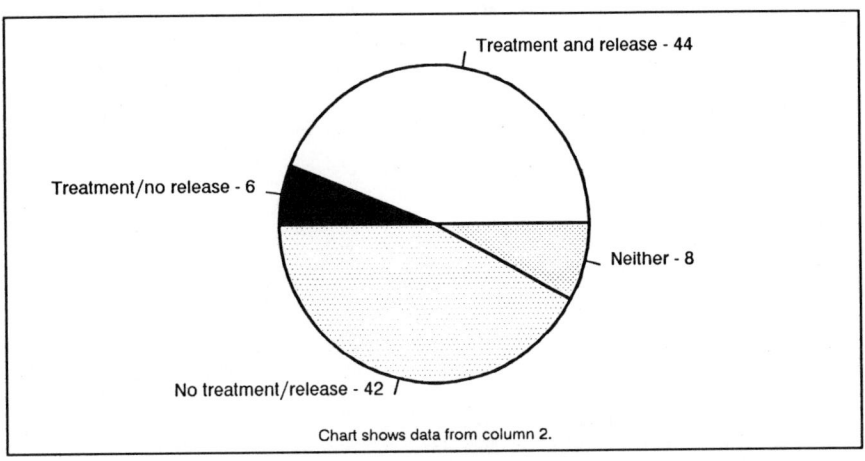

Chart shows data from column 2.

Data for 1987 are based on 74,152 Toxic Release Inventory (TRI) forms sent to EPA.

	Number of forms reporting	% of total
Treatment and release	32,482	44
No treatment/release	30,951	42
Treatment/no release	4,726	6
Neither	5,715	8

Source: The Toxic Release Inventory, A National Perspective, U.S. Environmental Protection Agency, Washington, D.C., June 1989, p. 19.

★ 205 ★

TRI Facilities and Discharges by State - Part I

Facilities that report toxic chemical releases to EPA's Toxic Release Inventory (TRI) database are called TRI facilities. Data are for 1987, by state.

State	TRI Facilities Number	Total TRI Air Emissions		Total TRI Surface Water Discharges		Total TRI Transfers to Public Sewage		Total TRI Releases/ Transfers in Pounds	Total TRI Releases/ Transfers by Rank
		Pounds	Percent	Pounds	Percent	Pounds	Percent		
Alabama	355	98,339,784	11.9	533,895,407	64.6	32,713,211	4.0	827,064,312	4
Alaska	7	31,707,083	85.8	5,221,865	14.1	35	0.0	36,944,052	42
American Samoa	2	56,250	78.1	15,750	21.9	0	0.0	72,000	53
Arizona	156	16,565,691	13.1	3000	0.0	9,236,876	7.3	126,071,984	31
Arkansas	293	54,559,906	14.6	171,220,328	45.7	4,325,937	1.2	374,781,464	18
California	1662	82,708,429	1.4	3,834,809,964	65.7	246,101,586	4.2	5,839,808,374	1
Colorado	172	11,010,395	31.2	3,325,009	9.4	3,125,396	8.8	35,330,997	43
Connecticut	383	26,078,031	30.2	25,225,312	29.2	9,544,587	11.1	86,374,380	34
Delaware	53	6,036,385	10.3	29,852,685	50.8	16,375,820	27.8	58,818,708	39
Florida	419	50,196,070	11.5	107,593,997	24.8	39,468,550	9.1	434,685,722	16
Georgia	636	93,586,285	14.1	473,506,462	71.6	47,093,822	7.1	661,730,868	8
Hawaii	33	1,064,495	21.0	2,542,000	50.2	973,250	19.2	5,063,453	49
Idaho	52	4,176,707	5.7	50,737,549	69.1	3,250,118	4.4	73,411,988	35
Illinois	1185	99,226,761	21.2	33,437,606	7.1	199,165,360	42.5	468,816,984	12
Indiana	720	112,870,299	15.4	105,987,418	14.5	95,899,156	13.1	731,729,004	6
Iowa	310	39,238,921	54.8	15,335,547	21.4	10,090,895	14.1	71,583,169	36
Kansas	184	24,738,143	13.5	7,578,737	4.1	6,647,139	3.6	183,390,807	27
Kentucky	298	51,666,181	20.6	76,869,713	30.6	13,649,364	5.4	250,942,142	22
Louisiana	259	138,254,193	8.0	775,836,211	45.0	1,334,641	0.1	1,725,933,233	3
Maine	83	14,607,382	6.7	195,803,966	89.2	5,071,706	2.3	219,560,564	24
Maryland	191	20,234,753	10.4	111,795,540	57.3	47,863,355	24.5	195,248,259	25
Massachusetts	560	30,061,360	28.7	2,116,295	2.0	36,142,507	34.5	104,826,800	33
Michigan	758	116,359,932	15.7	38,127,898	5.1	38,245,470	5.1	742,716,029	5
Minnesota	301	42,095,160	29.7	15,826,354	11.2	70,020,634	49.5	141,498,325	29
Mississippi	247	57,285,976	8.7	473,882,098	72.2	9,125,709	1.4	656,085,795	9
Missouri	503	50,623,710	17.3	36,406,436	12.4	112,489,998	38.5	292,426,658	21
Montana	27	5,255,856	13.7	791,946	2.1	28,109	0.1	38,437,649	41
Nebraska	139	14,403,622	68.1	2,754,398	13.0	1,213,294	5.7	21,149,589	46
Nevada	33	742,389	6.3	0	0.0	33,814	0.3	11,735,250	47
New Hampshire	129	12,983,935	19.9	42,428,961	65.1	2,802,094	4.3	65,131,279	37
New Jersey	875	41,983,116	13.6	55,063,498	17.8	123,413,118	40.0	308,585,011	20
New Mexico	32	3,831,726	17.0	9057	0.0	738,719	3.3	22,528,013	45
New York	765	89,399,757	27.4	56,110,261	17.2	65,294,934	20.0	326,074,780	19
North Carolina	820	94,568,576	21.4	217,090,591	49.2	54,537,779	12.4	441,345,879	14
North Dakota	28	933,275	33.4	393,600	14.0	94,217	3.4	2,803,582	52
Ohio	1261	172,685,650	23.9	68,219,055	9.4	131,193,018	18.1	723,893,016	7
Oklahoma	193	36,445,117	28.1	65,792,624	50.7	1,692,971	1.3	129,781,423	30
Oregon	217	20,941,392	17.4	63,362,600	52.5	13,900,170	11.5	120,604,568	32
Pennsylvania	1027	87,547,598	20.0	61,901,577	14.1	39,815,049	9.1	437,634,494	15
Puerto Rico	172	12,867,913	30.0	1,676,734	3.9	23,060,390	53.7	42,927,540	40
Rhode Island	166	5,927,841	22.3	13,187,892	49.5	2,998,055	11.3	26,622,622	44
South Carolina	394	64,215,277	12.4	340,939,102	65.8	51,090,961	9.9	518,127,600	11
South Dakota	37	2,441,359	69.4	3698	0.1	620,208	17.6	3,518,226	51
Tennessee	503	135,010,665	22.4	196,399,204	32.6	97,149,025	16.1	602,148,025	10
Texas	999	238,817,765	8.5	659,657,602	23.6	154,293,072	5.5	2,799,768,533	2
Utah	102	77,327,036	31.0	133,749	0.1	2,032,004	0.8	249,743,154	23
Vermont	52	1,379,661	28.2	1,113,799	22.8	298,037	6.1	4,889,666	50
Virgin Islands	1	2,033,873	27.4	5,303,250	71.4	0	0.0	7,424,628	48
Virginia	399	132,436,076	29.8	225,383,321	50.8	55,690,097	12.5	444,049,924	13
Washington	306	40,637,496	10.0	303,684,767	74.6	4,061,980	1.0	407,078,587	17
West Virginia	107	35,564,455	20.9	87,295,714	51.2	5,179,381	3.0	170,571,053	28
Wisconsin	645	48,656,361	26.3	16,563,741	9.0	46,313,952	25.0	184,957,138	26

[Continued]

★ 205 ★

TRI Facilities and Discharges by State - Part I
[Continued]

State	TRI Facilities Number	Total TRI Air Emissions		Total TRI Surface Water Discharges		Total TRI Transfers to Public Sewage		Total TRI Releases/ Transfers in Pounds	Total TRI Releases/ Transfers by Rank
		Pounds	Percent	Pounds	Percent	Pounds	Percent		
Wyoming	27	3,154,641	5.0	3,460,037	5.5	17,800	0.0	62,596,791	38
Total	19,278	2,655,542,710	11.8	9,615,673,925	42.7	1,935,517,370	8.6	22,519,044,09	1

Source: The Toxic Release Inventory, A National Perspective, U.S. Environmental Protection Agency, Washington, D.C., June 1989, p. 6.

★ 206 ★

TRI Facilities and Discharges by State - Part II

Facilities that report toxic chemical releases to EPA's Toxic Release Inventory (TRI) database are called TRI facilities. Data are for 1987, by state.

State	TRI Facilities Number	Total TRI On-Site Land Releases		Total TRI Underground Injection		Total TRI Off-Site Transfers		Total TRI Releases/ Transfers in Pounds	Total TRI Releases/ Transfers by Rank
		Pounds	Percent	Pounds	Percent	Pounds	Percent		
Alabama	355	98,091,692	11.9	1,443,591	0.2	62,580,627	7.6	827,064,312	4
Alaska	7	14,930	0.0	0	0.0	139	0.0	36,944,052	42
American Samoa	2	0	0.0	0	0.0	0	0.0	72,000	53
Arizona	156	97,102,866	77.0	0	0.0	3,163,551	2.5	126,071,984	31
Arkansas	293	108,534,294	29.0	13,016,449	3.5	23,124,550	6.2	374,781,464	18
California	1662	47,693,392	0.8	1,530,850,645	26.2	97,644,358	1.7	5,839,808,374	1
Colorado	172	12,547,494	35.5	1170	0.0	5,321,533	15.1	35,330,997	43
Connecticut	383	1,848,676	2.1	0	0.0	23,677,774	27.4	86,374,380	34
Delaware	53	2,565,876	4.4	250	0.0	3,987,692	6.8	58,818,708	39
Florida	419	190,827,201	43.9	29,437,389	6.8	17,162,515	3.9	434,685,722	16
Georgia	636	14,969,473	2.3	19,500	0.0	32,555,326	4.9	661,730,868	8
Hawaii	33	237,342	4.7	216,140	4.3	30,226	0.6	5,063,453	49
Idaho	52	14,988,307	20.4	0	0.0	259,307	0.4	73,411,988	35
Illinois	1185	11,209,153	2.4	14,221,970	3.0	11,556,134	23.8	468,816,984	12
Indiana	720	246,523,580	33.7	63,356,466	8.7	107,092,085	14.6	731,729,004	6
Iowa	310	768,722	1.1	0	0.0	6,149,084	8.6	71,583,169	36
Kansas	184	1,058,669	0.6	91,067,410	49.7	52,300,709	28.5	183,390,807	27
Kentucky	298	4,028,637	1.6	25,000,250	10.0	79,727,997	31.8	250,942,142	22
Louisiana	259	154,894,837	9.0	553,820,180	32.1	101,793,171	5.9	1,725,933,233	3
Maine	83	2,037,139	0.9	0	0.0	2,040,371	0.9	219,560,564	24
Maryland	191	4,318,725	2.2	750	0.0	11,035,136	5.7	195,248,259	25
Massachusetts	560	3,575,212	3.4	250	0.0	32,931,176	31.4	104,826,800	33
Michigan	758	3,979,327	0.5	6,472,752	0.9	539,530,650	72.6	742,716,029	5
Minnesota	301	1,722,105	1.2	250	0.0	11,833,822	8.4	141,498,325	29
Mississippi	247	15,252,731	2.3	46,433,140	7.1	54,106,141	8.2	656,085,795	9
Missouri	503	56,439,000	19.3	1,001,450	0.3	35,466,064	12.1	292,426,658	21
Montana	27	32,223,598	83.8	0	0.0	138,140	0.4	38,437,649	41
Nebraska	139	349,910	1.7	0	0.0	2,428,365	11.5	21,149,589	46
Nevada	33	10,817,492	92.2	0	0.0	141,555	1.2	11,735,250	47
New Hampshire	129	666,529	1.0	0	0.0	6,249,760	9.6	65,131,279	37
New Jersey	875	5,312,503	1.7	780	0.0	82,811,996	26.8	308,585,011	20
New Mexico	32	17,307,456	76.8	0	0.0	641,055	2.8	22,528,013	45
New York	765	17,598,716	5.4	500	0.0	97,670,612	30.0	326,074,780	19
North Carolina	820	30,157,949	6.8	250	0.0	44,990,734	10.2	441,345,879	14
North Dakota	28	1,100,500	39.3	0	0.0	279,990	10.0	2,803,582	52
Ohio	1261	47,664,590	6.6	71,850,645	9.9	232,280,058	32.1	723,893,016	7

[Continued]

167

★ 206 ★

TRI Facilities and Discharges by State - Part II
[Continued]

State	TRI Facilities Number	Total TRI On-Site Land Releases		Total TRI Underground Injection		Total TRI Off-Site Transfers		Total TRI Releases/ Transfers in Pounds	Total TRI Releases/ Transfers by Rank
		Pounds	Percent	Pounds	Percent	Pounds	Percent		
Oklahoma	193	2,482,881	1.9	7,171,133	5.5	16,196,697	12.5	129,781,423	30
Oregon	217	13,998,763	11.6	0	0.0	8,401,643	7.0	120,604,568	32
Pennsylvania	1027	70,957,429	16.2	74,000	0.0	177,338,841	40.5	437,634,494	15
Puerto Rico	172	184,150	0.4	988	0.0	5,137,365	12.0	42,927,540	40
Rhode Island	166	69,009	0.3	0	0.0	4,439,825	16.7	26,622,622	44
South Carolina	394	8,994,959	1.7	750	0.0	52,886,551	10.2	518,127,600	11
South Dakota	37	9	0.0	0	0.0	452,952	12.9	3,518,226	51
Tennessee	503	20,550,544	3.4	124,406,900	20.7	28,631,687	4.8	602,148,025	10
Texas	999	835,087,965	29.8	630,223,666	22.5	281,688,463	10.1	2,799,768,533	2
Utah	102	165,467,430	66.3	3	0.0	4,782,932	1.9	249,743,154	23
Vermont	52	168,696	3.5	0	0.0	1,929,473	39.5	4,889,666	50
Virgin Islands	1	87,505	1.2	0	0.0	0	0.0	7,424,628	48
Virginia	399	6,949,712	1.6	250	0.0	23,590,468	5.3	444,049,924	13
Washington	306	25,105,014	6.2	500	0.0	33,588,830	8.3	407,078,587	17
West Virginia	107	11,638,215	6.8	1,719,219	1.0	29,174,069	17.1	170,571,053	28
Wisconsin	645	7,535,521	4.1	1500	0.0	65,886,063	35.6	184,957,138	26
Wyoming	27	24,183,539	38.6	30,651,671	49.0	1,129,103	1.8	62,596,791	38
Total	19,278	2,451,889,964	10.9	3,242,462,757	14.4	2,617,957,365	11.6	22,519,044,09	1

Source: The Toxic Release Inventory, A National Perspective, U.S. Environmental Protection Agency, Washington, D.C., June 1989, p. 6.

Trace Metals

★ 207 ★

Atmospheric Emissions of Trace Metals Worldwide

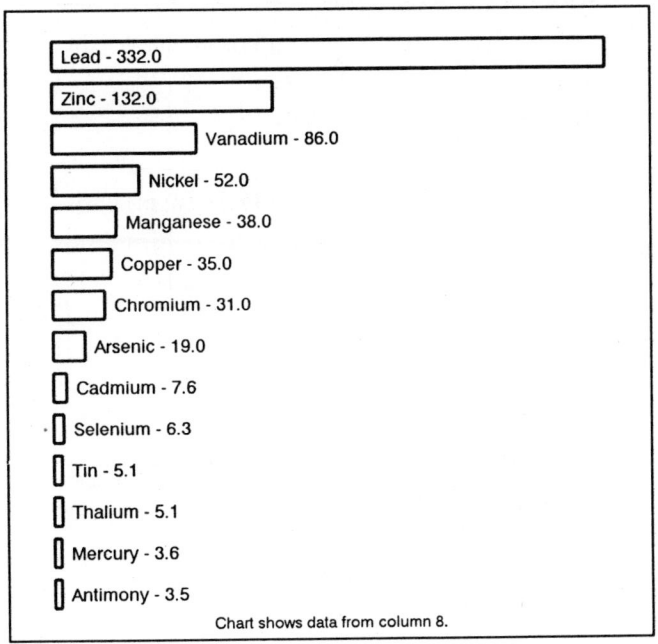

Chart shows data from column 8.

Data shown are in thousands of tons a year.

Element	Energy production	Mining	Smelting and refining	Manufac- turing processes	Com- mercial uses[1]	Waste incin- eration	Trans- portation	Total[2]
Antimony	1.30	0.10	1.42			0.67		3.5
Arsenic	2.22	0.06	12.30	1.95	2.02	0.31		19.0
Cadmium	0.79		5.43	0.60		0.75		7.6
Chromium	12.70			17.00		0.84		31.0
Copper	8.04	0.42	23.20	2.01		1.58		35.0
Lead	12.70	2.55	46.50	15.70	4.50	2.37	248.0	332.0
Manganese	12.10	0.62	2.55	14.70		8.26		38.0
Mercury	2.26		0.13			1.16		3.6
Nickel	42.00	0.80	3.99	4.47		0.35		52.0
Selenium	3.85	0.16	2.18			0.11		6.3
Thalium	1.13		4.01					5.1
Tin	3.27		1.06			0.81		5.1
Vanadium	84.00		0.06	0.74		1.15		86.0
Zinc	16.80	0.46	2.00	33.40	3.25	5.90		132.0

Source: Environment, September 1990, p. 9, from J.O. Nriagu and J.M. Pacyna, "Quantitative Assessment of Worldwide Contamination of Air, Water and Soils with Trace Metals," *Nature* 333 (1988): 134-139. *Notes:* 1. Includes agricultural uses. 2. Totals are rounded.

★ 208 ★

Heavy Metals and Trace Elements in Cow Manure

Data compare trace elements in cow manure obtained from a herd in Potter County, PA which was bedded on waste paper and on straw. The object of the test was to see if heavy metals and other trace elements in paper would enter the food chain.

	Paper-Bedded	Straw-Bedded
	Percent, dry weight	
Total Nitrogen	3.2	4.4
Phosphate(P205)	1.4	1.6
Potash(K20)	3.4	5.1
	Mg/kg (ppm) basis	
Copper	30.0	41.0
Zinc	157.0	174.0
Lead	1.0	11.0
Chromium	1.0	3.0
Mercury	0.0	0.0
Nickel	5.0	7.0
Cadmium	0.3	0.3

Source: BioCycle, September 1990, p. 61. Submitted by Samuel Crossley, Senior Extension Agent, Potter County Extension and analyzed by the P.S.U. Soil and Environmental Chemistry Laboratory, 104 Res. Bldg. A, University Park, PA, March, 1989.

★ 209 ★

Heavy Metals and Trace Elements in Newspaper

The Pennsylvania's Department of Environmental Resources (DER) estimates that 3,527,076 tons of paper are available in the state each year; the dairy/beef animal bedding market could potentially use one third of the paper produced in the state.

		Element (mg/kg, dry weight basis [equivalent to ppm.])						
		Copper	Zinc	Lead	Chromium	Nickel	Cadmium	Mercury
Centre Daily Times	(Glossy print Ad.) Blue	114	14.0	10.0	1.0	5.0	0.1	0
	Mixed colors	141	14.0	10.0	1.0	7.0	0.2	0
	Blue Head-lines	101	1.0	4.0	0.0	1.0	0.1	0
	Black and White	2	0.0	4.0	0.0	1.0	0.0	0

[Continued]

★ 209 ★

Heavy Metals and Trace Elements in Newspaper
[Continued]

		Element (mg/kg, dry weight basis [equivalent to ppm.])						
		Copper	Zinc	Lead	Chromium	Nickel	Cadmium	Mercury
Collegian	Black Pictures	3	3.0	5.0	1.0	2.0	0.2	0
	Black and White	2	8.0	4.0	1.0	1.0	0.1	0
USA Today	Mixed Colors	53	9.0	3.0	1.0	1.0	0.3	0
	Blue	132	12.0	2.0	1.0	2.0	0.4	0
	Black and White	2	19.0	3.0	1.0	1.5	0.4	0
Xerox Print		6	7	7.0	1.0	2.0	0.0	0
Computer Print		1	6	7.0	0.0	2.0	0.1	0
Livestock Feed Maxs[1]		100	500	30.0	3000.0	50.0	0.5	NS[4]
Vitamin-Mineral Pill[2]		1342	9880	16.5	12.1	11.1	0.2	0
DER/NE Maxs[3]		1000	2500	1000	1000	200	25.0	10

Source: BioCycle, September 1990, p. 61. All analyses performed by Penn State University Soil and Environmental Chemistry Laboratory, 104 Res. Buildg. A, University Park, PA. Jan/Feb., 1989. *Notes:* 1. Mineral tolerances in domestic animals. National Research Council, National Academy of Science, Washington, D.C. 1980. 2. Centrum vitamin-mineral pill analysis. 3. D.E. Baker, et. al. Criteria and Recommendations for Land Application of Sludges in the Northeast bull. 851, PA Agr. Exp. Sta., 1985. Guidelines for the Agricultural Utilization of Sewage Sludge, PA Dept. of Environ. Resources, Chapter 275, May 1988. 4. Not Specified.

★ 210 ★

Inputs of Trace Metals Into Soils Worldwide
Values are shown in thousands of metric tons per year.

Source	Trace Elements												
	Antimony	Arsenic	Cadmium	Chromium	Copper	Lead	Manganese	Mercury	Molybdenum	Nickel	Selenium	Vanadium	Zinc
Agricultural and animal wastes	4.90	5.80	2.20	82.00	67.0	26.0	158.0	0.85	34.00	45.0	4.60	19.00	316.0
Logging and wood wastes	2.80	1.70	1.10	10.00	28.0	7.40	61.0	1.10	1.60	13.0	1.60	5.50	39.0
Urban refuse	0.76	0.40	4.20	20.00	26.0	40.0	24.0	0.13	2.30	6.10	0.33	0.20	60.0
Municipal sewage and organic waste	0.18	0.25	0.18	6.50	13.0	7.10	8.10	0.44	0.43	15.0	0.11	1.30	39.0
Solid wastes from metal fabrication	0.08	0.11	0.04	1.50	4.30	7.60	2.60	0.04	0.08	1.70	0.10	0.12	11.0
Coal ashes	12.00	22.00	7.20	298.00	214.0	144.0	1076.0	2.60	44.00	168.0	32.00	39.00	298.0
Fertilizers and peat	0.25	0.28	0.20	0.32	1.40	2.90	12.0	0.01	0.46	2.20	0.27	0.97	2.50
Discarded manufactured products[1]	2.40	38.00	1.20	458.00	592.0	292.0	300.0	0.68	1.90	19.0	0.15	1.70	465.0

[Continued]

★ 210 ★

Inputs of Trace Metals into Soils Worldwide
[Continued]

Source	Trace Elements												
	Antimony	Arsenic	Cadmium	Chromium	Copper	Lead	Manganese	Mercury	Molybdenum	Nickel	Selenium	Vanadium	Zinc
Atmospheric fallout	2.50	13.00	5.30	22.00	25.0	232.0	27.0	2.50	2.30	24.0	2.00	60.00	92.0
Total input[2]	26.00	82.00	22.00	898.0	971.0	759.0	1669.0	8.30	87.00	294.0	41.00	128.0	1322.0

Source: Environment, September 1990, p. 11, from J.O. Nriagu and J.M. Pacyna, "Quantitative Assessment of Worldwide Contamination of Air, Water and Soils with Trace Metals," *Nature* 333 (1988): 134-139. These inputs exclude mine tailings and slags at the smelter sites. *Notes:* 1. Metal used for industrial installations and "durable" goods are assumed to have a definite life span and to be released into the environment at a constant rate. 2. Totals are rounded.

★ 211 ★

Trace Metal Emissions From Natural Sources Worldwide

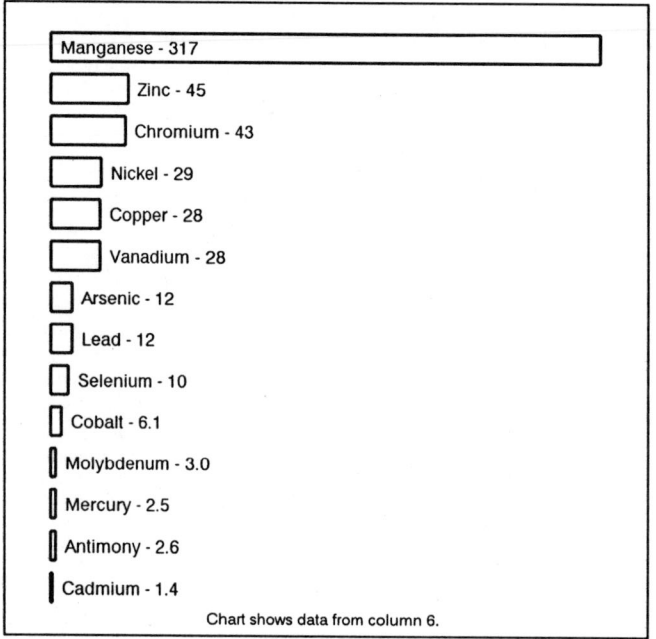

Manganese - 317
Zinc - 45
Chromium - 43
Nickel - 29
Copper - 28
Vanadium - 28
Arsenic - 12
Lead - 12
Selenium - 10
Cobalt - 6.1
Molybdenum - 3.0
Mercury - 2.5
Antimony - 2.6
Cadmium - 1.4

Chart shows data from column 6.

Data shown are in thousands of metric tons per year.

Element	Wind-borne soil particles	Sea salt spray	Volcanoes	Forest fires	Biogenic sources	Total[1]
Antimony	0.78	0.56	0.71	0.22	0.29	2.6
Arsenic	2.6	1.7	3.8	0.19	3.9	12
Cadmium	0.21	0.06	0.82	0.11	0.24	1.4
Chromium	27	0.07	15	0.09	1.1	43
Cobalt	4.1	0.07	0.96	0.31	0.66	6.1
Copper	8.0	3.6	9.4	3.8	3.3	28
Lead	3.9	1.4	3.3	1.9	1.7	12
Manganese	221	0.86	42	23	30	317
Mercury	0.05	0.02	1.0	0.02	1.4	2.5

[Continued]

★ 211 ★

Trace Metal Emissions from Natural Sources Worldwide
[Continued]

Element	Wind-borne soil particles	Sea salt spray	Volcanoes	Forest fires	Biogenic sources	Total[1]
Molybdenum	1.3	0.22	0.40	0.57	0.54	3.0
Nickel	11	1.3	14	2.3	0.73	29
Selenium	0.18	0.55	0.95	0.26	8.4	10
Vanadium	16	3.1	5.6	1.8	1.2	28
Zinc	19	0.44	9.6	7.6	8.1	45

Source: Environment, September 1990, p. 8. Primary source: J.O. Nriagu, "Global Assessment of Natural Sources of Atmospheric Trace Metals," *Nature* 338 (1989), pp. 47-49. *Note:* 1. Totals are rounded.

★ 212 ★

Trace Metal Releases Into Water Worldwide

Values are shown in thousands of metric tons per year.

Source	Antimony	Arsenic	Cadmium	Chromium	Copper	Lead	Manganese	Mercury	Molybdenum	Nickel	Selenium	Vanadium	Zinc
Domestic wastewaters	2.20	9.2	1.70	46.0	28.0	6.80	110	0.30	2.20	62.0	3.80	2.30	48.0
Electric power plants	0.18	8.2	0.12	5.7	13.0	0.72	11.0	1.80	0.65	11.0	18.00	0.30	18.0
Base metal mining and smelting	3.80	7.4	2.00	12.0	14.0	7.00	40.0	0.10	0.51	13.0	12.00	0.60	29.0
Manufacturing processes	9.30	7.0	2.40	51.0	34.0	14.0	21.0	2.10	4.20	7.4	4.30	0.55	85.0
Atmospheric fallout	1.10	5.6	2.20	9.1	11.0	100.00	12.0	2.00	0.95	10.0	0.82	26.00	40.0
Sewage discharges	1.50	4.1	0.69	19.0	12.0	9.40	69.0	0.16	2.90	11.0	2.00	3.50	17.0
Total input[1]	18.00	42.0	9.10	143.0	112.0	138.00	263.0	6.50	11.00	114.0	41.0	33.00	237.0

Source: Environment, September 1990, p. 10, from J.O. Nriagu and J.M. Pacyna, "Quantitative Assessment of Worldwide Contamination of Air, Water and Soils with Trace Metals," *Nature* 333 (1988): 134-139. *Note:* 1. Totals are rounded.

Water Pollution

★ 213 ★

Pesticides and Nitrates in U.S. Wells

Data are the results of the EPA National Survey of Drinking Water Wells, which tested more than 1,300 wells. Data show percentage of wells in which pesticides were detected and percentage in which pesticide levels exceeded a health standard.

Category	Detected	Exceeding Standard
Pesticides		
Urban	10.4	0.8
Rural	4.2	0.6
Nitrates		
Urban	52.1	1.2
Rural	57.0	2.4

Source: Farm Journal, January 1991, p. A1, from the EPA.

★ 214 ★

Phosphorous Emissions to the Great Lakes by Source

Estimates of industrial, municipal and tributary phosphorous loading to the Great Lakes shown in metric tons per year.

Phosphorus Source	Lake Superior	Lake Michigan	Lake Huron	Lake Erie	Lake Ontario	St. Lawrence River
Point:						
Direct Industrial Discharge	81	60	23	38	29	14
Indirect Industrial Discharge	79	79	35	30	27	0
Direct Municipal Discharge	78	367	134	1,689	1,384	146
Indirect Municipal Discharge	60	488	305	724	365	27
Point Subtotal	298	995	496	2,481	1,805	188
Nonpoint:						
Tributary:Monitored	1,206	2,646	1,505	5,446	1,985	93
Adjustment for Unmonitored Area	1,064	881	803	1,753	652	90
Nonpoint Subtotal	2,269	3,527	2,308	7,199	2,637	182
Within Lake Totals	2,567	4,522	2,805	9,680	4,441	370

Source: Council on Environmental Quality, *20th Annual Report 1990*, Washington, D.C., p. 353, from Great Lakes Water Quality Board, *1986 Report on Water Quality: Report to the IJC*, International Joint Commission. Totals may not sum due to rounding.

★ 215 ★

Phosphorus Load Reduction in the Great Lakes

Phosphorous reduction goals and progress toward reduction, shown in metric tons per year.

Body of Water	Phosphorus Element
Lake Erie	
1990 Goal	1,700
1988 Reductions	330
Reduction Needed to Meet 1990 Goal	1,370
Lake Ontario	
1990 Goal	235
1988 Reductions	106
Reduction Needed to Meet 1990 Goal	129
Saginaw Bay	
1990 Goal	225
1988 Reductions	208
Reduction Needed to Meet 1990 Goal	17

Source: Council on Environmental Quality, *20th Annual Report 1990*, Washington, D.C., p. 351, from EPA Great Lakes National Program Office, *U.S. Progress in Implementing the Great Lakes Water Quality Agreement*, EPA, Chicago, (1989), pp. 4-5.

★ 216 ★

Pollutants Associated With Fish Kills

| Biological Oxygen Demand/Dissolved Oxygen - 19 |
| Oil and gas - 14 |
| Pesticides - 14 |
| Ammonia - 8 |
| Chlorine - 8 |
| Temperature - 8 |
| Acidity - 6 |
| Inorganics - 5 |
| Nutrients - 5 |

Pollutant	Number of States Reporting
Biological Oxygen Demand/Dissolved Oxygen	19
Oil and gas	14
Pesticides	14
Ammonia	8
Chlorine	8
Temperature	8
Acidity	6
Inorganics	5
Nutrients	5

Source: National Water Quality Inventory, 1988, Report to Congress, U.S. Environmental Protection Agency, Washington, D.C., April 1990, p. 116, from 1988 State Section 305(b) reports.

★ 217 ★

Pollutants Associated With Fishing Restrictions

Pollutant	Number of States Reporting
PCBs	22
Chlordane	17
Mercury	15
Dioxin	9
Other metals	9
DDT	7

[Continued]

★ 217 ★

Pollutants Associated With Fishing Restrictions
[Continued]

Pollutant	Number of States Reporting
Organics (unspecified)	5
Dieldrin	4
Pesticides (unspecified)	4

Source: National Water Quality Inventory, 1988, Report to Congress, U.S. Environmental Protection Agency, Washington, D.C., April 1990,p. 108, from 1988 State Section 305(b) reports.

★ 218 ★

Pollution Sources Associated With Fishing Restrictions

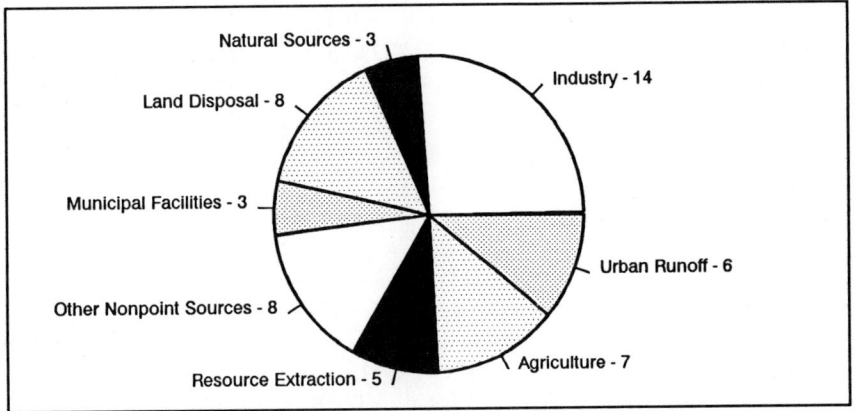

Number of states reporting industrial activities, institutions, and other sources causing the imposition of fishing restrictions.

Source	Number of States Reporting
Industry	14
Land Disposal	8
Other Nonpoint Sources	8
Agriculture	7
Urban Runoff	6
Resource Extraction	5
Municipal Facilities	3
Natural Sources	3

Source: National Water Quality Inventory, 1988, Report to Congress, U.S. Environmental Protection Agency, Washington, D.C., April 1990, p. 108, from 1988 State Section 305(b) reports.

★ 219 ★

Regulated Pollutants in Wastewater Treatment Plants

Data shown are the results of the EPA National Sewage Sludge Survey, which sampled 209 wastewater treatment plants randomly selected to ascertain quality of wastewater sludges.

Pollutant	Number of Times Detected	Mean (mg/kg)	Minimum (mg/kg)	Maximum (mg/kg)
4,4'-DDD	1	0.391	0.391	0.391
4,4'-DDE	4	0.100	0.030	0.190
4,4'-DDT	7	0.051	0.015	0.121
Aldrin	8	0.029	0.019	0.046
Arsenic	194	12.390	0.300	315.600
Benzene	4	0.098	0.012	0.220
Benzo(a)pyrene	7	10.785	0.671	24.703
Beryllium	64	0.660	0.100	3.900
Bis(2-ethylhexyl)phthalate	189	107.233	0.510	89.129
Cadmium	194	65.460	0.700	8220.000
Chlordane	1	0.489	0.489	0.489
Chromium	231	258.515	2.000	3750.000
Copper	239	665.300	6.800	3120.000
Dieldrin	6	0.024	0.013	0.047
Dimethyl nitrosamine	0	[1]	[1]	[1]
Heptachlor	1	0.023	0.023	0.023
Hexachlorobenzene	0	[1]	[1]	[1]
Hexachlorobutadiene	0	[1]	[1]	[1]
Lead	213	195.230	9.400	1670.000
Lindane (Gamma-BHC)	2	0.074	0.072	0.076
Mercury	184	4.120	0.200	47.000
Molybdenum	148	13.120	2.000	67.900
Nickel	201	77.010	2.000	976.000
PCB-1016	0	[1]	[1]	[1]
PCB-1221	0	[1]	[1]	[1]
PCB-1232	0	[1]	[1]	[1]
PCB-1242	0	[1]	[1]	[1]
PCB-1248	23	0.740	0.043	5.203
PCB-1254	13	1.765	0.312	9.347
PCB-1260	20	0.671	0.031	4.006
Selenium	163	6.240	0.500	70.000
Toxaphene	0	[1]	[1]	[1]
Trichloroethylene	7	0.848	0.024	3.302
Zinc	239	1692.760	37.800	68000.000

Source: BioCycle, July 1990, p. 60 *Note:* 1. Pollutants always below detection limits.

Chapter 3
EFFECTS

Deaths

★ 220 ★

Death From Asbestos Related Diseases

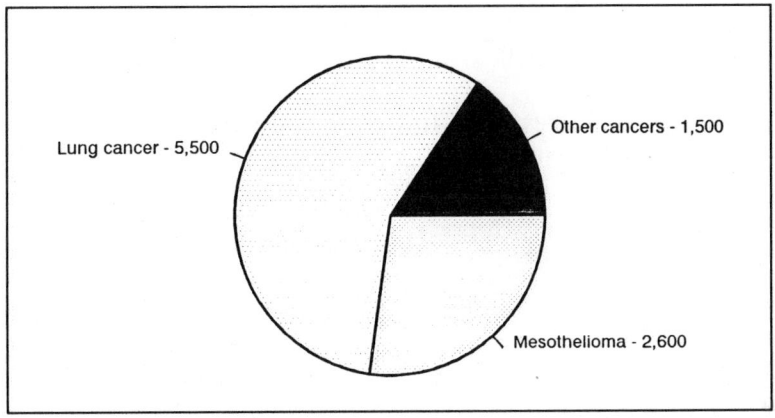

Occupational exposures are primarily responsible for deaths related to asbestos. Data show projected deaths in 1990.

	Number of expected deaths
Lung cancer	5,500
Mesothelioma[1]	2,600
Other cancers	1,500

Source: Garbage, March/April 1990, p. 16, from *American Journal of Industrial Medicine. Note:* 1. Primarily cancer of the lung's lining.

★ 221 ★

Estimated Deaths From Indoor Air Pollution

The values represent at-home exposure over the course of a lifetime.

Pollutant	Estimated deaths
Radon	5000-20000[1]
Second-hand tobacco smoke	6000
Benzene	460
Five other suspected carcinogens[2]	<780

Source: Garbage, March/April 1990, p. 16, from EPA and Air and Waste Management Association. *Notes:* 1. Estimate based on mortality for smokers exposed to radon; the number of non-smokers estimated to die from radon exposure each year is 3,000. 2. Chloroform, carbon tetrachloride, paradichlorobenzene, tetrachloroethylene, trichlorobenzene.

Deforestation

★ 222 ★

Forest Conditions in the U.S.

Damage and reforestation are shown in millions of acres.

Year	Wildfire Damage	Reforestation
1930	52.3	0.14
1940	25.9	0.52
1950	15.5	0.50
1951	10.8	0.45
1952	14.2	0.52
1953	10.0	0.71
1954	8.8	0.81
1955	8.1	0.78
1956	6.6	0.89
1057	3.4	1.14
1958	3.3	1.53
1959	4.2	2.12
1960	4.5	2.14
1961	3.0	1.76
1962	4.1	1.37
1963	7.1	1.33
1964	4.2	1.31
1965	2.7	1.29
1966	4.6	1.28
1967	4.7	1.37

[Continued]

★ 222 ★

Forest Conditions in the U.S.
[Continued]

Year	Wildfire Damage	Reforestation
1968	4.2	1.44
1969	6.7	1.43
1970	3.3	1.60
1971	4.3	1.69
1972	2.6	1.68
1973	1.9	1.75
1974	2.9	1.60
1975	1.8	1.93
1976	5.1	1.89
1977	3.2	1.98
1978	3.9	2.09
1979	3.0	2.06
1980	5.3	2.27
1981	4.8	1.93
1982	2.4	2.37
1983	5.1	2.45
1984	3.0	2.55
1985	5.2	2.70
1986	3.2	2.75
1987	5.0	3.03
1988	5.7	3.39
1989	1.5[1]	[2]

Source: Council on Environmental Quality, *20th Annual Report 1990*, Washington, D.C., p. 439, from U.S. Department of Agriculture, Forest Service. Wildfire statistics, annual. Washington, DC; U.S. Department of Agriculture, Forest Service, U.S. forest planting report, annual. Washington, DC. Reforestation refers to acres planted in seedings and directed seeded. *Notes:* 1. Preliminary estimates reported to the Boise Interagency Fire Center as of September 1989. 2. Not available.

★ 223 ★

Present and Future Demand on Timberland

Timber demand, exports, and demand on timberland in the United States. Data are shown in billions of cubic feet.

	Historical					Projections					
	1952	1962	1970	1976	1986	1990	2000	2010	2020	2030	2040
Demand by Product											
Sawlogs[1]	6.1	5.9	6.0	6.8	9.0	8.6	8.2	8.9	9.5	9.6	9.6
Veneer logs[2]	0.4	0.9	1.2	1.5	1.8	1.6	1.3	1.4	1.5	1.6	1.7
Pulpwood[3]	2.7	3.3	4.4	4.4	5.8	5.9	7.4	8.8	9.6	10.3	10.8
Miscellaneous products[4]	0.7	0.5	0.4	0.4	0.5	0.7	0.8	1.0	1.2	1.3	1.4
Fuelwood	1.0	0.5	0.3	0.3	3.3	3.6	4.3	5.6	5.7	5.4	5.1
Total[5]	10.9	11.1	12.3	13.5	20.5	20.3	22.9	25.7	27.6	28.2	28.6

[Continued]

★ 223 ★

Present and Future Demand on Timberland
[Continued]

	Historical					Projections					
	1952	1962	1970	1976	1986	1990	2000	2010	2020	2030	2040
Exports	0.2	0.5	1.5	1.9	1.9	2.1	2.2	2.3	2.4	2.5	2.5
Imports	1.4	1.9	2.4	2.8	4.4	4.2	3.7	4.1	4.4	4.1	4.0
Harvest from U.S. Forestland	9.7	9.7	11.4	12.6	18.0	18.2	20.5	23.9	25.6	26.5	27.1

Source: Resource Recycling, November 1989, p. 44, from U.S. Department of Agriculture, Forest Service. *Notes:* 1. Lumber products 2. Plywood products 3. Includes both pulpwood and the pulpwood equivalent of the net imports of pulp, paper and board. 4. Includes cooperage logs, poles, piling, fence posts, round mine timbers, box bolts, shingle bolts, roundwood used in waferboard, oriented strand board, particleboard manufacture, and other miscellaneous items. 5. Includes imported logs not shown by product use.

Erosion

★ 224 ★

Cropland Erosion in the U.S.
Erosion shown in average tons per acre per year.

Year	Sheet and rill erosion			Wind erosion		
	Cultivated cropland	Uncultivated cropland	Average	Cultivated cropland	Uncultivated cropland	Average
1977	5.1	3.4	4.7	6.0	1.9	5.3
1982	4.7	0.8	4.3	3.4	0.4	3.1
1987	4.1	0.9	3.8	3.6	0.7	3.3

Source: Council on Environmental Quality, *20th Annual Report 1990*, Washington, D.C., p. 476, from U.S. Department of Agriculture, Soil Conservation Service. *National Resources Inventory: 1977, 1982, and 1987.* Washington, D.C. Data for 1977 are not strictly comparable with data for 1982 and 1987 because of different reporting categories.

Global Warming

★ 225 ★

Global Climate Change - Coastal Wetland Loss

Loss of coastal wetlands for one-meter rise in sea level.

Area	Current Wetlands Area (sq. mi.)	All Dryland Protected (percent)	Current Development Protected (percent)	No Protection (percent)
Northeast	600	16.0	10.0	2.0
Mid-Atlantic	746	70.0	46.0	38.0
South Atlantic	3,813	64.0	44.0	39.0
Southwest Florida	1,869	44.0	8.0	7.0
Louisiana[1]	4,835	77.0	77.0	77.0
Other Gulf	1,218	85.0	76.0	75.0
West	64	56.0	gain[2]	gain[2]
USA	13,145	50.0-82.0	29.0-69.0	26.0-66.0

Source: Environmental Protection Agency, "The Potential Effects of Global Climate Change on the United States, Draft Report to Congress," October 1988 (executive summ.), EP1.2: G51/Draft/ Exec. Summ. Adapted from Park et al. *Notes:* 1. Louisiana projections do not consider potential benefits of restoring flow of sediment and freshwater. 2. Potential gain in wetland acreage not shown because principal author suggested that no confidence could be attributed to those estimates. West coast sites constituted less than 0.5% of wetlands in study sample.

★ 226 ★

Global Climate Change - Impacts of Sea Level Rise

Consequences due to a rise in the sea level by 50, 100, and 200 centimeters.

Impact	50 cm	100 cm	200 cm
If Densely Developed Areas Are Protected			
Shore protection costs (bill. dols.)	32-43	73-111	169-309
Dryland lost (sq. mi.)	2,200-6,100	4,100-9,200	6,400-13,500
Wetlands lost (percent)	20-45	29-69	33-80
If No Shores Are Protected			
Dryland lost (sq. mi.)	3,300-7,300	5,100-10,300	8,200-15,400
Wetlands lost (percent)	17-43	26-66	29-76
If All Shores Are Protected			
Wetlands lost (percent)	38-61	50-82	66-90

Source: Environmental Protection Agency, "The Potential Effects of Global Climate Change on the United States, Draft Report to Congress," October 1988 (executive summary), EP1.2: G51/Draft/Exec.Summ. Assembled by Titus and Greene.

Habitats and Species

★ 227 ★

Endangered and Threatened Species Worldwide

An endangered species is in danger of becoming extinct throughout all or in significant part of its natural range; a threatened species is likely to become endangered in the foreseeable future.

Item	Mammals	Birds	Reptiles	Amphibians	Fishes	Snails	Clams	Crustaceans	Insects	Plants
Endangered species, total	290	221	74	13	58	4	34	8	10	159
U.S. only	31	61	8	5	45	3	32	8	10	152
U.S. and foreign	19	15	7	-	2	-	-	-	-	6
Foreign only[1]	240	145	59	8	11	1	2	-	-	1
Threatened species, total	30	10	32	4	30	5	-	1	7	48
U.S. only	5	7	14	4	24	5	-	1	7	40
U.S. and foreign	2	3	4	-	6	-	-	-	-	6
Foreign only[1]	23	-	14	-	-	-	-	-	-	2

Source: U.S. Department of Commerce, Bureau of the Census, *Statistical Abstract of the United States 1990 (110th ed.)*, Superintendent of Documents, Washington, D.C., p. 208, from U.S. Fish and Wildlife Service, *Endangered Species Technical Bulletin*, April 1989, Vol. XIII, No. 4. *Notes:* - Represents zero. 1. Species outside U.S. and outlying areas as determined by Fish and Wildlife Service.

★ 228 ★

Endangered Freshwater Fish - Midwest

Endangered or threatened species include pallid sturgeon, catfish, ciscoes, and paddle fish.

State	Number of Endangered Threatened, or of Special Concern
Illinois	12
Indiana	9
Iowa	7
Kansas	9
Michigan	7
Minnesota	7
Missouri	14
Nebraska	6
North Dakota	5
Ohio	8

[Continued]

★ 228 ★

Endangered Freshwater Fish - Midwest
[Continued]

State	Number of Endangered Threatened, or of Special Concern
South Dakota	5
Wisconsin	8

Source: *Field and Stream*, August 1990, p. 62.

★ 229 ★

Estimated World Elephant Population
The numbers are estimates of elephants in the world.

Country	Number of Elephants
Angola	18,000
Bangladesh	200-350
Benin	2,100
Bhutan	60-150
Botswana	68,000
Burkina Faso	4,500
Cambodia	2,000
Cameroon	22,000
Central African Republic	23,000
Chad	2,100
Congo	42,000
Cote D'Ivoire	3,000
Equatorial Guinea	500
Ethiopia	8,000
Gabon	74,000
Ghana	2,800
Guinea	560
Guinea Bissau	40
India	17,000-22,000
Indonesia	2,900-5,500
Laos	2,000-3,000
Liberia	1,300
Malawi	2,800
Malaysia	1,300-3,000
Mali	840
Mauritania	100
Mozambique	1,700
Myanmar	3,000-10,000
Namibia	5,700

[Continued]

★ 229 ★

Estimated World Elephant Population
[Continued]

Country	Number of Elephants
Nepal	50-90
Niger	440
Nigeria	1,300
Rwanda	50
Senegal	140
Sierra Leone	380
Somalia	2,000
South Africa	7,800
Sri Lanka	2,700-3,200
Sudan	22,000
Tanzania	61,000
Thailand	1,300-2,000
Togo	380
Uganda	1,000
Vietnam	1,500-2,000
Zaire	112,000
Zambia	32,000
Zimbabwe	52,000

Source: National Geographic, Volume 179, No. 5, May 1991.

★ 230 ★

Fish Kill Distribution Nationwide

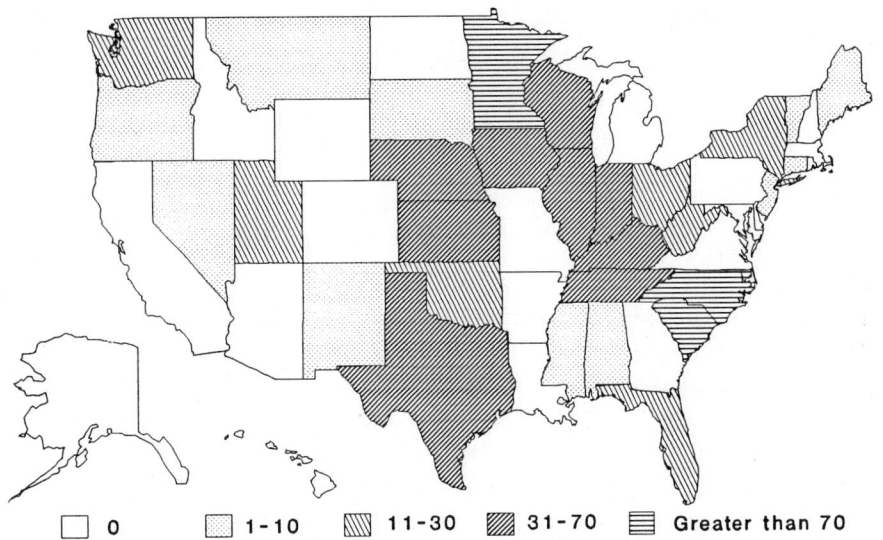

☐ 0   ▦ 1-10   ▨ 11-30   ▧ 31-70   ☰ Greater than 70

Source: The Quality of Our Nation's Water: A Summary of the 1988 National Water Quality Inventory, U.S. Environmental Protection Agency, EPA 440/4-90-005, May 1990, p. 5, from 1988 State Section 305(b) Reports.

★ 231 ★

Fish Kills Caused by Pollution

Data refer to the 1986-1988 reporting period. When a breakout was possible, fill kills due to natural causes have been excluded from the count.

State	Number of Fish Kills	Number Fish Killed	Kills Caused by Toxic Pollutants		Kills Caused by Conventional Pollutant	
			Kills	Fish	Kills	Fish
Alabama	8	43,370	6	33,370	2	10,000
Connecticut	6	2,820	2	1,710	4	1,110
Delaware	1	124,588	-	-	1	124,588
District of Columbia	3	-	0	-	3	-
Florida	25	5,500,000	-	-	-	-
Hawaii	0	0	-	-	-	-
Illinois	49	561,049	-	-	-	-
Indiana	41	428,331	-	-	-	-
Iowa	45	286,601	10	119,324	35	167,277
Kansas	51	174,263	11	133,708	40	40,555
Kentucky	53	359,143	6	19,155	47	339,988
Maine	6	6,450	-	-	6	6,450
Maryland	40	-	8	-	32	-
Minnesota	80	112,419	11	5,663	69	106,756
Mississippi	6	70,400	4	69,500	2	900
Montana	9	3,000	9	3,000	-	-

[Continued]

★ 231 ★

Fish Kills Caused by Pollution
[Continued]

State	Number of Fish Kills	Number Fish Killed	Kills Caused by Toxic Pollutants		Kills Caused by Conventional Pollutant	
			Kills	Fish	Kills	Fish
Nebraska	52	-	-	-	-	-
Nevada	4	-	-	-	-	-
New Jersey	9	-	1	-	8	-
New Mexico	5	-	2	-	3	-
New York	24	21,980	13	12,530	11	9,450
North Carolina	88	4,052,000	4	1,200	84	4,050,800
North Dakota	0	0	-	-	-	-
Ohio	28	608,042	4	30,720	24	577,322
Oklahoma	16	74,160	1	2,000	15	72,160
Oregon	2	200	1	-	1	200
Puerto Rico	16	-	2	-	14	-
South Carolina	144	-	14	20,382	130	-
South Dakota	3	-	-	-	-	-
Tennessee	33	-	6	-	27	-
Texas	69	23,225,000	-	-	-	-
Utah	13	-	7	-	6	-
Vermont	1	-	1	-	-	-
Virgin Islands	2	-	-	-	2	-
Washington	13	-	-	-	-	-
West Virginia	17	52,322	6	24,739	11	27,583
Wisconsin	34	411,394	6	43,365	28	368,029
Totals	996	36,117,532	135	520,366	605	5,903,168

Source: National Water Quality Inventory, 1988, Report to Congress, U.S. Environmental Protection Agency, Washington, D.C., April 1990, p. 115, from 1988 State Section 305(b) reports. A - represents figures not reported.

★ 232 ★

Major U.S. Species Threatened by Air Pollution

Type	Location	Effects
High-elevation spruce and fir	Appalachian Mountains, eastern United States	Decreased growth rate; mortality
Southern pines	Southeastern United States	Decreased growth rate
Sugar maples	Northeastern United States, southeastern Canada	Death of top branches; less syrup production
Ponderosa, Jeffrey pines	Southern and central California	Mortality; decreased growth rate and regeneration

Source: The New York Times, May, 15, 1991, p. A10, from National Acid Precipitation Assessment Program.

★ 233 ★

Sources Associated With Fish Kills

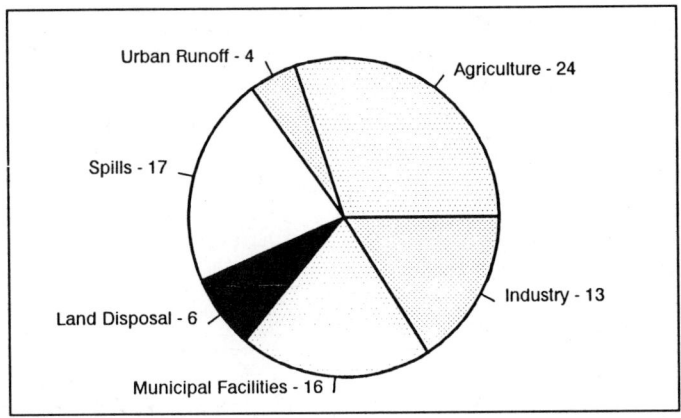

Pollutant	Number of States Reporting
Agriculture	24
Spills	17
Municipal Facilities	16
Industry	13

[Continued]

★ 233 ★

Sources Associated with Fish Kills
[Continued]

Pollutant	Number of States Reporting
Land Disposal	6
Urban Runoff	4

Source: National Water Quality Inventory, 1988, Report to Congress, U.S. Environmental Protection Agency, Washington, D.C., April 1990, p. 116, from 1988 State Section 305(b) reports.

★ 234 ★

Stellar Sea Lion Population in Alaska
Population data refer to an area from the West Gulf of Alaska to the Aletians.

Year	Population
1956-60	140,000
1975	105,000
1985	68,000
1989-90	25,000

Source: Christian Science Monitor, April 24, 1991, p. 10, from International Pacific Halibut Commission; 1991 Pacific Fishing Yearbook; City of Unalaska.

★ 235 ★

Threatened & Endangered Species in the U.S.
An endangered species is in danger of becoming extinct throughout all or a significant part of its natural range; a threatened species is likely to become endangered in the forseeable future. Numbers shown are cumulative.

Group	Threatened				Endangered			
	1980	1985	1987	1989	1980	1985	1987	1989
Mammals	3	4	7	6	32	20	50	32
Birds	3	3	10	7	66	59	76	61
Reptiles	10	8	18	14	13	8	15	9
Amphibians	3	3	4	4	5	5	5	6
Fishes	12	14	30	25	34	30	47	49
Snails	5	5	5	6	2	3	3	3
Crustaceans	0	1	1	1	1	3	7	8
Insects	6	4	7	7	7	8	10	10
Arachnids	0	0	0	0	0	0	3	3
Clams	0	0	0	0	23	22	30	34

[Continued]

★ 235 ★

Threatened & Endangered Species in the U.S.
[Continued]

Group	Threatened				Endangered			
	1980	1985	1987	1989	1980	1985	1987	1989
Plants	7	10	44	42	51	67	158	163
Total	49	52	126	112	234	225	404	378

Source: Council on Environmental Quality, *20th Annual Report 1990*, Washington, D.C., p. 490, from U.S. Department of the Interior, Fish and Wildlife Service, Division of Endangered Species and Habitat Conservation, unpublished data. Washington, D.C.

Health Effects

★ 236 ★

Annual Radiation Exposure

Annual radiation exposure, in millirem, of an average American. The federal government permits an exposure of 5,000 milirem annually in the workplace.

	Millirem of Radiation	Percent of Exposure
Manmade radiation		
Medical X-rays	39	11
Nuclear medicine	14	4
Consumer products	10	3
Miscellaneous	-	<1
Natural radiation		
Radon	200	55
From inside human body	40	11
Rocks and soil	28	8
Cosmic	27	8
Total	358	100

Source: The Bulletin of the Atomic Scientists, September 1990, p. 13 from National Council on Radiation Protection and Measurements.

★ 237 ★

Cancer Deaths and Pollution

Factor or Class of Factors	Percent of All Cancer Deaths
Tobacco	30.0
Alcohol	3.0
Diet	35.0
Food additives[1]	<1.0
Reproductive and sexual behavior	7.0
Occupation	4.0
Pollution	2.0
Industrial products	<1.0
Medicines and medical procedures	1.0
Geophysical factors[2]	3.0
Infection	about 10.0
Unknown	??

Source: Consumer's Research, April 1990, p. 36, from Dell and Peto, "The Causes of Cancer: Quantitative Estimates of Avoidable Risks of Cancer in the United States Today," *Journal of the National Cancer Institute*, 1981. *Notes:* 1. Allowing for a possibly protective effect of antioxidants and other preservatives. 2. Geophysical factors also cause much greater proportion of non-fatal cancers (up to 30% of all cancers, depending on ethnic mix and latitude) because of the importance of UV light in causing the relatively non-fatal basal cell and squamous cell carinomas of sunlight exposed skin.

★ 238 ★

Carcinogens - Top Ten

Environmental distribution of Toxic Release Inventory (TRI) releases and transfers for the top state for the top 10 carcinogens, 1988.

Chemical	State	Total Releases and Transfers (Pounds)	Air (Percent)	Water (Percent)	Land (Percent)	Underground (Percent)	Public Sewage (Percent)	Off-Site (Percent)	Rank
Dichloromethane	NY	17,359,940	84.40	0.12	0.69	0.00	8.60	6.18	1
Styrene	OH	5,005,040	59.17	0.01	0.35	0.00	1.16	39.31	2
Tetrachloroethylene	CA	5,054,221	91.00	0.00	0.47	0.00	0.02	8.51	3
Benzene	TX	6,962,482	73.05	0.26	2.39	8.19	3.28	12.83	4
Formaldehyde	TX	6,881,160	19.80	0.10	0.07	78.42	0.70	0.92	5
Chloroform	AL	2,389,139	97.02	2.66	0.21	0.00	0.00	0.11	6
Acetonitirle	LA	12,087,240	1.22	0.02	0.00	98.45	0.00	0.30	7
Asbestos (friable)	TN	5,885,555	0.18	0.00	0.00	0.00	0.00	99.82	8
Lead	TX	3,253,111	22.78	0.18	91.25	0.00	0.12	5.67	9
Chromium	OH	4,760,916	2.03	0.06	68.57	0.00	0.41	28.92	10

Source: Toxics in the Community: National and Local Perspectives, U.S. Environmental Protection Agency, EPA 560/4-90-017, September 1990, p. 104.

★ 239 ★

Changing Radiation Standards in the U.S.

Recommended maximum permissible whole-body doses of external radiation, above natural background.

Year	Doses/Year
Occupational exposure	
1934	30.00
1949	15.00
1957	5.00
1960	5.00
1977	5.00
1987	5.00
1990[1]	2.00
General public exposure	
1956	0.50
1960	0.17
1987	0.10

Source: The Bulletin of the Atomic Scientist, September 1990, p. 14, from National Council on Radiation Protection and Measurements, *Recommendations on Limits for Exposure to Ionizing* (1987); J. Shapiro, *Radiation Protection: A Guide for Scientists and Physicians* (Cambridge, Mass: Harvard University Press, 1990).

★ 240 ★

Death Risks From Various Causes

Cause	Voluntary (V) or Invol- untary (I)	Lifetime Risk of Premature Death (per 100,000)
Smoking (all causes)	V	21,900
Smoking (cancer only)	V	8,800
Motor vehicle	I	1,600
Frequent airline passenger	V/I	730
Coal mining accidents	I/V	441
Indoor radon	V/I	400
Motor vehicle - pedestrian	I	290
Environmental tobacco smoke / living with a smoker	I/V	200
Diagnostic X-rays	I	75
Cycling deaths	I/V	75
Consuming Miami or New Orleans drinking water	I	7
Lightning	I	3

[Continued]

★ 240 ★

Death Risks from Various Causes
[Continued]

Cause	Voluntary (V) or Involuntary (I)	Lifetime Risk of Premature Death (per 100,000)
Hurricanes	I	3
Asbestos in school buildings	I	1

Source: *Consumer's Research*, July 1990, p. 12, from Commins (1985), Well and Hughes (1986), Wilson and Crouch (1982).

★ 241 ★

Disabling Work Injuries

| Overexertion - 28.2 |
| Struck by or against object - 25.9 |
| Falls - 16.4 |
| Non-impact strains - 7.4 |
| Caught in or between objects - 6.0 |
| Other - 4.7 |
| Contact with radiation, caustics - 3.5 |
| Motor-vehicle accident - 3.0 |
| Rub or abrasion - 2.6 |
| Contact with extreme temperature - 2.3 |

Environmentally-related injuries accounted for 3.5 percent of work injuries, all industries.

	% of Injuries
Overexertion	28.2
Struck by or against object	25.9
Falls	16.4
Non-impact strains	7.4
Caught in or between objects	6.0
Contact with radiation, caustics	3.5
Motor-vehicle accident	3.0
Rub or abrasion	2.6
Contact with extreme temperature	2.3
Other	4.7

Source: *The Wall Street Journal*, March 29, 1991, p. B1, from National Safety Council.

★ 242 ★

Exposures to Ozone Levels

Estimated exposures to ozone levels above 0.12 ppm.[1] Estimates are based on hourly ozone data for the period 1983-85.

Exercise level	People Exposed Per Year (millions)	% of People Living in Areas Exceeding 0.12 ppm[1]	Hours of Exposure Per Person Exposed Per Year
Nationwide except Los Angeles:			
Low	24.0	20	3.7
Moderate	16.0	13	4.6
Heavy	10.0	8	3.2
Very heavy	0.6 <	0.1	2.1
Los Angeles:			
Low	9.7	97	22
Moderate	4.6	46	24
Heavy	3.0	30	14
Very heavy	0.2	0.2	10

Source: Consumers' Research, March 1990, p. 14, from Office of Technology Assessment, "Catching Our Breath: Next Steps for Reducing Ozone," July 1989. Estimates take into account people's activity patterns (e.g., time commuting, time indoors, etc.) and location throughout the day. The estimates are broken down according to exercise levels. Those exercising at the higher levels are most apt to be susceptible to health impacts. The total number of people residing in areas where ozone concentrations exceeded 0.12 ppm at least one hour per year, on average during this time period, was approximately 130 million. *Note:* 1. PPM stands for parts per million.

★ 243 ★

Health and Environmental Effects From Toxic Chemicals

The following are the chemicals with the largest releases and transfers in 1988.

Chemical	Type of toxicity					1988 Rank
	Health/Terrestrial		Aquatic		Carcino-genicity[5]	
	Acute[1]	Chronic[2]	Acute[3]	Chronic[4]		
Ammonium sulfate	-	-	-	-	-	1
Hydrochloric acid	Moderate	-	Low	-	-	2
Methanol	Low	-	Low	-	-	3
Sulfuric acid	Moderate	-	Moderate	-	-	4
Ammonia	Moderate	Moderate	High	-	-	5
Toluene	Low	Moderate	Moderate	-	-	6
Acetone	-	Moderate	Low	-	-	7
Phosphoric acid	Low	-	Low	-	-	8
Zinc compounds	High	Moderate	High	High		9
Xylene (mixed isomers)	Low	-	Moderate	-	-	10
1,1,1-Trichloroethane	Low	Moderate	Moderate	-	-	11

[Continued]

★ 243 ★

Health and Environmental Effects from Toxic Chemicals
[Continued]

| Chemical | Type of toxicity | | | | | 1988 Rank |
| | Health/Terrestrial | | Aquatic | | Carcino-genicity[5] | |
	Acute[1]	Chronic[2]	Acute[3]	Chronic[4]		
Methyl ethyl ketone	Low	Moderate	Low	-	-	12
Chlorine	High	-	High	High	-	13
Dichloromethane	Low	Moderate	Low	-	High	14
Manganese compounds	-	High	High	High	-	15
Ammonium nitrate	-	-	-	-	-	16
Carbon disulfide	Moderate	High	Low	-	-	17
Nitric acid	Moderate	-	Moderate	-	-	18
Freon 113	-	-	-	-	-	19
Zinc (fume or dust)	-	Moderate	-	High	-	20
Glycol ethers	-	-	-	-	-	21
Ethylene glycol	-	Low	-	-	-	22
Copper compounds	Moderate	Moderate	High	High	-	23
Trichloroethylene	Low	Moderate	Moderate	Low	-	24
N-Butyl alcohol	Low	-	-	-	-	25

Source: Toxics in the Community: National and Local Perspectives, U.S. Environmental Protection Agency, EPA 560/4-90-017, September 1990, p. 98 Based on data from *The Toxic Chemical Release Inventory Risk Screening Guide (version 1.0)*, Volume 2:Appendices, EPA 560/2-89-002 (Washington, DC:U.S. Environmental Protection Agency, July 1989). *Notes:* 1. Indicates toxic effects to humans or terrestrial animals associated with inhalation or ingestion of relatively high levels of the chemical over a short period of time. Based on threshold planning quantities (TPQs) and reportable quantities for acute toxicity (RQ Acute). 2. Indicates toxic effects to humans or terrestrial animals associated with inhalation or ingestion of moderate or low levels of the chemical over a long period of time. Based on reportable quantities for chronic (RQCH), inhalation reference doses (RFDI), and oral reference doses (RQ Acute). 3. Indicates toxic effects to aquatic organisms associated with exposure to relatively high levels of the chemical over a short period of time. Based on reportable quantities for aquatic toxicity (RQ AQTX) and water quality criteria for acute toxicity (WQC Acute). 4. Indicates toxic effects to aquatic organisms associated with exposure to moderate or low levels of the chemical over a long period of time. Based on water quality criteria for aquatic toxicity (WQC CTX). 5. According to the carcinogen list used for TRI reporting.

★ 244 ★

Lead Exposure for the Two-Year-Old Child

Sources	Percent
Dust	45
Food	45
Water	9
Air	1

Source: FDA Consumer, December 1988-January 1989, p. 25, from U.S. Environmental Protection Agency, 1986.

★ 245 ★

Respiratory Symptoms and Woodstove Use

Results of a study which measured frequency and severity of upper respiratory symptoms in relation to hours of woodstove use. The subjects were 59 children ranging from 13 to 67 months of age.

Symptoms	T-ratio
Wheeze frequency	4.24[1]
Wake up with cough	3.30[1]
Wheeze severity	2.92[1]
Cough frequency	2.89[1]
Cough severity	2.50[2]
Runny nose frequency	1.19
Fever severity	1.10
Fever frequency	0.77
Shortness of breath	0.44
Nasal drainage severity	0.00

Source: Journal of Environmental Health, November/December 1989, p. 173. *Notes:* 1. 0.01 level of significance T-ratio of 2.58. 2. 0.05 level of significance T-ratio of 1.96.

★ 246 ★

Safe-Level Concentration of Tetrachloro-P-Dibenzodioxin

Lifetime cancer risk is one in a million in the general population.

	Calculated TCDD equivalent[5] (in ppt)		
	Female	Male	Measured
Bleached pulps	-	-	5[1]
Communication paper	-	-	13[2]
Clerical worker	9,000	9,100	-
Manager	4,200	4,300	-
Personal care products			
Disposable diapers	-	-	0[3]
Conventional	540,000	540,000	-
Superabsorbent	2,000,000	2,000,000	-
Facial tissue	-	-	-
Normal use	66,000,000	79,000,000	-
Make-up	230,000	-	-
Toilet tissue	27,000,000	65,000,000	-
Sanitary pads	63,000,000	-	-
Paper towels	7,900,000	9,500,000	-
Composite personal care products[4]	160,000	510,000	-
Combined communication paper and personal care products	-	-	4

[Continued]

★ 246 ★

Safe-Level Concentration of Tetrachloro-P-Dibenzodioxin
[Continued]

	Calculated TCDD equivalent[5] (in ppt)		
	Female	Male	Measured
Clerical worker	8,500	8,900	-
Manager	4,100	4,200	-

Source: Technologies for Reducing Dioxin in the Manufacture of Bleached Wood Pulp, U.S. Congress, Office of Technology Assessment, OTA-BP-054, May 1989, p. 36, from National Council of the Paper Industry for Air and Stream Improvement, *Assessment of Potential Health Risks From Dermal Exposure to Dioxin in Paper Products*, Technical Bulletin No. 534 (New York, NY: 1987), p. 107. *Notes:* 1. Measured in 7 pulps with levels of dioxin from less than 1 ppt to 51 ppt, with a median of 4.9 ppt. 2. Measured in bond paper. 3. No TCDD detected in disposable diapers at detection limits of 2.1 and 2.6 ppt. 4. Excluding superabsorbent disposable diapers. 5. Tetrachloro-P-Dibenzodioxine.

Oil Spills

★ 247 ★

Comparisons of the Largest Oil Spills

Characteristic	Sea Island	Exxon Valdez
Location	Persian Gulf	Prince William Sound
Cause	Act of war	Accident
Size	294 mil. gal. (estimate)	11 mil. gal.
Date	1/25/92	3/24/89
Rate of water exchange	3-5 years	28 days
Wave height	<10 feet	>10 feet
Average depth	110 feet	300+ feet
Water temperature	80 F	38 F
Salinity	High	Low
Shoreline	Shallow, wetlands, sandy beaches	Cliffs, cobblestone-sized rocks

Source: Journal of Environmental Health, Spring 1991, p. 20.

★ 248 ★

Large Oil Spills

List of 66 oil spills with volume in excess of 2 million gallons, 1967 to present. Numbers are shown in millions of gallons.

Spill	Date	Location	Volume
Ixtoc I, Well Blowout	1979-1980	Mexico	139-428[1]
Nowruz Oil Field, Well Blowout	1983	Persian Gulf	80-185
Castillo de Bellver/Broke, Fire	1983	S. Africa	50-80[1]
Amoco Cadiz/Grounding	1978	France	67-76
Aegean Captain/Atlantic Empress	1979	off Tobago	49.0[1]
D-103 Libya, Well Blowout	1980-1981	Libya	42.0
Atlantic Empress/Fire	1979	Barbados	41.5[1]
Torrey Canyon/Grounding	1967	England	35.7-38.6[1]
Irenes Serenade/Fire	1980	Greece	12.3-36.6[1]
Sea Star/Collision, Fire	1972	Gulf of Oman	35.3[1]
Kuwait Nat'l Petroleum Tank	1981	Kuwait	31.2
Urquiola/Grounding	1976	Spain	27-30.7[1]
Othello/Collision	1970	Sweden	18.4-30.7
Hawaiian Patriot/Fire	1977	N. Pacific	30.4[1]
Independenta	1979	Turkey	28.9
No. 126 Well/Pipe	1978	Iran	28.0
Jakob Maersk	1975	Portugal	25.0[1]
BP Storage Tank	1985	Nigeria	23.9
Nova/Collision	1985	Iran	21.4
BP, Shell Fuel Dept.	1978	Zimbabwe	20.0
Wafra	1971	S. Africa	19.6[1]
Kharg 5, Explosion	1989	Morocco	19.0
Metula/Grounding	1974	Chile	16.0
Assimi/Fire	1983	off Oman	15.8[1]
Polycommander	1970	Spain	3-15.3
Tohoku Storage Tanks, Earthquake	1978	Japan	15.0
Andros Patria	1978	Spain	14.6
Pericles GC	1983	Qatar	14.0
Ranger, TX, Well Blowout	1985	Texas	6.3-13.7
World Glory/Hull Failure	1968	S. Africa	13.5
Ennerdale/Struck Granite	1970	Seychelles	12.6
Mizushima Refinery, Tank Rupture	1974	Japan	11.3
Napier	1973	SE Pacific	11.0[1]
Juan A. Lavalleja	1980	Algeria	11.0
Exxon Valdez/Grounding	1989	Alaska	10.8
Turkish Petroleum Corporation	1978	Turkey	10.7
Burmah Agate/Collision, Fire	1979	Texas	1.3-10.7[1]
Texaco Oklahoma, 120 mi. offshore	1971	N. Carolina	9.2-10.7
Trader	1972	Mediterranean	10.4
St. Peter	1976	SE Pacific	10.4
Irene's Challenge	1977	Pacific	10.4
Golden Drake	1972	NW Atlantic	9.5
Chryssi	1970	NW Atlantic	9.5
Pacocean/Broke in two	1969	NW Pacific	9.2
Caribbean Sea	1977	E. Pacific	9.2

[Continued]

★ 248 ★

Large Oil Spills
[Continued]

Spill	Date	Location	Volume
Grand Zenith/Disappearance	1976	NW Atlantic	8.9
Cretan Star	1976	Indian Ocean	8.9
Keo/Hull failure	1969	Massachusetts	8.8
Storage Tank	1969	New Jersey	8.4
Ekofisk Bravo, Well Blowout	1977	North Sea	4.6-8.2
Giuseppi Guilietti	1972	NE Atlantic	8.0
Venpet and Venoil/Collision	1977	S. Africa	7.4-8.0
Argo Merchant/Grounding	1976	Massachusetts	7.7
Humble Oil Pipeline, Offshore Leak	1967	Louisiana	6.7
Jawacta	1973	Baltic Sea	6.1
R.C. Stoner	1967	Wake Island	6.0
Marlena	1970	Sicily	4.3
Pipeline	1970	Saudi Arabia	4.2
Oil Well	1971	Persian Gulf	4.2
Tanio/Broke amidships	1980	France	4.2
Ashland Storage Tank, Rupture	1988	Pennsylvania	3.8
Santa Barbara Channel, Well Blowout	1969	California	1.4-3.4
Arrow/Grounding	1970	Nova Scotia	1.5-3.1
Storage Tank	1970	Pennsylvania	3.0
Alvenus/Grounding	1984	Louisiana	2.8
Offshore Platform, Well Blowout	1970	Louisiana	2.7

Source: "Coping With An Oiled Sea: An Analysis of Oil Spill Response Technologies," U.S. Congress, Office of Technology Assessment, March 1990, p. 4, from Exxon Corp. and Office of Technology Assessment. Tanker spills from the Iran/Iraq war were not generally available. *Note:* 1. Fire burned part of spill.

★ 249 ★

Oil Spills in the U.S.

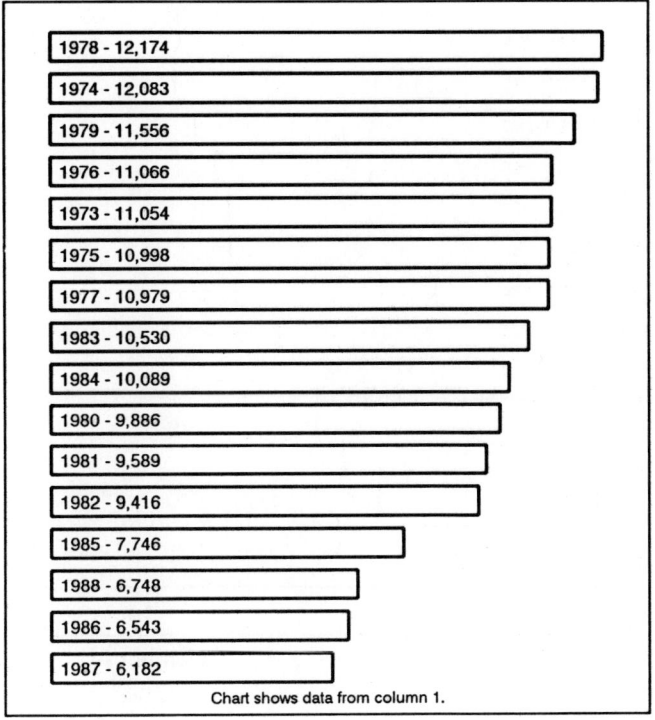

1978 - 12,174
1974 - 12,083
1979 - 11,556
1976 - 11,066
1973 - 11,054
1975 - 10,998
1977 - 10,979
1983 - 10,530
1984 - 10,089
1980 - 9,886
1981 - 9,589
1982 - 9,416
1985 - 7,746
1988 - 6,748
1986 - 6,543
1987 - 6,182

Chart shows data from column 1.

Item	Incidents	Gallons
1973	11,054	15,289,188
1974	12,083	15,739,792
1975	10,998	21,528,444
1976	11,066	18,517,384
1977	10,979	8,188,398
1978	12,174	11,035,890
1979	11,556	10,051,271
1980	9,886	12,638,848
1981	9,589	8,919,789
1982	9,416	10,404,646
1983	10,530	8,378,719
1984	10,089	16,254,974
1985	7,746	18,675,137
1986	6,543	4,451,343
1987	6,182	4,331,612
1988[1]	6,748	5,493,397

Source: U.S. Department of Commerce, Bureau of the Census, *Statistical Abstract of the United States 1990 (110th ed.),* Superintendent of Documents, Washington, D.C., p. 202, from U.S. Coast Guard. Based on unpublished data from the *Marine Safety Information System,* March 1989. *Note:* 1. Preliminary.

★ 250 ★

Oil Spills Since 1978

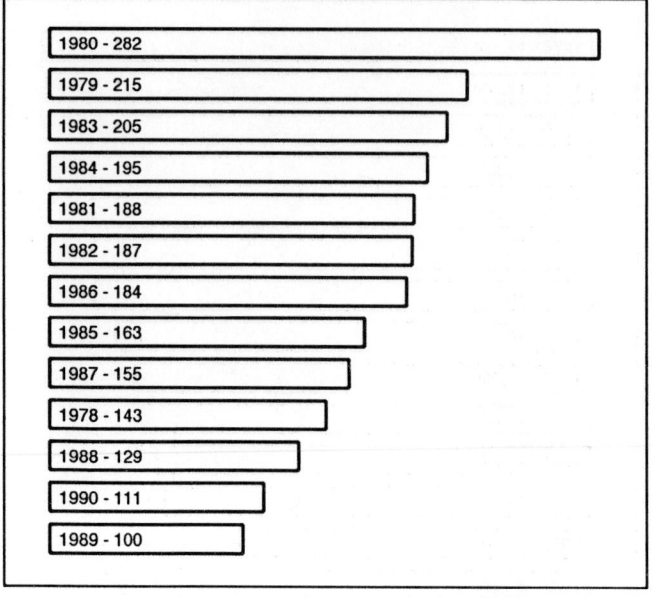

Year	Number of spills
1978	143
1979	215
1980	282
1981	188
1982	187
1983	205
1984	195
1985	163
1986	184
1987	155
1988	129
1989	100
1990	111

Source: Consumer's Research, January 1991, p.15, from *The Oil Spill Intelligence Report*. 1989 and 1990 figures are estimates. Numbers may be changed upward with newer data.

Toxic Accidents

★ 251 ★

Hazardous Materials Transportation Accidents

Casualty and Year	1970	1975	1980	1981	1982	1983	1984	1985	1986	1987	1988
Accidents	(NA)	10,951	15,737	10,070	6,636	5,845	5,776	6,014	5,760	6,135	6,141[1]
Deaths	(NA)	27	19	25	12	8	7	8	16	10	16[1]
Injuries	(NA)	648	626	643	130	193	257	253	316	331	158

Source: U.S. Department of Commerce, Bureau of the Census, *Statistical Abstract of the United States 1990 (110th ed.)*, Superintendent of Documents, Washington, D.C., p. 598, from U.S. Dept. of Transportation Systems Center, Cambridge, MA, *Transportation Safety Information Report.* NA stands for not available. *Notes:* 1. Data on deaths are from U.S. National Highway Traffic Safety Administration and are based on 30 day definition. Other data are from National Safety Council.

★ 252 ★

Oil and Hazardous Waste Spills

Data are for spills in and around U.S. waters, 1970-1986. Spills reported include any spill, however small, required to be reported to the Coast Guard [Ed.].

Year	Oil spills (thousands of spills)	Oil spills (millions of gallons)	Hazardous waste spills (number of spills)	Hazardous waste spills (millions of pounds)
1970	3.71	15.25	[1]	[1]
1971	8.74	8.84	[1]	[1]
1972	9.93	18.81	[1]	[1]
1973	13.23	22.11	[1]	[1]
1974	14.43	19.42	42	1.12
1975	12.78	22.24	42	3.08
1976	13.93	36.61	54	13.16
1977	15.33	11.25	57	0.85
1978	14.50	17.56	49	0.24
1979	13.13	13.66	47	1.74
1980	11.16	15.09	63	0.27
1981	10.56	19.77	102	0.55
1982	10.41	23.15	175	8.66
1983	11.35	30.08	1,031	3.41
1984	13.02	18.16	1,433	3.80
1985	10.99	23.97	[1]	[1]
1986	9.21	5.53	[1]	[1]

Source: Council on Environmental Quality, *20th Annual Report*, 1990, Washington, DC, p. 464, from U.S. Coast Guard, COMDTINST M16450 series. *Note:* 1. Not available.

★ 253 ★

Toxic Rail Accident Trends in the U.S.

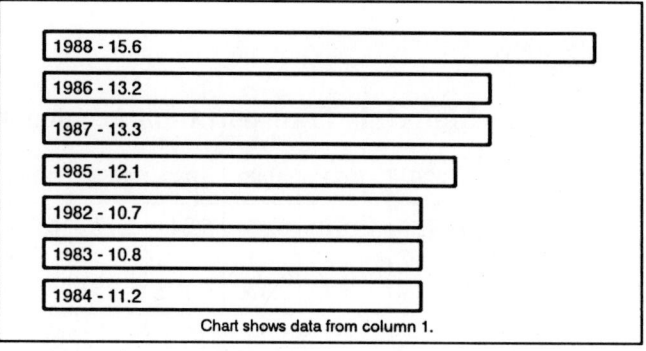

| 1988 - 15.6 |
| 1986 - 13.2 |
| 1987 - 13.3 |
| 1985 - 12.1 |
| 1982 - 10.7 |
| 1983 - 10.8 |
| 1984 - 11.2 |

Chart shows data from column 1.

Year	Percentage of all accidents Involving hazardous materials	Number of accidents with evacuations
1982	10.7	13
1983	10.8	16
1984	11.2	17
1985	12.1	22
1986	13.2	32
1987	13.3	28
1988	15.6	32

Source: Transportation of Hazardous Materials by Rail: Hearings Before the Government Activities and the Transportation Subcommittee of the Committee on Government Operations, House of Representatives, 101st Congress, and Session, February 28, 1990, p. 87, from the Federal Railroad Administration.

★ 254 ★

Toxic Rail Accidents by Carrier

Number, rate, and trend of toxic rail accidents involving Class I carriers in 1988.

Carrier	1988 Toxic Accidents	Rate[1]	Change 1987-88
Amtrak	0	.00	0
Santa Fe	41	.82	17
Springfield Term.	11	9.17	7
Burlington Northern	41	.46	19
Chicago & NW	1	.06	1
Conrail	25	.50	8
CSX	66	.93	8
DE & Hudson	2	1.33	(4)

[Continued]

★ 254 ★

Toxic Rail Accidents by Carrier
[Continued]

Carrier	1988 Toxic Accidents	Rate[1]	Change 1987-88
Denv & Rio Grande	0	.00	(1)
Elgin, Joliet & EIL	4	2.22	3
Florida East Coast	3	.91	3
Grand Trunk	4	.75	(4)
Illinois Central	9	1.06	(6)
KC Southern	3	.28	(1)
LA & AK	3	.64	2
MO - KA - TX	6	1.46	4
Norfolk Southern	46	.91	46
Soo Line	36	3.96	9
Southern Pacific	26	.73	(7)
St. Louis SW	2	.25	(9)
Union Pacific	78	1.11	74
Total Class I Lines	407	.76	175

Source: Transportation of Hazardous Materials by Rail: Hearings Before the Government Activities and the Transportation Subcommittee of the Committee on Government Operations, House of Representatives, 101st Congress, and Session, February 28, 1990, p. 93, from the Federal Railroad Administration. Note: 1. Per million total train miles.

★ 255 ★

Toxic Rail Accidents by Cause
Figures shown are for 1988.

Reported Cause	Number of Accidents
Railroad Defects and Failures	(51.5%)
Roadbed defects	8
Track geometry defects	61
Rail and joint bar defects	43
Frogs, switches and track appliances	47
Signal and communication failures	6
Brake failures	17
Trailure/container defects	1
Body defects	2
Coupler and draft system	14
Truck, axels, journal bearings and wheels	53
Locomotives	4
Employee Error	(34.4%)
Brakes, use of	32
Employee physical condition	3
Flagging, fixed, hand and radio signals	7

[Continued]

★ 255 ★

Toxic Rail Accidents by Cause
[Continued]

Reported Cause	Number of Accidents
Other rules and instructions	45
Speed	18
Switches, use of	45
Miscellaneous	42
Miscellaneous Factor	(14.1%)
Collision with highway users	25
Vandalism and other interference	4
Loaded shifted or fell	2
Interaction of lateral/vertical forces	12
Acts of God/weather/other	27

Source: Transportation of Hazardous Materials by Rail: Hearings Before the Government Activities and the Transportation Subcommittee of the Committee on Government Operations, House of Representatives, 101st Congress, and Session, February 28, 1990, p. 96, from the Federal Railroad Administration.

★ 256 ★

Toxic Rail Accidents in the U.S.

Toxic rail accidents in 1988, by state.

State	FRA Accidents[1]			HMS[2] Spills	Track[3] Miles
	Consists	Releases	Evacuated		
Alabama	16	2	420	52	3,832
Alaska	0	0	0	7	[4]
Arizona	12	5	200	1	1,757
Arkansas	7	4	22	28	2,712
California	22	3	4,720	45	6,438
Colorado	3	0	0	10	3,388
Connecticut	0	0	0	4	464
Delaware	1	0	0	1	213
District of Columbia	0	0	0	0	48
Florida	9	1	450	26	3,230
Georgia	14	7	650	55	5,119
Hawaii	0	0	0	0	[4]
Idaho	6	0	0	5	2,180
Illinois	78	6	1,020	59	8,380
Indiana	12	0	0	35	5,069
Iowa	10	2	1,000	8	3,646
Kansas	8	1	0	28	7,509
Kentucky	6	4	4,030	23	3,175
Louisiana	28	2	15	54	3,050
Maine	7	0	0	11	46
Maryland	1	0	0	10	908

[Continued]

★ 256 ★

Toxic Rail Accidents in the U.S.
[Continued]

State	FRA Accidents[1]			HMS[2] Spills	Track[3] Miles
	Consists	Releases	Evacuated		
Massachusetts	3	0	0	10	1,077
Michigan	9	0	400	38	3,579
Minnesota	14	5	1,750	6	5,592
Mississippi	5	0	200	3	1,744
Missouri	19	1	0	27	5,741
Montana	6	1	0	3	3,326
Nebraska	5	1	0	5	4,579
Nevada	2	0	0	2	1,451
New Hampshire	0	0	0	1	409
New Jersey	1	0	0	19	1,268
New Mexico	6	1	250	19	2,062
New York	9	1	0	24	3,565
North Carolina	9	3	7	21	3,334
North Dakota	0	0	0	2	4,597
Ohio	14	5	30	64	6,238
Oklahoma	11	0	0	7	3,289
Oregon	8	0	0	6	2,889
Pensylvania	11	1	100	41	5,232 [4]
Rhode Island	0	0	0	0	
South Carolina	6	6	150	11	2,579
South Dakota	0	0	0	0	1,953
Tennessee	8	0	100	42	2,597
Texas	63	9	165	151	12,853
Utah	1	0	0	5	1,493
Vermont	3	1	125	3	102
Virginia	13	0	10	18	3,766
Washington	5	2	0	7	3,927
West Virginia	4	0	0	14	3,209
Wisconsin	16	0	350	2	3,752
Wyoming	6	0	0	2	1,993

Source: Transportation of Hazardous Materials by Rail: Hearings Before the Government Activities and the Transportation Subcommittee of the Committee on Government Operations, House of Representatives, 101st Congress, and Session, February 28, 1990, p. 114 *Notes:* 1. FRA Accidents: Includes consists carrying hazardous materials (Consists); number of cars releasing hazardous materials (Releases); and number of people evacuated (Evacuations); from U.S. Department of Transportation, Federal Railroad Administration, Office of Safety, "Accident/Incident Bulletins," for calendar year 1988 (No. 157), p. 42. 2. HMS Spills: Incidents reported by U.S. Department of Transportation, Hazardous Material Information System, *"Hazmat Summaries,"* for 1988. 3. Track Miles: Class I operated track mileage from Association of American Railroads, "Yearbook of Railway Facts," 1986. 4. Class I operated track miles only.

★ 257 ★

U.S. Toxic Accidents in Transportation

Severity of toxic accidents for all railroad classes.

Year	Cars Involved	Cars w/HAZMAT[1]	Damaged w/HAZMAT[1]	Releasing HAZMAT[1]
1987	26,251	2,292	495	89
1988	32,821	13,841	630	74
Change	+6,570 (+25%)	+1,549 (+68%)	+135 (+27%)	-15 (-17%)

Source: Transportation of Hazardous Materials by Rail: Hearings Before the Government Activities and the Transportation Subcommittee of the Committee on Government Operations, House of Representatives, 101st Congress, and Session, February 28, 1990, p. 85, from the Federal Railroad Administration. *Note:* 1. Hazardous materials.

Chapter 4
COSTS, BUDGETS, AND EXPENDITURES

Air Pollution Control

★ 258 ★

Acid Rain Control Expenditures by States

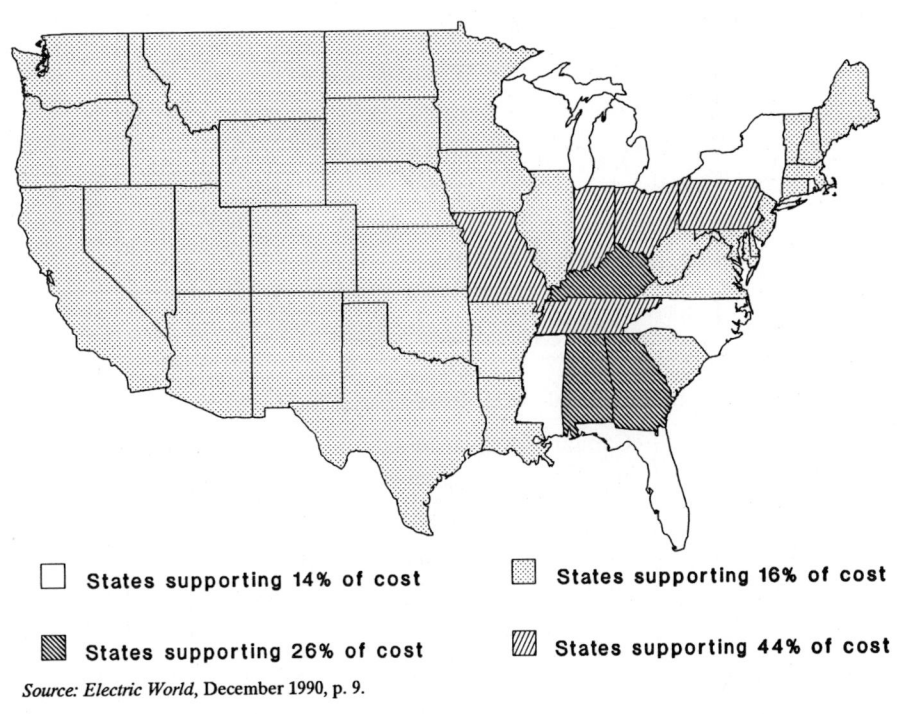

☐ States supporting 14% of cost ▦ States supporting 16% of cost

▨ States supporting 26% of cost ▨ States supporting 44% of cost

Source: Electric World, December 1990, p. 9.

★ 259 ★

Costs of the Clean Air Act

```
Total - 26,451

          Petroleum & Coal - 6,081

        Primary Metals - 5,010

      Chemicals - 4,690

    Paper - 2,749

   Transportation - 1,307

   Stone, Clay, Glass - 1,201

   Food - 1,173

  Electrical Machinery - 898

  Fabricated Metals - 750

  Printing & Publishing - 630

  Lumber & Wood - 489

  Nonelectrical Machinery - 369

  Rubber & Plastics - 350

  Furniture - 246

  Instruments - 176

  Textiles - 162

  Tobacco - 70

  Miscellaneous - 57

  Leather - 45

            Chart shows data from column 7.
```

Pollution Engineering Clean Air Act cost estimates in millions of 1990 dollars.

Industry	Capital Spending % by industry	Capital Spending % of total	Replacement Capital [$]	Maintenance Spending % by industry	Maintenance Spending % of total	Annual Maintenance [$]	Total Costs [$]
Food	0.066	0.384	634	0.035	0.616	539	1,173
Tobacco	0.002	0.200	10	0.003	0.800	60	70
Textiles	0.005	0.258	32	0.007	0.742	130	162
Lumber & Wood	0.021	0.276	145	0.019	0.724	344	489
Furniture	0.013	0.370	120	0.008	0.630	126	246
Paper	0.153	0.385	1,473	0.083	0.615	1,276	2,749
Printing & Publishing	0.037	0.438	405	0.016	0.562	225	630
Chemicals	0.244	0.344	2,098	0.158	0.656	2,591	4,690
Petroleum & Coal	0.137	0.150	514	0.262	0.850	5,568	6,081
Rubber & Plastics	0.014	0.259	91	0.014	0.741	259	350
Leather	0.003	0.400	30	0.001	0.600	15	45
Stone, Clay, Glass	0.001	0.145	4	0.056	0.855	1,197	1,201
Primary Metals	0.110	0.147	404	0.216	0.853	4,606	5,010
Fabricated Metals	0.030	0.250	188	0.030	0.750	563	750
Nonelectrical Machinery	0.014	0.244	85	0.015	0.756	284	369

[Continued]

★ 259 ★

Costs of the Clean Air Act
[Continued]

Industry	Capital Spending % by industry	Capital Spending % of total	Replacement Capital [$]	Maintenance Spending % by industry	Maintenance Spending % of total	Annual Maintenance [$]	Total Costs [$]
Electrical Machinery	0.053	0.466	617	0.021	0.534	280	898
Transportation	0.058	0.283	410	0.050	0.717	896	1,307
Instruments	0.010	0.405	101	0.005	0.595	74	176
Miscellaneous	0.003	0.286	21	0.002	0.714	36	57
Total	0.974		7,383	1.001		19,069	26,451

Source: Pollution Engineering, July 1990, p. 20, from Clean Air Act Amendments, Cost Comparisons, Office of Air and Radiation, U.S. Environmental Protection Agency, Jan. 23, 1990 (and later revisions). Manufacturers' Pollution Abatement Capital Expenditures and Costs, U.S. Department of Commerce. Bureau of the Census. Advanced Report of 1988. Cahners Economics. Apparel industries are excluded. Percent of total column data do not add to 1.0 because of rounding, partial withholding of data, and exclusion of apparel and certain textile data.

★ 260 ★

Projected Clean Air Costs

1999 - 8.9	
1998 - 3.2	
1996 - 3.2	
	1995 - 1.1
	1993 - 0.8
	1994 - 0.8
	1997 - 0.4

Data show estimated capital expenditures that will be required in the years 1993 through 1999 to meet clean air legislation requirements.

Year	Cost (billion $)
1993	0.8
1994	0.8
1995	1.1
1996	3.2
1997	0.4
1998	3.2
1999	8.9

Source: Electric Light and Power, January 1991, p. 25., from Edison Electric Institute.

★ 261 ★

Sulfur Dioxide Removal Costs

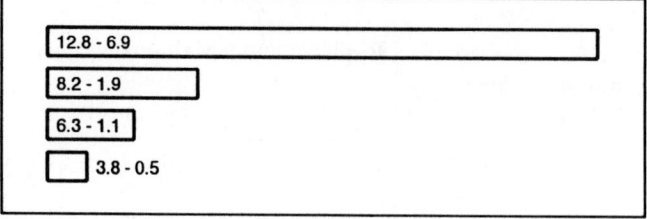

Data show, in 1987 dollars, the costs of removing sulfur dioxide from smokestacks at four levels by the year 2000. Thus the removal of 3.8 million tons would cost $500 million ($132 per ton); removal of 12.8 million tons would cost $6.9 billion ($539 per ton).

Tons of emissions reduced in millions	Cost (in billions of dollars)
3.8	0.5
6.3	1.1
8.2	1.9
12.8	6.9

Source: U.S. News & World Report, July 25, 1988, p. 44, from *USN&WR* - Basic data: Environmental Protection Agency.

★ 262 ★

Utility Air Pollution Control Spending

Breakdown of investments in air pollution control for investor-owned utilities. Values, for each year as of December 31, are in billions of dollars.

Year	Amount
1985	16.7
1986	16.7
1987	19.4
1988	20.5
1989	21.6

Source: Energy Information Administration, *Financial Statistics of Selected Investor-Owned Electric Utilities 1989*, January 1991, pp. 560-568, from Federal Energy Regulatory Commission, FERC Form 1, "Annual Report of Major Electric Utilities, Licensees and Others."

Construction and Maintenance

★ 263 ★

America's Infrastructure Maintenance Costs

Annual capital expenditures (shown in 1988 dollars) required to fix deficiencies and to meet current standards.

	Billion of dollars
Streets	25-35
Transit	4-6
Water supply	4-6
Wastewater treatment	60
Solid waste disposal	1
Airports	24

Source: American City & County, April 1989, p. 10.

★ 264 ★

Construction Contracts Forecast - 1991

Construction contracts in current dollars for the year.

Type of work	1989	Actual 1990	Forecast 1991	Percent change	
				1989-90	1990-91
Total construction[1]	175,366	154,603	147,359	-12	-5
Heavy construction, total	49,090	48,815	48,900	-1	0
Water use and control	16,111	14,740	14,850	-9	+1
Waterworks	4,270	4,273	4,250	0	-1
Sewerage/waste disposal	7,824	6,320	6,400	-19	+1
Dams, reservoirs, waterways	4,017	4,147	4,200	+3	+1
Transportation	21,873	21,193	22,300	-3	+5
Highways, streets	15,958	15,958	16,700	0	+5
Bridges	5,915	5,234	5,600	-12	+7
Electricity, gas, communications	4,515	4,128	4,300	-9	+4
Other heavy construction[2]	6,591	8,754	7,450	+33	-15
Nonresidential buildings	98,906	86,039	80,373	-13	-7
Manufacturing	12,608	7,302	7,083	-42	-3
Commercial	48,112	39,019	33,548	-19	-14
Offices, banks	22,354	16,395	14,154	-27	-14
Stores, mercantile	14,074	13,331	10,844	-5	-19
Warehouses	7,673	5,957	5,808	-22	-3
Garages, service stations	4,011	3,336	2,742	-17	-18
Educational	14,511	15,316	15,568	+6	+2
Hospitals, health treatment	8,853	8,947	8,945	+1	0

[Continued]

★ 264 ★

1991 Construction Contracts Forecast
[Continued]

Type of work	1989	Actual 1990	Forecast 1991	Percent change	
				1989-90	1990-91
Government service	5,218	5,321	5,523	+2	+4
Other (leisure, religious, misc.)[3]	9,604	10,135	9,705	+6	-4
Multiunit residential	27,370	19,750	18,087	-28	-8
Apartments	20,705	15,217	13,721	-27	-10
Hotels, motels, dormitories	6,665	4,533	4,366	-32	-4

Source: ENR, January 28, 1991, p. 30, from ENR-F.W. Dodge Division. *Notes:* 1. Excludes 1-2 family houses. 2. Includes military, space, airport paving. 3. Includes airport buildings.

★ 265 ★

Material Handling Equipment Costs

	New costs	Used costs
Horizontal baler	40-250,000	20-100,000
Vertical baler	6-12,000	3-7,000
Glass crusher	2-5,000	1-3,000
Can separator	2-4,000	1-2,000
Can flattener	3-7,000	1-3,000
Can densifier	12-25,000	8-15,000
Forklift	20-35,000	8-18,000
Front loader	20-35,000	8-18,000

Source: World Wastes, October 1989, p. 31.

★ 266 ★

Park Waste and Site Waste Removal Construction
The figures refer to 12-month cumulative contract awards, 1990 vs. 1989, in top 20 major 1990 construction markets.

States	Millions of dollars	% Change
California	479	-12
New York	271	+1
Florida	168	-5
Ohio	152	+25
Pennsylvania	152	+24
Michigan	116	+95

[Continued]

★ 266 ★

Park Waste and Site Waste Removal Construction
[Continued]

States	Millions of dollars	% Change
Texas	116	-6
Hawaii	113	+130
New Jersey	112	+28
Massachusetts	106	+49
Colorado	105	+8
Washington	90	+82
Maryland	85	-25
Illinois	69	-55
Arizona	64	-6
Virginia	62	-39
Kentucky	57	-1
Georgia	48	+5
Alabama	47	+188
Indiana	46	-31
Total U.S.	3,036	0

Source: ENR, January 28, 1991, p. 34, from *ENR*- F.W. Dodge Division.

★ 267 ★

Utility Environmental Construction

Construction work in progress (CWIP) and environmental protection investments for investor-owned utilities. Data are shown for each year as of December 31.

Year	Environmental investments (000 dols.)	Electric Utility Plant[1] (000 dols.)	Percent of Electric Utility Plant	Environmental CWIP (000 dols.)	Electric Utility CWIP[2] (000 dols.)	Percent of Electric Utility CWIP
1985	36,405,745	312,913,885	11.6	9,124,216	83,970,176	10.9
1986	36,335,874	344,133,244	10.6	8,340,504	75,334,698	11.1
1987	44,818,600	383,532,411	11.7	5,485,970	51,029,217	10.8
1988	47,005,176	409,092,233	11.5	4,548,741	40,298,296	11.3
1989	49,370,594	428,700,561	11.5	4,454,276	33,714,555	13.2

Source: Energy Information Administration, *Financial Statistics of Selected Investor-Owned Electric Utilities 1989*, January 1991, p. 11, from Federal Energy Regulatory Commission, FERC Form 1, "Annual Report of Major Electric Utilities, Licensees and Others." CWIP stands for "Construction Work in Progress." *Notes:* 1. Excludes cost of nuclear fuel. 2. Excludes other utility plant CWIP.

Consumer Costs

★ 268 ★

Annual Fuel Costs for 1991 Model Year

Estimates are based on 15,000 miles per year. The Department of Energy suggests that you use the chart to figure your costs by first calculating the cost for the estimated highway mpg for your car and then the cost for the estimated city mpg. Multiply each value by the percent of your total driving that is done in the city and percent that is done on the highway and add the two values together to yield the total cost. Simply averaging the mpg for city and highway driving and then looking up a single value in the table will yield an incorrect answer.

Estimated miles per gallon	Dollars Per Gallon					
	1.90	1.70	1.50	1.30	1.10	1.05
50	570	510	450	390	330	315
49	582	520	459	398	337	321
48	594	531	469	406	344	328
47	606	543	479	415	351	335
46	620	554	489	424	359	342
45	633	567	500	433	367	350
44	648	580	511	443	375	358
43	663	593	523	453	384	366
42	679	607	536	464	393	375
41	695	622	549	476	402	384
40	713	638	563	488	413	394
39	731	654	577	500	423	404
38	750	671	592	513	434	414
37	770	689	608	527	446	426
36	792	708	625	542	458	438
35	814	729	643	557	471	450
34	838	750	662	574	485	463
33	864	773	682	591	500	477
32	891	797	703	609	516	492
31	919	823	726	629	532	508
30	950	850	750	650	550	525
29	983	879	776	672	569	543
28	1018	911	804	696	589	563
27	1056	944	833	722	611	583
26	1096	981	865	750	635	606
25	1140	1020	900	780	660	630
24	1188	1063	938	813	688	656
23	1239	1109	978	848	717	685
22	1295	1159	1023	886	750	716
21	1357	1214	1071	929	786	750
20	1425	1275	1125	975	825	788
19	1500	1342	1184	1026	868	829
18	1583	1417	1250	1083	917	875

[Continued]

★ 268 ★

Annual Fuel Costs for 1991 Model Year
[Continued]

Estimated miles per gallon	Dollars Per Gallon					
	1.90	1.70	1.50	1.30	1.10	1.05
17	1676	1500	1324	1147	971	926
16	1781	1594	1406	1219	1031	984
15	1900	1700	1500	1300	1100	1050
14	2036	1821	1607	1393	1179	1125
13	2192	1962	1731	1500	1269	1212
12	2375	2125	1875	1625	1375	1313
11	2591	2318	2045	1773	1500	1432
10	2850	2550	2250	1950	1650	1575
9	3167	2833	2500	2167	1833	1750

Source: 1991 Gas Mileage Guide, U.S. Department of Energy, October 1990. One gallon is equivalent to 3.785 liters.

★ 269 ★

Consumer Costs for Diapers

	Single use disposables (in dollars)	Cotton diapers (with service) (in dollars)	Proposed flushable diaper (in dollars)
Diaper cost/use	.22	.13	.16
Unit cost/diaper	.20	18.98[1]	.15

All numbers below in millions

Air pollution prevention[2]	.04	-	-
Water	-	-	121.50
Landfill[3]	339.40	-	2.40
Net energy	(3.60)	-	(.20)
Incineration tip fee	25.70	-	0.20
Subtotal	361.50	-	124.00
Life Cycle Costs	3,961.50	227.80	2,824.00

Source: Recycling Today, August 1989, p. 130, from Diapers in the Waste Stream 1988. *Notes:* 1. Unit cost includes diaper service costs: assumes 150 uses in a life cycle. 2. Air pollution Prevention: additional costs of pollution control equipment for incineration. 3. Landfill costs include disposal of all diaper waste.

★ 270 ★

Cost of Water in Selected Cities

The water use is in gallons per month per household.

	Gallons	Cost per 100 gallons (cents)
Santa Barbara	4,488	14.6[1]
Tucson	8,600[2]	13.7[1]
New York City	7,650[2]	12.6
Miami	8,750[2]	10.3-11.9[1]
Chicago	7,480	8.93

Source: Garbage, March/April 1991, p. 66. *Notes:* 1. Rate varies with season and/or water usage. 2. Averaged between house and apartment usage.

★ 271 ★

Electrical Costs and Household Rate Increase

State	Value
West Virginia	590
Indiana	306
Missouri	268
Tennessee	255
Ohio	223
Kentucky	222
Alabama	204
Georgia	175
Pennsylvania	141
South Carolina	115
Illinois	96
North Carolina	96
Florida	61
Virginia	56
Michigan	54

Chart shows data from column 2.

Estimated cost increase for state and annual rate increase per household resulting from acid rain control measures.

State	Total Cost (Millions of Dollars)	Dollars Per Household
Alabama	303	204
Florida	294	61
Georgia	396	175
Illinois	410	96
Indiana	626	306
Kentucky	304	222
Michigan	180	54
Missouri	520	268
North Carolina	230	96
Ohio	898	223
Pennsylvania	626	141
South Carolina	129	115
Tennessee	464	255
Virginia	121	56
West Virginia	417	590

Source: Consumers' Research, March 1990, p. 19, from The Edison Electric Institute. Additional data from Warren Brookes.

★ 272 ★

Energy Expenditures in the Average U.S. Household

Data include electric appliances only and assume an average cost of 7 cents per kilowatt hour.

Household appliance/item	Annual energy cost (dollars)
Space heating	350
Refrigerator/freezer	239
Water heating	154
Air-conditioning	109
Lighting	84
Washer/dryer	77
Furnace fan	46
Range/oven	42
Color TV	22
Dishwasher	12
Microwave	7
Other appliances	22

Source: Changing by Degrees: Steps to Reduce Greenhouse Gases, U.S. Congress, Office of Technology Assessment, OTA-O-482, Washington, D.C., February 1991, p. 117, from Office of Technology Assessment, 1991, adapted from U. S. Department of Energy, Energy Information Administration, *Household Energy Consumption and Expenditure* (Washington, DC: 1989). Lighting data provided by A. Mejer, Lawrence Berkeley Laboratory.

★ 273 ★

Lawn-Care Spending

Dollars spent on lawn-care per year.

	Dollars spent
Chemical pesticides	1.5 billion
Chemical fertilizers	956 million
Federal research into organic lawn-care	0

Source: Garbage, July/August 1990, p. 26, from USDA, Harvey J. Stengel and Associates.

Cost/Benefit

★ 274 ★

Control Cost to Revenue Comparison

| Subcategory | Capacity | Service Fee | | Revenue | | | Control cost | | |
		Defined	Amount	Category	($000)	Period	($000)	Period	As % of fee
Incinerator	18,000 MT/Y	High ($/MT)	3,300	High	0	Annually		Annually	1.4
		Average	1,000	Average	0	Annually	854	Annually	4.7
		Low	26	Low	0	Annually		Annually	182.5
Landfill	62 Acres	High ($/MT)	41	High	30,700	Life		Life	11.2[1]
Municipal		Average	13	Average	9,700	Life	3,444	Life	35.5[1]
		Low	3	Low	2,300	Life		Life	149.7[1]
Hazardous	62 Acres	High ($/MT)	658	High	495,630	Life		Life	0.7[1]
Waste		Average	120	Average	90,000	Life	3,444	Life	3.8[1]
Landfill		Low	76	Low	57,000	Life		Life	6.0[1]
Aqueous	45,500 GPD	High($/G)	6	High	71,000	Annually		Annually	0.8
Treater	for 260 D/Y	Average	1.6	Average	18,900	Annually	569	Annually	3.0
		Low	0.12	Low	1,400	Annually		Annually	40.6

Source: Preliminary Data Summary for the Hazardous Waste Industry (PB 90-126517), U.S. Environmental Protection Agency, Washington, D.C., September 1989, p. 149 Abbreviations Used: MT/Y - metric tons per year; MT - metric ton; GPD - gallons per day; D/Y - days per year. *Notes:* 1. Comparing life cycle cost with initial revenue (assuming a discount rate of 10% in 20 years).

★ 275 ★

Cost Effectiveness of Alternative Fuel Use

Table compares uses of gasoline to methanol and compressed natural gas alone or in blends.

	Fuel price ($ per gallon of of gasoline equivalent)	New vehicle differential ($)	Fleet cost-effectiveness ($/ton)	General cost-effectiveness ($/ton)
Methanol blends			8,700-51,000	8,700-66,000
Straight methanol	1.15-1.51	0-1,000	3,200-18,000	3,200-22,000
Dual-fuel CNG[1,2]			400-12,000	3,900-22,000
Exclusive CNG[2]	0.85-0.95	500-1,500	0-7,400	1,600-14,000

Source: Catching Our Breath: Next Steps for Reducing Urban Ozone, U.S. Congress, Office of Technology Assessment, OTA-F-412, Washington, D.C., July 1989, p. 190 from Office of Technology Assessment, 1989. A retail gasoline price of $1.25 per gallon is used to calculate fuel cost differentials. *Notes:* 1. Compressed Natural Gas. 2. Assumes 75 percent operation on CNG, 25 percent on gasoline.

★ 276 ★

Environmental Costs of Polystyrene and Paper Cups

Comparison of the environmental cost of producing and disposing of 10,000 cups, without recycling.

Category	Poly-styrene	Wax-coated paper
Energy		
Millions of BTUs	5.50	8.78
Solid Waste		
Weight in pounds	96.9	287.9
Volume in cubic yards	0.54	0.36
Selected Air Pollutants (in pounds)		
Particulates	0.8	4.0
Nitrogen Oxides	1.8	4.6
Hydrocarbons	5.7	2.4
Sulfur Oxides	2.6	8.6
Carbon Monoxide	0.8	1.8
Selected Water Pollutants (in pounds)		
Dissolved Solids	1.4	1.7
Suspended Solids	0.2	1.1
Acid	0.2	0.9

Source: The Wall Street Journal, February 28, 1991, p. B1, from Franklin Associates, Ltd.

★ 277 ★

Lifetime Energy Costs of U.S. Appliances

Estimated costs shown in dollars.

Appliance	Average Model	Efficient Model
Electric water heater	3,237	1,618
Refrigerator	1,824	274
Central air conditioner	4,560	2,280
Clothes washer	1,264	632
Electric dryer	983	772
Gas dryer	421	351
Dishwasher	706	454
Color television	252	101
Light	56	13

Source: World Watch, May/June 1988, p. 30, from American Council for an Energy-Efficient Economy data.

Financial Incentives

★ 278 ★

Environmental Investment Funds

Amounts invested are shown in millions of dollars.

Fund	Amount invested	
U.S. College Retirement Equity Fund/ Teacher's Insurance Annuity Association[1]		80,000
Interfaith Center for Corporate Responsibility	25,000	
U.S. Trust	800	
Calvert Group	600	
Franklin Research and Development	200	
Shearson Lehman Hutton	95	
Pax World Fund	92	
Environmental Awareness Fund	1.5	

Source: Chemical Week, April 18,1990, p. 30, from Fund Management. *Note:* 1. Pending study completion.

★ 279 ★

Grants to Recycling Firms

State grants are funding recycling proposals by businesses in the industry.

State	Description	Maximum Available (in dollars)
Illinois	Processors & Manufacturers	N/A
Michigan	Manufacturers	5,000,000
	Processors & Collectors	500,000
	Research & Development	250,000
	Marketing	50,000
Minnesota	Feasibility Study (general)	50,000

[Continued]

223

★ 279 ★

Grants to Recycling Firms
[Continued]

State	Description	Maximum Available (in dollars)
	Feasibility Study (tires)	30,000
New York	Feasibility Study	100,000[1]
Wisconsin	Feasibility Study	75,000[2]
	R&D or Pilot Program (tires only)	50,000[3]

Source: *BioCycle*, May 1990, p. 55. N/A stands for not available. *Notes:* 1. or 80% of study costs. 2. or 50% of eligible costs. 3. or 50% of project costs.

★ 280 ★

Loans to Recycling Firms

State low interest loans are funding recycling ventures by businesses in the industry.

State	Loan Use	Maximum Eligible Amount in Dollars
Illinois	Business Development	N/A
Michigan	Fixed Assets[1]	1,000,000
	Fixed Assets[2]	5,000,000
	Product Marketing	100,000
	Market R&D	500,000
Minnesota	Fixed Assets[3]	1,500,000[5]

[Continued]

★ 280 ★

Loans to Recycling Firms
[Continued]

State	Loan Use	Maximum Eligible Amount in Dollars
New Jersey	Fixed Assets	50,000-3,000,000[4]
New York	Fixed Assets	500,000[6]
Pennsylvania	Equipment	100,000[6]

Source: BioCycle, May 1990, p. 55. N/A stands for not available. *Notes:* 1. For processors. 2. For manufacturers. 3. For waste tires only. 4. Depending upon the type of material processed. 5. or 90% of eligible costs. 6. or 50% of eligible costs.

★ 281 ★

Recycling Program Funding by State

State	Type of Funding	Current Rate	Annual Amount
Alabama	Appropriation	-	-
Arkansas	Disposal Fee	$1.00/ton[1]	-
California	Disposal Fee	$.25/ton[1]	-
Connecticut	Disposal Fee	$1.00/ton[2]	-
District of Columbia	Disposal Fee	$5.00/ton	-
Florida	[3]	-	-
Georgia	Appropriation	-	-
Illinois	Disposal Fee	$.65/CY	$16,000,000
Iowa	Disposal Fee	$2.00/ton[1]	-
Kansas	Appropriation	-	-
Louisiana	Approp.[4]	-	-
Maine	Disposal Fee	$4.00/ton[1]	-
Maryland	Appropriation	-	-
Massachusetts	Approp.[5]	-	-
Michigan	Bond Funds	-	-
Minnesota	Coll. Tax	6%[6]	$15,000,000
Mississippi	Appropriation	-	-
Missouri	Appropriation	-	-
Nebraska	Litter Tax	-	$240,000
Nevada	Import. Tax	$3.00/ton[1]	-
New Jersey	Disposal Fee	$1.50/ton[1]	$12,000,000 +
New York	Approp.[5]	-	-
North Carolina	Approp.[7]	-	-
Ohio	Litter Tax	-	-
Oregon	Disposal Fee	$.50/ton	-

[Continued]

★ 281 ★

Recycling Program Funding by State
[Continued]

State	Type of Funding	Current Rate	Annual Amount
Pennsylvania	Disposal Fee	$2.00/ton[1]	$23,000,000
Rhode Island	Disposal Fee	[8]	-
Texas	Disposal Fee	$.50/ton[1]	-
Vermont	Disposal Fee	$6.00/ton	$1,300,000
Virginia	Litter Tax	-	-
Washington	Coll. Tax	1%[9]	$3,200,000
Wisconsin	Appropriation	-	-

Source: BioCycle, April 1990, p. 41. CY stands for cubic yard. *Notes:* 1. Only a portion of the fee goes to recycling. 2. Also has used bond monies and oil overcharge funds. 3. Uses advanced disposal fees. 4. Has authority to impose a disposal fee starting July 1, 1990. 5. Also uses bond funds. 6. Tax is on garbage collection. 7. Also uses funds from tire tax. 8. Monies come from the fee charges at the state-owned landfill. 9. Tax is on residential collection only.

★ 282 ★

State Financial Incentives to Produce Recycled Goods

State	Tax Credits	Loans		Grants		Sales/Tax Exemption
California	Yes					
Florida						Yes
Illinois			Yes	Yes		
Iowa						Yes
Maine			Yes			
Michigan		Yes	Yes			
Minnesota		Yes	Yes			
New Jersey	Yes			Yes	Yes	Yes
New York					Yes	
North Carolina	Yes					
Oregon	Yes[1]					
Pennsylvania		Yes	Yes			
Vermont					Yes	
Wisconsin						Yes

Source: BioCycle, April 1990, p. 39. *Notes:* 1. Oregon has three separate tax credits that pertain to market development.

Hazardous Waste Management

★ 283 ★

Construction Projects for Solid Waste and Resource Recovery

The figures refer to 12-month cumulative contract awards, 1990 vs. 1989, in top 20 major 1990 construction markets.

State	Million of dollars	% percent
Massachusetts	67	+447
Florida	44	-89
New York	35	-88
North Carolina	34	+...
Pennsylvania	28	-91
Connecticut	26	-59
Maine	25	2675
New Jersey	19	+48
Tennessee	15	+117
Minnesota	11	-23
Ohio	9	-62
Illinois	8	+42
Wisconsin	8	+138
California	7	-33
Maryland	7	+134
Texas	7	+211
Colorado	6	+...
Michigan	6	-22
Indiana	5	-7
Louisiana	5	-78
Total U.S.	402	-69

Source: ENR, January 28, 1991, p. 34, from ENR-F.W. Dodge Division. *Notes:* +... stands for a percent change greater than 1,000 .

★ 284 ★

Medical Waste Treatment Costs

Values are in dollars per pound per hour.

Type of Treatment	Operation and Maintenance	Capital Equipment
Incineration	0.04	500[1]
Hydropulping	0.06	200
Microwaving	0.15	750
Sterilization	0.07	300
Sterilization/Compaction	0.08	400
Sterilization/Grinding	0.08	500

Source: Pollution Engineering, September, 1990, p. 73. *Note:* 1. Controlled Air Incinerator.

★ 285 ★

Model Facilities and Costs

Detailed economic and technical data were not available; models are only for preliminary economic assessment. The land cost was estimated at 20 percent of the capital costs, and annual monitoring costs were estimated at $5,000.

Subcategory	Model Capacity	Capacity	Investment ($ 000)	Control Cost ($1,000)			
				Land	O&M[2]	Monitor	Annual[1]
Incinerator	18,000	MT/Y	1,501	300	381	5	854
Landfill							
Municipal	62	Acres	806	161	286	5	542
Hazardous Waste Landfill	62	Acres	806	161	286	5	542
Aqueous Treater	45,500	GPD					
	260	DPY	767	153	325	5	569

Source: Preliminary Data Summary for the Hazardous Waste Industry (PB 90-126517), U.S. Environmental Protection Agency, Washington, D.C., September 1989, p. 147. Abbreviations Used: MT/Y - metric tons per year; GDP - gallons per day; D/Y - days per year. *Notes:* 1. Capital recovery factor is 0.26 corresponding to a discount rate of 10 percent and 5 years. 2. Operations and Maintenance.

★ 286 ★

Superfund Sites Cleanup Costs

	No. of potential sites	Estimated cost (billions of dollars)
Superfund sites	60,000	50
Sites of RCRA cleanups	2,400	23
State-funded cleanup sites	22,000	45
Defense Dept. sites	7,200	11-15
Energy Dept. sites	NA[1]	66-110

Source: ENR, March 9, 1989, p. 35, from Salomon Brothers Inc.; Wertheim Schroder & Co.; Smith Barney, Harris Upham & Co. *Note:* 1. NA stands for not available.

Nuclear Waste Management

★ 287 ★

Economical Effect on Unit Disposal Costs

Data show the cost added to nuclear waste disposal if private financing is used.

Financing	Facility capacity in thousands of cubic feet/year		
	10	60	230
Shallow-land burial:			
Public	360	90	33
Private	460	110	40
Incremental cost of private financing in percent	28	22	18
Below- grade vaults:			
Public	450	110	50
Private	590	140	55
Incremental cost of private financing in percent	31	27	10

Source: Partnerships Under Pressure: Managing Commercial Low-Level Radioactive Waste, U.S. Congress, Office of Technology Assessment, OTA-F-426, Washington, D.C. November 1989, p. 146, from U.S. Department of Energy, "Conceptual Design Report: Alternative Concepts for Low-Level Radioactive Waste Disposal," prepared by Rogers & Associates Engineering Corp. for the National Low-Level Waste Management Program, DOE/LLW-60T, June 1987, pp. 12-24; EG&G Idaho, "Facility Life Cycle Costs and Average User Fee Projections for Small-Volume Low-Level Radioactive Waste Disposal Facilities," DOE Contract No. DE-ACO7-76IDO157, February 1989.

★ 288 ★

Immediate Dismantlement Costs of Boiling Water Reactor

Cost Category	Estimated 1978 Costs (million dollars)	Cost Adjustment Factor	Estimated 1984 Costs (million dollars)	Percent of Total Estimated Costs Before Contingency Allowance
Disposal of Radioactive Material				
Neutron-Activated	2.300	2.0	4.498	-
Contaminated	4.909	3.2	15.900	-
Radioactive Wastes	1.469	2.0	2.979	-
Total Disposal Costs	8.678	2.4	23.377	44.2
Staff Labor	17.561	1.6	28.098	27.6
Energy	3.519	[1]	10.688	17.5
Tools and Equipment	2.016	1.5	3.024	2.4
Miscellaneous Supplies	1.859	1.5	2.789	4.5
Specialty Contractors	.356	1.6	.570	1.7
Nuclear Insurance	.800	1.4	1.120	2.1
License Fees	.051	[1]	0[2]	0
Subtotal	34.840	-	69.666	100.0
Contingency	8.710	-	17.417	-
Total Costs	43.550	2.0	87.083	-

Source: *Commercial Nuclear Power 1990: Prospects for the United States and the World*, U.S. Department of Energy, DOE/EIA-0348(89), Washington, D.C., January 1991, p. 31, from Electric Power Research Institute, *Updated Costs for Decommissioning Nuclear Power Facilities*, EPRI NP-4012 (Palo Alto, CA, May 1985), p. 12. Cost adjustment factors are rounded to nearest tenths. *Notes:* 1. Cost adjustments for energy are based on cost adjustment factors of 2.6 for electricity and 3.4 for fuel oil. 2. Not included in costs.

★ 289 ★

Immediate Dismantlement Costs of Pressure Water Reactor

Cost Category	Estimated 1978 Costs (million dollars)	Cost Adjustment Factor	Estimated 1984 Costs (million dollars)	Percent of Total Estimated Costs Before Contingency Allowance
Disposal of Radioactive Material				
Neutron-Activated	2.734	2.2	5.995	-
Contaminated	5.183	3.0	15.356	-
Radioactive Wastes	.693	2.3	1.613	-
Total Disposal Costs	8.610	2.7	22.964	44.2
Staff Labor	8.986	1.6	14.378	27.6
Energy	3.500	2.6	9.100	17.5
Tools and Equipment	.822	1.5	1.233	2.4
Miscellaneous Supplies	1.559	1.5	2.339	4.5
Specialty Contractors	.544	1.6	.870	1.7
Nuclear Insurance	.800	1.4	1.120	2.1
License Fees	0	-	0	0
Subtotal	24.821	-	52.004	100.0
Contingency	6.205	-	13.001	-
Total Costs	31.026	2.1	65.005	-

Source: Commercial Nuclear Power 1990: Prospects for the United States and the World, U.S. Department of Energy, DOE/EIA-0348(89), Washington, D.C., January 1991, p. 30, from Electric Power Research Institute, *Updated Costs for Decommissioning Nuclear Power Facilities*, EPRI NP-4012 (Palo Alto, CA, May 1985), p. 12. Cost adjustment factors are rounded to nearest tenths.

★ 290 ★

Low-Level Radioactive Waste Disposal Costs

Site location	Volume disposed (cu ft 1988)	Disposal charge (in dollars)	Surcharge (in dollars)	Total cost
Richland, WA	403,303	18	20	38.00
Barnwell, SC	931,602	26	20	46.00
Beatty, NV	100,852	24	20	44.00
Total	1,435,757		Average	42.67

Source: Partnerships Under Pressure: Managing Commercial Low-Level Radioactive Waste, U.S. Congress, Office of Technology Assessment, OTA-F-426, Washington, D.C. November 1989, p. 145, from Lawrence P. Matheis, Nevada State Health Division, letter to Leonard Slosky, Rocky Mountain Low-Level Radioactive Waste Board, Feb. 29, 1988. U.S. Department of Energy, Draft, "Integrated Data Base for 1988: Spent Fuel and Radioactive Waste Inventories, Projections, and Characteristics," DOE/RW-0006, Rev. 5, August 1989 p. 157.

★ 291 ★

Low-Level Radioactive Waste Disposal Without Surcharge

The data show dollars per cubic foot; costs assume public financing of the disposal facility.

Disposal facility	Facility capacity in thousands of cubic feet/year				
	10	60	50	230	350
Below-grade facilities					
Shallow-land burial	460	110	55	40	30
Concrete containers and concrete vaults	590	140	80	55	40
Above-grade, earth-covered facilities					
Concrete containers and concrete vaults	670	160	90	65	50
Above-ground vaults (no earth cover)					
Earth-mounded concrete bunkers	780	180	105	75	55

Source: Partnerships Under Pressure: Managing Commercial Low-Level Radioactive Waste, U.S. Congress, Office of Technology Assessment, OTA-F-426, Washington, D.C. November 1989, p. 145, from U.S. Department of Energy, "Conceptual Design Report: Alternative Concepts for Low-Level Radioactive Waste Disposal," prepared by Rogers & Associates Engineering Corp. for the National Low-Level Waste Management Program, DOE/LLW-60T, June 1987, pp. 12-24, p. 25; U.S. Department of Energy, "1987 Annual Report on Low-Level Radioactive Waste Management Program," August 1988, pp. 17-19; EG&G Idaho, "Facility Life Cycle Cost and Average User Fee Projections for Small-Volume Low-Level Radioactive Waste Disposal Facilities," DOE Contract No. DE-ACO7-76IDO1570, February 1989; Rogers & Associates Engineering Corp., "Conceptual Designs and Preliminary Economic Analyses of Four Low-Level Radioactive Waste Disposal Facilities," October 1987; US Ecology, Inc., "Proposal for Development and Operation of the Appalachian States Low-Level Radioactive Waste Compact Regional Disposal Facility," prepared for the Commonwealth of Pennsylvania, Vol. II: Executive Summary, p. 18, and Vol. III: Technical Presentation, October 1988; Julie Conner, EG&G Idaho, personal communication, May 1989.

★ 292 ★

Nuclear Weapons Facilities Cleanup Costs

According to the Department of Energy, it will cost an estimated $30 billion to restore nearly 100 plants within its nuclear weapons complex, 60% higher than the cost reported last year. Estimated amounts to be spent by each regional field office are shown in millions of dollars.

DOE regional field office	1990	1991	1992	1993	1994	1995
Albuquerque	256	360	807	802	751	661
Chicago	28	62	73	61	73	68
Headquarters	76	143	379	529	526	398
Idaho	300	369	718	657	601	520
Nevada	11	24	67	88	127	122
Oak Ridge	417	567	1,214	1,408	1,637	1,634
Richland	430	627	1,302	1,385	1,514	1,460
Rocky Flats	136	89	167	193	196	189
San Francisco	48	51	138	161	127	90
Savannah River	475	585	822	777	888	872
Technology Development	186	206	280	353	359	359
Total	2,363	3,083	5,967	6,414	6,800	6,372

Source: ENR, July 12, 1990, p. 8, from Department of Energy.

★ 293 ★

Restoration Project Cost Ranges

Cost ranges for environmental restoration of nuclear waste disposal facilities based on 11 case studies conducted by the U.S. Department of Energy.

Type of project	Cost ranges from OTA case studies			
	Cost	Project	Cost	Project
Installation of groundwater monitoring well (per foot)	$150	Pinellas	$417	Hanford
Annual sample analysis (per well)	$1,333	LLNL	$20,500	INEL
Excavation of soil and sludge (per cubic yard)	$8	Savannah River	$260	Oak Ridge
Off-site soil disposal (per ton)	$110	Pinellas	$146	Kansas City
Installation of groundwater recovery well (per foot)	$159	Savannah River	$400	LLNL
Cap installation (per square foot)	$5	Oak Ridge	$8	Oak Ridge

Source: Complex Cleanup: The Environmental Legacy of Nuclear Weapons Production, U.S. Congress, Office of Technology Assessment, OTA-O-484, Washington, D.C., February 1991, p. 59.

★ 294 ★

Safe Storage Preparation Costs for Boiling Water Reactor

Cost Category	Estimated 1978 Costs (million dollars)	Cost Adjustment Factor	Estimated 1984 Costs (million dollars)	Percent of Total Estimated Costs Before Contingency Allowance
Disposal of Radioactive Material (Radioactive Waste)	1.216	2.0	2.401	7.9
Staff Labor	11.254	1.6	18.006	59.4
Energy	2.122	[1]	6.297	20.8
Tools and Equipment	.351	1.5	.527	1.7
Miscellaneous Supplies	1.361	1.5	2.042	6.8
Specialty Contractors	.196	1.6	.314	1.0
Nuclear Insurance	.500	1.4	.700	2.3
License Fees	.038	1.0	.038	.1
Subtotal	17.038	-	30.325	100.0
Contingency	4.260	-	7.581	-
Total Costs	21.298	1.8	37.906	-

Source: Commercial Nuclear Power 1990: Prospects for the United States and the World, U.S. Department of Energy, DOE/ EIA-0348(89), Washington, D.C., January 1991, p. 32, from Electric Power Research Institute, Updated Costs for Decommissioning Nuclear Power Facilities, EPRI NP-4012 (Palo Alto, CA, May 1985), p. 12. These estimates do not include dismantling costs. Cost adjustment factors rounded to nearest tenths. Notes: 1. Cost adjustments for energy are based on cost adjustment 2.6 for electricity and 3.4 for fuel oil.

★ 295 ★

Safe Storage Preparation Costs for Pressure Water Reactor

Cost Category	Estimated 1978 Costs (million dollars)	Cost Adjustment Factor	Estimated 1984 Costs (million dollars)	Percent of Total Estimated Costs Before Contingency Allowance
Disposal of Radioactive Material (Radioactive Wastes)	0.544	2.3	1.262	8.7
Staff Labor	3.651	1.6	5.842	40.9
Energy	1.865	2.6	4.849	33.9
Tools and Equipment	.075	1.5	.113	.8
Miscellaneous Supplies	.892	1.5	1.338	9.4
Specialty Contractors	.305	1.6	.488	3.4
Nuclear Insurance	.294	1.4	.412	2.9

[Continued]

★ 295 ★

Safe Storage Preparation Costs for Pressure Water Reactor
[Continued]

Cost Category	Estimated 1978 Costs (million dollars)	Cost Adjustment Factor	Estimated 1984 Costs (million dollars)	Percent of Total Estimated Costs Before Contingency Allowance
License Fees	0	-	-	-
Subtotal	7.626	-	14.304	100.0
Contingency	1.907	-	3.576	-
Total Costs	9.533	1.9	17.880	-

Source: Commercial Nuclear Power 1990: Prospects for the United States and the World, U.S. Department of Energy, DOE/EIA-0348(89), Washington, D.C., January 1991, p. 31, from Electric Power Research Institute, *Updated Costs for Decommissioning Nuclear Power Facilities*, EPRI NP-4012 (Palo Alto, CA, May 1985), p. 12. These estimates do not include dismantling costs. Cost adjustment factors rounded to nearest tenths.

Pollution Control

★ 296 ★

Air & Water Pollution Abatement Expenditures

Data are shown in millions of 1982 dollars.

Year	Air							Water				
	Total	Mobile sources[1]			Total[2]	Stationary sources		Total[4]	Industrial		Public sewer systems[5]	
		Total	Cars	Trucks		Industrial						
						Facilities	Operations[3]		Facilities	Operations[3]	Facilities	Operations[3]
1975	20,768	9,324	7,419	1,904	11,444	6,669	4,348	22,840	4,200	2,950	8,997	3,428
1980	24,744	11,764	8,818	2,946	12,980	5,946	6,304	24,647	3,725	4,081	8,942	4,694
1981	35,850	13,401	10,564	2,837	12,448	5,446	6,299	21,984	3,259	4,180	6,882	4,880
1982	24,961	13,464	10,530	2,934	11,496	5,086	5,675	21,199	3,080	4,022	6,148	5,156
1983	26,367	15,581	12,274	3,307	10,785	4,104	5,990	21,543	2,811	4,509	5,551	5,475
1984	28,591	17,561	13,481	4,081	11,030	4,115	6,260	23,257	2,900	4,795	6,387	5,649
1985	29,665	18,697	14,209	4,488	10,968	3,935	6,452	24,724	2,995	5,035	7,005	6,016
1986	30,580	19,508	14,804	4,704	10,073	3,884	6,660	26,386	2,853	5,319	7,774	6,691
1987, prel.	28,253	16,746	12,392	4,354	11,508	3,955	7,039	27,933	3,131	5,987	8,256	7,081

Source: U.S. Department of Commerce, Bureau of the Census, *Statistical Abstract of the United States 1990 (110th ed.)*, Superintendent of Documents, Washington, D.C., p. 207, from U.S. Bureau of Economic Analysis, *Survey of Current Business*, June 1989. *Notes:* 1. Excludes expenditures to reduce emissions from sources other than cars and trucks. 2. Includes other expenditures not shown separately. 3. Operation facilities. 4. Includes nonpoint sources not shown separately. 5. Includes expenditures for private connectors to sewer systems, by owners of animal feedlots, and by government enterprises.

★ 297 ★

Chemical Industry Pollution Abatement Expenditures

Data are shown in millions of dollars.

Year	Chemicals and allied products							
	Capital expenditures				Operating costs			
	Total	Air	Water	Solid waste	Total	Air	Water	Solid waste
1973	395.9	164.4	214.6	16.8	502.3	174.1	247.6	80.2
1974	539.2	250.6	264.4	24.1	643.3	203.8	335.6	104.0
1975	780.2	359.5	387.7	35.0	807.4	249.9	430.9	126.7
1976	942.0	319.8	577.4	44.7	983.5	295.6	514.7	173.2
1977	982.5	339.9	593.1	49.6	1,238.3	335.5	685.2	217.6
1978	827.5	376.3	385.9	65.1	1,473.0	398.8	794.1	280.1
1979	770.9	314.6	360.7	95.6	1,667.5	485.3	895.2	287.0
1980	780.7	325.9	350.0	104.8	1,851.8	539.9	942.9	368.8
1981	752.8	335.0	322.2	95.6	2,047.8	571.7	1,069.1	406.9
1982	627.6	272.8	256.5	98.3	2,106.5	556.1	1,112.3	438.2
1983	395.4	159.0	187.4	49.0	2,198.2	624.9	1,106.0	467.4
1984	418.1	142.9	212.4	32.7	2,345.4	622.0	1,206.3	517.1
1985	738.1	193.7	271.5	272.5	2,540.0	672.9	1,267.7	599.4
1986	624.4	197.8	325.5	101.0	2,654.3	646.5	1,301.8	705.9

Source: Council on Environmental Quality, *20th Annual Report 1990*, Washington, D.C., p. 432, from U.S. Department of Commerce, Bureau of the Census. *Pollution Abatement Costs and Expenditures*, annual. Current industrial reports, MA-200. Washington, D.C. Statistics cover manufacturing establishments with 20 employees or more. Capital expenditures are new capital expenditures for pollution abatement. Operating costs are related to pollution abatement activities (including payments to government for the costs of pollution removal). Totals may not agree because of independent rounding.

★ 298 ★

Electric Utility Environmental Operating Costs by States

Data represent environmental protection expenditures by investor-owned electric utilities within each state for the year ending December 31, 1989. Values are shown in thousands of dollars.

State and Utility	Depreciation Expenses	Labor, Maintenance, Materials, and Supplies	Operation of Facilities	Fly Ash and Sulfur Removal	Differences in Cost of Environmentally Clean Fuel	Replacement Power Costs	Taxes and Fees	Administrative and General	Other Environmental Protection Expenses	Total
Total	651,927	570,398	50,467	166,983	535,311	38,587	42,042	39,361	146,076	2,241,152
Alabama										
Alabama Power Co.	0	10,821	0	7,650	0	0	0	0	42,546	61,016
Southern Electric Generating Co.	0	425	0	1,603	0	0	1	0	2,490	4,520
Arizona										
Arizona Public Service Co.	31,055	28,348	77	2,429	46	0	6.536	815	2,266	71,573
Century Power Corp.	6,438	1,780	3,317	842	0	0	646	0	0	13,024
Tucson Electric Power Co.	10,121	2,648	834	765	0	0	1,774	185	0	16,328
Arkansas										
Arkansas Power & Light Co.	0	0	0	0	0	0	0	0	0	0

[Continued]

★ 298 ★

Utility Environmental Operating Costs by States
[Continued]

State and Utility	Depreci- ation Expenses	Labor, Maintenance, Materials, and Supplies	Operation of Facilities	Fly Ash and Sulfur Removal	Differen- ces in Cost of En- vironmen- tally Clean Fuel	Replace- ment Power Costs	Taxes and Fees	Adminis- trative and General	Other Environ- mental Protection Expenses	Total
California										
Pacific Gas & Electric Co.	0	0	0	0	0	0	0	0	0	0
San Diego Gas & Electric Co.	0	550	368	0	0	0	0	28	0	946
Southern California Edison Co.	0	0	0	0	0	0	0	0	0	0
Colorado										
Public Service Co. of Colorado	0	4,100	779	2,367	207	1,327	0	0	0	8,781
Connecticut										
Citizens Utilities Co.	0	0	0	0	0	0	0	0	0	0
Connecticut Light & Power Co.	0	0	0	0	0	0	0	0	0	0
Connecticut Yankee Atom Power Co.	0	0	0	0	0	0	0	0	0	0
Holyoke Power & Electric Co.	0	0	0	0	0	0	0	0	0	0
United Illuminating Co.	0	0	0	0	0	0	0	0	0	0
Delaware										
Delmarva Power & Light	0	0	0	0	0	0	0	0	0	0
District of Columbia										
Potomac Electric Power Co.	0	0	0	0	0	0	0	0	0	0
Florida										
Florida Power & Light Co.	0	0	0	0	0	0	0	0	0	0
Florida Power Corp.	13,022	0	0	368	36,925	0	0	0	12	50,327
Gulf Power Co.	8,263	3,159	1,780	2,073	6,054	7,545	826	3,226	1,000	33,926
Tampa Electric Co.	0	0	0	0	0	0	0	0	0	0
Georgia										
Georgia Power Co.	55,259	23,743	0	5,666	23,207	0	763	4,898	0	113,537
Savannah Electric & Power Co.	470	187	0	206	0	312	0	0	0	1,176
Hawaii										
Hawaiian Electric Co. Inc.	0	0	0	0	40,600	0	0	0	0	40,600
Maui Electric Co. Ltd.	0	0	0	0	0	0	0	0	0	0
Idaho										
Idaho Power Co.	0	4,616	484	1,232	0	499	0	131	732	7,695
Illinois										
Central Illinois Light Co.	0	3,924	0	1,464	0	0	0	186	0	5,573
Central Illinois Public Service Co.	8,440	11,403	0	689	0	0	38	1,820	52	22,442
Commonwealth Edison Co.	56,258	88,799	1	0	190,622	0	4,290	2,163	37,034	379,167
Electric Energy Inc.	1,169	172	0	0	0	422	0	0	0	1,763
Illinois Power Co.	21,503	1,058	0	0	0	0	0	1,949	0	24,510
Mt. Carmel Public Utility Co.	0	0	0	0	0	0	0	0	0	0
Indiana										
Alcoa Generating Corp.	1,026	1,609	0	0	0	0	0	0	0	2,636
AEP Generating Co.	0	0	0	0	0	0	0	0	0	0
Commonwealth Edison Co. of IN, Inc.	2,290	448	0	0	7,146	0	0	189	1,847	11,919
Indiana Michigan Power Co.	0	0	0	0	0	0	0	0	0	0
Indianapolis Power & Light Co.	15,131	2,233	907	9,208	0	0	8	0	0	27,487
Northern Indiana Public Service Co.	0	13,057	461	1,307	0	0	0	685	104	15,613
Public Service Co. of IN, Inc.	7,059	5,275	0	7,252	0	0	0	1,335	0	20,922
Southern Indiana Gas & Electric Co.	0	0	0	0	0	0	0	0	0	0
Iowa										
Interstate Power Co.	0	141	0	782	0	0	1	0	0	924
Iowa Electric Light & Power Co.	1,707	1,418	0	0	0	0	0	0	0	3,125
Iowa Power & Light Co.	2,755	1,264	253	14	0	0	0	0	0	4,285
Iowa Public Service Co.	0	1,364	0	808	0	0	0	0	2,263	4,436
Iowa Southern Utilities Co.	799	259	172	106	0	0	428	55	0	1,819
Iowa-Illinois Gas & Electric Co.	3,811	3,717	653	17	0	0	397	192	0	8,786
Kansas										
Centel Corp.	0	0	0	0	0	0	0	0	0	0
Kansas Gas & Electric Co.	0	1,726	11	720	706	0	0	0	1,065	4,227
Kansas Power & Light Co.	0	0	0	0	0	0	0	0	0	0
Kentucky										
Kentucky Power Co.	740	702	619	0	0	0	16	0	0	2,076
Kentucky Utilities Co.	5,935	1,073	0	0	16,903	0	199	0	0	24,109
Louisville Gas & Electric Co.	14,712	16,395	1,861	6,385	0	0	614	0	0	39,967
Ohio Valley Transmission Co.	0	0	0	0	0	0	0	0	0	0

[Continued]

★ 298 ★

Utility Environmental Operating Costs by States
[Continued]

State and Utility	Depreci-ation Expenses	Labor, Maintenance, Materials, and Supplies	Operation of Facilities	Fly Ash and Sulfur Removal	Differen-ces in Cost of En-vironmen-tally Clean Fuel	Replace-ment Power Costs	Taxes and Fees	Adminis-trative and General	Other Environ-mental Protection Expenses	Total
Union Light Heat & Power Co.	1	-53	0	0	0	0	0	0	0	-51
Louisiana										
Central Louisiana Electric Co. Inc.	1,713	0	0	294	0	0	0	0	0	2,007
Louisiana Power & Light Co.	0	1,109	0	0	0	0	0	247	0	1,356
New Orleans Public Service Inc.	343	0	0	0	0	0	0	120	0	463
Southwestern Electric Power Co.	5,185	3,205	0	8	0	0	0	0	103	8,500
Maine										
Bangor Hydro-Electric Co.	0	13	0	1	116	0	48	0	0	179
Central Maine Power Co.	0	1,321	0	91	820	0	610	0	0	2,842
Maine Electric Power Co. Inc.	0	0	0	0	0	0	0	0	0	0
Maine Public Service Inc.	0	5	0	1	46	0	19	0	0	72
Maine Yankee Atomic Power Co.	0	0	0	0	0	0	0	0	0	0
Maryland										
Baltimore Gas & Electric Co.	0	0	0	0	0	0	0	0	0	0
Potomac Edison Co.	0	0	0	0	0	0	0	0	0	0
Massachusetts										
Boston Edison Co.	0	7,808	0	94	27,000	0	0	0	0	34,902
Cambridge Electric Light Co.	0	66	4	0	0	0	0	0	0	71
Canal Electric Co.	778	1,519	22	133	0	231	0	0	0	2,684
Commonwealth Electric Co.	0	69	113	26	0	9	0	0	0	217
Eastern Edison Co.	0	0	0	0	0	0	0	0	0	0
Fitchburg Gas & Electric Light Co.	0	0	0	0	0	0	0	0	0	0
Holyoke Water Power Co.	0	0	0	0	0	0	0	0	0	0
Massachusetts Electric Co.	0	0	0	0	0	0	0	46	0	46
Montaup Electric Co.	0	880	11	67	27	115	11	0	0	1,113
New England Power Co.	0	522	0	6,879	0	0	0	820	0	8,221
Western Massachusetts Electric Co.	583	817	0	199	1,494	0	201	0	0	3,295
Yankee Atomic Electric Co.	383	644	0	0	0	0	0	0	0	1,027
Michigan										
Consumers Power Co.	0	0	0	1,081	0	0	0	0	0	1,081
Detroit Edison Co.	72,659	9,909	14,690	2,400	0	0	0	0	0	99,659
Edison Sault Electric Co.	0	0	0	0	0	0	0	0	0	0
Michigan Power Co.	0	0	0	0	0	0	0	0	0	0
Upper Peninsula Power Co.	80	135	0	29	0	0	0	0	12	256
Minnesota										
Minnesota Power & Light Co.	6,013	2,368	0	1,417	0	4,535	0	0	0	14,334
Northern States Power Co.	405	256	0	0	0	0	0	0	0	662
Otter Tail Power Co.	0	0	0	0	0	0	0	0	0	0
Mississippi										
Mississippi Power & Light Co.	2,271	507	0	0	0	0	515	0	0	3,292
Mississippi Power Co.	0	885	83	74	0	0	0	0	3,954	4,996
System Energy Resources Inc.	0	0	0	0	0	0	0	0	0	0
Missouri										
Empire District Electric Co.	0	16	0	1	0	0	0	0	10	27
Kansas City Power & Light Co.	0	3,852	38	978	736	0	0	0	0	5,604
St. Joseph Light & Power Co.	0	67	53	402	0	0	0	0	0	522
Union Electric Co.	0	0	0	0	0	0	0	482	0	482
UtiliCorp United Inc.	0	0	0	0	0	0	0	0	0	0
Montana										
Montana Power Co.	0	925	0	4,607	0	0	1,178	0	0	6,710
Nevada										
Nevada Power Co.	0	5,504	0	0	0	0	0	0	0	5,504
Sierra Pacific Power Co.	1,176	746	0	0	0	499	1	123	0	2,545
New Hampshire										
James River-NH Electric Inc.	0	0	0	0	0	0	0	0	0	0
New England Electric Transmission Corp.	0	0	0	0	0	0	0	0	0	0
Public Service Co. of NH	2,508	2,240	0	0	0	0	1,429	0	387	6,563
New Jersey										
Atlantic City Electric Co.	6,135	3,121	355	707	5,637	41	0	79	1,370	17,445
Jersey Central Power & Light Co.	8,316	0	0	0	0	0	231	585	0	9,132
Public Service Electric & Gas Co.	0	0	0	0	0	0	0	0	0	0

[Continued]

★ 298 ★

Utility Environmental Operating Costs by States
[Continued]

State and Utility	Depreciation Expenses	Labor, Maintenance, Materials, and Supplies	Operation of Facilities	Fly Ash and Sulfur Removal	Differences in Cost of Environmentally Clean Fuel	Replacement Power Costs	Taxes and Fees	Administrative and General	Other Environmental Protection Expenses	Total
Rockland Electric Co.	0	754	25	132	0	0	0	1	35	946
New Mexico										
Public Service Co. of NM	0	0	0	0	0	0	0	0	0	0
New York										
Central Hudson Gas & Electric Corp.	0	0	0	0	0	0	0	0	0	0
Consolidated Edison Co.-NY Inc.	0	0	0	0	0	0	0	0	0	0
Long Island Lighting Co.	0	0	0	0	0	0	0	0	0	0
Long Sault Inc.	0	0	0	0	0	0	0	0	0	0
New York State Electric & Gas Corp.	6,683	12,369	5,555	4,296	8,450	4,968	0	1,442	0	43,763
Niagara Mohawk Power Co.	14	12	12	2	0	9	12	0	0	49
Orange & Rockland Utilities Inc.	0	2,386	61	322	0	0	0	2	81	2,853
Rochester Gas & Electric Corp.	0	0	0	0	94,773	0	0	0	0	94,773
North Carolina										
Carolina Power & Light Co.	63,303	1,963	0	0	0	0	0	0	0	65,266
Duke Power Co.	0	0	0	0	0	0	0	0	0	0
Nantahala Power & Light Co.	0	0	0	0	0	0	0	0	0	0
Yadkin Inc.	0	0	0	0	0	0	0	0	0	0
North Dakota										
MDU Resources Group Inc.	2,483	2,179	0	0	0	0	0	0	0	4,661
Ohio										
Cincinnati Gas & Electric Co.	12,752	7,072	1,070	7,208	0	0	586	69	0	28,758
Cleveland Electric Illumination Co.	0	0	0	0	0	0	0	0	0	0
Columbus Southern Power Co.	7,403	1,871	33	12,359	15,476	52	817	392	150	38,553
Dayton Power & Light Co.	7,719	3,959	486	3,128	2,602	0	0	244	0	18,138
Indiana-Kentucky Electric Corp.	4,997	2,610	2,197	0	0	138	0	23	956	10,921
Ohio Edison Co.	29,500	23,544	80	3,160	27,579	2,176	475	0	0	86,516
Ohio Power Co.	0	0	0	0	0	0	0	0	0	0
Ohio Valley Electric Corp.	4,890	1,125	2,231	0	0	119	18	460	1,098	9,940
Toledo Edison Co.	0	0	0	0	0	0	0	0	0	0
Oklahoma										
Oklahoma Gas & Electric Co.	0	5,744	0	0	0	0	0	0	0	5,744
Public Service Co. of Oklahoma	0	0	0	0	0	0	0	0	0	0
Oregon										
Fale-Safe Inc.	0	0	0	0	0	0	0	0	0	0
PacifiCorp	13,058	15,159	2,478	8,510	0	0	0	0	0	39,205
Portland General Electric Co.	0	0	0	0	0	0	0	0	0	0
Warm Springs Power Enterprises	36	0	0	0	0	0	0	0	0	36
Pennsylvania										
Duquesne Light Co.	15,185	17,788	695	6,431	0	0	282	582	34,005	74,968
Metropolitan Edison Co.	0	0	0	0	0	0	305	0	0	305
Pennsylvania Electric Co.	0	0	0	0	0	0	0	0	0	0
Pennsylvania Power & Light Co.	0	13	0	2	0	0	0	1	1	17
Pennsylvania Power Co.	4,590	3,464	427	585	0	530	118	0	0	9,714
Philadelphia Electric Co.	48,365	54,447	4,057	6,766	27,822	5,058	7,816	219	0	154,550
Safe Harbor Water Pump Corp.	0	0	0	0	0	0	0	0	0	0
Susquehanna Electric Co.	0	0	0	0	0	0	0	0	0	0
UGI Corp.	129	217	0	220	0	0	0	28	0	595
West Penn Power Co.	0	0	0	0	0	0	0	0	0	0
York Haven Power Co.	0	0	0	0	0	0	0	0	0	0
Rhode Island										
Blackstone Valley Electric Co.	0	0	0	0	0	0	0	0	0	0
Narragansett Electric Co.	0	19	0	0	0	0	0	15	0	35
Newport Electric Corp.	0	0	0	0	0	0	0	0	0	0
South Carolina										
Lockhart Power Co.	0	0	0	0	0	0	0	0	0	0
South Carolina Electric & Gas Co.	0	656	0	848	0	2,295	0	0	0	3,799
South Carolina Generating Co. Inc.	0	85	0	418	0	751	0	0	0	1,254
South Dakota										
Black Hills Corp.	1,009	0	213	70	0	0	186	0	0	1,478
Northwestern Public Service Co.	1,026	457	134	397	0	158	309	0	0	2,480

[Continued]

★ 298 ★

Utility Environmental Operating Costs by States
[Continued]

State and Utility	Depreci-ation Expenses	Labor, Maintenance, Materials, and Supplies	Operation of Facilities	Fly Ash and Sulfur Removal	Differen-ces in Cost of En-vironmen-tally Clean Fuel	Replace-ment Power Costs	Taxes and Fees	Adminis-trative and General	Other Environ-mental Protection Expenses	Total
Tennessee										
Kingsport Power Co.	0	121	0	0	0	0	0	0	0	121
Tapoco Inc.	2,295	0	0	0	0	0	0	0	0	0
Texas										
Central Power & Light Co.	0	1,978	1	218	0	0	106	320	0	2,623
El Paso Electric Co.	0	795	5	352	0	0	0	0	0	1,152
Gulf States Utilities Co.	0	1,284	0	128	0	0	275	0	0	1,687
Houston Lighting & Power Co.	0	0	0	0	0	0	0	0	0	0
Southwestern Electric Service Co.	0	0	0	0	0	0	0	0	12	12
Southwestern Public Service Co.	0	0	0	0	0	0	0	0	0	0
Texas Utilities Electric Co.	18,933	88,107	0	20,526	0	0	6,213	12,015	0	145,794
Texas-New Mexico Power Co.	0	0	0	0	0	0	0	0	0	0
West Texas Utilities Co.	0	0	0	0	0	0	0	0	0	0
Vermont										
Central Vermont Public Service Corp.	13	137	0	0	0	0	12	70	0	233
Green Mountain Power Corp.	28	196	0	0	0	0	22	0	0	245
Vermont Electric Power Co. Inc.	0	0	0	0	0	0	0	0	0	0
Vermont Yankee Nuclear Power Corp.	528	2,458	0	0	0	0	194	185	931	4,296
Virginia										
Appalachian Power Co.	0	8,856	0	6	0	0	0	1,097	0	9,958
Virginia Electric & Power Co.	0	0	0	0	0	0	0	0	0	0
Washington										
Puget Sound Power & Light Co.	0	1,167	50	4,064	0	0	0	0	1,476	6,758
Washington Water Power Co.	0	0	0	0	0	0	0	0	0	0
West Virginia										
Monongahela Power Co.	0	0	0	0	0	0	0	0	0	0
Wheeling Power Co.	7	81	0	0	0	0	0	0	0	88
Wisconsin										
Consolidated Water Power Co.	0	0	0	0	0	0	0	0	0	0
Madison Gas & Electric Co.	0	0	0	0	0	0	0	0	0	0
Northern States Power Co.	405	256	0	0	0	0	0	0	0	662
Northwestern Wisconsin Electric Co.	0	0	0	0	0	0	0	0	0	0
South Beloit Water Gas & Electric Co.	20	0	0	0	0	0	0	0	0	20
Superior Water Light & Power Co.	0	0	0	0	0	0	0	0	0	0
Wisconsin Electric Power Co.	6,428	9,021	1,997	5,889	0	0	0	538	123	23,995
Wisconsin Power & Light Co.	5,063	2,043	61	124	316	818	130	166	0	8,721
Wisconsin Public Service Corp.	0	0	0	0	0	0	0	0	0	0
Wisconsin River Power Co.	0	0	0	0	0	0	0	0	0	0

Source: Energy Information Administration, *Financial Statistics of Selected Investor-Owned Electric Utilities 1989*, January 1991, pp. 570-578, from Federal Energy Regulatory Commission, FERC Form 1, "Annual Report of Major Electric Utilities, Licensees and Others." Totals may not equal sum of components because of independent rounding. CWIP stands for "Construction Work in Progress."

★ 299 ★

Electric & Electronics Industry Pollution Abatement Expenditures
Data are shown in millions of dollars.

| Year | Electric, electronic equipment | | | | | | | |
| | Capital expenditures | | | | Operating costs | | | |
	Total	Air	Water	Solid waste	Total	Air	Water	Solid waste
1973	52.7	27.0	22.2	3.5	87.2	20.2	38.9	28.1
1974	55.6	24.6	28.0	3.1	88.6	22.7	39.8	26.2
1975	52.3	22.7	26.2	3.3	97.3	27.6	43.1	26.7
1976	58.4	23.0	31.3	4.1	109.9	26.8	50.8	32.3
1977	63.8	23.0	36.0	4.9	128.1	28.0	63.2	37.1
1978	72.2	32.9	36.0	3.3	148.6	30.7	71.7	46.1
1979	90.9	41.8	42.0	7.1	182.3	46.7	82.8	52.8
1980	79.0	43.5	27.1	8.4	205.0	45.2	87.8	71.9
1981	97.1	48.7	41.0	7.4	247.1	51.8	106.2	88.8
1982	105.9	58.1	40.9	6.9	260.2	55.1	116.6	88.7
1983	97.0	43.8	45.1	8.0	353.8	77.3	142.0	134.5
1984	112.4	38.3	59.5	14.6	364.0	74.6	150.3	139.1
1985	137.7	45.4	74.1	18.3	428.2	78.0	174.0	176.3
1986	125.1	46.6	61.5	17.0	530.8	88.3	210.9	231.5

Source: Council on Environmental Quality, *20th Annual Report 1990*, Washington, D.C., p. 435, from U.S. Department of Commerce, Bureau of the Census: Pollution abatement costs and expenditures, annual. Current industrial reports, MA-200. Washington, D.C. Statistics cover manufacturing establishments with 20 employees or more. Capital expenditures are new capital expenditures for pollution abatement. Operating costs are related to pollution abatement activities (including payments to government for the costs of pollution removal). Totals may not agree because of independent rounding.

★ 300 ★

Fabricated Metal Industry Pollution Abatement Expenditures
Data are shown in millions of dollars.

| Year | Fabricated metal products | | | | | | | |
| | Capital expenditures | | | | Operating costs | | | |
	Total	Air	Water	Solid waste	Total	Air	Water	Solid waste
1973	63.7	39.6	21.5	2.7	84.8	27.0	35.7	22.2
1974	90.5	56.4	28.2	5.9	110.1	34.5	44.9	30.7
1975	77.5	46.9	29.0	1.7	109.5	32.6	45.7	31.3
1976	72.9	35.5	34.1	3.4	124.3	35.4	52.7	36.1
1977	76.7	32.5	39.2	5.0	149.2	40.3	66.1	42.8
1978	61.6	33.1	26.2	2.3	168.7	42.1	73.8	52.8
1979	66.1	36.7	24.5	4.9	220.9	57.0	99.7	64.2
1980	76.4	37.5	34.8	4.2	219.2	49.0	88.2	81.9
1981	75.7	37.5	30.4	7.6	230.5	51.6	93.4	85.0
1982	95.9	57.9	43.3	6.7	223.5	48.6	103.4	71.5

[Continued]

★ 300 ★

Fabricated Metal Industry Pollution Abatement Expenditures
[Continued]

Year	Fabricated metal products							
	Capital expenditures				Operating costs			
	Total	Air	Water	Solid waste	Total	Air	Water	Solid waste
1983	70.6	27.0	32.9	10.6	366.3	81.9	137.8	146.6
1984	125.3	25.2	82.5	17.6	348.5	64.9	128.2	155.4
1985	116.9	40.4	59.7	16.8	408.1	79.4	163.2	165.5
1986	135.8	36.7	80.9	18.2	502.5	95.6	187.7	219.2

Source: Council on Environmental Quality, *20th Annual Report 1990*, Washington, D.C., p. 434, from U.S. Department of Commerce, Bureau of the Census. *Pollution Abatement Costs and Expenditures*, annual. Current industrial reports, MA-200. Washington, D.C. Statistics cover manufacturing establishments with 20 employees or more. Capital expenditures are new capital expenditures for pollution abatement. Operating costs are related to pollution abatement activities (including payments to government for the costs of pollution removal). Totals may not agree because of independent rounding.

★ 301 ★

Federal Environmental Spending Allocations

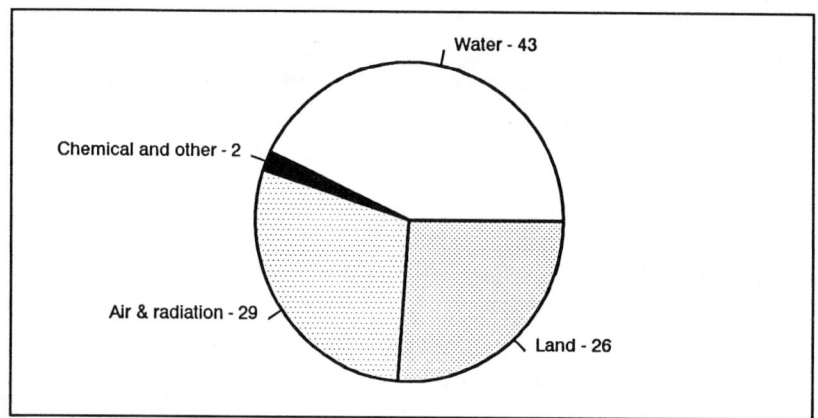

Allocation of environmental spending, by issue, shown as percent of total. Data refers to 1987.

Issue	Percent
Water	43
Air & radiation	29
Chemical and other	2
Land	26

Source: Science, March 8, 1991, p. 1182, from *Environmental Investments: The Costs of a Clean Environment*.

★ 302 ★

Federal Government Spending - 1990

Breakdown by function, of how a family's tax dollar will be spent by the federal government. The example assumes a two-earner family with two dependent children and a household income of $45,000 per year.

Function	Family's Share		
	Amount $	% of Total	Spending (Billions)
Income Security[1]	4,237	32.75	418.5
National Defense	3,070	23.73	303.3
Net interest	1,751	13.54	173.0
Health[2]	1,643	12.70	162.3
Education, Training, Employment, Social Services	415	3.21	41.0
Veteran's Benefits and Services	307	2.37	30.3
Transportation	302	2.33	29.8
Environmental and Natural Resources	184	1.42	1.82
International Affairs	184	1.42	18.2
Commerce and Housing Credit	174	1.35	17.2
General Science, Space, and Technology	168	1.30	16.6
Agriculture	151	1.17	14.9
Administration of Justice	128	0.99	12.6
General Government	114	0.88	11.3
Community and regional Development	79	0.61	7.8
Energy	30	0.23	3.0
Total[3]	12,938	100.00	1,233.3

Source: Consumers' Research, April 1990, p. 27, from Tax Foundation computations based on FiscYear 1991 U.S. Budget presented January 29, 1990, and 1990 tax laws from U.S. Department of Treasury. *Notes:* 1. Primarily Social Security. Includes federal employee retirement, unemployment compensation, and nutrition assistance. Excludes veteran's income security. 2. Primarily Medicare and Medicaid. Excludes veteran's health care. 3. After deduction $44.7 billion in undistributed and offsetting receipts not classified by function.

★ 303 ★

Federal Spending by Year

Source or Function	1980	1982	1983	1984	1985	1986	1987	1988	1989, est.	Percent Distribution	
										1980	1989
Natural resources and environment[1]	13.9	13.0	12.7	12.6	13.4	13.6	13.4	14.6	16.5	2.35	1.45
Water resources	4.2	3.9	3.9	4.1	4.1	4.0	3.8	4.0	4.4	0.71	0.39
Conservation and land management	1.0	1.1	1.5	1.3	1.5	1.4	1.5	2.2	3.3	0.18	0.29
Recreational resources	1.7	1.4	1.5	1.6	1.6	1.5	1.6	1.7	1.7	0.28	0.15
Pollution control and abatement	5.5	5.0	4.3	4.0	4.5	4.8	4.9	4.8	5.1	0.93	0.45
Other natural resources	1.4	1.5	1.5	1.6	1.7	1.9	1.7	1.8	2.0	0.24	0.18
Energy[1]	10.2	13.5	9.4	7.1	5.7	4.7	4.1	2.3	4.1	1.72	0.36
Supply	8.4	8.3	6.1	3.3	2.6	2.8	2.3	0.7	2.4	1.42	0.21
Conservation	0.6	0.5	0.5	0.5	0.5	0.5	0.3	0.3	0.3	0.10	0.03

[Continued]

★ 303 ★

Federal Spending by Year
[Continued]

Source or Function	1980	1982	1983	1984	1985	1986	1987	1988	1989, est.	Percent Distribution	
										1980	1989
Emergency preparedness	0.3	3.9	1.9	2.5	1.8	0.6	0.8	0.6	0.7	0.06	0.06
Information, policy, and regulation	0.9	0.9	0.9	0.8	0.7	0.8	0.7	0.6	0.7	0.15	0.06

Source: U.S. Department of Commerce, Bureau of the Census, *Statistical Abstract of the United States 1990 (110th ed.),* Superintendent of Documents, Washington, D.C., p. 311, from U.S. Office of Management and Budget, *Historical Tables, Budget of the United States Government, annual. Notes:* 1. Totals reflect interfund and intragovernmental transactions and/or other functions, not shown separately.

★ 304 ★

Federal Spending to Protect Environment - 1991
The budget provides over $2 billion in new spending to protect the environment. Figures are in millions of dollars.

Summary of Major Initiatives	1990	1991	Increases
America the Beautiful	361	630	+269
Reforestation	(-)	(175)	(+175)
Protecting America's Wetlands	372	460	+88
EPA Operating Budget	1,936	2,166	+230
Maintaining Environmental Infrastructure (DOI)	488	579	+91
Superfund	1,530	1,740	+210
Federal Facility Cleanup:			
Department of Energy	2,190	2,791	+601
Department of Defense	1,402	1,520	+118
Other Agencies	116	175	+59
Global Change Research	659	1,034	+375
Natural Resources Research	710	814	+104
Proposed Increase for Major Initiatives	-	-	+2,032[1]

Source: Budget of the United States Government, Fiscal Year 1991, p. 119 *Note:* 1. Total has been adjusted to eliminate double counting.

★ 305 ★

Food Industry Pollution Abatement Expenditures

Data are shown in millions of dollars.

Year	Food and kindred products							
	Capital expenditures				Operating costs			
	Total	Air	Water	Solid waste	Total	Air	Water	Solid waste
1973	196.7	77.6	104.8	14.3	203.1	39.1	110.4	53.6
1974	199.2	73.4	111.7	14.3	268.9	48.8	143.5	76.8
1975	180.9	75.6	93.9	11.4	294.2	53.2	153.7	87.7
1976	207.5	102.5	97.6	7.4	345.9	57.7	187.5	100.5
1977	183.9	67.9	103.6	12.5	357.1	56.2	211.6	89.5
1978	175.0	67.7	94.4	12.9	412.0	69.4	243.2	99.4
1979	182.7	57.9	111.1	13.6	504.2	91.0	297.9	115.3
1980	208.2	61.7	133.0	13.5	519.4	81.6	314.3	123.6
1981	173.5	53.9	104.8	14.8	579.1	78.3	343.3	157.5
1982	169.3	47.4	110.9	11.0	522.1	77.1	328.1	116.2
1983	153.8	37.7	105.1	10.9	649.6	96.1	402.3	151.3
1984	154.5	50.6	91.8	12.2	714.4	101.3	458.1	155.0
1985	155.1	66.2	77.4	11.7	832.1	106.3	525.2	201.0
1986	185.8	61.9	108.2	15.7	932.1	126.0	559.9	246.1

Source: Council on Environmental Quality, *20th Annual Report 1990*, Washington, D.C., p. 437, from U.S. Department of Commerce, Bureau of the Census: Pollution abatement costs and expenditures, annual. Current industrial reports, MA-200. Washington, D.C. Statistics cover manufacturing establishments with 20 employees or more. Capital expenditures are new capital expenditures for pollution abatement. Operating costs are related to pollution abatement activities (including payments to government for the costs of pollution removal). Totals may not agree because of independent rounding.

★ 306 ★

Instrumentation Industry Pollution Abatement Expenditures

Data are shown in millions of dollars.

Year	Instruments and related products							
	Capital expenditures				Operating costs			
	Total	Air	Water	Solid waste	Total	Air	Water	Solid waste
1973	11.8	3.0	5.6	3.2	21.9	2.0	11.3	8.6
1974	15.7	3.6	6.7	5.5	34.1	4.9	15.0	14.3
1975	29.6	11.2	17.3	1.1	38.5	5.9	19.5	13.2
1976	32.3	10.9	12.2	9.3	45.7	8.7	22.3	14.8
1977	24.4	14.5	8.5	1.4	47.3	9.0	23.0	15.4
1978	16.9	6.8	9.5	0.6	55.8	7.3	26.9	21.6
1979	23.2	13.0	7.7	2.5	69.2	10.6	30.7	27.9
1980	27.2	11.3	12.7	3.2	77.1	11.3	33.7	32.1
1981	40.1	14.4	23.7	2.1	90.4	12.8	40.0	37.9
1982	30.0	18.7	9.8	1.4	80.2	12.9	33.9	33.3

[Continued]

★ 306 ★

Instrumentation Industry Pollution Abatement Expenditures
[Continued]

Year	Instruments and related products							
	Capital expenditures				Operating costs			
	Total	Air	Water	Solid waste	Total	Air	Water	Solid waste
1983	21.1	10.4	9.5	1.2	163.8	25.0	53.9	85.0
1984	23.7	10.9	11.1	1.7	161.9	23.6	67.3	70.8
1985	24.8	13.8	7.8	3.1	165.1	24.2	71.8	69.1
1986	18.8	10.8	5.1	2.9	164.4	19.9	78.6	66.0

Source: Council on Environmental Quality, *20th Annual Report 1990*, Washington, D.C., p. 436, from U.S. Department of Commerce, Bureau of the Census: Pollution abatement costs and expenditures, annual. Current industrial reports, MA-200. Washington, D.C. Statistics cover manufacturing establishments with 20 employees or more. Capital expenditures are new capital expenditures for pollution abatement. Operating costs are related to pollution abatement activities (including payments to government for the costs of pollution removal). Totals may not agree because of independent rounding.

★ 307 ★

Lumber Industry Pollution Abatement Expenditures
Data are shown in millions of dollars.

Year	Lumber and wood products							
	Capital expenditures				Operating costs			
	Total	Air	Water	Solid waste	Total	Air	Water	Solid waste
1973	62.7	41.5	11.7	9.6	61.6	14.9	18.5	28.2
1974	81.1	58.4	7.6	15.0	64.2	19.5	14.0	30.8
1975	75.1	46.4	7.7	21.0	70.5	22.7	19.6	28.3
1976	51.1	29.5	9.2	12.5	81.3	26.6	21.1	33.6
1977	59.9	33.9	19.1	6.9	73.4	20.4	19.2	33.9
1978	84.5	46.9	25.6	12.0	90.7	27.7	19.4	43.7
1979	93.6	67.5	12.3	13.8	115.4	40.2	25.5	49.7
1980	81.5	55.8	15.6	10.1	129.1	39.6	32.9	56.4
1981	78.5	49.2	10.5	18.8	134.7	43.2	26.9	64.6
1982	33.2	20.0	11.7	1.5	87.1	26.4	23.4	37.3
1983	25.2	18.0	4.0	3.2	102.8	31.1	27.8	43.9
1984	48.5	24.1	18.8	5.7	114.2	41.2	30.7	42.4
1985	34.5	15.2	6.3	13.0	139.1	41.8	35.3	62.0
1986	33.3	17.8	11.0	4.6	178.9	61.7	42.6	74.7

Source: Council on Environmental Quality, *20th Annual Report 1990*, Washington, D.C., p. 438, from U.S. Department of Commerce, Bureau of the Census: Pollution abatement costs and expenditures, annual. Current industrial reports, MA-200. Washington, D.C. Statistics cover manufacturing establishments with 20 employees or more. Capital expenditures are new capital expenditures for pollution abatement. Operating costs are related to pollution abatement activities (including payments to government for the costs of pollution removal). Totals may not agree because of independent rounding.

★ 308 ★

Machinery Industry Pollution Abatement Expenditures

Electrical machinery is not included in this industry. Data are shown in millions of dollars.

Year	Machinery, except electrical							
	Capital expenditures				Operating costs			
	Total	Air	Water	Solid waste	Total	Air	Water	Solid waste
1973	56.3	36.6	15.6	4.1	72.5	19.7	23.0	29.9
1974	67.7	41.9	17.6	8.1	91.7	24.3	29.1	38.2
1975	60.5	37.5	20.8	2.3	98.0	28.4	33.7	36.0
1976	69.4	44.8	21.8	2.9	117.9	30.8	37.7	49.6
1977	90.2	42.3	42.4	5.5	135.4	33.1	49.8	52.6
1978	81.5	41.2	27.8	12.6	158.8	41.0	54.4	63.1
1979	84.5	38.5	38.2	7.8	200.2	50.1	69.0	81.1
1980	74.5	34.0	34.9	5.6	206.4	48.0	73.0	85.3
1981	67.1	30.9	28.0	8.2	220.9	47.3	81.6	91.7
1982	78.2	29.2	42.2	6.8	207.6	46.6	85.3	75.7
1983	51.0	17.7	19.0	14.3	290.5	58.0	105.0	127.5
1984	43.1	22.6	6.7	314.4	68.4	115.7	130.3	301.7
1985	69.0	21.2	35.1	12.7	344.0	76.0	119.9	147.7
1986	48.7	16.7	25.7	6.3	358.8	81.4	128.3	149.1

Source: Council on Environmental Quality, *20th Annual Report 1990*, Washington, D.C., p. 435, from U.S. Department of Commerce, Bureau of the Census. *Pollution Abatement Costs and Expenditures*, annual. Current industrial reports, MA-200. Washington, D.C. Statistics cover manufacturing establishments with 20 employees or more. Capital expenditures are new capital expenditures for pollution abatement. Operating costs are related to pollution abatement activities (including payments to government for the costs of pollution removal). Totals may not agree because of independent rounding.

★ 309 ★

Paper Industry Environmental Spending by Region

Reported spending for 1990-92 by region and facility type. Data for the U.S. are shown in thousands of dollars; data for Canada are shown in thousands of Canadian dollars.

	Environmental Quality Spending						Totals					
	Water	Percent	Air	Percent	Solid waste	Percent	Production	Percent	Environmental	Percent	Grand Total	Percent
U.S.												
New England	44,670	4	20,920	3	9,150	12	1,127,900	7	74,740	4	1,202,640	7
Mid-Atlantic	15,709	1	19,907	3	1,409	2	409,648	3	37,025	2	446,673	3
East North Central	109,905	10	20,135	3	7,785	11	1,862,990	12	137,825	7	2,000,815	12
West North Central	6,480	1	6,480	1	540	1	621,550	4	13,500	1	635,050	4
South Atlantic	390,176	37	272,105	36	27,713	37	4,178,432	28	689,994	37	4,868,426	29
East South Central	326,994	31	211,910	28	18,896	25	3,978,800	26	557,800	30	4,536,600	927
West South Central	20,820	2	130,043	17	7,738	10	1,401,151	9	158,301	8	1,559,452	9
Mountain/Pacific	140,735	13	76,850	10	1,200	2	1,558,003	10	218,785	12	1,776,788	10
Total	1,055,489		758,350		74,131		15,138,474		1,887,970		17,026,444	
Canada												
Maritimes	63,575	3	59,000	11	6,325	9	102,677	1	128,900	5	231,577	2

[Continued]

★ 309 ★

Paper Industry Environmental Spending
[Continued]

	Environmental Quality Spending						Totals					
	Water	Percent	Air	Percent	Solid waste	Percent	Production	Percent	Environmental	Percent	Grand Total	Percent
Quebec	319,129	17	69,135	12	35,071	52	2,348,584	31	423,335	17	2,771,919	27
Ontario	119,601	6	16,020	3	510	1	1,391,209	18	136,131	5	1,527,340	15
Central	0	0	0	0	0	0	0	0	0	0		
West	1,391,379	73	417,675	74	25,929	38	3,786,893	50	1,834,983	73	5,621,876	55
Total	1,893,684		561,830		67,835		7,629,363		2,523,349		10,152,712	

Source: *Pulp & Paper*, January 1991, p. 103 and 106.

★ 310 ★

Paper Industry Environmental Spendings
Production capacity and resources of the top paper producers worldwide.

Company	Production capacity		% of Production From Owned Timberland	Environmental Spending (in millions of dollars)
	Market Pulp/Paper (1000 short tons)	Wood Products (in millions)		
International Paper	9,854	Lumber 887 Panels 722[1]	45[2]	
James River[3]	3,700	None	15	70[4]
Kimberly-Clark	2,589	None	67	18
Scott Paper	3,500	None	75[3]	8
Noranda	2,323	Lumber 1,033 Panels 4,881	70	31
Champion International	5,103	Lumber 1,599 Panels 2,412	46	25
Stone Container	4,908	Lumber 600 Panels 780	20[2]	NA
Great Northern Nekoosa	4,405	Lumber 294 Panels 160	35[2]	NA
Georgia-Pacific	5,310	Lumber 2,603 Panels 9,860	40[2]	43
Weyerhaeuser	4,887	Lumber 3,209 Panels 3,834	80[3]	53
Mo Och Domsjo	2,318	(See note 5)	24	49
OJI Paper[4]	2,186	None	NA	4
Stora Kopparbergs	3,804	Lumber 400	35	NA
Honshu Paper[4]	1,347	None	NA	NA
Svenska Cellulosa	1,727	Lumber 233	60	7
Jujo Paper[6]	1,786	None	NA	11
Boise Cascade	3,475	Lumber 938 Panels 1,901	42	25
Daishowa Paper MFG.[6]	2,163	None	0	12

[Continued]

★ 310 ★

Paper Industry Environmental Spendings
[Continued]

Company	Production capacity		% of Production From Owned Timberland	Environmental Spending (in millions of dollars)
	Market Pulp/Paper (1000 short tons)	Wood Products (in millions)		
Canadian Pacific Forest Prod.	2,900	Lumber 605	60	7
Mead	2,250	Lumber 565 Panels 235	19	4

Source: Financial World, February 20, 1990, from companies, industry analysts. Lumber is in Bd. ft. and panels are in Sq. ft. *Notes:* 1. Plywood and veneer. 2. Analysts' estimates. 3. Year end 4/24/88. 4. Fiscal 1989. 5. Produced 200,000 cu. meters of timber in 1988. 6. As of 3/31/89. NA means not available. Figures as of 12/31/88 unless otherwise noted.

★ 311 ★

Paper Industry Pollution Abatement Expenditures

Data are shown in millions of dollars.

Year	Paper and allied products							
	Capital expenditures				Operating costs			
	Total	Air	Water	Solid waste	Total	Air	Water	Solid waste
1973	339.6	166.4	161	12.1	220.5	59.2	118.1	43.2
1974	476.9	270.8	193.2	12.9	289.0	81.2	152.0	55.7
1975	605.3	323.0	266.0	16.3	344.0	100.9	185.5	57.5
1976	486.6	180.6	278.6	27.3	430.3	123.3	239.1	67.3
1977	427.4	134.1	261.7	31.6	529.0	133.5	309.0	86.4
1978	341.6	123.9	189.0	28.7	622.0	158.4	357.6	105.6
1979	426.4	207.0	180.6	38.8	698.2	176.6	400.5	121.1
1980	339.6	197.4	111.2	31.0	762.1	196.2	436.7	129.1
1981	285.5	168.0	86.5	31.1	829.7	211.8	469.9	148.0
1982	313.4	190.0	93.7	29.7	796.0	206.7	455.2	0.0
1983	216.1	122.3	65.9	27.9	919.1	226.5	508.9	183.6
1984	262.3	151.9	68.2	42.1	1,060.1	280.7	566.1	213.2
1985	332.4	190.9	106.0	35.6	1,120.8	313.0	573.4	234.4
1986	271.3	137.1	96.9	37.3	1,154.6	319.2	565.7	269.7

Source: Council on Environmental Quality, *20th Annual Report 1990*, Washington, D.C., p. 438, from U.S. Department of Commerce, Bureau of the Census: Pollution abatement costs and expenditures, annual. Current industrial reports, MA-200. Washington, D.C. Statistics cover manufacturing establishments with 20 employees or more. Capital expenditures are new capital expenditures for pollution abatement. Operating costs are related to pollution abatement activities (including payments to government for the costs of pollution removal). Totals may not agree because of independent rounding.

★ 312 ★

Petroleum & Coal Industry Pollution Abatement Expenditures

Data are shown in millions of dollars.

Year	Petroleum and coal products							
	Capital expenditures				Operating costs			
	Total	Air	Water	Solid waste	Total	Air	Water	Solid waste
1973	321.8	222.5	96.1	3.2	337.8	192.5	125.4	19.9
1974	462.3	341.3	119.7	1.3	420.1	238.3	153.3	28.5
1975	555.7	398.2	155.7	1.7	563.1	339.4	192.1	31.7
1976	441.4	236.5	199.8	5.2	774.8	466.1	263.3	45.3
1977	368.5	167.7	195.6	5.3	948.0	601.3	289.3	57.4
1978	419.3	311.2	100.5	7.6	997.4	636.4	304.1	57.0
1979	534.3	397.8	119.4	17.1	1,173.8	750.7	370.8	25.3
1980	531.9	402.3	114.2	15.4	1,415.0	910.1	406.9	101.0
1981	590.6	440.8	131.7	18.2	1,685.5	1,118.0	437.2	130.2
1982	712.1	533.2	165.7	13.1	1,800.8	1,195.1	472.0	133.7
1983	485.0	308.2	164.7	12.0	1,893.7	1,203.6	552.3	137.9
1984	311.7	195.1	96.8	19.8	2,083.5	1,327.9	583.8	171.1
1985	290.4	175.0	88.4	27.0	2,063.4	1,278.5	586.5	198.5
1986	424.3	273.6	121.5	29.2	2,005.2	1,230.9	578.0	196.4

Source: Council on Environmental Quality, *20th Annual Report 1990*, Washington, D.C., p. 432, from U.S. Department of Commerce, Bureau of the Census. *Pollution Abatement Costs and Expenditures*, annual. Current industrial reports, MA-200. Washington, D.C. Statistics cover manufacturing establishments with 20 employees or more. Capital expenditures are new capital expenditures for pollution abatement. Operating costs are related to pollution abatement activities (including payments to government for the costs of pollution removal). Totals may not agree because of independent rounding.

★ 313 ★

Pollution Abatement Capital Expenditures and Operating Costs

Values are shown in millions of dollars based on a sample of 20,000 manufacturing establishments.

Year and Industry Group	Pollution Abatement Capital Expenditures					Pollution Abatement Gross Operating Costs[1]				
	Total	Air	Water	Solid Waste		Total	Air	Water	Solid Waste	
				Hazardous	Nonhazardous				Hazardous	Nonhazardous
1980	3,502.9	2,105.5	1,146.5	251.0		8,141.8	3,297.8	3,193.1	1,650.6	
1981	3,484.9	2,193.6	1,028.4	263.1		9,109.9	3,697.8	3,554.3	1,855.7	
1982	3,024.1	1,828.2	977.0	218.5		8,565.0	3,455.9	3,488.5	1,619.9	
1983	2,045.0	1,029.0	819.0	60.9	136.0	9,925.1	3,806.9	3,943.2	573.5	1,601.6
1984	2,171.8	1,037.8	887.8	89.7	156.7	10,888.1	4,189.3	4,296.4	770.3	1,632.2
1985	2,809.7	1,292.3	1,017.9	326.2	172.9	11,677.9	4,330.2	4,609.5	943.0	1,795.3
All industries, 1986[2]	2,846.9	1,462.8	1,038.7	168.7	176.0	12,258.1	4,261.0	4,820.2	1,135.5	2,041.4
Food	185.8	61.9	108.2	2.9	12.8	932.1	126.0	560.0	5.8	240.4
Lumber and wood	33.4	17.8	11.0	1.7	2.8	178.9	61.7	42.6	13.5	61.2
Paper	271.3	137.1	96.9	4.8	32.5	1,154.6	319.2	565.7	32.0	237.7
Chemicals	624.4	197.9	325.5	57.3	43.6	2,654.3	646.5	1,301.9	350.0	355.9
Petroleum	424.3	273.6	121.5	22.9	6.2	2,005.2	1,230.9	578.0	109.7	86.6

[Continued]

★ 313 ★

Pollution Abatement Capital Expenditures and Operating Costs
[Continued]

Year and Industry Group	Pollution Abatement Capital Expenditures					Pollution Abatement Gross Operating Costs[1]				
	Total	Air	Water	Solid Waste		Total	Air	Water	Solid Waste	
				Hazardous	Nonhazardous				Hazardous	Nonhazardous
Stone, clay, glass	84.4	53.1	13.7	3.8	13.8	423.6	237.0	68.3	19.0	99.4
Primary metal	225.9	102.8	74.6	23.9	24.5	1,741.9	968.5	509.4	100.5	163.6
Fabricated metals	135.8	36.7	80.9	9.6	8.6	502.5	95.6	187.7	99.6	119.6
Machinery exc. electrical	48.7	16.7	25.7	3.8	2.5	487.0	209.7	128.2	60.8	88.3
Electrical machinery	125.1	46.6	61.5	13.9	3.0	530.8	88.3	210.9	114.1	117.4
Transportation equipment	541.1	432.4	81.8	18.4	8.4	770.0	195.7	269.4	127.4	177.5

Source: U.S. Department of Commerce, Bureau of the Census, *Statistical Abstract of the United States 1990 (110th ed.)*, Superintendent of Documents, Washington, D.C., p. 208, from U.S. Bureau of the Census, *Current Industrial Reports*, series MA-200, Annual. *Notes:* 1. Includes payments to governmental units. 2. Includes industries not shown separately.

★ 314 ★

Pollution Abatement Expenditures
Expenditures by type of pollution, shown in billions of current and 1982 constant dollars.

Year	Air		Water		Solid Waste		Other	
	Current	Constant	Current	Constant	Current	Constant	Current	Constant
1978	15.7	23.8	19.0	26.6	6.5	9.5	-1.1	-1.5
1979	18.6	24.5	20.8	36.5	7.8	10.2	-1.3	-1.6
1980	21.9	24.7	21.3	24.7	8.8	10.7	-1.5	-1.7
1981	25.1	25.9	20.8	22.0	10.0	10.7	-1.6	-1.6
1982	25.0	25.0	21.2	21.2	9.6	9.6	-1.3	-1.3
1983	26.6	26.4	22.4	21.5	10.2	9.7	-1.2	-1.2
1984	29.6	28.6	25.2	23.3	11.8	10.8	-1.3	-1.3
1985	31.2	29.7	27.6	24.7	13.1	11.5	-1.0	-1.0
1986	31.2	30.6	29.7	26.4	14.7	12.3	-1.0	-1.1
1987	30.1	28.3	32.1	27.9	16.2	13.2	-1.5	-1.5

Source: Council on Environmental Quality, *20th Annual Report 1990*, Washington, D.C., p. 431, from Fraber, K.D. & G. L. Rutledge, 1986, "Pollution abatement and control expenditures." Survey of Current Business, table 9, pp. 100-103 (July 1986). U. S. Department of Commerce, Bureau of Economic Analysis, Washington, D.C. Fraber, K.D. & G.L Rutledge, 1989, "Pollution abatement and control expenditures, 1984-87." Survey of Current Business, table 6, pp. 24-25 (June, 1989). U.S. Department of Commerce, Bureau of Economic Analysis. Washington, D.C. Expenditures are attributed to the sector that performs the air or water pollution abatement or solid waste collection and disposal. Other includes expenditures for abatement of noise, radiation, and pesticide pollution, and business expenditures not assigned to another media. Totals may not agree with detail because of independent rounding.

★ 315 ★

Pollution Abatement & Control Expenditures, 1980 - 1987

In millions of dollars, except percent. Excludes agricultural production of crops and livestock, except feedlots.

Type	1980	1982	1983	1984	1985	1986	1987, prel.			
							Total[1]	Air	Water	Solid waste
Total expenditures	53,538	57,680	61,779	68,929	74,636	78,712	81,057	32,273	32,987	16,655
Percent Government	25.3	21.8	20.7	20.7	21.3	22.6	23.2	3.0	35.8	31.6
Pollution abatement	50,491	54,500	58,060	65,230	70,945	74,607	76,890	30,087	32,065	16,225
Personal consumption	6,589	8,318	9,771	10,767	11,839	12,276	10,905 1	0,905	-	-
Business	32,283	35,610	37,589	42,191	45,097	46,743	49,368	18,811	20,966	11,361
Government	11,620	10,571	10,700	12,273	14,900	15,588	16,618	372	11,099	4,865
Federal	494	550	795	944	1,225	1,346	1,237	80	707	250
State and local	2,778	3,274	3,547	3,886	4,324	4,788	5,138	15	426	4,615
Govt. enterprise fixed capital	8,347	6,747	6,358	7,443	8,460	9,454	10,243	277	9,966	-
Regulation and montoring	1,296	1,397	1,385	1,362	1,279	1,532	1,519	410	583	300
Research and development	1,751	1,783	2,335	2,337	2,412	2,573	2,648	1,776	339	129
Constant (1982) Dollars										
Total expenditures	62,046	57,680	60,007	64,713	68,121	71,800	71,366	30,136	28,700	13,509
Pollution abatement	58,421	54,500	56,453	61,326	64,846	68,218	67,827	28,253	27,933	13,158
Personal consumption	7,164	8,318	9,731	10,565	11,336	12,228	10,333	10,333	-	-
Business	37,885	35,610	36,533	39,495	41,282	42,718	43,780	17,573	18,743	9,223
Government	13,372	10,571	10,188	11,266	12,228	13,272	13,713	348	9,190	3,935
Regulation and montoring	1,533	1,397	1,315	1,230	1,104	1,291	1,234	332	474	239
Research and development	2,092	1,783	2,239	2,157	2,171	2,292	2,306	1,551	293	112

Source: U.S. Department of Commerce, Bureau of the Census, *Statistical Abstract of the United States 1990 (110th ed.)*, Superintendent of Documents, Washington, D.C., p. 207, from U.S. Bureau of Economic Analysis, Survey of Current Business, June 1989. *Notes:* - Represents zero 1. Includes "other and unallocated" expenditures (such as for noise, radiation, and pesticide pollution and business expenditures not assigned to media) which may be either positive or negative; therefore, data may not add.

★ 316 ★

Pollution Abatement - New Capital Expenditures

Pollution abatement expenditures shown in billions of dollars.

Selected Industry	Pollution abatement expenditures (billion dollars)								1988[1] planned	Percent of Total Capital Outlays by Business[2]		
	1975	1980	1985	1986	1987					1975	1980	1988[2]
					Total	Air	Water	Solid waste				
Nonfarm business total[3]	6.81	9.19	8.61	8.45	9.12	4.18	3.58	1.36	9.02	4.2	2.9	1.9
Manufacturing[3]	4.66	5.35	5.13	5.33	6.22	2.63	2.69	0.89	6.51	8.7	4.8	4.1
Food, incl. beverage	0.30	0.26	0.25	0.27	0.28	0.08	0.15	0.04	0.32	6.8	3.2	2.6
Paper	0.47	0.46	0.58	0.55	0.45	0.26	0.08	0.11	0.72	16.0	7.1	6.3
Chemicals	0.76	0.69	0.74	0.98	0.86	0.30	0.41	0.14	1.26	10.7	5.9	7.1
Petroleum	1.21	1.54	1.25	1.28	2.11	0.90	0.95	0.26	1.65	13.3	7.9	8.7
Primary metals	0.92	0.94	0.89	0.76	0.88	0.45	0.37	0.06	0.91	16.9	13.9	9.2
Machinery, except electrical	0.09	0.12	0.15	0.10	0.15	0.05	0.09	0.02	0.18	1.9	1.1	1.2
Electrical machinery	0.09	0.22	0.18	0.25	0.32	0.07	0.20	0.05	0.20	2.9	2.3	1.2

[Continued]

★ 316 ★

New Capital Expenditures for Pollution Abatement
[Continued]

Selected Industry	Pollution abatement expenditures (billion dollars)								1988[1] planned	Percent of Total Capital Outlays by Business[2]		
	1975	1980	1985	1986	1987					1975	1980	1988[2]
					Total	Air	Water	Solid waste				
Transportation equipment	0.15	0.48	0.55	0.60	0.46	0.21	0.17	0.08	0.50	2.7	3.2	3.1
Public utilities	1.56	3.05	2.87	2.50	2.28	1.32	0.65	0.31	1.75	7.7	8.1	3.8

Source: U.S. Department of Commerce, Bureau of the Census, *Statistical Abstract of the United States 1990 (110th ed.)*, Superintendent of Documents, Washington, D.C., p. 207, from U.S. Bureau of Economic Analysis, Survey of Current Business, November 1988. *Notes:* 1. Expenditures planned as of January and February 1988 2. Based on outlays reported in source 3. Includes industries not shown separately.

★ 317 ★

Pollution Control Costs by Sector

Chart shows data from column 3.

	1972	1980	1987	2000
Percent of Total				
Private	61	63	63	60
Local	29	22	22	22
State	6	4	4	3
EPA	3	8	8	7
Non-EPA federal	1	3	3	8
Total costs (billions of $)	26.5	58	85.3	147.9

Source: C&EN, February 18, 1991, p. 26, from Environmental Protection Agency.

★ 318 ★

Primary Metal Industry Pollution Abatement Expenditures
Data are shown in millions of dollars.

| Year | Primary metal industries | | | | | | | |
| | Capital expenditures | | | | Operating costs | | | |
	Total	Air	Water	Solid waste	Total	Air	Water	Solid waste
1973	498.6	397.2	84.7	16.8	466.8	264.7	148.3	53.8
1974	646.8	5.1	132.7	12.5	590.2	339.6	181.2	69.5
1975	833.5	640.6	187.5	5.4	715.2	429.9	209.4	75.9
1976	833.7	632.5	197.8	575.7	229.5	90.7	24.0	34.0
1977	874.6	616.0	250.2	8.4	1,122.3	721.6	268.3	132.3
1978	791.8	563.3	219.1	9.4	1,321.4	809.6	333.0	178.9
1979	823.1	588.8	227.3	6.9	1,587.2	981.7	442.0	163.5
1980	740.0	539.7	180.7	19.6	1,677.3	998.2	463.2	215.3
1981	728.2	567.2	144.1	16.9	1,911.8	1,111.9	549.2	250.7
1982	569.8	423.1	133.7	13.0	1,513.6	897.2	488.4	167.6
1983	225.3	147.6	100.2	7.5	1,615.6	904.3	454.6	256.7
1984	274.0	175.2	72.9	26.0	1,769.7	1,017.3	450.7	301.7
1985	252.9	142.9	84.3	25.6	1,863.0	1,067.0	517.4	278.7
1986	225.9	102.8	74.6	48.4	1,721.9	968.5	509.4	264.1

Source: Council on Environmental Quality, *20th Annual Report 1990*, Washington, D.C., p. 434, from U.S. Department of Commerce, Bureau of the Census. *Pollution Abatement Costs and Expenditures*, annual. Current industrial reports, MA-200. Washington, D.C. Statistics cover manufacturing establishments with 20 employees or more. Capital expenditures are new capital expenditures for pollution abatement. Operating costs are related to pollution abatement activities (including payments to government for the costs of pollution removal). Totals may not agree because of independent rounding.

★ 319 ★

Rubber & Plastics Industry Pollution Abatement Expenditures
Data are shown in millions of dollars.

| Year | Rubber and miscellaneous plastic products | | | | | | | |
| | Capital expenditures | | | | Operating costs | | | |
	Total	Air	Water	Solid waste	Total	Air	Water	Solid waste
1973	24.2	13.5	7.3	3.3	42.6	12.2	10.1	20.4
1974	37.9	22.2	13.5	2.2	58.8	15.7	15.1	28.2
1975	31.9	22.2	6.6	3.1	64.8	20.7	18.4	25.7
1976	37.4	24.2	10.0	3.1	80.3	22.3	24.0	34.0
1977	36.6	17.4	13.8	5.4	73.8	19.8	18.9	35.1
1978	27.7	18.7	5.5	3.4	84.9	17.7	23.9	43.3
1979	25.1	12.9	9.3	2.9	111.7	32.2	29.6	49.9
1980	21.7	12.6	6.9	2.3	108.2	30.4	27.6	50.2
1981	21.8	15.3	5.9	6.5	118.3	29.8	29.4	58.8

[Continued]

★ 319 ★

Rubber & Plastics Industry Pollution Abatement Expenditures
[Continued]

| Year | Rubber and miscellaneous plastic products | | | | | | | |
| | Capital expenditures | | | | Operating costs | | | |
	Total	Air	Water	Solid waste	Total	Air	Water	Solid waste
1982	25.2	14.8	7.7	2.7	90.2	22.2	28.2	39.8
1983	23.6	12.0	3.8	7.8	165.8	50.9	52.8	62.0
1984	33.4	20.5	7.0	5.8	168.0	51.1	48.7	68.1
1985	29.7	21.3	3.2	5.2	193.1	46.7	55.6	90.8
1986	36.0	20.1	9.7	6.2	226.2	50.9	52.0	123.3

Source: Council on Environmental Quality, *20th Annual Report 1990*, Washington, D.C., p. 433, from U.S. Department of Commerce, Bureau of the Census. *Pollution Abatement Costs and Expenditures*, annual. Current industrial reports, MA-200. Washington, D.C. Statistics cover manufacturing establishments with 20 employees or more. Capital expenditures are new capital expenditures for pollution abatement. Operating costs are related to pollution abatement activities (including payments to government for the costs of pollution removal). Totals may not agree because of independent rounding.

★ 320 ★

Stone, Clay & Glass Industry Pollution Abatement Expenditures
Data are shown in millions of dollars.

| Year | Stone, clay, and glass products | | | | | | | |
| | Capital expenditures | | | | Operating costs | | | |
	Total	Air	Water	Solid waste	Total	Air	Water	Solid waste
1973	150.7	131.6	14.4	4.7	117.0	73.7	16.4	27.0
1974	208.8	185.8	13.1	10.0	152.9	98.7	24.7	29.4
1975	173.5	152.7	16.7	4.1	171.8	109.7	28.3	33.8
1976	104.7	82.2	18.9	3.6	192.1	122.8	30.3	39.0
1977	133.4	85.8	39.1	8.6	214.5	141.7	28.0	44.5
1978	123.8	98.1	28.0	3.7	251.1	163.7	33.2	54.2
1979	145.6	110.2	25.4	10.0	293.6	188.0	45.1	60.5
1980	1,510.0	123.1	17.9	10.0	301.7	1,821.1	48.2	71.4
1981	188.5	165.5	13.8	9.2	310.7	191.0	47.3	72.5
1982	105.2	84.9	14.0	6.3	260.2	142.8	44.0	39.8
1983	95.9	57.9	9.8	28.2	320.4	179.9	55.8	84.6
1984	84.0	65.6	13.1	5.2	377.9	215.0	64.2	98.7
1985	61.9	44.4	9.9	7.5	393.2	217.2	66.7	109.3
1986	84.4	53.1	13.7	17.6	423.6	237.0	68.2	118.3

Source: Council on Environmental Quality, *20th Annual Report 1990*, Washington, D.C., p. 433, from U.S. Department of Commerce, Bureau of the Census. *Pollution Abatement Costs and Expenditures*, annual. Current industrial reports, MA-200. Washington, D.C. Statistics cover manufacturing establishments with 20 employees or more. Capital expenditures are new capital expenditures for pollution abatement. Operating costs are related to pollution abatement activities (including payments to government for the costs of pollution removal). Totals may not agree because of independent rounding.

★ 321 ★

Textile Industry Pollution Abatement Expenditures

Data are shown in millions of dollars.

Year	Textile mill products							
	Capital expenditures				Operating costs			
	Total	Air	Water	Solid waste	Total	Air	Water	Solid waste
1973	29.2	10.3	17.7	1.2	38.8	6.3	23.5	9.0
1974	32.0	12.7	17.7	1.7	54.0	9.4	31.3	13.3
1975	43.0	19.7	22.2	1.1	50.7	9.4	29.4	12.0
1976	53.3	9.2	42.6	1.6	65.3	9.2	41.8	14.3
1977	36.7	20.7	14.7	1.4	75.0	10.9	46.4	-31.0
1978	59.7	42.7	15.4	1.6	92.5	19.0	51.6	21.9
1979	39.2	21.9	15.2	2.1	101.7	19.0	60.2	22.5
1980	59.5	32.5	23.6	3.5	115.8	16.6	59.3	39.9
1981	48.0	27.2	16.2	4.6	108.5	18.9	60.2	29.4
1982	22.0	12.2	6.2	3.6	74.7	14.8	41.4	18.3
1983	18.7	9.4	8.4	0.9	101.1	21.3	54.5	25.4
1984	20.9	12.8	6.3	1.8	122.2	25.8	68.4	28.0
1985	24.7	12.2	10.3	2.1	148.9	30.9	82.6	35.4
1986	25.5	12.3	10.5	2.6	161.6	28.5	94.9	38.2

Source: Council on Environmental Quality, *20th Annual Report 1990*, Washington, D.C., p. 437, from U.S. Department of Commerce, Bureau of the Census: Pollution abatement costs and expenditures, annual. Current industrial reports, MA-200. Washington, D.C. Statistics cover manufacturing establishments with 20 employees or more. Capital expenditures are new capital expenditures for pollution abatement. Operating costs are related to pollution abatement activities (including payments to government for the costs of pollution removal). Totals may not agree because of independent rounding.

★ 322 ★

Transportation Equipment Industry Pollution Abatement Expenditures

Data are shown in millions of dollars.

Year	Transportation equipment							
	Capital expenditures				Operating costs			
	Total	Air	Water	Solid waste	Total	Air	Water	Solid waste
1973	101.2	52.6	41.7	6.9	129.8	35.2	51.1	43.4
1974	103.4	52.7	41.5	9.2	154.8	44.8	59.5	50.5
1975	75.4	32.1	36.4	6.8	168.3	52.2	66.4	49.7
1976	78.5	21.1	53.6	3.8	197.9	56.9	83.5	57.6
1977	82.6	36.9	39.4	6.3	233.9	60.6	97.3	76.1
1978	139.5	71.0	57.9	10.7	280.5	77.3	110.2	93.0
1979	189.5	120.1	59.5	99.9	331.8	96.4	126.3	109.1
1980	275.0	201.4	60.7	12.9	401.5	110.7	137.4	153.2
1981	283.3	209.2	60.0	14.2	426.1	117.5	150.7	157.7
1982	108.3	59.7	36.5	12.1	396.5	105.6	153.5	137.6

[Continued]

★ 322 ★

Transportation Equipment Industry Pollution Abatement Expenditures
[Continued]

Year	Transportation equipment							
	Capital expenditures				Operating costs			
	Total	Air	Water	Solid waste	Total	Air	Water	Solid waste
1983	98.3	33.0	55.0	10.2	560.3	157.5	224.2	178.6
1984	207.6	71.3	116.9	19.4	685.6	192.9	280.1	212.6
1985	456.5	254.5	165.1	36.9	738.8	194.5	283.9	260.3
1986	541.1	432.4	81.8	26.8	839.0	195.7	338.5	304.9

Source: Council on Environmental Quality, *20th Annual Report 1990*, Washington, D.C., p. 436, from U.S. Department of Commerce, Bureau of the Census: Pollution abatement costs and expenditures, annual. Current industrial reports, MA-200. Washington, D.C. Statistics cover manufacturing establishments with 20 employees or more. Capital expenditures are new capital expenditures for pollution abatement. Operating costs are related to pollution abatement activities (including payments to government for the costs of pollution removal). Totals may not agree because of independent rounding.

★ 323 ★

Utility Environmental Spending by State

Data represent environmental protection investments by investor-owned electric utilities within each state for the year ending December 31, 1989. Values are shown in thousands of dollars.

State and Utility	Air Pollution Control	Water Pollution Control	Solid Waste Disposal	Noise Abatement Equipment	Esthetic	Additional Plant Capacity	Miscellaneous Environmental Protection	Total	Construction Work in Progress
Total	21,591,928	11,124,380	4,352,827	279,108	9,286,210	1,690,086	1,046,056	49,370,594	4,454,276
Alabama									
Alabama Power Co.	491,905	116,386	93,795	81	89,328	22,167	5,987	819,650	116,539
Southern Electric Generating Co.	38,315	2,182	0	0	0	0	0	40,497	12
Arizona									
Arizona Public Service Co.	307,761	146,208	424,542	1,237	53,694	20,819	54,802	1,009,063	8,651
Century Power Corp.	94,423	27,329	5,549	0	0	0	0	127,301	0
Tucson Electric Power Co.	149,555	33,715	7,537	2,392	69,154	2,214	150	264,717	174,830
Arkansas									
Arkansas Power & Light Co.	125	100	33	9	26	1	6	300	4
California									
Pacific Gas & Electric Co.	304,000	253,000	42,000	3,000	883,000	3,000	246,000	1,734,000	184,000
San Diego Gas & Electric Co.	25,637	18,254	1,058	1,341	558,846	0	435	605,571	0
Southern California Edison Co.	361,517	185,114	203,512	9,707	1,849,541	3,746	237,455	2,850,592	45,119
Colorado									
Public Service Co. of Colorado	221,610	45,635	2,061	0	165,902	36,312	0	471,520	2,252
Connecticut									
Citizens Utilities Co.	3	76	23	25	332	32	0	491	0
Connecticut Light & Power Co.	15,921	19,388	2,594	90	2,503	0	6,764	47,261	4,881
Connecticut Yankee Atom Power Co.	42	1,209	0	102	7	0	364	1,723	0
Holyoke Power & Electric Co.	0	0	0	0	0	0	3	3	0
United Illuminating Co.	4,609	12,139	17,137	1,593	5,777	1,416	420	43,090	0
Delaware									
Delmarva Power & Light	155,400	27,521	35,376	1,596	9,087	427	2,782	232,189	9,363
District of Columbia									
Potomac Electric Power Co.	223,918	65,691	21,298	61,032	670,208	127	0	1,042,274	35,057
Florida									
Florida Power & Light Co.	365,227	524,107	21,681	44,983	8,212	2,561	3,915	970,684	20,479
Florida Power Corp.	244,401	133,004	3,388	4,053	526	12,588	0	397,959	0
Gulf Power Co.	121,911	55,943	40,711	541	690	0	0	219,796	28
Tampa Electric Co.	317,323	23,517	56,132	316	37	6,146	6,985	410,346	1,527

[Continued]

★ 323 ★

Utility Environmental Spending by State
[Continued]

State and Utility	Air Pollution Control	Water Pollution Control	Solid Waste Disposal	Noise Abatement Equipment	Esthetic	Additional Plant Capacity	Miscellaneous Environmental Protection	Total	Construction Work in Progress
Georgia									
Georgia Power Co.	709,436	724,525	173,964	0	92,470	3,604	13,846	1,717,845	62,885
Savannah Electric & Power Co.	13,691	2,500	9,596	0	0	0	0	25,787	0
Hawaii									
Hawaiian Electric Co. Inc.	18,850	24,209	0	1,479	1,669	0	235	46,442	0
Maui Electric Co. Ltd.	0	0	0	0	0	0	0	0	0
Idaho									
Idaho Power Co.	126,679	15,228	1,677	168	340	6,181	11,626	161,899	9,238
Illinois									
Central Illinois Light Co.	71,004	21,370	20,100	32	30,160	0	0	142,666	301
Central Illinois Public Service Co.	231	25	16	0	1	0	3	276	0
Commonwealth Edison Co.	432,712	1,014,023	11,612	6,157	47,674	601,080	6,658	2,119,916	56,209
Electric Energy Inc.	20,852	0	1,247	0	0	0	0	22,099	0
Illinois Power Co.	227,953	422,371	95,128	195	5,084	2,217	6,320	759,268	6,716
Mt. Carmel Public Utility Co.	0	0	0	0	0	0	0	0	0
Indiana									
Alcoa Generating Corp.	13,485	5,993	0	0	0	0	0	19,478	595
AEP Generating Co.	180	49	10	0	0	0	0	240	1
Commonwealth Edison Co. of IN, Inc.	4,898	47,307	45	0	134	123,480	0	175,863	1,932
Indiana Michigan Power Co.	336	107	13	0	10	0	0	465	2
Indianapolis Power & Light Co.	264	89	40	0	15	51	0	458	5
Northern Indiana Public Service Co.	374,214	115,077	11,286	1,335	3,051	57,600	1,759	564,323	6,401
Public Service Co. of IN, Inc.	153,661	22,572	31,123	1,251	101	25,130	0	233,838	6,756
Southern Indiana Gas & Electric Co.	92,446	28,266	19,994	0	23	0	0	140,729	841
Iowa									
Interstate Power Co.	44,982	1,961	4,487	22	52	559	0	52,069	0
Iowa Electric Light & Power Co.	31,872	19,121	35	89	399	2,755	29	54,300	1,632
Iowa Power & Light Co.	65,528	8,188	11,805	0	616	7,997	0	94,134	0
Iowa Public Service Co.	51,918	5,757	6,550	102	39,730	5,823	0	109,880	0
Iowa Southern Utilities Co.	19,028	192	3,920	14	104	1,171	24	24,454	0
Iowa-Illinois Gas & Electric Co.	74,351	24,949	18,601	138	7,358	14,402	1,329	141,127	992
Kansas									
Centel Corp.	18,652	0	0	0	0	0	0	18,652	0
Kansas Gas & Electric Co.	114,953	163,247	150,837	0	15,160	5,007	0	449,204	423
Kansas Power & Light Co.	139,483	8,335	5,104	35	36,516	30,284	240	219,997	0
Kentucky									
Kentucky Power Co.	12,259	1,023	5,568	0	0	1,742	0	20,592	50
Kentucky Utilities Co.	136	28	28	0	0	0	0	191	2
Louisville Gas & Electric Co.	256,230	34,547	40,810	19	1,915	0	109	333,630	208,673
Ohio Valley Transmission Co.	0	0	0	0	0	0	0	0	0
Union Light Heat & Power Co.	0	0	0	79	6	0	0	85	0
Louisiana									
Central Louisiana Electric Co. Inc.	34,765	6,804	9,182	0	0	0	13	50,764	211
Louisiana Power & Light Co.	3,886	2,147	414	0	25,191	0	0	31,639	0
New Orleans Public Service Inc.	1,232	1,941	411	0	24,637	0	0	28,221	0
Southwestern Electric Power Co.	114,031	15,919	26,377	351	699	0	3,561	160,938	0
Maine									
Bangor Hydro-Electric Co.	1,496	730	30	389	19	126	13	2,803	0
Central Maine Power Co.	15,307	11,149	1,440	3,649	1,098	915	3,398	36,956	520
Maine Electric Power Co. Inc.	0	0	0	0	0	0	0	0	0
Maine Public Service Inc.	530	199	11	136	7	44	5	930	0
Maine Yankee Atomic Power Co.	811	11,249	5,328	71	347	0	0	17,806	286
Maryland									
Baltimore Gas & Electric Co.	168,650	159,845	17,928	4,610	129,736	261	1,288	482,318	103,517
Potomac Edison Co.	89,882	33,320	28,014	102	54,850	0	2,176	208,345	3,548
Massachusetts									
Boston Edison Co.	45,983	62,678	8,207	4,201	25,888	0	42,246	189,204	9,472
Cambridge Electric Light Co.	620	595	0	396	33	0	0	1,645	0
Canal Electric Co.	12,461	2,698	1,930	221	25	0	0	17,335	28,017
Commonwealth Electric Co.	1,199	513	23	109	380	0	0	2,224	0
Eastern Edison Co.	0	0	0	0	0	0	0	0	0
Fitchburg Gas & Electric Light Co.	0	0	0	0	0	0	0	0	0
Holyoke Water Power Co.	434	95	405	0	0	0	3,359	4,294	0

[Continued]

★ 323 ★

Utility Environmental Spending by State
[Continued]

State and Utility	Air Pollution Control	Water Pollution Control	Solid Waste Disposal	Noise Abatement Equipment	Esthetic	Additional Plant Capacity	Miscellaneous Environmental Protection	Total	Construction Work in Progress
Massachusetts Electric Co.	209	0	967	34	10,954	0	0	12,163	162
Montaup Electric Co.	50,995	3,063	569	389	4	26	3	55,049	21,669
New England Power Co.	128,459	52,794	24,625	843	3,508	0	13	210,242	6,624
Western Massachusetts Electric Co.	2,224	568	525	15	471	0	12,322	16,125	1,143
Yankee Atomic Electric Co.	24	1,241	0	0	0	0	3,456	4,721	162
Michigan									
Consumers Power Co.	182,423	228,494	36,310	695	27,596	13,460	8,509	497,487	6,262
Detroit Edison Co.	1,815,211	540,894	65,295	11,162	19,131	0	0	2,451,693	4,527
Edison Sault Electric Co.	0	0	0	0	0	0	0	0	0
Michigan Power Co.	0	6	0	0	0	0	5	11	0
Upper Peninsula Power Co.	1,631	129	16	100	0	0	47	1,924	0
Minnesota									
Minnesota Power & Light Co.	147,071	38,433	39,167	7,693	3,093	9,594	521	245,573	409
Northern States Power Co.	26,049	251	0	1,820	267	0	182	28,569	3
Otter Tail Power Co.	44,842	29,954	3,748	0	13,750	2,477	317	95,088	57
Mississippi									
Mississippi Power & Light Co.	26,752	23,363	3,431	0	0	0	735	54,281	14
Mississippi Power Co.	32,245	28,137	11,254	583	11,894	6,051	1,362	91,526	255
System Energy Resources Inc.	112,578	422,606	101,224	0	0	0	0	636,407	844
Missouri									
Empire District Electric Co.	13,579	387	3,172	211	13,234	873	216	31,671	787
Kansas City Power & Light Co.	141,377	183,478	158,333	648	99,542	8,320	0	591,698	0
St. Joseph Light & Power Co.	9,833	57	1,620	61	0	266	0	11,837	0
Union Electric Co.	261,805	305,943	30,876	2,970	179,306	0	10,962	791,861	5,975
UtiliCorp United Inc.	25,675	4,571	4,378	743	10,338	0	258	45,963	0
Montana									
Montana Power Co.	97,099	72,429	44,301	2,600	2,854	8,189	503	227,975	280
Nevada									
Nevada Power Co.	69,330	35,636	12,189	42	1,939	1,494	507	121,137	484
Sierra Pacific Power Co.	37,824	7,622	0	161	0	0	0	45,607	351
New Hampshire									
James River-NH Electric Inc.	0	0	0	0	0	0	0	0	0
New England Electric Transmission Corp.	0	16	0	0	0	0	0	16	0
Public Service Co. of NH	36,952	13,245	3,357	1,348	17,911	2,124	5,591	80,529	445,038
New Jersey									
Atlantic City Electric Co.	123,845	47,482	1,328	810	25,050	69	797	199,381	6,732
Jersey Central Power & Light Co.	137,662	110,745	17,679	2,116	1,987	128	7,416	277,732	4,189
Public Service Electric & Gas Co.	717,478	159,384	13,218	11,735	89,320	302	10,521	1,001,958	18,809
Rockland Electric Co.	0	0	0	0	0	0	0	0	0
New Mexico									
Public Service Co. of NM	397,524	94,862	74	0	0	0	0	492,460	1,552
New York									
Central Hudson Gas & Electric Corp.	45,928	29,303	20,992	764	14,537	0	2,438	113,963	2,838
Consolidated Edison Co.-NY Inc.	149,256	54,858	31,714	4,184	2,580,390	0	867	2,821,269	91,568
Long Island Lighting Co.	57,120	39,232	2,083	10,914	54,228	0	23,638	187,216	571,486
Long Sault Inc.	0	0	0	0	0	0	0	0	0
New York State Electric & Gas Corp.	147,042	27,941	15,279	2,927	78,856	0	4,636	276,681	363,948
Niagara Mohawk Power Co.	171,342	165,356	63,073	2,184	29,978	0	35,625	467,558	7,952
Orange & Rockland Utilities Inc.	41,075	5,150	3,792	1,173	23,023	0	1,056	75,268	1,449
Rochester Gas & Electric Corp.	35,733	67,568	12,114	87	63,434	0	9,548	188,484	326
North Carolina									
Carolina Power & Light Co.	761,575	844,842	371,630	3,698	62,365	62,536	863	2,107,507	5,749
Duke Power Co.	99,156	125,799	182,554	5,166	23,269	3,246	2,741	441,930	36,171
Nantahala Power & Light Co.	0	0	0	0	0	0	0	0	0
Yadkin Inc.	0	0	0	0	0	0	0	0	0
North Dakota									
MDU Resources Group Inc.	37,124	5,732	2,280	17	11,119	441	319	57,032	1,187
Ohio									
Cincinnati Gas & Electric Co.	180,655	55,185	57,597	2,542	2,489	23,428	377	322,273	127,593
Cleveland Electric Illumination Co.	550,293	318,842	32,654	22	14,074	14,796	886	931,567	101,056
Columbus Southern Power Co.	136,895	21,243	23,840	148	29,775	15,134	2,030	229,066	80,374
Dayton Power & Light Co.	117,304	51,765	47,719	902	9,462	15,604	412	243,166	72,292
Indiana-Kentucky Electric Corp.	99,253	3,973	0	0	0	0	0	103,227	3,317

[Continued]

★ 323 ★

Utility Environmental Spending by State
[Continued]

State and Utility	Air Pollution Control	Water Pollution Control	Solid Waste Disposal	Noise Abatement Equipment	Esthetic	Additional Plant Capacity	Miscellaneous Environmental Protection	Total	Construction Work in Progress
Ohio Edison Co.	704,246	145,081	124,063	797	6,347	8,345	2,333	991,212	120,491
Ohio Power Co.	384,880	73,714	60,894	606	595	36,500	0	557,190	2,572
Ohio Valley Electric Corp.	70,249	648	0	0	0	0	0	70,898	0
Toledo Edison Co.	275,492	83,744	29,465	273	9,262	4,399	1,193	403,827	46,580
Oklahoma									
Oklahoma Gas & Electric Co.	106,740	43,197	41,921	141	109,394	10,595	5,412	317,400	140
Public Service Co. of Oklahoma	137,034	30,797	611	1,399	21,614	0	54,097	245,551	102
Oregon									
Fale-Safe Inc.	0	0	0	0	0	0	0	0	0
PacifiCorp	634,724	60,341	96,577	188	47,545	61,260	8,338	908,973	31,086
Portland General Electric Co.	197,546	79,659	12,155	2,149	2,307	8,177	17,469	319,460	600
Warm Springs Power Enterprises	0	0	0	0	0	0	1,744	1,744	0
Pennsylvania									
Duquesne Light Co.	383,851	127,867	56,073	750	21,223	45,299	1,500	636,563	2,775
Metropolitan Edison Co.	151,974	103,935	5,569	509	87	227	990	263,290	6,336
Pennsylvania Electric Co.	254,622	51,855	972	358	424	3,861	672	312,766	5,231
Pennsylvania Power & Light Co.	189,180	121,332	69,542	2,257	54,760	31,089	36,046	504,206	10,067
Pennsylvania Power Co.	121,598	24,253	13,946	330	105	1,278	488	161,997	19,523
Philadelphia Electric Co.	908,968	253,071	36,990	2,165	10,110	433	0	1,211,737	23,520
Safe Harbor Water Pump Corp.	0	79	0	0	0	0	626	705	0
Susquehanna Electric Co.	0	0	0	0	0	0	0	0	0
UGI Corp.	2,293	1,515	116	6	0	0	0	3,930	226
West Penn Power Co.	215,233	61,258	65,434	217	10,935	0	2,922	355,998	3,223
York Haven Power Co.	0	19	0	0	0	0	0	19	0
Rhode Island									
Blackstone Valley Electric Co.	0	0	0	0	0	0	0	0	0
Narragansett Electric Co.	482	356	1,702	0	4,291	0	0	6,832	95
Newport Electric Corp.	0	0	0	0	0	0	0	0	0
South Carolina									
Lockhart Power Co.	0	9	0	0	0	0	0	9	0
South Carolina Electric & Gas Co.	69,608	10,264	4,140	0	0	0	0	84,012	8,022
South Carolina Generating Co. Inc.	38,656	4,501	0	0	0	0	0	43,157	125
South Dakota									
Black Hills Corp.	28,504	0	0	0	0	0	0	28,504	0
Northwestern Public Service Co.	17,347	12,760	2,951	27	112	719	437	34,352	1,082
Tennessee									
Kingsport Power Co.	0	10	1	0	1,434	0	0	1,445	37
Tapoco Inc.	0	0	0	0	0	0	0	0	0
Texas									
Central Power & Light Co.	168,914	230,520	11,408	931	3,190	0	985	415,948	0
El Paso Electric Co.	57,780	32,891	123,160	0	0	0	13,951	227,782	2,537
Gulf States Utilities Co.	82	135	18	0	36	0	0	271	1
Houston Lighting & Power Co.	0	0	0	0	0	0	9,009	9,009	0
Southwestern Electric Service Co.	0	0	0	0	0	0	5	5	0
Southwestern Public Service Co.	84,175	23,810	11,223	3,959	0	0	0	123,166	5,490
Texas Utilities Electric Co.	330,180	62,051	171,829	6,790	19,308	47,936	580	638,673	944,266
Texas-New Mexico Power Co.	0	0	0	0	0	0	0	0	0
West Texas Utilities Co.	33,133	12,703	4,785	14	687	0	654	51,976	302
Vermont									
Central Vermont Public Service Corp.	0	18	14	74	444	0	7	556	0
Green Mountain Power Corp.	0	67	0	42	834	0	41	984	0
Vermont Electric Power Co. Inc.	0	0	0	0	3,059	0	0	3,059	0
Vermont Yankee Nuclear Power Corp.	11,975	11,950	306	0	252	0	149	24,632	0
Virginia									
Appalachian Power Co.	273,383	51,456	34,148	37	44,542	89,913	148	493,627	1,225
Virginia Electric & Power Co.	379,291	189,737	84,215	2,545	75,745	0	58,756	790,289	98,606
Washington									
Puget Sound Power & Light Co.	164,560	21,096	15,179	2,970	155,168	8,479	10,053	377,505	103
Washington Water Power Co.	57,196	4,075	1,379	46	5,486	1,119	636	69,937	0
West Virginia									
Monongahela Power Co.	107,548	36,305	27,081	105	3,435	0	2,522	176,997	1,451
Wheeling Power Co.	0	284	0	0	0	0	0	284	0

[Continued]

★ 323 ★

Utility Environmental Spending by State
[Continued]

State and Utility	Air Pollution Control	Water Pollution Control	Solid Waste Disposal	Noise Abatement Equipment	Esthetic	Additional Plant Capacity	Miscellaneous Environmental Protection	Total	Construction Work in Progress
Wisconsin									
Consolidated Water Power Co.	6	0	0	0	0	0	0	6	0
Madison Gas & Electric Co.	19,432	4,887	2,917	0	0	1,126	0	28,361	68
Northern States Power Co.	26,049	251	0	1,820	267	0	182	28,569	3
Northwestern Wisconsin Electric Co.	0	0	0	0	0	0	0	0	0
South Beloit Water Gas & Electric Co.	0	0	0	0	701	0	0	701	0
Superior Water Light & Power Co.	464	14	473	0	0	0	0	951	0
Wisconsin Electric Power Co.	152,697	48,144	18,808	3,341	163,793	1,681	310	388,774	7,964
Wisconsin Power & Light Co.	70,485	13,494	17,376	235	45,150	2,365	0	149,106	1,141
Wisconsin Public Service Corp.	64,051	34,254	6,569	0	0	0	0	104,874	830
Wisconsin River Power Co.	0	0	0	0	0	0	0	0	0

Source: Energy Information Administration, *Financial Statistics of Selected Investor-Owned Electric Utilities 1989*, January 1991, pp. 560-568, from Federal Energy Regulatory Commission, FERC Form 1, "Annual Report of Major Electric Utilities, Licensees and Others." Totals may not equal sum of components because of independent rounding. CWIP stands for "Construction Work in Progress." *Notes:* 1. Excludes cost of nuclear fuel. 2. Excludes other utility plant CWIP.

★ 324 ★

Utility Water Pollution Control Expenditures

1989 - 11.1
1988 - 10.6
1987 - 9.8
1986 - 6.9
1985 - 7.1

Average of total investments in water pollution control for investor-owned utilities. Values, for each year ending December 31, are in billions of dollars.

Year	Amount
1985	7.1
1986	6.9
1987	9.8
1988	10.6
1989	11.1

Source: Energy Information Administration, *Financial Statistics of Selected Investor-Owned Electric Utilities 1989*, January 1991, pp. 560-568, from Federal Energy Regulatory Commission, FERC Form 1, "Annual Report of Major Electric Utilities, Licensees and Others."

Prices

★ 325 ★

Can Prices and Recycling

Can pricing effects on recycling rates from 1980 through 1989.

Year	Average price per pound in cents[1]	Average price per can in cents	Recycling rate (%)	Cans per pound
1980	48.8	2.01	37.3	24.23
1981	46.8	1.91	53.2	24.45
1982	46.2	1.83	55.5	25.21
1983	45.0	1.75	52.9	25.70
1984	45.3	1.74	52.8	26.00
1985	35.2	1.32	51.0	26.60
1986	38.6	1.43	49.0	27.00
1987	50.4	1.84	50.5	27.40
1988	69.8	2.47	54.6	28.30
1989[2,3]	70.4	2.44	58.0	28.90

Source: Resource Recycling, November 1989, p. 24, from Aluminum Association; Can Manufacturers Institute; and Resource Recycling. *Notes:* 1. American Metal Market; American National Can. 2. 1989 pricing data are based on seven months. 3. 1989 cans per pound extrapolated from previous years.

★ 326 ★

Future Fuel Prices

Figures represent dollars per million Btu, shown in 1987 constant dollars for 2010 and 2015.

	1987	2010	2015
Oil			
Residual	2.83	6.50	8.00
Distillate fuel	3.83	8.30	10.00
Gasoline (retail)	7.65	13.20	14.90
Natural gas			
Residential	5.40	9.60	11.40
Commercial	4.58	8.80	10.50
Industrial	2.48	7.30	9.00
Utility	2.23	6.70	8.30
Coal			
Utility	1.50	2.20	2.30

[Continued]

★ 326 ★

Future Fuel Prices
[Continued]

	1987	2010	2015
Industrial	1.63	2.60	2.90
Electricity			
Residential	21.83	25.70	28.80
Commercial	20.46	22.40	24.20
Industrial	14.11	17.40	19.20
Average	18.74	21.60	23.80

Source: Changing by Degrees: Steps to Reduce Greenhouse Gases, U.S. Congress, Office of Technology Assessment, OTA-O-482, Washington, D.C., February 1991, p. 322, from Gas Research Institute, *Baseline Projection of U.S. Energy Supply and Demand to 2010* (Washington, DC: 1988). Prices for 2015 extrapolated by OTA.

★ 327 ★

Recyclable Cash Value in Waste Stream

Source	Cash Value in Dollars (per ton separated)
Aluminum Cans	600-1,000
Plastic Bottles (HDPE)[1]	160-200
Plastic Bottles (PET)[2]	160-200
Plastic Bottles (PVC)[3]	120-200
Steel	50-80
Glass	15-60
Paper	0-20

Source: Packaging, February 1991, p. 27 *Notes:* 1. High density polyethylene. 2. Polyethylene terephthalate. 3. Polyvinyl chloride.

★ 328 ★

Recycled Resin Prices

The prices are in cents per pound.

Resin	Baled	Regrind	Pellet
High Density Polyethylene			
Natural	8-11	28-31	32-39
Mixed colors	5-8	22-23	28-31
Low Density Polyethylene	5-9	-	19-23

[Continued]

★ 328 ★

Recycled Resin Prices
[Continued]

Resin	Baled	Regrind	Pellet
Polyethylene terephtalate			
Clear	8-10	33-35	42-45
Green	7-8	17	-
Polystyrene	-	16-23	26-40
Polyvinyl chloride	6-10	12-25	-
Polypropylene	-	8-20	20-30
Mixed Bottles	5-8	-	-

Source: BioCycle, January 1991, p. 70, from *Plastic News* with additions from *BioCycle*.

★ 329 ★

Sludge Compost Selling Price in Selected Locations

The figures refer to compost selling price by the owner and the final price to the
end user. Not all compost is sold at all facilities; in some cases, it is utilized for
municipal purposes or given away.

Location	Selling price by owner	Final selling price
Akron, OH	$16 (less than 60 cubic yards) $5 (60-180 cy) $4 (more than 180 cy)	$16-20 per cubic yard
Clayton County, GA	$6 per cy	$6-12 per cy
Metropolitan Denver Sewage Disposal District, CO.	$8 (delivered, to 20 miles) $16 (to 100 miles)	$2.50 for 1.25 cu. ft. bag
East Bay Municipal Utility	$8 (1988)	$10-25 $4/$5 for 2 ft. bag
Hampton Roads Sanitation	$12 (less than 10 cy) $8 (10-500 cy) $6 (more than 500 cy) $1.35 (1 cu. ft. bag)	$30 (pickup) $40 (delivered) $3.00-$3.50 per bag
Los Angeles County Sanitation District, CA	$1 cy	See note.
Nashville, TN	$5 cy	N.A.
Sarasota, FL		City pays $7.50 for removal
Scranton, PA	$3 cy	$5-$15 cy
Washington Suburban Sanitary Commission, MD	$7.50	$20-25 (pickup) $30-$40 (delivered) $4.50 cu. ft. bag

Source: BioCycle, February 1990, p. 45. N.A. means not available. The Los Angeles County Sanitation
Districts sells all of its compost to Kellogg Supply Company. Kellogg sells compost or compost blends in
bags ranging from 0.5 to 4.0 cu. ft. each. Typical price range for 2 cu. ft. bag is $4-$5.

★ 330 ★

Used Beverage Can Pricing

Date	Price ($/lb.)[1]
4/02/79	.388
7/02/79	.428
10/01/79	.468
4/01/80	.508
7/07/80	.488
6/22/81	.468
10/04/81	.428
1/04/82	.408
3/01/82	.380
5/05/82	.400
6/13/83	.420
7/04/83	.460
7/11/83	.490
8/11/83	.540
8/29/83	.570
10/28/83	.540
11/15/83	.510
1/19/84	.540
3/15/84	.520
4/16/84	.500
5/28/84	.470
6/20/84	.450
7/15/84	.430
8/03/84	.400
9/05/84	.380
5/31/85	.350
6/25/85	.310
12/18/85	.340
1/05/86	.380
2/25/86	.420
3/26/86	.440
4/17/86	.420
5/02/86	.400
6/10/86	.380
11/04/86	.360
1/15/87	.390
2/13/87	.420
3/19/87	.450
5/04/87	.470
5/13/87	.490
6/09/87	.520
7/17/87	.550
9/21/87	.580
10/12/87	.610
10/20/87	.560

[Continued]

★ 330 ★

Used Beverage Can Pricing
[Continued]

Date	Price ($/lb.)[1]
12/01/87	.590
12/21/87	.620
1/08/88	.670
1/21/88	.680
1/22/88	.690
2/16/88	.730
8/25/88	.680
9/20/88	.650
10/24/88	.620
12/16/88	.700
1/16/89	.760
2/06/89	.730
2/22/89	.760
3/22/89	.700
5/09/89	.730
6/02/89	.700
6/12/89	.660
6/27/89	.630
7/07/89	.600
7/17/89	.560

Source: Resource Recycling, November 1989, p. 21, from Recycling Processor Survey; American National Can; *American Metal Market*; American Recycling Market Inc. surveys. *Notes:* 1. These prices represent the toll price paid for truckload quantities, and larger, of baled used aluminum beverage cans. The data represent industry-wide price shifts only.

★ 331 ★

Value of Recyclables in Waste

Material	Percent in Waste Stream	Value per Ton ($)[1]
Aluminum	1.40	1,000
Paper		
Newsprint	7.40	2 - 17
Corrugated Paper	12.90	15 -59
Office Paper	4.10	215 - 235
Mixed Paper Waste	-	0 - 25
Glass	7.00	
Clear/Flint	-	35 - 43
Green	-	10 - 17
Amber	-	25 - 40
Mixed	-	0 - 30
Plastics	8.00	-

[Continued]

★ 331 ★

Value of Recyclables in Waste
[Continued]

Material	Percent in Waste Stream	Value per Ton ($)[1]
High density polyethylene (e.g. milk jugs)	2.10	220 - 320
Polyethylene (e.g. soda bottles)	0.50	140 - 180
Steel (cans, etc.)	6.50	10 - 40

Source: World Wastes, October 1990, p. 39, from *Curbing Waste in a Throwaway World*, National Governor's Association, Washington, D.C. *Note:* 1. Prices as of July 1989.

Research and Development

★ 332 ★

Applications of Industrial Biotechnology

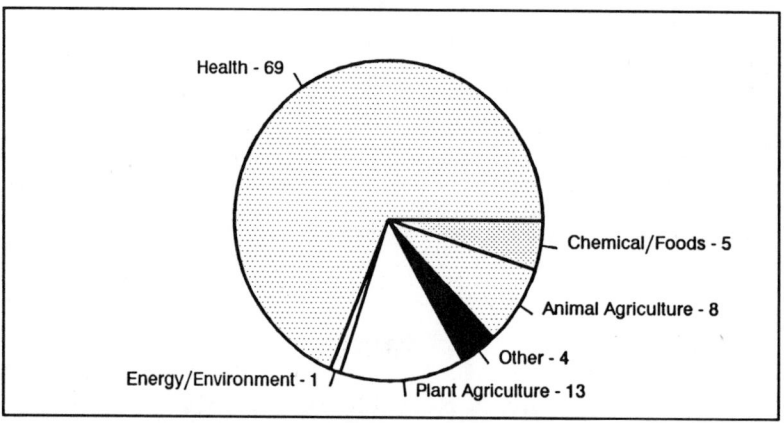

Percent of biotechnological R&D spending by industry, by application. Total spending in fiscal year 1990 was $2.0 billion.

Application	Percent of spending
Health	69
Energy/Environment	1
Other	4
Chemical/Foods	5
Animal Agriculture	8
Plant Agriculture	13

Source: Science, March 8, 1991, p. 1183, from the Office of Technology.

★ 333 ★

Department of Energy Conservation Budget

Item	Budget Authority (in millions)	
	FY 1990 Estimate	FY 1991 Request
Respecting the Environment		
Environment, Safety and Health	2,388.2	2,975.5
Nuclear Waste Disposal	300.1	293.5
Subtotal, Respecting the Environment	2,688.3	3,269.0
Use of Prior Year Balances and Other Adjustments	(4.0)	-
Total, Respecting the Environment	2,684.3	3,269.0
Increasing Energy Efficiency		
Building Technologies	38.8	46.0
Transportation Technologies	64.9	56.6
Industrial Technologies	50.9	40.1
Multi-Sector Research and Development	36.0	32.5
In-House Energy Management	19.5	20.5
Facilities, Policy and Management	3.4	7.5
Total Increasing Energy Efficiency	213.5	203.2
Securing Future Energy Supplies		
Power Marketing Administrations	607.5	555.0
Electric Energy Systems and Storage	29.8	40.2
Nuclear Energy	347.0	390.7
Fusion Energy	320.3	325.3
Renewable Technologies	109.4	136.7
Fossil Technologies	969.5	656.0
Subtotal, Securing Future Energy Supplies	2,383.5	2,103.9
Use of Prior Year Balances and Other Adjustments	(10.0)	(53.8)
Total, Securing Future Energy Supplies	2,373.5	2,050.1

Source: Energy, Special Issue 1990, p. 28.

★ 334 ★

Department of Energy Research and Development Funds

The values are in millions of dollars.

	1992[1]	1991[1]	1990[2]	% Change 1991-1992
Energy R&D	4,135.0	3,847.3	3,492.8	7
General science and research	1,542.5	1,144.9	1,056.2	35
High energy physics	666.4	588.7	576.3	13
Superconducting Super Collider	533.7	242.9	192.7	119
Nuclear physics	342.4	313.3	287.2	9
Basic energy sciences[3]	569.7	572.5[4]	450.8	0
Materials sciences	257.1	274.9	196.2	-7
Chemical sciences	158.3	157.6	138.5	0
Other research	154.3	140.0	116.1	10
Nuclear	398.0	305.0	334.9	30
Fusion	337.1	273.6	316.5	23
Clean coal technology	315.0	391.0	334.9	-20
Biological, environmental	312.6	368.6	305.2	-15
Conservation	274.1	214.6	158.8	28
Fossil	184.0	378.8	393.4	-51
Solar and other renewables	202.0	198.3	142.1	2
Defense R&D	2,565.0	2,506.9	2,550.6	2
Weapons R&D, testing	1,764.0	1,737.1	1,908.6	1
Naval reactor development	801.0	769.8	642.0	4
Total	6,700.0	6,354.2	6,043.4	5

Source: C&EN, February 18, 1991, p. 11, from Department of Energy, Office of Management & Budget. *Notes:* 1. Actual. 2. Estimates. 3. Operating expense. 4. Includes $59.2 million for congressionally directed projects for which no funding is requested in 1992.

★ 335 ★

EPA Research Funds by Category

Total - 491.5

Multimedia - 150.7

Air - 112.4

Superfund - 68.6

Hazardous waste - 43.6

Water quality - 28.9

Toxic substances - 26.3

Drinking water - 22.2

Pesticides - 15.0

Energy/acid rain - 13.7

Management & support - 5.3

Radiation - 4.0

Leaking underground storage tanks - 0.8

Chart shows data from column 1.

	Millions of Dollars			% Change 1991-
	1992[1]	1991[1]	1990[2]	1992
Multimedia	150.7	124.2	84.0	21
Air	112.4	86.6	77.9	30
Superfund	68.6	73.6	78.7	-7
Hazardous waste	43.6	39.2	43.9	11
Water quality	28.9	27.7	26.9	4
Toxic substances	26.3	25.5	27.2	3
Drinking water	22.2	20.7	20.9	7
Pesticides	15.0	12.6	12.7	19
Energy/acid rain	13.7	13.6	33.3	0
Management & support	5.3	5.2	14.7	0
Radiation	4.0	4.0	3.6	0
Leaking underground storage tanks	0.8	0.8	0.7	0
Total	491.5	433.7	424.5	13

Source: C&EN, February 18, 1991, p. 13, from Environmental Protection Agency. *Notes:* 1. Estimates 2. Actual.

★ 336 ★

Global Change Research Program

Budget appropriations received from Congress in 1991 and requested amounts for 1992, shown in millions of dollars.

Global Change Research Program	1991 Appropriated	1992 Requested	% Change
Climate Modeling	60	95	+59.5
Global Water & Energy Cycles	417	521	+24.9
Global Carbon Cycle	130	163	+25.3
Ecosystems and Population Dynamics	106	147	+38.8
Other Research Activities	241	259	+7.6
Total	954	1,185	+24.3

Source: Science, February 15, 1991, p. 737.

Resource Recovery

★ 337 ★

Existing Materials Recovery Facilities Capital Costs

The average capital cost per ton of daily capacity of existing material recovery projects is approximately $20,900.

Capacity	Cost/Ton of Daily Capacity	
	Range of Capital Costs (dollars)	Average Capital Costs (dollars)
100 tpd & less	10,000-40,000	18,100
100 to 200 tpd	20,000-26,700	22,500
200 tpd	n/a	21,7100
All	10,000-40,000	20,900

Source: BioCycle, May 1990, p. 29. *Notes:* tpd - tons per day. n/a - not available. .

★ 338 ★

Newsprint Manufacturer Operating Cost

Operating cost comparison between use of virgin pulp and recycled materials. Comparison does not include investment-related costs.

	Costs ($/metric ton)	
	Virgin pulp	100 percent old newspaper
Raw material	66	91
Power	157	66
Other process costs	164	158
Total cost newsprint	387	315

Source: Resources Recycling, July 1989, p. 35, from Andover International Associates.

★ 339 ★

Wastepaper Repulping Process Costs

Projected operating and capital costs of a new process for steam-explosion pulping of different types of wastepaper. The process was developed by Chesapeake Corp., Richmond, VA and Stake Technology, Toronto, ON.

Type of paper waste	Corrugated cardboard	Newsprint	Tissue
Capacity tons per day	600	600	300
Processing costs, $ per ton	107	175	322
Capital investment, $ millions	23	120	65

Source: C&EN, January 7, 1991, p. 22, from Recoupe Recycling Technologies.

Soil Conservation

★ 340 ★

Conservation and Pollution Abatement Practices

Values are shown in thousands of dollars of assistance to farmers for carrying out conservation and pollution abatement practices in the U.S. and Caribbean area.

Year	Agricultural Conservation Program[1]	Emergency Conservation Program	Total
1975	138,700	7,405	146,105
1976	134,731	15,142	149,873
1977	175,347	18,952	194,299
1978	180,940	16,318	197,258
1979[2]	245,843	23,418	269,261
1980	183,686	21,818	205,504
1981	193,209	15,410	208,619
1982	168,339	4,251	172,590
1983	184,986	10,300	195,286
1984	160,278	12,638	172,916
1985	178,801	10,700	189,501
1986	137,305	7,410	144,715
1987	137,297	3,900	141,197
1988	198,665	4,378	203,043
1989	179,244	7,226	186,470

Source: Agricultural Conservation and Forestry Statistics, 1989, U.S. Government Printing Office, Washington, D.C., 1989, p. 439, from Agricultural Stabilization and Conservation Service. Totals are from unrounded data. *Notes:* 1. Excludes administrative expenses. Includes Long-Term Agreements from 1975. 2. Because of the change to fiscal year funding in 1979, data for the period October 1, 1978-December 31, 1978 is included in the 1978 program year and the 1979 fiscal year.

★ 341 ★

Soil Conservation Fund Appropriations by State

Data for fiscal year ending September 30, 1989 is shown in thousands of dollars.

State or Territory	Actual appropriation
Alabama	5,013
Alaska	74
Arizona	1,582
Arkansas	2,742

[Continued]

★ 341 ★

Soil Conservation Fund Appropriations by State
[Continued]

State or Territory	Actual appropriation
California	4,405
Colorado	1,500
Connecticut	3,950
Delaware	5,025
Florida	7,896
Georgia	5,720
Hawaii	10,764
Idaho	2,506
Illinois	9,878
Indiana	15,040
Iowa	18,228
Kansas	12,053
Kentucky	8,080
Louisiana	3,385
Maine	1,093
Maryland	16,595
Massachusetts	802
Michigan	6,422
Minnesota	54,554
Mississippi	3,876
Missouri	21,769
Montana	5,705
Nebraska	31,405
Nevada	178
New Hampshire	285
New Jersey	6,865
New Mexico	977
New York	19,553
North Carolina	17,163
North Dakota	1,854
Ohio	11,311
Oklahoma	6,381
Oregon	2,190
Pennsylvania	5,429
Rhode Island	50
South Carolina	4,554
South Dakota	1,144
Tennessee	2,592
Texas	99,296
Utah	8,211
Vermont	468
Virginia	10,990
Washington	8,072
West Virginia	5,631
Wisconsin	20,228

[Continued]

★ 341 ★

Soil Conservation Fund Appropriations by State
[Continued]

State or Territory	Actual appropriation
Wyoming	4,159
Caribbean[1]	9,277
Pacific Basin[2]	511
Total	507,431

Source: Agricultural Conservation and Forestry Statistics, 1989, U.S. Government Printing Office, Washington, D.C., 1989, p. 447, from Soil Conservation Service. *Notes:* 1. Puerto Rico and Virgin Islands. 2. Guam and Northern Marianas.

Solid Waste Management

★ 342 ★

Municipal Bonds Issued for Waste Management

Year	Millions of Dollars
1984	4.50
1985	3.80
1986	2.40
1987	1.30
1988	3.00
1989	2.60
1990	1.66[1]

Source: American City & County, January 1991, p. 6, from FGIC. *Note:* 1. First nine months.

★ 343 ★

Tire Piles Management State Funding Programs

Summary of state tire pile management and recycling programs that are funded by per-tire fees, taxes or surcharges; vehicle title transaction surcharges; or general fund monies. Amounts are shown in dollars, except where noted.

Funding mechanism	State	Amount
Retail sales tax	Arizona	2 percent
Per-tire fee	California	0.25
Per-tire surcharge	Florida	1.00
Per-vehicle title fee	Illinois	0.50
Permit fee on tire pile operators	Indiana	varies
Per-tire excise tax	Kansas	0.50
Per-tire retail sales tax	Kentucky	1.00
Per-tire fee	Maine	1.00
General fund	Maryland	-
Per-vehicle title transaction surcharge	Michigan	0.50
Per-vehicle title transfer surcharge	Minnesota	4.00
Per-tire surcharge	Missouri	0.50
Per-tire fee on retail sales	Nebraska	1.00
Retail tire tax	North Carolina	1 percent
Per-tire sales surcharge	Oklahoma	1.00
Per-tire fee	Oregon	1.00
Per-tire tax	Rhode Island	0.50
Per-tire sales tax	Utah	1.00-2.00[1]
Per-tire sales tax	Virginia	0.50
Per-vehicle title fee	Washington	1.00
Per-vehicle title fee	Wisconsin	2.00

Source: Resource Recycling, December 1990, p. 64, from National Tire Dealers and Retreaders Association, 1990; *Scrap Tire News*, 1990. *Note:* 1. Varies by size of tire.

Wastewater Treatment

★344★

Federal Aid & Water Treatment Facilities Construction

The values are in millions of dollars for the fiscal year ending Sept. 30, 1988.

Division, State, and Outlying Areas	Federal Aid[1] Total	Federal Aid[1] Per capita[2] (dollars)	OE[3] compensatory education[4]	EPA[5] waste treatment facilities construction	HHS[6] Family Support[7] Administration	HHS[6] Medicaid	HUD[8] Lower income housing assistance[9]	HUD[8] Community development	ETA[10] employment/training	Dept. of Transportation, highway trust fund
Total[11]	114,610	460	4,016	2,511	13,211	30,321	6,541	3,050	2,966	13,819
New England	6,901	532	199	193	837	2,093	584	171	132	791
Maine	665	551	21	14	91	223	40	19	13	66
New Hampshire	398	363	9	26	26	96	32	8	7	61
Vermont	324	582	11	10	46	80	17	5	7	45
Massachusetts	3,328	567	100	89	431	1,063	293	95	63	262
Rhode Island	644	647	14	20	68	187	71	11	12	99
Connecticut	1,542	476	44	34	175	444	131	33	30	258
Middle Atlantic	21,615	574	750	579	2,583	7,455	1,433	578	445	1,588
New York	12,494	698	427	345	1,525	5,014	795	294	208	674
New Jersey	3,328	431	125	87	390	947	316	85	87	229
Pennsylvania	5,793	482	198	147	668	1,494	322	199	150	685
East North Central	17,794	422	597	527	2,753	5,070	979	531	612	1,633
Ohio	4,693	432	135	199	676	1,475	280	140	156	383
Indiana	1,960	352	60	77	60	667	104	59	79	243
Illinois	4,670	405	189	111	634	1,031	310	189	159	518
Michigan	4,243	456	155	84	923	1,194	174	92	160	325
Wisconsin	2,228	459	57	56	460	703	111	51	58	164
West North Central	7,758	437	204	193	865	1,985	396	207	178	1,132
Minnesota	2,120	492	45	52	291	678	118	51	43	253
Iowa	1,199	423	31	32	163	312	41	33	29	199
Missouri	1,942	378	60	56	201	438	115	64	56	239
North Dakota	462	697	9	7	33	121	25	7	9	85
South Dakota	443	620	11	7	29	93	26	10	10	78
Nebraska	712	445	19	21	63	152	35	17	12	111
Kansas	880	354	30	18	85	191	36	25	19	167
South Atlantic	16,991	400	631	387	1,398	4,111	961	458	427	2,303
Delaware	319	483	13	14	23	55	27	7	7	61
Maryland	2,004	442	64	70	192	499	146	52	48	338
District of Columbia	1,615	2,605	19	18	73	197	55	32	17	68
Virginia	1,961	327	73	43	172	420	144	53	51	327
West Virginia	1,056	561	34	60	117	239	55	19	27	184
North Carolina	2,299	352	90	35	195	690	136	64	76	224
South Carolina	1,354	388	58	41	109	366	69	37	41	180
Georgia	2,964	463	100	42	247	755	135	70	56	445
Florida	3,419	276	179	64	270	890	194	124	104	476
East South Central	7,036	459	289	108	466	1,967	370	170	224	884
Kentucky	1,766	474	67	25	152	514	95	46	56	188
Tennessee	2,225	452	77	36	141	730	111	44	64	270
Alabama	1,721	417	75	20	84	359	97	53	67	294
Mississippi	1,324	504	70	27	89	364	67	27	37	132
West South Central	9,720	362	469	158	628	2,645	558	300	257	1,244
Arkansas	1,011	417	48	15	61	322	51	24	31	101
Louisiana	2,135	483	94	26	165	692	107	62	56	269
Oklahoma	1,406	431	39	27	109	394	90	33	32	198
Texas	5,168	308	288	89	293	1,237	310	181	138	676
Mountain	5,781	434	163	78	427	1,004	296	120	153	973
Montana	546	679	12	9	45	104	30	10	13	101
Idaho	477	477	14	9	31	91	16	11	13	105
Wyoming	448	950	6	8	18	28	10	2	7	61

[Continued]

★ 344 ★

Federal Aid & Water Treatment Facility Construction
[Continued]

Division, State, and Outlying Areas	Federal Aid[1]		OE[3] compensatory education[4]	EPA[5] waste treatment facilities construction	HHS[6]		HUD[8]		ETA[10] employment/ training	Dept. of Transportation, highway trust fund
	Total	Per capita[2] (dollars)			Family Support[7] Adminis- tration	Medicaid	Lower income housing assistance[9]	Community development		
Colorado	1,241	377	39	12	102	260	66	26	28	225
New Mexico	831	550	28	8	55	170	45	15	19	97
Arizona	1,177	339	42	9	89	140	80	27	48	212
Utah	725	429	14	11	71	160	21	21	14	118
Nevada	336	317	8	12	16	51	28	8	11	54
Pacific	16,238	435	557	245	3,075	3,911	801	396	443	1,600
Washington	2,170	470	56	32	315	518	73	48	61	372
Oregon	1,322	482	41	19	141	252	55	24	39	148
California	11,676	415	435	165	2,525	2,985	601	312	319	904
Alaska	593	1,156	13	10	44	64	46	9	12	114
Hawaii	477	436	12	19	50	92	26	3	12	62
Outlying Areas	2,717	6,558	130	40	83	80	144	123	98	51

Source: U.S. Department of Commerce, Bureau of the Census, *Statistical Abstract of the United States 1990 (110th ed.)*, Superintendent of Documents, Washington, D.C., p. 277, from U.S. Bureau of the Census, Federal Expenditures by State for Fiscal Year, annual. *Notes:* 1. Includes other amounts not shown separately. 2. Based on Bureau of the Census estimated resident population as of July 1. 3. Office of Education. 4. For the disadvantaged. 5. Environmental Protection Agency. 6. Department of Health and Human Services. 7. Includes work incentives, family support payments (Aid to Families with Dependent Children), community service block grant, low income home energy assistance, refugee assistance, and assistance for legalized aliens. 8. Department of Housing and Urban Development. 9. Includes public housing, housing payments (section 8) to public agencies, and college housing. 10. Employment and Training Administration, Job Training Partnership Act. 11. includes $2,058 million undistributed by State; programs not shown here which are affected are compensatory education ($28 million), family support administration ($98 million), public housing ($17 million), lower income housing assistance ($18 million), community development ($5 million), employment/training ($1 million), and a highway trust fund ($1,621 million).

★ 345 ★

Regulatory Options for Controlling Volatile Organic Chemicals

	Regulatory Options		
	1 microgram per liter	5 micrograms per liter	10 micrograms per liter
Number of Systems Impacted	3,800	1,300	800
Cost of Control			
Total cost ($M)	1,300	280	150
Annual cost ($M)	100	21	11
Cost of Monitoring			
Compliance($M)	-	9	-
Unregulated ($M) (1445)	-	2	-
Annual cost per family ($)			
very small (25-500)	96	91	90
small (501-3300)	47	41	40
medium (3301-50k)	12	12	11
large (>50k)			
Annual Cancer Cases Avoided	42	32	31

Source: Risk Assessment, Management and Communication of Drinking Water Contamination, U.S. Environmental Protection Agency, EPA/625/4-89/024, Washington, D.C., 1989, p. C-22, from *Federal Register*, November 13, 1985, p. 46927.

★ 346 ★

Wastewater Treatment Investments by Sector

As regulators mandate cleaner wastewater, the chemicals industry is buying more wastewater treatment equipment. The values are in millions of 1987 dollars.

Sector	1987	1989	1991	1993	1995
Chemicals and chemical industry wastewater expenses	160	190	206	238	263
Iron and steel	98	97	95	91	88
Metal finishing	59	58	56	56	50
Petroleum refining	37	55	78	83	88
Design/engineering	49	58	63	73	80
Equipment	160	190	206	238	263
Instruments	34	40	44	51	56
Construction	414	465	503	544	611
Total for industry	662	745	845	907	958
Total	657	754	816	906	1,010

Source: Chemical Week, April 1991, p. 39, from William T. Lorenz & Co.

Wetlands Protection

★ 347 ★

Capital Cost of Subsurface Flow Wetlands

Location	Flow (in mill. gal. per day)	Area (in acres)	Cost (in $/acre)
Bear Creek, AL	0.02	0.5	72,532
Hardin, KY	0.10	1.6	84,373
Pembroke, KY	0.09	1.8	95,555
Kingston, TN	0.02	0.6	100,000
Smackover, AK	0.50	8.7	91,954
Denham Springs, LA	3.00	15.2	98,552
Haughton, LA	0.35	1.5	86,000
Benton, LA	0.31	1.2	89,600
Hornbeck, LA	0.06	0.2	86,020
Clarks, LA	0.19	0.74	91,000
Provencal, LA	0.09	0.35	87,000
Converse, LA	0.06	0.22	80,000
Crowley, LA	3.50	18.00	72,222
Tatum, NM	0.09	0.60	97,000
El Dorado, NM	0.01	0.23	87,120
Maysville, OK	0.14	0.36	88,000

[Continued]

★ 347 ★

Capital Cost of Subsurface Flow Wetlands
[Continued]

Location	Flow (in mill. gal. per day)	Area (in acres)	Cost (in $/acre)
Colbert, OK	0.08	0.29	88,000
Binger, OK	0.10	0.36	75,000
Mean			87,218
Maximum			100,000
Minimum			72,222

Source: Biocycle, January 1991, p. 45.

★ 348 ★

Capital Costs of Free Water Surface Wetlands

Location	Flow (MGD)[1]	Area (Acre)	Cost ($/Acre)
Spencer, MA	0.54	4.6	54,347
Orlando, FL	20.00	1200.0	17,517
Orange Co., FL	14.00	1400.0	2,071
Ft. Deposit, AL	0.24	15.0	24,933
West Jackson, MS	0.60	22.0	15,909
Lucedale, MS	0.50	6.0	65,000
Vermontville, MI	0.10	15.0	6,000
Crowley, LA	3.50	26.0	13,846
Columbia, MO	19.50	94.0	23,179
Minot, ND	7.50	125.0	15,200
Mellette, SD	0.06	2.8	18,000
McIntosh, SD	0.06	9.0	19,333
Hoven, SD	0.23	28.5	18,596
Eureka, SD	0.28	17.4	27,000
Gustine, CA	1.00	24.0	36,750
Mountain View, CA	1.60	20.3	4,630
Arcata, CA	2.32	38.0	13,542
Incline Vill., NV	1.30	300.0	10,947
Mt. Angel, OR	2.00	10.0	35,000
		Mean:	22,200
		Maximum:	65,000
		Minimum:	2,071

Source: BioCycle, January 1991, p. 46. *Note:* 1. Millions of gallons per day.

★ 349 ★

Wetlands Research, Protection and Enhancement

The fundings for wetlands will increase by 24 percent, figures are in millions of dollars.

Wetlands Funding	1989	1990	1991
Department of the Interior	95	122	155[1]
Department of Agriculture	49	83	97
Environmental Protection Agency	9	12	21
Army Corp of Engineers	109	130	159
National Oceanic and Atmospheric Administration	19	25	28
Total	281	372	460

Source: Budget of the United States Government, Fiscal Year 1991, p. 123 *Notes:* 1. Includes about $100 million categorized as part of America the Beautiful.

Chapter 5

TOOLS, METHODS, AND SOLUTIONS

Acid Rain Control

★ 350 ★

Technologies for Acid Rain Reduction

	Removal Sulfur Dioxide Percent	Efficiency Nitrogen Oxide Percent	Applies to		Status
			Retrofit/ Repowering	New Facilities	
Pre-Combustion Technology					
Fuel Changing	50-80	0-50	Yes	Yes	Available
Coal Benefication					
Physical Cleaning	10-50	0	Yes	Yes	Available
Chemical Cleaning	10-30	0	Yes	Yes	Available
Bacterial Cleaning	10-30	0	Yes	Yes	Available
Fuel Cells	90+	90+	Yes	Yes	Commercial Demo
Combustion-Stage Technology					
Fluidized-Bed Combustion (FBC)					
Atmospheric FBC	85-90	Moderate	Yes	Yes	Commercial Demo
Pressurized FBC	90-95	Moderate	Yes	Yes	Commercial Demo
Integrated Gas Combined Cycle (IGCC)	95-99	Moderate	Yes	Yes	Commercial Demo
Furnace Sorbent Injection (FSI)	50-70	0	Yes	Yes	Available
Gas Reburning	15-25	40-70	Yes	Yes	Commercial Demo
Slagging Combustor	50-90	Moderate	Yes	Yes	Commercial Demo
Oven Fire Air & Low-NO_x Burners	0	15-50	Yes	Yes	Limited Availability
NO_x Combustion Modification	0-20	50-70	Yes	Yes	Commercial Demo
UREA/Ammonia Injection	0	40-80	Yes	Yes	Commercial

[Continued]

283

★ 350 ★

Technologies for Acid Rain Reduction
[Continued]

	Removal Sulfur Dioxide Percent	Efficiency Nitrogen Oxide Percent	Applies to		Status
			Retrofit/ Repowering	New Facilities	
					Demo
Post-Combustion Technology					
Wet Flue-Gas Desulfurization	90-95	0	Yes	Yes	Available
Dry Flue-Gas Desulfurization	70-90	0	Yes	Yes	Available
Dry Flue-Gas Desulfurization w/Sodium	70-90	20-40	Yes	Yes	Commercial
					Demo
Advanced Flue-Gas Desulfurization	90+	40-90	Yes	Yes	Development
Wellman-Lord (Dravo Wellman)	95+	0	Yes	Yes	Available
Sorbent Injection	40-70	0	Yes	Yes	Commercial
					Demo
Selective Catalytic NO$_x$ Reduction (SCR)	0	65-80	Yes	Yes	Available (Foreign)

Source: Electric Light and Power, June 1990, p. 19.

Air Pollution Control

★ 351 ★

Alternative Refrigerant Applications in Domestic Appliances

Fluids	Concerns
R-134a	Energy Penalty Soluble/Compatible Lubricant PAGs Lubrication Effect of Moisture
Blend R-22/15a/114	Intermediate ODP, Mixture Handling
Blend R-22/152a/124	R-124 Availability, Mixture Handling
R-22	High Pressure, High Discharge Temperature
R-152a	Moderate Flammability, High Discharge Temperature, Lubricant
R-22/142b	Moderate Flammability, Equipment Redesign Flammability
R-290 (propane) R-717 (Ammonia)	Toxicity, Flammability

Source: ASHRAE Journal, February 1991, p. 24. *Notes:* PAG stands for Polyalkylene glycol; ODP stands for Ozone Depletion Potentials.

★ 352 ★

Alternative Refrigerant Applications - Auto Air Conditioning

Fluids	Concerns
R-123 for R-11	Energy Penalty, Suitable Lubricant, Polymer Compatibility, Motor Insulation Compatibility
R-134a for R-12	Energy Penalty, Suitable Lubricant, Material Compatibility
Blend R-22/152a/124 for R-12	Availability of R-124, Material Compatibility Mixture Handling
R-152a for R-12	Flammability, Suitable Lubricant

Source: ASHRAE Journal, February 1991, p. 26. *Notes:* 1. Polyalkylene glycols 2. Ozone depletion potential.

★ 353 ★

Alternative Refrigerant Applications - Centrifugal Chillers

Fluids	Concerns
R-123 for R-11	Energy Penalty, Suitable Lubricant, Polymer Compatibility, Motor Insulation Compatibility
R-134a for R-12	Energy Penalty, Suitable Lubricant, Material Compatibility
Blend R-22/152a/124 for R-12	Availability of R-124, Material Compatibility, Mixture Handling
R-152a for R-12	Flammability, Suitable Lubricant

Source: ASHRAE Journal, February 1991, p. 26.

★ 354 ★

Carbon Emissions Reduction Measures

Numbers are expressed as percentage of 1987 total emissions.

	Reductions in 2015	
	Moderate (in percent)	Tough (in percent)
Demand-Side Measures		
Residential buildings		
New investments		
Shell efficiency	1.3	2.0
Heating and cooling equipment	0.1	0.4 to 0.6
Water heaters and appliances	1.2	1.5 to 2.3
O&M, retrofits:[1]		
Shell efficiency	0.8	0.9
Lights	0.6	0.8
All residential measures together	4.0	5.6 to 6.6
Commercial buildings		
New investments		
Shell efficiency	2.3	4.0
Heating and cooling equipment	1.0	1.2 to 1.9
Lights	2.1	3.0
Office equipment	1.6	2.1
Water heater and appliances	0.1	0.1
Cogeneration	0.2	1.5 to 2.3
O&M, retrofits		
Shell efficiency	0.8	0.8
Lights	0.5	0.5
All commercial measures together	8.5	13.0 to 15.0
Transportation		
New investments		
New auto efficiency	0.8	3.5 to 3.8
New light truck efficiency	0.5	2.5 to 2.7
New heavy truck efficiency	0.4	2.4 to 2.4
Non-highway efficiency	0.5	1.2
O&M, retrofits		
Improved public transit	0.2	3.5
Truck inspection & maintenance	0.3	0.4
Traffic flow improvements/55 mph speed limit	1.2	1.4
Ridesharing/parking controls	0.4	1.0
All transportation measures together	4.0	14.0 to 15.0
Industry		
New investments		
Efficient motors	1.2	3.7 to 4.0
Lighting	0.5	0.7 to 0.8
Process change, top 4 industries	3.0	8.2
Fuel switch to gas	0.0	2.4 to 2.7
Cogeneration	0.8	5.2 to 5.8
O&M, retrofits		

[Continued]

★ 354 ★

Carbon Emissions Reduction Measures
[Continued]

	Reductions in 2015	
	Moderate (in percent)	Tough (in percent)
Housekeeping	1.9	2.0
Lighting	0.1	0.2
All industrial measures together	8.0	17.0 to 18.0
Electric Utility Supply-Side Measures		
Existing plant measures		
Improved nuclear utilization	4.1	4.1
Fossil efficiency improvements	1.7	1.7
Upgraded hydroelectric plants	0.5	0.5
Natural gas co-firing	-	3.7
New plant measures		
No new coal; higher fraction of new nonfossil sources	-	0.0 to 4.7
CO_2 emission rate standards	0.4	0.0 to 0.1
All utility supply-side measures together	6.6	9.9 to 14.0
Forestry Measures		
Afforestation		
Conservation Reserve Program	0.2	0.2
Urban trees	-	0.7
Additional tree planning	-	2.3
Increased timber productivity	-	3.1
Increased use of biomass fuels	-	1.2
All forestry measures together	0.2	7.5

Source: *Changing by Degrees: Steps to Reduce Greenhouse Gases*, U.S. Congress, Office of Technology Assessment, OTA-O-482, Washington, D.C., February 1991, p. 11, from Office of Technology Assessment 1 percent of 1987 emissions =13 million metric tons. Carbon = 0.7 percent of 2015 emissions. - means not available. *Note:* 1. Operating and maintenance.

★ 355 ★

CFC Phase-Out Impact

Data show the impact of moving from chlorofluorocarbon-based refrigerants to others by type of application.

Product Category	Refrigerant		
	From	To	Impact
Domestic Appliances	R-12	R-134a, R-22, R-152a Blends, Mixtures, R-290, R-717	Major
Residential Air Conditioner	R-22	R-22	N/C[2]

[Continued]

★ 355 ★

CFC Phase-Out Impacts on Products
[Continued]

Product Category	Refrigerant		
	From	To	Impact
Automotive Air Conditioner	R-12	R-134a, R-22, Blends	Major
Chillers, Positive Displacement	R-22	R-22	N/C[2]
Chillers, Centrifugal	R-11 (80%) R-12 (10%) R-114	R-123, R-134a Blends, R-124	Major
Heat Pumps, Non-Industrial	R-22	R-22	N/C[2]
Industrial Incl. Food Storage	R-22, R-717, R-12, R-502	R-22, R-717	Minor[3]
Commercial Stores and Supermarkets	R-502, R-22 R-12	R-22, R-125	Minor

Source: ASHRAE Journal, February 1991, p. 24 *Notes:* 1. New working fluids (refrigerants and lubricants) and perhaps other changes as required. 2. No changes required. 3. Some equipment modification will be needed.

★ 356 ★

CFCs and Alternative Refrigerants
Data show alternative refrigerants to chlorofluorocarbons (CFCs).

Present Refrigerants	Leading Candidates	Future Prospects	Long Range
NH_3	R-123	R-23	Fluorinated
R-11	R-124	R-32	Cyclics
R-12	R-134a	R-125	
R-22	R-142b	R-134	Fluorinated
R-113	R-152a	R-143a	Polyethers
R-114	R-22/142b		
R-115	R-22/152a/114		
R-500	R-22/152a/124		3C Halo- carbons
R-502			
Hydrocarbons	Mixtures		Mixtures

Source: ASHRAE Journal, February 1991, p. 23.

★ 357 ★

Chemical Flame-Retardant System and Smoke Suppressant Sales

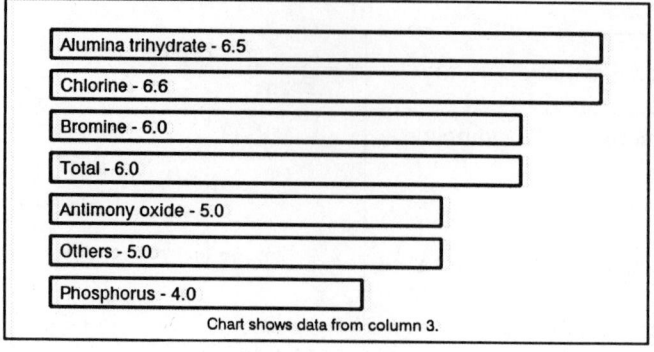

Chart shows data from column 3.

Type	Millions of Pounds		Average growth, %/yr, 1989-94
	1989 Sales	1994 Sales	
Alumina trihydrate	317	435	6.5
Antimony oxide	50	63	5.0
Bromine	59	80	6.0
Chlorine	90	123	6.6
Phosphorus	195	242	4.0
Others	46	60	5.0
Total	757	1003	6.0

Source: Modern Plastics, May 1990, p. 44, from *Business Communications*.

★ 358 ★

Commercial Flue Gas Desulfurization Systems

Level of development/Major features	Process	Reagent	Additive	Byproduct/ Disposal	% Sulfur Dioxide Removal

Widely used in the U.S.
  Low cost
  Good space utilization
  Improved waste dewatering
  Decreased waste processing costs
	Limestone/ Forced Oxida- tion(LSFO)	Limestone	None	Gypsum/ landfill (potentially salable)	95

Installed in several U.S. units; extensive foreign experience
  Marketable product
  No landfill costs
  Increased capital costs
	Wallboard LSFO	Limestone	None	Wallboard grade gypsum/sale	95

12 full-scale installations
  Reduced scaling problems
  Increased waste-handling and operating costs
	Inhibited LS (thisosul- fate)	Limestone	Sulfur emulsion (thisosul-	Fixated calcium sulfite/land-	95

[Continued]

★ 358 ★

Commercial Flue Gas Desulfurization Systems
[Continued]

Level of development/Major features	Process	Reagent	Additive	Byproduct/ Disposal	% Sulfur Dioxide Removal

Retrofit instal. at older units to improve SO₂ removal
  High SO₂ removal
  Low scaling and plugging
	Organic Acid (DBA) Enhanced LSFO	Limestone	Dibasic, formate or alternate organic acid	Gypsum/ landfill	95 +

13 installed in Japan; development proceeding in U.S.
  Single vessel
  Vessel size could limit applications
	Chiyoda 121	Limestone	None	Gypsum/ landfill or wallboard sale	95 +

Many installations in Japan and Europe
  Combined absorber/reaction tank reduces size
  Maximizes conversion to sulfate
	Pure Air	Limestone	None	Gypsum/ landfill or wallboard sale	95

Many full scale installations in U.S.
  High SO₂ removal
  Low scale and plugging
	Magnesium- Enhanced Lime (Maglime)	4-8% MgO Lime	None	Fixated calcium sulfate/landfill	98

3000 MW installed in Japan; several in U.S.
  High SO₂ removal
  Low maintenance
  Requires lime and flyash for sludge fixation
	Lime Dual Alkali (LDA)	Soda Ash & Slakable Lime	None	Fixated calcium sulfate/landfill	95 +

Widely used, especially in western U.S.
  Limited experience on high sulfur coal
  Lower SO₂ removal
  Upgrade likely
	Lime Spray Dryer (LSD)	Lime	None	Calcium sulfite-sulfate/ landfill	85-90

Source: Electric Light and Power, March 1991, p. 19.

★ 359 ★

Nitrogen Oxide Emissions Reductions in 1994

Potential nitrogen oxide emissions reductions and remaining emissions in 1994 as a percentage of 1985 emissions in nonattainment cities.

Emission source	Percent
Emissions reductions	
Enhanced inspection and maintenance	2.6
Electric utility boiler	11.2
Other large stationary[1]	3.5
Remaining emissions	
Air, rail, marine	10.3
Electric utility boiler	15.6
Commercial and Institutional boiler, industrial processes, and other minor sources	5.5
Small industrial and other boilers	13.1

[Continued]

★ 359 ★

Nitrogen Oxide Emissions Reductions in 1994
[Continued]

Emission source	Percent
Highway vehicles	30.1
Other large stationary[1]	8.0

Source: Catching Our Breath: Next Steps for Reducing Urban Ozone, U.S. Congress, Office of Technology Assessment, OTA-F-412, Washington, D.C., July 1989, p. 161, from Office of Technology Assessment, 1989. *Notes:* 1. Other large stationary includes: Industrial boilers, stationary engines, gas turbines, and process heaters.

★ 360 ★

Nitrogen Oxide Emissions Reductions in 2004

Potential nitrogen oxide emissions reductions and remaining emissions in 2004 as a percentage of 1985 emissions in nonattainment cities.

Emission source	Percent
Emissions reductions	
Enhanced inspection and maintenance	2.8
Electric utility boiler	12.7
New mobile standards	7.5
Enhanced I/M[2]	2.8
Other large stationary[1]	4.7
Remaining emissions	
Highway vehicles	21.1
Electric utility boiler	14.3
Small industrial and other boilers	14.2
Air, rail, marine	9.4
Commercial and Institutional boiler, industrial processes, and other minor sources	4.8
Other large stationary[1]	8.5

Source: Catching Our Breath: Next Steps for Reducing Urban Ozone, U.S. Congress, Office of Technology Assessment, OTA-F-412, Washington, D.C., July 1989, p. 161, from Office of Technology Assessment, 1989. *Notes:* 1. Other large stationary includes: Industrial boilers, stationary engines, gas turbines, and process heaters. 2. I/M = Inspection and maintenance.

★ 361 ★

Steam-Electric Plants With Environmental Equipment

Number and nameplate capacity of fossil-fueled steam-electric generators in plants that have environmental equipment.

Environmental Equipment	Scrubbers		Particulate Collectors		Cooling Towers		Total[2]	
	Number of Generators	Capacity (megawatts)	Number of Generators	Capacity (megawatts)	Number of Generators	Capacity (megawatts)	Number of Generators	Capacity (megawatts)
1989[1]	160	68,911	1,211	348,652	555	175,033	1,433	379,954
1988	158	68,396	1,211	349,227	498	164,202	1,419	377,870
1987	156	67,257	1,211	346,415	537	170,676	1,431	377,742
1986	155	65,261	1,221	344,946	537	168,898	1,444	376,498
1985	148	60,440	1,220	340,115	540	163,177	1,452	371,927

Source: Energy Information Administration, Electric Power Annual, January 1991, p. 74, from Energy Information Administration, Form EIA-767, "Steam-Electric Plant Operation and Design Report." Data include petrolum coke. These data are estimates derived from Form EIA-767, "Steam-Electric Plant Operation and Design report." Data for 1985 through 1988 are revised. *Notes:* 1. Data for 1989 are preliminary. 2. Components are not additive since some generators are included in more than one category and not all units have environmental equipment.

★ 362 ★

Volatile Organic Compound Emission Reductions in 1994

Potential volatile organic compound (VOC) emissions reductions and remaining emissions in 1994, shown as a percentage of 1985 emissions in nonattainment cities.

Emission source	Percent
Emissions reductions	
Gasoline volatility	12.0
Expected reductions without further control	6.8
TSDFs	5.7
RACT/New CTGs[1,2]	4.8
Enhanced I/M[4]	2.0
Stage II	1.8
Methanol fuels	0.2
Remaining emissions	
Small stationary	37.1
Mobile	23.1
Large stationary	6.2

Source: Catching Our Breath: Next Steps for Reducing Urban Ozone, U.S. Congress, Office of Technology Assessment, OTA-F-412, Washington, D.C., July 1989, p. 129, from Office of Technology Assessment, 1989. *Notes:* 1. RACT = Reasonably Available Control Technology. 2. CTG = Control Technique Guidelines. 3. TSDFs = Treatment, Storage, and Disposal Facilities. 4. I/M = Inspection and Maintenance.

★ 363 ★

Volatile Organic Compound Emission Reductions in 2004

Potential volatile organic compound (VOC) emissions reductions and remaining emissions in 2004 as a percentage of 1985 emissions in nonattainment cities.

Emission source	Percent
Emissions reductions	
Gasoline volatility	13.3
TSDFs	7.5
RACT/New CTGs[1,2]	5.2
Stage II + Onboard	2.5
Enhanced I/M[4]	1.5
New mobile standards	1.3
Expected reductions without further control	1.2
Arch. coatings	0.4
Methanol fuels	0.1
Remaining emissions	
Small stationary	40.8
Mobile	19.8
Large stationary	6.2

Source: Catching Our Breath: Next Steps for Reducing Urban Ozone, U.S. Congress, Office of Technology Assessment, OTA-F-412, Washington, D.C., July 1989, p. 129, from Office of Technology Assessment, 1989. *Notes:* 1. RACT = Reasonably Available Control Technology. 2. CTG = Control Technique Guidelines. 3. TSDFs = Treatment, Storage, and Disposal Facilities. 4. I/M = Inspection and Maintenance.

Alternative Fuels

★ 364 ★

Alternative Fuel Vehicle Gas Emissions

Values shown represent the difference in greenhouse gas emissions if alternative fuel is used rather than gasoline.

Fuel and feedstock	Percent change from present
Methanol	
M85, current natural gas conversion technology	-2
M100, improved vehicle and gas conversion technology	-17
M100, improved vehicle and best coal conversion technology	+25-+30

[Continued]

★ 364 ★

Alternative Fuel Vehicle Gas Emissions
[Continued]

Fuel and feedstock	Percent change from present
Natural gas	
Compressed, from domestic sources	-14 to 0
Biomass fuels	
Ethanol from corn using coal for process heat	-10- +30
Synthetic natural gas from woody biomass	-70 to -60
Methanol from woody biomass	-70
Electricity	
Recharging from coal-fired plant	+5
Recharging from current electricity mix	-23
Recharging from best gas turbine	-45
Recharging from nuclear plants	-80
Recharging from solar or hydropower	-85
Hydrogen	
Hydride vehicle, nuclear electrolytic hydrogen	-55
Liquid hydrogen, all solar hydrogen	-85

Source: Changing by Degrees: Steps to Reduce Greenhouse Gases, U.S. Congress, Office of Technology Assessment, OTA-O-482, Washington, D.C., February 1991, p. 160, from M.A. DeLuchi, *State-of-the-art Assessment of Emissions of Greenhouse Gases From the Use of Fossil and Nonfossil Fuels, With Emphasis on Alternative Transportation Fuels*, draft report (Davis, CA: University of California, June 3, 1990), table 10. Estimates recalculated by M.A. DeLuchi, Dec. 11, 1990.

★ 365 ★

Cleaner Cars for Tomorrow

Engines

Reduced friction and improved combustion for existing designs	8% to 10% better fuel economy
New multivalve designs	5% to 10% better fuel economy
Two-cycle engines	20% to 40% better economy; also allows smaller, lighter cars

Transmissions

Electronic four-speed automatics	Extra 1 to 2 miles per gallon

Body and styling

Sleeker undercarriage, rear end	Extra 2 to 3 miles per gallon
Lightweight plastic and metal panels and structures	Each 250-pound reduction saves 1 mile per gallon

Catalytic converters

Metal replacing ceramic honey-comb, addition of electric preheaters	30% less hydrocarbon emission, 10% less nitrogen oxide, 60% less carbon monoxide

Fuel tank

Improved canisters for trapping vapors	15% to 20% decline in vapors

Source: Business Week, September 4, 1989, p. 103, from Data:BW. *Note:* 1. Better fuel economy lowers CO_2 emissions.

★ 366 ★

Electricity From Electric Utilities by Renewable Energy Resources

Year	Geothermal		Wood and Waste		Wind and Other[1]	
	Net Summer Capacity[2] (thousand kilowatts)	Net Generation (million kilowatt-hours)	Net Summer Capacity[2] (thousand kilowatts)	Net Generation (million kilowatt-hours)	Net Summer Capacity[2] (thousand kilowatts)	Net Generation (million kilowatt-hours)
1949	[3]	[3]	13	386	0	0
1950	[3]	[3]	13	390	0	0
1951	[3]	[3]	13	391	0	0
1952	[3]	[3]	37	482	0	0
1953	[3]	[3]	37	389	0	0

[Continued]

★ 366 ★

Electricity from Electric Utilities by Renewable Energy Resources
[Continued]

Year	Geothermal		Wood and Waste		Wind and Other[1]	
	Net Summer Capacity[2] (thousand kilowatts)	Net Generation (million kilowatt-hours)	Net Summer Capacity[2] (thousand kilowatts)	Net Generation (million kilowatt-hours)	Net Summer Capacity[2] (thousand kilowatts)	Net Generation (million kilowatt-hours)
1954	[3]	[3]	37	263	0	0
1955	[3]	[3]	37	276	0	0
1956	[3]	[3]	37	152	0	0
1957	[3]	[3]	64	177	0	0
1958	[3]	[3]	64	175	0	0
1959	[3]	[3]	64	153	0	0
1960	11	33	64	140	NA	NA
1961	11	94	64	126	NA	NA
1962	11	100	64	128	NA	NA
1963	24	168	64	128	NA	NA
1964	24	204	64	148	NA	NA
1965	24	189	64	269	NA	NA
1966	24	188	72	334	NA	NA
1967	51	316	72	316	NA	NA
1968	78	436	72	375	NA	NA
1969	78	615	72	320	NA	NA
1970	78	525	72	356	NA	NA
1971	184	548	72	311	NA	NA
1972	290	1,453	77	331	NA	NA
1973	396	1,966	77	328	NA	NA
1974	396	2,453	77	251	NA	NA
1975	502	3,246	77	191	NA	NA
1976	502	3,616	77	266	NA	NA
1977	502	3,582	77	481	NA	NA
1978	502	2,978	77	338	NA	NA
1979	667	3,889	78	498	NA	NA
1980	909	5,073	78	433	NA	NA
1981	909	5,686	78	368	[4]	NA
1982	1,022	4,843	79	321	6	NA
1983	1,207	6,075	212	379	6	3
1984	1,231	7,741	321	886	17	12
1985	1,580	9,325	350	1,383	18	16
1986	1,558	10,308	343	1,177	19	18
1987	1,549	10,775	401	1,477	25	14

[Continued]

★ 366 ★

Electricity from Electric Utilities by Renewable Energy Resources
[Continued]

Year	Geothermal		Wood and Waste		Wind and Other[1]	
	Net Summer Capacity[2] (thousand kilowatts)	Net Generation (million kilowatt-hours)	Net Summer Capacity[2] (thousand kilowatts)	Net Generation (million kilowatt-hours)	Net Summer Capacity[2] (thousand kilowatts)	Net Generation (million kilowatt-hours)
1988	1,667	10,300	421	1,674	7	10
1998[5]	1,667	9,428	421	1,964	8	3

Source: Annual Energy Review 1989, U.S. Department of Energy, DOE/EIA-0384 (89), May 24, 1990, p. 238, from *Net Summer Capability at End of Year*. 1960 through 1984-Energy Information Administration estimates.1985 and forward - Energy Information Administration, form EIA-860, "Annual Electric Generator Report." *Net Generation*: 1949 through September 1977-Federal Power Commission, Form FPC-4, "Monthly Power Plant Report." October 1977 through 1981-Federal Energy Regulatory Commission, Form FPC-4, "Monthly Power Plant Report." 1982 and forward-Energy Information Administration, Form EIA-759, "Monthly Power Plant Report." NA = Not available *Notes:* 1. Includes photovoltaic and solar thermal energy. 2. At end of year. 3. No geothermal capacity prior to 1960. 4. Less than 500 kilowatts. 5. Preliminary.

★ 367 ★

Vehicle Storage of Alternative Fuels

Weight and volume of alternative fuels or power systems compared with petrol (gasoline) for use in automobiles. Data are indexes with petrol defined as 100. Values above 100 indicate more weight or volume than petrol.

	Weight Index (Petrol = 100)	Volume Index (Petrol = 100)
Petrol	100	100
Diesel	100	90
Ethanol	165	118
Methanol	190	125
Liquefied hydrogen	270	500
Sodium-Sulfur battery	3,455	2,100
Lead battery	11,520	3,000

Source: The Economist, October 13, 1990, p. 81, from Volkswagen.

Conservation

★ 368 ★

Selected Conservation and Pollution Abatement Measures

Data refer to the U.S. and the Carribean area.

Practice	Unit	1980	1981	1982	1983	1984	1985	1986	1987	1988	1989	Total 1936-89[1]
Terrace systems[2]	1,000 acres	491	454	427	513	388	442	342	572	964	841	41,155
Sod waterways[2]	do	740	727	489	453	207	230	176	133	224	167	17,151
Conservation tillage systems	do	377	717	733	919	1,009	1,076	631	423	445	330	7,081
Stripcropping systems	do	112	120	125	127	102	131	92	82	139	123	116,252
Establishing permanent vegetative cover	do	900	817	714	964	667	772	542	522	646	615	75,037
Cropland protective cover	do	1,281	1,495	1,115	1,100	791	798	637	601	750	636	509,279
Improving permanent vegetative cover	do	1,958	1,961	1,728	1,828	1,337	1,519	1,011	1,014	1,373	1,170	164,322
Planting trees or shrubs	do	49	53	55	66	55	87	98	130	156	132	6,808
Timber stand improvement	do	62	75	54	38	25	34	27	21	38	40	5,466
Permanent wildlife habitat[2]	do	36	46	46	40	23	23	20	15	24	21	5,367
Water impoundment reservoirs	Number	11,865	12,271	7,423	7,020	5,987	5,756	4,783	5,626	8,480	6,520	2,473,755
Grazing land protection	do	11,573	13,977	9,411	9,151	7,701	8,764	6,664	6,801	12,502	13,764	565,970
Contour farming	1,000 acres	27	24	24	20	29	35	21	21	20	23	140,138
Diversions[2]	do	136	128	123	111	112	95	71	66	102	85	7,164
Sediment retention, erosion, or water control structures	Number	14,266	15,968	12,142	12,646	12,462	14,081	12,655	10,427	16,007	12,281	3,468,562

Source: Agricultural Conservation and Forestry Statistics, 1989, U.S. Government Printing Office, Washington, D.C., 1989, p. 443, from Agriculture Stabilization and Conservation Service Totals are from unrounded data. *Notes:* 1. In 1974, the data include the Regular, Long-Term Agreement, and Forestry Incentive Programs. From 1975, the data include the Regular and Long-Term Agreement Programs. 2. In area served.

★ 369 ★

Soil Conservation - Watershed Protection & Flood Prevention

The projects were carried out with the assistance of the Soil Conservation Service with watershed protection and flood prevention funds for year ending September 30, 1989.

Item	Watershed[1] and flood prevention projects[2]
Flood prevention subwatersheds in operation during year	333
Watershed projects in operation during year	770
Land protected from erosion (in acres):	
Cropland	536,116
Pasture and hayland	1,174,500
Range and native pasture	1,074,892
Woodland	15,987
Wildlife	86,262

[Continued]

★ 369 ★

Soil Conservation - Watershed Protection & Flood Prevention
[Continued]

Item	Watershed[1] and flood prevention projects[2]
Recreation	9,031
Other	16,232
Total land[3]	2,913,020

Source: Agricultural Conservation and Forestry Statistics, 1989, U.S. Government Printing Office, Washington, D.C., 1989, p. 452, from Soil Conservation Service *Notes:* 1. As authorized by the Soil Conservation Act of 1935 (Public law 46, 74th Congress) and Watershed Protection and Flood Prevention Act. P.L. 566, as amended. 2. All of the 11 watersheds were approved Dec. 22, 1944; however, flood control funds did not become available for works of improvement until 1946. As of Sept. 30, 1985, work in two watersheds was completed. 3. Land protected data included in Table "Land Protected From Erosion by Soil Conservation Practices."

Energy Conservation

★ 370 ★

Emissions From High-Efficiency Fluorescent Lamps
Results from replacing the lights in an Environmental Protection Agency office.

	Using incandescent bulbs	Using Fluorescent bulbs	Savings
Kilowatt-hours a year	184,766	78,734	106,032
Annual electric cost	$12,934	$5,511	$7,422
Carbon dioxide emissions (lbs per year)	415,724	177,152	238,572
Sulphur dioxide emissions (lbs per year)	3,231	1,377	1,854
Nitrogen oxide emissions (lbs per year)	1,522	649	873

Source: The New York Times, from Environmental Protection Agency, January 16, 1991, p. C16.

★ 371 ★

Lamp Efficiency by Type

The 400 watt High-Pressure Sodium (HPS) lamp emits 50,000 lumens for a lumen per watt (LPW) rating of 125, where a typical 500 watt incandescent bulb provides 10,850 initial lumens for an LPW of only 22.

Lamp Types	Wattage	Approximate Initial Lumens
Incandescent	100	1,750
	150	2,850
	300	6,360
	500	10,850
	1,000	23,740
	1,500	34,400
Mercury (coated)	100	4,200
	175	8,500
	250	12,100
	400	22,500
	1,000	63,000
Metal Halide	100	8,500
	175	16,600
	250	20,500
	400	36,000
	1,000	110,000
High-Pressure Sodium	100	9,500
	150	16,000
	250	27,500
	400	50,000
	1,000	140,000

Source: Electric Light and Power, September 1990, p. 37.

Hazardous Waste Management

★ 372 ★

Chemical Industry Waste Disposal by Method

Shares, by method, of solid hazardous waste disposed of by the chemical industry. Percentages are based on a total of 6.6 million tons of waste in 1988.

Disposal method	Percent
Material reclaimed/reused/recovered	64.3
Burned for energy recovery	11.4
Incineration	10.2
Other treatment	2.4
Landfill	6.8
Surface impoundment	2.8
Waste pile	0.6
Underground injection	0.6
Other disposal	0.7
Storage at year's end	0.2

Source: Chemical Week, August 22, 1990, p. 36, from "Chemical Manufacturers Association Hazardous Waste Survey".

★ 373 ★

Hazardous Household Waste Treatment Methods

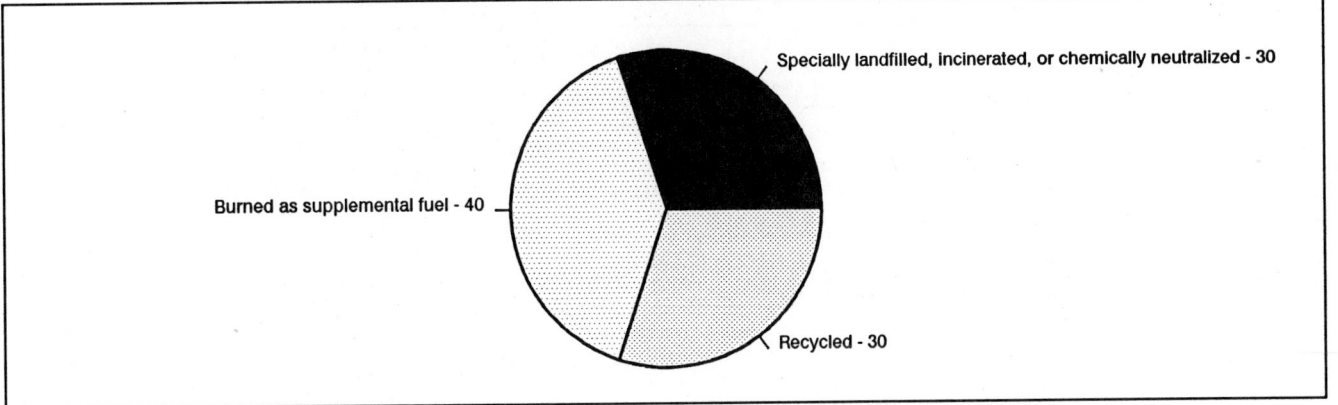

Methods of treatment, shown as percentage of all household waste treated.

Method	Percent of total waste
Burned as supplemental fuel	40
Recycled	30
Specially landfilled, incinerated, or chemically neutralized	30

Source: Garbage, March/April 1990, p. 16, from Chemical Waste Management Company; GSX Chemical Services, Inc.

★ 374 ★

Hazardous Solid Waste Treatment - 1988

Method	Company-owned facilities		Commercial facilities	
	Tons	Number of Plants	Tons	Number of Plants
Incineration	611,806	105	69,143	309
Chemical Treatment	40,212	8	4,528	17
Physical Treatment	83,983	4	130	2
Biological Treatment	11	3	5,187	3
Thermal Treatment	3,614	3	1,231	3
Solidification	246	2	3,804	12
Combination of above methods	12,419	7	5,230	10

[Continued]

★ 374 ★

Hazardous Solid Waste Treatment - 1988
[Continued]

Method	Company-owned facilities		Commercial facilities	
	Tons	Number of Plants	Tons	Number of Plants
Not specified	994	4	936	8
Total	753,285		90,189	

Source: Chemicalweek, August 22, 1990, p. 40, from Chemical Manufacturers Association Hazardous Waste Survey.

★ 375 ★

Hazardous Solids Management

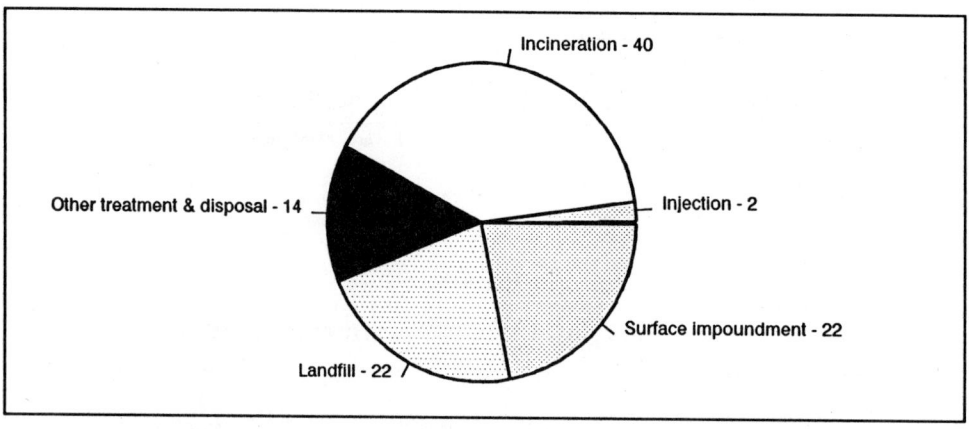

Data show prevalence of methods in the chemical industry for handling hazardous solid waste.

Type of treatment	Percent
Incineration	40
Landfill	22
Surface impoundment	22
Injection	2
Other treatment & disposal	14

Source: C&EN, July 31, 1989, p. 44, from Chemical Manufacturers Association. Based on a survey of selected chemical plants.

★ 376 ★

Hazardous Waste Disposal Sites

The sites that are eligible for cleanup under Superfund program are considered the worst hazardous waste sites in the nation.

States	Superfund Sites[1]	Other Hazardous Waste Sites[2]
Alabama	12	70
Alaska	1	-
Arizona	9	250
Arkansas	10	13
California	88	250
Colorado	16	74
Connecticut	14	-
Delaware	21	137
Florida	51	760
Georgia	13	350
Hawaii	6	-
Idaho	4	-
Illinois	39	64
Indiana	37	32
Iowa	23	300
Kansas	11	203
Kentucky	17	26
Louisiana	11	-
Maine	8	36
Maryland	10	30
Massachusetts	22	351
Michigan	81	910
Minnesota	40	83
Mississippi	3	200
Missouri	21	84
Montana	10	26
Nebraska	5	160
Nevada	-	-
New Hampshire	15	172
New Jersey	110	400[3]
New Mexico	10	376
New York	76	420
North Carolina	21	88
North Dakota	2	3
Ohio	32	108
Oklahoma	11	11
Oregon	7	80
Pennsylvania	97	40
Rhode Island	9	20
South Carolina	21	75
South Dakota	1	2
Tennessee	13	255

[Continued]

★ 376 ★

Hazardous Waste Disposal Sites
[Continued]

States	Superfund Sites[1]	Other Hazardous Waste Sites[2]
Texas	28	352
Utah	11	75
Vermont	8	102
Virginia	22	25
Washington	43	131
West Virginia	6	-
Wisconsin	39	321
Wyoming	2	16
Puerto Rico	9	2
Guam	1	-
Total	1,177	7,483

Source: Editorial Research Reports, July 29, 1988, p. 379, from Environmental Protection Agency, Association of State and Territorial Solid Waste Management Officials. *Notes:* 1. Final and proposed sites as of June 1988.l 2. Data are for Oct. 1986, the most recent available. 3. As of July 1988.

★ 377 ★

Hazardous Waste Generation and Disposal
The values are in millions of tons.

	1977	1988	1993	2000	Average annual growth (percent) 1977-1988	Average annual growth (percent) 1988-1993
Total by type of waste	131	291	380	510	7.5	5.5
Heavy metals	51	114	149	196	7.6	5.5
Organic chemicals	42	100	132	180	8.2	5.7
Petroleum derived	16	33	44	60	6.8	5.9
Inorganic chemicals	17	35	43	55	6.8	4.2
Other hazardous waste	5	9	13	19	5.5	7.6
By method of disposal						
Landfill/surface impound	12	200	225	165	29.1	2.4
Treatment/stabilization	2	13	50	150	18.5	30.9
Incineration	Neg	15	35	95	-	18.5
Resource recovery	2	12	30	75	17.7	20.1
Deep-well injection	5	14	15	10	9.8	1.4

[Continued]

★ 377 ★

Hazardous Waste Generation and Disposal
[Continued]

	1977	1988	1993	2000	Average annual growth (percent)	
					1977-1988	1988-1993
Illegal disposal	110	35	20	5	-9.9	-10.6
Other methods	Neg	2	5	10	-	20.1

Source: C&EN, July 31, 1989, p. 16. Neg stands for negligible.

★ 378 ★

Hazardous Waste Incinerators

Source of Data	Estimated Number			
	Commercial Facilities	Noncate-gorical[1] Facilities	Categorical Industries	Total
OSW Report on RCRA Permit Activities[2]	-	-	-	230
EPA's Directory of Commercial Facilities[3]	42	-	-	-
Mitre Corporation Survey of Manufacturers[4]	-	-	-	342
HWDMS Data base[5]	42	170	164	376
Directory of Industrial & Hazardous Waste Management Firms[6]	40	-	-	-
Average				316

Source: Preliminary Data Summary for the Hazardous Waste Industry (PB 90-126517), U.S. Environmental Protection Agency, Washington, D.C., September 1989, p. 32 *Notes:* 1. Does not include commercial facilities. 2. U.S. EPA. 1987. "Summary Report on RCRA Permit Activities for January 1987." Office of Solid Waste. February 17, 1987. 3. U.S. EPA. 1985. "Directory of Commercial Hazardous Waste Treatment and Recycling Facilities," EPA/530-SW-85-019. December 1985. 4. Keitz, E., et al. 1984. "Profile of Existing Hazardous Waste Incineration Facilities and Manufacturers in the United States." EPA-600/2-84-052. Mitre Corporation. February 1984. 5. HWDMS stands for Hazardous Waste Data Management Systems. 6. Environmental Information Ltd., 1986. *Industrial and Hazardous Waste Management Firms 1987*. Minneapolis, Minnesota.

★ 379 ★

Hazardous Waste Management Methods

Data show methods in use and quantities managed by each method in millions of metric tons per year.

Type of technology/process	Waste volume managed (million metric tons)
Incineration	0.85-0.95
Reuse as fuel	1.0-1.2
Fuel blending	0.45-0.6
Solidification/stabilization	0.5-0.6
Solvent recovery	0.7-0.8
Metal recovery	0.4-0.5
Wastewater treatment	350-450
Other treatment processes	1.5-3.0
Waste pile	0.4-0.5
Surface impoundment	150-225
Landfill	1.7-2.0
Land treatment	0.3-0.4
Underground injection	11.5-13.5

Source: C&EN, February 6, 1989, p. 20.

★ 380 ★

Hazardous Waste Management - 1988

The total waste managed was 272 million metric tons; of this total the top 50 facilities managed 90%, 269.28 million metric tons.

	Percentage	Metric tons
Top 50 facilities	90	269.28
Other 2921 facilities	10	2.72

Source: C&EN, February 6, 1989, p. 19.

★ 381 ★

Hazardous Wastewater Management - Chemical Industry

Data show prevalence of treatment methods in the chemical industry for handling hazardous wastewater.

Type	Percent
Treat & discharge directly to surface waters[1]	81
Pretreat & discharge to public treatment plant	9
Injection	8
Other	2

Source: C&EN, July 31, 1989, p. 44, from Chemical Manufacturers Association Based on a survey of selected chemical plants. *Notes:* 1. Treated by plant with a National Pollution Discharge Elimination System permit.

★ 382 ★

On-Site Releases to Land

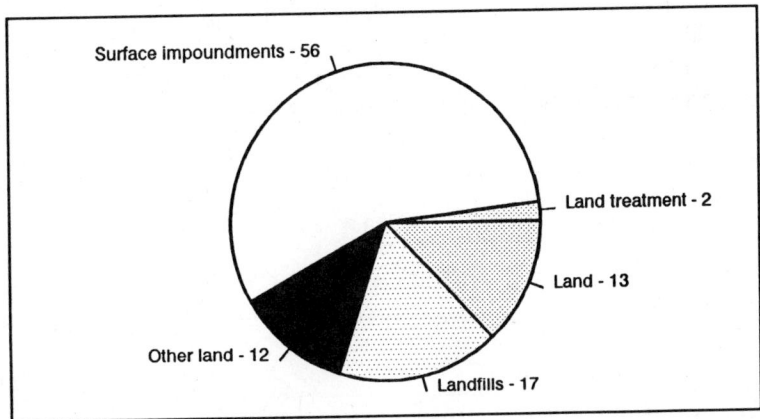

Percentage, by type, of on-site land releases totaling 2.5 billion pounds in 1987.

	Percentage
Surface impoundments	56
Landfills	17
Land	13
Other land	12
Land treatment	2

Source: The Toxic Release Inventory, A National Perspective, U.S. Environmental Protection Agency, Washington, D.C., June 1989, p. 173.

★ 383 ★

Superfund Site Cleanup Technologies

The values show frequency of selection and use in Superfund records of decision between 1982 and 1989.

Technologies	Percent
Established technologies	63.0
Solidification/stabilization	24.6
On-site incineration	19.0
Off-site incineration	16.0
Other	2.4
Innovative technologies	37.0
Vacuum extraction	12.0
Bioremediation	8.3
Thermal desorption	5.0
In situ soil flushing	4.0
Soil washing	2.8
Chemical extraction	2.4
Chemical treatment	1.6
In situ vitrification	0.8

Source: ENR, March 11, 1991, p. 15, from U.S. Environmental Protection Agency.

★ 384 ★

Superfund Sites

	Number or dollars
Number of Superfund sites	1,173
Potential Superfund sites	30,844
Number of emergency cleanups	1,837
Number of sites cleaned up	50
Number of Superfund sites deleted from the National Priority List	26
Remedial Investigation (RI)/feasibility studies (FS) underway	681
Record of decisions (or RI/FS completed)	438
Remedial action at Superfund sites underway	174
Completed (at portions of sites)	103
Total Superfund money authorized by law	$10.1 billion
Amount spent to date	$4.5 billion
Number of judicial settlements	101
Amount of settlement recoveries	$128 million

[Continued]

★ 384 ★

Superfund Sites
[Continued]

	Number or dollars
Total of cost recovery action initiated at 273 sites	$343 million
Enforcement actions	702
Amount of enforcement actions	$2.21 billion
Administrative orders to responsible parties	660

Source: C&EN, May 29, 1989, p. 19.

★ 385 ★

Treatment Technologies at Superfund Sites

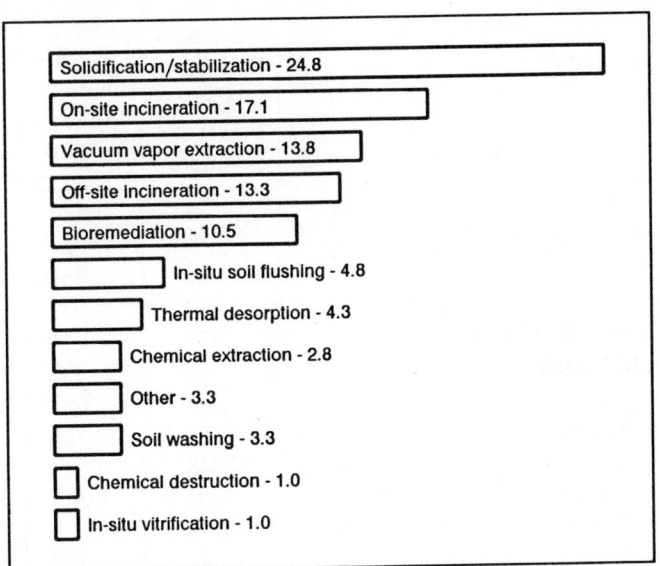

Treatment technologies	Percent
On-site incineration	17.1
Off-site incineration	13.3
Soil washing	3.3
Chemical extraction	2.8
Bioremediation	10.5
In-situ soil flushing	4.8
Vacuum vapor extraction	13.8
In-situ vitrification	1.0
Chemical destruction	1.0
Thermal desorption	4.3

[Continued]

★ 385 ★

Treatment Technologies at Superfund Sites
[Continued]

Treatment technologies	Percent
Solidification/stabilization	24.8
Other	3.3

Source: Environment Today, January/February 1991, p. 27, from EPA. Based on 210 treatment technologies specified in 165 Records of Decision during fiscal years 1987 through 1989. Sources include only solids, soils, sludges and liquid wastes.

★ 386 ★

TRI Facilities Reporting On-Site Treatment

Number of Toxic Release Inventory (TRI) facilities in 1987 reporting on-site waste treatment, shown by industry group.

Industry	SIC Code	TRI Facilities Reporting Waste Treatment Number	TRI Facilities in the Industry Number	Percent of Facilities in the Industry Reporting Waste Treatment
Food Products	20	678	1,576	43.02
Tobacco Manufacturers	21	9	24	37.50
Textile Mill Products	22	217	469	46.27
Apparel	23	13	37	35.14
Lumber and Wood Products	24	189	644	29.35
Furniture and Fixtures	25	98	332	29.52
Paper Products	26	399	663	60.18
Printing, Publishing	27	144	287	50.17
Chemical Products	28	2,048	3,849	53.21
Petroleum Refining	29	201	343	58.60
Rubber and Plastic Products	30	373	1,125	33.16
Leather Products	31	44	117	37.61
Stone, Clay, Glass Products	32	267	629	42.45
Primary Metals	33	724	1,305	55.48
Fabricated Metals	34	1,430	2,393	59.76
Machinery, except Electrical	35	334	787	42.44
Electric and Electronic Equip.	36	875	1,426	61.36
Transportation Equipment	37	469	908	51.65
Measuring, Photographic Goods	38	145	306	47.39
Misc. Manufacturing	39	134	337	39.76
Multiple SIC codes in 20-39		790	1,317	59.98
No SIC codes in 20-39		144	404	35.64
Total		9,725	19,278	50.45

Source: The Toxic Release Inventory, A National Perspective, U.S. Environmental Protection Agency, Washington, D.C., June 1989, p. 249.

★ 387 ★

Underground Injection Toxic Releases

About 97% of the total toxic substances are released by 25 counties.

County	State	TRI Underground Injection releases (pounds)	Percent of Underground Injection Releases in the State
San Bernardino	CA	1,530,705,635	99.99
St. Charles	LA	224,967,781	40.62
Jefferson	LA	216,257,250	39.05
Jefferson	TX	180,655,474	28.67
Brazoria	TX	177,803,200	28.21
Calhoun	TX	108,271,200	17.18
Sedgwick	KS	91,067,160	100.00
Galveston	TX	80,457,940	12.77
Ascension	LA	74,770,693	13.50
Humphreys	TN	62,200,000	50.00
Maury	TN	60,191,200	48.38
Allen	OH	58,588,750	81.54
Harrison	MS	39,600,000	85.28
Harris	TX	33,394,993	5.30
Laramie	WY	30,651,671	100.00
La Porte	IN	30,071,815	47.46
Jefferson	KY	25,000,000	100.00
Escambia	FL	22,397,400	76.08
Porter	IN	21,256,667	33.55
Victoria	TX	18,691,650	2.97
Lake	IN	12,026,924	18.98
St. James	LA	10,106,253	1.82
Harrison	TX	9,859,130	1.56
Scioto	OH	8,973,595	12.49
Union	AR	8,951,344	68.77
Subtotal		3,136,917,725	
Percent of grand total		96.74	
Total for all others		105,545,032	
Grand total		3,242,462,757	

Source: The Toxic Release Inventory, A National Perspective, U.S. Environmental Protection Agency, Washington, D.C., June 1989, p. 202.

Incineration

★ 388 ★

Municipal Solid Waste Combustion

The estimated values are in millions of tons and percent.

	1988	1995	2000
Generation of MSW	179.6	199.8	216.0
Combustion with energy recovery	24.5	45.0	55.0
Combustion without energy recovery	1.0	0.5	0.1
Total combustion	25.5	45.5	55.1
Percent of generation	14.2	22.8	25.5

Source: Characterization of Municipal Solid Waste in the United States: 1990 Update, U.S. Environmental Protection Agency, EPA/530-SW-90-042, Washington, D.C., June 1990, p. 74, from Franklin Associates, Ltd. Residues from combustion of MSW are not classified as MSW in this report. Details may not add to totals due to rounding.

★ 389 ★

U.S. Incinerators by Type

Operating plants and operating capacity Incinerator type	Capacity, as of 3/1/89		Additions, through[2] 1/1/91	
	Number	Capacity, million lb.	Number	Capacity, million lb.
Waste-to-energy plants				
Mass-burn[3]	43	10.9	18	7.0
Refuse-derived fuel[4]	13	5.6	3	2.2
Modular[5]	56	2.2	2	0.1
Volume-reducing plant:				
Refuse-derived fuel[6]	19	2.6	-	-
Other	50	3.7	-	-
Total	181	25.0	23	9.3

Source: Modern Plastics, April 1990, p. 68, from National Solid Waste Management Association, Washington, D.C. Notes: 1. Operating capacity is defined as 85% of nameplate capacity. 2. Includes projects in which engineering and construction work has actually begun. Proposed plants at earlier stages of development are not included. 3. Facilities burn undifferentiated trash mix, with minimal pre-sorting of non-combustibles. 4. Resource-derived fuel plants with upfront operation for separation of combustibles used as fuel for on-site steam generation boilers. 5. Modular (generally small-scale and older technology). 6. Refuse-derived fuel processing facilities. These separate and process combustibles for use as fuel off-site.

Mine Waste Management

★ 390 ★

Surface Mining Reclamation

```
1981 - 129,746
1980 - 126,917
1972-1974 - 52,300
1978 - 47,106
1984 - 239,285
1983 - 172,528
1979 - 105,135
1986 - 168,592
1974-1977 - 22,203
1965-1972 - 676,500
          1985 - 201,718
       1982 - 198,351
```

Figures are shown in number of acres.

Year	Total land reclaimed
1965-1972	676,500
1972-1974	52,300
1974-1977	22,203
1978	47,106
1979	105,135
1980	126,917
1981	129,746
1982	198,351
1983	172,528
1984	239,285
1985	201,718
1986	168,592

Source: Council on Environmental Quality, *20th Annual Report 1990*, Washington, D.C., p. 441, from the U.S. Department of Agriculture, Soil Conservation Service, 1979. "The status of land disturbed by mining in the United States: Basic statistics by State and County as of July, 1977," pp. 3, 4, 11; U.S. Department of the Interior, Office of Surface Mining Reclamation and Enforcement, 1987. "Surface coal mining reclamation: 10 years of progress, 1977-1987," Table 3, pp. 44-45; and U.S. Department of the Interior, Office of Surface Mining Reclamation and Enforcement, 1987. "The abandoned mine program: 1977-1987," p. 25, Washington, DC. Data for 1965-1986 are not strictly comparable because of different methods of data collection. Data for 1965-1977 refer to reclamation of surface coal, sand, and gravel, and other mined areas and were compiled from national inventories. Data for 1978-1986 refer to acreages of surface coal mined areas released from reclamation bonds after reclamation was completed. In addition to data reported above, 5,600 abandoned mine sites, encompassing 55,615 acres across the Nation, have been reclaimed since 1977.

Nuclear Waste Management

★ 391 ★

Commercial Low-Level Radioactive Waste Disposal

No mixed low-level radioactive waste (LLW) is included since none was shipped for disposal after 1985.

	LLW volumes (cubic feet)
Compacts[1]	
Southeast (NC, GA, FL, TN, AL, SC, MS, VA)	522,000
Appalachian (PA, WV, MD, DE)	172,000
Northwest (WA, ID, OR, UT, AK, HI, MT)	129,000
Central Midwest (IL, KY)	128,000
Southwestern (CA, SD, ND, AZ)	102,000
Midwest (MI, WI, IN, IA, OH, MN, MO)	96,000
Northeast (CT, NJ)	78,000
Central Interstate (NE, AR, LA, KS, OK)	71,000
Rocky Mountain (CO, NV, NM, WY)	4,000
Unaffiliated States[2]	
New York[2]	65,000
Massachusetts[2]	47,000
Texas[2]	9,000
Vermont	7,000
Maine[2]	6,000
Rhode Island	1,000
District of Columbia	<1,000
New Hampshire[3]	<1,000
Puerto Rico	<1,000
Total	1,440,000

Source: Partnerships Under Pressure: Managing Commercial Low-Level Radioactive Waste, U.S. Congress, Office of Technology Assessment, OTA-F-426, Washington, D.C. November 1989, p. 8, from data taken from tables prepared by EG&G Idaho in May 1989 for the U.S. Department of Energy, DRAFT Integrated Data Base for 1989: Spent Fuel and Radioactive Waste Inventories, Projections, and Characteristics, DOE/RW-006, Rev. 5, 1989. LLW stands for low-level radioactive waste. *Notes:* 1. Host States that are operating, or scheduling to operate, a disposal facility are listed first. 2. Unaffiliated States that are planning to develop a disposal facility. 3. LLW volumes will increase once the Seabrook power plant is operational.

★ 392 ★

Effect of Delayed Decommissioning of Nuclear Plants

Effects on low-level radiation wastes generated by delaying the decommissioning of commercial nuclear power plants. Long deferral of decommissioning is shown to reduce risks to workers by reducing radioactivity and volume of wastes.

Plant type [1.175 gigawatts]	No delay	30-year delay	50-year delay
Radoactivity of all LLW in thousands of curies:			
Boiling water	6,600	180	140
Pressurized-water	4,900	210	160
Volume of all LLW in thoudsands of cubic feet:			
Boiling water	670	670[1]	60[1]
Pressurized-water	630	630[1]	65[1]

Source: Partnership Under Pressure: Managing Commercial Low-Level Radio Waste, November 1988, p. 153 from U.S. Department of Energy, Integrated Data Base for 1988: Spent Fuel anRadioactive Waste Inventories, Projections, and Characteristics, DOE/RW-0006, Rev. 4, September 1988, p. 185. *Note:* 1. Includes wastes from both preparation and decommissioning.

★ 393 ★

Low-Level Radioactive Waste Disposal

The table presents an estimation of potential for further volume reduction if currently available waste minimization and treatment techniques are more widely applied. The approach is based on maximizing decontamination with material reuse and further incineration.

	Volume (cubic feet)[1]	Possible volume (cubic feet)
LLW volume shipped for disposal		
Utility (58%)	840,000	-
Industrial (35%)	500,000	-
Other (7%)	100,000	-
Total	1,440,000	-
Utility	-	
Combustible[2]	-	360,000
Recyclable	-	240,000
Total utility reduction (42% of total shipped)	-	600,000
Industry		
Combustible + recyclable = 20% reduction (7% of total shipped)[3]	-	100,000
Possible total volume reduction (49% total volume reduction)	-	700,000

Source: Partnership Under Pressure: Managing Commercial Low-Level Radioactive Waste, November 1989, p. 90, from Office of Technology Assessment, 1989. LLW stands for Low-Level Radioactive Waste. *Notes:* 1. Volume figures are based on 1988 shipment data. 2. Figure deduced from Electric Power Research Institute, *Radwaste Generation Survey Update*, prepared by Analytical Resources, Inc., Sinking Spring, PA, February 1988. 3. Conservative estimate representing a 20% reduction of industrial disposal of LLW.

★ 394 ★

Low-Level Waste Disposal Sites

Disposal sites for cumulative amounts of commercial low-level radioactive wastes.

Disposal Site	Years in operation	Cumulative amounts in 10 cubic[6] feet	Approx-imate percent
Barnwell, SC	1971-present	20.60	45
Richland, WA	1965-present	10.80	24
Maxey Flats, KY	1963-1977	4.80	10
Beatty, NV	1962-present	4.00	9
Sheffield, IL	1967-1978	3.10	7
West Valley, NY	1963-1975	2.50	5
Total		45.80	100

Source: Partnerships Under Pressure: Managing Commercial Low-Level Radioactive Waste, Office of Technology Assessment, November 1989, p. 124, from U.S. Department of Energy, Draft, *Integrated Data Base for 1989: Spent Fuel and Radioactive Waste Inventories, Projections, and Characteristics*, DOE/RW-0006, Rev. 5, August 1989.

Radon Detection

★ 395 ★

Top Five Radon Detection Kits

Product	Type	Price (dollars)
Air check	Charcoal	9.95
Radon Project	Charcoal	12.00
Key Rad Kit	Charcoal	19.99
Key Track kit	Alpha	21.70
RadTrack	Alpha	25.00

Source: Money, January 1989, p. 147.

Resource Recovery

★ 396 ★

Aluminum Can Recycling

Amount of aluminum cans collected each year, shown in millions of pounds and as a percentage of all aluminum beverage cans produced in the same time period.

Year	Million pounds collected	Total in percent
1978	340	27.4
1979	360	25.7
1980	609	37.3
1981	1,107	53.2
1982	1,124	55.5
1983	1,144	52.9
1984	1,226	52.8
1985	1,245	51.0
1986	1,233	48.7
1987	1,335	50.5
1988	1,500	54.6

Source: Resource Recycling, May/June 1989, p. 67, from Aluminum Association; U.S. Department of Commerce and U.S. Bureau of Mines.

★ 397 ★

Aluminum Can Recycling

Year	Can sheet[1]	Cans Shipped[2]	Cans Collected[3]	Can weight Collected	Cans Per Pound	Recycling Rate (%)
1972	1,139	7.8	1.2	53	21.75	15.4
1973	1,307	9.9	1.5	68	22.25	15.2
1974	1,540	13.1	2.3	103	22.70	17.5
1975	1,411	15.2	4.1	180	23.00	26.9
1976	1,851	19.7	4.9	212	23.30	24.9
1977	2,051	25.0	6.6	280	23.47	26.4
1978	2,349	29.2	8.0	340	23.65	25.7
1979	2,445	33.1	8.5	360	23.69	25.7
1980	2,583	39.7	14.8	360	2.23	37.3
1981	2,725	46.8	24.9	1,017	24.45	53.2
1982	2,858	51.0	28.3	1,124	25.21	55.5
1983	3,140	55.6	29.4	1,144	25.70	52.9

[Continued]

★ 397 ★

Aluminum Can Recycling
[Continued]

Year	Can sheet[1]	Cans Shipped[2]	Cans Collected[3]	Can weight Collected	Cans Per Pound	Recycling Rate (%)
1984	3,251	60.4	31.9	1,226	26.00	52.8
1985	3,381	64.9	33.1	1,245	26.60	51.0
1986	3,502	68.0	33.3	1,233	27.00	49.0
1987	3,732	72.5	36.6	1,335	27.40	50.5
1988	3,698	77.8	42.5	1,505	28.30	54.6
1989[3]	1,984	42.6	24.7	785	28.90	58.0

Source: Resource Recycling, p. 23, November 1989, from Aluminum Association; Can Manufacturers Institute; and Resource Recycling. *Notes:* 1. In million pounds. 2. In billion units. 3. Data are for January through June.

★ 398 ★

Appliance Recycling Profile of the U.S.
Availability and recycling rate of appliances in the United States in 1986.

	Value
Population of United States (millions)	238.00
Quantity (million tons)	2.80
Units (millions)	32.70
Per capita (pounds/per person/year)	23.50
Per capita (units/per person/year)	0.14
Weight of appliance (pounds)	171.00
Recycling rate (percent)	7.10

Source: Resource Recycling, October 1989, p. 30, from *Characterization of Municipal Solid Waste in the United States 1960 to 2000*, U.S. Environmental Protection Agency, 1988.

Container and Packaging Recovery From Municipal Wastestream

Recovery of postconsumer wastes; does not include converting/fabrication scrap.

Products	Millions of tons						
	1960	1965	1970	1975	1980	1985	1988
Durable Goods	0.4	0.9	0.9	1.0	1.3	1.4	1.9
Nondurable Goods	2.4	2.8	3.8	3.8	4.8	5.6	7.4
Containers and Packaging							
Glass Packaging							
Beer and Soft Drink Bottles	0.1	0.1	0.1	0.4	0.8	1.0	1.1
Wine and Liquor Bottles	0.0	0.0	0.0	0.0	0.0	0.1	0.1
Food and Other Bottles & Jars	0.0	0.0	0.0	0.0	0.0	0.0	0.3
Total Glass Packaging	0.1	0.1	0.2	0.4	0.8	1.1	1.5
Steel Packaging							
Beer and Soft Drink Cans	0.0	0.0	0.0	0.0	0.1	0.0	0.0
Food and Other Cans	0.0	0.1	0.1	0.1	0.1	0.1	0.4
Other Steel Packaging	0.0	0.0	0.0	0.0	0.0	0.0	0.0
Total Steel Packaging	0.0	0.1	0.1	0.1	0.2	0.1	0.4
Aluminum Packaging							
Beer and Soft Drink Cans	0.0	0.0	0.0	0.1	0.3	0.6	0.8
Other Cans	0.0	0.0	0.0	0.0	0.0	0.0	0.0
Foil and Closures	0.0	0.0	0.0	0.0	0.0	0.0	0.0
Total Aluminum Packaging	0.0	0.0	0.0	0.1	0.3	0.6	0.8
Paper & Paperboard Packaging							
Corrugated Boxes	2.5	2.2	2.7	3.6	6.3	7.2	10.5
Milk Cartons	0.0	0.0	0.0	0.0	0.0	0.0	0.0
Folding Cartons	0.0	0.0	0.0	0.0	0.5	0.2	0.3
Other Paperboard Packaging	0.3	0.4	0.5	0.5	0.0	0.0	0.0
Bags and Sacks	0.0	0.0	0.0	0.0	0.3	0.1	0.2
Wrapping Papers	0.0	0.0	0.0	0.0	0.0	0.0	0.0
Other Paper Packaging	0.2	0.3	0.4	0.4	0.0	0.0	0.0
Total Paper & Board Packaging	3.0	2.9	3.6	4.5	7.1	7.5	11.0
Plastics Packaging							
Soft Drink Bottles	0.0	0.0	0.0	0.0	0.0	0.1	0.1
Milk Bottles	0.0	0.0	0.0	0.0	0.0	0.0	0.0
Other Containers	0.0	0.0	0.0	0.0	0.0	0.0	0.0
Bags and Sacks	0.0	0.0	0.0	0.0	0.0	0.0	0.0
Wraps	0.0	0.0	0.0	0.0	0.0	0.0	0.0
Other Plastics Packaging	0.0	0.0	0.0	0.0	0.0	0.0	0.0
Total Plastics Packaging	0.0	0.0	0.0	0.0	0.0	0.1	0.1

[Continued]

★ 399 ★

Container and Packaging Recovery from Municipal Waste Stream
[Continued]

Products	Millions of tons						
	1960	1965	1970	1975	1980	1985	1988
Wood Packaging	0.0	0.0	0.0	0.0	0.0	0.0	0.0
Other Miscellaneous Packaging	0.0	0.0	0.0	0.0	0.0	0.0	0.0
Total Containers & Packaging	3.1	3.1	3.9	5.1	8.4	9.4	13.8
Total Nonfood Product Wastes	5.9	6.8	8.6	9.9	14.5	16.4	23.1
Other Wastes							
Food Wastes	0.0	0.0	0.0	0.0	0.0	0.0	0.0
Yard Wastes	0.0	0.0	0.0	0.0	0.0	0.0	0.5
Miscellaneous Inorganic Wastes	0.0	0.0	0.0	0.0	0.0	0.0	0.0
Total Other Wastes	0.0	0.0	0.0	0.0	0.0	0.0	0.5
Total MSW Recovered-Weight	5.9	6.8	8.6	9.9	14.5	16.4	23.5

Source: Characterization of Municipal Solid Waste in the United States: 1990 Update, U.S. Environmental Protection Agency, EPA/530-SW-90-042, Washington, D.C., June 1990, p. 44, from Franklin Associates, Ltd. Details may not add to totals due to rounding.

★ 400 ★

Containers and Packaging Recovery as Percent of Waste Generated
Recovery of postconsumer wastes; does not include converting/fabrication scrap.

Products	Percent of Generation of Each Product						
	1960	1965	1970	1975	1980	1985	1988
Durable Goods	4.3	8.1	6.0	5.7	6.6	6.5	7.5
Nondurable Goods	13.6	12.6	14.9	14.8	13.2	13.1	14.6
Containers and Packaging							
Glass Packaging							
Beer and Soft Drink Bottles	7.1	3.8	2.6	6.3	11.9	17.5	20.0
Wine and Liquor Bottles	0.0	0.0	0.5	0.0	0.0	4.5	5.0
Food and Other Bottles and Jars	0.0	0.0	0.5	0.0	0.0	0.0	8.1
Total Glass Packaging	1.6	1.2	1.5	3.1	5.7	9.1	13.3
Steel Packaging							
Beer and Soft Drink Cans	1.6	1.7	1.3	3.9	9.7	7.5	15.2
Food and Other Cans	0.5	1.2	1.8	2.7	5.2	4.3	15.0
Other Steel Packaging	0.0	0.0	0.0	0.0	0.0	0.0	0.0
Total Steel Packaging	0.6	1.3	1.6	2.9	5.5	4.2	13.8
Aluminum Packaging							
Beer and Soft Drink Cans	0.0	0.0	5.1	27.0	37.0	51.0	55.0

[Continued]

★ 400 ★

Containers and Packaging Recovery as Percent of Waste Generated
[Continued]

Products	Percent of Generation of Each Product						
	1960	1965	1970	1975	1980	1985	1988
Other Cans	0.0	0.0	0.0	0.0	0.0	0.0	0.0
Foil and Closures	0.0	0.0	0.0	0.0	0.0	0.0	4.9
Total Aluminum Packaging	0.0	0.0	0.0	17.3	27.1	37.5	44.1
Paper and Paperboard Packaging							
Corrugated Boxes	34.2	22.0	21.3	26.7	37.1	37.9	45.4
Milk Cartons	0.0	0.0	0.0	0.0	0.0	0.0	0.0
Folding Cartons	0.0	0.0	0.0	0.0	13.5	5.0	7.7
Other Paperboard Packaging	7.9	8.9	10.4	11.4	0.0	0.0	0.0
Bags and Sacks	0.0	0.0	0.0	0.0	8.8	3.2	7.0
Wrapping Papers	0.0	0.0	0.0	0.0	0.0	0.0	0.0
Other Paper Packaging	6.9	9.1	10.5	12.1	0.0	0.0	0.0
Total Paper & Board Packaging	21.4	16.3	16.9	21.2	27.3	26.4	33.5
Plastics Packaging							
Soft Drink Bottles	0.0	0.0	0.0	0.0	4.6	18.7	21.0
Milk Bottles	0.0	0.0	0.0	0.0	0.0	0.0	0.5
Other Containers	0.0	0.0	0.0	0.0	0.0	0.0	0.0
Bags and Sacks	0.0	0.0	0.0	0.0	0.0	0.0	0.0
Wraps	0.0	0.0	0.0	0.0	0.0	0.0	0.0
Other Plastics Packaging	0.0	0.0	0.0	0.0	0.0	0.0	0.0
Total Plastics Packaging	0.0	0.0	0.0	0.0	0.3	1.5	1.6
Wood Packaging	0.0	0.0	0.0	0.0	0.0	0.0	0.0
Other Misc. Packaging	0.0	0.0	0.0	0.0	0.0	0.0	0.0
Total Containers and Packaging	11.4	9.1	8.9	11.5	16.6	18.1	24.3
Total Nonfood Product Wastes	10.9	10.1	10.2	11.3	13.6	14.2	17.5
Other Wastes							
Food Wastes	0.0	0.0	0.0	0.0	0.0	0.0	0.0
Yard Wastes	0.0	0.0	0.0	0.0	0.0	0.0	1.6
Miscellaneous Inorganic Wastes	0.0	0.0	0.0	0.0	0.0	0.0	0.0
Total Other Wastes	0.0	0.0	0.0	0.0	0.0	0.0	1.0
Total MSW Recovered-Percent	6.7	6.6	7.0	7.7	9.7	10.1	13.1

Source: Characterization of Municipal Solid Waste in the United States: 1990 Update, U.S. Environmental Protection Agency, EPA/530-SW-90-042, Washington, D.C., June 1990, p. 45, from Franklin Associates, Ltd. Details may not add to totals due to rounding.

★ 401 ★

Containers for Separate Collections

Results of a side-by-side test of popular types of containers used for separate collection of recyclables conducted by the Gildea Resource Center, Santa Barbara, California.

	Blue Boxes	Stacking	Sacks	Buckets
Participation rates				
Average weekly set out rate (percent)[1]	56	42	36	40
Overall participation rate (percent)[2]	88	62	55	78
Average pounds per set out	14.40	18.46	13.94	16.47
Average pounds per week per household	8.11	7.90	5.09	6.69
Average number of set outs per household	6.42	6.16	6.24	5.18
Frequency of set outs per household (1 set out/# weeks)	1.40	1.46	1.44	1.74
Container handling time (seconds/set out)[3]				
Driver	23.52	24.17	26.78	25.00
Collector	32.39	15.78	31.65	22.04
Driver and collector average	27.95	19.97	29.21	23.52
Container costs[4]				
Capital per household	5.50	17.00	0.86	3.80
Capital costs for 38,000 homes	209,000.00	646,000.00	32,680.00	144,000.00
Approximate container lifetime[5]	10 years	5 years	1 year	3 years
Percent containers replaced annually[6]	5	5	100	5
Annual replacement cost	10,450.00	32,300.00	32,680.00	7,220.00
Annual amortization costs[7]	34,014	170,000	-	58,065
Total annual cost	44,464	202,713	32,680	65,285

Source: Resource Recycling, January/February 1989, p. 21, from Gildea Resource Center, Santa Barbara, California *Notes:* 1. The average percentage of homes placing a set out on the curb in any given week. 2. The percentage of home participating at least twice during the nine week study. 3. Measured as the time from first touching the container(s), sorting the material into the truck bins, and replacing the container(s) on the ground. The highest and lowest of 25 measurements for driver and collector were dropped. 4. These prices are offered for comparative purposes only and may vary due to the percentage of recycled plastic used, quantities ordered, and customization of the container. For current prices, contact the manufacturers directly. 5. The stated lifetimes are based on manufacturers' claims and may vary due to extremes of heat and cold, exposure to sunlight, and abuse of the container. 6. The 5 percent figure is based on the experience of many communities and accounts for loss and theft of containers, and people moving and taking their containers. The 100 percent figure in the Sack neighborhood includes the factors stated above and sacks wearing out. 7. Amortization figures are based on a 10 percent annual interest rate.

★ 402 ★

Durable Goods Recovery as Percent of Waste Generated

Recovery of postconsumer wastes does not include converting/fabrication scrap.

Products	Percent of Generation of Each Product						
	1960	1965	1970	1975	1980	1985	1988
Durable Goods							
Major Appliances	0.0	0.0	0.0	0.0	3.6	7.4	7.0
Furniture and Furnishings	0.0	0.0	0.0	0.0	0.0	0.0	0.0
Rubber Tires	36.4	21.8	15.8	8.0	3.8	5.3	4.8
Batteries, lead acid	0.0	88.6	75.0	66.7	66.7	66.7	90.0
Miscellaneous Durables	0.0	0.0	0.0	0.0	1.3	1.0	0.7
Total Durable Goods	4.3	7.9	6.0	5.7	6.6	6.5	7.5
Nondurable Goods	13.6	12.6	14.9	14.8	13.2	13.1	14.6
Containers and Packaging	11.4	9.1	9.0	11.5	16.6	18.1	24.3
Total Nonfood Product Wastes	10.9	10.0	10.2	11.3	13.6	14.2	17.5
Other Wastes							
Food Wastes	0.0	0.0	0.0	0.0	0.0	0.0	0.0
Yard Wastes	0.0	0.0	0.0	0.0	0.0	0.0	1.6
Miscellaneous Inorganic Wastes	0.0	0.0	0.0	0.0	0.0	0.0	0.0
Total Other Wastes	0.0	0.0	0.0	0.0	0.0	0.0	1.1
Total MSW Recovered-Percent	6.7	6.6	7.1	7.7	9.7	10.1	13.1

Source: Characterization of Municipal Solid Waste in the United States: 1990 Update, U.S. Environmental Protection Agency, EPA/530-SW-90-042, Washington, D.C., June 1990, p. 33, from Franklin Associates, Ltd. Details may not add to totals due to rounding.

★ 403 ★

Durable Goods Recovery From Municipal Wastestream

Recovery of postconsumer wastes does not include converting/fabrication scrap.

Products	Millions of tons						
	1960	1965	1970	1975	1980	1985	1988
Durable Goods							
Major Appliances	0.0	0.0	0.0	0.0	0.1	0.2	0.2
Furniture and Furnishings	0.0	0.0	0.0	0.0	0.0	0.0	0.0
Rubber Tires	0.4	0.3	0.3	0.2	0.1	0.1	0.1
Batteries, lead acid	0.0	0.6	0.6	0.8	1.0	1.0	1.5
Miscellaneous Durables	0.0	0.0	0.0	0.0	0.1	0.1	0.1
Total Durable Goods	0.4	0.9	0.9	1.0	1.3	1.4	1.9

[Continued]

★ 403 ★

Durable Goods Recovery from Municipal Waste Stream
[Continued]

Products	Millions of tons						
	1960	1965	1970	1975	1980	1985	1988
Nondurable Goods	2.4	2.8	3.8	3.8	4.8	5.6	7.4
Containers and Packaging	3.1	3.1	3.9	5.1	8.4	9.4	13.8
Total Nonfood Product Wastes	5.9	6.8	8.6	9.9	14.5	16.4	23.1
Other Wastes							
Food Wastes	0.0	0.0	0.0	0.0	0.0	0.0	0.0
Yard Wastes	0.0	0.0	0.0	0.0	0.0	0.0	0.5
Miscellaneous Inorganic Wastes	0.0	0.0	0.0	0.0	0.0	0.0	0.0
Total Other Wastes	0.0	0.0	0.0	0.0	0.0	0.0	0.5
Total MSW Recovered-Weight	5.9	6.8	8.6	9.9	14.5	16.4	23.5

Source: Characterization of Municipal Solid Waste in the United States: 1990 Update, U.S. Environmental Protection Agency, EPA/530-SW-90-042, Washington, D.C., June 1990, p. 33, from Franklin Associates, Ltd. Details may not add to totals due to rounding.

★ 404 ★

Energy Saved by Recycling

Aluminum - 95
Plastics - 88
Newsprint - 34
Corrugated - 24
Glass - 5

Chart shows data from column 2.

Materials	Energy required to produce from virgin (million Btu/ton)	Energy saved by using recyclables (percentage)
Aluminum	250.0	95
Plastics	98.0	88
Newsprint	29.8	34
Corrugated	26.5	24
Glass	15.6	5

Source: Resource Recycling, January/February 1989, p. 59. These are only rough estimates provided for illustrative purposes.

★ 405 ★

Ferrous Scrap Metal Exports From the U.S.

Data shown for 1988.

Grade	Net tons
Carbon steel	
No. 1 heavy melting steel	2,400,415
No. 2 heavy melting steel	690,515
No. 1 bundles	74,496
No. 2 bundles	370,573
Borings, shovelings	515,015
Shredded steel and iron	2,910,096
Iron scrap	851,582
Miscellaneous	1,252,222
Total carbon steel	9,491,483
Stainless steel	243,344
Alloy steel	362,730
Total ferrous scrap exports	10,097,557

Source: Resource Recycling, May/June 1989, p. 66, from U.S. Department of Commerce; *Resource Recycling*; Institute of Scrap Recycling Industries.

★ 406 ★

Glass Processing by Method

The table shows the weight of glass in pounds related to its volume and method of crushing.

Volume	Whole Bottles (10 oz.)	Semi-Crushed (Manually Broken)	1 1/2 in. Max. Size (Mechanically Broken)	1/4 in. Max. Size Ready for Furnace
1 cu. yard	600.0	1,000.0	1,800.0	2,700.0
5 cu. yards	3,000.0	5,000.0	9,000.0	13,500.0
10 cu. yards	6,000.0	10,000.0	18,000.0	27,000.0
15 cu. yards	9,000.0	15,000.0	27,000.0	40,500.0
20 cu. yards	12,000.0	20,000.0	36,000.0	54,000.0
30 cu. yards	18,000.0	30,000.0	54,000.0	81,000.0
40 cu. yards	24,000.0	40,000.0	74,000.0	108,000.0
50 cu. yards	30,000.0	50,000.0	90,000.0	135,000.0
55 gal. drum	175.0	300.0	550.0	800.0
1 gallon	3.2	5.5	10.0	14.5
Cubic foot	22.0	37.0	67.0	100.0

Source: BioCycle, April 1990, p. 91.

★ 407 ★

Hospital Waste Recycling

Type of Waste	Total Amount of Waste		Recycle (%)	Amount recycled	Percent for disposal	Amount for disposal (lbs)
	Percent	(lb/day)				
Regulated medical waste	9.5	475	-	-	100	475
Aluminum cans	5.0	250	100	250	-	-
Batteries	<1	-	100	all	-	-
Plastics	5.0	250	100	250	-	-
Food waste	30.0	1500	100	1500	-	-
				Compost		
Bond paper	25.0	1250	-	-	100	1250
Green bar paper	14.0	700	100	700	-	-
Glass	1.0	50	-	-	100	50
Cardboard	9.5	475	-	-	100	475

Source: Pollution Engineering, September 1990, p. 72.

★ 408 ★

Household Mixed Wastepaper Management

Methods of recovery in U.S. programs, based on a survey of 25 recycling collection programs.

Type	Numbers	Percent
Curbside[1]	7	28
Drop-off site	3	12
Curbside, drop-off site	10	40
Curbside, multi-family[2]	1	4
Curbside, multi-family, drop-off site	4	16

Source: Resource Recycling, January 1991, p. 84, from Sound Resource Management Group, Inc., *Household Mixed Wastepaper Recycling*, February 1990. *Notes:* 1. Curbside recycling collection is offered to single-family through fourplex residences. 2. Recycling collection is offered to residences with more than four units.

★ 409 ★

Materials Recovery Facilities Development Status

	Number of Facilities
Operational	47
Under Construction	12
In Procurement	23
Design	17
Total	99[1]

Source: BioCycle, May 1990, p. 26. *Notes:* 1. Does not include seven projects that will upgrade smaller existing projects.

★ 410 ★

Materials Recovery, Food and Yard Waste Composting - I

Values shown reflect recovery of postconsumer wastes and do not include converting/fabrication scrap.

Materials	Millions of Tons						
	1960	1965	1970	1975	1980	1985	1988
Paper and paperboard	5.4	5.7	7.4	8.2	11.9	13.1	18.4
Glass	0.1	0.1	0.2	0.4	0.8	1.0	1.5
Metals							
Ferrous	0.1	0.1	0.1	0.2	0.4	0.4	0.7
Aluminum	0.0	0.0	0.0	0.1	0.3	0.6	0.8
Other nonferrous	0.0	0.3	0.3	0.4	0.5	0.5	0.7
Total metals	0.1	0.4	0.4	0.7	1.2	1.5	2.2
Plastics	0.0	0.0	0.0	0.0	0.0	0.1	0.2
Rubber and leather	0.3	0.3	0.3	0.2	0.1	0.2	0.1
Textiles	0.0	0.0	0.0	0.0	0.0	0.0	0.0
Wood	0.0	0.0	0.0	0.0	0.0	0.0	0.0
Other[1]	0.0	0.3	0.3	0.4	0.5	0.5	0.7
Total nonfood product wastes	5.9	6.8	8.6	9.9	14.5	16.4	23.1
Other Wastes							
Food wastes	0.0	0.0	0.0	0.0	0.0	0.0	0.0
Yard wastes	0.0	0.0	0.0	0.0	0.0	0.0	0.5
Miscellaneous inorganic wastes	0.0	0.0	0.0	0.0	0.0	0.0	0.0
Total other wastes	0.0	0.0	0.0	0.0	0.0	0.0	0.5
Total MSW recovered-weight	5.9	6.8	8.6	9.9	14.5	16.4	23.5

Source: Characterization of Municipal Solid Waste in the United States: 1990 Update, U.S. Environmental Protection Agency, EPA/530-SW-90-042, Washington, D.C., June 1990, p. 11, from Franklin Associates, Ltd. Details may not add to totals due to rounding. *Note:* 1. Recovery of electrolytes in batteries; probably not recycled.

★ 411 ★

Materials Recovery, Food and Yard Waste Composting - II

Values shown reflect recovery of postconsumer wastes by type, as percent of total generation.
Materials recovery does not include converting/fabrication scrap.

Materials	Percent of Generation of Each Material						
	1960	1965	1970	1975	1980	1985	1988
Paper and paperboard	18.1	15.0	16.7	19.1	21.8	21.3	25.6
Glass	1.5	1.1	1.6	3.0	5.3	7.6	12.0
Metals							
Ferrous	1.0	1.0	0.8	1.6	3.4	3.7	5.8
Aluminum	0.0	0.0	0.0	9.1	16.7	26.1	31.7
Other nonferrous	0.0	60.0	42.9	44.4	45.5	50.0	65.1
Total metals	1.0	3.6	2.8	4.9	8.3	10.6	14.6
Plastics	0.0	0.0	0.0	0.0	0.0	0.9	1.1
Rubber and leather	15.0	11.5	9.4	5.1	2.3	5.3	2.3
Textiles	0.0	0.0	0.0	0.0	0.0	0.0	0.6
Wood	0.0	0.0	0.0	0.0	0.0	0.0	0.0
Other	0.0	80.4	36.8	21.5	17.4	14.0	21.7
Total nonfood product wastes	10.9	10.1	10.2	11.3	13.6	14.2	17.5
Other wastes							
Food wastes	0.0	0.0	0.0	0.0	0.0	0.0	0.0
Yard wastes	0.0	0.0	0.0	0.0	0.0	0.0	1.6
Miscellaneous inorganic wastes	0.0	0.0	0.0	0.0	0.0	0.0	0.0
Total other wastes	0.0	0.0	0.0	0.0	0.0	0.0	1.1
Total MSW recovered-percent	6.7	6.6	7.1	7.7	9.7	10.1	13.1

Source: Characterization of Municipal Solid Waste in the United States: 1990 Update, U.S. Environmental Protection Agency, EPA/530-SW-90-042, Washington, D.C., June 1990, p. 11, from Franklin Associates, Ltd. Details may not add to totals due to rounding.

★ 412 ★

Municipal Waste Recovery by Type

Municipal solid waste recovery shown as percentage of total discards.

Year	Paper	Glass	Metal	Aluminum	Plastics	Rubber & leather	Textiles	Wood	Food & yard
1960	30.0	7.8	12.3	0.5	0.5	2.1	2.1	3.7	39.4
1965	33.5	8.8	10.6	0.5	1.5	2.3	2.0	3.6	35.4
1970	32.4	11.1	11.3	0.7	2.7	2.7	1.8	3.6	32.0
1975	29.6	11.4	10.6	0.9	3.8	3.2	1.9	3.8	33.2
1980	32.5	11.0	9.0	1.1	5.9	3.2	2.0	3.8	29.7

[Continued]

★ 412 ★

Municipal Waste Recovery by Type
[Continued]

Year	Paper	Glass	Metal	Alum- inum	Plastics	Rubber & leather	Textiles	Wood	Food & yard
1985	35.5	8.9	7.8	1.2	2.5	2.0	2.0	3.9	29.4
990	36.8	8.3	7.6	1.3	2.3	2.0	2.0	3.6	28.2

Source: Council on Environmental Quality, *20th Annual Report 1990,* Washington, D.C., p. 492, from U.S. Environmental Protection Agency, Office of Solid Waste and Emergency Reponse. "Characterization of municipal solid waste in the United States, 1960 to 2000." Prepared by Franklin associates, Prairie Village, KS. Data refer to waste discarded after materials recovery has taken place. Data for 1990 are projections.

★ 413 ★

Nondurable Goods Recovery as Percent of Waste Generated

The values are percent of generation of each product in the municipal waste stream. Recovery of postconsumer wastes; does not include converting/fabrication scrap.

Products	1960	1965	1970	1975	1980	1985	1988
Durable Goods	4.3	8.1	6.0	5.7	6.6	6.5	7.5
Nondurable Goods							
Newspapers	25.4	24.1	24.2	27.3	27.3	28.0	33.3
Books and Magazines	5.3	4.5	12.0	8.7	11.8	10.6	13.2
Office Papers	20.0	18.2	25.9	26.9	25.0	19.3	22.5
Commercial Printing	7.7	11.1	14.3	14.3	12.9	15.6	14.6
Tissue Paper and Towels	0.0	0.0	0.0	0.0	0.0	0.0	0.0
Paper Plates and Cups	0.0	0.0	0.0	0.0	0.0	0.0	0.0
Plastic Plates and Cups	0.0	0.0	0.0	0.0	0.0	0.0	0.0
Disposable Diapers	0.0	0.0	0.0	0.0	0.0	0.0	0.0
Other Nonpackaging Paper	3.7	2.6	5.6	5.7	0.0	0.0	0.0
Clothing and Footwear	0.0	0.0	0.0	0.0	0.0	0.0	0.6
Other Miscellaneous Nondurables	0.0	0.0	0.0	0.0	0.0	0.0	0.0
Total Nondurables	13.6	12.6	14.9	14.8	13.2	13.1	14.6
Containers and Packaging	11.4	9.1	9.0	11.5	16.6	18.1	24.3
Total Nonfood Product Wastes	10.9	10.1	10.2	11.3	13.6	14.2	17.5
Other Wastes							
Food Wastes	0.0	0.0	0.0	0.0	0.0	0.0	0.0
Yard Wastes	0.0	0.0	0.0	0.0	0.0	0.0	1.6
Miscellaneous Inorganic Wastes	0.0	0.0	0.0	0.0	0.0	0.0	0.0
Total Other Wastes	0.0	0.0	0.0	0.0	0.0	0.0	1.1
Total MSW Recovered-Percent	6.7	6.6	7.1	7.7	9.7	10.1	13.1

Source: Characterization of Municipal Solid Waste in the United States: 1990 Update, U.S. Environmental Protection Agency, EPA/530-SW-90-042, Washington, D.C., June 1990, p. 37, from Franklin Associates, Ltd. Details may not add to total due to rounding.

★ 414 ★

Nondurable Goods Recovery From Municipal Waste Stream

Recovery of postconsumer wastes; does not include converting/fabrication scrap.

Products	Millions of Tons						
	1960	1965	1970	1975	1980	1985	1988
Durable Goods	0.4	0.9	0.9	1.0	1.3	1.4	1.9
Nondurable Goods							
Newspapers	1.8	2.0	2.3	2.4	3.0	3.5	4.4
Books and Magazines	0.1	0.1	0.3	0.2	0.4	0.5	0.7
Office Papers	0.3	0.4	0.7	0.7	1.0	1.1	1.6
Commercial Printing	0.1	0.2	0.3	0.3	0.4	0.5	0.6
Tissue Paper and Towels	0.0	0.0	0.0	0.0	0.0	0.0	0.0
Paper Plates and Cups	0.0	0.0	0.0	0.0	0.0	0.0	0.0
Plastic Plates and Cups	0.0	0.0	0.0	0.0	0.0	0.0	0.0
Disposable Diapers	0.0	0.0	0.0	0.0	0.0	0.0	0.0
Other Nonpackaging Paper	0.1	0.1	0.2	0.2	0.0	0.0	0.0
Clothing and Footwear	0.0	0.0	0.0	0.0	0.0	0.0	0.0
Other Miscellaneous Nondurables	0.0	0.0	0.0	0.0	0.0	0.0	0.0
Total Nondurable Goods	2.4	2.8	3.8	3.8	4.8	5.6	7.4
Containers and Packaging	3.1	3.1	3.9	5.1	8.4	9.4	13.8
Total Nonfood Product Wastes	5.9	6.8	8.6	9.9	14.5	16.4	23.1
Other Wastes							
Food Wastes	0.0	0.0	0.0	0.0	0.0	0.0	0.0
Yard Wastes	0.0	0.0	0.0	0.0	0.0	0.0	0.5
Miscellaneous Inorganic Wastes	0.0	0.0	0.0	0.0	0.0	0.0	0.0
Total Other Wastes	0.0	0.0	0.0	0.0	0.0	0.0	0.5
Total MSW Recovered-Weight	5.9	6.8	8.6	9.9	14.5	16.4	23.5

Source: Characterization of Municipal Solid Waste in the United States: 1990 Update, U.S. Environmental Protection Agency, EPA/530-SW-90-042, Washington, D.C., June 1990, p. 37, from Franklin Associates, Ltd. Details may not add to total due to rounding.

★ 415 ★

Non-Ferrous Scrap Export Value

Values are shown in millions of dollars. The value of nickel and tin exports combined was $52.8 million.

Grade	Value
Aluminum	774.3
Copper	445.5
Lead	23.2
Zinc	62.7
Total	1,305.7

Source: Resource Recycling, May/June 1990, p. 67, from U.S. Department of Commerce and Resource Recycling.

★ 416 ★

Non-Ferrous Scrap Exports

Market shares of the leading foreign buyers of non-ferrous scrap, shown in percent.

Grade	Principal buyers	Percent marketshare
Aluminum	Japan	57
	Taiwan	13
	Mexico	7
Copper	South Korea	20
	Taiwan	17
	Canada	17
Lead	Brazil	20
	Canada	15
	Mexico	14
Zinc	Taiwan	88
	South Korea	4
	Belgium	2

Source: Resource Recycling, May/June 1989, p. 67, from U.S. Department of Commerce and Resource Recycling.

★ 417 ★

Non-Ferrous Scrap Exports From the U.S.

Data are shown in net tons.

Grade	1987	1988	Percent change
Aluminum	338,940	434,731	+28.3
Copper	324,372	352,432	+8.7
Lead	57,785	90,063	+55.9
Zinc	90,815	104,826	+15.4

Source: Resource Recycling, May/June 1989, p. 66, from Institute of Scrap Recycling Industries.

★ 418 ★

Old Newspaper Supply and Demand

Supply and demand in the U.S. in 1987, shown in thousands of metric tons per year.

Region	Newsprint consumption	ONP domestic use[1]		Net ONP exports	Total ONP recovered	Recovery rate (percent)
		Total	Newsprint manufacturing			
New England	746	139	0	0.3	139	19
Mid-Atlantic	2,414	634	241	83.0	717	30
East north Central	1,908	669	122	0.8	670	35
West north central	678	54	0	0.8	54	8
South Atlantic	2,185	439	220	18	457	21[2]
East south central	409	76	0	0	76	18
West south central	1,216	128	0	204	332	27
Mountain and Pacific	2,761	810	592	457	1,267	46
Total U.S.	12,323	3,220[3]	1,260	764	3,984[3]	32[3]

Source: Resource Recycling, July 1989, p. 71, from Andover International Associates. *Notes:* 1. ONP stands for Old Newspaper and includes newsprint manufacture plus others (recycled board and fiber). 2. Southeast Paper Manufacturing Co. is installing a second newsprint machine at Dublin, Georgia. The additional ONP demand (220,000 tons per year) will increase the recovery rate to about 32 percent. 3. Includes 270,000 tons per year used for insulation manufacture. This additional amount is not distributed on a regional basis by the American Paper Institute.

★ 419 ★

Paperboard and Recycled Paperboard Growth Trends

Additions to production capacity in 1980-89 and 1990-92 shown as thousands of short tons and percent. Recycled paperboard capacity is included in total paperboard capacity.

	Additions 1980-1989		Additions 1990-1992	
	Ten-year increase	Average annual growth	Three-year increase	Average annual growth
Total paperboard	7,683	2.1	4,357	3.4
Recycled paperboard	855	0.9	1,193	4.0

Source: Pulp & Paper, February 1990, p. 177, from American Paper Institute.

★ 420 ★

Potential Benefits of Resource Recovery

Potential environmental benefits from substituting secondary materials for virgin resources.

Environmental benefit	Aluminum	Steel	Paper	Glass	Plastic
Reduction (%) of					
Energy use	90-97	47-74	23-74	4-32	85-90
Air pollution	95	85	74	20	-
Water pollution	97	76	35	-	-
Mining wastes	-	97	-	80	-
Water use	-	40	58	50	-

Source: Resources, Conservation and Recycling, Volume 4, No. 1, 2, August 1990, p. 18. - stands for not available.

★ 421 ★

Potential Recovery Rates for Wastepaper

Type	Recovery rate 1988 (percent)	Projected Recovery rate 1995 (percent)
Newspaper	35	52
Corrugated	52	66
Mixed	13	20
Pulp Subs	100	100
High Grade Deinking	37	50
Overall	31	40 (goal)

Source: American City & County, April 1990, p. 16, from American Paper Institute & Franklin Associates, Ltd.

★ 422 ★

Potential Wastepaper Recovery Rates

Source	Percent Recovered in 1988	Potential Recovery (percent)
Newspaper	35	50-55
Corrugated	52	63-68
Mixed	13	15-25
Pulp Subs	100	100
High Grade Deinking	37	50
Overall	31	37-42

Source: Water Environment & Technology, September 1990, p. 84, from American Paper Institute and Franklin Associates, Ltd.

★ 423 ★

Product Recovery, Food and Yard Waste Composting - I

The values are in millions of tons.

Products	Millions of Tons						
	1960	1965	1970	1975	1980	1985	1988
Durable Goods	0.4	0.9	0.9	1.0	1.3	1.4	1.9
Nondurable Goods	2.4	2.8	3.8	3.8	4.8	5.6	7.4
Containers and Packaging	3.1	3.1	3.9	5.1	8.4	9.4	13.8
Total Nonfood Product Wastes	5.9	6.8	8.6	9.9	14.5	16.4	23.1
Other Wastes							
Food Wastes	0.0	0.0	0.0	0.0	0.0	0.0	0.0
Yard Wastes	0.0	0.0	0.0	0.0	0.0	0.0	0.5
Miscellaneous Inorganic Wastes	0.0	0.0	0.0	0.0	0.0	0.0	0.0
Total Other Wastes	0.0	0.0	0.0	0.0	0.0	0.0	0.5
Total MSW Recovered-Weight	5.9	6.8	8.6	9.9	14.5	16.4	23.5

Source: Characterization of Municipal Solid Waste in the United States: 1990 Update, U.S. Environmental Protection Agency, EPA/530-SW-90-042, Washington, D.C., June 1990, p. 29, from Franklin Associates, Ltd. Details may not add to totals due to rounding.

★ 424 ★

Product Recovery, Food and Yard Waste Composting - II

The values are percent of total in the waste stream.

Products	Percent of Generation of Each Product						
	1960	1965	1970	1975	1980	1985	1988
Durable Goods	4.3	8.1	6.0	5.7	6.6	6.5	7.5
Nondurable Goods	13.6	12.6	14.9	14.8	13.2	13.1	14.6
Containers and Packaging	11.4	9.1	9.0	11.5	16.6	18.1	24.3
Total Nonfood Product Wastes	10.9	10.1	10.2	11.3	13.6	14.2	17.5
Other Wastes							
Food Wastes	0.0	0.0	0.0	0.0	0.0	0.0	0.0
Yard Wastes	0.0	0.0	0.0	0.0	0.0	0.0	1.6
Miscellaneous Inorganic Wastes	0.0	0.0	0.0	0.0	0.0	0.0	0.0
Total Other Wastes	0.0	0.0	0.0	0.0	0.0	0.0	1.1
Total MSW Recovered-Percent	6.7	6.6	7.1	7.7	9.7	10.1	13.1

Source: Characterization of Municipal Solid Waste in the United States: 1990 Update, U.S. Environmental Protection Agency, EPA/530-SW-90-042, Washington, D.C., June 1990, p. 29, from Franklin Associates, Ltd. Details may not add to totals due to rounding.

★ 425 ★

Recovery of Selected Materials in Municipal Solid Wastes

In millions of tons, except as indicated. Covers post-consumer residential and commercial solid wastes which comprise the major portion of typical municipal collections. Excludes mining, agricultural and industrial processing, demolition and construction wastes, sewage sludge, and junked autos and obsolete equipment wastes. Based on material-flows estimating procedure and wet weight as generator.

Item and material	1970	1975	1980	1981	1982	1983	1984	1985	1986
Gross waste generated:									
Paper and paperboard	43.9	42.6	53.9	55.0	52.4	57.7	62.5	61.7	64.7
Ferrous metals	12.6	12.3	11.6	11.4	11.3	11.4	11.3	10.7	11.0
Aluminum	.9	1.1	1.8	1.9	1.9	2.1	2.2	2.3	2.4
Glass	12.7	13.9	14.9	15.0	14.5	14.2	13.8	13.2	12.9
Plastics	3.0	4.4	7.6	7.8	8.4	9.1	9.7	9.8	10.3
Materials Recovered:									
Paper and paperboard	7.4	8.2	11.8	11.4	11.1	12.0	13.2	13.0	14.6
Ferrous metals	.2	.2	.4	.3	.3	.3	.3	.3	.4
Aluminum	(NA)	.1	.3	.5	.6	.6	.6	.6	.6
Glass	.2	.4	.8	.8	.8	.9	1.0	1.1	1.1
Plastics	(NA)	(NA)	(NA)	(NA)	(NA)	(NA)	.1	.1	.1
Percent of gross discards recovered:									
Paper and paperboard	16.9	19.2	21.9	20.7	21.2	20.8	21.1	21.1	22.6
Ferrous metals	1.6	1.6	3.4	2.6	2.6	2.6	2.7	2.8	3.6
Aluminum	(NA)	9.1	16.7	26.3	31.6	28.6	27.3	26.1	25.0
Glass	2.3	2.9	5.4	5.3	5.5	6.3	7.2	8.3	8.5
Plastics	(NA)	(NA)	(NA)	(NA)	(NA)	(NA)	1.0	1.0	1.0

Source: U.S. Department of Commerce, Bureau of the Census, *Statistical Abstract of the United States 1990 (110th ed.),* Superintendent of Documents, Washington, D.C., p. 206, from Franklin Associates Ltd., Prairie Village, KS. Characterization of Municipal Solid Waste in the United States, 1960 to 2000. Prepared for the U.S. Environmental Protection Agency. *Note:* NA stands for not available.

★ 426 ★

Recyclable Materials in Commercial Waste

Recyclable material in the commercial waste stream, by type of business, in percent.

Waste Component	Retail Trade	Restaurant	Office	School	Government
Paper	41.5	36.6	64.2	47.8	53.8
Newspaper	2.9	2.5	3.6	3.3	6.7
Corrugated	22.0	15.6	11.5	11.6	8.4
High grade white	1.4	0.0	10.6	6.3	7.2
Mixed recyclable	10.3	4.4	29.0	21.6	25.0
Nonrecyclable	4.9	14.1	9.5	5.0	6.5
Plastic	12.0	13.7	4.3	5.1	3.5
Polyethylene	0.1	0.0	0.1	0.1	0.1
High density polyethylene	0.0	0.1	0.0	0.0	0.0

[Continued]

★ 426 ★

Recyclable Materials in Commercial Waste
[Continued]

Waste Component	Retail Trade	Restaurant	Office	School	Government
Other	11.9	13.6	4.2	5.0	3.4
Glass	2.5	5.9	3.9	3.2	2.7
Containers	2.3	5.8	2.9	1.0	2.4
Nonrecyclable glass	0.2	0.1	1.0	2.2	0.3
Metal	20.5	4.9	2.9	5.8	9.8
Aluminum cans	0.2	0.5	0.5	0.8	0.5
Tin/steel cans	0.2	3.8	0.2	0.2	0.4
Other ferrous	19.5	0.4	2.2	3.7	8.6
Other nonferrous	0.6	0.2	0.0	1.1	0.3
Organics	18.8	36.6	10.8	35.0	23.2
Food waste	8.1	36.0	3.0	14.0	3.2
Yard debris and wood	10.7	0.6	7.8	21.0	20.0
Other	4.7	2.3	13.9	3.1	7.0
Totals	100.0	100.0	100.0	100.0	100.0

Source: Resource Recycling, November 1990, p. 50, from Washington State Department of Ecology, *Best Management Practices for Solid Waste: Recycling and Waste Stream Survey*, 1987.

★ 427 ★

Recycled Content Products - Paper

Survey data for paper and paperboard mills producing recycled content products.

Product category	Percent of input		Input fibers used in each product category (Percentage distribution)									
	Recycled	Post-consumer	MWP	BXB	ONP	OCC	BLK	LDG	CBS	OTH	RGS	PLP
Paper products												
Newsprint	100	100	0	0	100	0	0	0	0	0	0	0
Printing and writing	6	N.A	0	0	0	0	4	0	0	3	19	75
Packaging	58	50	0	5	0	52	0	0	0	0	0	43
Tissue and toweling	100	25	4	0	17	8	0	33	21	17	0	0
Paperboard products												
Semichemical corrugating medium	33	N.A	0	0	0	20	13	0	0	0	0	67
Recycled boxboard, chipboard and tubing	98	73	13	15	28	36	1	6	0	0	0	1
Recycled corrugating medium	100	94	0	0	0	100	0	0	0	0	0	0
Recycled gypsum wallboard facing	100	48	7	0	32	61	0	0	0	0	0	0
Construction paper and board	80	68	33	0	20	28	0	0	0	0	0	20
Molded pulp products	100	9	0	4	34	0	6	0	0	57	0	0
Total/Average	85	65	8	6	20	37	3	6	2	3	0	14

Source: Resource Recycling, January 1991, p. 91. MWP = mixed waste paper; BXB = boxboard cuttings (non-corrugated cardboard); ONP = old newspapers (including other mechanical pulp content paper); OCC = old corrugated cardboard (including other unbleached kraft paper); BLK = bleached kraft paper; LDG = ledger and computer printout; CBS = coated book stock; OTH = Speciality grades (Including magazines and polycoated milk cartons); RGS = rags;PLP = wood pulp. N.A. = Data not available.

★ 428 ★

Recycled Plastic Consumption

Data refer to the U.S. and are shown in millions of dollars. Growth rates are shown in percent.

Resin	1990 in dollars	1995[1] in dollars	Compounded rate (percent)
Homogeneous			
PET[2]	150	400	10
Others[3]	90	400	16
Subtotal	240	800	13
Commingled	10	50	17
Total	250	850	13

Source: Chemicalweek, December 19/26, 1990, p. 46, from Strategic Analysis (Reading, PA) *Notes:* 1. In constant 1990 dollars. 2. Polyethylene Terephthalate 3. Includes high-density and low-density polyethylene, polypropylene, polystyrene, and polyvinyl chloride.

★ 429 ★

Scrap Exports, 1989-1990

Table compares U.S. exports of scrap material, by type, for January through June, 1989 and 1990. Value is shown in dollars per unit of measure.

	Unit of Measure	Weight		Value	
		1989	1990	1989	1990
Plastic scrap					
Ethylene scrap	Kilogram	4,574,652	6,346,021	0.72	0.42
Styrene scrap	Kilogram	5,377,507	4,457,503	0.95	0.77
Vinylchloride	Kilogram	5,117,801	4,297,691	0.49	0.49
Miscellaneous plastics	Kilogram	57,653,538	65,323,559	0.67	0.66
Wastepaper					
Corrugated and kraft	Metric ton	1,270,272	1,202,252	124.26	106.08
Deink grades	Metric ton	364,999	471,578	191.65	178.34
Pulp substitutes	Metric ton	106,807	171,151	165.24	219.18
Newspaper	Metric ton	375,166	404,694	76.02	59.88
Mechanical pulp	Metric ton	253,743	124,942	176.31	376.29
Mixed waste paper	Metric ton	405,321	790,646	138.16	104.53
Ferrous scrap[1]					
Cast iron	Metric ton	459,064	522,070	121.98	132.12
Stainless steel	Metric ton	151,214	102,630	1,306.29	854.71
Alloy steel	Metric ton	344,746	183,493	189.64	185.08
Tinned steel	Metric ton	68,556	115,285	153.62	119.81
No. 1 bundles	Metric ton	42,707	111,259	137.90	120.34

[Continued]

★ 429 ★

Scrap Exports, 1989-1990
[Continued]

	Unit of Measure	Weight		Value	
		1989	1990	1989	1990
No. 2 bundles	Metric ton	175,635	230,921	103.15	91.05
Borings, turnings	Metric ton	240,263	162,421	74.72	80.82
Shavings, chips	Metric ton	39,918	55,271	109.42	95.27
No. 1 melting steel	Metric ton	8,014,139	1,377,568	19.11	117.85
No. 2 melting steel	Metric ton	490,212	511,298	116.78	112.16
Cut plate/structural	Metric ton	3,473,594	466,321	11.34	136.20
Shredded scrap	Metric ton	1,757,876	1,998,610	142.31	128.46
Other scrap	Metric ton	118,094	411,795	168.49	111.79
Remelt ingot	Metric ton	7,667	36,422	238.76	131.13
Non-ferrous scrap					
Refined copper scrap	Kilogram	82,905,812	69,180,794	1.69	1.66
Brass scrap	Kilogram	16,968,924	12,134,592	1.55	1.48
Copper scrap	Kilogram	82,774,551	76,346,010	1.51	1.50
Nickel scrap	Kilogram	7,340,549	9,243,883	3.51	2.30
Aluminum ingot	Kilogram	23,645,072	42,789,662	1.43	1.49
Used aluminum cans	Kilogram	9,895,671	1,564,404	1.60	1.22
Aluminum scrap	Kilogram	248,448,383	206,801,493	1.40	1.22
Lead battery scrap	Kilogram	1,887,333	4,325,908	0.29	0.28
Other lead scrap	Kilogram	23,494,447	28,132,026	0.40	0.41
Zinc scrap	Kilogram	44,622,614	40,464,643	0.72	0.77
Tin scrap	Kilogram	11,355,702	7,911,547	0.70	0.54

Source: Resource Recycling, October 1990, p. 70, from U.S. Department of Commerce. *Notes:* 1. The value of shipments to South Korea from Los Angeles in 1989 of No. 1 heavy melting steel and cut plate and structural steel may be incorrect.

★ 430 ★

Secondary Fibers Recovery Rates - Paper and Paperboard

Region	Total paper and paperboard production[1]		Secondary fiber consumption[1]		Percent secondary fiber utilization	
	1988	2001	1988	2001	1988	2001
North America	86,737	115,198	19,778	36,030	22.8	31.3
Western Europe	57,633	78,844	19,881	31,228	34.4	39.6
E.F.T.A[2,3]	(22,350)	(30,400)	(2,967)	(5,198)	13.3	17.1
European Community[3]	(35,283)	(48,444)	(16,844)	(26,031)	47.7	53.7
Eastern Europe and USSR	17,988	22,193	4,868	8,746	27.1	39.4
Oceania	2,487	3,864	702	1,271	28.2	32.9
Latin America	10,506	15,909	4,757	7,801	45.3	49.0
Japan	24,624	34,892	12,538	19,415	50.9	55.6
China	12,645	19,760	3,084	8,305	24.4	42.0

[Continued]

★ 430 ★

Recovery Rates of Secondary Fibers - Paper and Paperboard
[Continued]

Region	Total paper and paperboard production[1]		Secondary fiber consumption[1]		Percent secondary fiber utilization	
	1988	2001	1988	2001	1988	2001
Rest of Asia	12,218	22,431	8,369	15,877	68.5	70.8
Africa	2,524	3,578	679	1,092	26.9	30.5
World total	227,362	316,669	74,586	129,766	32.8	41.0

Source: Resource Recycling, November 1990, Secondary Fiber Supplement, p. 91, from Jaakko Poyry, 1990. *Notes:* 1. In thousands of metric tons. 2. E.F.T.A. stands for European Free Trade Association. 3. E.F.T.A. and European Community figures sum to Western Europe figures.

★ 431 ★

Selected Products Recovery and Composting Rates in 1995

The estimated values are in millions of tons and percent of generation of each material.

Products	Million tons		% of generation	
	Low	High	Low	High
Paper and paperboard				
Newspapers	6.8	8.3	45.0	55.0
Books and magazines	1.0	1.7	15.0	25.0
Office papers	2.0	2.9	20.0	30.0
Commercial printing	0.9	1.4	15.0	25.0
Corrugated boxes	15.2	17.4	55.0	63.0
Other paper and paperboard	0.6	0.9	2.9	4.4
Total paper and paperboard	26.5	32.6	31.0	38.0
Glass containers				
Beer and soft drink bottles	1.3	1.7	35.0	45.0
Other glass containers	0.8	1.4	13.0	17.5
Total glass containers	2.1	3.1	22.0	32.0
Ferrous metals				
Beer and soft drink cans	<0.1	<0.1	45.0	55.0
Other steel containers	1.0	1.2	45.0	55.0
Ferrous in durables	0.5	1.1	6.8	16.8
Total ferrous metals	1.5	2.4	12.8	20.5
Aluminum				
Beer and soft drink cans	1.1	1.4	60.0	75.0
Other aluminum packaging	<0.1	<0.1	6.5	17.5
Total aluminum packaging	1.1	1.4	50.0	64.0
Plastics				
Soft drink bottles	0.1	0.2	25.0	40.0

[Continued]

★ 431 ★

Selected Products Recovery and Composting Rates in 1995

[Continued]

Products	Million tons		% of generation	
	Low	High	Low	High
Milk/water bottles	<0.1	0.1	10.0	25.0
Other plastic packaging	0.2	0.7	3.8	11.5
Total plastic packaging	0.4	1.1	6.0	15.0
Batteries (lead only)	0.8	0.9	85.0	95.0
Composting				
Food wastes	0.0	1.0	0.0	7.6
Yard wastes	6.6	11.0	20.0	33.3
Other materials[1]	1.2	2.2	-	-
Total recovery	40.1	55.3	20.0	27.7

Source: Characterization of Municipal Solid Waste in the United States: 1990 Update, U.S. Environmental Protection Agency, EPA/530-SW-90-042, Washington, D.C., June 1990, p. 65, from Franklin Associates Ltd. *Note:* 1. Plastic and other materials in batteries; rubber; wood; textiles.

★ 432 ★

Sludge Composting Facilities in the U.S.

State/Plant Name	Status	Type	Sludge Volume
Alabama			
Dothan City	Operational	I-V[1]	4
Alaska			
Homer	Construction	A-SP	28/yr
Arizona			
Phoenix: 23rd Ave. plant	Operational	Windrow[2]	-
Phoenix: 91st Ave. plant	Operational	Windrow[2]	50,000/yr
Arkansas			
Fayetteville/Northwest Arkansas Waste Management	Permitting[5]	A-SP	100 cu.yd/day
California			
Chino Basin	Consid. pilot	-	156 wtd[24]
Encina WPCF	Consideration	I-V	8,500/yr
Escondido	Planning	I-V[4]	7-8
Fallbrook	Operational	[6]	1-1.5
Hayward	Oper. (DC)	A-SP	10
Los Alisos/El Toro	Operational	A-SP	1,500 cyy
Los Angeles	Constr. (SJC)	Windrow	60
Los Angeles County	Operational	Windrow[7]	300 wtd
Los Virgenes	Pre-design	I-V	10
Oakland: East Bay	Operational	A-SP	60

[Continued]

★ 432 ★

Sludge Composting Facilities in the U.S.
[Continued]

State/Plant Name	Status	Type	Sludge Volume
Oceanside	Planning	I-V[3]	6
Orange County	Operational	Windrow/SP	64.8
Oxnard	Design[8]	I-V[9]	30
Riverside County	Design (RI)	Windrow	600 wtd
San Diego	Pilot	Windrow	2
	Consideration	I-V	-
Santa Paula WWTP	Pilot	SP	200/yr
Santa Rosa	Planning	I-V/A-SP	21
Simi Valley	Pilot (1990)	P-E	10[24]
South San Francisco/			
Tillo Products Co.	Operational	Windrow	10,000/yr
Thousand Oaks	Design	A-SP	4
Colorado			
Breckenridge	Pilot	A-SP	-
Denver Metro	Operational	A-W	10
Ft. Collins	Operational	A-W	2
Longmont	Construction	A-SP	8.5
Silver Thorne/Dillon	Operational	A-SP	50/yr
Summit County	Oper. (TLC)	A-SP	500/yr
Connecticut			
Bristol	Operational	A-SP	50-60 cyd
Fairfield	Operational	I-V (IPS)	3
Farmington	Design	I-V	20 yd/day
Glastonbury	Consideration	I-V (IPS)	1.5
Greenwich	Operational	A-SP	2,500 cyy
Groton	Consid.[14]	I-V (IPS)	-
Hartford	Construction	I-V (ABT)	60
Norwich	Consideration	[10]	-
Ridgefield	Operational	Windrow	1-1.5
Windham	Consid.[14]	I-V	1.7
Delaware			
Middletown/Odessa	Operational	I-V[16]	.5
Seaford	Operational	A-SP	500/yr
Wilmington/Delaware			
Reclamation Project	Operational	I-V[17]	109
Florida			
Brooksville	Design[5]	I-V (BB)	.5 min.
Cooper City Utilities	Operational	Windrow	.75
Daytona Beach	Consideration		10
Fort Lauderdale	Operational	I-V[19]	14
Hillsborough County Utilities	Design	I-V	35
Jacksonville: Buckman Plant	Operational	A-SP[20]	2.26
Lee County	Design	A-SP or I-V	-
Meadowood Utility	Operational	Windrow	4/mo.
Melbourne	Planning	I-V[21]	30 wtd

[Continued]

★ 432 ★

Sludge Composting Facilities in the U.S.
[Continued]

State/Plant Name	Status	Type	Sludge Volume
Orange County	Pilot	Windrow	[11]
Palm Beach County	Consideration	I-V (A-B)	+/- 30
Reedy Creek	Operational	I-V[1]	9
Royal Palm Beach	Construction	Windrow	1.7
Sarasota	Operational	I-V[19]	6-10
Georgia			
Northeast Clayton Co. WPCP	Operational	I-V[1]	1.7
Hawaii			
Waimanalo WWTP	CLP	A-SP	17
Idaho			
Coeur d'Alene	Construction	A-SP	1
Illinois			
Woodridge-Greene Valley	Oper./Consid.	A-SP/I-V	5
Indiana			
Bloomington: Blucher Poole WWTF	Operational	Windrow	2
Iowa			
Davenport	Pilot	Windrow	6
Des Moines	Pilot[5]	Windrow	25 wtd-pilot
Ft. Madison/Lee County	Operational	A-SP	15/wk.
Kansas			
Mission	Consideration	Windrow/I-V	20
Topeka: Oakland WWTP	Operational	Windrow	10-12
Wichita: WPCP #1 & #2	Operational	Windrow	10
Maine			
Bangor	Operational	A-SP	2.4
Bar Harbor	Operational	A-SP	365/yr
Gardiner	Operational	A-SP	1
Kennebunkport	Operational	A-SP	50/yr
Kittery	Operational	A-SP	35/yr
Lincoln	Operational	Windrow	.164
Lisbon	Consideration	Windrow	.40
Old Orchard Beach & Saco	Operational	A-SP	3.4
Portland	Design	A-SP	12/wk.
	Pilot	I-V[12]	
Rumford & Mexico	Operational	A-SP	-
Scarborough	Operational	A-SP	.75
South Portland	Operational	Windrow	1.8
Unity Plantation (including Belfast, Augusta, Camden & Kennebec)	Consideration	Windrow[13]	5.3
Yarmouth	Operational	Windrow	.5
Maryland			
Aberdeen	Design	A-SP	2.2
Baltimore: Back River	Operational	I-V (Paygro)	48.3
Cambridge	Operational	A-SP	300 cym
Elkton	Operational	A-SP	2

[Continued]

★ 432 ★

Sludge Composting Facilities in the U.S.
[Continued]

State/Plant Name	Status	Type	Sludge Volume
Havre de Grace	Operational	A-SP	2-3
Montgomery County	Operational	A-SP	40
Perryville	Operational	A-SP	2.5
Queen Anne's County	Operational	A-SP	60 cym
Massachusetts			
Amherst	Planning	I-V	8
Barre	Operational	A-SP	5 yd/wk.
Northern Berkshire County	Consid.[5]		
Southern Berkshire County	Consid.[5]	[15]	59 wtd
Billerica WWTP	Construction	A-SP	2
Bridgewater	Operational	A-SP	1.5
Dartmouth	Design	I-V	7,300 lbs/day
Deer Island	Pilot	A-SP	3
Edgartown	Planning	A-SP	1
Franklin County	Consid.[5]		56
Gloucester	Pilot[18]	A-SP	800/yr[24]
Haverhill WWTP	Design	I-V (A-S-H)	10-14
Leicester WWTP	Operational	A-SP	.75/wk.
Lowell & Chelmsford	Consid.[5]		35
Mansfield	Operational	A-SP	143 yds/wk.
Marlborough East Plant	Operational	A-SP	10
Medfield	Design	A-SP	3
Nantucket	Construction	A-W	-
Northampton (with 11 communities in Hampshire County)	Consid.[5]		48
Orleans	Construction	A-SP	3.9
Pepperell	Pilot	A-SP	8 yds/wk.
Rockport	[18]	A-SP	1
Somerset	Construction	A-SP	2
Southbridge	Operational	A-SP	18 cyd
Springfield	Construction	I-V[1]	8,800/yr
Swampscott	Operational	A-SP	1.4/wk.
Westborough/Shrewsbury	Operational	A-SP	3
Williamstown/Hoosac	Operational	A-SP	120 cyd
Yarmouth	Design[22]	I-V (A-B)	3
Michigan			
Battle Creek	Consideration	I-V	20
Mackinac Island	Design[5]	I-V	-
Trenton	Consideration	All options	2
Minnesota			
St. Cloud	Oper.[5]	I-V[23]	17.5 wtd
St. Paul (Southwest area)	Consid. pilot	I-V (A-S-H)	.5
Missouri			
Joplin Landfill	Pilot	I-V	-
Springfield	Operational	Windrow	20[24]

[Continued]

★ 432 ★

Sludge Composting Facilities in the U.S.

[Continued]

State/Plant Name	Status	Type	Sludge Volume
Montana			
Missoula	Operational	A-SP[24]	7
Nebraska			
Beatrice	Operational	Windrow	1.5
Grand Island	Operational	A-SP	7-10
Holdredge	Consideration	Windrow	.5
Kearney	Operational	Windrow	6/wk.
Nevada			
Clark County San. District	Pilot	A-W	37[24]
New Hampshire			
Bristol	Operational	A-SP	100 cyy
Claremont	Operational	A-SP	2.2
Dover	Design	A-SP	5
Durham	Operational	A-SP	1.97
Hampton	Consideration	I-V	600/yr
Lebanon	Operational	A-SP	1.5
Merrimack	Operational	A-SP	21
	Consideration	I-V[5]	-
Milford	Operational	A-SP	.8
Plymouth	Operational	A-SP	.25
	Designed	I-V (IPS)	2
Sunapee	Operational	A-SP	-
New Jersey			
Buena Borough	Operational	A-SP	3.5
Burlington County	Design	I-V (H-B)	30
Camden/Delaware #1 WPCF	Design	I-V (A-S-H)	50
Cape May County MUA	Operational	I-V[19]	20
Middletown Twp.	Operational	A-SP	4.5
Musconetcong	Design	I-V[1]	3
Pennsville	Operational	Windrow	1
Sussex County MUA	Operational	A-SP	6
New Mexico			
Albuquerque	Bidding	A-W	15+
New York			
Binghampton/Johnson	Construction	I-V[1]	10
Clinton County/Plattsburgh	Operational	I-V[17]	25
Endicott	Operational	I-V[1]	2
Gowanda	Pilot	A-SP	1.3 cyd
Guilderland	Operational	A-SP	1
LeRoy[14]	Consideration	A-SP	6
Lawrence STP	Operational	A-SP	0.5
Lewiston	Consideration	A-SP	16
Lloyd STP	Pilot	A-SP	1.5 (capac.)
Lockport	Construction	I-V (IPS)	14
Manchester/Shortavl	Operational	A-SP	1

[Continued]

★ 432 ★

Sludge Composting Facilities in the U.S.
[Continued]

State/Plant Name	Status	Type	Sludge Volume
Minoa/V	Operational	Windrow	0.2
Monroe County[5]	Pilot	All options	100[24]
Rennselaer County/Eastern	Planning[5]	I-V	1;10,000 gds
Schenectady	Operational	I-V (ABT)	15
Thompson	Permitting	A-SP	1.5
Tompkins County	Pilot	A-SP	4 cyw
Tri-Municipal Sewage/			
Woppinger Falls & Poughkeepsie	Operational	A-SP	2
Yorktown Heights	Operational	Windrow	1
North Carolina			
Charlotte	Bid Stage	I-V	30
Hickory[14]	Construction	I-V (A-S-H)	20
Lexington	Planning	I-V	400/yr
Morgantown/Catawba River Plant	Operational	A-SP	4.5
Raleigh/Neuse River WWTP	Design	I-V(A-S-H)[1]	25
Valdese	Operational	A-SP	1
Ohio			
Akron	Operational	I-V[25]	24
Columbus	Operational	A-SP	20
Hamilton WWTP	Operational	I-V (A-S-H)	17
Lake County	Operational	A-W	7
Oklahoma			
Tulsa	Pilot	A-SP	-
Oregon			
Newburg	Operational	I-V (A-S-H)	3.5
Portland	Operational	I-V[1]	30
Pennsylvania			
Bristol Twp.	Pilot	A-SP	-
Evans City/RBW Industries -			
Regional project	Design	A-SP	50 wtd
Hampden Twp.	Design	A-SP	-
Lackawana River Basin	Consideration	Mod.-W	5,000 wty
Lancaster	Operational	I-V[1]	32
Lancaster/A&M	Operational	A-SP	70 wet cyy
Philadelphia	Operational	A-SP	300
Scranton	Operational	A-SP	18 (5-days)
Springettsbury Twp.	Operational	A-SP	358/yr
Rhode Island			
Bristol	Planning	I-V	3
Jamestown	Operational	Windrow	350 cyy
South Kingston	Consideration	I-V (IPS)	4
West Warwick	Operational	A-SP	5
South Carolina			
East Richland County PSD: Gills Creek	Operational	I-V[1]	5
Hilton Head/Broad Creek Plant	Construction	I-V[26]	2

[Continued]

★ 432 ★

Sludge Composting Facilities in the U.S.
[Continued]

State/Plant Name	Status	Type	Sludge Volume
Myrtle Beach	Operational	A-SP	5
Tennessee			
Bristol	Construction	I-V[1]	14.3
Chattanooga/Moccasin Bend WWTP	Pilot	A-SP	10-20/yr
Nashville: Central Treatment Plant	Operational	A-SP	30-40
Texas			
Austin	Operational	Windrow	10
Dallas	Pilot Pln[27]	I-V	-
Fredericksburg	Operational	Windrow	-
San Antonio	Operational	Windrow	600 cyw
Trinity River Authority/Grand Prairie	Design	A-W	10
Vermont			
Bennington	Design	I-V (IPS)	2
Burlington	Planning	I-V	782/yr
Central Vermont Region (including Barre & Montpelier)	Consideration		10
Champlain Basin Region (including Burlington)	Consideration		20
Connecticut River Valley Region (incl. White River Junction & Brattleboro)	Consideration		15
Rutland Region	Consideration		15
Springfield/interim project within Connecticut River Valley	Design	A-SP	1.25
Virginia			
Hampton Roads/Peninsula Compost Facility	Operational	A-SP	12
Henrico County	Construction	I-V[19]	18
Moores Creek WWTP/Charlottesville	Operational	A-SP	9
Upper Occoquan	Operational	A-W	7.5-10
Washington			
Monroe	Operational	A-SP	45-50/mo
Seattle METRO	Oper. (GroCo)	A-SP	20
Southwest Suburban Sewer District/ Miller Creek & Salmon Creek	Oper. (NWC)	SP	10 wet yd/wk.
West Virginia			
Charleston	Pilot		
Wisconsin			
Portage	Oper.[5]	I-V	2.4
District of Columbia			
Blue Plains	Operational	A-SP	40

[Continued]

★ 432 ★

Sludge Composting Facilities in the U.S.

[Continued]

State/Plant Name	Status	Type	Sludge Volume
Puerto Rico			
Aricebo	Construction	A-SP	15

Source: Biocycle, December 1989, p. 29. Sludge volume listed in dry tons per days unless otherwise noted. A minus sign (-) represents a value not available. A-SP stands for Aerated Static Pile. SP - Static Pile. I-V - In-Vessel. TLC - Twin Landfill Corp. SJC - San Joaquin Composting. IPS - International Process Systems. RI - Recyc, Inc. ABT - American Bio-Tech. BB - Bedminster Bioconversion. DC - Darling's Compost. NWC - Northwest Cascade. A-S-H - Ashbrook, Simon, Hartley. P-E - Pasteurization & Windrow. A-W - Aerated Windrow. Mod.- W - Modified Windrow. A-B - agitated bin. H-B - horizontal bin. WTD - wet tons/day. CYD - cubic yards/day. CYW - cubic yards/week. CYM - cubic yards/month. CYY - cubic yards/year. GDS - gallons/day septage. CLP - Consideration, low priority. *Notes:* 1. Taulman. 2. Solar drying. 3. Pilot-tested tunnel reactor. 4. Full-scale. 5. Co-composting. 6. Vermicomposting. 7. I-V under consideration. 8. Site selection. 9. With windrow curing. 10. In-Vessel (IPS), A-SP, Windrow. 11. 200-300/mo. (planned). 12. W/Comtek Eng. 13. Private facility by RCS. 14. Regional facility. 15. Sludge & septage. 16. Laidig. 17. Fairfield. 18. Operated by Agrisource, Inc. 19. Purac. 20. Compost for odor filter. 21. Favored. 22. w/septage. 23. Recomp. 24. EKO-Compost. 25. Compost Systems. 26. Dynatherm. 27. 1995 + .

★ 433 ★

Soda Bottle and Paper Recycling

Number of 2-liter PET soda bottles in a cubic yard	217
Number of stepped-on PET soda bottles in a cubic yard	343
Energy saved if all paper had 50% recycled content	11.5 billion kwh
Money saved if all paper had 50% recycled content	$1.8 billion
Proportion of nonrequested items in NYC recycling bins	5.0%
Proportion of nonrequested items in Seattle recycling bins	1.4%

Source: Garbage, March/April 1991, p.66. *Note:* PET stands for polyethylene terephthalate; NYC stands for New York City; and kwh stands for kilowatt hours.

★ 434 ★

Solid Waste Processing - Generation

The values are percent of total municipal solid waste generation.

	Percent of Total Generation						
	1960	1965	1970	1975	1980	1985	1988
Generation	100.0	100.0	100.0	100.0	100.0	100.0	100.0
Recovery for Recycling	6.7	6.6	7.1	7.7	9.7	10.1	12.9
Recovery for Composting	0.0	0.0	0.0	0.0	0.0	0.0	0.3
Total Materials Recovery	6.7	6.6	7.1	7.7	9.7	10.1	13.1
Discards after Recovery[1]	93.3	93.4	92.9	92.3	90.3	89.9	86.9
Combustion with Energy Recovery	0.0	0.2	0.3	0.5	1.8	4.7	13.6
Combustion without Energy Recovery	30.8	25.9	20.3	13.9	7.4	2.5	1.5

[Continued]

★ 434 ★

Solid Waste Processing - Generation
[Continued]

	Percent of Total Generation						
	1960	1965	1970	1975	1980	1985	1988
Total Combustion	30.8	26.1	20.6	14.4	9.2	7.2	14.2
Discards to Landfill, Other Disposal[2]	62.5	67.3	72.4	77.8	81.1	82.6	72.7

Source: Characterization of Municipal Solid Waste in the United States: 1990 Update, U.S. Environmental Protection Agency, EPA/530-SW-90-042, Washington, D.C., June 1990, p. 55, from Franklin Associates, Ltd. Details may not add to totals due to rounding. *Notes:* 1. Does not include residues from recycling/composting processes. 2. Does not include residues from recycling, composting, or combustion processes.

★ 435 ★

Solid Waste Processing - Tonnage
The values are in millions of tons.

	Millions of Tons						
	1960	1965	1970	1975	1980	1985	1988
Generation	87.8	103.4	121.9	128.1	149.6	161.6	179.6
Recovery for Recycling	5.9	6.8	8.6	9.9	14.5	16.4	23.1
Recovery for Composting	0.0	0.0	0.0	0.0	0.0	0.0	0.5
Total Materials Recovery	5.9	6.8	8.6	9.9	14.5	16.4	23.5
Discards After Recovery[1]	81.9	96.6	113.3	118.2	135.1	145.2	156.0
Combustion with Energy Recovery	0.0	0.2	0.4	0.7	2.7	7.6	24.5
Combustion without Energy Recovery	27.0	26.8	24.7	17.8	11.0	4.1	1.0
Total Combustion	27.0	27.0	25.1	18.5	13.7	11.7	25.5
Discards to Landfill, Other Disposal[2]	54.9	69.6	88.2	99.7	121.4	133.5	130.5

Source: Characterization of Municipal Solid Waste in the United States: 1990 Update, U.S. Environmental Protection Agency, EPA/530-SW-90-042, Washington, D.C., June 1990, p. 55, from Franklin Associates, Ltd. Details may not add to totals due to rounding. *Notes:* 1. Does not include residues from recycling/composting processes. 2. Does not include residues from recycling, composting, or combustion processes.

★ 436 ★

Solid Waste Recovery by Material

```
┌─────────────────────────────────────────────────────┐
│  ┌─────────────────────────────────────────────┐    │
│  │ Aluminum - 28.6                             │    │
│  └─────────────────────────────────────────────┘    │
│  ┌───────────────────────────────────────┐          │
│  │ Paper and paperboard - 20.7           │          │
│  └───────────────────────────────────────┘          │
│  ┌─────────────────────────┐                        │
│  │ Total - 14.3            │                        │
│  └─────────────────────────┘                        │
│  ┌──────────────┐                                   │
│  │ Glass - 7.2  │                                   │
│  └──────────────┘                                   │
│  ┌──────┐  Rubber and leather - 3.0                 │
│  └──────┘                                           │
│  ┌──────┐  Iron and steel - 2.7                     │
│  └──────┘                                           │
│  ┌──┐ Plastics - 1.0                                │
│  └──┘                                               │
│               Chart shows data from column 3.       │
└─────────────────────────────────────────────────────┘
```

Annual discard and recovery of municipal solid waste in the U.S. in 1984.

Material	Annual discards, million ton ton[1]	Post-consumer recovery, million ton	Recovery rate %
Aluminum	2.1	0.6	28.6
Paper and paperboard	62.3	12.9	20.7
Glass	13.9	1.0	7.2
Rubber and leather	3.4	0.1	3.0
Iron and steel	11.3	0.3	2.7
Plastics	9.7	0.1	1.0
Total	100.6	14.4	14.3

Source: Modern Plastics, April 1990, p. 10, from Franklin Associates, Ltd., Prairie Village, KS.
Note: 1. Municipal solid waste system figures for 1984.

★ 437 ★

Solvent Recycling by Type

Volumes are shown in billions of gallons.

Item	1990	1995	2000	% Annual Growth 95/90
Solvent recycling (billions of $)	15.2	18.0	20.0	3.4
$/gallon	0.24	0.29	0.34	3.9
Solvents demanded	159.9	153.4	145.4	-0.8
% recyclable	50.0	48.9	48.1	
Potentially recycled solvents	80.0	75.0	70.0	-1.3
% recycled	78.1	82.0	85.0	-
Solvent recycled (total)	62.5	61.5	59.5	-0.3
Halogenated hydrocarbons	16.0	14.0	12.0	-2.6
Hydrocarbons	14.7	14.0	13.0	-1.0
Alcohols	12.3	13.5	14.0	1.9

[Continued]

★ 437 ★

Solvent Recycling by Type
[Continued]

Item	1990	1995	2000	% Annual Growth 95/90
Esters and ethers	10.0	10.4	10.8	0.8
Ketones	9.5	9.6	9.7	0.2
On-site	51.0	49.2	46.8	-0.7
Commercial	11.5	12.3	12.7	1.4

Source: Chemical Engineering, June 1991, p. 45, from The Freedonia Group.

★ 438 ★

U.S. Waste Exports to China and Hong Kong

Grade	China		Hong Kong	
	Tons	Value in $	Tons	Value in $
Wastepaper				
Newspaper	10,706	1,565,008	3,524	348,080
Deink high grades	32,584	5,078,120	1,751	313,583
Pulp substitutes	2,276	284,838	2,135	236,851
Corrugated	52,165	4,897,276	12,216	1,354,971
Mixed/other	18,913	2,394,548	6,041	759,273
Ferrous Scrap				
No. 1 bundles	120	10,000	-	-
Shredded	1,584	151,940	1,092	149,835
Iron	5,121	1,054,069	898	396,915
Miscellaneous	23,353	3,717,177	1,984	1,099,838
Stainless	-	-	2,043	1,077,794
Alloy	386	76,330	3,694	649,592
Non-ferrous Scrap	Pounds		Pounds	
Alloyed copper	2,293,055	837,795	454,299	211,626
Unalloyed copper	940,381	496,233	3,158,360	1,148,647
Secondary aluminum ingot	-	-	156,299	150,704
Aluminum cans	10,803	3,673	362,628	570,678
Nickel	-	-	250,651	130,700
Tin	174,884	31,084	896,111	161,496
Lead	877,118	88,677	-	-
Zinc	-	-	59,077	9,895

Source: Resource Recycling, July 1989, p. 26, from the U.S. Department of Commerce.

★ 439 ★

U.S. Wastepaper Consumption

Projected consumption in 1990 by paper and board mills, shown in thousands of short tons.

Total	Mixed paper	Newspaper	Corrugated	Pulp sub-stitutes	High grade deinking
22,568	2,341	3,690	11,424	3,087	2,025
6,596	254	1,955	474	2,157	1,746
1,754	9	1,744	-	-	-
1,517	15	-	45	1,089	368
253	17	9	81	144	2
3,072	223	202	348	924	1,376
15,020	1,718	1,401	10,763	881	258
2,694	-	-	2,511	102	81
2,063	59	10	1,932	62	-
2,343	49	16	2,275	3	-
7,921	1,610	1,375	4,045	714	177
953	360	335	188	50	21

Source: Pulp & Paper, February 1990, p. 23.

★ 440 ★

Voluntary Drop-Off Programs

Type of voluntary drop-off programs in 63 communities.

Type	Number
Drop-off satellite centers (materials are donated)	20
Buy-back satellite centers	2
One central center collection center (materials donated)	42
One central buy-back center	3
Some other type of facility	4
Total	71[1]

Source: Resource Recycling, January 1991, p. 74, from David H. Folz and Joseph M. Hazlett, *Recycling Solid Wastes: A National Survey of Local Government Programs*, 1990. *Notes:* 1. The total exceeds 63 because eight communities have more than one type of drop-off facility. Four have one central center and satellite centers for materials; the other four have combinations of buy-back and central centers for donations.

★ 441 ★

Voluntary Drop-off Programs - Participation

Participation rates at voluntary drop-off programs in 63 communities. Data are shown in percent.

Type	Program number	Participation			
		Mean	Median	High	Low
All programs	63	25.0	15	92	1
Drop-off satellite centers only	20	16.3	10	40	1
One central collection center (materials donated)	42	27.0	20	95	1
Combination of satellite and central center facilities	4	26.2	30	5	

Source: *Resource Recovery*, January 1991, p. 74, from David H. Foltz and Joseph M. Hazlett, *Recycling Solid Wastes: A National Survey of Local Government Programs*, 1990.

★ 442 ★

Voluntary Drop-off Programs - Waste Diversion

Diversion rates for voluntary drop-off programs in 63 communities. Data are shown in percent.

Type	Program number	Diversion			
		Mean	Median	High	Low
All programs	63	12.0	10	35	1
Drop-off satellite centers only	20	10.0	6	35	1
One central collection center (materials donated)	42	13.3	12	35	1
Combination of satellite and central center facilities	4	20.0	19	35	1

Source: *Resource Recovery*, January 1991, p. 74, from David H. Foltz and Joseph M. Hazlett, *Recycling Solid Wastes: A National Survey of Local Government Programs*, 1990.

★ 443 ★

Wastepaper Collections

Collection of wastepaper including consumption at plants making molded pulp and insulation products. Data are shown in thousands of short tons.

Grade	19987	1988	Percent change
Newspaper	4,312.7	4,535.4	+5.2
Corrugated	11,098.4	12,024.7	+8.3
Mixed	2,854.3	3,065.0	+7.4
High grades	5,358.0	6,084.4	+13.6
Total	23,623.4	25,709.5	+8.8

Source: *Resource Recycling*, May/June 1989, p. 31, from the American Paper Institute.

★ 444 ★

Wastepaper Consumption in the U.S.

Wastepaper consumption includes consumption at plants making molded pulp and insulation products. Data are shown in thousands of short tons.

Grade	1987	1988	Percent change
Newspaper	3,442.5	3,526.7	+2.4
Corrugated	9,176.7	9,747.5	+6.2
Mixed	2,116.2	2,180.2	+3.0
High grades	4,465.7	4,615.0	+3.3
Total	19,201.1	20,069.4	+4.5

Source: Resource Recycling, May/June 1989, p. 30, from the American Paper Institute.

★ 445 ★

Wastepaper Consumption - 1988-1992

Data are shown in thousands of short tons.

Source	1988	1989[1]	1990[2]	1991[2]	1992[2]
Total all grades	19,886	20,878	22,570	23,740	24,982
Total paper	5650	5960	6596	7087	7397
Newsprint	1431	1498	1754	1831	1965
Printing, writing, and related	1461	1447	1517	1608	1635
Packaging and industrial converting	265	253	253	255	259
Tissue	2538	2762	3072	3393	3538
Total paperboard	13,371	14,034	15,021	15,671	16,594
Kraft, bleached, and unbleached	2042	2311	2694	2830	3035
Semichemical	1845	1935	2063	2093	2294
Recycled corrugating	2081	2165	2343	2436	2483
Other recycled	7403	7623	7921	8312	8782
Construction paper & board	885	884	953	982	991

Source: Pulp & Paper, April 1990, p. 31, from API capacity survey, 1989. *Notes:* 1. Estimated actual consumption. 2. Estimated consumption of full capacity operations.

★ 446 ★

Wastepaper Exports From the U.S.

Exports of wastepaper in 1987 and 1988, shown in thousands of short tons.

Grade	1987	1988	Percent change
Newspaper	870.2	1,088.7	+25.1
Corrugated	1,921.7	2,277.2	+18.5
Mixed	738.1	884.8	+19.9
High grades	892.3	1,469.4	+64.7
Total	4,422.3	5,640.1	+27.5

Source: Resource Recycling, May/June 1989, p. 30, from the American Paper Institute.

★ 447 ★

Wastepaper Recovery and Consumption

U.S. - 20,100	
Japan - 12,590	
Fed. Rep. Germany - 4,310	
People's Rep. China - 2,900	
Rep. Korea - 2,630	
France - 2,460	
Taiwan - 2,385	
Italy - 2,360	
U.K. - 2,300	
Spain - 2,220	
Mexico - 2,070	
Brazil - 1,600	
Netherlands - 1,480	
Canada - 830	
Australia - 605	
Venezuela - 400	
Portugal - 325	
Belgium - 260	
Denmark - 250	
Colombia - 245	

Chart shows data from column 2.

The figures are for 1987-88, and are metric tons except U.S.

Country	Wastepaper recovered (000 tons)	Wastepaper consumed (000 tons)	Recovery rate (%)	Utilization rate (%)
U.S.	26,000	20,100	31	24
Canada	1,400	830	23	5
Mexico	1,250	2,070	47	65
Brazil	1,570	1,600	34	31
Venezuela	320	400	35	50
Colombia	225	245	42	50
U.K.	2,700	2,300	30	56
France	2,550	2,460	35	42
Denmark	345	250	29	69
Fed. Rep. Germany	4,735	4,310	41	43
Netherlands	1,410	1,480	55	68
Belgium	610	260	35	24
Italy	1,600	2,360	26	44
Spain	1,660	2,220	41	58
Portugal	305	325	44	44

[Continued]

★ 447 ★

Wastepaper Recovery and Consumption
[Continued]

Country	Wastepaper recovered (000 tons)	Wastepaper consumed (000 tons)	Recovery rate (%)	Utilization rate (%)
Japan	12,000	12,590	48	49
People's Rep. China	2,600	2,900	20	25
Rep. Korea	1,420	2,630	43	68
Taiwan	1,140	2,385	40	87
Australia	690	605	30	36

Source: Pulp & Paper, June 1989, p. 144, from American Paper Institute; Canadian Pulp & Paper Assn.; European Confederation of Pulp, Paper & Board Industries; Food & Agricultural Organization of the United Nations; Pulp & Paper International.

★ 448 ★

Wastepaper Use in 1988

Total - 19,770

Corrugated - 9,747

Newspaper - 3,227

Pulp substitute - 2,901

Mixed paper - 2,180

Deinking - 1,714

Chart shows data from column 1.

Category	Usage (000 tons)	Percent
Deinking	1,714	9
Mixed paper	2,180	11
Pulp substitute	2,901	15
Newspaper	3,227	16
Corrugated	9,747	49
Total	19,770	100

Source: Pulp & Paper, November 1989, p. 70, from the National Association of Recycling Industries, Inc.

★ 449 ★

Wastepaper Utilization and Recovery

Utilization values are in millions of short tons, and recovery rate is the ratio of wastepaper recovered to new supply.

Item	1970	1975	1980	1981	1982	1983	1984	1985	1986	1987	1988
Paper and paperboard, production[1]	51.70	51.00	63.50	64.30	61.00	66.80	70.30	68.70	72.50	76.00	78.10
Wastepaper consumption	11.80	11.70	14.90	15.00	14.40	15.60	16.70	16.40	17.90	18.70	19.60
Wastepaper utilization rate (percent)	22.80	23.00	23.40	23.40	23.70	24.40	23.80	23.80	24.70	24.60	25.00
Other wastepaper uses[2]	.42	.54	.47	.48	.49	.48	.46	.48	.49	.51	.51
Wastepaper exports	.41	.86	2.66	2.21	2.13	2.57	3.24	3.29	3.75	4.42	5.64
Total wastepaper recovered	12.60	13.10	18.00	17.70	17.00	18.60	20.30	20.00	22.10	23.50	25.50
Paper and board, new supply[3]	56.00	54.10	67.20	68.00	64.70	71.20	77.00	76.10	79.70	83.60	85.60
Recovery rate (percent)	22.40	24.20	26.80	26.00	26.20	26.10	26.40	26.30	27.70	28.10	29.90

Source: U.S. Department of Commerce, Bureau of the Census, *Statistical Abstract of the United States 1990 (110th ed.)*, Superintendent of Documents, Washington, D.C., p. 676, from American Paper Institute, Inc., New York, NY, *Statistics of Paper, Paperboard and Woodpulp* annual and unpublished. *Notes:* 1. Excludes hard pressed board; includes construction paper and board, and wet machine board. 2. Estimated. 3. Excludes production of hard pressed board.

★ 450 ★

Wastewood and Refuse-Derived Fuel for Boilers

Table compares waste wood and municipal refuse characteristics when burned. Refused derived fuel (RDF) can be combusted in boilers of similar design as those used for wastewood.

Constituent	Pine bark (%)	Hardwood bark (%)	Municipal refuse (%)
Ash	-1.5	5.3	14.4
Sulfur	0.1	0.1	0.2
Hydrogen	5.5	5.4	5.7
Carbon	55.3	49.7	42.5
Oxygen and Nitrogen	37.6	39.5	37.2
Total	100.0	100.0	100.0
HHV on ash- and moisture-free basis[1]	9,300 Btu/lb	8,830 Btu/lb	8,600 Btu/lb

Source: Pulp & Paper, September 1989, p. 203 *Note:* 1. HHV stands for higher heating value and Btu for British thermal units.

★ 451 ★

Waste-to-Energy Plants in the U.S.

The data show the result of a 1987 survey.

Towns with operating plants	State	# Operating waste-to-energy plants	Total capacity of the plants (tpd)	Future plants (through yr. 2000)	Statewide resource recovery plan	Year state-wide plan enacted	Does plan address re-cycling?	Total MSW generated in in state (tpd)	Wastepaper consuming paper mills	Mills' waste-paper con-sumption (tpd
Tuscaloosa	Ala.	1	300	3	N	-	-	8,000	6	1,076
	Alaska	0	-	0	N	-	-	2,000	0	0
(Hospital)	Ariz.	1	25	0	N	-	-	8,750	1	750
Batesville, N. Little Rock	Ark.	2	150	n.a	N	-	-	5,897	2	194
Commerce	Calif.	1	300	6	N	-	-	97,200	10	2,380
	Colo.	0	-	0	Y	1983	N	9,500	0	0
Windham	Conn.	1	108	8	Y	1985	Y	7,293	2	300
Newcastle	Del.	1	1000	n.a.	Y	1978	N	1,848	0	0
Dade Co., Miami, Mayport, Lakeland, Pinellas Co., Tampa	Fla.	6	7,408	12	Y	1986	N	27,500	2	120
Savannah	Ga.	1	500	0	N	-	-	12,000	4	1,025
	Hawaii	0	-	1	Y	1983	N	2,200	0	0
Heyburn	Idaho	1	50	3	Y	1982	N	2,740	0	0
Chicago	Ill.	1	1,200	1	Y	1986	Y	30,680	3	267
	Ind.	0	-	1	Y	1980	Y	68,493	5	1,410
Ames	Iowa	1	160	n.a	Y	1987	N	5,205	1	50
	Kans.	0	-	3	N	-	-	4,657	2	305
	Ky.	0	-	n.a.	N	-	-	8,767	1	225
	La.	0	-	1	Y	1980	-	-	4	370
Auburn	Maine	1	200	3	N	-	-	2,000	1	130
City of Baltimore, Smith Is., Baltimore Co.	Md.	3	2,050	3	Y	1977	Y	17,000	0	0
Sangus, Haverhill, N. Andover, Pittsfield	Mass.	4	3,840	3	Y	1985	Y	16,400	4	345
	Mich.	0	-	4	Y	1979	Y	32,000	9	1,945
Thief River Falls, Rochester, Perham, Duluth, Savage, Red Wing (2)	Minn.	7	1,585	11	Y	1984	Y	10,000	0	0
Jackson Co.	Miss.	1	150	n.a	N	-	-	3,200	2	173
Ft. Leonard Wood	Mo.	1	75	n.a.	N	-	-	n.a.	3	255
Livingston/Park County	Mont.	1	75	3-5	Y	1976	N	1,400	0	0
	Nebr.	0	-	1	N	-	-	4,657	0	0
	Nev.	0	-	2	N	-	-	2,250	0	0
Claremont, Durham, Portsmouth	N.H.	3	550	2	Y	1981	N	1,600	4	154
Ft. Dix, Atlantic Co.	N.J.	2	200	17	Y	1985	Y	26,000	6	1,660
	N.Mex.	0	-	1	N	-	-	2,440	0	0
Glen Cove, Westchester Co., Dutchess Co., Albany, Oneida Co., Oswego Co., Cuba, Niagara Falls	N.Y.	8	6,208	14	Y	1987	Y	48,000	11	1,410
	N.C.	1	200	3-5	N	-	-	16,000	1	25
	N. Dak.	0	-	0	N	-	-	1,305	0	0
Columbus, Akron	Ohio	2	4,200	n.a.	N	-	-	27,400	8	962
Miami, Tulsa	Okla.	2	500	0	N	-	-	5,000	2	340
Salem	Ore.	1	550	1	N	-	SRP[1]	5,500	6	1,700
Harrisburgh, Westmoreland Co.	Pa.	2	770	10	Y	1982	Y	25,000	7	360
	R.I.	0	-	4	Y	1986	Y	2,740	0	0
Hampton Co.	S.C.	1	225	1	N	-	-	6,125	3	1,340
	S.Dak.	0	-	2	N	-	-	1,500	0	0
Nashville, Lewisburg, Gallatin, Dyersburg Center, Carthage, Cleburne, Gatesville,	Tenn.	4	1,420	0	N	-	-	n.a.	5	1,260
Beto, Waxahachie, Houston, Huntsville	Texas	8	430	6-7	Y	1983	N	41,000	4	845
Davis Co.	Utah	1	400	3	N	-	-	4,165	0	0
	Vt.	0	-	2	Y	1987	Y	975	2	59
Salem, Harrisonburg, Ft. Eustis, Norfolk, Hampton, Portsmouth, Alexandria	Va.	7	2,900	10	N	-	-	-	5	1,030
	Wash.	0	-	3	Y	1970	Y	12,054	1	30
	W.Va.	0	-	1	N	-	-	4,200	0	0
Barron Co., city of Waukesha, Madison	Wis.	3	455	25	Y	1986	Y	10,130	14	1,833
	Wyo.	0	-	0	N	-	-	n.a.	0	0

Source: Pulp & Paper, February 1988, p. 65. *Notes:* n.a. stands for not available. Y = yes. N= no. Co. = County. 1. SRP means separate recycling program.

Soil Conservation

★ 452 ★

Soil Conservation by Method

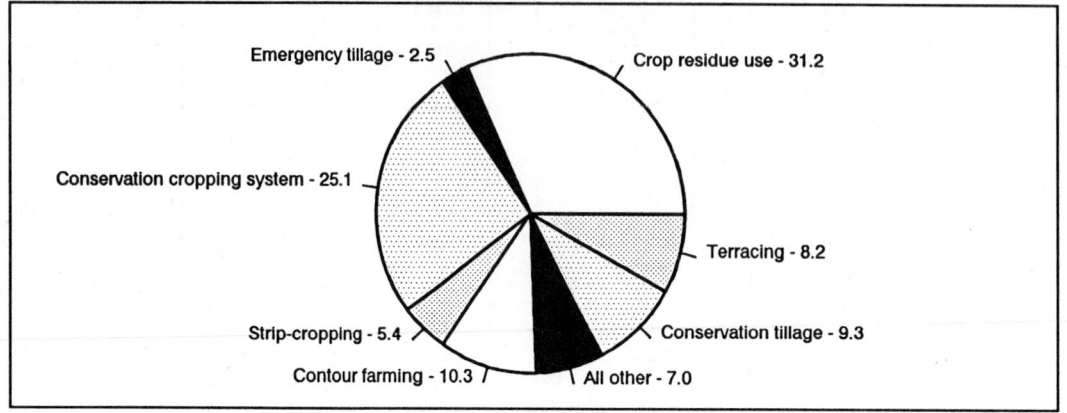

Values shown are percentages of total acres enrolled in conservation plans across the U.S.

Erosion type	Percent
Crop residue use	31.2
Conservation cropping system	25.1
Contour farming	10.3
Conservation tillage	9.3
Terracing	8.2
Strip-cropping	5.4
Emergency tillage	2.5
All other	7.0

Source: Farm Journal, May 1990, p. 17.

★ 453 ★

Soil Conservation - Type of Land Protected From Erosion Control

The data, shown in acres, show land protected from erosion in newly established conservation districts with Soil Conservation Service assistance, for fiscal years 1985-89.

Land protected from erosion	1985	1986	1987	1988	1989
Cropland	15,051,298	15,900,000	20,317,696	22,883,640	23,038,757
Pasture and hayland	4,894,898	5,100,000	5,184,482	6,167,604	5,401,220
Range and native pasture	31,227,673	32,200,000	26,186,535	28,184,587	29,249,034
Woodland	1,650,995	2,000,000	1,790,156	1,818,494	2,191,268
Wildlife	1,493,655	1,700,000	1,655,329	1,648,216	2,311,863
Recreation	88,588	100,000	62,348	42,728	42,811

[Continued]

★ 453 ★

Soil Conservation - Type of Land Protected from Erosion Control
[Continued]

Land protected from erosion	1985	1986	1987	1988	1989
All others	157,267	300,000	375,958	1,085,027	456,473
Total land protected	54,564,374	57,300,000	55,572,504	61,830,296	62,691,426

Source: Agricultural Conservation and Forestry Statistics, 1989, U.S. Government Printing Office, Washington, D.C., 1989, p. 449, from Soil Conservation Service.

Solid Waste Management

★ 454 ★

Animal Manures for Co-Composting
Animal manure, by animal and amount, available for composting with yard waste in the state of Florida.

Confined animals	Numbers[1]	Dry manure Solids (tons per year)
Beef Cattle	30,000	21,100
Dairy Cattle	144,000	355,000
Swine	90,000	11,800
Layers (chicken)	1,800,000	17,600
Horses	75,000	128,000

Source: BioCycle, April 1990, p. 53. *Notes:* 1. Estimates made by Extension Specialists, Florida Cooperative Extension Service, University of Florida, Gainesville, based on average animal weights.

★ 455 ★

Ash Treatment and Reuse

Reuse and disposal options, by type of ash.

Type of Ash	Preparation	Uses
Bottom Ash	Particle-size screening	Coarse highway aggregate, concrete products
Bottom Ash		Asphalt paving
Combined Ash		Artificial reefs
Combined Ash	Particle-size screening	Aggregate for paving
Flyash	Particle-size screening	Aggregate for paving
Flyash	Particle-size screening	Fine cement aggregate

Source: Power, March 1990, p. S-4.

★ 456 ★

Combustion of Municipal Waste

	1960	1965	1970	1975	1980	1985	1988
Generation of MSW[1]	87.8	103.4	121.9	128.1	149.6	161.6	179.6
Combustion with energy recovery							
Millions of tons	-	0.2	0.4	0.7	2.7	7.6	24.5
Percent of generation	-	0.2	0.3	0.5	1.8	4.7	13.6
Combustion without energy recovery							
Million tons	27.0	26.8	24.7	17.8	11.0	4.1	1.0
Percent of total generation	30.8	25.9	20.3	13.9	7.4	2.5	0.6

Source: Characterization of Municipal Solid Waste in the United States: 1990 Update, U.S. Environmental Protection Agency, EPA/530-SW-90-042, Washington, D.C., June 1990, p. 52, from Franklin Associates, Ltd. *Note*: Data do not include residues from combustion of municipal solid waste (MSW). Details may not add to totals due to rounding. *Note*: 1. Municipal Solid Waste.

★ 457 ★

Composting Facilities by Status

Type of Facility	In Opera-tion	Under Construc-tion	Planning, Design, Bid Bidding, Permitting	Pilot Plant Stage	Under Conside-ration
Aerated static pile	68	7	11	10	3.0
In-vessel	21	8	25	2	9.5
Windrow	24	3	1	5	3.5
Aerated windrow	4	1	2	1	-
Static pile	1	-	-	1	-
Vermicomposting	1	-	-	-	-
Unspecified	-	-	-	2	13
Co-composting	-	-	-	-	5
Survey totals	119	19	39	21	29
Grand Total	227				

Source: BioCycle, December 1989, p.32.

★ 458 ★

Composting Facilities for Municipal Solid Waste

Location	Year opened	Processing capacity (TPD of MSW)[3]	Type of composting system	Co-compost with sludge
Wilmington, DE	1984	1350	In-vessel	Yes
Sumpter County, FL	1988	65-100	Windrow	NA[2]
Dodge City, KS	1987[1]	30	Windrow	NA
St. Cloud, MN	1987	50	In-vessel	Yes
Fillmore County, MN	1987	25	Windrow	No
Portage, WI	1986	30	In-vessel	Yes

Source: Facing America's Trash: What Next for Municipal Solid Waste, U.S. Congress, Office of Technology Assessment, OTA-O-412, Washington, D.C., July 1989., p. 189, from Cal Recovery Systems, Inc., "Composting Technologies, Costs, Programs, and Markets," contract report prepared for U.S. Congress, Office of Technology Assessment (Richmond, CA: January 1989); Ron Albrecht Associates, Inc., "Composting Technologies, Costs, Programs and Markets," contract report prepared for U.S. Congress, Office of Technology Assessment (Annapolis, MD: December 1988). *Notes:* 1. Not commercially operating; run for research and demonstration by vendor. 2. Information not available. 3. TPD stands for tons per day; MSW for Municipal Solid Waste.

★ 459 ★

Discarded Waste in Landfills

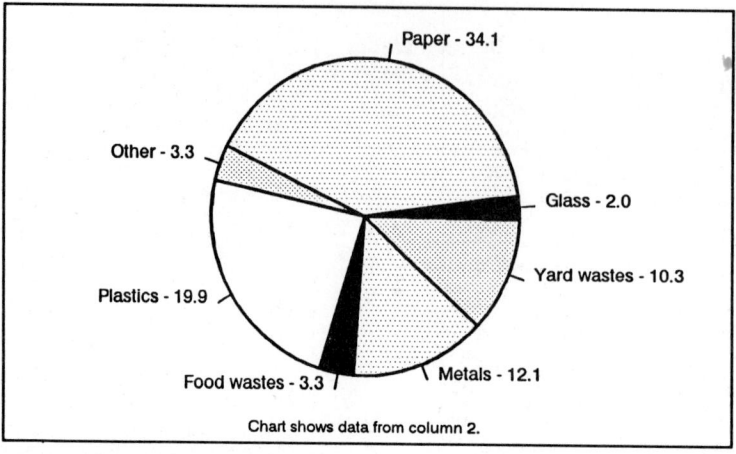

Chart shows data from column 2.

The total volume of municipal solid waste discarded in landfills in 1988 was 400 million cubic yards.

Material	Volume Discarded (cubic yards)	Percent
Paper	136.2	34.1
Plastics	79.7	19.9
Metals	48.3	12.1
Yard wastes	41.3	10.3
Food wastes	13.2	3.3
Glass	7.9	2.0
Other	13.2	3.3

Source: Characterization of Municipal Solid Waste in the United States: 1990 Update, U.S. Environmental Protection Agency, EPA/530-SW-90-042, Washington, D.C., June 1990, p. ES-10.

★ 460 ★

Incineration in the U.S.

	Year	Number
Number of incinerators in the U.S. and Canada	1914	300
Number in the U.S.	1974	160
Number today (1991)		128
Number in planning stages		70
Number under construction		19

Source: Garbage, March/April 1991, p. 66, from *Garbage in the Cities,* Texas A&M University Press; National Solid Wastes Management Assoc.

★ 461 ★

Incineration of Solid Waste - Post-Recycling

These figures refer to incineration after recycling.

Country	Percent Incinerated	Year
Denmark	55	1985
France	37	1983
Italy	11	1983
Japan	67	1987
Netherlands	38-42	1985
Sweden	51-55	1985, 1987
Switzerland	75	1985
United Kingdom	9	1983
United States	15	1986
West Germany	22-34	1985, 1986

Source: Facing America's Trash: What Next for Municipal Solid Waste, U.S. Congress, Office of Technology Assessment, OTA-O-412, Washington, D.C., July 1989., p. 220, from Franklin Associates, Ltd., *Characterization of Municipal Solid Waste in the United States, 1960 to 2000 (Update 1988)*, final report prepared for the U.S. Environmental Protection Agency (Prairie Village, KS: March 1988); A. Hershkowitz, "International Experiences in Solid Waste Management", contract prepared for U.S. Congress, Office of Technology Assessment (Elmsford, NY: Municipal Recycling Associates, October 1988); Institute for Local Self-Reliance, *Garbage in Europe: Technologies, Economics, and Trends* (Washington, DC: 1988); C. Pollock, "Mining Urban Wastes: The Potential For Recycling", Worldwatch Paper 76 (Washington, DC: Worldwatch Institute, April 1987); Swedish Association of Public Cleansing and Solid Waste Management, *Solid Waste Management in Sweden* (Malmo, Sweden: February 1988).

★ 462 ★

Landfill Capacity in Twenty Years

The figures refer to municipal landfills projected to remain in operation over the next twenty years.

Year	Number of landfills
1988	5,499[1]
1993	3,332
1998	2,720
2003	1,594
2008	1,234

Source: Facing America's Trash: What Next for Municipal Solid Waste, U.S. Congress, Office of Technology Assessment, OTA-O-412, Washington, D.C., July 1989., p. 273, from U.S. Evironmental Protection Agency, *Report to Congress: Solid Waste Disposal in the United States, Vol. II.* EPA/530-SW-88-011B (Washington, DC: Oct. 1988). *Note:* 1. 1988 figures reflect projected closings of 535 landfills during 1987.

★ 463 ★

Landfill Liners - Polymeric Geomembranes

Landfill liners are used to prevent moisture from reaching drinking water sources. Leachate collected by membranes must be extracted and treated.

Market	Volume, million lb.	
	1985	1990
Solid waste containment		
Hazardous landfill[1]	4	20
Landfill capping	8	32
Sanitary landfill	9	50
Liquid containment		
Canal[2]	7	15
Chemical/brine pond	3	6
Earthen dam	2	5
Fish farm	2	5
River/coastal bank	2	4
Wastewater[3]	7	16
Recreation[4]	8	12
Mining		
Heap leach pads[5]	10	25
Tailing ponds	2	4
Specialties		
Floating reservoir caps	3	5
Secondary containment[6]	6	10
Tunnel	2	4
Vapor barrier	2	3
Export	7	14
Total	84	230

Source: Modern Plastics, November 1990, p. 62, from Industrial Fabrics Association, International, St. Paul, MN, and other sources. *Notes:* 1. Federal regulations require double groundliner systems for hazardous waste sites. 2. Includes irrigation and shipping canals. 3. Primarily sewage settling ponds. 4. Includes golf course ponds and artificial lakes. 5. To contain cyanide-laced water used to extract alluvial mineral deposits. 6. Primarily for gasoline storage tanks, oil reserve pits, chemical plants.

★ 464 ★

Landfill Liners - Soil or Synthetic Membrane

Type of liner	Percentage of landfill units[1] with given type			Percentage used in combination with another type at active units.
	Closed	Active	Planned	
In-situ soil	34	28	30	9
Engineered soil	35	39	36	15
Synthetic membrane	<1	1	6	<1
Other	8	7	8	2
None or unknown	39	40	35	-

Source: *Facing America's Trash: What Next for Municipal Solid Waste*, U.S. Congress, Office of Technology Assessment, OTA-O-412, Washington, D.C., July 1989., p. 279, Adapted from U.S. Environmental Protection Agency, *Survey of State and Territorial Subtitle D Municipal Landfill Facilities*, draft final report prepared by Westat, Inc., Oct. 13, 1987. *Notes:* 1. Totals add more than 100 percent because some units have more than one type.

★ 465 ★

On-Site Waste Treatment

Number of TRI (Toxic Release Inventory) facilities reporting in 1987, by state.

State	No. of Facilities Reporting Waste Treatment (Rank)	TRI Facilities Reporting Waste Treatment (Number)	TRI Facilities Reporting in the State (Number)	Percent of TRI Total in the State that Reported Waste Treatment	Rank for Proportion of Facilities Reporting Waste Treatment
Alabama	21	173	355	48.73	34
Alaska	51	6	7	85.71	2
American Samoa	53	0	2	0.00	53
Arizona	29	97	156	62.18	6
Arkansas	26	119	293	40.61	48
California	1	895	1,662	53.85	18
Colorado	34	78	172	45.35	43
Connecticut	17	222	383	57.96	11
Delaware	41	34	53	64.15	4
Florida	18	205	419	48.93	33
Georgia	13	278	636	43.71	44
Hawaii	48	10	33	30.30	50
Idaho	42	29	52	55.77	15
Illinois	3	602	1,185	50.80	26
Indiana	9	360	720	50.00	29
Iowa	25	147	310	47.42	38

[Continued]

★ 465 ★

On-Site Waste Treatment
[Continued]

State	No. of Facilities Reporting Waste Treatment (Rank)	TRI Facilities Reporting Waste Treatment (Number)	TRI Facilities Reporting in the State (Number)	Percent of TRI Total in the State that Reported Waste Treatment	Rank for Proportion of Facilities Reporting Waste Treatment
Kansas	30	96	184	52.17	22
Kentucky	23	163	298	54.70	16
Louisiana	22	166	259	64.09	5
Maine	40	51	83	61.45	8
Maryland	31	90	191	47.12	39
Massachusetts	12	298	560	53.21	20
Michigan	6	423	758	55.80	14
Minnesota	24	152	301	50.50	27
Mississippi	27	119	247	48.18	35
Missouri	15	262	503	52.09	24
Montana	46	16	27	59.26	10
Nebraska	35	70	139	50.36	28
Nevada	44	23	33	69.70	3
New Hampshire	36	69	129	53.49	19
New Jersey	7	406	875	46.40	42
New Mexico	45	19	32	59.38	9
New York	8	397	765	51.90	25
North Carolina	10	351	820	42.80	46
North Dakota	50	8	28	28.57	51
Ohio	2	621	1,261	49.25	31
Oklahoma	32	80	193	41.45	47
Oregon	28	101	217	46.54	40
Pennsylvania	5	492	1,027	47.91	37
Puerto Rico	33	80	172	46.51	41
Rhode Island	38	60	166	36.14	49
South Carolina	16	244	394	61.93	7
South Dakota	49	10	37	27.03	52
Tennessee	14	263	503	52.29	21
Texas	4	521	999	52.15	23
Utah	39	55	102	53.92	17
Vermont	43	26	52	50.00	30
Virgin Islands	52	1	1	100.00	1
Virginia	19	173	399	43.36	45
Washington	20	173	306	56.54	13
West Virginia	37	62	107	57.94	12
Wisconsin	11	316	645	48.99	32
Wyoming	47	13	27	48.15	36
Total		9,725	19,278	50.45	

Source: The Toxic Release Inventory, A National Perspective, U.S. Environmental Protection Agency, Washington, D.C., June 1989, p. 246.

★ 466 ★

On-Site Waste Treatment by Method

| Total - 100.00 |
| Combination - 32.84 |
| Chemical - 21.06 |
| Unknown - 11.84 |
| Air Emissions - 9.57 |
| Sequential - 8.54 |
| Recovery/Reuse - 5.72 |
| Physical - 4.67 |
| Incineration - 2.91 |
| Biological - 2.42 |
| Solidification - 0.43 |

Chart shows data from column 2.

Number of TRI (Toxic Release Inventory) facilities and forms reported in 1987.

	TRI Facilities		TRI Forms	
	Number	Percent	Number	Percent
Air Emissions	931	9.57	4,419	11.88
Biological	235	2.42	1,430	3.84
Chemical	2,048	21.06	8,859	23.81
Incineration	283	2.91	1,359	3.65
Physical	454	4.67	1,989	5.35
Recovery/Reuse	556	5.72	1,647	4.43
Solidification	42	0.43	134	0.36
Combination	3,194	32.84	7,249	19.48
Sequential	831	8.54	6,233	16.75
Unknown	1,151	11.84	3,889	10.45
Total	9,725	100.00	37,208	100.00

Source: The Toxic Release Inventory, A National Perspective, U.S. Environmental Protection Agency, Washington, D.C., June 1989, p. 200.

★ 467 ★

Projected Resource Recovery, Combustion, and Disposal

```
Generation - 100.0

Discards after Recovery - 75.8

Landfill, Other Disposal - 53.1

        Total Materials for Recovery - 24.2

        Total Combustion - 22.8

        Combustion with Energy Recovery - 22.5

        Recovery for Recycling - 19.4

   Rceovery for Composting - 4.8

 Combustion without Energy Recovery - 0.3
           Chart shows data from column 4.
```

The estimated values are in millions of tons and percent of total generation.

	Millions of tons		% of generation	
	1988	1995	1988	1995
Generation	179.6	199.8	100.0	100.0
Recovery for Recycling	23.1	38.8	12.9	19.4
Rceovery for Composting	0.5	9.5	0.3	4.8
Total Materials for Recovery[1]	23.5	48.3	13.1	24.2
Discards after Recovery[2]	156.0	151.5	86.9	75.8
Combustion with Energy Recovery	24.5	45.0	13.6	22.5
Combustion without Energy Recovery	1.0	0.5	1.5	0.3
Total Combustion	25.5	45.5	14.2	22.8
Landfill, Other Disposal[3]	130.5	106.0	72.7	53.1

Source: Characterization of Municipal Solid Waste in the United States: 1990 Update, U.S. Environmental Protection Agency, EPA/530-SW-90-042, Washington, D.C., June 1990, p. 74 from Franklin Associates, Ltd. Details may not add to totals due to rounding. *Notes:* 1. Mid-range recovery estimates 2. Does not include residues from recycling/composting processes. 3. Does not include residues from recycling, composting, or combustion processes.

★ 468 ★

Sludge Disposal in the U.S.

Dumped in landfills - 42.3	
Incinerated - 21.4	
Used to fertilize farms/parks/forests - 15.7	
Composted (for use as a soil conditioner) - 9.1	
Dumped at sea - 5.5	
Other - 6.0	

Sludge containing heavy metals and organic chemicals from industrial wastewater is unsuitable for agricultural use.

Methods	Percent
Dumped in landfills	42.3
Incinerated	21.4
Used to fertilize farms/parks/forests	15.7
Composted (for use as a soil conditioner)	9.1
Dumped at sea	5.5
Other	6.0

Source: Garbage, January/February 1990, p. 12, from EPA.

★ 469 ★

Solid Waste Disposal - Post-Recycling

The figures refer to landfilling after recycling of source-separated glass, paper, and metals has occurred.

Country	Percent landfilled	Year
Denmark	44	1985
France	54	1983
Greece	100	1983
Ireland	100	1985
Italy	85	1983
Japan	33	1987
Netherlands	56-61	1985
Sweden	35-49	1985, 1987
Switzerland	22-25	1985
United Kingdom	90	1983

[Continued]

★ 469 ★

Post-Recycling Municipal Solid Waste Landfillings
[Continued]

Country	Percent landfilled	Year
United States	90	1986
West Germany	66-74	1985, 1986

Source: *Facing America's Trash: What Next for Municipal Solid Waste*, U.S. Congress, Office of Technology Assessment, OTA-O-412, Washington, D.C., July 1989., p. 273, from Franklin Associates, Ltd., *Characterization of Municipal Solid Waste in the United States, 1960 to 2000 (Update 1988)*, final report prepared for U.S. Environmental Protection Agency (Prairie Village, KS: March 1988); A. Hershkowitz, "International Experiences in Solid Waste Management," contract prepared for U.S. Congress, Office of Technology Assessment (Elmsford, NY: Municipal Recycling Associates, October 1988); Institute for Local Self-Reliance (ILSR), *Garbage in Europe: Technologies, Economics, and Trends* (Washington, DC: 1988); C. Pollock, "Mining Urban Wastes: The Potential for Recycling," Worldwatch Paper 76 (Washington, D.C.: Worldwatch Institute, April 1987); Swedish Association of Public Cleansing and Solid Waste Management, *Solid Waste Management in Sweden* (Malmo, Sweden: February 1988).

★ 470 ★

Solid Waste Generation, Recovery, and Disposal

In millions of tons, except as indicated. Covers post-consumer residential and commercial wastes which comprise the major portion of typical municipal collections. Excludes mining, agricultural and industrial processing, demolition and construction wastes, sewage sludge, and junked autos and obsolete equipment wastes. Based on material-flows estimating procedure and wet weight as generated.

Item and material	1970	1975	1980	1981	1982	1983	1984	1985	1986
Gross waste generated	120.5	125.3	142.6	144.8	142.0	148.3	153.6	152.5	157.7
Per person per day (lb)	3.22	3.18	3.43	3.45	3.35	3.47	3.56	3.49	3.58
Materials recovered	8.0	9.1	13.4	13.2	12.9	13.9	15.3	15.3	16.9
Per person per day (lb)	.21	.23	.32	.31	.30	.32	.35	.35	.39
Processed for energy recovery	.4	.7	2.7	2.3	3.5	5.0	6.5	7.6	9.6
Per person per day(lb)	.01	.02	.06	.05	.08	.12	.15	.17	.22
Net waste disposed of	112.1	115.5	126.5	129.3	125.6	129.5	131.8	129.7	131.2
Per person per day (lb)	3.00	2.93	3.04	3.08	2.96	3.03	3.05	2.97	2.98
Percent distribution of net discards[1]									
Paper and paperboard	32.4	29.6	32.5	33.1	32.1	34.1	35.7	35.5	35.6
Glass	11.1	11.4	11.0	10.9	10.7	9.9	9.3	8.9	8.4
Metals	12.0	11.5	10.1	9.8	9.7	9.6	9.3	9.0	8.9
Plastics	2.7	3.8	5.9	5.9	6.5	6.8	6.9	7.1	7.3
Rubber and leather	2.7	3.2	3.2	3.1	2.9	2.5	2.4	2.5	2.8
Textiles	1.8	1.9	2.0	2.6	2.2	2.1	2.0	2.0	2.0
Wood	3.6	3.8	3.8	3.3	3.9	3.9	3.7	3.9	4.1
Food wastes	11.4	11.5	9.2	9.2	9.3	8.9	8.8	9.0	8.9

[Continued]

★ 470 ★

Solid Waste Generation, Recovery, & Disposal
[Continued]

Item and material	1970	1975	1980	1981	1982	1983	1984	1985	1986
Yard wastes	20.6	21.7	20.5	20.3	20.9	20.4	20.1	20.4	20.1
Other wastes	1.6	1.7	1.7	1.7	1.8	1.8	1.7	1.8	1.8

Source: U.S. Department of Commerce, Bureau of the Census, *Statistical Abstract of the United States 1990 (110th ed.)*, Superintendent of Documents, Washington, D.C., p. 206, from Franklin Associates Ltd., Prairie Village, KS, Characterization of Municipal Solid Waste in the United States, 1960 to 2000. Prepared for the U.S. Environmental Protection Agency. *Notes:* NA stands for not available 1. Net discards after materials recovery and before energy recovery.[1]

★ 471 ★

Solid Waste Management Worldwide

Data from selected countries over the globe show total generation of municipal solid waste (MSW) and its disposition by management method.

Country	Year	MSW (mill. metr. tons/yr.)	Weight Percent			
			Landfill	Incineration	Composting	Recycling[1]
Austria	1988	2.6	51.0	12.0	37.0	
Canada	1987	12.7	90.0	10.0		
Denmark	1983	3.4	22.0	70.0	8.0	
France	1983	17.8	54.0[2]	37.0	9.0	
W. Germany	1983	23.1	70.0	27.0	3.0	
Greece	1983		100.0[2]			
Ireland	1985		100.0[2]			
Italy	1983	14.0	85.0[2]	11.0	3.0	
Japan	1983	40.5	30.0	68.0	2.0	(50.0)
Netherlands	1983	7.3	53.0	37.0	10.0	
Norway	1984	2.0	69.0	27.0	4.0	
Spain	1986	10.6	81.0[2]	14.0	5.0	
Sweden	1985	2.5	40.0	55.0	5.0	
Switzerland	1986	2.5	20.0	80.0		
United Kingdom	1983	32.3	90.0	9.0	1.0	(3.0)
United States	1985	144.0	94.0	6.0		(10.0)

Source: Resources, Conservation and Recycling, August 1990, p. 9. *Notes:* 1. Data show percent of total solid waste not requiring disposal due to volume reduction through recycling. 2. Significant percentage (more than 10%) went to uncontrolled landfills.

★ 472 ★

Solid Waste Management - Municipal

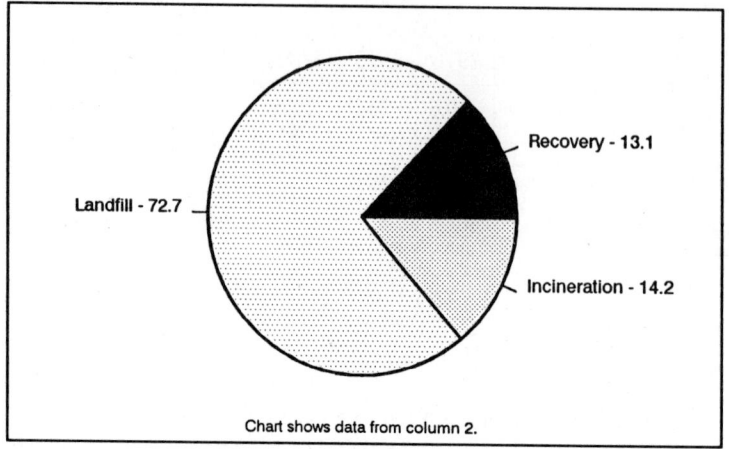

Chart shows data from column 2.

Methods used for management of 179.6 million tons of municipal solid waste (MSW) in the U.S. in 1988. Data are shown in millions of tons and as percent of total waste.

Material	Weight (Million Tons)	Percent of total MSW
Landfill	130.5	72.7
Incineration	25.5	14.2
Recovery	23.5	13.1

Source: Characterization of Municipal Solid Waste in the United States: 1990 Update, U.S. Environmental Protection Agency, EPA/530-SW-90-042, Washington, D.C., June 1990, p. ES-6.

★ 473 ★

Waste Reduction by Method

Data are drawn from the Environmental Protection Agency's Toxic Release Inventory (TRI) reporting system.

Method	TRI Waste Generation			Amount of TRI Wastes Reduced	Percent Change
	Forms Number	1987 Pounds	1986 Pounds		
Recycling/Reuse On-Site	224	18,707,656	39,797,950	21,090,294	53
Equip./Technology Modifications	115	14,095,067	22,556,259	8,461,192	38
Other Techniques	61	4,576,129	12,731,974	8,155,845	64
Process Procedure Modifications	104	15,929,784	20,717,421	4,787,637	23
Recycling/Reuse Off-Site	126	7,620,462	12,102,795	4,482,333	37
Product Reformulation/Redesign	29	3,566,733	5,932,720	2,365,987	40
Substitution of Raw Materials	33	2,151,481	4,423,236	2,271,755	51

[Continued]

★ 473 ★

Waste Reduction by Method
[Continued]

Method	TRI Waste Generation			Amount of TRI Wastes Reduced	Percent Change
	Forms Number	1987 Pounds	1986 Pounds		
Improved Housekeeping, etc.	110	2,301,528	3,087,751	786,223	25
Total	802	68,948,840	121,350,106	52,401,266	

Source: The Toxic Release Inventory, A National Perspective, U.S. Environmental Protection Agency, Washington, D.C., June 1989, p. 273.

Spill Response Equipment

★ 474 ★

U.S. Coast Guard Spill Response Equipment

Equipment description	Atlantic team	Pacific team
Spilled oil recovery equipment:		
Open Water Oil Containment and Recovery Systems:		
Skimming barriers	5	19
Fast surface delivery systems	11	11
Pumping subsystem	7	17
Dracone barges (various sizes)	8	4
Expandi harbor boom (1,600 feet)	1	0
Pumping equipment:		
Air Deliverable Anti-Pollution Transfer Systems (ADAPTS):		
Prime movers	7	13
Submersible pumps	11	15
Hydraulic hose (5,000 ft.)	1	1
Discharge hose (4,000 ft.)	1	1
Fuel bladders	NA	8
Viscous oil pumping systems:		
Prime movers	2	1
Submersible pumps	NA	8
Chemical transfer systems	2	NA
Nonsubmersible pumps	9	16
Ancillary equipment:		
Command posts	3	2
Tractors	4	2
Boats (various small boats)	10	6
All purpose vehicles	7	5
Trailers	3	12

[Continued]

377

★ 474 ★

U.S. Coast Guard Spill Response Equipment
[Continued]

Equipment description	Atlantic team	Pacific team
Radios	42	36
Computers	3	NA
Monitoring equipment	NA	yes
Testing equipment	NA	yes

Source: *Coping With An Oiled Sea: An Analysis of Oil Spill Response Technologies*, U.S. Congress, Office of Technology Assessment, March 1990, p. 4, from the U.S. Navy, 1989. NA stands for not available.

★ 475 ★

U.S. Navy Spill Response Equipment

Equipment description	Quantities by location		
	Williams-burg, VA	Stockton, CA	Pearl Harbor, HI
Spilled oil recovery equipment:			
Skimmer vessel system (36-foot aluminum hull)	12	11	1
Skimming system (sorbent belt voss)	1	1	0
Skimming system (screw pump voss)	2	2	0
Skimmer, sorbent rope mop (36-inch)	2	1	0
Boom vans (42-inch by 1980-foot boom)	6	7	0
Boom mooring system	37	34	4
Boom handling boat (24-inch 260 hp)	8	6	2
Boom tending boats (19- by 23-foot, inflatable)	2	2	1
Boom tending boats (18-foot rigid hull)	4	4	1
136,000-gallon oil storage bladder	6	4	0
26,000-gallon oil storage bladder	4	3	1
Pumping equipment:			
Pump, 6-inch submersible	11	8	2
Floating hose (6-inch by 100-foot)	65	0	0
Hot tap system	4	3	0
Boarding kit	1	2	0
Firefighting system	3	2	0
Ancillary equipment:			
Command trailer (40-foot communications/command center)	1	1	0
Command van (20-foot communications/command center)	3	2	0
Fender system (8- by 12-foot, foam)	16	4	0
Fender system (14- by 60-foot, lp air)	8	0	0
Fender system (10- by 50-foot, lp air)	24	0	0
Shop vans	3	2	0
Rigging vans	2	3	0
Personnel bunk van	2	0	0
Beach transfer system (4-wheel drive vehicle)	1	0	0
Communication system (SAT phone, land)	1	0	0

[Continued]

★ 475 ★

U.S. Navy Spill Response Equipment
[Continued]

Equipment description	Quantities by location		
	Williams-burg, VA	Stockton, CA	Pearl Harbor, HI
Communication system (SAT phone, ship)	1	0	0
Oil/water separator (parallel plate, 100 gal./min.)	2	1	0
Cleaning system van	1	2	0

Source: Coping With An Oiled Sea: An Analysis of Oil Spill Response Technologies, U.S. Congress, Office of Technology Assessment, March 1990, p. 4, from the U.S. Navy, 1989.

Wastewater Treatment

★ 476 ★

Municipal Wastewater Treatment Levels

Municipal treatment facilities receive wastewater from residential sources, industry groundwater infiltration, and storm run-off.

Treatment Level	Number of facilities			Design capacity (MGD)			Population served		
	1984	1986	1988	1984	1986	1988	1984	1986	1988
Raw	202	149	118	-	-	-	1.3	1.6	1.5
L.T. Secondary	2,617	2,112	1,789	6,510	5,529	5,030	33.7	28.8	26.5
Secondary	8,070	8,403	8,536	14,603	15,714	16,087	70.7	72.2	78.0
G.T. Secondary	2,965	3,115	3,412	13,874	14,373	15,488	59.5	54.9	65.7
No discharge	1,726	1,762	1,854	938	973	1,034	5.5	5.7	6.1
Totals	15,580	15,541	15,709	35,925	36,589	37,639	170.7	163.2	177.8

Source: National Water Quality Inventory, 1988, Report to Congress, U.S. Environmental Protection Agency, Washington, D.C., April 1990, p. 148, from U.S. EPA. *1988 Needs Survey Report to Congress*.

★ 477 ★

Population Served by Waste Water Treatment Plants

The values represent percentage of population served from 1970 to 1987 in selected countries.

Country	Percentage of Population Served, Total				Primary Treatment Only				Primary and Secondary and/ or Tertiary Treatment			
	1970	1980	1985	1987	1970	1980	1985	1987	1970	1980	1985	1987
United States[1]	42.0	70.0	74.0[2]	(NA)	(NA)	17.0	15.0[2]	(NA)	(NA)	53.0	59.0[2]	(NA)
Belgium	3.8	22.9[3]	(NA)	(NA)	-	-[3]	(NA)	(NA)	3.8	22.9[3]	(NA)	(NA)
Canada[4]	(NA)	56.0	57.0	62.6	(NA)	13.0	10.0	14.7	(NA)	43.0	47.0	51.5
France	19.0	43.0	49.7[2]	(NA)	(NA)	(NA)	(NA)	(NA)	(NA)	(NA)	(NA)	(NA)
Italy	14.5[5]	30.0	(NA)	(NA)	8.0[5]	(NA)	(NA)	(NA)	6.0[5]	(NA)	(NA)	(NA)
Japan	16.0	30.0	36.0[2]	39.0	(NA)	(NA)	(NA)	(NA)	16.0[6]	30.0[6]	36.0[2,6]	39.0[6]
Netherlands	(NA)	68.0	85.0	90.0	(NA)	7.0	7.0	7.0	(NA)	61.0	78.0	83.0
Spain	(NA)	17.9	29.0	(NA)	(NA)	8.8	13.2	(NA)	(NA)	9.1	15.8	(NA)
Sweden[7]	78.0	99.0	100.0	100.0	23.0	1.0	1.0	1.0	55.0	98.0	99.0	99.0
Switzerland	35.0	70.0	81.0	85.0	-	-	-	-	35.0	70.0	81.0	85.0
United Kingdom[8]	(NA)	82.0	83.0	84.0	(NA)	6.0	6.0	6.0	(NA)	76.0	77.0	78.0
West Germany	61.8[9]	81.8	86.5[10]	(NA)	20.5[9]	10.2	7.5[10]	(NA)	41.3[9]	71.6	79.0[10]	(NA)

Source: U.S. Department of Commerce, Bureau of the Census, *Statistical Abstract of the United States 1990 (110th ed.)*, Superintendent of Documents, Washington, D.C., p. 843, from Organization for Economic Cooperation and Development, Paris, France Environmental Data Compendium, 1989. *Notes:* - Represents zero. NA stands for not available. 1. Beginning 1980, data not comparable with 1970 data and data for secondary treatment include 1 percent and 2 percent of non-discharge treatment. Primary treatment may provide some biological treatment. Secondary is preliminary treatment plus biological process with no additional treatment except disinfection. 2. 1984 data. 3. 1979 data. 4. Secondary usually includes private treatment and includes waste stabilization ponds. Tertiary refers to secondary treatment with phosphorus removal. 5. 1971 data. 6. Data for secondary category may include data for primary treatment only. 7. Urban population only (85 percent of total). Primary: Removal of sediments; Secondary: Chemical or biological treatment; Tertiary: Chemical, biological and complementary treatment. 8. England and Wales only. Primary: Removal of gross solids; Secondary: Aerobic removal of organic material or bacteria; Tertiary: Removal of suspended solids following secondary treatment. 9. 1969 data. 10. 1983 data.

★ 478 ★

Publicly Owned Wastewater Treatment Facilities

Based on the latest *Needs Survey*, $36.9 billion is needed for upgrading or constructing secondary wastewater treatment facilities, correcting infiltration/ inflow problems, or building new interceptor sewers. Figures are shown in January 1988 dollars.

Needs category	Current 1988 Needs (billions)	Design Year 2008 Needs (billions)
I Secondary Treatment	20.2	26.8
II Advanced Treatment	3.9	5.0
IIIA Infiltration/Inflow Correction	2.9	2.9
IIIB Replacement/Rehabilitation	3.7	3.7
IVA New Collector Sewers	10.9	13.8
IVB New Interceptor Sewers	9.9	14.9
V Combined Sewer Overflow	16.4	16.4
Categories I-V	67.9	83.5

[Continued]

★ 478 ★

Publicly Owned Wastewater Treatment Facilities
[Continued]

Needs category	Current 1988 Needs (billions)	Design Year 2008 Needs (billions)
Treatment Categories I and II	24.1	31.8
Categories I, II, IIIA, and IVB	36.9	49.6

Source: National Water Quality Inventory, 1988, Report to Congress, U.S. Environmental Protection Agency, Washington, D.C., April 1990, p. 150, from U.S. Environmental Protection Agency, *1988 Needs Survey Report to Congress.*

★ 479 ★

Selected Wastewater Sludge Composting Facilities

Location	Type of Sludge	Type of Dewatering	Type of Composting	Design Capacity (dry tons/ day)	Composting Date Start
Akron, OH	Raw	Belt Filter Press	In-Vessel (Paygro)	73	1987
Clayton County, GA	Raw	Belt Filter Press	In-Vessel (Taulman)	3	1986
Metropolitan Denver Sewage Disposal District No. 1, CO	Digested	Centrifuge	Covered Aerated Wind-row	100	1986
East Bay Municipal Utility District, CA	Digested	Centrifuge	Static Pile	10	1983
Hampton Roads Sanitation District, VA	Digested	Belt Filter Press	Static Pile	12	1981
Los Angeles County Sanitation District, CA	Digested	Centrifuge	Windrow	100	1972
Nashville, TN	Raw	Belt Filter Press	Static Pile	40	1985
Sarasota, FL	Raw	Belt Filter Press	In-Vessel (Purac)	6	1987
Scranton, PA	Raw	Vacuum Filter	Static Pile	25	1984
Washington Suburban Sanitary Commission, MD	Raw	Centrifuge	Enclosed Static Pile	70	1983

Source: BioCycle, February 1990, p. 44.

★ 480 ★

U.S. Sewage Treatment by Method

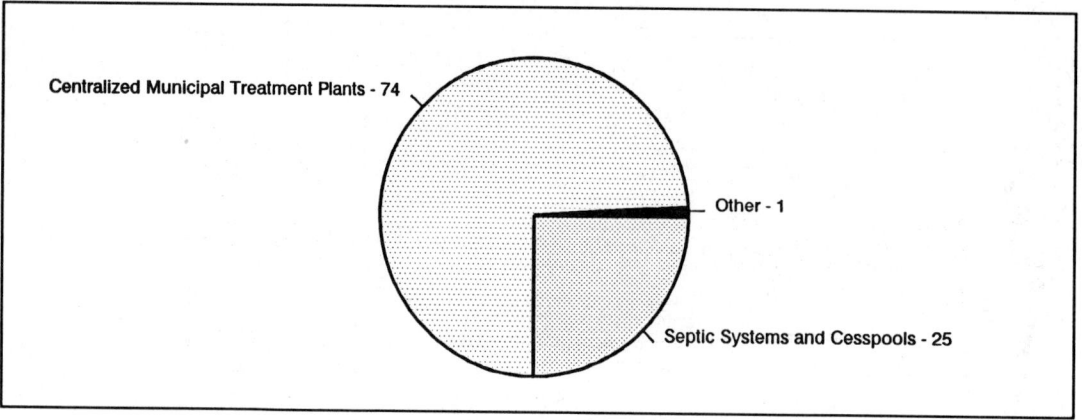

Treatments	Percent
Centralized Municipal Treatment Plants	74
Septic Systems and Cesspools	25
Other	1

Source: Garbage, January/February 1990, p. 12, from *Detailed Housing Characteristics,* U.S. Census 1980.

★ 481 ★

Waste Treatment Efficiencies

Unknown - 94.86
Liquid - 95.13
Water - 94.10
Air - 94.26
Solid - 89.40

Wastestream Type	Percent Efficiency
Air	94.26
Water	94.10
Liquid	95.13
Solid	89.40
Unknown	94.86

Source: The Toxic Release Inventory, A National Perspective, U.S. Environmental Protection Agency, Washington, D.C., June 1989, p. 254.

★ 482 ★

Wastewater Irrigation

Irrigated area in selected cities worldwide, shown in numbers of acres.

City	Irrigated Are (acres)
Melbourne, Australia	24,700
Braunschweig, Germany	7,400
Calcutta, India	30,900
Mexico City, Mexico	222,300
Lima, Peru	16,800
Riyadh, Saudi Arabia	7,000
Tunis, Tunisia	11,000[1]
Chandler, Arizona, U.S.A.	6,900

Source: World Watch, March/April 1989, p. 27, from C.R. Bartone and Arlosoroff, *Water Science Technology. Note:* 1. Includes planned extension.

★ 483 ★

Wastewater Treatment Process Effectiveness

Measure of Effectiveness	Primary treatment percent	Primary and secondary treatment percent	"Old" advanced primary treatment (alum-lime) percent	"New" advanced primary treatment (polymer-ferr chloride) percent
Percent of biological oxygen demand (BOD) removed	35	85	50	50-55
Percent of suspended solids removed	60	85	70	80-85
Amount of sludge produced[1]		1.9	2.2	1.5

Source: Technology Review, April 1990, p. 64 *Note:* 1. Weight of sludge produced, dry weight per day.

Wetlands Management

★ 484 ★

Water Bank Programs by Year

Summary of status of agreements carried out under the Water Bank Program, 1980 through September 30, 1989, by years.

Program year	Number of agreements[1]	Designated acres			Annual payment (Dollars)
		Total	Wetlands	Adjacent	
1980	542	60,929	17,155	43,774	987,123
1981	274	26,251	8,309	17,942	388,966
1982	523	44,115	15,650	28,465	679,614
1983	506	52,843	16,656	36,187	819,721
1984	589	59,167	22,829	36,338	849,218
1985	577	61,310	22,691	38,619	861,681
1986	316	35,451	12,481	22,970	544,394
1987	475	53,108	18,749	34,359	835,485
1988	486	61,670	24,902	36,768	949,577
1989	456	52,749	24,241	28,508	926,819
1990[1]	12	1,444	447	997	20,893
Total	4,756	509,037	184,110	324,927	7,863,491

Source: Agricultural Conservation and Forestry Statistics, 1989, U.S. Government Printing Office, Washington, D.C., 1989, p. 444, from Agricultural Stabilization and Conservation Service. *Notes:* 1. The agreements were entered into in 1989. Since compliance could not be rendered during 1988, the agreements were given the beginning date of January 1, 1990.

Chapter 6
POLLUTION CONTROL INDUSTRY

Coal

★ 485 ★

Clean Coal Technology by Company

Companies working on technological systems for controlling emissions from coal fired power plants.

Companies and project	Cost ($ 000)
American Electric Power Service Corp.	
Pressurized fluidized-bed combustion	185,000
Coal Tech Corp.	
Advanced combustor	984
Babcock & Wilcox Co.	
Limestone injection multistage burner	19,405
Energy & Environmental Research Corp.	
Gas burning/sorbent injection	30,000
Ohio-Ontario Coal Fuels Inc.	
Oil coprocessing	225,675
Colorado-Ute Electric Assoc. Inc.	
Circulating atmospheric fluidized-bed combustion	54,087
TRW Inc.	
Advanced slagging combustor	49,000
CQ Inc./Combustion Engineering Co.[1]	
Coal quality expert	17,382
Western Energy Co.	
Advanced coal cleaning	
City of Tallahassee	
Circulating fluidized-bed combustion	
Bethlehem Steel Corp	
Coke oven gas cleanup	45,000
Southern Co. Services Inc.	
Low-Nitrogen oxides technique for wall-fired boilers	11,711
Combustion Engineering Co.[1]	
WSA-SNOX flue-gas cleanup	31,438
Babcock & Wilcox Co.	
SNRB flue-gas cleanup	10,641

[Continued]

★ 485 ★

Clean Coal Technology by Company
[Continued]

Companies and project	Cost ($ 000)
Passamaquoddy Tribe	
Scrubbing system for cement kilns	10,166
Pure Air	
Advanced flue-gas desulfurization	150,497
American Electric Power Service Corp.	
Pressurized fluidized-bed combustion	659,860
Babcock & Wilcox Co.	
Coal reburning for cyclone boiler NO_x control	10,655
Southern Co. Services Inc.	
Advanced limestone scrubber	35,844
Southern Co. Services Inc.	
Selective catalytic reduction for NO_x control	15,574
TransAlta Corp.	
Low-nitrogen oxides/Sulfuric oxides burner retrofit	15,300
Southern Co. Services Inc.	
Low-NO_x for tangentially-fired boilers	-
Southwestern Public Service Co.	
Circulating fluidized-bed combustion	-
Otisca Industries Ltd.	
Water-slurry production/test burn	-
Combustion Engineering Co.[1]	
Gasification repowering	-
Bethlehem Steel Corp.	
Blast furnace granulated-coal injection	-
Bechtel Corp.	
Confined-zone dispersion flue-gas desulfurization	-
Babcock & Wilcox Co.	
Low-NO_x cell burner retrofit	-
AirPol Inc.	
Gas suspension-absorption flue-gas desulfurization	-
Alaska Industrial Development & Export Authority	
Healy cogeneration	-
Public Service Co. of Colorado	
Integrated dry-sorbent injection and NO_x control	-
CP-SS Capital Inc./TECO Power Services Corp.	
Integrated gasification combined-cycle	-
LIFAC North America	
LIFAC flue-gas desulfurization	-
Air Products & Chemical/Dakota Gasification Co.	
Liquid-phase methanol	-
Emcoal Corp.	
Mild gasification	-
MK-Ferguson Co.	
NOX SO SO_2/NO_x removal flue-gas cleanup	-
Dairyland Power Cooperative	

[Continued]

★ 485 ★

Clean Coal Technology by Company
[Continued]

Companies and project	Cost ($ 000)
Pressurized circulating fluidized-bed Energy & Environmental Research Corp.	-
Wall-fired boiler gas reburning and low-NO$_x$ burner	-

Source: Electric Light and Power, June 1990, p. 20, from DOE. Note: 1. Now part of the ABB Group.

Compensation

★ 486 ★

Average 1989 Salary Increases

Employee	Environmental firms	Design, construction firms	All industries
Executives	7.4	5.9	5.8
Middle managers	6.7	5.6	5.3
Professionals	7.1	5.6	5.3
Lab/office positions	6.4	5.1	5.1
Field positions	6.8	5.1	5.1

Source: ENR, November 30, 1989, p. 9, from Mercer Meidinger Hansen Inc. Figures do not include increases resulting from promotion.

★ 487 ★

Engineer's Median Income by Type

Type of engineer	Median income ($)
Petroleum	65,600
Nuclear	58,664
Architectural	56,250
Cost/value	54,325
Civil (structural)	54,000
Environmental	54,000

[Continued]

★ 487 ★

Engineer's Median Income by Type
[Continued]

Type of engineer	Median income ($)
Electrical	53,904
Chemical	53,700
Mechanical	52,722
Manufacturing	52,021
Civil (general)	51,250
Civil (surveying)	46,800
All types	53,000

Source: ENR, August 31,1989, p. 15, from National Society of Professional Engineers.

★ 488 ★

Salaries of Hazardous Waste Managers

Corporate Managers - 64,888
Scientists - 49,771
Compliance Managers - 47,392
Consultants - 46,611
Environmental Managers - 46,041
Other - 43,063
Health/Safety Managers - 42,575
First Responders - 39,390
Purchasing Agents - 37,759
Technicians - 35,516

Survey of *Hazmat World* subscribers soliciting information on their job functions and salaries.

Position	Base Salary ($)
Environmental Managers	46,041
Compliance Managers	47,392
Health/Safety Managers	42,575
Corporate Managers	64,888
Scientists	49,771
Technicians	35,516
Purchasing Agents	37,759
First Responders	39,390

[Continued]

★ 488 ★

Salaries of Hazardous Waste Managers
[Continued]

Position	Base Salary ($)
Consultants	46,611
Other	43,063

Source: Hazmat World, December 1990, p. 37.

Consultants

★ 489 ★

Leading Environmental Consulting Firms

Leading U.S. companies that provide environmental consulting, engineering design, and regulatory compliance services. Dollar amount headers refer to fiscal year revenues from such services.

Company Name	Headquarters City	Employees	Year Founded
$200 million			
American Capital & Research Technologies	Fairfax, VA	4,000	1987
Camp, Dresser & McKee Inc.	Cambridge, MA	2,000	1947
CH2M Hill Inc.	Denver, CO	4,500	1946
Dames & Moore Inc.	Los Angeles, CA	3,200	1938
EBASCO Environmental Inc.	Lyndhurst, NJ	1,000	1975
Fluor Daniel Inc. Environmental Services Div.	Irvine, CA	1,000	1986
International Technology Corp.	Torrance, CA	3,000	1926
Metcalf & Eddy Cos. Inc.	Wakefield, MA	2,200	1907
OHM Corp.	Findlay, OH	1,900	1969
Roy F. Weston, Inc.	West Chester, PA	2,500	1957
$100 million			
Bechtel Environmental Inc.	San Francisco CA	9,000 1	898
Clean Harbors Environmental Engineering Corp.	Quincy, MA	1,200	1986
Du Pont Safety & Environmental Resources Div.	Wilmington, DE	300	1802
ENSR Corp.	Acton, MA	1,500	1968
Environmental Science & Engineering Inc.	Peoria, IL	1,400	1965
ERM Group	Exton, PA	1,200	1977
Harding Lawson Associates Inc.	Novato, CA	900	1957

[Continued]

★ 489 ★

Leading Environmental Consulting Firms
[Continued]

Company Name	Headquarters City	Employees	Year Founded
J.M. Montgomery Consulting Engineers Inc.	Pasadena, CA	1,200	1945
Malcolm Pirnie Inc.	White Plains, NY	850	1929
NUS Corp.	Gaithersburg, MD	1,000	1960
Radian Corp.	Austin, TX	1,650	1969
$50 million			
Advanced Environmental Technology Corp.	Indianapolis, IN	1,500	1958
BCM Engineers Inc.	Plymouth Meeting, PA	1,000	1890
Black & Veatch	Kansas City, MO	1,000	1915
Brown & Caldwell	Pleasant Hill, CA	800	1947
Ecology & Environment Inc.	Lancaster, NY	1,200	1970
ERC Environmental & Energy Services Co.	Fairfax, VA	940	1972
Geraghty & Miller Inc.	Plainview, NY	900	1957
Groundwater Technology Inc.	Norwood, MA	1,360	1975
HDR Engineering Inc.	Omaha, NE	550	1917
Law Companies Group Inc.	Atlanta, GA	2,600	1948
McLaren Environmental Engineering	Rancho Cordova, CA	400	1977
Versar Inc.	Springfield, VA	800	1969

Source: Environment Today, July/August 1990, Vol. 1, No. 5.

★ 490 ★

Leading Firms in Water Pollution Control
The top 30 firms in the U.S. Total billings for the group in 1990 were $1.2 billion.

	Rank
Fluor	1
CH2M Hill Cos. Ltd.	2
Camp Dresser & McKee Inc.	3
Metcalf & Eddy Cos. Inc.	4
James M. Montgomery Consulting Engineers Inc.	5
Black & Veatch	6
Roy F. Weston, Inc.	7

[Continued]

★ 490 ★

Leading Sewage Design Firms
[Continued]

	Rank
Louis Berger International Inc.	8
Malcolm Pirnie Inc.	9
Engineering-Science Inc.	10
EMCON Associates	11
Brown & Caldwell Consultants	12
BCM Engineers Inc.	13
Post, Buckley, Schuh & Jernigan Inc.	14
Greeley & Hansen	15
Hazen & Sawyer P.C.	16
Donohue & Associates Inc.	17
Blasland & Bouck Engineers P.C.	18
The ERM Group	19
Law Cos. Group Inc./Sir Alexander Gibb	20
HDR Inc.	21
Woodward-Clyde Consultants Inc.	22
Hill Group Inc.	23
John Carollo Engineers	24
Golder Associates Corp.	25
URS Consultants Inc.	26
Killam Associates	27
Greenhorne & O'Mara Inc.	28
R.W. Beck and Associates	29
Boyle Engineering Corp.	30

Source: ENR, April 8 ,1991, p. 39.

★ 491 ★

Top Design Firms in Hazardous Waste

Firm	Rank 1990	Type of firm	Percent of billings[1] in hazardous waste[2]
International Technology Corp.	24	EC	100
Roy F. Weston Inc.	50	CE	78
Bechtel Group Inc.	1	EC	12
Dames & Moore	16	CE	49
CH2M Hill Cos. Ltd.	10	CE	35
Parsons/Main	5	EC	21
ICF Kaiser Engineers Inc.	20	EC	44
Groundwater Technology Inc.	57	CE	100
The ERM Group	46	CE	84
Geraghty & Miller Inc.	89	CE	90

[Continued]

★ 491 ★

Top Design Firms in Hazardous Waste
[Continued]

Firm	Rank 1990	Type of firm	Percent of billings[1] in hazardous waste[2]
Law Cos. Group Inc./Sir Alexander Gibb	25	CE	29
McLaren/ Hart Environmental Engineering	150	CE	100
Burns & Roe Enterprises Inc.	7	EC	24
Camp Dresser & McKee Inc.	21	CE	34
Ebasco Services Inc.	9	EC	16
NUS Corp.	37	EA	40
Ecology & Environment Inc.	79	CE	92
Environmental Science & Engineering Inc.	[3]	CE	71
Metcalf & Eddy Cos. Inc.	22	EA	30
ABB Environmental Services Inc.	87	CE	96
Harding Associates	59	CE	67
Engineering-Science Inc.	60	CE	46
United Engineers & Constructors Intl. Inc.	6	EC	10
HIH USA Inc.	64	GE	45
The Earth Technology Corp.	119	CE	100
ATEC Associates Inc.	70	CE	54
Woodward-Clyde Consultants Inc.	38	CE	26
PRC Environmental Management Inc.	[3]	CE	21
James M. Montgomery Consulting Engineers Inc.	52	CE	29
Malcolm Pirnie Inc.	62	CE	40

Source: ENR, April 8, 1991, p. 36. Key to type of firm: A = architect; AE=architect-engineer; CE=consulting engineer; EA=engineer-architect; GE=soils or geotechnical engineer; P=planner; PM=project manager; EC=engineer-contractor; ENV=environmental engineer. Firms classified themselves. *Notes:* 1. Billings estimated by *ENR* 2. Hazardous waste=solid, liquid, chemical, toxic waste,and nuclear waste. 3. Not ranked among the top 500 in 1990.

Education and Training

★ 492 ★

Certificates/Degrees in Hazardous Waste Management

Wayne State University, under a contract from U.S. Department of Health and Human Services, conducted a survey of organizations/universities that provide education in hazardous waste management.

Course	Undergraduate	Graduate	Non-credit
Any HW Credit Course[1]	117	116	-
Required HW Courses	34	35	-
Option or Minor	3	13	-
B.S. or A.S. in HW	2	-	-

[Continued]

★ 492 ★

Certificates/Degrees in Hazardous Waste Management
[Continued]

Course	Undergraduate	Graduate	Non-credit
Certificate in HW	-	3	10
M.S. in HW	-	4	-

Source: Evaluating Hazardous Waste Education & Training, U.S. Department of Health and Human Services, U.S. Government Printing Office: 1991-281-821:44112, 1991, p. 31 *Note:* 1. Hazardous Waste.

★ 493 ★

Departments Offering Credit Courses in Hazardous Waste
Data represent results of a survey of 799 institutions, conducted by Wayne State University.

Course	Number of Courses for Graduate	Number of Courses for Undergraduate
Civil Engineering	49	36
Environmental Engineering	25	23
Chemical Engineering	16	10
Environmental Science	14	10
Environmental Health	9	11
Allied & Public Health	11	3
Agriculture	3	2
Chemistry	0	9
Other	11	11

Source: Evaluating Hazardous Waste Education & Training, U.S. Department of Health and Human Services, U.S. Government Printing Office: 1991-281-821:44112, 1991, p. 30.

★ 494 ★

Institutions Offering Hazardous Waste Education by Type

Institution	Type of Education[1]
University of Alabama	U, G, N
Arizona State University	U, N
Auburn University at Montgomery	N
Baldwin-Wallace College	N
Baylor University	U, G
Berry College	U

[Continued]

★ 494 ★

Institutions Offering Hazardous Waste Education by Type
[Continued]

Institution	Type of Education[1]
Boise State University	U, G
Boston University	U, G
Bowling Green State University	U
Bradley University	U, G
Brown University	U, G, N
Bryant College	U
Bucknell College	U, G
Butler University	N
California Institute of Technology	G
California Polytechnic State University	U
California State University-Fresno	U, G, N
California State University-Long Beach	N
California State University-Northridge	U, G
California State University-Sacramento	U, G
University of California-Berkeley	U, G, N
University of California-Davis	U, G, N
University of California-Irvine	N
University of California-Los Angeles	U, G, N
University of California-Riverside	U, N
University of California-San Diego	N
University of California-San Francisco	N
University of California-Santa Barbara	N
University of California-Santa Cruz	N
Carnegie-Mellon University	G
Carroll College	U
University of Central Florida	U, G
Central State University	U
Christopher Newport College	N
University of Cincinnati	U, G, N
Clarkson University	U, G
Clemson University	U, N
Cleveland State University	N
Colorado School of Mines	U, G
Colorado State University	N
University of Connecticut	U, G
Cornell University	U, G, N
Corpus Christi State University	U, N
Cumberland College	N
University of Dayton	U
University of Delaware	U, G
Delaware Valley College of Science and Agriculture	U
DePaul University	U
Detroit College of Law	G
Drexel University	U, G

[Continued]

★ 494 ★

Institutions Offering Hazardous Waste Education by Type

[Continued]

Institution	Type of Education[1]
Duke University	U, G, N
East Carolina University	U
East Central University	U
East Tennessee State University	N
Eastern Kentucky University	U
Eastern Michigan University	N
Edinboro University of Pennsylvania	U
Emory University	U, G, N
Ferris State University	U
University of Findlay	U, N
Florida Institute of Technology	U, G
University of Florida	U, G, N
Front Range Community College	U, N
George Washington University	N
Georgetown University	N
Georgia Institute of Technology	U, G, N
Georgia State University	N
Glenville State College	N
Grand Valley State University	U
Hamline University	G
Hampshire College	U, G
Harvard University	G, N
University of Hawaii	G
University of Houston-Clear Lake	U, G
Howard University	G
Idaho State University	U, G
University of Idaho	U, G, N
Illinois Institute of Technology	U, G, N
Illinois State University	U
University of Illinois-Chicago	U, G
University of Illinois-Urbana-Champaign	G, N
Indiana State University	U, G, N
Indiana University	U, G, N
Indiana University-Purdue University at Indianapolis	G
Indiana University of Pennsylvania	U
Iowa State University	G
University of Iowa	U, G
Jersey City State College	U
John Hopkins University	N
Kansas State University	U, G, N
University of Kansas	N
Lamar University	G, N
Lehigh University	U, G
Loma Linda University	G

[Continued]

★ 494 ★

Institutions Offering Hazardous Waste Education by Type
[Continued]

Institution	Type of Education[1]
Louisiana State University-Baton Rouge	U, G, N
Louisiana State University-Shreveport	U, N
Louisiana Technological University	U, G
University of Louisville	N
Loyola Marymount University	G
Luther College	U
Maine Maritime Academy	N
University of Maine	U
Manhattan College	G
University of Maryland	N
University of Massachusetts	N
Massachusetts Institute of Technology	U, G
McNeese University	U, G
Medical College of Ohio	G
University of Medicine and Dentistry in New Jersey	N
Memphis State University	G
Mercy College	U
Miami University at Oxford	U, G
Michigan State University	G, N
Michigan Technological University	U, G
University of Michigan	U, G, N
University of Minnesota	G, N
University of Minnesota-Duluth	U, G
University of Missouri-Columbia	N
University of Missouri-St. Louis	N
Montana College of Mineral Science and Technology	U, G
Montana State University	U, G
University of Nevada	U, G
New Hampshire College	U
New Jersey Institute of Technology	G, N
New York University	N
North Carolina State University	U, G
University of North Carolina- Chapel Hill	G, N
University of North Carolina-Charlotte	G
Northeastern Illinois University	U, G
Northeastern State University	G
University of Northern Colorado	G
Northern Michigan University	U
University of Notre Dame	U, G
Ohio Northern University	U, G
Ohio University	U, G, N
Oklahoma State University	G, N
University of Oklahoma	G
Oregon State University	U, G, N

[Continued]

★ 494 ★

Institutions Offering Hazardous Waste Education by Type
[Continued]

Institution	Type of Education[1]
Pennsylvania State University	U, G
University of Pennsylvania	G
University of Pittsburgh	N
Point Park College	U
Purdue University	U, G, N
Rampo College	U, N
Rensselaer Polytechnic Institute	U, G
University of Rhode Island	U, G
Rice University	G
Roane State Community College	U
Roosevelt University	U
Rutgers the State University of New Jersey	U
San Diego State University	G
University of San Francisco	G
Slippery Rock University	U
University of South Carolina-Aiken	U
University of South Carolina-Columbia	G
South Dakota School of Mines and Technology	G
University of Southern California	U, G
University of Southern Maine	N
Stanford University	U, G
State University of New York - Buffalo	G
State University of New York-Syracuse	U, G
Sumter Area Technical College	U, N
SUNY Empire State College	U, G
Syracuse University	G
University of Tennessee-Chattanooga	N
University of Tennessee-Knoxville	N
Tennessee Technical University	N
Texas A&M University	U, G, N
Texas Tech University	G
University of Texas-Arlington	G
University of Texas-Austin	G, N
University of Texas-Houston	G
Thomas M. Cooley Law School	G
University of Toledo	U, G, N
University of Toledo-Community College	U
Tufts University	G, N
Union University	U
Unity College	N
Utah State University	U, G
University of Utah	N
Vanderbilt University	U, G, N
Villanova University	U, G

[Continued]

★ 494 ★

Institutions Offering Hazardous Waste Education by Type
[Continued]

Institution	Type of Education[1]
Virginia Polytechnic Institute	U, G
University of Virginia	N
Virginia Commonwealth University	N
Washington State University	U, G
University of Washington	U, G, N
Wayne State University	U, G, N
West Chester University of Pennsylvania	U, G
University of West Virginia	G
West Virginia University	G
Western Kentucky University	U
Western Michigan University	U
University of Wisconsin-Green Bay	G, N
University of Wisconsin-Madison	G, N
University of Wisconsin-Milwaukee	N
University of Wisconsin-Whitewater	G, N
Worchester Polytechnic Institute	G
Wright State University	U
Yale School of Medicine	G
York College	U

Source: Evaluating Hazardous Waste Education & Training, U.S. Department of Health and Human Services, U.S. Government Printing Office: 1991-281-821:44112, 1991, p. 33. *Note:* 1. U = Undergraduate. G = Graduate, and N = non-credit.

★ 495 ★

Non-Degree Short Courses Offered by Subject
The following short courses are offered by different organizations in hazardous waste management training.

Courses	Number
Law and Administration	148
Asbestos	91
Safety and Toxicology	67
General Overview	53
Emergency Response	49
Risk and Contingency	44
Ground/Surface Water	40
OSHA Training	36
Sampling/Testing	24
Waste Minimization	21
Incineration	19
Solid Waste	15
Underground Storage	14

[Continued]

★ 495 ★

Non-Degree Short Courses Offered by Subject
[Continued]

Courses	Number
Biological Disposal	13
Hospital/Infectious	9
Radiation Safety	5
Other	27
Total	675

Source: Evaluating Hazardous Waste Education & Training, U.S. Department of Health and Human Services, U.S. Government Printing Office: 1991-281-821:44112, 1991, p. 18.

★ 496 ★

Top Twenty Organizations Offering Hazardous Waste Courses

Organization Names	Number of Different Courses Offered Per Year	Total Number of Courses (including multiples) Offered Per Year
U.S. EPA, Office of Solid Waste and Emergency Response (OSWER)	36	600
Executive Enterprises, Inc.	43	92
Georgia Institute of Technology, Environmental Science and Technology Laboratory	41	109
Texas A&M University System, Texas Engineering Extension Service	23	257
National Institute for Occupational Safety and Health (NIOSH), Educational Resource Centers	33	100
University of Florida, Continuing Education Center for Training, Research and Education	30	129
Eastern Michigan University, Corporate Services	22	113
University of California System, Departments of Continuing Education	31	39
American Institute of Chemical Engineers (AIChE) Continuing Education	23	74
Government Institutes, Inc.	27	32
University of Wisconsin System, Department of Engineering Professional Development	25	36
University of Cincinnati, Institute of Environmental Health	18	38
University of Kansas, Division of Continuing Education	12	56
Hazardous Materials Control Research Institute	22	25
New Jersey/New York Hazardous Material Worker Training Center	5	59
DuPont Safety and Environmental Resources	7	51
Center for Professional Advancement	16	20
Tufts University, Center for Environmental Management	10	35
Engineering Society of Detroit	14	15

[Continued]

★ 496 ★

Top Twenty Organizations Offering Hazardous Waste Courses
[Continued]

Organization Names	Number of Different Courses Offered Per Year	Total Number of Courses (including multiples) Offered Per Year
J.T. Baker, Inc.	7	23
Total	442	1894

Source: Evaluating Hazardous Waste Education & Training, U.S. Department of Health and Human Services, U.S. Government Printing Office: 1991-281-821:44112, 1991, p. 17.

Hazardous Waste Management

★ 497 ★

Hazardous Waste Management Facilities
Number of facilities by major industrial categories.

Industry	Number of TSDR[1] Facilities
Industrial organic chemicals	150
Petroleum refining	96
National security	85
Electric services	63
Plastic materials/resins	57
Industrial inorganic chemicals	54
Plating and polishing	45
Refuse systems (commercial TSDR facility)	45
Wood preserving	44
Blast furnaces/steel mills	37

Source: C&EN, February 6, 1989, p. 20. *Note:* 1. Transportation, storage, disposal, or recycling.

★ 498 ★

Hazardous Waste Management Facilities by Ownership

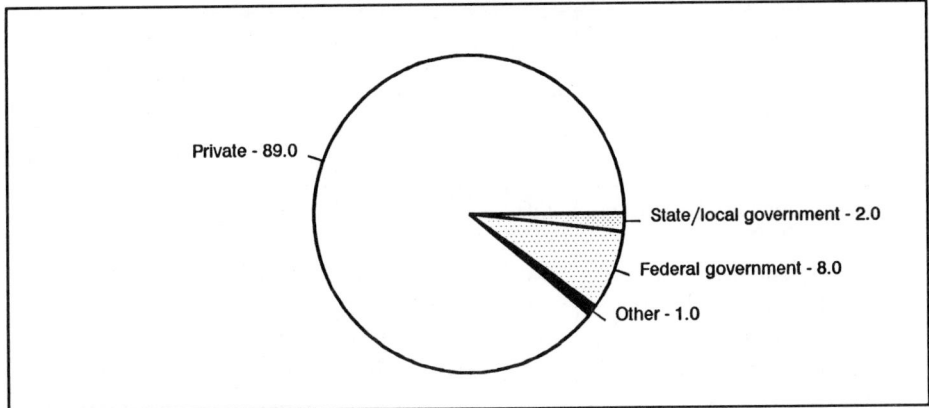

Percentages are based on a total of 2,971 facilities.

Type of facility	Percent
Private	89.0
Federal government	8.0
State/local government	2.0
Other	1.0

Source: C&EN, February 6, 1989, p. 20.

★ 499 ★

Hazardous Waste Management Market

In billions of dollars for 1989. Total market was $32 billion. The commercial segment of the market is $14 billion.

	Billions of dollars
On-site treatment and disposal at market price (excluding aqueous)	18.0
Off-site treatment and disposal	3.0
Commercial market	14.0
Collection and transfer	3.0
Site cleanup[1]	4.0
Products, auxiliarry services, and capital expenditures	1.0
Specific service segments[2]	3.0

Source: Chemicalweek, August 22, 1990, p. 46, Booz-Allen & Hamilton. Notes: 1. Site cleanup includes Superfund and private sector spending. 2. Asbestos removal, transformer services, nuclear waste.

★ 500 ★

Hazardous Waste Product and Service Revenues

The values are in millions of dollars.

| | 1977 | 1988 | 1993 | 2000 | Average annual growth (percent) | |
					1977-1988	1988-1993
Hazardous waste products	120	3,500	9,300	23,000	35.9	21.6
Treatment chemicals	40	520	2,550	9,000	26.3	37.4
Incineration equipment	40	1,600	4,000	8,500	39.8	20.1
Processing equipment	10	340	1,020	2,700	37.8	24.6
Analytical instruments	25	390	700	1,100	28.4	12.4
Other products	5	650	1,030	1,700	55.7	9.6
Hazardous waste services	385	6,200	10,900	20,000	28.7	11.9
Transportation	185	2,560	3,770	4,700	27.0	8.0
Consulting/engineering	5	700	1,400	3,500	56.7	14.9
Remediation/cleanup	Neg	645	1,290	3,400	-	14.9
Incineration services	10	370	920	2,500	38.9	20.0
Analytical testing	35	610	1,070	2,300	29.7	11.9
Landfill disposal	15	605	1,370	2,000	39.9	17.8
Other services	135	710	1,080	1,600	16.3	8.8
Total	505	9,700	20,200	43,000	30.8	15.8

Source: C&EN, July 31,1989, p. 14, from the Freedonia Group. Neg stands for negligible.

★ 501 ★

Hazardous Waste Treatment Facilities

Subcategory Name	Total	Facility Prod. Waste	Direct Discharger	Discharge to POTW[1]	Handled by Hauling	Other Discharge
Landfills						
Commercial	67	67				
Non-Commercial	301	240				
Subtitle D landfill	16,416	604				
Total	16,784	911	173	355	128	255
Percent			19	39	14	28
Incinerators						
Commercial	42					
Non-Commercial	274					

[Continued]

★ 501 ★

Hazardous Waste Treatment Facilities
[Continued]

Subcategory Name	Total	Facility Prod. Waste	Direct Discharger	Discharge to POTW[1]	Handled by Hauling	Other Discharge
Total	316	273	137	27	27	82
Percent			50	10	10	30
Aqueous waste treaters						
Commercial	125	125				
Non-commercial	600	600				
Total	725	725	87	515	51	72
Percent			12	71	7	10

Source: Preliminary Data Summary for the Hazardous Waste Industry (PB 90-126517), U.S. Environmental Protection Agency, Washington, D.C., September 1989, p. 39 *Note:* 1. Publicly-Owned Treatment Works.

★ 502 ★

Leading Waste Management Companies

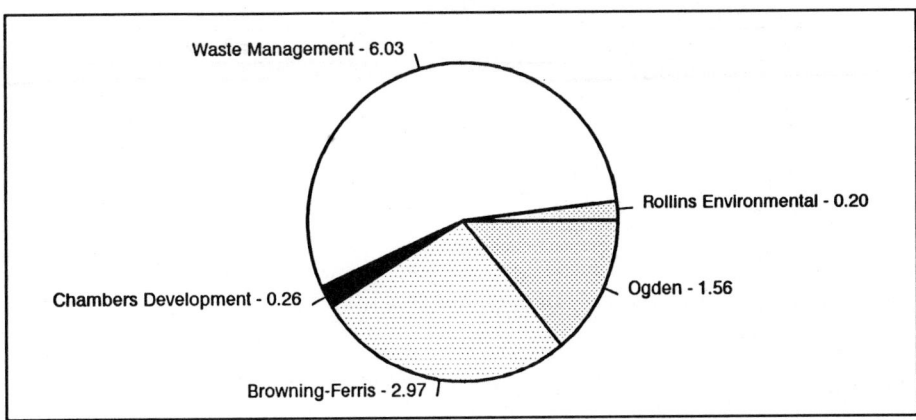

Companies	1990 Revenue in Billions of Dollars
Waste Management	6.03
Browning-Ferris	2.97
Ogden	1.56
Chambers Development	0.26
Rollins Environmental	0.20

Source: The Wall Street Journal, May 1, 1991, p. A4.

★ 503 ★

Waste Management Inc. Subsidiaries

Company	Percent Owned by Waste Management Inc.
Waste Management of North America	100
Chemical Waste Management	76
Brand[1]	56
Wheelabrator Technologies	55
Waste Management International	100
ServiceMaster Consumer Services L.P.	20

Source: The Wall Street Journal, May 1, 1991, p. A4. *Notes:* 1. Brand is in the asbestos abatement business. Data show share owned by Chemical Waste Management.

Hazardouse Waste Management

★ 504 ★

Asbestos Abatement Contractors

Firm	Rank	Revenues ($ million)	Reno-vation (%)
Speciality Systems Inc., Indianapolis, Ind.	1	29.8	100
Young Sales Corp., St. Louis, MO.	2	21.7	75
Baker Pacific Corp., Long Beach, Calif.	3	19.8	60
Ogden Allied Abatement and Decontamination Service, Inc., New York, New York	4	16.8	0
Barsotti's Inc., Santa Fe Springs, Calif	5	13.1	90
Project Development Group Inc. Pittsburgh, PA	6	12.1	0
Kimmins Environmental Service Corp., Tampa, Fla.	7	11.8	40
Burdco Environmental Inc., Traverse City, Mich	8	11.4	0
Eastern Environmental Services of the Southeast Inc., Tampa, Fla	9	10.6	95
Anson Industries Inc., Melrose Park, Ill.	10	10.6	7
Power Master Inc., Portland, Ore.	11	10.2	60
Cleveland Wrecking Co., Los Angeles, Calif	12	10.0	40
Speciality Waste Services Inc., Alton, Ill.	13	7.8	80
J.F. Walton & Co. Inc., Chelsea, Mass	14	5.9	100
Acmat Corp., E. Hartford, Conn.	15	5.8	100
Ralco Inc., Weymouth, Mass.	16	5.2	30
Davis Cos., Troy, N.Y.	17	4.8	40
Invirex Demolition Inc., Huntington Station, N.Y.	18	4.3	3

[Continued]

★ 504 ★

Asbestos Abatement Contractors
[Continued]

Firm	Rank	Revenues ($ million)	Reno- vation (%)
Michael T. Robinson & Associates, Madison, Wis.	19	4.2	90
Envirocon International Corp., Tampa, Fla.	20	4.0	20

Source: ENR, August 24, 1989, p. 84.

Insurance

★ 505 ★

Asbestos Liability Insurance Markets

Market	Limit Available (millions of dollars)	Policy Form[1]	Minimum Premium (dollars)
American Empire Surplus Lines Insurance Co.	4.0	CM	42,500
American Safety Risk Retention Group	5.0	O,RO,CM	50,000
Asbestos Abatement Assoc. (also utilizes ERIC)	1.0	O (shared limit)	15,000
Environmental Risk Insurance Co. (ERIC)	5.0	O	15,000
Fidelity Environmental Insurance Co.	2.0	O	15,000
London (Lloyd's, Weavers, ILU)	15.0	OS,CM	N/A
National Union Fire Insurance Company (AIG)	5.0	O, OS, CM	100,000[1]
Reliance National	5.0	O,OS,CM	100,000[1]
United Capitol Insurance Co.	1.0	CM	40,000
United Coastal Insurance Co.	4.0	O, RO, CM	40,000

Source: ENR, July 13, 1989, p. A-9. *Notes:* 1. O = Occurrence. OS = Occurrence with a Sunset. RO = Reported Occurrence. CM = Claims-Made. N/A means not available. 1. Minimum premium for occurrence coverage only.

Investment

★ 506 ★

Environmental Profiles of Investment Funds

Fund	Inception Date	Minimum Investment/ subsequent (dollars)	Front-end Load (percent)	Net Assets (millions)	Expense Ratio (percent)	Return	
						1/90-6/90 (percent)	8/87-6/90 (percent)
Socially Responsible Funds; Screen Polluters							
Calvert Social Investment-Managed Growth	1982	1000/250	4.5	215	1.30	1.04	16.59
Calvert Social Investment-Equity	9/87	1000/250	4.5	22	0.50	1.72	[7]
Dreyfus Third Century	1972	2500/100	0	189	1.05	20.57	26.80
Parnassus	1985	2000/500	3.5	26	1.65	3.15	-3.10
Pax World	1971	250/50	0[1]	108	1.10	6.01	24.98
Working Assets	1983	1000/100	0[1]	215	1.13	3.06	20.10
Environmental Funds; Screen Polluters							
Merrill Lynch Eco-logical Trust[6]	4/90	1000/10	4.0	7	1.60[2,3]	23.41[3]	[7]
New Alternatives	1982	2650/500	6.0	16	1.12	2.27	26.81
Schield Progressive Environmental	2/90	1000/100	4.5[1]	2	2.50[2,3]	31.20	[7]
Environmental Funds; Do Not Screen Polluters							
Fidelity Select Environmental Services	6/89	1000/250	2.0[5]	126	2.25[3]	8.20	[7]
Freedom Environmental	10/89	1000/100	4.5[1]	62	1.76[3,4]	3.58	[7]
Kemper Environmental	4/90	1000/100	5.75[1]	69	1.50[2]	0.00	[7]
Oppenheimer Global Environmental	3/90	1000/25	4.75[1,2]	34	1.50[2]	10.76	[7]
SFT Environmental Awareness	11/88	1000/100	5.0	3	1.12	10.12	[7]

Source: Garbage, September/October 1990, p. 50, from Lipper Analytical Services, Inc.; Merrill Lynch. All information as of 6/29/90 except where noted. *Notes:* 1. 12b-1 fee (see source). 2. Estimated. 3. Annualized. 4. From inception. 5. 1% redemption fee (back-end load). 6. Some socially responsible investments. 7. Long-term results not available.

★ 507 ★

Environmental Stock Prices Trend

Environmental stock price changes in 1988 are compared with Standard and Poor's 500.

Company	Stock price (percent)
Gundle Environmental Systems Inc.	+126
Calgon Carbon Corp.	+58
Clean Harbors Inc.	+57
Chambers Development Co.	+54
Geraghty & Miller Inc.	+40
TRC Cos. Inc.	+39
The Brand Cos. Inc.	+38
Groundwater Technology Inc.	+37
Canonie Environmental Services Corp.	+35
Allwaste Inc.	+20

[Continued]

★ 507 ★

Environmental Stock Prices Trend
[Continued]

Company	Stock price (percent)
Enviromental Treatment & Technology Corp. (Now OHM Corp.)	+16
Wheelabrator Technologies Inc.	+14
Environmental Control Group Inc.	+13
S&P 500	+12
Roy F. Weston Inc.	+11
Waste Management Inc.	+10
Chemical Waste Management	+2
Browning Ferris Industries, Inc.	-2
Rollins Environmental Services Inc.	-22

Source: ENR, March 9, 1989, p. 35, from Alex Brown & Sons Inc.

Pollution Control

★ 508 ★

Environmental Markets in the U.S.

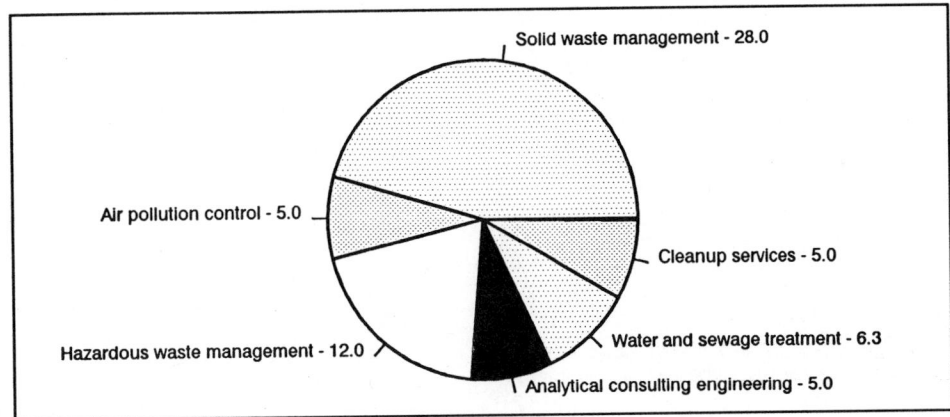

Market totals shown are for 1990.

Market	Billions of dollars
Solid waste management	28.0
Hazardous waste management	12.0
Water and sewage treatment	6.3
Cleanup services	5.0

[Continued]

407

★ 508 ★

Environmental Markets in the U.S.
[Continued]

Market	Billions of dollars
Analytical consulting engineering	5.0
Air pollution control	5.0

Source: ENR, June 3, 1991, p. 11, from Booz Allen & Hamilton Inc.

Resource Recovery

★ 509 ★

Leading Recycled Paperboard Producers
Top 10 producers in the U.S.

Company	Annual capacity (000 tons/ year)[1]	Market share (percent)
Jefferson Smurfit Corp.	1,330	13.3
The Newark Group, Inc.	875	8.7
Sonoco Products Co.	850	8.5
Caraustar Industries Inc.	550	5.5
Rock-Tenn Co.	532	5.3
Inland Container Corp.	475	4.7
Waldorf Corp.	395	3.9
U.S. Gypsum Co.	332	3.3
National Gypsum Co.	220	2.2
Packaging Corp. of America	210	2.1
Total	5,769	57.5

Source: Resource Recycling, January 1991, p. 33, from *Pulp & Paper*, June 1990. *Note:* 1. Total U.S. capacity in 1990 was estimated at 10.029 million tons.

★ 510 ★

Materials Recovery Facilities in the U.S.

Location Sponsor	Status	Operator	Throughput (Tons Per Day)
Arizona			
Phoenix City of Phoenix	O	St. Vincent de Paul Society	11 (a); 25 (d)
California			
Anaheim Taormina Industries	O	Taormina Industries	50 (a); 200 (d)[1]
Fremont Oakland Scavenger/WMI	O	WMI	40 (a); 50 (d)
Los Angeles City Fibers	O	City Fibers	N/A
Los Angeles Bestway Recycling Co.	O	Bestway	10 (a) 80 (d)
Modesto Gilton Solid Waste Management	C	Gilton	N/A
San Francisco City of San Francisco	O	West Coast Salvage	45 (a) 200 (d)
Stanton CR&R	O	CR&R	Up to 100 (a)
Connecticut			
Brookfield (Area) Housatonic Resource Recovery Authority	D	N/A	N/A
Groton SE Ct. Regional Resources Recovery Authority	O	Resource Recovery Systems	25 (a) 40 (d)
Hartford Capitol Region Cog/Connecticut Res. Rec. Auth.	P	N/A	400 (d)[2]
Manchester REI Distributors, Inc.	O	REI	80 (d)
South Central Conn.	D	N/A	160 (d)

[Continued]

★ 510 ★

Materials Recovery Facilities in the U.S.
[Continued]

Location Sponsor	Status	Operator	Throughput (Tons Per Day)
South Central Regional Cog.			
Strafford Sw Ct Reg'l Recycling Operating Comm.	P	Fairfield County Recycling	250 (d)
District of Columbia			
Washington Washington	D	N/A	N/A
Florida			
Broward County Broward County	D	N/A	N/A
Hialeah Dade County	P	Attwoods, Inc. (IWF)	300+ (d)
Jacksonville Browning Ferris Industries (BFI)	C	-	25 (d)
Lee County Lee County	O	Goodwill	10 (a)
Orange County Orange County	C	Waste Mgmt of Florida	180-250 (d)
Palm Beach County Palm Beach County Solid Waste Authority	P	RRT-Empire Returns	250 (d)
Palm Beach County Palm Beach County Solid Waste Authority	O	Authority	125 (a)
Pinellas Park Recycle America (WMI)	C	Recycle America (WMI)	200 (d)
Illinois			
Carol Stream Dupage County	P	NECRinc or Waste Mgmt. Inc.	150 (d)
Champaign County	P	N/A	N/A

[Continued]

★ 510 ★

Materials Recovery Facilities in the U.S.
[Continued]

Location Sponsor	Status	Operator	Throughput (Tons Per Day)
Intergovernmental SW Disposal Authority			
Dupage County Dupage County	P	NECRinc or Waste Mgmt Inc.	150 (d)
Romeoville Land & Lakes Co.	D	Land & Lakes	450 (d)[2]
Iowa Carrol County Carrol Co. Solid Waste Commission	P	Carrol Enter- prises	50 (d)
Sheldon Northwest Iowa Area Solid Waste Agency	O	Authority	3 (a) 8 (d)
Maryland Anne Arundel County Anne Arundel County	O	County	8-10 (a)
Halethorpe Eastern Waste Industries	D	Eastern Waste	300-400(d)[3]
Landover Prince Georges County	P	N/A	270 (d)
Montgomery County Montgomery County	P	CRinc-Well	200 (d)[2]
Massachusetts			
Milbury Recovery Comm.	D	N/A	N/A
Mills (Area) Mills Consortium	P	N/A	N/A
Springfield Commonwealth of Massachusetts	O	Resource Recovery Systems	150 (a) 240 (d)
Michigan			
Auburn Hills	P	N/A	260 (d)

[Continued]

★ 510 ★

Materials Recovery Facilities in the U.S.

[Continued]

Location Sponsor	Status	Operator	Throughput (Tons Per Day)
Oakland County			
Minnesota			
Lyon County Lyon County	D	N/A	10 (d)
Switt County Switt County	C	County	10 (d)
New Hampshire			
Hookset Resource Conservation Services, Inc.	D	RCS	100 (d)
Keene (Area) Southwest Solid Waste Mgmt District	P	N/A	80 (d)
New Jersey			
Boundbrook Somerset County	O	County	100-150 (a) 190 (d)[1]
Camden County Camden County	O	Resource Recovery Systems	75 (a)
Deerfield Twp. Cumb. Co Cumberland County Improvement Authority	C	CCIA	80 (d)
Lakewood Twp. Ocean Co Ocean County	C	RRT-Empire	300 (d)
Long Branch Monmouth Recycling Corp.	O	Monmouth Recycling	43 (a) 80 (d)
Mercer County Mercer County Improvement Authority	D	N/A	300 (d)
Newark REI Distributors, Inc.	O	REI	250 (a)
Ocean Monmouth Processing	O	Monmouth Processing	235 (a) 270 (d)[3]

[Continued]

★ 510 ★

Materials Recovery Facilities in the U.S.

[Continued]

Location Sponsor	Status	Operator	Throughput (Tons Per Day)
Pleasantville Atlantic County Utilities Authority	O	Authority	50 (a) 150 (d)[1]
Toms River Rosetto Recycling Inc.	O	Rosetto Recycling	80 (a) 250 (d)[1]
West Paterson W.P.A.R.	O	W.P.A.R.	40-80 (a)
Woodbine Cape May County Municipal Util. Auth.	C	RRT-Empire Returns	225 (d)[2]
New York			
Babylon Town of Babylon	D	Town	80-90 (d)[8]
Brookhaven Town of Brookhaven	P	NECRinc	300 (d)
Columbia County Columbia County	O	County	6-7 (a)
East Harlem New York City	O	Resource Recovery Systems	46 (d)[4]
Fort Edwards North American Recycling	O	North Amer- ican	100 (a) 200 (d)[3]
Goshen Orange County	D	County	80 (d)
Islip Town of Islip	O	Town	600 (a)[8] 1500 (a)[8]
Lincoln Madison County	C	Assoc. of Retarded Citizens	50 (d)
Lowville Lewis County	C	County	25 (d)
Ontario County	P	N/A	15 (min) (d)

[Continued]

★ 510 ★

Materials Recovery Facilities in the U.S.
[Continued]

Location Sponsor	Status	Operator	Throughput (Tons Per Day)
Ontario County			
Peekskill Karta Container and Recycling	O	Karta	260 (a)[3]
Potsdam Waste Stream Management	O	Waste Stream	10 (a) 80 (d)[1]
Poughkeepsie Dutchess Co. Resource Recovery Agency	P	NECRinc-Well	70 (d)
Rochester Monroe County	P	N/A	500 (d)
Smithtown Town of Smithtown	O	Town	130 (a)
St. Lawrence County St. Lawrence Co. SW Disposal Authority	O	Authority	5-6 (a) 20 (d)
Staten Island New York City	P	N/A	300 (d)
Syracuse RRT-Empire Returns Corp.	O	RRT-Empire Returns	300 (d)
Utica Oneida-Herkimer SW Mgmt. Authority	C	Authority	200 (d)
Volney Oswego County	D	Assoc. of Retarded Citizens	220+ (d)
Westbury Omni Recycling of Westbury (NY)	O	Omni	85[4]
Yonkers Westchester County	D	N/A	200 (d)
North Carolina			
Charlotte Mecklenberg County	O	Fairfield County Recycling	70 (a) 130 (d)

[Continued]

★ 510 ★

Materials Recovery Facilities in the U.S.

[Continued]

Location Sponsor	Status	Operator	Throughput (Tons Per Day)
Ohio			
Akron wTe	O	wTe	5 (a) 35 (d)
Oregon			
Portland Wastech	O	Wastech	N/A[5]
Pennsylvania			
Bristol Otter Recycling	O	Otter	50 (a) 80+ (d)
College Twp. Centre Co. Centre County Solid Waste Authority	O	Authority	15 (a) 75 (d)[5]
Cumru Twp. Berks Co Berks County	D	N/A	N/A
Pen Argyl Grand Central Recycling	O	Grand Central	6-8 (a) 25 (d)
Philadelphia National Temple Recycling	O[6]	National Temple	100 (d)
Philadelphia Waste Management, Inc.	O	Waste Mgmt. Inc.	60 (a)
Scranton Lackawanna County SWM Authority	C	Authority	125 (d)
Windsor Twp. York Co. Recycle America-York	O	Recycle Am- erica (WMI)	40 (a) 100 (d)
York York Waste Disposal	O	York Waste Disposal	35 (a)[3]
Rhode Island			
Johnston Rhode Island SWM Corporation	O	NECRinc	200 (a)[7]

[Continued]

★ 510 ★

Materials Recovery Facilities in the U.S.
[Continued]

Location Sponsor	Status	Operator	Throughput (Tons Per Day)
Quonset Point Rhode Island SWM Corporation	P	NECRinc	160 (d)
South Carolina			
Charleston Charleston County	P	N/A	60 (d)
Tennessee			
Davidson County Metro Nashville	P	N/A	100+ (d)
Knox County Metro Knox Solid Waste Authority	P	Waste Mgmt., Inc.	N/A
Washington			
Seattle City of Seattle	O	Recycle America (WMI)	110 (a)[2]
Seattle City of Seattle	O	Rabanco Recycling	140 (a) 200 (d)
Tumwater City of Olympia	O	Exceptional Forresters	8 (a) 20 (d)
Wisconsin			
Milwaukee City of Milwaukee	O	Waste Mgmt. Inc., et al	20-25 (a) 50 (d)[1]
Milwaukee City of Milwaukee	D	N/A	50 (d)
Waukesha County Waukesha County	D	N/A	100-130 (d)

[Continued]

★ 510 ★

Materials Recovery Facilities in the U.S.
[Continued]

Location Sponsor	Status	Operator	Throughput (Tons Per Day)
Waukesha County Waukesha County	P	N/A	N/A

Source: BioCycle, May 1990, p. 27. In the Status column, the following abbreviations have been used: P=Procurement; O=Operational; D=Design; C=Construction. In the Throughput column, (a) stands for Actual Throughput and (d) stands for Design Capacity. N/A means Not determined or unavailable. *Notes:* 1. Capacity of Upgraded Facility to be Built. 2. Two shifts Per Day. 3. Includes Recyclables from Commercial Sector. 4. 1 1/2 Shifts Per Day. 5. Primary Source Separated Material, But Does Have Commingled Capacity. 6. Currently Not Processing Commingled Material. 7. Paper is Processed on Two Shifts. 8. Tons Per Week.

★ 511 ★

Old Newspaper Deinking Facilities

The deinking and newsprint manufacturing facilities in North America include both existing and proposed.

Type of Facility	Start-up Date	Deinking Capacity (000 tons)	Existing/ New Site	Type of Facility
Stone Container	1989	Nominal	Existing	Conversion
Smurfit Newsprint	1989	Nominal	Existing	Conversion
Southeast Paper Co.	1989	240	Existing	New
Atlantic Packaging	1990-91	180	Existing	New
North Pacific Paper Corp.	1990-91	180	Existing	New
Alabama River Newsprint	1991	140	Existing	New
Newstech Recycling	1991	140	Existing	New
Canadian Pacific Forest Products Ltd.	1991	347	Existing	New
Weyerhaeuser Paper Co.	1991	220	Existing	New
Inland Empire Paper Co.	1991	40	Existing	New
Daishowa Forest Products, Ltd.	1991	130	Existing	New
Cascades, Inc.	1992	110	Existing	New
Champion International Corp.	1992	175	Existing	New
Augusta Newsprint Co.	-	100	Existing	New
Georgia-Pacific Corp.	-	100	Existing	New
Daishowa America Co.	-	65	Existing	New
Champion International Corp.	-	175	Existing	New
Boise Cascade	-	110	Existing	New
Jefferson Smurfit	-	300	New	-
Kruger, Inc.	-	N/A	-	
Smurfit Newsprint	-	220	-	
Garden State		220	-	-
Golden State	-	220	Existing	New
Great Northern	-	180[1]	Existing	New
Bowater Corp.	-	180[1]	Existing	

[Continued]

417

★ 511 ★

Old Newspaper Deinking Facilities
[Continued]

Type of Facility	Start-up Date	Deinking Capacity (000 tons)	Existing/ New Site	Type of Facility
	-	88[1]	Existing	
Bear Island Paper Co.	-	180[1]	Existing	New
MacMillan Bloedel	-	140[1]	Not Specified	New
Abitibi-Price		140[1]	Not Specified	New
Fletcher Challenge		140[1]	Existing	New
Soucy		140[1]	Existing	New
Donahue, Inc.		55		

Source: Waste Age, February 1991, p. 64, from published information and NSWMA estimates. N/A not available *Note:* 1. Estimated.

★ 512 ★

Scrap Plastic Bottle Reclaimers

Major reclaimers in Canada and the U.S. in 1991.

Company	Location[1]	Estimated annual capacity in million pounds
Clean Tech	Dundee, MI	12
Day Products	Bridgeport, NJ	40
Eaglebrook Plastics	Chicago, IL	35
Graham Recycling	York, PA	20
Johnson Controls	Novi, MI	20
M.A. Industries	Peachtree City, GA	N.A.
Midwest Plastics	Edgerton, WI	10
Orion Pacific	Odessa, TX	7
Partek	Vancouver, WA	5
Pelo Plastique	Berthier-vill, PQ	15
Plastic Recycling Alliance	Philadelphia, PA	40
Plastic Recycling Alliance	Chicago, IL	40
Star Plastics	Albany, NY	32
St. Jude Polymer	Frackville, PA	25
Union Carbide	Piscataway, NJ	50

[Continued]

★ 512 ★

Scrap Plastic Bottles Reclaimers
[Continued]

Company	Location[1]	Estimated annual capacity in million pounds
United Resource Recovery	Findlay, OH	8
Wellman	Johnsonville, SC	175

Source: Resource Recycling, January 1991, p. 40. N.A. means not available. *Notes:* 1. Processing plant location. Corporate headquarters may be at another location.

★ 513 ★

U.S. Recycled Containerboard Projects

Company/mill site	Startup	Capacity (000 tpy)	Grade[4,5]	Recycled content (percent)
Macon Kraft Co.	1990	107[1]	L[4]	40
Stone Container Corp.	1990	55	M[5]	100
Green Bay Packaging Inc.	1990	216[1]	L/M[4,]	60-70
Temple-Inland Inc.	1990	42[1]	M[5]	100
Visy Recycle/Hartford City, Ind.	1990	53[2]	M[5]	100
Cascades Inc.	1990	35[1]	M[5]	100
Corrugated Services Inc.	1990	27[1]	L/M[4,5]	100
Virginia Fibre Corp.	1990	60[1]	M[5]	20-25
Menasha Corp.	1991	50[1]	M[5]	50
Temple Inland/Ontario, Calif.	1991	70	L[4]	100
Weston Paper & Manufacturing Co.	1991	64[1]	M[5]	100
Weyerhaeuser Paper Co.	1992	80[1]	L[4]	25
Stone Container Corp.	1992	420[2]	L[4]	100
Temple-Inland/Maysville, KY	1993	214[3]	L/M[4,5]	100
Smurfit-CCA/ ernandina, Fla.[6]	1992	211[2]	L[4]	100
Dunkirk Container/Dunkirk, N.Y.[6]	1992	250[3]	L[4]	100
Northampton Paperboard[6]	na	300[3]	L[4]	100
Clinch River Corp.[6]	na	105[2]	M[5]	100
Daishowa-Trans Rim/Stockton, Calif.[6]	na	350[3]	L[4]	100

Source: Pulp & Paper, October, 1990, p.31. *Notes:* 1. Adding or expanding OCC recycling or deinking facilities (estimated recycled fiber content based on total mill production). 2. Restart or conversion of existing machine. 3. New paper machine at existing or greenfield mills. 4. Linerboard 5. Medium 6. Proposed sites 7. Not anailable.

★ 514 ★

Waste-To-Energy Companies

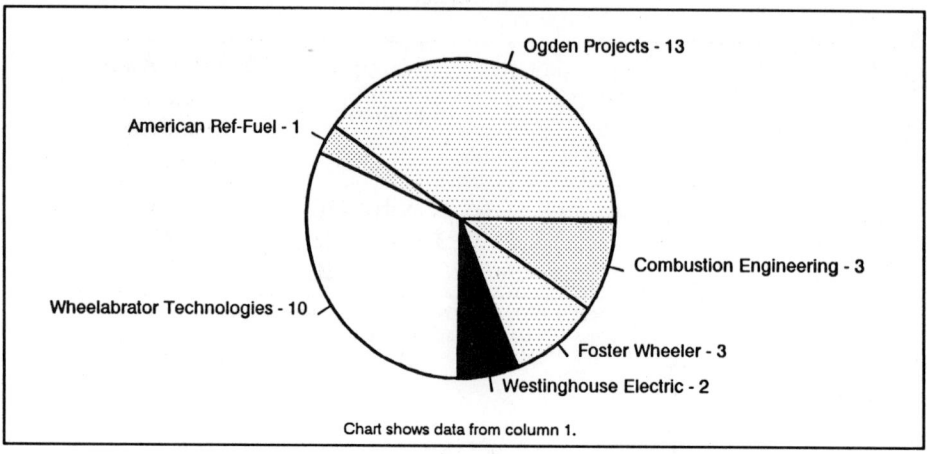

Chart shows data from column 1.

Company	In Operation	Under Construction Contract
Ogden Projects	13	14
Wheelabrator Technologies	10	4
Foster Wheeler	3	6
Combustion Engineering	3	2
Westinghouse Electric	2	6
American Ref-Fuel	1	2

Source: Fortune, December 18, 1989, p. 9.

★ 515 ★

Waste-To-Energy Facility Ownership in the U.S.

Type of ownership	Percent of response[1]
Private sector	43.6
Public authority	20.5
City/Town/Township	15.4
Joint venture of private firms	7.7
County	5.1
Joint public/private owner	5.1
Joint public sector owner	2.6

Source: American City & County, March 1991, p. 12 *Notes:* 1. No information was available from 16 facilities where a decision regarding ownership is currently pending.

★ 516 ★

Waste-To-Energy Leaders in the U.S.

```
Wheelabrator - 25,625
Ogden Martin - 18,725
            American Ref-Fuel - 9,169
            Combustion Engineering - 8,850
        Montenay Power - 6,673
        Westinghouse - 6,323
        Foster Wheeler - 5,901
      Consumat - 3,215
    Blount - 2,310
            Chart shows data from column 7.
```

The values are in tons per day.

Primary Operator/ Developer	Advanced Palnning		Construction		Operational		Total	
	Tons/ Day	Number of Companies	Tons/ Day	Number of Companies	Tons/ Day	Number of Companies	Tons/ Day	Number of Companies
Wheelabrator	3,800	2	5,875	4	15,950	10	25,625	16
Ogden Martin	750	1	8,613	7	9,362	9	18,725	17
American Ref-Fuel	4,000	2	5,169	3	0		9,169	5
Combustion Engineering	1,550	2	2,000	1	5,300	2	8,850	5
Montenay Power	1,200	1	518	1	4,955	5	6,673	7
Westinghouse	1,375	2	4,038	2	910	2	6,323	6
Foster Wheeler	1,471	2	2,050	3	2,380	2	5,901	7
Consumat	375	2	0		2,840	24	3,215	26
Blount	710	1	1,200	1	400	1	2,310	3

Source: World Wastes, June 1989, p. 25 from telephone survey, April 1989.

★517★

Waste-To-Energy Projects - Market Share in Capacity

Total - 100.0

Other Firms - 30.6

Wheelabrator Technologies - 18.1

Ogden Martin - 17.2

American Ref-Fuel - 7.8

Combustion Engineering - 6.8

Foster Wheeler - 4.5

Westinghouse - 4.9

Dravo Res. Energy Sys. - 2.5

Vicon - 1.9

Blount - 1.5

Consumat Systems - 2.1

Montenay Power - 2.0

Chart shows data from column 9.

Capacity is shown in tons per day. Market share is in percent.

Primary Developer	Advanced Planning		Construction		Operational		Total		Market Share (percent)
	Capacity	No. Plants	Capacity	No. Plants	Capacity	No. Plans	Capacity	No. Plants	
Wheelabrator Technologies[1]	8,825	5	5,000	3	13,350	8	27,175	16	18.1
Ogden Martin	11,190	8	9,187	6	5,400	6	25,777	20	17.2
American Ref-Fuel	9,377	6	2,319	1	-		11,696	7	7.8
Combustion Engineering	4,150	3	4,000	1	2,000	1	10,150	5	6.8
Westinghouse	4,703	3	1,862	2	710	2	7,275	7	4.9
Foster Wheeler	3,350	4	644	1	2,760	3	6,754	8	4.5
Dravo Res. Energy Sys.[2]	1,890	2	1,880	2	-		3,770	4	2.5
Consumat Systems	405	2	-		2,739	24	3,144	26	2.1
Montenay Power	-		-		3,000	1	3,000	1	2.0
Vicon[3]	980	2	780	2	1,080	3	2,840	7	1.9
Blount	710	1	1,600	2	-		2,310	3	1.5
Other Firms	12,921	34	8,022	9	24,966	55	45,909	98	30.6
Total	58,501	62	35,294	29	56,005	111	149,800	202	100.0

Source: World Wastes, June 1989, p. 24. Market share *Notes:* 1. Waste Management Energy Systems now owns portions of Wheellabrator 2. Dravo's projects have been purchased by Montenay Power 3. Vicon filed for bankruptcy in 1988.

★ 518 ★

Waste-To-Energy Projects - Market Share in Dollars

```
┌─────────────────────────────────────────────────┐
│  ┌───────────────────────────────────────────┐  │
│  │ Total - 100.0                             │  │
│  └───────────────────────────────────────────┘  │
│  ┌──────────────────────┐                        │
│  │                      │ Other Firms - 26.7     │
│  └──────────────────────┘                        │
│  ┌────────────────┐                              │
│  │                │ Wheelabrator Technologies - 18.8 │
│  └────────────────┘                              │
│  ┌──────────────┐                                │
│  │              │ Ogden Martin - 18.0            │
│  └──────────────┘                                │
│  ┌──────────┐                                    │
│  │          │ American Ref-Fuel - 10.5           │
│  └──────────┘                                    │
│  ┌──────┐                                        │
│  │      │ Combustion Engineering - 6.6           │
│  └──────┘                                        │
│  ┌────┐                                          │
│  │    │ Foster Wheeler - 5.1                     │
│  └────┘                                          │
│  ┌────┐                                          │
│  │    │ Westinghouse - 5.2                       │
│  └────┘                                          │
│  ▯ Dravo Resource Energy Systems - 2.4           │
│  ▯ Blount - 1.6                                  │
│  ▯ Vicon - 2.1                                   │
│  ▯ Montenay Power - 1.9                          │
│  ▮ Consumat Systems - 1.1                        │
│              Chart shows data from column 9.     │
└─────────────────────────────────────────────────┘
```

Value of projects is shown in millions of dollars. Market share is in percent.

Primary Developer	Advanced Planning		Construction		Operational		Total		Market Share (percent)
	Value	No. Plants	Value	No. Plants	Value	No. Plans	Value	No. Plants	
Wheelabrator Technologies[1]	867.79	5	476.29	3	907.61	8	2,251.69	16	18.8
Ogden Martin	1,024.43	8	649.65	6	487.25	6	2,161.33	20	18.0
American Ref-Fuel	992.87	6	264.25	1	-		1,257.12	7	10.5
Combustion Engineering	387.95	3	233.06	1	168.00	1	789.01	5	6.6
Westinghouse	447.00	3	131.31	2	50.27	2	628.58	7	5.2
Foster Wheeler	376.00	4	56.75	1	177.19	3	609.94	8	5.1
Dravo Resource Energy Systems[2]	142.50	2	147.50	2	-		290.00	4	2.4
Vicon[3]	85.00	2	57.09	2	103.96		246.05	7	2.1
Montenay Power	-		-		228.23		228.23	1	1.9
Blount	72.00	1	120.00	2	-		192.00	3	1.6
Consumat Systems	25.40		-		111.68	24	137.00	26	1.1
Other Firms	984.61		608.71	9	1,612.04	55	3,205.36	98	26.7
Total	5,405.55	62	2,744.61	29	3,846.15	111	11,996.31	202	100.0

Source: World Wastes, June 1989, p. 25 from Government Advisory Associates. Market share *Notes:* 1. Waste Management Energy Systems now owns portions of Wheellabrator 2. Dravo's projects have been purchased by Montenay Power 3. Vicon filed for bankruptcy in 1988.

Solid Waste Management

★ 519 ★

Closed Body Collection Truck Manufacturers
The noted capacity is in cubic yards.

Manufacturer	Model Name	Rated Capacity	Loading Height Min-Max (inches)	Estimated Base Price ($ 000)
Amertek	RBM	27, 31	58 - 80	60.0
	RBA (Hydraulic)	31	50	70.0
Dempster	Recycle King I	31	54 - 96	61.5
	Recycle King II /hydraulic	31	46 - 48	68.5
Frink	MR 1800	18	50 - 83	40.0
	MR 3000	27, 30, 32	50 - 83	55.0
	PR 3000 (Hydraulic)	31	45	70.0-75.0
Impact	Modular Recycler (Body only)	20-35	48-92	-
Jeager	ML	30-34	54-84	60.0-63.0
	PL (Hydraulic)	32	40-44	80.0
Labrie	MRT	31	48-72	62.0
	Top Select 2000 (Hydraulic)	31	42	76.0-78.0
Lodal	ECO-3000	28	49-71	63.5
	ECO-3030	31	42-71	64.5
	ECO-Bi-Loader (Hydraulic)	31	49	68.5
Perkins	Rendacycler	25,30	43	25.0-28.0[1]
RTI	Amrep (Hydraulic)	28,30	36	61.9

[Continued]

★ 519 ★

Closed Body Collection Trucks
[Continued]

Manufacturer	Model Name	Rated Capacity	Loading Height Min-Max (inches)	Estimated Base Price ($ 000)
Summit	- (Hydraulic)	25	36	53.0
Walinga	Champion	31	52-100	68.0
	Champion (Hydraulic)	31	46	72.0

Source: BioCycle, June 1989, p. 38.

★ 520 ★

Open Top Collection Truck Manufacturers
Waste collection vehicles. Rated capacity is in cubic yards.

Manufacturer	Model Name	Rated Capacity	Loading Heights Min-Max (in.)	Estimated Base Price ($ 000)
Able Body	CRRC	Varies	Varies	23.5[1]
Eager Beaver	Recycler	15,23	48-78	35.0-40.0
Holden	Flexi-Dump	11,15,20,23	42-75 48-78	34.1-39.6
	Flexi-Dump EZ	30	42	72.0
Kann	Curbsorter	16,20,22	48-75	8.0-11.0[1]
	Side Dump	Up to 22	49	6.0-20.0[1]
Peerless	MMRB	Up to 21	40-56 72-84	15.0-19.0[1]
Pm/Rudco	Std-Dump	21,25	63-94	38.5-40.5
	Hi-Lift	15	67-94	38.5
RTI	Peerless	18-22	44-64	61.9
	Bowles	18-22	48-76	59.9
WASP[2]	Curbside Col. unit	20	60-63	15.0[1]

Source: Biocycle, June 1989, p. 37. *Notes:* 1. Body only. 2. WASP Unit is a combination truck and trailer.

★ 521 ★

Trailers for Curbside Collection

The rated capacity is in cubic yards.

Manufacturer	Model Name	Rated Capacity	Loading Height (inches)	Estimated Base Price ($ 000)
All Season	ASR25	Varies	38	7.0-20.0
Eager Beaver	Recycler	15	54 - 76	13.4
Holden	Flexi-dump	15,20,23	52 - 76	13.7-18.0
Kann	Curb-sorter	16,20,22	48 - 75	13.5-15.0
	Side Dump	14-19	42	14.0-22.0
Labrie	RT	15	48	11.0
Mobile Equip.		Up to 24	Varies	10.0-16.0[1]
Multi-Tek	Recycle	15,18,20	50 - 79	12.5-13.0
	Wagon	22, 23		
Norcia	Side Dump	Varies	38	11.0-15.0
WASP	Curbside Col. Unit	10.5	60	6.6

Source: Biocycle, June 1989, p. 38. *Note:* 1. Excludes bins.

Transportation

★ 522 ★

Interstate Hauling of Toxic Waste

Leading importers and exporters of toxic waste via interstate trucking in 1988. Volumes are shown in number of tons of toxic waste.

State	Volume Transported
Importers	
Ohio	15,131
Louisiana	11,599
Alabama	7,925
South Carolina	6,214
Tennessee	5,623
Exporters	
New Jersey	13,549
Pennsylvania	7,179

[Continued]

★ 522 ★

Interstate Hauling of Toxic Waste
[Continued]

State	Volume Transported
Kentucky	6,804
Massachusetts	6,728
West Virginia	6,671

Source: Garbage, January/February 1991, p. 58, from the EPA.

Wastewater Treatment

★ 523 ★

Selected Wastewater Sludge Composting Markets

Location	Volume (Cubic Yards)	Product Name	Method of Distribution	Typical Users
Akron, OH	32,000	Organix	Fairfield Serv. Company	Dept. Natural Resources-70% Landscapers Topsoil Nursery
Clayton County, GA	5,000	None	North American Soils	Landscapers-75% Nursery- 10%
Metropolitan Denver Sewage Disposal District No. 1, CO	20,000	METROGRO	Direct sale and Perma-green Co.	Farmland-50% General Public-40%
East Bay Municipal Utility District, CA	25,000	CompGro	Ten Brokers	Landscapers
Hampton Roads Sanitation District, VA	11,000	Nutri-Green	Direct Sales	Landscapers-40% Municipal-30% General Public-20%
Los Angeles County Sanitation District, CA	250,000- 300,000	Nitrohumus, Topper, Gromulch, Amend and Others	Kellogg Supply Company	General Public and Nurseries
Nashville, TN	9,000	Nitro Humus	Soil Products Inc.-90%	Landscapers and Nurseries
Sarasota, FL	6,000	None	Single Company	Agriculture Right-of-Way

[Continued]

★ 523 ★

Selected Waste Water Sludge Composting Markets
[Continued]

Location	Volume (Cubic Yards)	Product Name	Method of Distribution	Typical Users
Scranton, PA	15,000	Pay Dirt	Direct Sale and Single Broker	Landscapers-25% Municipal Give-Away-25%
Washington Suburban Sanitary Commission, MD	40,000	Com PRO	Maryland Environmental Service	Landscapers-25% General Public-40% Topsoil Dealers-25%

Source: *BioCycle*, February 1990, p. 45.

★ 524 ★

U.S. Water Treatment Chemical Demand

Values for the U.S. show market in millions of dollars per year for 1989 and projected growth, 1989-1994 per annum. World market is shown in millions of dollars for 1989.

Chemicals	U.S. Market		Worldwide ($ Mil.)
	Total ($ Mil.)	Growth (%/year 1989-1994)	
Activated carbon	65	5.0	125
Ion exchange resins	100	2.0	175
Polyacrylamides	160	6.5	320
Polyamines	40	3.5	60
Quaternary ammonium compounds	45	5.7	45
Subtotal	410	4.8	725
Water treatment services (corrosion and scale inhibitors)	1,055	5.2	1,555
Total market	1,465	5.1	2,280

Source: *Chemicalweek*, May 16, 1990, p. 20, from SRI International (Menlo Park, CA).

★ 525 ★

U.S. Water Treatment Chemicals Market

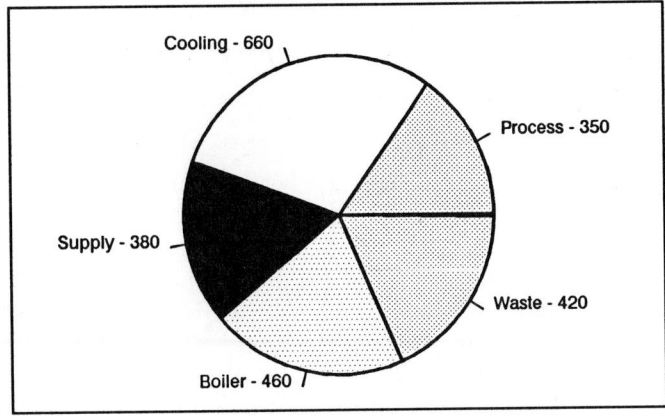

Values shown in millions of dollars. Total market is $2.27 billion.

Chemical Type	Millions of dollars
Process	350
Supply	380
Waste	420
Boiler	460
Cooling	660

Source: Chemicalweek, May 16, 1990, p. 20, from Kline & Co. (Fairfield, NJ), 1989.

★ 526 ★

Water Treatment Chemicals Market in Western Europe

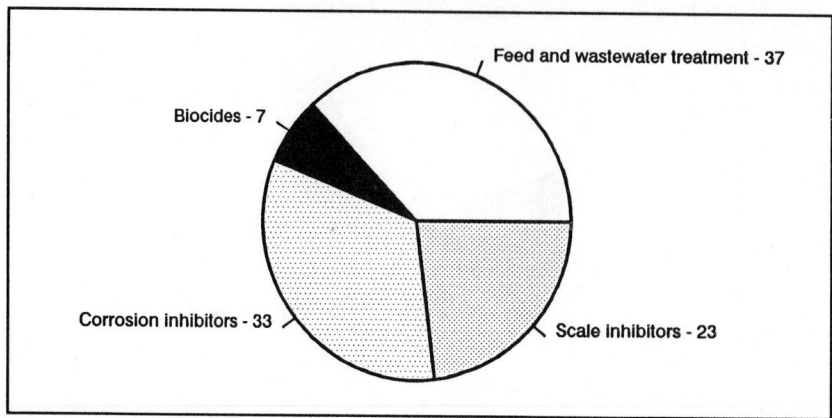

The total water treatment chemical market in Western Europe was $400-$450 million in 1989.

Chemical	Percent
Scale inhibitors	23
Corrosion inhibitors	33
Feed and wastewater treatment	37
Biocides	7

Source: Chemicalweek, May 16,1990, p. 32, from SRI International (Zurich).

Chapter 7

GENERAL INDUSTRY AND GOVERNMENT DATA

Asbestos

★ 527 ★

Asbestos Industry in the U.S.

Two firms in California and Vermont accounted for 100 percent of domestic production in 1988.
Values shown in thousands of metric tons.

Item	1984	1985	1986	1987	1988[1]
Production (sales), mine	57	57	51	51	18
Imports for consumption	210	142	108	94	93
Exports	40	46	47	60	30
Consumption, apparent	226	162	120	84	83
Price, average value, dol./ton, f.o.b. mine	422	357	338	340	434
Stocks, producer, yearend	23	14	6	6	4
Employment, mine and mill[1]	190	200	250	230	58
Net import reliance as percent of apparent consumption[2]	75	65	58	40	78

Source: U.S. Department of Commerce, Bureau of the Census, *Statistical Abstract of the United States 1990 (110th ed.),* Superintendent of Documents, Washington, D.C., p. 699, Table No. 1229, from U.S. Bureau of Mines, *Mineral Commodity Summaries, 1989. Notes:* 1. Estimated. 2. Reliance defined as imports minus exports plus adjustments for Government and industry stock changes.

★ 528 ★

Asbestos Production in the U.S.

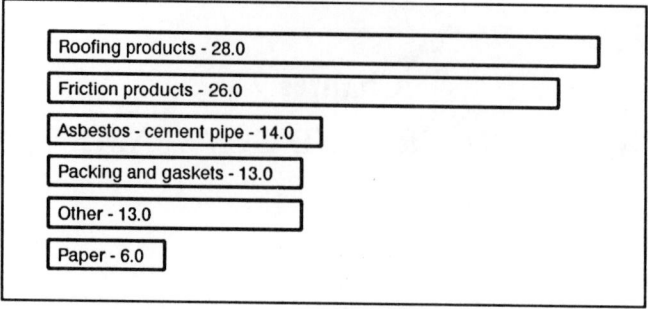

Product shares of asbestos production in 1988, shown in percent. Total production was 18,000 metric tons and 100% of this amount was produced by two firms in California and Vermont.

Product	Share
Roofing products	28.0
Friction products	26.0
Asbestos - cement pipe	14.0
Packing and gaskets	13.0
Paper	6.0
Other	13.0

Source: U.S. Department of Commerce, Bureau of the Census, *Statistical Abstract of the United States 1990 (110th ed.)*, Superintendent of Documents, Washington, D.C., p. 699, from U.S. Bureau of Mines, Mineral Commodity Summaries, 1989.

Automobiles

★ 529 ★

Auto Facts

	Ratio and $/gallon
Ratio of people to cars	
New York City	4 to 1
Denver	1.5 to 1
Los Angeles County	2 to 1
Tax per gallon of gasoline	
Denmark	2.51

[Continued]

★ 529 ★

Auto Facts
[Continued]

	Ratio and $/gallon
United Kingdom	1.55
United States	0.33

Source: Garbage, July/August 1990, p. 26, from Organization for Economic Cooperation and Development (OECD).

★ 530 ★

Automobile Mileage, 1978-1990

Average miles per gallon achieved by manufacturers of U.S. and foreign automobiles.

Year	Average MPG
1978	19.9
1979	20.3
1980	23.5
1981	25.1
1982	26.0
1983	25.9
1984	26.3
1985	27.0
1986	27.9
1987	28.1
1988	28.6
1989[1]	28.1
1990[1]	27.8

Source: The Christian Science Monitor, March 18, 1991, p. 6, from the Environmental Protection Agency. *Note:* 1. Preliminary figure.

★ 531 ★

Automotive Ingredient by Material

Values are shown in pounds of material per U.S. passenger vehicle.

Material	1977	1985	1987	1989	1990
Steel	2,202	1,781	1,775	1,728	1,717
Iron	540	468	480	459	454
Plastic	168	211	222	225	229
Glass	86	85	86	85	87

Source: The Wall Street Journal, April 30, 1991, p. B1, from *American Metal Market* newspaper.

★ 532 ★

Average U.S. Family Auto Travel

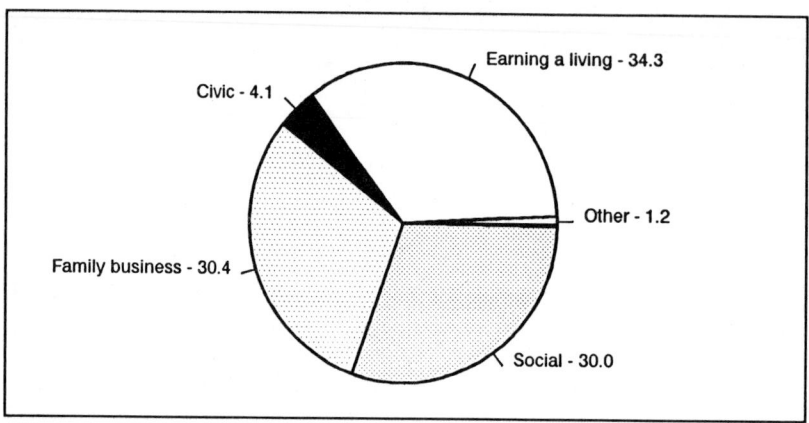

Purpose	Percent
Earning a living	34.3
Family business	30.4
Social	30.0
Civic	4.1
Other	1.2

Source: Consumer's Research, January 1989, p. 21, from U.S. Department of Transportation, Federal Highway Administration 1983 to 1984 National Transportation Study.

★ 533 ★

Population per Automobile

```
China - 1,074.0
India - 544.4
                Ghana - 217.0
            Nigeria - 141.0
            Egypt - 123.6
            Thailand - 94.0
            Senegal - 88.8
        South Korea - 50.2
        Tanzania - 44.9
    Brazil - 15.5
    Malaysia - 12.4
    Venezuela - 11.4
    Japan - 4.1
    France - 2.6
    United States - 1.8
```

The data refer to selected countries in 1987.

Country	Persons per Automobile
United States	1.8
France	2.6
Japan	4.1
Venezuela	11.4
Malaysia	12.4
Brazil	15.5
Tanzania[1]	44.9
South Korea	50.2
Senegal	88.8
Thailand	94.0
Egypt	123.6
Nigeria	141.0
Ghana	217.0
India	544.4
China[1]	1,074.0[2]

Source: World Watch, January/February 1990, p. 31, from Worldwatch Institute, based on Motor Vehicle Manufacturers Association, *Facts and Figures '89* (Detroit, Mich:1989). *Notes:* 1. 1985 2. Refers to all automobiles; population per privately owned automobiles was 74,000 in 1988.

★ 534 ★

World Auto Registration

Values shown are for 1987.

Continent/Country	Cars (thousands)	Population per car
North and South America		
Canada	11,500	2.2
Honduras	30,000	170.0
Mexico	5,402	16.0
U.S.A.	137,323	1.8
Total	156,776	2.6
South America		
Argentina	4,060	8.0
Brazil	9,527	16.0
Colombia	579	55.0
Peru	390	56.0
Total	17,165	17.0
Asia		
China	995	1,075.0
India	1,471	566.0
Indonesia	974	193.0
Japan	29,478	4.2
Pakistan	272	404.0
Total	43,782	65.0
Oceania		
Total	8,666	2.4
Africa		
Egypt	417	131.0
Nigeria	774	149.0
South African Republic	3,078	12.0
Total	7,860	80.0
Europe		
France	21,950	2.5
Germany, East	3,462	4.8
Germany, West	28,304	2.1
Italy	22,800	2.5
Turkey	1,193	46.0
U.S.S.R.	13,000	22.0
United Kingdom	20,096	2.8
Total	159,958	5.2
World total	394,209	13.0

Source: Changing by Degrees: Steps to Reduce Greenhouse Gases, U.S. Congress, Office of Technology Assessment, OTA-O-482, Washington, D.C., February 1991, p. 153, from Motor Vehicle Manufacturer's Association, *Facts and Figures '89* (Detroit, MI: 1990).

Chemicals

★ 535 ★

Agrichemicals Use in the U.S.

Year	Corn			Wheat			Soybeans		
	Fertilizer	Herbicides	Insecticides	Fertilizer	Herbicides	Insecticides	Fertilizer	Herbicides	Insecticides
Number of acres treated (1,000)									
1971	69,728	58,601	25,963	31,217	22,067	3,768	8,695	29,654	3,478
1980	80,681	78,160	36,138	54,128	(NA)	(NA)	25,874	64,336	7,692
1984	78,127	76,516	33,828	60,202	(NA)	(NA)	23,037	63,690	5,420
1985	81,779	80,110	37,552	58,193	(NA)	(NA)	20,202	59,974	4,419
1986	73,607	73,607	31,436	56,934	33,872	5,045	19,927	57,970	2,415
1987	63,076	63,076	26,939	52,667	40,817	4,608	17,386	55,057	1,739
1988	65,590	64,914	23,667	54,389	34,730	2,621	18,838	56,515	4,710
Percent of acres treated									
1971	94	79	35	58	41	7	20	68	8
1980	96	93	43	67	(NA)	(NA)	37	92	11
1984	97	95	42	76	(NA)	(NA)	34	94	8
1985	98	96	45	77	(NA)	(NA)	32	95	7
1986	96	96	41	79	47	7	33	96	4
1987	96	96	41	80	62	7	30	95	3
1988	97	96	35	83	53	4	32	96	8

Source: U.S. Department of Commerce, Bureau of the Census, *Statistical Abstract of the United States 1990 (110th ed.)*, Superintendent of Documents, Washington, D.C., p. 655, from U.S. Dept. of Agriculture, Economic Research Service, *Agricultural Resources: Situation and Outlook Report*, February 1988 and previous issues. NA Stands for not available.

★ 536 ★

CFCs by Enduse

| Solvents - 26.0 |
| Refrigeration/air conditioning - 25.0 |
| Rigid foams - 19.0 |
| Others - 13.0 |
| Fire extinguishing - 12.0 |
| Flexible foams - 5.0 |

Use of chlorinated fluorocarbons (CFCs) by end use. CFCs are suspected of causing ozone-depletion in the atmosphere.

Source	Percent of depletion
Solvents	26.0
Refrigeration/air conditioning	25.0
Rigid foams	19.0
Fire extinguishing	12.0
Flexible foams	5.0
Others	13.0

Source: Power, March 1990, p. 28.

★ 537 ★

Chlorofluorocarbon Market in the Future

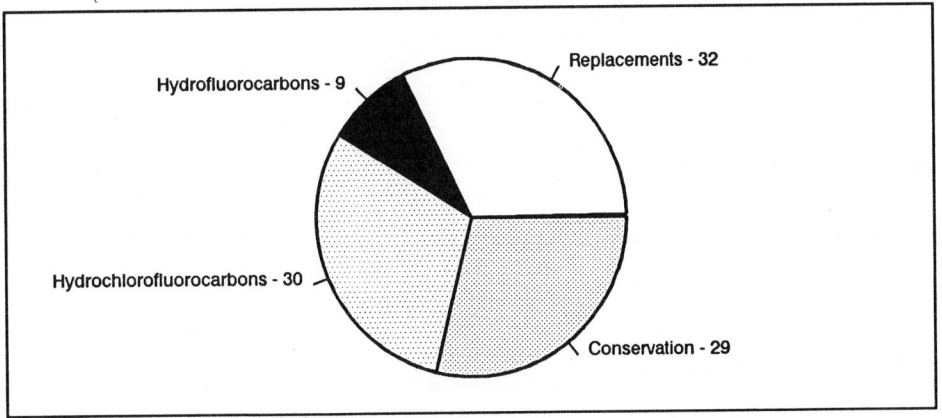

The percent values represent market projections by DuPont, to determine how the current markets that use chlorofluorocarbons (CFCs) will be satisfied in the year 2000.

Type	Percent
Replacements	32
Hydrochlorofluorocarbons	30
Conservation	29
Hydrofluorocarbons	9

Source: Science, July 6, 1990, p. 32.

★ 538 ★

Evolution of Refrigerants and Refrigeration

Event/Issue	Year	Experimenter
Demonstrated evaporation of ethyl ether by reducing pressure.	1750	W. Cullen
Latent heat phenomena studied; theory developed.	1761-64	J. Black
Ice produced artificially using sulfuric acid/water as absorption pair.	1810	J. Leslie
Concept of vapor compression machine based on ethyl ether demonstrated and patented.	1834	J. Perkins
Commercially viable air cycle machine developed and placed in service.	1844	J. Gorrie
Viable ammonia/water absorption machines developed and commercialized.	1850	F. Caree
Initial commercial applications of vapor compression cycle technology based on ethyl ether.	1853-56	Twining and Harrison

[Continued]

★ 538 ★

Evolution of Refrigerants and Refrigeration
[Continued]

Event/Issue	Year	Experimenter
Vapor compression machines using carbon dioxide.	1866	T.S.C. Lowe
Vapor compression machines using ammonia.	1873	Boyle & Linde
Vapor compression using sulfur dioxide.	1876	Pictet
Methyl chloride used as a vapor compression refrigerant in France.	1898	
Automatic household refrigerator based on sulfur dioxide.	1918	
Successful centrifugal compressor using $C_2H_2Cl_2$ Isobutane used in refrigerators.	1922	W. Carrier
Fluorine containing molecules, including CFCs, proposed and demonstrated.	1930	Midgley et al.
CFC/Ozone Hypothesis.	1974	S. Rowland and M. Molina
Montreal Protocol.	1987	
U.S. environmental legislation (Clean Air Act provisions impacting refrigerants).	1990	

Source: *ASHRAE Journal*, February 1991, p. 34.

★ 539 ★

Farm Pesticide Use

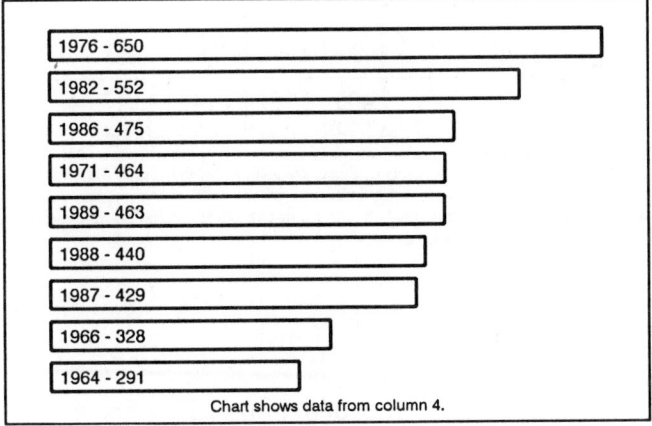

| 1976 - 650 |
| 1982 - 552 |
| 1986 - 475 |
| 1971 - 464 |
| 1989 - 463 |
| 1988 - 440 |
| 1987 - 429 |
| 1966 - 328 |
| 1964 - 291 |

Chart shows data from column 4.

Figures are shown in millions of pounds of active ingredients.

Year	Herbicides	Insecticides	Other	Total
1964	76	143	72	291
1966	112	138	78	328
1971	207	127	130	464
1976	374	130	146	650
1982	451	71	30	552
1986	410	59	6	475
1987	365	57	7	429
1988	372	60	8	440
1989	394	61	8	463

Source. Council on Environmental Quality, *20th Annual Report 1990*, Washington, D.C., Appendix E, Table 55, from U.S. Department of Agriculture, Economic Research Service. "Agricultural resources: Inputs outlook and situation report," periodic. Washington, DC. For the years 1964, 1966, 1972, and 1976, estimates of pesticide use are for total use on all crops and livestock in the United States. The 1982 estimates are for major field and forage crops only and represent 33 major producing states, excluding California. The 1986-1989 estimates are for 10 major field crops.

★ 540 ★

Synthetic Organic Pesticide Production

Data include a small quantity of soil conditioners.

Item	Unit	1978	1979	1980	1981	1982	1983	1984	1985	1986	1987
Production total	Mil. lb	1,416	1,429	1,468	1,430	1,113	1,017	1,189	1,235	1,180	1,040
Herbicides	Mil. lb	664	657	806	839	623	570	716	756	725	556
Insecticides	Mil. lb	605	617	506	448	379	324	350	370	342	379
Fungicides	Mil. lb	147	155	156	143	111	123	123	109	113	105
Production value[1]	Mil. $	3,342	3,685	4,269	5,136	4,331	3,993	5,056	5,360	5,305	4,725

[Continued]

★ 540 ★

Synthetic Organic Pesticide Production

[Continued]

Item	Unit	1978	1979	1980	1981	1982	1983	1984	1985	1986	1987
Sales, total	Mil. lb	1,300	1,369	1,406	1,291	1,147	1,017	1,108	1,022	940	911
Sales value	Mil. $	3,041	3,631	4,078	4,652	4,432	4,054	4,730	4,437	4,234	4,171

Source: U.S. Department of Commerce, Bureau of the Census, *Statistical Abstract of the United States 1990 (110th ed.),* Superintendent of Documents, Washington, D.C., p. 206, from U.S. Dept. of Agriculture, Agricultural Stablization and Conservation Service, The Pesticide Review, 1978; and unpublished data. Based on data from U.S. International Trade Commission, Synthetic Organic Chemicals, annual. *Note:* 1. Manufacturers unit value multiplied by production.

★ 541 ★

U.S. Chlorofluorocarbon (CFC) Uses

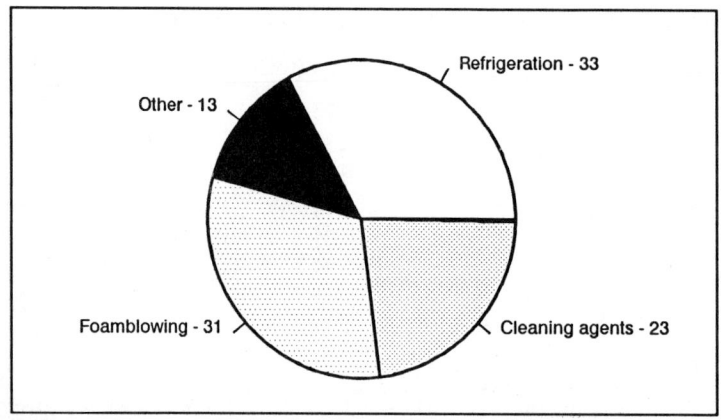

Data show end uses of chlorofluorocarbons (CFCs) as percent by end use.

CFC use	Percent
Refrigeration	33
Foamblowing	31
Cleaning agents	23
Other	13

Source: C&EN, July 24, 1989, p. 11, from Alliance for Responsible CFC Policy.

Coal

★ 542 ★

Coal Resources, Consumption, and Trade Worldwide

Values shown are percentages of worldwide totals.

Country	Reserves 1989	Production 1989	Consumption 1989	Imports 1987	Exports 1987
United States	24.1	23.9	21.2	-	22.6
U.S.S.R.	22.1	13.9	12.9	2.3	7.6
China	15.4	22.9	22.6	-	2.1
Australia	8.4	4.4	-	-	29.7
India	5.7	4.1	4.1[1]	-	-
West Germany	5.4	3.3	3.3	2.8	3.0
South Africa	5.1	-	3.4[1]	-	10.9
Poland	3.7	5.0	5.7[1]	-	7.3
East Germany	1.9	2.9	3.0[1]	-	-
United Kingdom	0.6	2.7	2.8	-	0.8
Czechoslovakia	-	1.8	-	-	-
Japan	-	-	3.4	27.0	-
South Korea	-	-	-	7.4	-
Italy	-	-	-	5.7	-
Canada	-	-	-	4.3	8.3
France	-	-	-	3.9	-
Netherlands	-	-	-	3.6	-
Belgium/Luxembourg	-	-	-	3.0	-
Denmark	-	-	-	2.9	-
Colombia	-	-	-	-	2.4
Other	7.6	15.1	17.6	37.1	5.3
Total	100.0	100.0	100.0	100.0	100.0

Source: Changing by Degrees: Steps to Reduce Greenhouse Gases, U.S. Congress, Office of Technology Assessment, OTA-O-482, Washington, D.C., February 1991, p. 82, from the British Petroleum Company, *BP Statistical Review of World Energy* (London, UK: British Petroleum, June 1990), unless otherwise specified. Data on imports and exports are derived from U.S. Department of Energy, Energy Information Administration, *International Energy Annual, 1988* DOE/EIA-0219(88) (Washington, DC: November 1989). Approximately 10 percent of coal production/consumption is traded internationally. *Notes:* 1. Apparent consumption for Poland, India, South Africa, and East Germany is obtained from U.S. Department of Energy (1989). It represents their share of world apparent consumption in 1987 (not 1989).

★ 543 ★

Lignite Production Worldwide

1989 production values are shown in millions of metric tons.

Country	Hard coal	Lignite	% Lignite
U.S.S.R.	497.7	164.7	N/A
Bulgaria	0.2	31.5	18
Czechoslovakia	25.1	91.8	41
Eastern Germany	-	305.0	75
Hungary	2.2	18.2	16
Poland	178.0	71.5	11
Romania	9.8	52.3	11
Yugoslavia	0.3	78.3	N/A
U.K.	99.9	-	-
West Germany	77.8	109.1	-
U.S.	608.0	283.8	-

Source: Chemical Engineering, February 1991, p. 33, from Gilges. N/A stands for not available.

Construction

★ 544 ★

Federal Building Construction

	General Services Administration
	Federal building parking
	Federal Bureau of Investigation
	Navy
	Courthouse annex
	Dept. of Transportation - 2,000,000
	Internal Revenue Service
	Dept. of Defense - 1,800,000
	Dept. of Justice
	Environmental Protection Agency

Chart shows data from column 1.

	Sq. ft.	Cost ($ mil)	Need
Navy (Northern Va.)	3,000,000	742.4	Lease Cons[1]
Dept. of Transportation	2,000,000	624.3	Headquarters
Dept. of Defense	1,800,000	317.6	
Environmental Protection Agency (Washington)	1,120,000	226.0	Headquarters
Internal Revenue Service (Washington area)	885,000	212.7	Lease Cons[1]
General Services Administration (Washington)	650,000	170.0	Headquarters
Dept. of Justice (Washington)	400,000	106.4	Lease Cons[1]
Federal building parking (Newark, N.J.)	256,000	18.6	Parking
Federal Bureau of Investigation (Washington)	248,000	101.5	Field office
Courthouse annex (Minneapolis)	168,000	46.5	Expansion

Source: ENR, September 21, 1989, p. 15, from the General Services Administration and the Office of Management and Budget, report to Congress, September 7, 1989. *Note:* 1. Lease consolidation.

★ 545 ★

Global Construction Contracts

Shares of $204.5 billion dollars in contracts that were awarded worldwide in 1990.

Type	Percent
General building	31
Petroleum	24
Industrial process	13
Transportation	9
Power	7
Manufacturing plant	7
Hazardous waste	4
Sewer/waste control	2
Water supply	1
Other	2

Source: ENR, May 27, 1991, p. 35.

Consumer Products

★ 546 ★

Aerosol Product Consumption in the U.S.

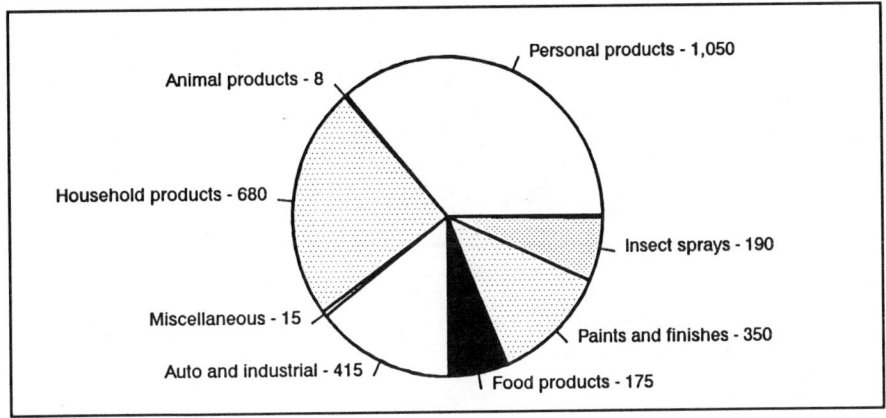

	Millions of Units
Personal products	1,050
Household products	680
Auto and industrial	415
Paints and finishes	350
Insect sprays	190
Food products	175
Miscellaneous	15
Animal products	8

Source: Chemical Week, May 8, 1991, p. 18, from Chemical Specialties Manufacturers' Association (Washington).

★ 547 ★

Consumer Spendings for Toxic Beauty Products

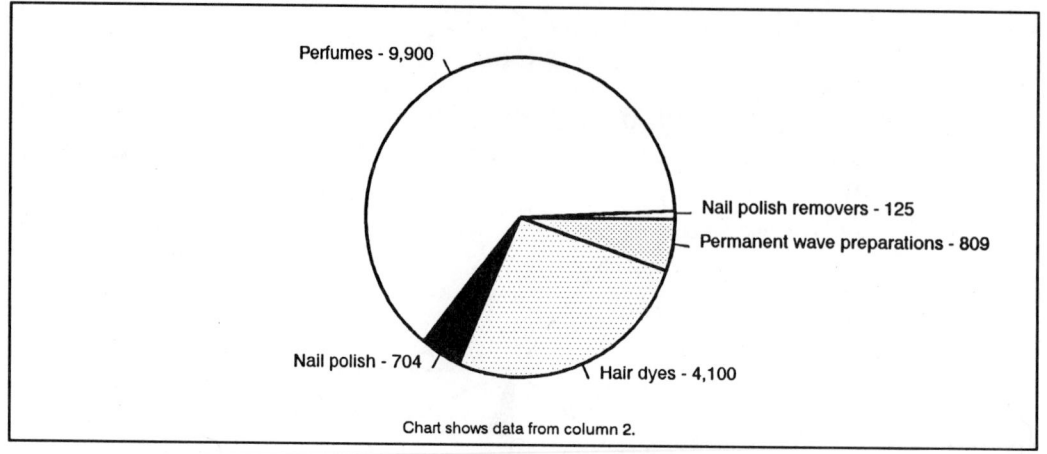

Chart shows data from column 2.

Toxicity definitions: slightly toxic—from 1 pt. to 1 qt.—equals a lethal human dose; extremely toxic—from 7 drops to 1 tsp. equals a lethal human dose.

Beauty product	Toxicity levels[1]	Spending ($ million)
Hair dyes	S - M	4,100
Nail polish	M - V	704
Nail polish removers	M - V	125
Perfumes	M	9,900
Permanent wave preparations	M - X	809

Source: Garbage, July/August 1990, p. 26, from U.S. Census Bureau. *Notes:* 1. Codes used to mark toxicity ranges are as follows: *S:* slightly toxic; *M:* moderately toxic; *V:* very toxic; *X:* extremely toxic.

★ 548 ★

Diaper Market in the U.S.

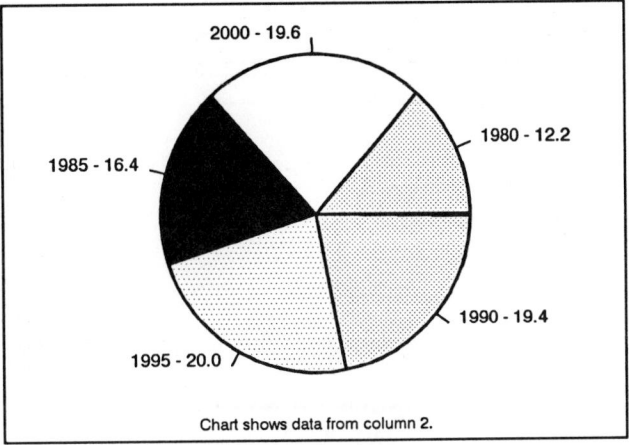

Chart shows data from column 2.

Projected unit growth of disposable infant diapers.

	Market share (%)[1]	Billions of units
1980	60.0	12.2
1985	75.5	16.4
1990	83.9	19.4
1995	90.8	20.0
2000	93.3	19.6

Source: Pulp & Paper, March 1988, p. 79, from Marketing/Technology Service Inc. *Notes:* 1. Market share is defined as the percentage of the total potential market for diapers if all 30-month infants were to use disposable diapers at the rate of 6.6 changes per day.

★ 549 ★

Green Products Introduced by Year

Chart shows data from column 1.

Green products claim on their label on in advertising to address environmental concerns.

Year	Green Products Introduced	% Share of Total Introductions
1985	24	0.5
1986	60	1.1
1987	122	2.0
1988	160	2.8
1989	262	4.5
1990	308	9.2

Source: Environmental Action, November/December 1990, p. 20, from Marketing Intelligence Service. Numbers for 1990 reflect the first 6 months.

Energy

★ 550 ★

Energy Consumption in Average U.S. Households

Annual expenditures are shown for 1987. The energy cost refers to electric appliances only, based on an assumed average cost of 7 cents per kilowatt hour.

Item	Cost (dollars)
Space heating	350
Refrigerator/freezer	239
Water heating	154
Air-conditioning	109
Lighting	84
Washer/dryer	77

[Continued]

★ 550 ★

Energy Consumption in Average U.S. Households
[Continued]

Item	Cost (dollars)
Furnace fan	46
Range/oven	42
Color TV	22
Dishwasher	12
Microwave oven	7
Other appliances	22
Total annual expenditures	1,164

Source: Changing by Degrees: Steps to Reduce Greenhouse Gases, U.S. Congress, Office of Technology Assessment, OTA-O-482, Washington, D.C., February 1991, p. 117, from Office of Technology Assessment, 1991, adapted from U.S. Department of Energy, Energy Information Administration, *Household Energy Consumption and Expenditure* (Washington, DC: 1989, Lighting data provided by A. Mejer, Lawrence Berkeley Laboratory. *Notes:* Five major end-uses—space heating, refrigerating, water heating, air-conditioning, and lighting—account for 80 percent of average household expenditures. .

★ 551 ★

Energy Consumption in Manufacturing
Values are 1985 manufacturing energy intensities.

	1,000 BTUs per dollar of Value of Shipments[1]
Stone, clay, and glass products	16.6
Primary metal industries	14.6
Paper and allied products	13.9
Chemicals and allied products	12.4
Textile mill products	4.8
Petroleum and coal products	4.4
Rubber and miscellaneous plastics	3.1
Food and kindred products	2.7
Fabricated metal products	2.3
Furniture and fixtures	1.6
Other manufacturing	1.4
Electrical and electronic equipment	1.2
Instruments and related equipment	1.2
Transportation equipment	1.1
Printing and publishing	0.9

[Continued]

★ 551 ★

Energy Consumption in Manufacturing
[Continued]

	1,000 BTUs per dollar of Value of Shipments[1]
Machinery, except electrical	0.9
All manufacturing	4.4

Source: *Changing by Degrees: Steps to Reduce Greenhouse Gases*, U.S. Congress, Office of Technology Assessment, OTA-O-482, Washington, D.C., February 1991, p. 179, from U.S. Department of Energy, Energy Information Agency, *Manufacturing Energy Consumption Survey: Changes in Energy Efficiency 1980-1985*, DOE/EIA-0516(85) (Washington, DC: January 1990), table ES1, p. viii. *Note:* 1. Based on constant 1980 dollars.

★ 552 ★

Industrial Energy Use by Function

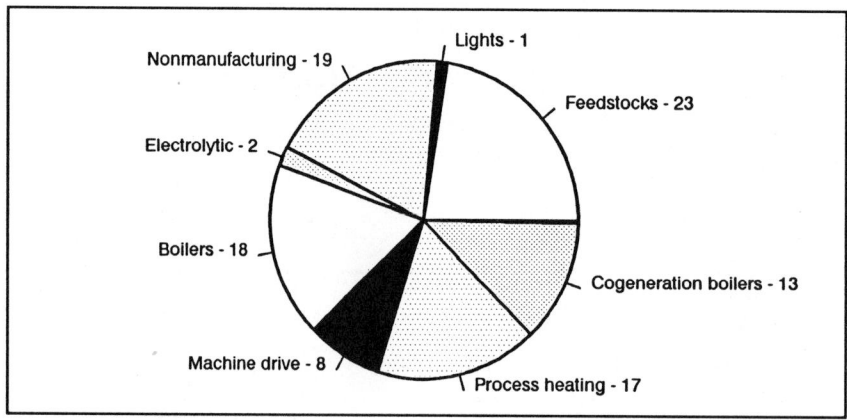

Values shown refer to 1987 experience and represent percent of total energy use by industry.

Energy use	Percent
Feedstocks	23
Nonmanufacturing	19
Boilers	18
Process heating	17
Cogeneration boilers	13
Machine drive	8
Electrolytic	2
Lights	1

Source: *Changing by Degrees: Steps to Reduce Greenhouse Gases*, U.S. Congress, Office of Technology Assessment, OTA-O-482, Washington, D.C., February 1991, p. 181, from Gas Research Institute, *Industrial Natural Gas Markets: Facts, Fallacies, and Forecasts* (Washington, DC: 1989).

★ 553 ★

Non-Utility Power Generation Projects by Fuel

Data shown are for the U.S. and are current as of August, 1989.

Primary energy source	Projects (Number)	Capacity (Megawatts)
Natural gas	902	12,685
Oil	43	412
Coal	82	3,854
Waste fuel	50	1,904
Wood	137	2,379
Agricultural waste	21	181
Biomethane	98	481
Other (hydro, solid waste, solar, wind)	1,121	5,955
Total	2,454	27,851

Source: Electric Light and Power, February 1990, p. 22.

Forestry

★ 554 ★

Federal Tree-Cutting Versus Tree-Planting

Logging in 1989 on federally owned land, shown by region in number of acres.

Region	Logging (1989)	Planting (1991)
Northeast & Great Lakes	113,575	57,361
California & Pacific Northwest	445,057	19,328
The South	132,638	127,913
Rocky Mountain, Midwest, & Southwest	310,538	140,307
Total	1,001,808	344,909

Source: Garbage, January/February 1991, p. 58, from the U.S. Forest Service.

★ 555 ★

Forest Product Value in the U.S.

Volumes and values are shown in millions of board feet and thousands of dollars respectively, for fiscal years 1975-89.

Year	Total timber cut[2]		Value of miscellaneous forest products[4]	Total value including free-use timber
	Volume	Value[3]		
1975	9,174	365,952	1,369	368,423
1976	9,575	492,029	1,224	495,367[5]
[6]	(3,432)	(209,938)	(129)	(210,067)
1977	10,482	732,547	1,002	735,949
1978	10,080	854,682	1,174	858,474
1979	10,377	968,033	1,149	973,018
1980	9,178	729,829	1,064	736,641
1981	8,036	720,922	1,627	728,919
1982	6,747	339,215	2,020	348,708
1983	9,244	649,652	1,728	655,874
1984	10,549	759,577	1,669	763,889
1985	10,941	720,636	1,703	724,505
1986	11,786	786,906	1,592	789,878
1987	12,712	1,015,995	1,905	1,018,977
1988	12,649	1,239,788	2,031	1,242,988
1989	11,913	1,309,061	2,864	1,313,141

Source: Agricultural Conservation and Forestry Statistics, 1989, U.S. Government Printing Office, Washington, D.C., 1989, p. 450, from Forest Service *Notes:* 1. Fiscal years July 1-June 30 for 1975-76; Oct. 1-Sept. 30 for 1977-89. 2. Commercial and cost sales and land exchanges. 3. Includes collections for forest restoration or improvement under the Knutson-Vandenberg Act, 1930. 4. Includes materials not measurable in board feet, such as Christmas trees, tanbark, turpentine, seedlings, Spanish moss, etc. 5. Includes free-use timber for 15-month period ending Sept. 30, 1976. 6. Transition quarter July 1, 1976-Sept. 30, 1976.

★ 556 ★

Leading Timber Producers Worldwide

The top 15 producers worldwide in 1988. Production includes all wood products except fuelwood and charcoal.

Country	Volume (million cu. meters)	Share of Total (percent)
USA	417	25.0
USSR	305	18.0
Canada	173	10.0
China	98	6.0
Brazil	67	4.0
Sweden	48	3.0

[Continued]

★ 556 ★

Leading Timber Producers Worldwide
[Continued]

Country	Volume (million cu. meters)	Share of Total (percent)
Finland	46	3.0
Indonesia	40	2.0
Malaysia	36	2.0
France	32	2.0
W. Germany	31	2.0
Japan	28	2.0
India	24	2.0
Poland	20	1.0
Australia	18	1.0
Other	281	17.0
World Total	1,664	100.0

Source: World Watch, July/August 1990, p. 29, from FAO, *Forest Products Yearbook 1988* (Rome: 1990).

★ 557 ★

Livestock Grazing on National Forest Lands

Year	Number grazed[1,2]		Receipts from grazing[4] (Thousands of dollars)
	Cattle and horses[3] (Thousands)	Sheep and goats (Thousands)	
1975	1,626	1,549	7,665
1976	1,690	1,750	10,909
1977	1,587	1,473	11,443
1978	1,557	1,284	11,037
1979	1,540	1,251	12,520
1980	1,521	1,328	15,849
1981	1,535	1,341	14,889
1982	1,562	1,340	12,426
1983	1,609	1,242	10,182
1984	1,521	1,129	9,617
1985	1,565	1,183	9,040
1986	1,491	1,168	8,617
1987	1,410	1,134	8,104

[Continued]

★ 557 ★

Livestock Grazing on National Forest Lands
[Continued]

Year	Number grazed[1,2]		Receipts from grazing[4] (Thousands of dollars)
	Cattle and horses[3] (Thousands)	Sheep and goats (Thousands)	
1988	1,387	1,051	8,737
1989	1,313	1,067	10,950

Source: Agricultural Conservation and Forestry Statistics, 1989, U.S. Government Printing Office, Washington, D.C., 1989, p. 463, from Forest Service *Notes:* 1. Data for 1975-76 are for authorized use; 1977-89 are number actually grazed. 2. Calendar years through 1976; fiscal years Oct. 1-Sept. 30 for 1977-89. 3. Beginning 1977 includes burros. 4. Fiscal years July 1-June 30 for 1975-76; Oct. 1-Sept. 30 for 1977-89.

★ 558 ★

Lumber Production in the U.S.
Values are shown in millions of board feet for fiscal years 1975-89.

Year	Total	Softwoods	Hardwoods
1975	32,619	26,747	5,872
1976	36,997	30,571	6,427
1977	39,362	32,661	6,701
1978	40,498	33,467	7,031
1979	40,569	33,255	7,314
1980	35,354	28,239	7,115
1981	31,672	25,420	6,252
1982	30,010	24,949	5,061
1983	34,553	28,926	5,627
1984	37,065	30,801	6,264
1985	36,445	30,479	5,966
1986	41,999	34,815	7,184
1987	44,886	37,410	7,476
1988	44,576	36,845	7,731
1989[1]	43,576	36,040	7,536

Source: Agricultural Conservation and Forestry Statistics, 1989, U.S. Government Printing Office, Washington, D.C., 1989, p. 458, from Forest Service *Note:* 1. Preliminary.

★ 559 ★

National Forests - Assets & Revenues

Data show the value of resources in the national forests of the U.S. ($3.4 billion) and the revenues the national forests generate ($1.1 billion).

	Potential Value (Annual total $3.4 billion) (percent)	Receipts (Annual total $1.1 billion) (percent)
Fish and Wildlife	12	0
Grazing	1	1
Minerals	17	14
Recreation	41	3
Timber	27	82
Water	2	0

Source: The Economist, June 22, 1991, p. 23, from U.S. Forest Service.

★ 560 ★

Paper Production

Paper products that can be produced from one cord of wood. A cord is approximately 44 trees, 40 to 50 feet high, and five to six inches in diameter, yielding approximately 4,400 pounds of paper.

Product	Amount
Personal checks	460,000
Sheets of letterhead bond	89,000
No. 10 envelopes	61,370
1-gallon milk cartons	4,000
Issues of National Geographic	1,200
Hardback copies of Spycatcher by Peter Wright	603
Copies of Sunday New York Times	250

Source: U.S. News & World Report, February 29, 1988, p. 75, from the American Forest Council.

★ 561 ★

Pulpwood Consumption in the U.S.

Year	Pulpwood consump-tion[1] (1,000 cords)[4]	Woodpulp production (1,000 tons)	Paper and board[2]		
			Production (1,000 tons)	Consumption or new supply[3] (1,000 tons)	Per capita consumption (in pounds)
1975	65,373	43,084	50,738	54,134	501
1976	72,011	47,721	57,788	61,739	566
1977	73,935	49,132	60,485	64,940	590
1978	74,170	50,020	61,917	68,045	611
1979	77,594	51,177	64,023	69,940	621
1980	79,703	52,958	63,865	67,969	597
1981	79,350	52,790	64,582	68,793	598
1982	77,573	50,986	60,958	65,205	561
1983	83,493	54,055	66,761	71,611	610
1984	86,948	57,747	70,268	77,305	652
1985	84,840	57,693	68,658	76,316	638
1986	91,083	60,562	72,475	79,861	661
1987	92,386	62,392	75,908	83,764	687
1988	95,263	64,130	77,993	85,796	697
1989[5]	96,067	64,625	[6]	[6]	[6]

Source: Agricultural Conservation and Forestry Statistics, 1989, U.S. Government Printing Office, Washington, D.C., 1989, p. 465, from Forest Service compiled from U.S. Department of Commerce and American Paper Institute publications. *Notes:* 1. Includes changes in stocks. 2. Excludes hardboard 3. Production plus imports and minus exports (excludes products); changes in inventories not taken into account. 4. One cord equals 128 cubic feet. 5. Preliminary. 6. Not available.

★ 562 ★

Sawn Wood Consumption Worldwide

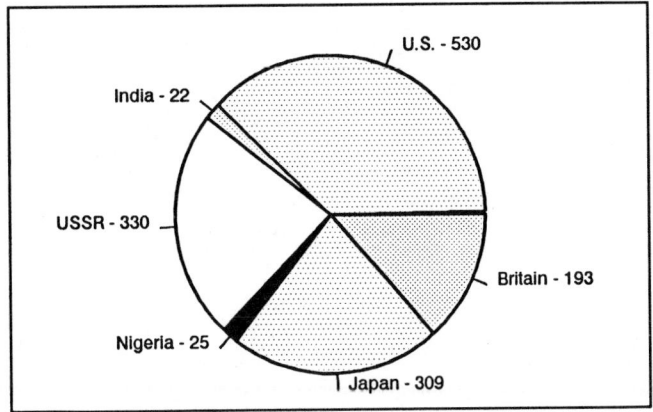

Annual consumption of sawn wood in selected countries. Data are shown in cubic meters per 1,000 people.

Country	Annual consumption
Nigeria	25
India	22
USSR	330
Britain	193
Japan	309
U.S.	530

Source: The Christian Science Monitor, March 15, 1991, p. 8, from Shell Briefing Service.

★ 563 ★

Sawtimber by Region

Data are shown in millions of board feet, as of January 1, 1987.

Region	Growing stock[1]			Sawtimber[2]		
	All species	Softwoods	Hardwoods	All species	Softwoods	Hardwoods
Northeast	109,135	31,391	77,744	252,183	80,476	171,707
North Central	77,905	16,009	61,896	207,088	45,255	161,833
Great Plains	3,380	1,912	1,468	11,742	6,807	4,935
North	190,420	49,312	141,108	471,013	132,538	338,475
Southeast	114,166	50,804	63,362	169,086	352,538	183,452
South Central	123,868	52,994	70,874	404,624	211,053	193,571
South	238,034	103,798	134,236	757,162	380,139	377,023

[Continued]

★ 563 ★

Sawtimber by Region
[Continued]

Region	Growing stock[1]			Sawtimber[2]		
	All species	Softwoods	Hardwoods	All species	Softwoods	Hardwoods
Pacific Northwest[3]	168,831	153,074	15,757	888,736	842,838	45,898
Pacific Southwest[4]	54,051	46,311	7,740	313,163	289,193	23,970
Rocky Mountains	104,599	98,386	6,213	399,196	386,904	12,292
West	327,481	297,771	29,710	1,601,095	1,518,935	82,160
All regions	755,935	450,881	305,054	2,829,270	2,031,612	797,658

Source: Agricultural Conservation and Forestry Statistics, 1989, U.S. Government Printing Office, Washington, D.C., 1989, p. 454, from Forest Service. *Notes:* Data may not add to totals because of rounding. 1. Live trees of commercial species meeting specified standards of quality or vigor. Cull trees are excluded. Includes only trees 5.0 inches diameter or larger at 4-1/2 feet above ground. 2. Live trees of commercial species containing at least one 12-foot sawlog or two noncontiguous 8-foot logs, and meeting regional specifications for freedom from defect. Softwood trees must be at least 9.0 inches diameter and hardwood trees must be at least 11.0 inches diameter at 4-1/2 feet above ground. 3. Includes Alaska. 4. Includes Hawaii.

★ 564 ★

Sawtimber in the East by Region
Values are shown in millions of board feet as of January 1, 1987.[1]

Species	Total East	North				South		
		Total	Northeast	North Central	Great Plains	Total	Southeast	South Central
Softwoods:								
Longleaf and slash pines	54,258	-	-	-	-	54,258	36,497	17,761
Loblolly and shortleaf pines	271,257	3,976	1,985	1,991	-	267,281	92,866	174,415
Other yellow pines	28,465	3,065	2,556	509	-	25,400	17,407	7,993
White and red pines	48,627	41,697	26,916	14,781	-	6,930	5,997	933
Jack pine	3,854	3,854	-	3,846	8	-	-	-
Spruce and balsam fir	37,773	37,699	26,099	11,362	238	74	74	-
Eastern hemlock	22,992	20,932	16,746	4,186	-	2,060	1,593	467
Cypress	22,112	157	-	157	-	21,955	13,778	8,177
Other	23,354	21,177	6,185	8,426	6,566	2,177	877	1,300
Total	512,692	132,557	80,487	45,258	6,812	380,135	169,089	211,046
Hardwoods:								
Select white oaks	71,577	31,501	10,461	20,371	669	40,076	18,273	21,803
Select red oaks	63,517	39,798	23,003	16,566	229	23,719	10,014	13,705
Other white oaks	47,075	13,806	9,585	4,182	39	33,269	15,553	17,716
Other red oaks	109,528	30,669	13,688	16,878	103	78,859	33,435	45,424
Hickory	40,616	12,751	4,956	7,680	115	27,865	9,432	18,433
Yellow birch	8,796	8,603	6,506	2,097	-	193	153	40
Hard maple	41,300	38,364	22,602	15,755	7	2,936	989	1,947
Soft maple	47,863	34,538	22,571	11,830	137	13,325	10,296	3,029
Beech	21,202	14,182	11,202	2,980	-	7,020	2,614	4,406
Sweetgum	39,571	1,556	1,141	415	-	38,015	18,563	19,452
Tupelo and black gum	30,960	1,243	967	276	-	29,717	20,098	9,619
Ash	26,142	16,104	7,814	7,837	453	10,038	4,288	5,750
Basswood	11,687	10,067	2,832	7,122	113	1,620	885	735
Yellow-poplar	52,949	12,611	8,462	4,149	-	40,338	28,136	12,202
Cottonwood and aspen	32,567	29,511	4,997	22,777	1,737	3,056	389	2,667
Black walnut	3,457	2,467	473	1,792	202	990	401	589

[Continued]

★ 564 ★

Sawtimber in the East by Region
[Continued]

Species	Total East	North				South		
		Total	Northeast	North Central	Great Plains	Total	Southeast	South Central
Black cherry	11,587	11,259	8,914	2,340	5	328	328	-
Other	55,123	29,475	11,544	16,800	1,131	25,648	9,601	16,047
Total	715,517	338,505	171,718	161,847	4,940	377,012	183,448	193,564
All species	1,228,209	471,062	252,205	207,105	11,752	757,147	352,537	404,610

Source: Agricultural Conservation and Forestry Statistics, 1989, U.S. Government Printing Office, Washington, D.C., 1989, p. 457, from Forest Service
Notes: 1. International 1/4-inch rule. Data may not add to totals because of rounding.

★ 565 ★

Sawtimber in the West by Species
Data are shown in millions of board feet, as of January 1, 1987.[1]

Species	Total West	Pacific Northwest[2]	Pacific Southwest[3]	Rocky Mountains
Softwoods:				
Douglas-fir	510,030	333,959	80,131	95,940
Ponderosa and Jeffrey pines	188,277	62,869	55,481	69,927
True fir	208,756	73,550	78,898	56,308
Western hemlock	195,902	192,080	206	3,616
Sugar pine	24,000	3,274	20,708	18
Western white pine	14,330	4,417	2,180	7,733
Redwood	30,504	583	29,921	-
Sitka spruce	65,390	65,190	200	-
Engelmann and other spruces	93,489	30,181	89	63,219
Western larch	34,388	12,386	-	22,002
Incense cedar	24,204	10,596	13,589	19
Lodgepole pine	76,280	15,604	5,260	55,416
Other	53,412	38,173	2,526	12,713
Total	1,518,962	842,862	289,189	386,911
Hardwoods:				
Cottonwood and aspen	19,604	7,292	74	12,238
Red alder	26,500	26,100	400	-
Oak	18,666	1,196	17,470	-
Other	17,397	11,320	6,025	52

[Continued]

★ 565 ★

Sawtimber in the West by Species
[Continued]

Species	Total West	Pacific Northwest[2]	Pacific Southwest[3]	Rocky Mountains
Total	82,167	45,908	23,969	12,290
All species	1,601,129	888,770	313,158	399,201

Source: *Agricultural Conservation and Forestry Statistics, 1989*, U.S. Government Printing Office, Washington, D.C., 1989, p. 455, from Forest Service. Data may not add to totals because of rounding. *Notes:* 1. International 1/4 inch rule. 2. Includes Alaska. Estimates of hardwood volume are not available for most National Forests in Oregon and Washington. 3. Includes Hawaii.

★ 566 ★

Timber Production, Imports, Exports, and Consumption in the U.S. - I
Values are shown in millions of cubic feet for the fiscal years 1975-88..

Year	Industrial roundwood used for											
	Lumber				Plywood and veneer				Pulp products			
	Production	Imports	Exports	Consumption	Production	Imports	Exports	Consumption	Production	Imports[2]	Exports[2]	Consumption
1975	4,890	930	255	5,565	1,165	170	70	1,265	3,485	1,105	715	3,875
1976	5,585	1,290	290	6,585	1,355	215	65	1,500	3,805	1,320	710	4,415
1977	5,950	1,675	260	7,365	1,425	210	35	1,600	3,645	1,395	725	4,320
1978	6,155	1,910	275	7,790	1,460	230	40	1,650	3,745	1,595	720	4,625
1979	6,115	1,800	340	7,580	1,370	195	45	1,520	4,110	1,635	805	4,935
1980	5,300	1,540	395	6,450	1,175	120	45	1,250	4,390	1,565	1,070	4,885
1981	4,780	1,490	380	5,885	1,180	140	70	1,250	4,125	1,515	995	4,645
1982	4,635	1,460	320	5,780	1,135	115	50	1,200	3,980	1,415	900	4,495
1983	5,370	1,915	360	6,925	1,365	160	65	1,460	4,165	1,605	965	4,805
1984	5,770	2,130	340	7,560	1,400	145	45	1,500	4,355	1,860	930	5,290
1985	5,665	2,345	305	7,700	1,420	165	40	1,550	4,165	1,810	920	5,055
1986	6,545	2,285	385	8,445	1,505	185	65	1,625	4,545	1,895	1,080	5,360
1987	6,990	2,380	510	8,860	1,650	190	80	1,760	4,670	1,985	1,195	5,465
1988[4]	6,920	2,225	720	8,425	1,630	165	100	1,695	4,885	2,045	1,345	5,585

Source: *Agricultural Conservation and Forestry Statistics, 1989*, U.S. Government Printing Office, Washington, D.C., 1989, p. 461, from Forest Service. *Notes:* 1. Data may not add to totals because of rounding. 2. Includes both pulpwood and the pulpwood equivalent of woodpulp, paper, and board. 3. Includes cooperage logs, poles and piling fence posts, hewn ties, round mine timbers, box bolts, excelsior bolts, chemical wood, shingle bolts, and miscellaneous items. 4. Preliminary.

★ 567 ★

Timber Production, Imports, Exports, and Consumption in the U.S. - II

The values are in million cubic feet for the fiscal years 1975-88.[1]

Year	Other industrial products[1] production and consumption	Logs		Pulpwood chip exports	Total				Fuelwood production and consumption	Production, all products	Consumption, all products
		Imports	Exports		Production	Imports	Exports	Consumption			
1975	385	15	455	195	10,575	2,215	1,685	11,105	570	11,145	11,675
1976	375	15	555	245	11,920	2,840	1,870	12,895	600	12,525	13,495
1977	385	30	525	250	12,185	3,310	1,800	13,700	1,000	13,185	14,700
1978	395	20	585	225	12,565	3,755	1,845	14,480	1,525	14,090	16,005
1979	405	25	670	280	12,950	3,655	2,135	14,465	2,205	15,155	16,670
1980	415	25	560	275	12,120	3,250	2,350	13,020	3,105	15,225	16,125
1981	425	20	425	220	11,150	3,165	2,090	12,225	3,180	14,330	15,405
1982	435	20	550	175	10,910	3,015	1,995	11,930	3,355	14,265	15,285
1983	445	30	565	155	12,065	3,710	2,110	13,665	3,235	15,300	16,900
1984	455	30	600	145	12,725	4,165	2,060	14,830	3,620	16,345	18,450
1985	465	20	655	145	12,515	4,340	2,070	14,785	3,450	15,965	18,235
1986	475	15	620	150	13,845	4,375	2,300	15,920	3,115	16,960	19,030
1987	495	15	705	160	14,670	4,575	2,650	16,595	3,150	17,820	19,745
1988[2]	510	15	825	215	14,985	4,445	3,200	16,230	3,360	18,345	19,590

Source: Agricultural Conservation and Forestry Statistics, 1989, U.S. Government Printing Office, Washington, D.C., 1989, p. 461, from Forest Service *Notes:* Data may not add to totals because of rounding. 1. Includes cooperage logs, poles and piling fence posts, hewn ties, round mine timbers, box bolts, excelsior bolts, chemical wood, shingle bolts, and miscellaneous items. 2. Preliminary.

★ 568 ★

U.S. Timberland by Ownership

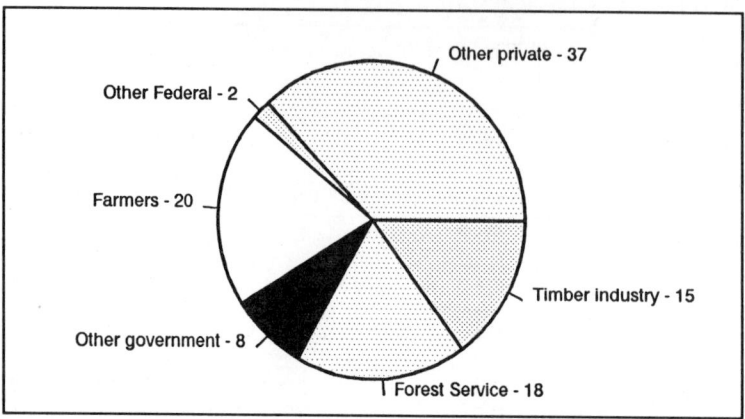

Percentages are based on a total of 196 million hectares of timberland in 1987.

Timberland Ownership	Percent
Farmers	20
Forest Service	18
Timber industry	15
Other private	37
Other Federal	2
Other government[1]	8

Source: Changing by Degrees: Steps to Reduce Greenhouse Gases, U.S. Congress, Office of Technology Assessment, OTA-O-482, Washington, D.C., February 1991, p. 209, from U.S. Forest Service, *An Analysis of the Land Situation in the United States: 1989-2040, A Technical Document Supporting the 1989 RPA Assessment*, General Technical Report RM-181 (Fort Collins, CO: U.S. Department of Agriculture, 1989); U.S. Forest Service, *An Analysis of the Timber Situation in the United States: 1989-2040, Part I: The Current Resource and Use Situation, Draft*, (Washington, DC: U.S. Department of Agriculture, 1989). *Notes:* 1. "Other government" refers to Bureau of Land Management, Native American, and State and local government lands.

★ 569 ★

U.S. Timberlands Reforestation by Ownership

Percentages are based on a total of 1.22 million intentionally planted hectares in 1989.

Ownership	Percent
Private nonindustry	43
Private industry	42
Federal Government	12
State and other government	3

Source: Changing by Degrees: Steps to Reduce Greenhouse Gases, U.S. Congress, Office of Technology Assessment, OTA-O-482, Washington, D.C., February 1991, p. 210, from U.S. Forest Service, *Report of the Forest Service, Fiscal Year 1989* (Washington, DC: U.S. Department of Agriculture, February 1990).

★ 570 ★

Visitor Days in National Forests by State in 1989

State or other area	Visitor Days[1] (thousands)
Alabama	686
Alaska	4,636
Arizona	18,998
Arkansas	2,377
California	63,685
Colorado	23,238
Florida	2,852
Georgia	2,715
Idaho	11,738
Illinois	950
Indiana	588
Kansas	48
Kentucky	2,327
Louisiana	513
Massachusetts	53
Michigan	4,725
Minnesota	5,148
Mississippi	1,237
Missouri	1,705
Montana	9,412
Nebraska	142
Nevada	3,082
New Hampshire	2,684
New Mexico	7,466
New York	22
North Carolina	5,036
North Dakota	184
Ohio	430
Oklahoma	341
Oregon	18,231
Pennsylvania	2,605
South Carolina	974
South Dakota	2,737
Tennessee	2,655
Texas	2,057
Utah	13,313
Vermont	1,352
Virginia	3,946
Washington	18,018
West Virginia	1,146
Wisconsin	1,979
Wyoming	6,068

[Continued]

★ 570 ★

Visitor Days in National Forests by State in 1989
[Continued]

State or other area	Visitor Days[1] (thousands)
Puerto Rico	396
Total[2]	252,495

Source: Agricultural Conservation and Forestry Statistics, 1989, U.S. Government Printing Office, Washington, D.C., 1989, p. 465, from Forest Service *Notes:* 1. Recreational use of national forest land and water that aggregates 12-hour visitors. This may entail one person for 12 hours, 12 persons for 1 hour, or any equivalent combination of individual or group use, either continuous or intermittent. Years ending September 30th. 2. Data may not add to total because of rounding.

★ 571 ★

Visitors to National Forests by Activity in 1989

1989 activity	Visitor Days[1] (thousands)	Percent
Mechanized travel and viewing scenery	81,266	32.2
Camping, picnicking, and swimming	72,263	28.6
Hiking, horseback riding and water travel	21,277	8.4
Winter sports	17,369	6.9
Hunting	16,053	6.4
Fishing	15,717	6.2
Resorts, cabins and organization camps	14,682	5.8
Nature studies	1,814	.7
Other[2]	12,054	4.8
Total[3]	252,495	100.0

Source: Agricultural Conservation and Forestry Statistics, 1989, U.S. Government Printing Office, Washington, D.C., 1989, p. 465, from Forest Service *Notes:* 1. Recreational use of national forest land and water that aggregates 12 visitor-hours. This may entail one person for 12 hours, 12 persons for 1 hour, or any equivalent combination of individual or group use, either continuous or intermittent. Years ending September 30th. 2. Includes team sports, gathering forest products, attending talks and programs, and other uses. 3. Data may not add to total because of rounding.

★ 572 ★

Visitors to National Forests by Year

Year and activity	Visitor Days[1] (thousands)
1981	235,709
1982	233,438
1983	227,708
1984	227,554
1985	225,407
1986	226,533
1987	238,458
1988	242,316

Source: Agricultural Conservation and Forestry Statistics, 1989, U.S. Government Printing Office, Washington, D.C., 1989, p. 465, from Forest Service *Notes:* 1. Recreational use of national forest land and water that aggregates 12 visitor-hours. This may entail one person for 12 hours, 12 persons for 1 hour, or any equivalent combination of individual or group use, either continuous or intermittent. Years ending September 30th.

Government

★ 573 ★

Computer Use in Local Government

Responses to the *American City & Country 1988 Annual Survey of Issues and Trends.*

Respondent	Total responses	Micro (%)	Mini (%)	Mainframe (%)
Building Maintenance/Security	49	49	27	24
Financial Planning/Budgeting	288	34	33	33
Fleet Management	96	47	29	24
Mapping/Engineering	86	60	27	13
Parks & Recreation	95	51	33	17
Personnel & Payroll	253	26	32	42
Police/Fire Services	182	40	35	25
Public Transit	21	52	38	10
Scheduling	35	57	29	14
Solid-Waste Collection/Disposal	54	46	22	31
Street Maintenance	76	50	24	26
Tax Records	140	21	31	49
Traffic Engineering/Control	70	56	23	21
Utility Billing/Maintenance	202	24	37	39

[Continued]

★ 573 ★

Computer Use in Local Government
[Continued]

Respondent	Total responses	Micro (%)	Mini (%)	Mainframe (%)
Water/Wastewater Operations	115	50	27	23
Word Processing	241	56	30	19
Other	39	31	44	25

Source: American City & County, July 1988, p. 36.

★ 574 ★

Weapons Complex Facilities

Type of facility	Facility	Location (State)	Size (Square miles)	Management and operations contractor	Approximate current employment
Weapons research and design	Los Alamos National Laboratory	NM	75.0	Univ. of California	7,400
	Sandia National Laboratory	NM	62.0	AT&T	8,500
	Lawrence-Livermore National Laboratory	CA	12.0	Univ. of California	8,500
Materials production	Hanford Plant	WA	570.0	Westinghouse	13,500
	Savannah River Site	SC	300.0	Westinghouse	20,000
	Fernald	OH	0.20	Westinghouse	1,000
	Idaho National Engineering Laboratory	ID	893.0	EG&G/ Westinghouse	10,500
Weapons manufacturing	Rocky Flats Plant	CO	14.0	EG&G	6,000
	Oak Ridge Reservation	TN	58.0	Martin-Marietta	16,500
	Mound Plant	OH	0.30	EG&G	2,400
	Pinellas Plant	FL	0.20	General Electric	2,000
	Kansas City Plant	MO	0.50	Allied Signal Corp.	7,800
	Pantex Plant	TX	14.0	Mason & Hanger-Silas	2,800

[Continued]

★ 574 ★

Weapons Complex Facilities

[Continued]

Type of facility	Facility	Location (State)	Size (Square miles)	Management and operations contractor	Approximate current employment
Warhead testing	Nevada Test Site	NV	1,350.0	Reynolds Electric	8,400
Waste disposal	Waste Isolation Pilot Plant	NM	16.0	Westinghouse	650

Source: Complex Cleanup: The Environmental Legacy of Nuclear Weapons Production, U.S. Congress, Office of Technology Assessment, OTA-O-484, Washington, D.C., February 1991, pp. 16-17, from U.S. Department of Energy.

Metals

★ 575 ★

Cadmium Demand by End Use

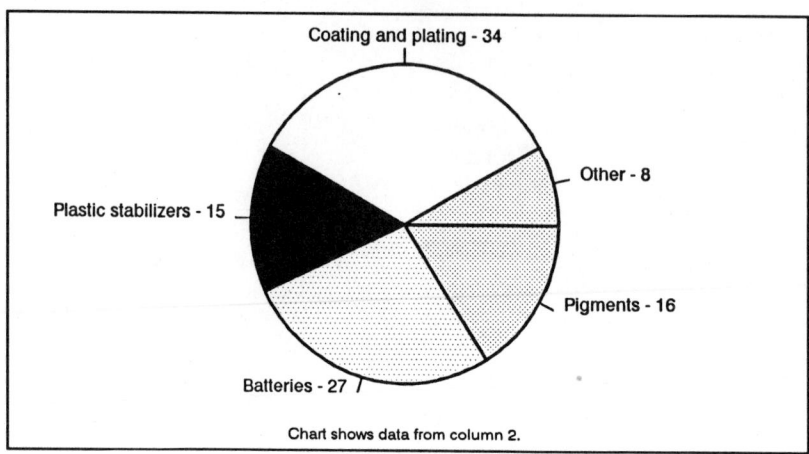

Chart shows data from column 2.

Data, for 1983, show distribution of cadmium by end use in tons and percent.

End use	Tons	Percent
Coating and plating	1,410	34
Batteries	1,120	27
Pigments	660	16
Plastic stabilizers	620	15
Other	330	8

Source: Facing America's Trash: What Next for Municipal Solid Waste, U.S. Congress, Office of Technology Assessment, OTA-O-412, Washington, D.C., July 1989., p. 102, from U.S. Department of the Interior, Bureau of Mines, *Mineral Facts and Problems 1985 Edition*, Bulletin 675 (Washington, DC: 1985); U.S. Department of the Interior, Bureau of Mines, *Minerals Yearbook* (Washington, DC: 1986).

★ 576 ★

Cadmium in Products

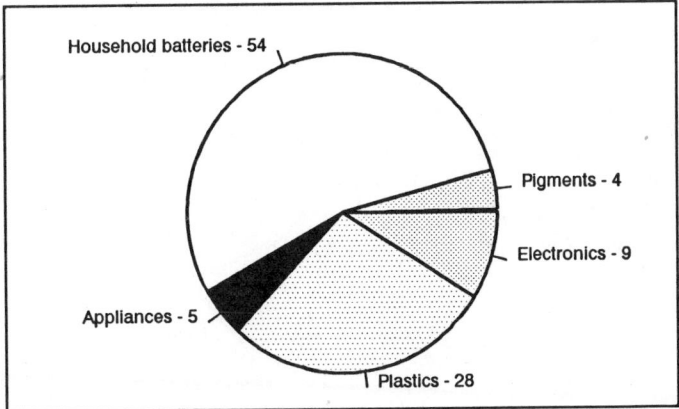

Distribution of cadmium in products that reach the municipal solid waste stream.

	Percent of total cadmium
Household batteries	54
Plastics	28
Electronics	9
Appliances	5
Pigments	4

Source: Facing America's Trash: What Next for Municipal Solid Waste, U.S. Congress, Office of Technology Assessment, OTA-O-412, Washington, D.C., July 1989., p. 103, from Franklin Associates, Ltd., *Characterization of Products Containing Lead and Cadmium in Municipal Solid Waste in the United States, 1970 to 2000, Executive Summary and Chapter 1,* Final report prepared for the U.S. Environmental Protection Agency, Municipal Solid Waste Program (Prairie Village, KS: January 1989).

★ 577 ★

Lead Demand by End Use

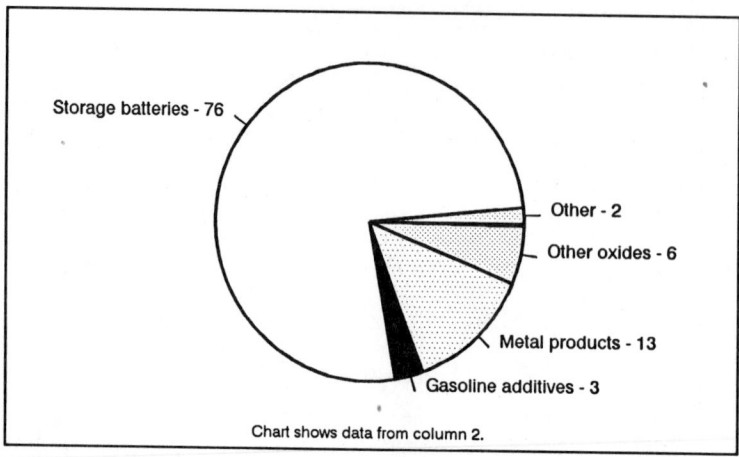

Chart shows data from column 2.

Data, for 1986, show distribution of lead by end use in tons and percent.

End use	Tons	Percent
Storage batteries	940,899	76
Metal products	160,949	13
Other oxides	76,619	6
Gasoline additives	31,452	3
Other	29,663	2

Source: Facing America's Trash: What Next for Municipal Solid Waste, U.S. Congress, Office of Technology Assessment, OTA-O-412, Washington, D.C., July 1989., p. 102, from U.S. Department of the Interior, Bureau of Mines, *Mineral Facts and Problems 1985 Edition*, Bulletin 675 (Washington, DC: 1985); U.S. Department of the Interior, Bureau of Mines, *Minerals Yearbook* (Washington, DC: 1986).

★ 578 ★

Lead in Products

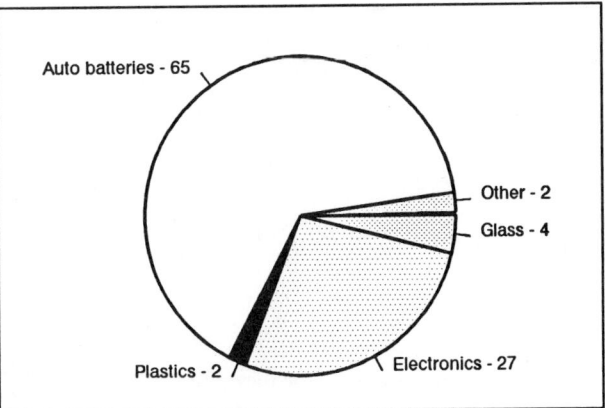

Distribution of lead in products that reach the municipal solid waste stream.

	Percent of total lead
Auto batteries	65
Electronics	27
Glass	4
Plastics	2
Other	2

Source: Facing America's Trash: What Next for Municipal Solid Waste, U.S. Congress, Office of Technology Assessment, OTA-O-412, Washington, D.C., July 1989., p. 103, from Franklin Associates, Ltd., *Characterization of Products Containing Lead and Cadmium in Municipal Solid Waste in the United States, 1970 to 2000, Executive Summary and Chapter 1*, Final report prepared for the U.S. Environmental Protection Agency, Municipal Solid Waste Program (Prairie Village, KS: January 1989).

★ 579 ★

Mercury Demand by End Use

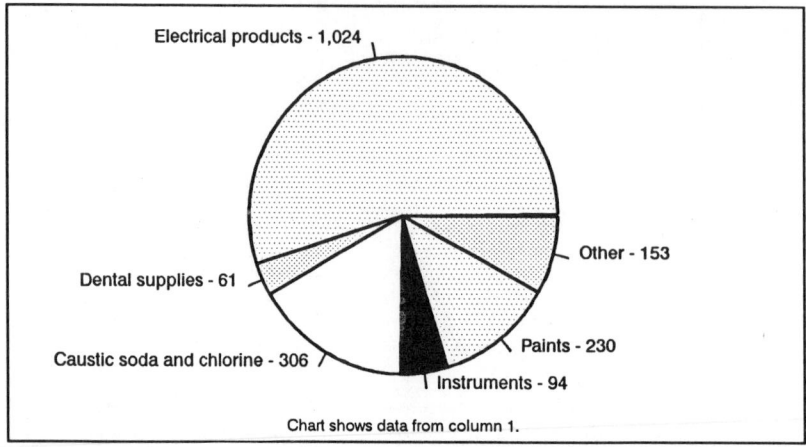

Chart shows data from column 1.

Data, for 1983, show distribution of mercury by end use in tons and percent.

End use	Tons	Percent
Electrical products	1,024	55
Caustic soda and chlorine	306	16
Paints	230	12
Instruments	94	5
Dental supplies	61	3
Other	153	8

Source: Facing America's Trash: What Next for Municipal Solid Waste, U.S. Congress, Office of Technology Assessment, OTA-O-412, Washington, D.C., July 1989., p. 102, from U.S. Department of the Interior, Bureau of Mines, *Mineral Facts and Problems 1985 Edition*, Bulletin 675 (Washington, DC: 1985); U.S. Department of the Interior, Bureau of Mines, *Minerals Yearbook* (Washington, DC: 1986).

Nuclear Weapons

★ 580 ★

Naval Nuclear Reactors Worldwide

Number of nuclear reactors on different types of naval vessels possessed by the five nuclear powers in 1990.

Nuclear-powered ship types	U.S.	Soviet	U.K.	France	China	Total
Ballistic missile submarines	33	122	4	6	2	167
Cruise missile submarines	0	78	0	0	0	78
Attack submarines	92	149	16	4	3	265
Aircraft carriers	18	0	0	0	0	18

[Continued]

★ 580 ★

Naval Nuclear Reactors Worldwide
[Continued]

Nuclear-powered ship types	U.S.	Soviet	U.K.	France	China	Total
Cruisers	18	6	0	0	0	24
Other	1	22	0	0	0	23
Total	162	377	20	10	5	575

Source: The Bulletin of the Atomic Scientists, September 1990, p. 49, adapted from Joshua Handler and William M. Arkin, Nuclear Warships and Naval Nuclear Weapons: A Complete Inventory, Neptune Paper No. 5 (Washington, D.C.: Greenpeace, 1990); Nuclear Weapons Databook Vol. IV: Soviet Nuclear Forces (1989); and Nuclear Weapons Databook Vol. I: U.S. Forces and Capabilities (forthcoming) *Notes:* 1. Reflects improved estimates, not increases or reductions from last year. 2. Totals may not add up due to rounding.

★ 581 ★

Naval Nuclear Weapons Worldwide

Nuclear warheads possessed by the naval forces of the five nuclear powers in 1990, shown by type.

Types of weapons	U.S.	Soviet	U.K.	France	China	Total
Strategic missile warheads	5,024	3,802	96[1]	416	26	9,400[2]
Nonstrategic warheads						
Cruise missiles	325	570	0	0	0	895
Aircraft bombs	1,350	450[1]	25	36	0[1]	1,861
Antisubmarine weapons	825	1,300	25	0	0	2,150
Anti-air weapons	0	188	0	0	0	188
Coastal missiles	0	100	0	0	0	100
Subtotal	2,500	2,608	50	36	0	5,200
Total	7,524	6,410	146	462	26	14,600

Source: The Bulletin of the Atomic Scientists, September 1990, p. 49, adapted from Joshua Handler and William M. Arkin, Nuclear Warships and Naval Nuclear Weapons: A Complete Inventory, Neptune Paper No. 5 (Washington, D.C.: Greenpeace, 1990); Nuclear Weapons Databook Vol. IV: Soviet Nuclear Forces (1989); and Nuclear Weapons Databook Vol. I: U.S. Forces and Capabilities (forthcoming) *Notes:* 1. Reflects improved estimates, not increases or reductions from last year. 2. Totals may not add up due to rounding.

★ 582 ★

Nuclear-Capable Naval Vessels Worldwide

Number of nuclear-capable ships and submarines possessed by the five nuclear powers in 1990.

Nuclear-capable ships and submarines	U.S.	Soviet	U.K.	France	China	Total
Submarines						
Ballistic missile	33	61	4	6	2	106
Cruise missile	0	60	0	0	0	60
Attack	50	178	0	0	0	228
Total submarines	83	299	4	6	2	394
Surface ships						
Aircraft carriers	19	4	3	2	0	28
Battleships	4	0	0	0	0	4
Cruisers	16	33	0	0	0	49
Destroyers	16	37	12	0	0	133
Frigates	0	118	15	0	0	133
Patrol combatants	0	74	0	0	0	74
Total surface ships	55	266	30	2	0	353
Total submarines and shipe	138	565	34	8	2	747

Source: The Bulletin of the Atomic Scientists, September 1990, p. 49, adapted from Joshua Handler and William M. Arkin, Nuclear Warships and Naval Nuclear Weapons: A Complete Inventory, Neptune Paper No. 5 (Washington, D.C.: Greenpeace, 1990); Nuclear Weapons Databook Vol. IV: Soviet Nuclear Forces (1989); and Nuclear Weapons Databook Vol. I: U.S. Forces and Capabilities (forthcoming) *Notes:* 1. Reflects improved estimates, not increases or reductions from last year. 2. Totals may not add up due to rounding.

Oil and Gas

★ 583 ★

Domestic Motor Fuel Consumption

Year	Fuel Consumption					Average Fuel Consumption per Vehicle (gal)				Average Mileage per Gallon			
	All vehicles (bill.gal)	Average annual percent change[1]	Cars[2] (bill.gal)	Buses[3] (bill.gal)	Trucks[4] (bill.gal)	All vehicles	Cars[2]	Buses[3]	Trucks[4]	All vehicles	Cars[2]	Buses[3]	Trucks[4]
1978	125.1	4.5	81.7	1.0	42.3	816	701	1957	1349	12.35	14.04	5.95	9.11
1979	122.1	-2.4	77.3	1.0	43.6	776	653	1891	1326	12.52	14.41	5.97	9.19
1980	115.0	-5.9	71.9	1.0	41.9	712	591	1926	1243	13.29	15.46	5.95	9.54
1981	114.5	-.4	71.0	1.1	42.2	697	576	1938	1219	13.57	15.94	5.92	9.59
1982	113.4	-.9	70.1	1.0	42.1	686	566	1756	1191	14.07	16.65	5.93	9.80
1983	116.1	2.4	69.9	.9	45.1	686	553	1507	1229	14.24	17.14	5.92	9.77
1984	118.7	2.3	68.7	.8	49.0	691	536	1359	1308	14.49	17.83	5.85	9.83

[Continued]

★ 583 ★

Domestic Motor Fuel Consumption

[Continued]

Year	Fuel Consumption					Average Fuel Consumption per Vehicle (gal)				Average Mileage per Gallon			
	All vehicles (bill.gal)	Average annual percent change[1]	Cars[2] (bill.gal)	Buses[3] (bill.gal)	Trucks[4] (bill.gal)	All vehicles	Cars[2]	Buses[3]	Trucks[4]	All vehicles	Cars[2]	Buses[3]	Trucks[4]
1985	121.3	2.2	69.3	.8	51.0	685	525	1407	1302	14.62	18.20	5.84	9.79
1986	125.2	3.2	71.4	.9	52.9	690	526	1463	1320	14.66	18.27	5.84	9.81
1987	127.7	2.0	71.0	.9	55.9	695	515	1502	1359	15.06	19.17	5.89	9.88

Source: U.S. Department of Commerce, Bureau of the Census, *Statistical Abstract of the United States 1990 (110th ed.)*, Superintendent of Documents, Washington, D.C., p. 610, from U.S. Federal Highway Administration, *Highway Statistics Summary to 1985*, and *Highway Statistics*, annual. Motor fuel comprises all fuels (gas, diesel, or other fuels) used for propulsion of vehicles under State motor fuels laws. Excludes Federal purchases for military use. See also *Historical Statistics, Colonial Times to 1970*, series Q 156-162. *Notes:* 1. From prior year, except 1970, change from 1965. 2. Includes taxicabs. 3. Includes school buses. 4. Includes combinations. - Indicates decrease.

★ 584 ★

Ethanol Use by State

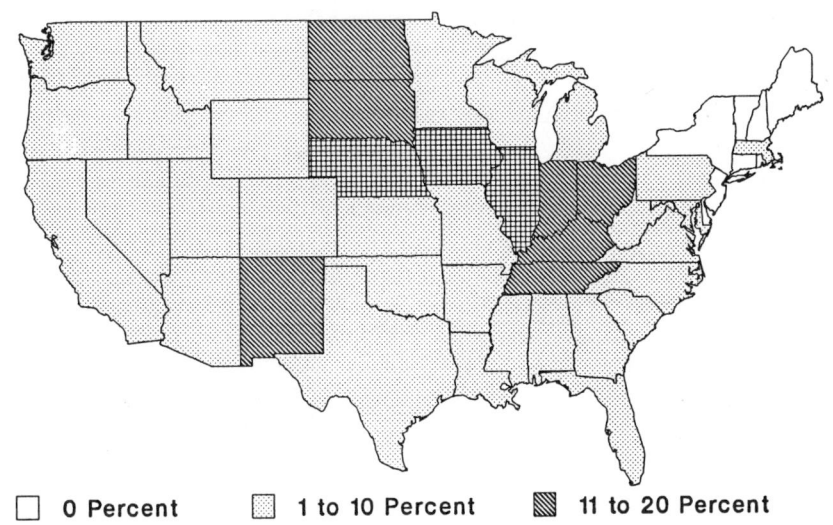

□ 0 Percent   ▦ 1 to 10 Percent   ▨ 11 to 20 Percent

▦ 21 to 35 Percent

Source: Farm Journal, August 1990, p. 28, from American Coalition for Ethanol, 1989. *Note:* Data are based on sales of gasoline blended with 10 percent ethanol.

★ 585 ★

Fossil Fuel Consumption and Stocks

Item	1989	1988	1987	1986	1985
Consumption					
Coal (thousand short tons)	766,888	758,372	717,894	685,056	693,841
Petroleum (thousand barrels)[1]	267,451	248,096	199,378	230,482	173,414
Gas (million cubic feet)	2,787,012	2,635,613	2,844,051	2,602,370	3,044,083
Stocks[2]					
Coal (thousand short tons)	135,860	146,507	170,797	161,806	156,376
Petroleum (thousand barrels)[1]	61,270	69,285	70,827	73,111	73,689

Source: Electric Power Annual 1989, Energy Information Administration, Office of Coal, Nuclear, Electric, and Alternate Fuels, U.S. Department of Energy, DOE/EIA-0348(89), Washington, D.C., January 1991, p. 45, from Energy Information Administration, Form EIA-759, "Monthly Power Plant Report." Totals may not equal sum of components because of independent rounding. *Notes:* 1. Does not include petroleum coke. 2. Stocks are shown as of December 31 of each year.

★ 586 ★

Gasohol Use on Highways
Values show gasohol as a percent of highway use gasoline in 1989.

State	Percent
Nebraska	37.00
Iowa	29.38
Illinois	26.45
Indiana	23.75
Kentucky	22.53
New Mexico	21.83
Ohio	19.33
South Dakota	15.74
Tennessee	14.96
Idaho	14.58
North Dakota	11.90
Michigan	9.62
Alabama	9.51
Minnesota	8.72
Virginia	8.53
Kansas	8.06
Nevada	6.12
Missouri	5.91
Colorado	4.77
South Carolina	4.75
Washington	2.87
California	2.85
Louisiana	2.76

[Continued]

★ 586 ★

Gasohol Use on Highways
[Continued]

State	Percent
Texas	2.60
Wisconsin	2.36
Florida	1.33
Wyoming	0.89
Georgia	0.87
District of Columbia	0.19
Utah	0.07
Montana	0.02
Alaska	0.01

Source: Highway Statistics 1989, U.S. Department of Transportation, Federal Highway Administration, Washington, D.C., 1989, p. 14.

★ 587 ★

Gasoline Use by State in 1989

Values are shown in thousands of gallons.

State	Highway				Non-highway			Total
	Private and Commercial	Public		Total	Private and Commercial	State,County Municipal	Total	Total
		Federal	State,County Municipal					
Alabama	2,025,266	3,370	28,640	2,057,276	52,413	9,547	61,960	2,119,236
Alaska	195,013	2,242	4,885	202,140	31,597	1,628	33,225	235,365
Arizona	1,677,140	6,083	16,469	1,699,692	39,370	5,490	44,860	1,744,552
Arkansas	1,205,031	1,893	13,833	1,220,757	34,976	4,611	39,587	1,260,344
California	12,721,883	29,427	224,759	12,976,069	281,698	74,920	356,618	13,332,687
Colorado	1,455,946	2,938	20,110	1,478,994	34,398	6,703	41,101	1,520,095
Connecticut	1,323,383	3,000	19,273	1,345,656	28,266	6,424	34,690	1,380,346
Delaware	331,208	566	4,582	336,356	11,204	1,527	12,731	349,087
District of Columbia	168,215	3,524	2,737	174,476	4,049	912	4,961	179,437
Florida	5,654,516	9,882	156,317	5,820,715	239,930	52,106	292,036	6,112,751
Georgia	3,410,905	5,061	49,748	3,465,714	96,128	16,583	112,711	3,578,425
Hawaii	355,676	1,177	6,635	363,488	19,043	2,212	21,255	384,743
Idaho	424,419	3,254	16,868	444,541	34,685	5,623	40,308	484,849
Illinois	4,772,918	7,080	53,142	4,833,140	92,870	17,714	110,584	4,943,724
Indiana	2,523,152	2,988	43,661	2,569,801	62,576	14,554	77,130	2,646,931
Iowa	1,282,643	2,027	29,090	1,313,760	72,395	9,697	82,092	1,395,852
Kansas	1,206,924	1,981	16,909	1,225,814	49,812	5,636	55,448	1,281,262
Kentucky	1,738,629	3,265	50,340	1,792,234	48,447	16,780	65,227	1,857,461
Louisiana	1,880,624	3,293	28,424	1,912,341	85,661	9,475	95,136	2,007,477
Maine	561,528	880	14,754	577,162	26,911	4,918	31,829	608,991
Maryland	2,005,954	4,926	20,350	2,031,230	63,865	6,783	70,648	2,101,878
Massachusetts	2,390,691	4,769	24,043	2,419,503	67,314	8,014	75,328	2,494,831
Michigan	4,097,647	5,601	82,925	4,186,173	117,563	27,642	145,205	4,331,378
Minnesota	1,926,789	3,138	24,470	1,954,397	118,784	8,157	126,941	2,081,338
Mississippi	1,171,532	2,587	17,546	1,191,665	48,189	5,849	54,038	1,245,703
Missouri	2,635,200	3,902	19,733	2,658,835	64,288	6,578	70,866	2,729,701
Montana	395,334	3,131	9,841	408,306	32,434	3,280	35,714	444,020
Nebraska	714,725	1,869	16,124	732,718	52,667	5,375	58,042	790,760
Nevada	595,185	4,421	10,421	610,027	13,434	3,474	16,908	626,935
New Hampshire	504,715	873	8,779	514,367	8,794	2,926	11,720	526,087

[Continued]

479

★ 587 ★

Gasoline Use by State in 1989
[Continued]

State	Highway				Non-highway			Total
	Private and Commercial	Public		Total	Private and Commercial	State,County Municipal	Total	Total
		Federal	State,County Municipal					
New Jersey	3,302,991	6,073	83,309	3,392,373	62,651	27,770	90,421	3,482,794
New Mexico	764,079	5,157	15,305	784,541	21,290	5,102	26,392	810,933
New York	5,456,140	13,592	71,185	5,540,917	141,737	23,728	165,465	5,706,382
North Carolina	3,137,723	3,693	75,304	3,216,720	89,825	25,101	114,926	3,331,646
North Dakota	309,912	1,445	7,813	319,170	38,196	2,604	40,800	359,970
Ohio	4,727,614	5,775	74,579	4,807,968	141,707	24,860	166,567	4,974,535
Oklahoma	1,548,065	3,370	40,054	1,591,489	62,840	13,351	76,191	1,667,680
Oregon	1,284,467	5,453	28,173	1,318,093	38,783	9,391	48,174	1,366,267
Pennsylvania	4,487,960	8,704	57,976	4,554,640	85,940	19,325	105,265	4,659,905
Rhode Island	360,762	651	4,854	366,267	12,958	1,618	14,576	380,843
South Carolina	1,707,586	3,525	26,374	1,737,485	80,310	8,791	89,101	1,826,586
South Dakota	347,994	1,842	9,260	359,096	31,019	3,087	34,106	,393,202
Tennessee	2,446,407	6,769	41,997	2,495,173	63,566	13,999	77,565	2,572,738
Texas	8,055,805	14,268	260,474	8,330,547	308,532	86,825	395,357	8,725,904
Utah	709,173	2,790	11,422	723,385	16,380	3,807	20,187	743,572
Vermont	265,386	416	4,658	270,460	8,641	1,553	10,194	280,654
Virginia	2,889,665	5,797	54,793	2,950,255	64,696	18,264	82,960	3,033,215
Washington	2,197,662	8,198	32,680	2,238,540	56,808	10,893	67,701	2,306,241
West Virginia	763,767	1,503	39,664	804,934	15,744	13,221	28,965	833,899
Wisconsin	1,977,544	2,954	34,120	2,014,618	77,881	11,373	89,254	2,103,872
Wyoming	228,536	1,744	8,155	298,435	23,310	2,718	26,028	324,463
Total	108,382,029	232,867	2,017,557	110,632,453	3,376,575	672,519	4,049,094	114,681,547

Source: Highway Statistics 1989, U.S. Department of Transportation, Federal Highway Administration, Washington, D.C., 1989, p. 6 Gasohol is included with gasoline. In order to make the data uniform and complete, non-highway uses of gasohol were estimated by the Federal Highway Administration or data were obtained from other sources.

★ 588 ★

Gasoline Use on Highways

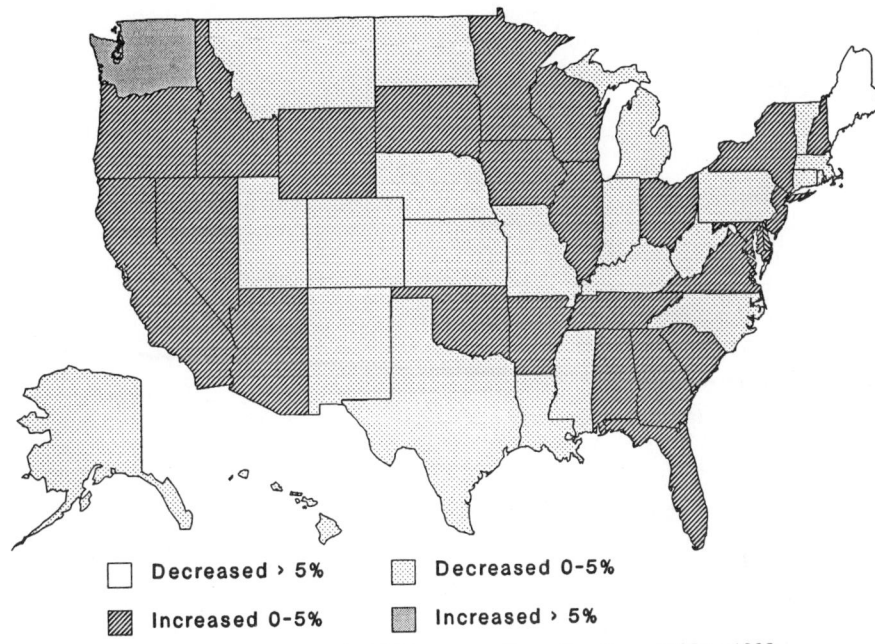

☐ Decreased › 5%	☐ Decreased 0-5%
▨ Increased 0-5%	▨ Increased › 5%

Values reflect percent change in highway use of gasoline from 1988 to 1989.

State	Percent change 1988-1989
Alabama	2.3
Alaska	-3.6
Arizona	2.1
Arkansas	0.9
California	3.3
Colorado	-1.8
Connecticut	-1.0
Delaware	-0.6
District of Columbia	-3.2
Florida	1.3
Georgia	0.9
Hawaii	4.2
Idaho	1.8
Illinois	0.6
Indiana	-2.9
Iowa	1.9
Kansas	-2.3
Kentucky	-0.7
Louisiana	-2.9
Maine	-7.4
Maryland	0.9
Massachusetts	-1.2
Michigan	-0.2

[Continued]

★ 588 ★

Gasoline Use on Highways
[Continued]

State	Percent change 1988-1989
Minnesota	0.6
Mississippi	-0.4
Missouri	-0.6
Montana	-0.9
Nebraska	0.0
Nevada	4.7
New Hampshire	0.6
New Jersey	0.9
New Mexico	-1.4
New York	3.2
North Carolina	-0.7
North Dakota	-0.4
Ohio	1.1
Oklahoma	1.0
Oregon	0.1
Pennsylvania	-0.7
Rhode Island	-3.7
South Carolina	0.3
South Dakota	0.4
Tennessee	2.2
Texas	-1.8
Utah	-3.7
Vermont	-2.8
Virginia	0.6
Washington	7.3
West Virginia	-0.5
Wisconsin	0.1
Wyoming	2.7

Source: Highway Statistics 1989, U.S. Department of Transportation, Federal Highway Administration, Washington, D.C., 1989, p. 12.

★ 589 ★

Natural Gas Resources, Consumption, and Trade Worldwide
Values shown are percentage shares of worldwide totals.

Country	Reserves 1989	Production 1989	Consumption 1989	Imports 1987	Exports 1987
U.S.S.R.	37.6	37.5	33.0	-	33.6
Iran	12.5	-	-	-	-
Abu Dhabi	4.6	-	-	-	-
Saudi Arabia	4.5	-	-	-	-

[Continued]

★ 589 ★

Natural Gas Resources, Consumption, and Trade Worldwide
[Continued]

Country	Reserves 1989	Production 1989	Consumption 1989	Imports 1987	Exports 1987
Qatar	4.1	-	-	-	-
United States	4.1	25.5	28.6	11.3	0.6
Algeria	2.9	2.3	-	-	9.8
Venezuela	2.5	-	-	-	-
Iraq	2.4	-	-	-	-
Canada	2.4	5.10	3.16	-	11.2
Netherlands	-	3.1	-	1.8	13.7
United Kingdom	-	2.2	2.6	4.9	-
Romania[1]	-	2.0	2.0	-	-
Indonesia	-	1.9	-	-	8.5
Norway	-	1.6	-	-	11.7
Mexico	-	1.3	-	-	-
West Germany	-	-	2.6	17.8	0.0
Japan	-	-	2.5	16.0	-
Italy	-	-	2.2	9.3	-
France	-	-	1.4	10.7	-
Belgium/Luxembourg	-	-	-	3.7	-
Poland	-	-	-	2.9	-
Czechoslovakia	-	-	-	2.9	-
East Germany	-	-	-	2.9	4.3
Malaysia	-	-	-	-	3.2
United Arab Emirates	-	-	-	-	1.2
Other	22.4	17.5	20.2	17.5	6.6
Total	100.0	100.0	100.0	100.0	100.0

Source: Changing by Degrees: Steps to Reduce Greenhouse Gases, U.S. Congress, Office of Technology Assessment, OTA-O-482, Washington, D.C., February 1991, p. 83, unless otherwise specified, data for resources/reserves/ production and consumption are from the British Petroleum Company, *BP Statistical Review of World Energy* (London, UK: British Petroleum, June 1990). Data on imports and exports are derived from U.S. Department of Energy, Energy Information Administration, *International Energy Annual, 1988* DOE/EIA-0219(88) (Washington, DC: November 1989). Approximately 13 percent of world natural gas production/consumption is traded internationally. *Notes:* 1. Romania's production and consumption are obtained from U.S. Department of Energy (1989).

★ 590 ★

Oil Consumption in the U.S.

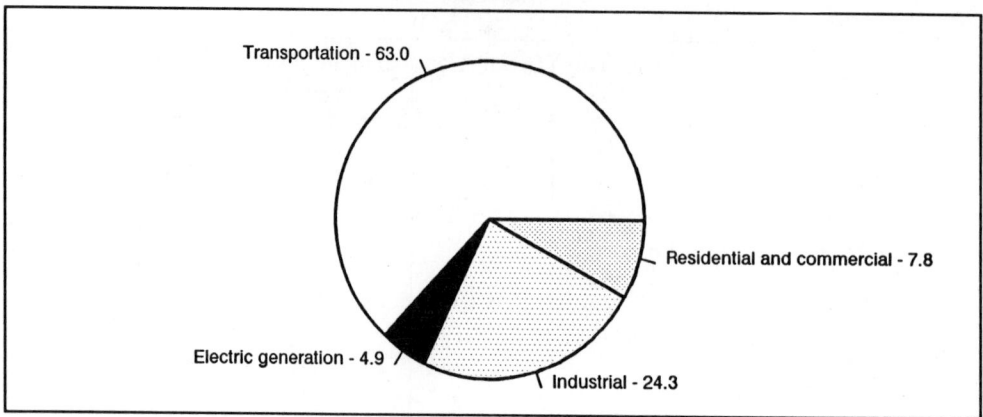

Figures shown are based on a total consumption of 17.3 million barrels per day in 1989.

Media	Percent consumed
Transportation	63.0
Industrial	24.3
Residential and commercial	7.8
Electric generation	4.9

Source: Business Week, August 27, 1990, p. 29, from American Petroleum Institute.

★ 591 ★

Oil Consumption in the U.S. by Fuel

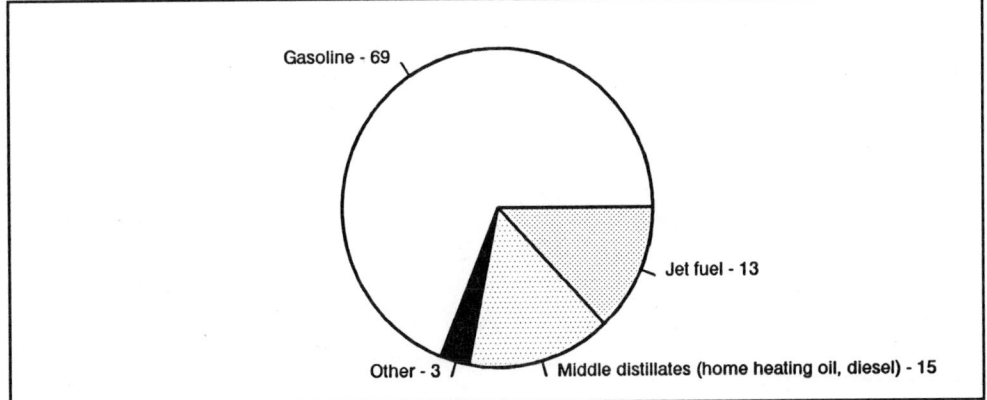

Values shown are percent shares of consumption by the transportation industry in 1988.

Fuel Type	Percent
Gasoline	69
Middle distillates (home heating oil, diesel)	15
Jet fuel	13
Other	3

Source: Business Week, August 27, 1990, p. 29, from American Petroleum Institute.

★ 592 ★

Petroleum Resources, Consumption, and Trade Worldwide

Values shown are percentage shares of worldwide totals.

Country	Reserves 1989	Production 1989	Consumption 1989	Imports 1987	Exports 1987
Saudi Arabia	25.2	8.3	-	-	10.5
Iraq	9.9	4.5	-	-	5.0
Kuwait	9.3	-	-	-	4.4
Iran	9.2	4.6	-	-	4.8
Abu Dhabi	9.1	-	-	-	-
U.S.S.R.	5.8	19.7	14.0	-	10.8
Venezuela	5.8	3.2	-	-	4.2
Mexico	5.6	4.6	-	-	4.0
United States	3.4	14.0	25.6	18.5	-
Libya	2.3	-	-	-	-
United Kingdom	-	3.0	2.6	2.8	5.7
Canada	-	2.6	2.5	-	-
Japan	-	-	7.5	12.5	-
China	-	-	3.8	-	-

[Continued]

★ 592 ★

Petroleum Resources, Consumption, and Trade Worldwide
[Continued]

Country	Reserves 1989	Production 1989	Consumption 1989	Imports 1987	Exports 1987
West Germany	-	-	3.5	6.5	-
Italy	-	-	3.0	5.6	-
France	-	-	2.9	5.4	-
Brazil[1]	-	-	2.0	-	-
Netherlands	-	-	-	4.8	-
Spain	-	-	-	2.9	-
Singapore	-	-	-	2.7	-
Belgium	-	-	-	2.2	-
United Arab Emirates	-	-	-	-	4.3
Nigeria	-	-	-	-	3.3
Other	14.4	31.0	32.6	36.1	43.0
Total	100.0	100.0	100.0	100.0	100.0

Source: Changing by Degrees: Steps to Reduce Greenhouse Gases, U.S. Congress, Office of Technology Assessment, OTA-O-482, Washington, D.C., February 1991, p. 82, unless otherwise specified, data for resources/reserves/ production and consumption are from the British Petroleum Company, *BP Statistical Review of World Energy* (London, UK: British Petroleum, June 1990). Data on imports and exports are derived from U.S. Department of Energy, Energy Information Administration, *International Energy Annual, 1988* DOE/EIA-0219(88) (Washington, DC: November 1989). Imports and exports include both crude oil and refined petroleum products. Nearly 40 percent of crude oil products was traded internationally in 1987; nearly 20 percent of production was traded internationally in the form of refined products. *Notes:* 1. Brazil's apparent consumption is obtained from U.S. Department of Energy (1989). It represents Brazil's share of world apparent consumption in 1987 (not 1989).

Packaging

★ 593 ★

Beverage Can U.S. Market Share
U.S. beverage can market, from 1975 to 1988, by type of can. Data are shown in billions of units.

Year	Aluminum cans	Bimetal cans	Total cans
1975	16.321	26.304	42.625
1976	20.928	25.509	46.437
1977	25.806	25.400	51.206
1978	30.064	24.309	54.373
1979	33.674	20.768	54.442
1980	41.577	13.662	55.239
1981	47.684	8.642	56.326
1982	51.700	6.234	57.934
1983	56.658	4.798	61.456
1984	61.501	4.143	65.644
1985	65.726	4.451	70.177

[Continued]

★ 593 ★

Beverage Can U.S. Market Share
[Continued]

Year	Aluminum cans	Bimetal cans	Total cans
1986	68.965	3.937	72.902
1987	73.747	3.026	76.773
1988	77.941	3.239	81.180

Source: Resource Recycling, November 1989, p. 22, from Can Manufacturers Institute. N.A. stands for not available.

★ 594 ★

Beverage Container Sales in California
Values shown are for 1989.

Beverage type and packaging material	Containers sold (millions)	Percent of total
Beer and soft drinks		
Aluminum	8,900	50.5
Glass (N.R.)	3,200	18.2
Glass, refillable	396	2.2
PET	530	3.0
Wine (glass bottles)	360	2.0
Liquor (glass bottles)	248	1.4
Juice		
Aluminum	52	0.3
Steel	302	1.7
Glass (N.R.)	175	1.0
HDPE	60	0.3
Aseptics[1]	847	4.8
Milk, water, other drinks		
HDPE	759	4.3
Paper cartons	1,800	10.2
Total	17,629	99.9

Source: Resource Recycling, July 1990, p. 22, from California Department of Conservation Division of Recycling, and California/Nevada Soft Drink Association, 1990. PET stands for polyethylene terephthalate. N.R. stands for non-returnable. HDPE stands for high-density polyethylene. *Notes:* 1. Fruit juice, wine and milk containers. Extrapolated from 1988 national data, assuming California represents 11 percent of the national market.

★ 595 ★

Beverage Containers by Type - 1964 to 1988

Historical container market shares in the United States, shown in billions of beverage units[1] sold and percent of total market.

Year	Refillable bottles		Nonrefillable (N.R.) bottles		Aluminum and steel cans		PET plastic bottles	
	Units	Percent	Units	Percent	Units	Percent	Units	Percent
1964[2]	25.4	87.0	1.0	3.4	2.8	9.6	-	-
1965	26.0	83.0	1.4	4.5	3.9	12.5	-	-
1970	19.1	45.8	8.6	20.6	14.0	33.6	-	-
1975	16.1	34.1	14.5	30.7	16.6	35.2	-	-
1980[3]	N.A.	32.2	N.A.	9.0	N.A.	41.5	N.A.	17.3[4]
1985	18.2	20.8	12.5	14.7	35.5	40.6	21.3	24.3
1986	19.5	20.1	12.7	13.1	36.8	38.0	27.9	28.8
1987	15.4	15.6	12.9	13.0	40.4	40.8	30.2	30.6
1988	10.8	10.7	13.2	13.1	44.9	44.5	32.0	31.7

Source: Resource Recycling, July 1990, p. 22, from *Beverage Industry*, 1990. N.A.=Not available. *Notes:* 1. Beverage units are 12-oz. equivalents. 2. The first year comparative data were compiled. 3. Only comparative market share data, not number of beverage units sold, are available for 1980. 4. PET was introduced in early 1976 and rapidly displaced other containers, expanding the increase from zero to 17 percent of the market between 1975 and 1980.

★ 596 ★

Materials Trends in Packaging

Increases and decreases in the use of materials in packaging for the 1980 to 1988 period, shown in percent.

	Percent
Plastics	63
Aluminum	50
Paper	27
Steel	-22
Glass	-21

Source: Environmental Action, March/April 1991, p. 26.

★ 597 ★

Packaging Facts

	Amount	Measure
Oil used for plastic packaging in 1989[1]	22,916,335	barrels
Natural gas used for plastic packaging in 1989[1]	34,848,000	cubic feet
"Brick packs" of fruit beverage sold in the U.S.[2]		
1983[3]	1.8	billion
1989[4]	4.3	billion

Source: Garbage, May/June 1990, p. 68. *Notes:* 1. Source: *Garbage* staff research. 2. Source: Beverage Marketing Corporation. 3. Introduced in 1983. 4. Projected.

★ 598 ★

Recyclable Packaging and Consumers

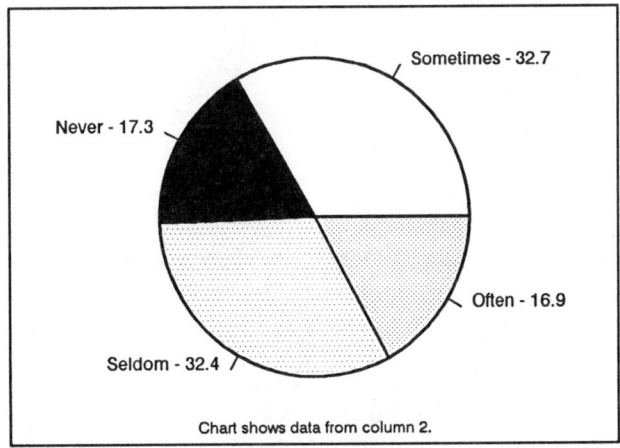

Chart shows data from column 2.

Percentage of consumers who purchase recyclable packages. Data are based on a survey of consumer attitudes in 1986 and 1989.

Response	1986	1989
Often	8.7	16.9
Sometimes	27.5	32.7
Seldom	34.0	32.4
Never	28.2	17.3

Source: Plastics World, September 1989, p. 21, from *Packaging*.

★ 599 ★

Types of Degradable Packaging

The average time for total degradation of cellulose film is 28 to 60 days for uncoated and 80 to 120 days for coated film.

Film Type	Film		Dis-integration Time (Days)
	Gauge	Yield	
Uncoated cellophane	90	215	10-14
Nitrocellulose coated cellophane			
1 side coated	100	195	14-28
2 side coated	100	195	14-28
2 side, non-sealing	85	220	28-56
Saran coated cellophane	80	250	28-56
Vinyl coated cellophane	100	195	56-84
Maple leaves	-	-	84-112
Polyethlylene coated cellophane	110	182	[1]
Regenerated cellulose portion	-	-	7-14
Polyethylene coating portion	-	-	[1]
Hydroxethyl cellulose	135	150	7-14
Nitrocellulose coated	100	195	14-28
Polyester (polyethylene terephthalate)	142	139	[1]
Polyvinyl chloride	150	158	[1]
Oriented polypropylene	100	306	[1]
Cotton cloth	3.2 oz	80 sq. cut	28-56

Source: Pollution Engineering. p. 72, May 1990. *Note:* 1. No detectable weight loss after one-year burial.

Plastics and Rubber

★ 600 ★

Common Thermoplastic Resin Sales by Type

Data reflect sales in 1989.

Type	Billion Lbs.
Low-density Polyethylene (LDPE)	10.64
Polyvinyl Chloride (PVC)	8.31
High-density Polyethylene (HDPE)	8.12
Polypropylene (PP)	7.25
Polystyrene (PS)	5.18
Polyethylene Terephthalate (PET)	1.91

Source: BioCycle, December 1990, p. 51, from *Modern Plastics,* January 1990.

★ 601 ★

Consumption of Polystyrene

Data for 1983 through 1990 (estimated) show decline in single-service polystyrene foam products after years of growth. These products are but a small fraction of the total polystyrene market (5 billion pounds per year).

Product	1983	1984	1985	1986	1987	1988	1989	1990[1]
Extrusion								
Egg cartons	66	70	81	80	80	80	68	60
Plates	57	75	90	114	138	157	153	140
Hinged cartons	35	55	65	76	105	146	140	130
Nonthermoformed cups	20	24	32	40	42	43	40	
Expanded polystyrene								
Cups/containers	145	150	158	154	160	160	160	153
Loose fill	24	31	37	36	42	58	78	75
Totals	347	405	463	500	567	643	642	598
Net change year to year, in percent		+14.0	+13.0	+8.0	+13.0	+13.0	0	-7.0

Source: Modern Plastics, January 1991, p. 75. *Note:* 1. Estimated.

★ 602 ★

Energy Requirements for Plastic Production

Plastic	Production energy (Btu/lb)	Feedstock (%)	Electricity (%)	Oil and natural gas (%)
Low-Density Polyethylene (Polymer)	38,500	73	17.0	10.0
High-Density Polyethylene (Plastics)	36,500	75	10.0	15.0
Polystyrene	34,300	69	4.5	26.5
Polyethylene terephthalate	48,700	51	10.0	39.0
Polyvinyl chloride	25,600	49	26.0	25.0

Source: Facing America's Trash: What Next for Municipal Solid Waste, U.S. Congress, Office of Technology Assessment, OTA-O-412, Washington, D.C., July 1989., p. 177, from Argonne National Laboratory, *Energy and Materials Use in the Production and Recycling of Consumer-Goods Packaging,* ANL/CNSV-TM-58, prepared for U.S. Department of Energy (Argonne, IL: February 1981).

★ 603 ★

High Density Polyethylene Consumption in 1990

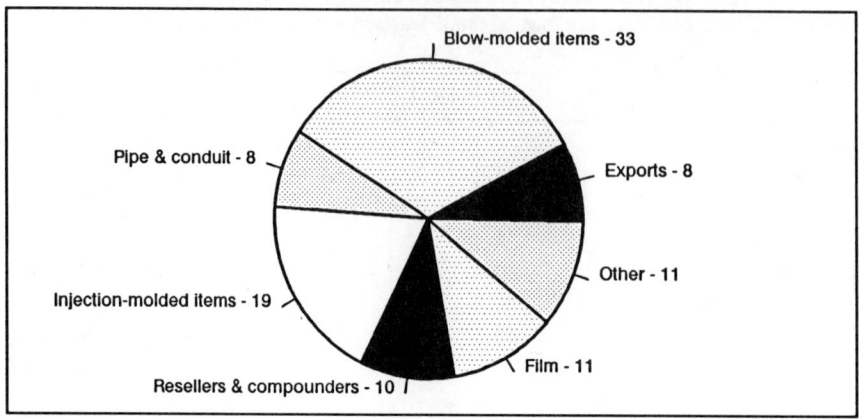

Percent shares are based on total sales and captive use of 8.7 billion pounds in 1990.

Type	Percent
Blow-molded items	33
Injection-molded items	19
Film[1]	11
Resellers & compounders	10
Pipe & conduit	8
Exports	8
Other[2]	11

Source: C&EN, June 10, 1991, p. 40, from Committee on Resin Statistics of the Society of the Plastics Industry. *Notes:* 1. Less than 0.012 inch. 2. Sheet (over 0.012 inch), wire and cable, rotomolding, and all other.

★ 604 ★

Leading States With Reinforced Plastics Plants

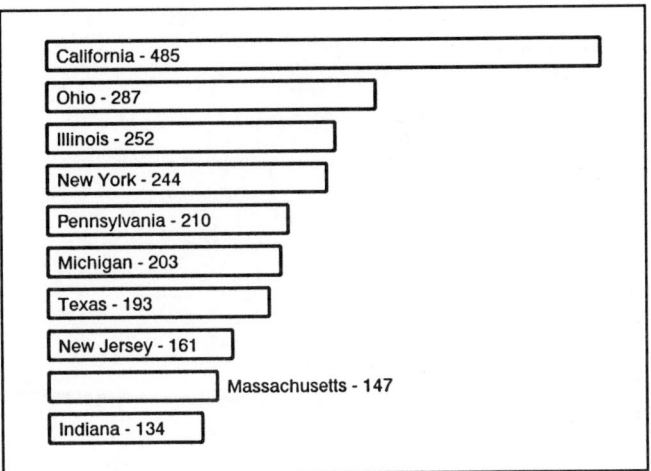

Data show number of plants.

States	Number of plants
California	485
Ohio	287
Illinois	252
New York	244
Pennsylvania	210
Michigan	203
Texas	193
New Jersey	161
Massachusetts	147
Indiana	134

Source: Plastics World, January 1989, p. 81.

★ 605 ★

Leading States With Thermoforming Plastics Plants

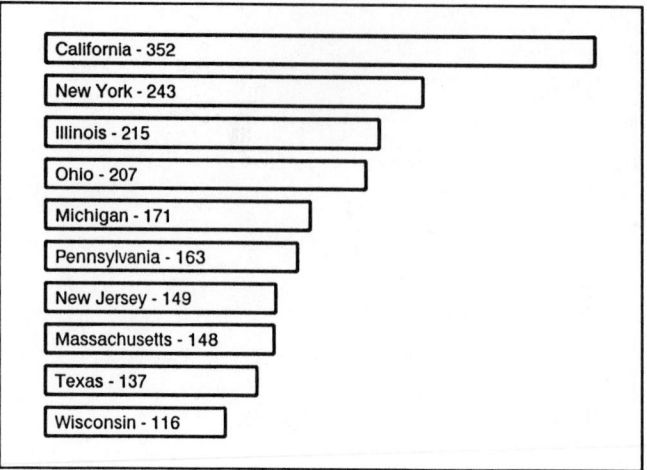

Data show number of plants.

States	Number of plants
California	352
New York	243
Illinois	215
Ohio	207
Michigan	171
Pennsylvania	163
New Jersey	149
Massachusetts	148
Texas	137
Wisconsin	116

Source: Plastics World, January 1989, p. 81.

★ 606 ★

Linear Low Density Polyethylene Consumption in 1990

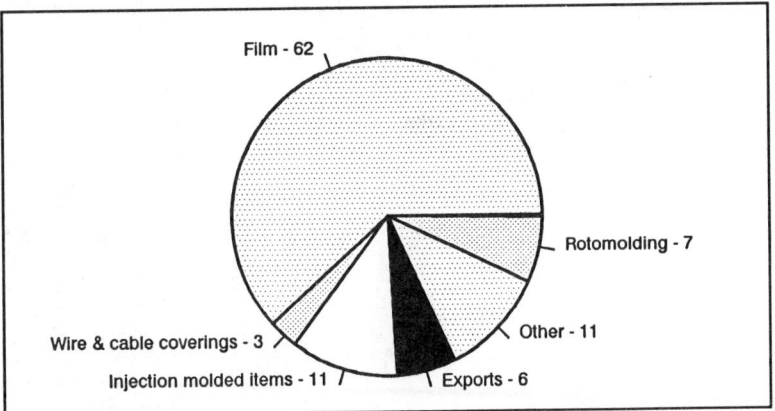

Percent shares are based on total sales and captive use of 4.7 billion pounds.

Type	Percent
Film[1]	62
Injection molded items	11
Rotomolding	7
Exports	6
Wire & cable coverings	3
Other[2]	11

Source: C&EN, June 10, 1991, p. 47, from Committee on Resin Statistics of the Society of the Plastics Industry, SRI International, Union Carbide, C&EN estimates. *Notes:* 1. Less than 0.012 inch. 2. Sheet (over 0.012 inch), blow molded items, pipe and conduit, resellers and compounders, and all other.

★ 607 ★

Low Density Polyethylene Consumption in 1990

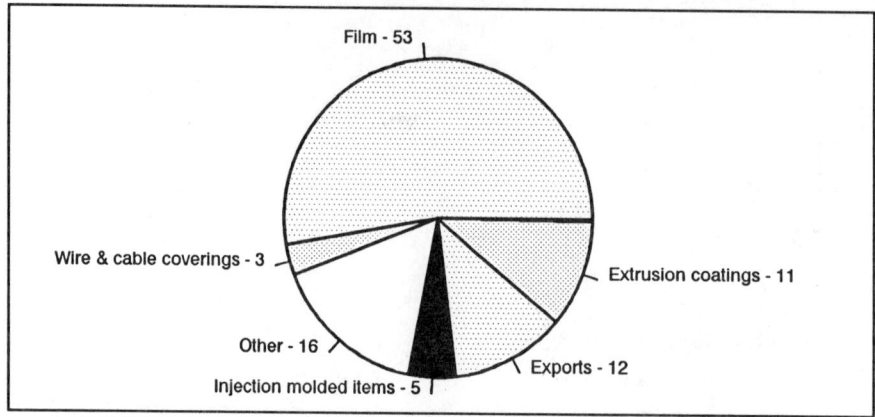

Percent shares are based on total sales and captive use of 7.2 billion pounds in 1990.

Type	Percent
Film[1]	53
Exports	12
Extrusion coatings	11
Injection molded items	5
Wire & cable coverings	3
Other[2]	16

Source: C&EN, June 10, 1991, p. 42, from Committee on Resin Statistics of the Society of the Plastics Industry, SRI International, Union Carbide, *C&EN* estimates. *Notes:* 1. Less than 0.012 inch. 2. Sheet (over 0.012 inch), blow molding, pipe and conduit, other extruded products, adhesives, and sealants, resellers and compounds, and all other.

★ 608 ★

Phenolics Consumption in 1990

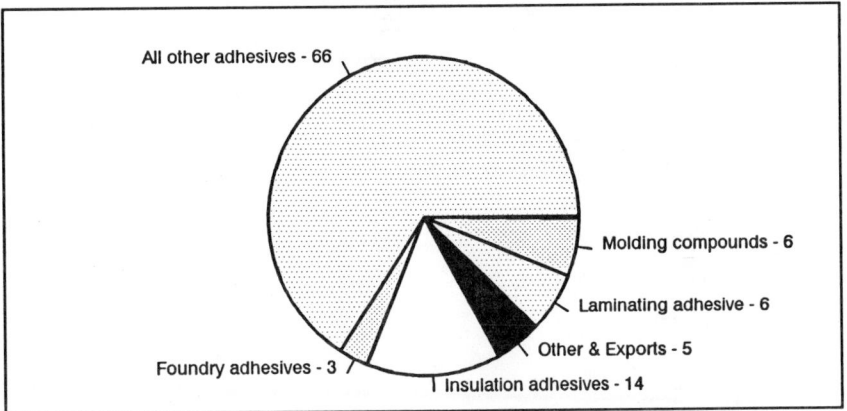

Percent shares are based on total sales and captive use of 2.9 billion pounds.

	Percent
Insulation adhesives	14
Molding compounds	6
Laminating adhesive	6
Foundry adhesives	3
Other & Exports	5
All other adhesives[1]	66

Source: C&EN, June 10, 1991, p. 66, from Committee on Resin Statistics of the Society of the Plastics Industry. *Notes:* 1. For disclosure reasons, plywood adhesives are not broken out; in 1989, plywood adhesives accounted for 51% of total sales and captive use.

★ 609 ★

Plastic Consumption

```
┌─────────────────────────────────────────────────┐
│  │Packaging - 30                              │    │
│  │Other - 21                          │            │
│  │Building - 20                       │            │
│  │              │ Housewares - 7                   │
│  │Electricals - 7│                                 │
│  │              │ Transport - 6                    │
│  │          │ Furniture - 4                        │
│  │      │ Engineering - 2                          │
│  │      │ Agriculture - 2                          │
│  │  │ Clothing - 1                                 │
└─────────────────────────────────────────────────┘
```

Consumption of plastics in Europe, North America, Japan, and India in 1989. Shares are shown, by industry, as percent of total volume.

Industry	Percent of Total Volume
Packaging	30
Building	20
Housewares	7
Electricals	7
Transport	6
Furniture	4
Engineering	2
Agriculture	2
Clothing	1
Other	21

Source: The Economist, July 21, 1990, p. 73, from British Plastics Waste Management Institute.

★ 610 ★

Plastic Consumption Worldwide by End Use

```
Packaging - 30
Other - 21
Building/Construction - 20
         Electrical devices - 7
         Housewares - 7
          Transportation - 6
     Furniture - 4
Agriculture - 2
Engineering - 2
Clothing - 1
```

The figures are percent of total plastic consumed in Europe, North America, Japan and India in 1989.

Type	% of total volume
Packaging	30
Building/Construction	20
Electrical devices	7
Housewares	7
Transportation	6
Furniture	4
Agriculture	2
Engineering	2
Clothing	1
Other	21

Source: The Economist, July 21, 1990, p. 73, from British Plastics Federation, Plastics Waste Management Institute.

★ 611 ★

Plastics Consumption by Life of Product

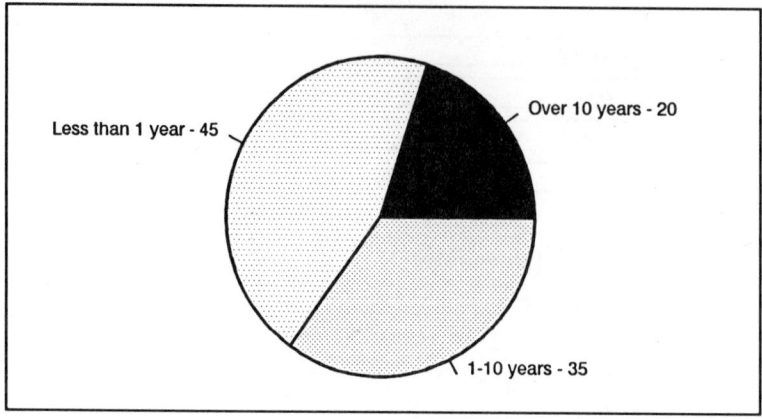

Breakdown of plastics by useful product life. Values refer to percent of total plastic consumption in Europe, North America, Japan, and India.

Number of years	% of total volume
Less than 1 year	45
1-10 years	35
Over 10 years	20

Source: The Economist, July 21, 1990, p. 73, from British Plastics Federation, Plastics Waste Management Institute.

★ 612 ★

Plastics in Packaging

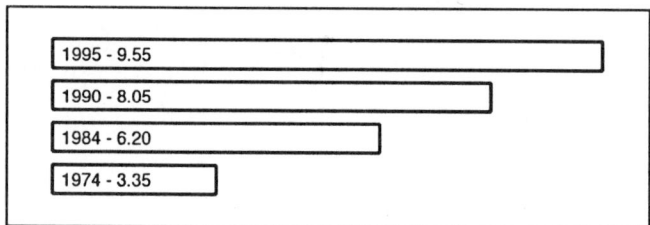

Year	Million Tons
1974	3.35
1984	6.20
1990	8.05[1]
1995	9.55[1]

Source: Garbage, May/June 1990, p. 68, from *Collision Course: Plastic Packaging vs. Solid Waste Solutions,* 1989, Environmental Action Coalition. *Note:* 1. Projected.

★ 613 ★

Polybutadiene Consumption in 1990

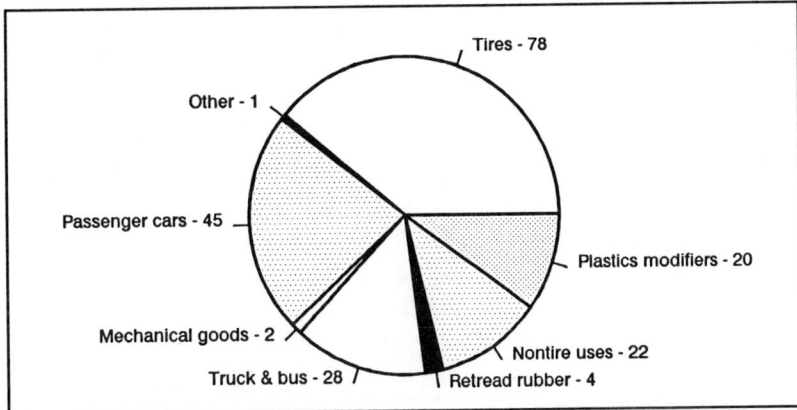

Percent shares are based on a total consumption of 652,000 metric tons in the U.S. in 1990.

Use	Percent
Tires	78
Passenger cars	45
Truck & bus	28
Nontire uses	22
Plastics modifiers[1]	20
Retread rubber	4
Mechanical goods	2
Other	1

Source: C&EN, May 13, 1991, p. 48, from *C&EN* estimates. *Notes:* 1. To give impact resistance to polystyrene and acrylonitrile-butadiene-styrene resins.

★ 614 ★

Polyester Consumption in 1990

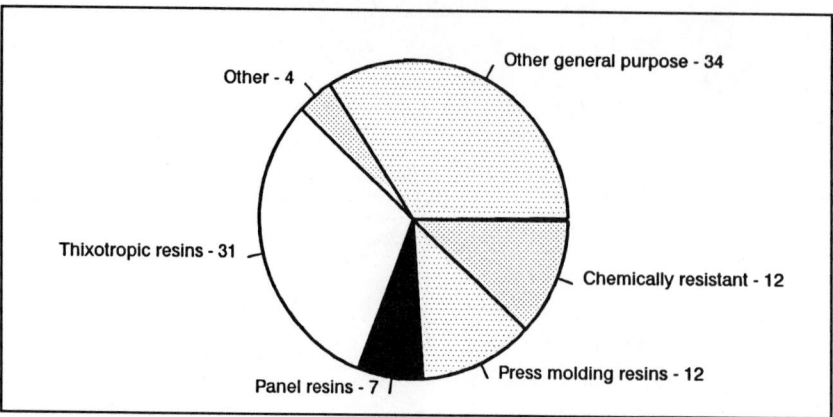

Percent shres are based on total sales and captive use of 1.2 billion pounds.

	Percent
Thixotropic resins	31
Press molding resins	12
Chemically resistant	12
Panel resins	7
Other general purpose	34
Other[1]	4

Source: C&EN, June 10, 1991, p. 67, from Committee on Resin Statistics of the Society of the Plastics Industry. *Note:* 1. Exports and flame-retardant resins.

★ 615 ★

Polypropylene Consumption in 1990

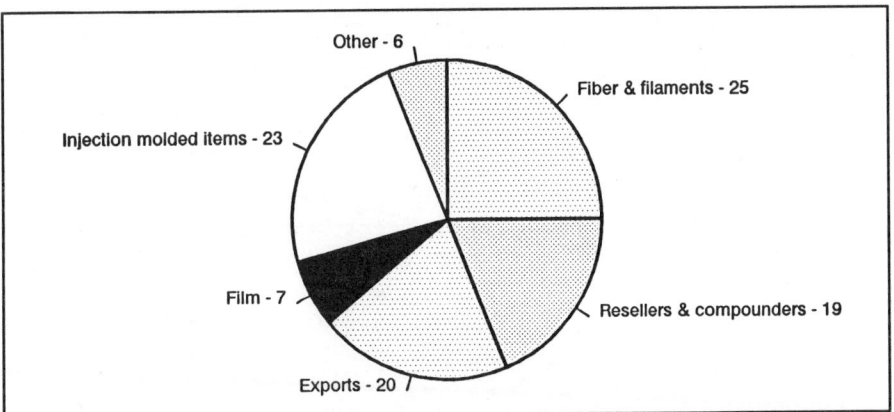

Percent shares are based on total sales and captive use of 8.2 billion pounds.

Type	Percent
Fiber & filaments	25
Injection molded items	23
Exports	20
Resellers & compounders	19
Film[1]	7
Other[2]	6

Source: C&EN, June 10, 1991, p. 50, from Committee on Resin Statistics of the Society of the Plastics Industry. *Notes:* 1. Less than 0.010 inch. 2. Blow molding, sheet (more than 0.010 inch), extrusion coatings, and all other.

★ 616 ★

Polystyrene Consumption in 1990

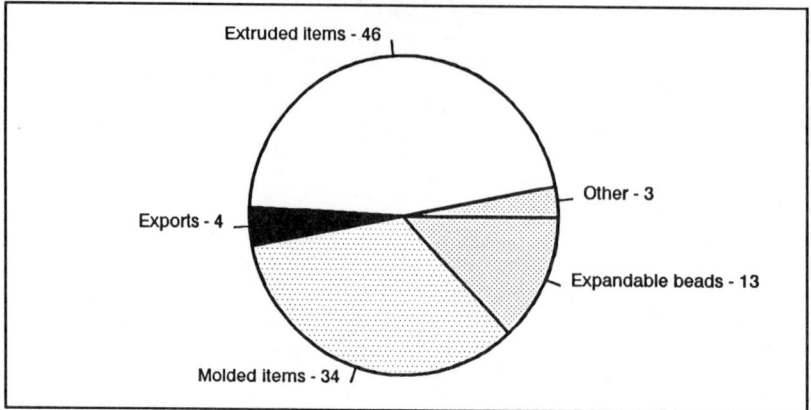

Percent shares are based on total sales and captive use of 5.1 billion pounds of crystal-and rubber-modified polystyrene.

	Percent
Extruded items	46
Molded items	34
Expandable beads	13
Exports	4
Other	3

Source: C&EN, June 10, 1991, p. 63, from Committee on Resin Statistics of the Society of the Plastics Industry.

★ 617 ★

Polyvinyl Chloride Consumption in 1990

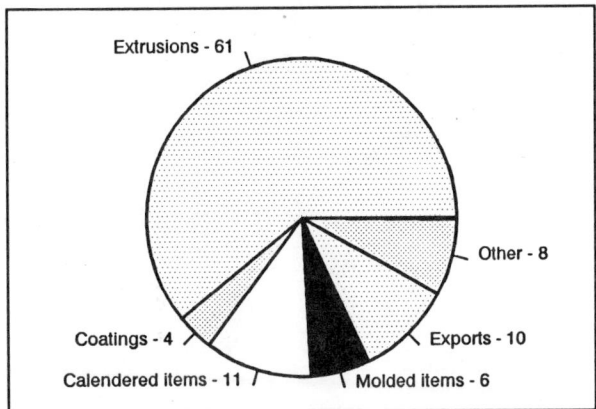

Percent shares are based on sales and captive use of 9.0 billion pounds.

Type	Percent
Extrusions[1]	61
Calendered items	11
Exports	10
Molded items	6
Coatings	4
Other[2]	8

Source: C&EN, June 10, 1991, p. 65, from Committee on Resin Statistics of the Society of the Plastics Industry. *Notes:* 1. Includes pipe and tubing, siding and accessories, wire and cable covering, and film and sheet. 2. Paste processes (except coatings), resellers and compounders, and all other.

★ 618 ★

Resin Sales in the U.S.

Data reflect sales in 1989.

Market	Billion Lbs.
Packaging	14.09
Construction	11.39
Electronics	2.02
Transportation	2.00
Housewares	1.36
Appliances	1.20
Furniture	1.19
Toys	.73

Source: BioCycle, December 1989, p. 50, from *Modern Plastics*.

★ 619 ★

Styrene-Butadiene Consumption

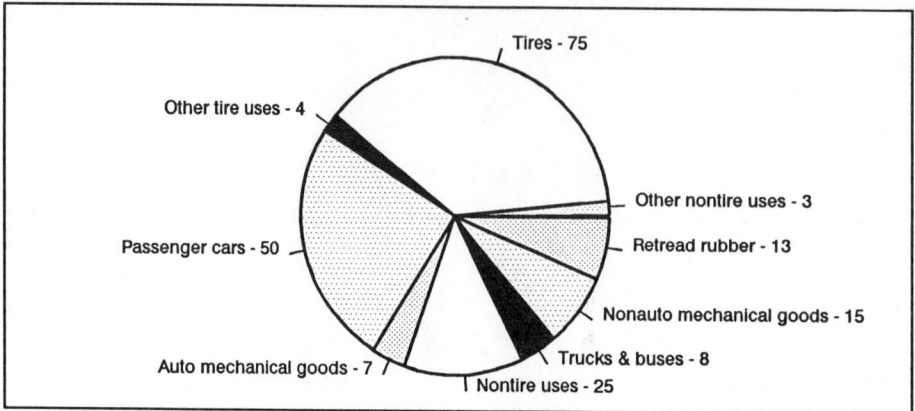

Percent shares are based on a total consumption of 365,000 metric tons in 1990.

Use	Percent
Tires	75
Passenger cars	50
Nontire uses	25
Nonauto mechanical goods	15
Retread rubber	13
Trucks & buses	8
Auto mechanical goods	7
Other tire uses	4
Other nontire uses	3

Source: C&EN, May 13, 1991, p. 48, from *C&EN* estimates.

★ 620 ★

Synthetic Rubber Use

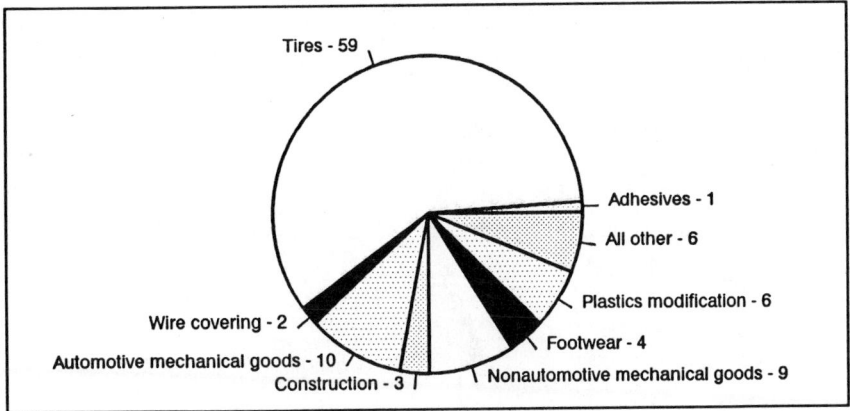

Percent distribution of synthetic rubber by end uses. The values shown are based on total worldwide consumption of 7.1 million metric tons in 1991.

Use	Percent
Tires	59
Automotive mechanical goods	10
Nonautomotive mechanical goods	9
Plastics modification	6
Footwear	4
Construction	3
Wire covering	2
Adhesives	1
All other	6

Source: C&EN, May 13, 1991, p. 44, from International Institute of Synthetic Rubber Producers.

★ 621 ★

Thermoplastic Consumption in 1989

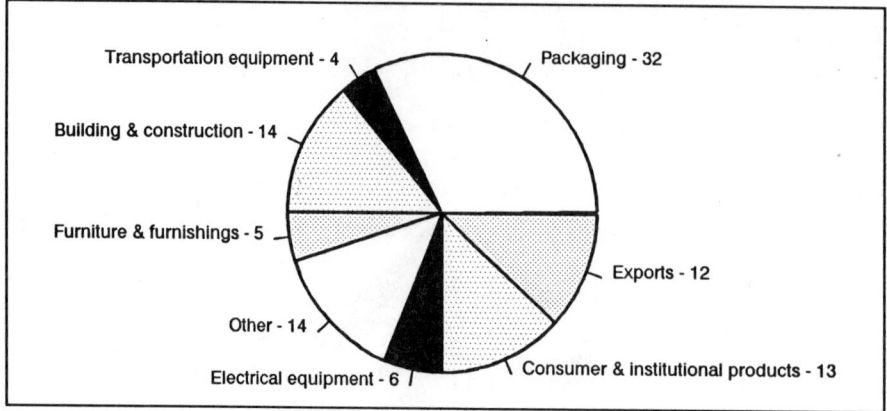

Percent shares are based on total sales and captive use of 46.3 billion pounds.

Type	Percent
Packaging	32
Building & construction	14
Consumer & institutional products	13
Exports	12
Electrical equipment	6
Furniture & furnishings	5
Transportation equipment	4
Other[1]	14

Source: C&EN, June 10, 1991, p. 56, from Committee on Resin Statistics of the Society of the Plastics Industry. Selected large-volume thermoplastics and thermosets; 1990 data not available yet. *Notes:* 1. Includes adhesives, inks, coatings; industrial equipment and machinery; volumes sold to resellers and compounders; and not classifiable elsewhere.

★ 622 ★

Thermoplastic Production in 1990

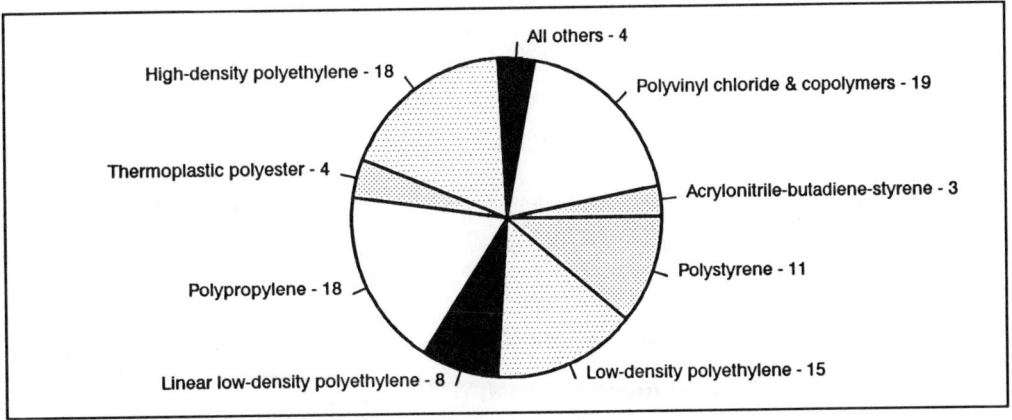

Percent shares are based on a total of 46.8 billion pounds produced in 1990.

Types	Percent
Polyvinyl chloride & copolymers	19
High-density polyethylene	18
Polypropylene	18
Low-density polyethylene	15
Polystyrene	11
Linear low-density polyethylene	8
Thermoplastic polyester	4
Acrylonitrile-butadiene-styrene	3
All others[1]	4

Source: C&EN, June 10, 1991, p. 54, from Committee on Resin Statistics of the Society of the Plastics Industry, U.S. International Trade Commission, *C&EN* estimates. *Notes:* 1. Production of less than 1 billion lb.; nylon, polyvinyl acetate, styrene-acrylonitrile, other styrenic plastics, other vinyls, and other thermoplastics.

★ 623 ★

Thermoplastics - Major Markets

Values for 1989 are shown in millions of pounds.

Market	LDPE[1]	PVC[2]	HDPE[3]	PP[4]	PS[5]	PET[6]
Packaging	4494	719	4073	1516	1707	1059
Construction	315	4826	491	32	365	-
Electronics	396	468	146	46	485	-
Transportation	-	197	-	319	-	-

[Continued]

★ 623 ★

Thermoplastics - Major Markets
[Continued]

Market	LDPE[1]	PVC[2]	HDPE[3]	PP[4]	PS[5]	PET[6]
Appliances	-	113	-	169	205	-
Housewares	415	67	241	265	228	-

Source: BioCycle, December 1990, p. 51, from *Modern Plastics. Notes:* 1. Low-density Polyethylene. 2. Polyvinyl Chloride. 3. High-density Polyethylene. 4. Polypropylene. 5. Polystyrene. 6. Polyethylene Terephthalate.

★ 624 ★

Thermosets Consumption in 1989

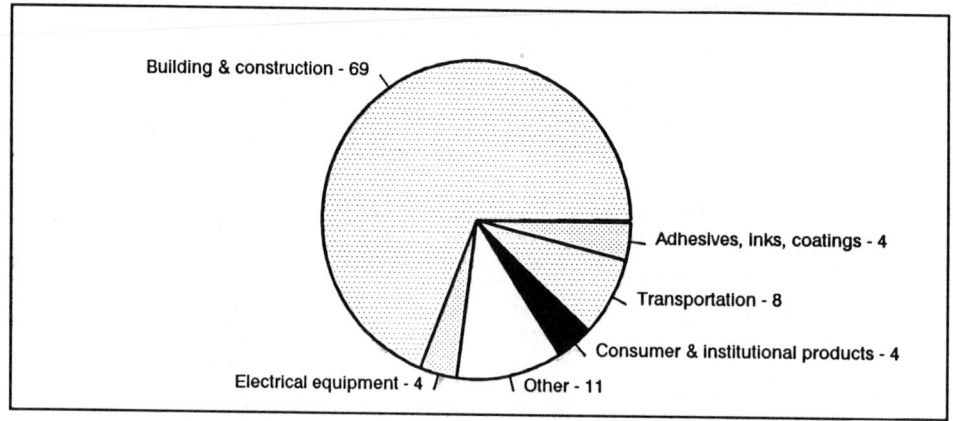

Percent shares are based on total sales and captive use of 6.3 billion pounds.

Type	Percent
Building & construction	69
Transportation	8
Adhesives, inks, coatings	4
Consumer & institutional products	4
Electrical equipment	4
Other[1]	11

Source: C&EN, June 10, 1981, p. 56, from Committee on Resin Statistics of the Society of the Plastics Industry. Selected large-volume thermoplastics and thermosets; 1990 data not available yet. *Notes:* 1. Includes furniture and furnishings, packaging; industrial equipment and machinery; exports; volumes sold to resellers and compounders; and not classified elsewhere.

★ 625 ★

Thermosets Production in 1990

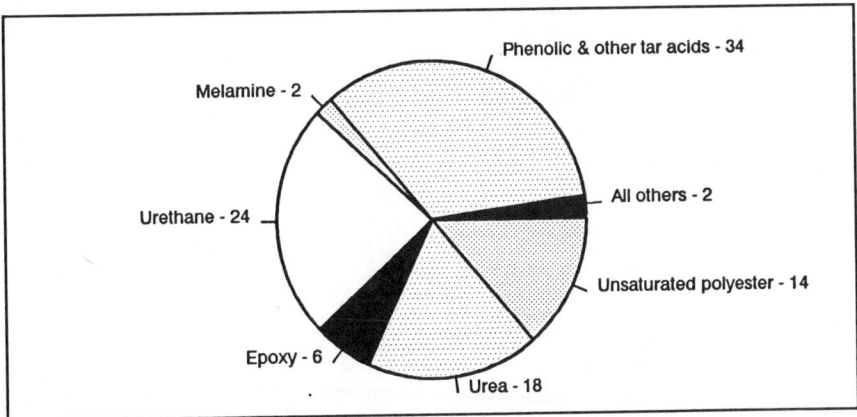

Percent shares are based on a total of 8.6 billion pounds produced in 1990.

	Percent
Phenolic & other tar acids	34
Urethane	24
Urea	18
Unsaturated polyester	14
Epoxy	6
Melamine	2
All others[1]	2

Source: C&EN, June 10, 1991, p. 54, from Committee on Resin Statistics of the Society of the Plastics Industry, U.S. International Trade Commission, C&EN estimates. *Notes:* 1. Includes other amino resins, furfural resins, glyoxal-formaldehyde resins, and silicone.

Power and Utilities

★ 626 ★

Coal-Fired Generator Capacity in Steam-Electric Plants

Number and nameplate capacity of coal-fired steam-electric generators in plants that have environmental equipment. Data are shown by state for 1989.

Census Division and State	Generating Units		Scrubbers		Particulate Collectors		Cooling Towers	
	Number of Generators	Capacity[2] (megawatts)	Number of Generators	Capacity[2] (megawatts)	Number of Generators	Capacity[2] (megawatts)	Number of Generators	Capacity[2] (megawatts)
New England	12	2,623	0	0	12	2,623	0	0
Connecticut	1	400	0	0	1	400	0	0
Maine	0	0	0	0	0	0	0	0
Massachusetts	9	1,764	0	0	9	1,764	0	0

[Continued]

★ 626 ★

Coal-Fired Generator Capacity in Steam-Electric Plants
[Continued]

Census Division and State	Generating Units		Scrubbers		Particulate Collectors		Cooling Towers	
	Number of Generators	Capacity[2] (megawatts)	Number of Generators	Capacity[2] (megawatts)	Number of Generators	Capacity[2] (megawatts)	Number of Generators	Capacity[2] (megawatts)
New Hampshire	2	459	0	0	2	459	0	0
Rhode Island	0	0	0	0	0	0	0	0
Vermont	0	0	0	0	0	0	0	0
Middle Atlantic	94	24,669	16	5,512	94	24,669	20	12,657
New Jersey	8	1,732	0	0	8	1,732	0	0
New York	25	3,743	1	655	25	3,743	0	0
Pennsylvania	61	19,194	15	4,857	61	19,194	20	12,657
East North Central	306	81,341	17	7,216	309	81,486	46	20,979
Illinois	55	17,123	4	1,439	55	17,123	3	671
Indiana	69	21,703	11	4,890	72	21,847	20	9,207
Michigan	55	12,659	0	0	55	12,659	7	536
Ohio	87	22,732	2	888	87	22,732	11	7,986
Wisconsin	40	7,126	0	0	40	7,126	5	2,579
West North Central	140	35,924	27	11,539	140	35,924	49	12,914
Iowa	31	5,857	1	160	31	5,857	9	1,912
Kansas	19	5,712	8	3,995	19	5,712	10	3,435
Minnesota	25	5,350	8	3,305	25	5,350	9	3,787
Missouri	38	11,517	3	1,099	38	11,517	12	1,019
Nebraska	14	3,038	0	0	14	3,038	4	429
North Dakota	12	3,994	7	2,981	12	3,994	5	2,332
South Dakota	1	456	0	0	1	456	0	0
South Atlantic	206	65,840	13	6,752	204	65,778	66	34,796
Delaware	6	1,034	0	0	6	1,034	1	442
District of Columbia	0	0	0	0	0	0	0	0
Florida	27	10,658	7	3,883	27	10,658	13	6,261
Georgia	38	12,957	0	0	38	12,957	12	8,862
Maryland	14	4,257	0	0	14	4,257	1	685
North Carolina	40	12,101	0	0	38	12,039	8	3,188
South Carolina	24	5,324	4	1,501	24	5,324	14	4,139
Virginia	24	4,549	0	0	24	4,549	3	713
West Virginia	33	14,958	2	1,368	33	14,958	14	10,506
East South Central	135	39,326	22	7,873	135	39,326	33	15,408
Alabama	39	11,943	4	1,591	39	11,943	6	3,535
Kentucky	53	15,212	16	5,882	53	15,212	23	10,724
Mississippi	6	2,150	2	400	6	2,150	4	1,150
Tennessee	37	10,020	0	0	37	10,020	0	0
West South Central	54	32,458	15	9,891	54	32,458	30	17,746
Arkansas	5	3,958	0	0	5	3,958	4	3,400
Louisiana	6	3,572	1	721	6	3,572	4	2,454
Oklahoma	10	5,210	1	520	10	5,210	8	4,072
Texas	33	19,719	13	8,650	33	19,719	14	7,820
Mountain	89	30,383	47	20,063	85	28,604	78	26,736
Arizona	13	5,297	8	2,425	13	5,297	11	4,894
Colorado	26	4,946	4	1,594	26	4,946	24	4,524
Idaho	3	3	3	3	3	3	3	3
Montana	5	2,464	4	2,273	5	2,464	4	2,273
Nevada	8	2,769	5	879	8	2,769	8	2,769
New Mexico	10	4,282	10	4,282	6	2,503	5	2,012
Utah	12	4,787	7	3,969	12	4,787	12	4,787
Wyoming	15	5,838	9	4,641	15	5,838	14	5,476
Pacific Contiguous	3	2,020	0	0	3	2,020	2	1,460
California	0	0	0	0	0	0	0	0
Oregon	1	561	0	0	1	561	0	0
Washington	2	1,460	0	0	2	1,460	2	1,460

[Continued]

★ 626 ★

Coal-Fired Generator Capacity in Steam-Electric Plants
[Continued]

Census Division and State	Generating Units		Scrubbers		Particulate Collectors		Cooling Towers	
	Number of Generators	Capacity[2] (megawatts)	Number of Generators	Capacity[2] (megawatts)	Number of Generators	Capacity[2] (megawatts)	Number of Generators	Capacity[2] (megawatts)
Pacific Noncontiguous	0	0	0	0	0	0	0	0
Alaska	0	0	0	0	0	0	0	0
Hawaii	0	0	0	0	0	0	0	0
U.S. Total	1,039	314,585	157	68,846	1,036	312,887	324	142,696

Source: Energy Information Administration, *Electric Power Annual 1989*, January 1991, p. 77, from Energy Information Administration, Form EIA-767, "Steam-Electric Plant Operation and Design Report." Totals may not equal sum of components because of independent rounding. These data are only for plants with a fossil-fueled steam-electric capacity of 100 or more megawatts. Data for 1989 are preliminary. Data include petroleum coke. *Notes:* 1. Components are not additive since some generators are included in more than one category and not all units have environmental equipment. 2. Nameplate capacity. 3. Not applicable.

★ 627 ★

Decommissioning Nuclear Power Reactors

Partial list of nuclear power reactors which are either waiting or undergoing decommissioning.

Reactor	Plant location	Year entered service	Number of years operated	Capacity (MW)
Shippingport	Pennsylvania	1957	25	72
Indian Point-1	New York	1962	12	257
Three Mile Island-2	Pennsylvania	1978	1	880
Windscale	United Kingdom	1962	19	33
Berkeley-1	United Kingdom	1962	27	138
Berkeley-2	United Kingdom	1962	27	138
G-2, Marcoule	France	1958	22	45
Chinon-A1	France	1963	10	70
Chinon-A2	France	1965	20	210
Garigliano	Italy	1964	14	160
Trino Vercellese	Italy	1965	24	260
Caorso	Italy	1981	8	875
Karlsruhe	West Germany	1965	19	58
Gundremmingen	West Germany	1966	11	250
Lingen	West Germany	1968	9	256

Source: World Watch, July/August 1989, p. 12.

★ 628 ★

Electricity From Nuclear Power in Selected Countries

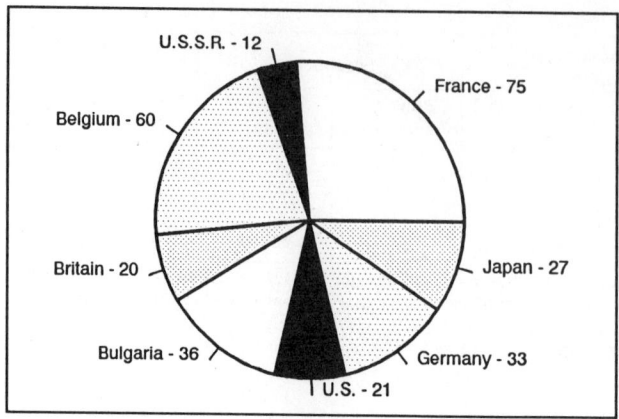

Percentage of electricity in each country obtained from nuclear power in 1990.

Country	Percent
France	75
Belgium	60
Bulgaria	36
Germany	33
Japan	27
U.S.	21
Britain	20
U.S.S.R.	12

Source: Time, April 29, 1991, p. 61, from International Atomic Energy Agency, U.S. Council for Energy Awareness.

★ 629 ★

Energy Generation

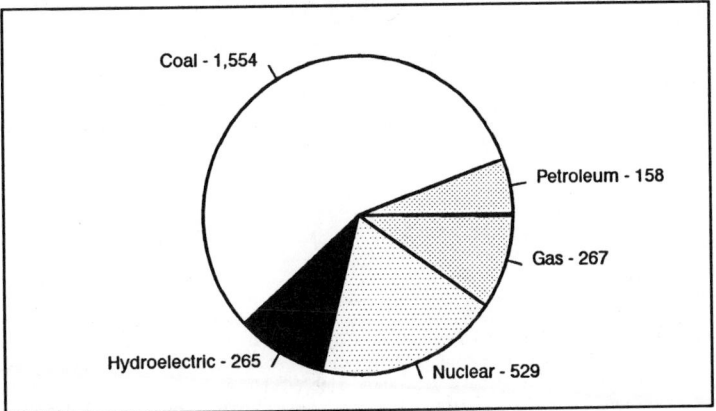

Net generation, by source, in 1989. Data are shown in billions of kilowatthours. Total net generation in 1989 was 2,784 billion kilowatthours.

Source	Net Generation
Coal	1,554
Petroleum	158
Gas	267
Nuclear	529
Hydroelectric	265

Source: Electric Power Annual 1989, Energy Information Administration, Office of Coal, Nuclear, Electric, and Alternate Fuels, U.S. Department of Energy, DOE/EIA-0348(89), Washington, D.C., January 1991, p. 14, from Energy Information Administration, Form EIA-759, "Monthly Power Plant Report." Total net generation value includes 11 billion kilowatthours of generation by other energy sources including geothermal, wood, wind, waste, and solar. Totals may not equal sum of components because of independent rounding.

★ 630 ★

Energy Generation Shares

Shares, by source, of net generation in 1989, shown in percent. Data are based on a total net generation of 2,784 billion kilowatthours.

Source	Percent of Total
Coal	56
Nuclear	19
Hydroelectric	10
Gas	10
Petroleum	6

Source: *Electric Power Annual 1989*, Energy Information Administration, Office of Coal, Nuclear, Electric, and Alternate Fuels, U.S. Department of Energy, DOE/EIA-0348(89), Washington, D.C., January 1991, p. 15, from Energy Information Administration, Form EIA-759, "Monthly Power Plant Report." Total value includes generation from other energy sources (geothermal, wood, wind, waste, and solar), which represents less than 1 percent of total generation. Totals may not equal sum of components because of independent rounding.

★ 631 ★

Fuel and Power Use and Cost Trends

	1987	Energy (trillion Btu)			Cost (billion 1987 $, 2015 prices)		
		Base 2015	Change		Base 2015	Change	
			Moderate 2015	Tough 2015		Moderate 2015	Tough 2015
Residential buildings							
Natural gas	4,462	4,198	-639	-1,320	48	-7	-15
Electricity	2,854	3,323	-597	-1,067	110	-20	-35
Oil	1,590	1,124	-174	-374	11	-2	-4
Coal	74	62	-8	-13	0	-0	-0
Wood	837	1,516	-353	-897	-	-	-
Total	8,980	8,707	-1,418	-2,774	169	-29	-54
Commercial buildings							
Natural gas	2,421	3,387	-416	387	36	-4	4
Electricity	2,525	4,264	-1,572	-2,922	119	-44	-81
Oil	1,086	922	-259	-649	9	-3	-6
Coal	107	114	-23	-43	0	-0	-0
Total	6,139	8,687	-2,270	-3,226	164	-51	-84
Industry							
Coal	2,678	4,598	-1,299	-3,088	13	-4	-9
Natural gas	7,044	7,685	-227	-24	69	-2	-0
Oil	4,725	5,041	-627	-1,742	40	-5	-14
Biomass	2,230	3,520	-298	-1,370	-	-	-

[Continued]

★ 631 ★

Fuel and Power Use and Cost Trends
[Continued]

	1987	Energy (trillion Btu)			Cost (billion 1987 $, 2015 prices)		
		Base 2015	Change		Base 2015	Change	
			Moderate 2015	Tough 2015		Moderate 2015	Tough 2015
Electric	2,679	4,398	-685	-1,686	97	-15	-37
Total	19,355	25,242	-3,136	-7,909	219	-26	-60
Transportation							
Gasoline	13,393	16,380	-2,008	-6,927	244	-30	-103
Distillate oil	3,338	5,140	-420	-1,586	51	-4	-16
Jet fuel	2,872	4,686	-317	-1,327	70	-5	-20
Aviation gas	45	48	0	0	1	0	0
Residual oil	817	1207	0	0	10	0	0
Natural gas	571	724	0	0	8	0	0
Electricity	17	28	0	104	1	0	3
Total	21,213	28,213	-2,745	-9,736	383	-39	-136
Exogenous electricity	0	2,527	-632	-1,263	69	-17	-35
All sectors							
Natural gas	14,497	15,994	-1,282	-957	160	-14	-11
Electricity	8,074	12,013	-2,855	-5,571	396	-96	-186
Oil	27,866	34,548	-3,805	-12,605	436	-48	-163
Coal	2,859	4,774	-1,330	-3,143	14	-4	-9
Biomass	3,067	5,036	-651	-2,267	-	-	-
Total	56,364	72,365	-9,923	-24,543	1,006	-162	-369

Source: Changing by Degrees: Steps to Reduce Greenhouse Gases, U.S. Congress, Office of Technology Assessment, OTA-O-482, Washington, D.C., February 1991, p. 321, from Office of Technology Assessment.

★ 632 ★

Generating Capability Shares

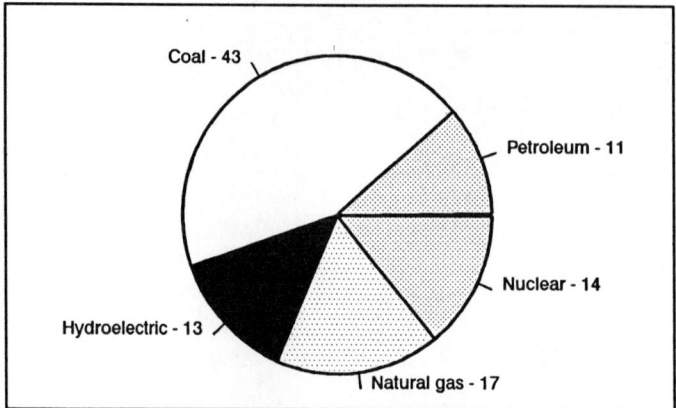

Shares, by source, of energy generation capability in 1989, shown in percent. Data are based on a total generating capability of 685 gigawatts.

Source	Percent of Total
Coal	43
Petroleum	11
Natural gas	17
Nuclear	14
Hydroelectric	13

Source: Electric Power Annual 1989, Energy Information Administration, Office of Coal, Nuclear, Electric, and Alternate Fuels, U.S. Department of Energy, DOE/EIA-0348(89), Washington, D.C., January 1991, p. 16, from Energy Information Administration, Form EIA-860, "Annual Electric Generator Report." Total capability value includes other generating capability (geothermal, refuse, waste heat, waste steam, solar, wind, and wood), which represents 1 percent of total capability.

★ 633 ★

Generation Capability

Generating capability, by source, shown in gigawatts. Total capability in 1989 was 685 gigawatts.

Source	Generating Capability
Coal	297
Petroleum	78
Gas	117
Nuclear	98
Hydroelectric	90

Source: Electric Power Annual 1989, Energy Information Administration, Office of Coal, Nuclear, Electric, and Alternate Fuels, U.S. Department of Energy, DOE/EIA-0348(89), Washington, D.C., January 1991, p. 16, from Energy Information Administration, Form EIA-860, "Annual Electric Generator Report." Total capability value includes 4 gigawatts of other generating capability (geothermal, refuse, waste, heat, waste steam, solar, wind, and wood).

★ 634 ★

Home Heating in the U.S. by Source

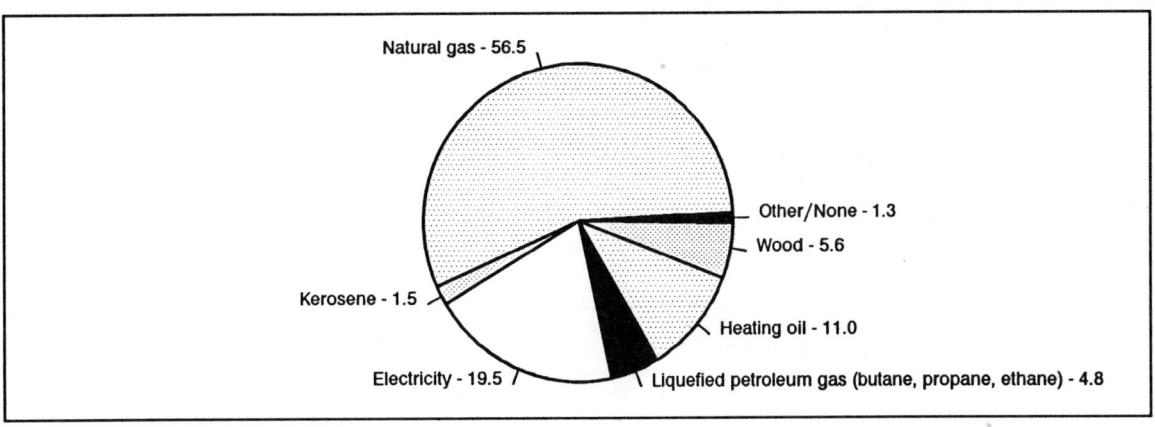

Source	Percent used
Natural gas	56.5
Electricity	19.5
Heating oil	11.0
Wood	5.6
Liquefied petroleum gas (butane, propane, ethane)	4.8
Kerosene	1.5
Other/None	1.3

Source: USA Today, October 30, 1990, p. 1B, from *USA Today* research.

★ 635 ★

Leading Users of Nuclear Power

```
Vermont - 75.8
South Carolina - 60.9
Maine - 59.7
Illinois - 59.0
Connecticut - 57.1
New Jersey - 56.0
Nebraska - 38.3
Mississippi - 37.2
North carolina - 33.5
Virginia - 32.9
```

The ten states that lead the nation in nuclear energy use.

State	Percent
Vermont	75.8
South Carolina	60.9
Maine	59.7
Illinois	59.0
Connecticut	57.1
New Jersey	56.0
Nebraska	38.3
Mississippi	37.2
North carolina	33.5
Virginia	32.9

Source: Energy, Fall Issue 1990, p. 16. Ten other states produced at least 20 per cent of their electricity from nuclear energy. These are: Kansas, Minnesota, Georgia, Arkansas, Pennsylvania, California, Wisconsin, Louisiana, Michigan and Tennessee.

★ 636 ★

Non-Utility Power Generating Projects by Type

The figures refer to annual survey of Compensation and Human Resources for the independent power producers industry by Gibson and Co., in 1990. The study had 42 participants with approximately 25,000 mw of capacity operating a total of 306 projects nationwide.

Type	Number of Projects	Percent of Total
Cogeneration: Coal	66	22
Cogeneration: Gas/Oil	56	18
Cogeneration: Waste Fuels	39	12
Geothermal	35	11

[Continued]

★ 636 ★

Non-Utility Power Generating Projects by Type
[Continued]

Type	Number of Projects	Percent of Total
Hydropower	35	11
Wind	32	10
Biomass	33	10
Other	10	3

Source: Independent Energy, March 1991, p. 24. Percent total may not be equal due to rounding.

★ 637 ★

Non-Utility Power Generation by Region
Values, shown in percent, are current as of August 1990.

Region	Natural Gas	Oil	Coal	Waste Fuel	Biomass
West-South Central	86	-	1	10	3
Pacific	73	2	4	5	16
South Atlantic	7	-	54	9	30
Mid-Atlantic	46	4	26	18	6
New England	17	10	2	-	71
East-North Central	16	7	47	17	13

Source: Electric Light and Power, February 1990, p. 22.

★ 638 ★

Nuclear Electricity Generation in OECD Area
Total and nuclear electric generation in the countries that belong to the Organization for Economic Cooperation and Development (OECD). Data are for 1988.

Country	Terawatt-hours[1]		Share of Nuclear %
	Total	Nuclear	
Australia	132.0	0.0	0.0
Austria	45.9	0.0	0.0
Belgium	61.9	40.9	66.1
Canada	487.0	78.2	16.1
Denmark	29.8	0.0	0.0
Finland	51.3	18.4	35.9
France	372.4	260.2	69.9

[Continued]

★ 638 ★

Nuclear Electricity Generation in OECD Area
[Continued]

Country	Terawatt-hours[1]		Share of Nuclear %
	Total	Nuclear	
Germany	402.5	137.8	34.2
Greece	30.5	0.0	0.0
Iceland	4.4	0.0	0.0
Ireland	12.2	0.0	0.0
Italy	196.8	0.0	0.0
Japan	641.8	174.8	27.2
Luxembourg	0.6	0.0	0.0
Netherlands	67.2	3.4	5.1
New Zealand	27.0	0.0	0.0
Norway	110.3	0.0	0.0
Portugal	21.4	0.0	0.0
Spain	133.3	48.3	36.2
Sweden	141.4	66.4	47.0
Switzerland	57.5	21.5	37.4
Turkey	64.8	0.0	0.0
United Kingdom	282.9	53.3	18.8
United States	2,701.0	527.0	19.5
OECD Total	6,075.9	1,430.2	23.5

Source: The OECD Observer, April/May 1990, p. 27, from *OECD Nuclear Energy Data 1989*, NEA/OECD, 1989. *Note:* 1. One terawatt-hour equals one thousand billion watt-hours.

★ 639 ★

Nuclear Energy Generating Unit Reactors Ordered in the U.S.

Unit Name and current status (12/31/1989)	Design Capacity (MWe)	Reactor Supplier[1]	Year of Order	Yearly Total	
				No. of Units Ordered	Design Capacity (MWe)
Shippingport Shut down, 1974. Resumed operation in 1977 as a light-water breeder reactor. Retired in 1982.	60	W	1953	1	60
Indian Point 1 Shut down, 1974. Operating license withdrawn in 1980.	265	B&W	1955	2	465
Dresden 1 Shut down, 1978. Decommissioning being planned.	200	GE	-	-	-
Yankee Rowe 1	175	W			

[Continued]

★ 639 ★

Nuclear Energy Generating Unit Reactors Ordered in the U.S.
[Continued]

Unit Name and current status (12/31/1989)	Design Capacity (MWe)	Reactor Supplier[1]	Year of Order	Yearly Total	
				No. of Units Ordered	Design Capacity (MWe)
Operating			1956	1	175
Humboldt Bay　Shut down, 1976.　Decommissioning being planned.	65	GE	1958	1	65
Big Rock Point　Operating	72	GE	1959	1	72
La Crosse　Retired	50	A-C	1962	2	632
Haddam Neck (Connecticut Yankee)　Operating	582	W	-	-	-
Malibu　Canceled, 1972	462	W	1963	5	3,018
San Onofre　Operating.	436	W	-	-	-
Hanford-N　Shut down[2]	850	GE	-	-	-
Nine Mile Point　Shut down. Restart planned for 8/89.	620	GE	-	-	-
Oyster Creek　Operating	650	GE	-	-	-
Dresden 2　Operating	794	GE	1965	7	4,475
Fort St. Vrain　Shutdown 1989	330	GA	-	-	-
Robert E. Ginna　Operating	470	W	-	-	-
Pilgrim 1　Operating	655	GE	-	-	-
Millstone 1　Operating	660	GE	-	-	-
Indian Point 2　Operating	873	W	-	-	-
Turkey Point 3　Operating	693	W	-	-	-
Dresden 3　Operating　Palisades	794	GE	1966	20	16,514

[Continued]

★ 639 ★

Nuclear Energy Generating Unit Reactors Ordered in the U.S.
[Continued]

Unit Name and current status (12/31/1989)	Design Capacity (MWe)	Reactor Supplier[1]	Year of Order	Yearly Total No. of Units Ordered	Yearly Total Design Capacity (MWe)
Operating	805	C-E	-	-	-
H.B. Robinson 2					
Operating	700	W	-	-	-
Point Beach 1					
Operating	497	W	-	-	-
Monticello					
Operating	545	GE	-	-	-
Quad-Cities 1					
Operating	789	GE	-	-	-
Browns Ferry 1					
Shut down. Restart unknown.	1,065	GE	-	-	-
Browns Ferry 2					
Shut down. Restart planned for 9/89.	1,065	GE	-	-	-
Oconee 1					
Operating	887	B&W	-	-	-
Oconee 2					
Operating	887	B&W	-	-	-
Quad-Cities 2					
Operating	789	GE	-	-	-
Peach Bottom 2					
Shut down.[3]	1,065	GE	-	-	-
Peach Bottom 3					
Shut down.[4]	1,065	GE	-	-	-
Salem 1					
Operating	1,090	W	-	-	-
Vermont Yankee					
Operating	514	GE	-	-	-
Fort Calhoun 1					
Operating	478	C-E	-	-	-
Surry 1					
Operating	788	W	-	-	-
Surry 2					
Operating	788	W	-	-	-
Diablo Canyon 1					
Operating	1,084	W	-	-	-
Three Mile Island 1					
Operating	819	B&W	-	-	-
Bell					
Canceled, 1972.	838	-	1967	31	26,470
Bailly					
Canceled, 1981	644	GE	-	-	-
Crystal River 3					

[Continued]

★ 639 ★

Nuclear Energy Generating Unit Reactors Ordered in the U.S.

[Continued]

Unit Name and current status (12/31/1989)	Design Capacity (MWe)	Reactor Supplier[1]	Year of Order	Yearly Total	
				No. of Units Ordered	Design Capacity (MWe)
Operating	825	B&W	-	-	-
Kewaunee					
Operating	535	W	-	-	-
Maine Yankee					
Operating	825	C-E	-	-	-
Prairie Island 1					
Operating	530	W	-	-	-
Point Beach 2					
Operating	497	W	-	-	-
Shoreham					
Operating license issued.[5]	820	GE	-	-	-
Zion 1					
Operating	1,040	W	-	-	-
Three Mile Island 2					
Shut down due to 1979 accident.	906	B&W	-	-	-
Arkansas Nuclear 1					
Operating	850	B&W	-	-	-
Cooper					
Operating	778	GE	-	-	-
Indian Point 3					
Operating	965	W	-	-	-
Turkey Point 4					
Operating	693	W	-	-	-
Calvert Cliffs 1					
Operating	845	C-E	-	-	-
Calvert Cliffs 2					
Operating	845	C-E	-	-	-
Oconee 3					
Operating	887	B&W	-	-	-
Salem 2					
Operating	1,115	W	-	-	-
Browns Ferry 3					
Shut down. Restart unknown.	1,065	GE	-	-	-
Prairie Island 2					
Operating.	530	W	-	-	-
Donald C. Cook 1					
Operating	1,030	W	-	-	-
Donald C. Cook 2					
Operating	1,100	W	-	-	-
Zion 2					
Operating	1,040	W	-	-	-
Rancho Seco 1					
Operating.[6]	918	B&W	-	-	-

[Continued]

★ 639 ★

Nuclear Energy Generating Unit Reactors Ordered in the U.S.
[Continued]

Unit Name and current status (12/31/1989)	Design Capacity (MWe)	Reactor Supplier[1]	Year of Order	Yearly Total	
				No. of Units Ordered	Design Capacity (MWe)
Beaver Valley 1					
Operating	835	W	-	-	-
Limerick 1					
Operating	1,065	GE	-	-	-
Limerick 2					
Operating	1,065	GE	-	-	-
North Anna 1					
Operating	907	W	-	-	-
Hatch 1					
Operating	777	GE	-	-	-
Millstone 2					
Operating	870	C-E	-	-	-
St. Lucie 1					
Operating	830	C-E	-	-	-
Verplanck 1					
Canceled, 1972.	1,115	GE	1968	16	15,167
Verplanck 2					
Canceled, 1972	1,115	GE	-	-	-
Brunswick 1					
Operating	821	GE	-	-	-
Brunswick 2					
Operating	821	GE	-	-	-
Duane Arnold 1					
Operating	538	GE	-	-	-
Sequoyah 1					
Operating	1,148	W	-	-	-
Sequoyah 2					
Operating	1,148	W	-	-	-
Midland 1					
Canceled, 1986.	492	B&W	-	-	-
Midland 2					
Canceled, 1986	818	B&W	-	-	-
Susquehanna 1					
Operating	1,065	GE	-	-	-
Susquehanna 2					
Operating	1,052	GE	-	-	-
Diablo Canyon 2					
Operating	1,084	W	-	-	-
Fermi 2					
Operating	1,093	GE	-	-	-
Davis-Besse 1					
Operating	906	B&W	-	-	-

[Continued]

★ 639 ★

Nuclear Energy Generating Unit Reactors Ordered in the U.S.

[Continued]

Unit Name and current status (12/31/1989)	Design Capacity (MWe)	Reactor Supplier[1]	Year of Order	Yearly Total	
				No. of Units Ordered	Design Capacity (MWe)
Trojan Operating	1,130	W	-	-	-
James A. Fitzpatrick Operating	821	GE	-	-	-
Joseph M. Farley 1 Operating	829	W	1969	7	7,203
Hope Creek 1 Operating	1,067	GE	-	-	-
Hope Creek 2 Canceled, 1981	1,067	GE	-	-	-
Zimmer 1 Canceled, 1984	810	GE	-	-	-
McGuire 1 Operating	1,180	W	-	-	-
McGuire 2 Operating	1,180	W	-	-	-
Forked River 1 Canceled, 1980	1,070	C-E	-	-	-
North Anna 2 Operating	907	W	1970	14	14,272
San Onofre 2 Operating	1,070	C-E	-	-	-
San Onofre 3 Operating	1,080	C-E	-	-	-
Hatch 2 Operating	784	GE	-	-	-
Arkansas Nuclear 2 Operating	912	C-E	-	-	-
LaSalle 1 Operating	1,078	GE	-	-	-
LaSalle 2 Operating	1,078	GE	-	-	-
North Coast 1 Canceled, 1978	538	W	-	-	-
Bellefonte 1 Indefinitely deferred	1,235	B&W	-	-	-
Bellefonte 2 Indefinitely deferred	1,235	B&W	-	-	-
Watts Bar 1 Under construction	1,165	W	-	-	-
Watts Bar 2					

[Continued]

★ 639 ★

Nuclear Energy Generating Unit Reactors Ordered in the U.S.
[Continued]

Unit Name and current status (12/31/1989)	Design Capacity (MWe)	Reactor Supplier[1]	Year of Order	Yearly Total	
				No. of Units Ordered	Design Capacity (MWe)
Under construction[7]	1,165	W	-	-	-
Waterford 3					
Operating	1,151	C-E	-	-	-
Joseph M. Farley 2					
Operating	829	W	-	-	-
Crystal River 4					
Canceled, 1972	897	W	1971	21	21,193
Stanislaus 1					
Canceled, 1979	1,200	GE	-	-	-
Stanislaus 2					
Canceled, 1979	1,200	GE	-	-	-
Summer 1					
Operating	900	W	-	-	-
WNP 2					
Operating	1,100	GE	-	-	-
Byron 1					
Operating	1,120	W	-	-	-
Byron 2					
Operating	1,120	W	-	-	-
Shearon Harris 1					
Operating	915	W	-	-	-
Shearon Harris 2					
Canceled, 1983	915	W	-	-	-
Shearon Harris 3					
Canceled, 1981	900	W	-	-	-
Shearon Harris 4					
Canceled, 1981	900	W	-	-	-
North Anna 3					
Canceled, 1982	907	B&W	-	-	-
North Anna 4					
Canceled, 1980	907	B&W	-	-	-
Fulton 1					
Canceled, 1975	1,160	GA	-	-	-
Fulton 2					
Canceled, 1975	1,160	GA	-	-	-
Beaver Valley 2					
Operating	852	W	-	-	-
Vogtle 1					
Operating	1,210	W	-	-	-
Vogtle 2					
Operating	1,210	W	-	-	-
Nine Mile Point 2					

[Continued]

★ 639 ★

Nuclear Energy Generating Unit Reactors Ordered in the U.S.
[Continued]

Unit Name and current status (12/31/1989)	Design Capacity (MWe)	Reactor Supplier[1]	Year of Order	Yearly Total	
				No. of Units Ordered	Design Capacity (MWe)
Operating	1,080	GE	-	-	-
Summit 1 Canceled, 1975	770	GA	-	-	-
Summit 2 Canceled, 1975	770	GA	-	-	-
Perryman 1 Canceled, 1972	845	C-E	1972	38	41,373
Perryman 2 Canceled, 1972	845	C-E	-	-	-
Fermi 3 Canceled, 1974	1,171	GE	-	-	-
Quanicassee 1 Canceled, 1974	1,150	W	-	-	-
Quanicassee 2 Canceled 1974	1,150	W	-	-	-
Vidal 1 Canceled, 1974	770	GA	-	-	-
Vidal 2 Canceled, 1974	770	GA	-	-	-
Grand Gulf 1 Operating	1,250	GE	-	-	-
Grand Gulf 2 Indefinitely deferred	1,250	GE	-	-	-
Pilgrim 2 Canceled, 1981	1,150	C-E	-	-	-
Greenwood 2 Canceled, 1980	1,264	B&W	-	-	-
Greenwood 3 Canceled, 1980	1,264	B&W	-	-	-
Perry 1 Operating	1,205	GE	-	-	-
Perry 2 Indefinitely deferred	1,205	GE	-	-	-
Seabrook 1 Operating license issued	1,198	W	-	-	-
Seabrook 2 Canceled, 1988[8]	1,198	W	-	-	-
Catawba 1 Operating	1,145	W	-	-	-
Catawba 2 Operating	1,145	W	-	-	-
Riverbend 1					

[Continued]

★ 639 ★

Nuclear Energy Generating Unit Reactors Ordered in the U.S.
[Continued]

Unit Name and current status (12/31/1989)	Design Capacity (MWe)	Reactor Supplier[1]	Year of Order	Yearly Total	
				No. of Units Ordered	Design Capacity (MWe)
Operating	934	GE	-	-	-
Atlantic 1					
Canceled, 1978	1,150	W	-	-	-
Atlantic 2					
Canceled, 1978	1,150	W	-	-	-
Braidwood 1					
Operating	1,120	W	-	-	-
Braidwood 2					
Operating	1,120	W	-	-	-
Douglas Point 1					
Canceled, 1977	1,146	GE	-	-	-
Douglas Point 2					
Canceled, 1977	1,146	GE	-	-	-
Surry 3					
Canceled, 1977	859	B&W	-	-	-
Surry 4					
Canceled, 1977	859	B&W	-	-	-
Comanche Peak 1					
Under construction	1,150	W	-	-	-
Comanche Peak 2					
Under construction	1,150	W	-	-	-
Clinch River Breeder					
Canceled, 1983	350	W	-	-	-
St. Lucies 2					
Operating	804	C-E	-	-	-
WNP 1					
Indefinitely deferred[9]	1,266	B&W	-	-	-
Barton 1					
Canceled, 1977	1,159	GE	-	-	-
Barton 2					
Canceled, 1977	1,159	GE	-	-	-
Hartsville A1					
Canceled	1,205	GE	-	-	-
Hartsville A2					
Canceled, 1984	1,205	GE	-	-	-
Hartsville B1					
Canceled, 1982	1,233	GE	-	-	-
Hartsville B2					
Canceled, 1982	1,233	GE	-	-	-
Tyrone 2					
Canceled, 1974	1,150	W	1973	41	46,975
Vogtle 3					

[Continued]

★ 639 ★

Nuclear Energy Generating Unit Reactors Ordered in the U.S.
[Continued]

Unit Name and current status (12/31/1989)	Design Capacity (MWe)	Reactor Supplier[1]	Year of Order	Yearly Total	
				No. of Units Ordered	Design Capacity (MWe)
Canceled, 1974	1,113	W	-	-	-
Vogtle 4					
Canceled, 1974	1,113	W	-	-	-
Clinton 1					
Operating	950	GE	-	-	-
Clinton 2					
Canceled, 1983	950	GE	-	-	-
Blue Hills 1					
Canceled, 1978	918	C-E	-	-	-
Millstone 3					
Operating	1,156	W	-	-	-
Pebble Springs 1					
Canceled, 1982	1,260	B&W	-	-	-
Allens Creek 1					
Canceled, 1982	1,150	GE	-	-	-
Allens Creek 2					
Canceled, 1976	1,150	GE	-	-	-
Cherokee 1					
Canceled	1,280	C-E	-	-	-
Cherokee 2					
Canceled, 1982	1,280	C-E	-	-	-
Cherokee 3					
Canceled, 1982	1,280	C-E	-	-	-
Perkins 1					
Canceled, 1982	1,280	C-E	-	-	-
Perkins 2					
Canceled, 1982	1,280	C-E	-	-	-
Perkins 3					
Canceled, 1982	1,280	C-E	-	-	-
Jamesport 1					
Rejected by New York State, 1980.	1,150	W	-	-	-
Callaway 1					
Operating	1,188	W	-	-	-
Callaway 2					
Canceled 1981.	1,120	W	-	-	-
Haven 1					
Canceled 1980	900	W	-	-	-
Haven 2					
Canceled 1978	900	W	-	-	-
South Texas 1					
Operating	1,250	W	-	-	-
South Texas 2					
Operating	1,250	W	-	-	-

[Continued]

★ 639 ★

Nuclear Energy Generating Unit Reactors Ordered in the U.S.
[Continued]

Unit Name and current status (12/31/1989)	Design Capacity (MWe)	Reactor Supplier[1]	Year of Order	Yearly Total	
				No. of Units Ordered	Design Capacity (MWe)
Sterling					
Canceled, 1980	1,150	W	-	-	-
Tyrone 1					
Canceled, 1979	1,100	W	-	-	-
Wolf Creek					
Operating	1,150	W	-	-	-
WNP 3					
Indefinitely deferred[9]	1,242	C-E	-	-	-
River Bend 2					
Canceled, 1984	934	GE	-	-	-
Palo Verde 1					
Operating	1,304	C-E	-	-	-
Palo Verde 2					
Operating	1,304	C-E	-	-	-
Palo Verde 3					
Operating	1,304	C-E	-	-	-
Atlantic 3					
Canceled, 1978	1,150	W	-	-	-
Atlantic 4					
Canceled, 1978	1,150	W	-	-	-
Black Fox 1					
Canceled, 1982	1,150	GE	-	-	-
Black Fox 2					
Canceled, 1982	1,150	GE	-	-	-
Davis-Besse 2					
Canceled, 1980	906	B&W	-	-	-
Davis-Besse 3					
Canceled, 1980	906	B&W	-	-	-
Skagit-Hanford 1					
Canceled, 1983	1,277	GE	-	-	-
South River 1					
Canceled 1978	1,150	B&W	-	-	-
South River 2					
Canceled, 1978	1,150	B&W	-	-	-
South River 3					
Canceled, 1978	1,150	B&W	-	-	-
Orange 1					
Canceled, 1975	1,300	C-E	1974	28	33,265
Orange 2					
Canceled, 1975	1,300	C-E	-	-	-
St. Rosalie 1					
Canceled, 1975	1,160	GA	-	-	-

[Continued]

★ 639 ★

Nuclear Energy Generating Unit Reactors Ordered in the U.S.
[Continued]

Unit Name and current status (12/31/1989)	Design Capacity (MWe)	Reactor Supplier[1]	Year of Order	Yearly Total	
				No. of Units Ordered	Design Capacity (MWe)
St. Rosalie 2 Canceled, 1975	1,160	GA	-	-	-
Somerset 1 Canceled, 1975	1,200	GE	-	-	-
Somerset 2 Canceled 1975	1,200	GE	-	-	-
Zimmer 2 Canceled 1978	1,170	GE	-	-	-
Jamesport 2 Rejected by New York State, 1980	1,150	W	-	-	-
Blue Hills 2 Canceled 1978	918	C-E	-	-	-
Nees 1 Canceled 1979	1,150	W	-	-	-
Nees 2 Canceled 1979	1,150	W	-	-	-
Pebble Springs 2 Canceled 1982	1,260	B&W	-	-	-
Greene County Canceled 1979	1,212	B&W	-	-	-
Montague 1 Canceled 1980	1,150	GE	-	-	-
Montague 2 Canceled 1980	1,150	GE	-	-	-
Skagit-Hanford 2 Canceled 1983	1,277	GE	-	-	-
WNP 4 Canceled 1982	1,218	B&W	-	-	-
WNP 5 Canceled 1982	1,240	C-E	-	-	-
Fort Calhoun 2 Canceled 1977	1,136	W	-	-	-
Marble Hill 1 Canceled 1985	1,130	W	-	-	-
Marble Hill 2 Canceled 1985	1,130	W	-	-	-
Phipps 1 Canceled 1982	1,233	GE	-	-	-
Phipps 2 Canceled 1982	1,233	GE	-	-	-
Yellow Creek 1 Canceled 1984	1,285	C-E	-	-	-
Yellow Creek 2					

[Continued]

★ 639 ★

Nuclear Energy Generating Unit Reactors Ordered in the U.S.
[Continued]

Unit Name and current status (12/31/1989)	Design Capacity (MWe)	Reactor Supplier[1]	Year of Order	Yearly Total	
				No. of Units Ordered	Design Capacity (MWe)
Canceled 1984	1,285	C-E	-	-	-
Barton 3					
Canceled 1975	1,159	GE	-	-	-
Barton 4					
Canceled 1975	1,159	GE	-	-	-
Sears Isle					
Canceled 1977	1,150	W	-	-	-
South Dade 1					
Canceled 1977	1,100	W	1975	4	4,148
South Dade 2					
Canceled 1977	1,100	W	-	-	-
Sundesert 1					
Canceled 1978	974	W	-	-	-
Sundesert 2					
Canceled 1978	974	W	-	-	-
Vandalia (Iowa 1)					
Canceled 1982	1,270	B&W	1976	3	3,804
Erie 1					
Canceled 1980	1,267	B&W	-	-	-
Erie 2					
Canceled 1980	1,267	B&W	-	-	-
NYSE&G 1					
Rejected by New York State, 1980	1,250	C-E	1977	4	5,040
NYSE&G 2					
Rejected by New York State, 1980	1,250	C-E	-	-	-
Palo Verde 4					
Canceled 1979	1,270	C-E	-	-	-
Palo Verde 5					
Canceled 1979	1,270	C-E	-	-	▪
Carroll County 1					
Canceled 1988	1,120	W	1978	2	2,240

[Continued]

★ 639 ★

Nuclear Energy Generating Unit Reactors Ordered in the U.S.

[Continued]

Unit Name and current status (12/31/1989)	Design Capacity (MWe)	Reactor Supplier[1]	Year of Order	Yearly Total	
				No. of Units Ordered	Design Capacity (MWe)
Carroll County 2 Canceled 1988	1,120	W	-	-	-

Source: Commercial Nuclear Power 1990: Prospects for the United States and the World, U.S. Department of Energy, DOE/EIA-0348(89), Washington, D.C., January 1991, p. 101, from Energy Information Administration, *U.S. Commercial Nuclear Power.* DOE/EIA-0315 (Washington, DC, November 1984); Energy Information Administration, *Nuclear Plant Cancellations: Causes, Costs, and Consequences,* DOE/EIA-0392 (Washington, DC, April 1983); Energy Information Administration, Form EIA-254, "Semiannual Report on Status of Reactor Construction"; Nuclear Regulatory Commission, *Licensed Operating Reactors,* NUREG-0020 (November 1986) *Notes:* 1. Reactor Suppliers: A-C, Allis-Chalmers; B&W, Babcock & Wilcox Co.; C-E, Combustion Engineering Inc.; GA, General Atomic Company; GE, General Electric Co.; W, Westinghouse Corp. 2. Unit placed in cold standby status by the Department of Energy, February 1988. 3. Resumed operation, June 1989. 4. Restart authorized. 5. A tentative agreement has been made between the State of New York and Long Island Lighting Company to close the plant. 6. Shutdown by referendum June 1989. 7. Unit is in an indefinite slowdown. No schedule exists for its completion. 8. Construction permit expired in October, 1988. 9. Extension of Construction Permit requested.

★ 640 ★

Nuclear Energy Generating Units in the U.S.

The generating units are listed operable as of December 31, 1989. Capacity is shown in megawatts.

Site	Unit Name	Capacity[1] (Net MWe)	Utility[2]	Reactor[3]		Date Operable
				Type	Supplier	
Region I - New England						
Connecticut						
Haddam Neck	Haddam Neck (Connecticut Yankee)	656	Connecticut L&P	PWR	W	8/67
Waterford	Millstone 1	652	Connecticut L&P	BWR	GE	11/70
Waterford	Millstone 2	863	Connecticut L&P	PWR	C-E	11/75
Waterford	Millstone 3	1,137	Connecticut L&P	PWR	W	1/86
Maine						
Wicasset	Maine Yankee	845	Maine Yankee Atomic Power	PWR	C-E	11/72
Massachusetts						
Plymouth	Pilgrim 1	667	Boston Edison	BWR	GE	7/72
Rowe	Yankee Rowe1	167	New England Power	PWR	W	11/60
Vermont						
Vernon	Vermont Yankee	496	Vermont Yankee Nuclear Power	BWR	GE	9/72

[Continued]

★ 640 ★

Nuclear Energy Generating Units in the U.S.
[Continued]

Site	Unit Name	Capacity[1] (Net MWe)	Utility[2]	Reactor[3] Type	Reactor[3] Supplier	Date Operable
Total Region I		5,391[4]				
Region II - New York/New Jersey						
New York						
Buchanan	Indian Point 2	849	Consolidated Edison	PWR	W	6/73
Buchanan	Indian Point 3	965	Power Authority of the State of New York	PWR	W	4/76
Rochester	Robert E. Ginna	470	Rochester Gas & Electric	PWR	W	12/69
Oswego	Nine Mile Point 1	610	Niagara Mohawk Power	BWR	GE	11/69
Oswego	Nine Mile Point 2	1,072	Niagara Mohawk Power	BWR	GE	7/87
Scriba	James A. Fitzpatrick	800	Power Authority of the State of New York	BWR	GE	2/75
New Jersey						
Forked River	Oyster Creek 1	620	Jersey Central P&L	BWR	GE	9/69
Salem	Salem 1	1,106	Public Service E & G and Philadelphia Electric	PWR	W	12/76
Salem	Salem 2	1,106	Public Service E&G and Philadelphia Electric	PWR	W	6/81
Salem	Hope Creek 1	1,031	Public Service E&G	BWR	GE	7/86
Total Region II		8,629				
Region III - Middle Atlantic						
Maryland						
Lusby	Calvert Cliffs 1	825	Baltimore G&E	PWR	C-E	1/75
Lusby	Calvert Cliffs 2	825	Baltimore G&E	PWR	C-E	12/76

[Continued]

★ 640 ★

Nuclear Energy Generating Units in the U.S.
[Continued]

Site	Unit Name	Capacity[1] (Net MWe)	Utility[2]	Reactor[3]		Date Operable
				Type	Supplier	
Pennsylvania						
Berwick	Susquehanna 1	1,050	Pennsylvania P&L	BWR	GE	11/82
Berwick	Susquehanna 2	1,050	Pennsylvania P&L	BWR	GE	6/84
Middletown	Three Mile Island 1	808	Metropolitan Edison	PWR	B&W	6/74
Lancaster	Peach Bottom 2	1,051	Philadelphia Electric	BWR	GE	2/74
Lancaster	Peach Bottom 3	1,035	Philadephia Electric and Public Service E&G	BWR	GE	9/74
Pottstown	Limerick 1	1,055	Philadelphia Electric	BWR	GE	8/85
Pottstown	Limerick 2	1,055	Philadelphia Electric	BWR	GE	8/89
Shippingport	Beaver Valley 1	810	Duquesne Light	PWR	W	6/76
Shippingport	Beaver Valley 2	833	Ohio Edison	PWR	W	8/87
Virginia						
Surry	Surry 1	781	Virginia Electric and Power	PWR	W	7/72
Surry	Surry 2	781	Virginia Electric and Power	PWR	W	3/73
Mineral	North Anna 1	915	Virginia Electric & Power	PWR	W	4/78
Mineral	North Anna 2	915	Virginia Electric & Power	PWR	W	8/80
Total Region III		13,789				
Region IV - South Atlantic						
Alabama						
Decatur	Browns Ferry 1	1,065	Tennessee Valley Authority	BWR	GE	10/73
Decatur	Browns Ferry 2	1,065	Tennessee Valley	BWR	GE	8/74

[Continued]

★ 640 ★

Nuclear Energy Generating Units in the U.S.

[Continued]

Site	Unit Name	Capacity[1] (Net MWe)	Utility[2]	Reactor[3]		Date Operable
				Type	Supplier	
Decatur	Browns Ferry 3	1,065	Authority Tennessee Valley	BWR	GE	9/76
Dothan	Joseph M. Farley 1	816	Authority Alabama Power	PWR	W	8/77
Dothan	Joseph M. Farley 2	825	Alabama Power	PWR	W	5/81
Florida						
Florida City	Turkey Point 3	666	Florida P&L	PWR	W	11/72
Florida City	Turkey Point 4	666	Florida P&L	PWR	W	6/73
Ft. Pierce	St. Lucie 1	839	Florida P&L	PWR	C-E	5/76
Ft. Pierce	St. Lucie 2	839	Florida P&L	PWR	C-E	6/83
Red Level	Crystal River 3	666	Florida Power Corp.	PWR	B&W	1/77
Georgia						
Baxley	Hatch 1	760	Georgia Power	BWR	GE	11/74
Baxley	Hatch 2	772	Georgia Power	BWR	GE	9/78
Waynesboro	Vogtle 1	1,086	Georgia Power	PWR	W	3/87
Waynesboro	Vogtle 2	1,086	Georgia Power	PWR	W	3/89
Mississippi						
Port Gibson	Grand Gulf 1	1,142	System Energy Resources, Inc.	BWR	GE	9/84
North Carolina						
Cowens Ford Dam	McGuire 1	1,129	Duke Power	PWR	W	9/81
Cowens Ford Dam	McGuire 2	1,129	Duke Power	PWR	W	5/83
New Hill	Shearon Harris 1	860	Carolina P&L	BWR	GE	1/87
Southport	Brunswick 1	790	Carolina P&L	BWR	GE	12/76
Southport	Brunswick 2	790	Carolina P&L	BWR	GE	4/75
South Carolina						
Clover	Catawba 1	1,129	North Carolina Electric Membership Corporation	PWR	W	1/85
Clover	Catawba 2	1,129	North Carolina Municipal	PWR	W	5/86

[Continued]

★ 640 ★

Nuclear Energy Generating Units in the U.S.
[Continued]

Site	Unit Name	Capacity[1] (Net MWe)	Utility[2]	Reactor[3]		Date Operable
				Type	Supplier	
Hartsville	H.B. Robinson 2	665	Power Carolina P&L	PWR	W	9/70
Jenkinsville	Summer 1	885	South Carolina E&G	PWR	W	11/82
Seneca	Oconee 1	846	Duke Power	PWR	B&W	5/73
Seneca	Oconee 2	846	Duke Power	PWR	B&W	12/73
Seneca	Oconee 3	846	Duke Power	PWR	B&W	9/74
Tennessee						
Daisy	Sequoyah 1	1,148	Tennessee Valley Authority	PWR	W	7/80
Daisy	Sequoyah 2	1,148	Tennessee Valley Authority	PWR	W	12/81
Total Region IV		26,697[4]				
Region V						
Braidwood	Braidwood 1	1,090	Commonwealth Edison	PWR	W	7/87
Braidwood	Braidwood 2	1,090	Commonwealth Edison	PWR	W	5/88
Byron	Byron 1	1,120	Commonwealth Edison	PWR	W	2/85
Byron	Byron 2	1,120	Commonwealth Edison	PWR	W	1/87
Clinton	Clinton 1	930	Illinois Power	BWR	GE	4/87
Cordova	Quad-Cities 1	769	Commonwealth Edison	BWR	GE	4/72
Cordova	Quad-cities 2	769	Commonwealth Edison	BWR	GE	5/72
Morris	Dresden 2	772	Commonwealth Edison	BWR	GE	4/70
Morris	Dresden 3	773	Commonwealth Edison	BWR	GE	7/71
Seneca	LaSalle 1	1,048	Commonwealth Edison	BWR	GE	9/82
Seneca	LaSalle 2	1,048	Commonwealth Edison	BWR	GE	3/84
Zion	Zion 1	1,040	Commonwealth Edison	PWR	W	6/73
Zion	Zion 2	1,040	Commonwealth Edison	PWR	W	12/73

[Continued]

★ 640 ★

Nuclear Energy Generating Units in the U.S.
[Continued]

Site	Unit Name	Capacity[1] (Net MWe)	Utility[2]	Reactor[3] Type	Reactor[3] Supplier	Date Operable
Michigan						
Bridgman	Donald C. Cook 1	1,030	Indiana & Michigan Electric	PWR	W	2/75
Bridgman	Donald C. Cook 2	1,100	Indiana & Michigan Electric	PWR	W	3/78
Charlevoix	Big Rock Point	67	Consumers Power	BWR	GE	12/62
Newport	Fermi 2	1,028	Detroit Edison	BWR	GE	7/85
South Haven	Palisades	755	Consumers Power	PWR	C-E	12/71
Minnesota						
Monticello	Monticello	541	Northern States Power	BWR	GE	3/71
Red Wing	Praire Island 1	504	Northern States Power	PWR	W	12/73
Red Wing	Prairie Island 2	504	Northern States Power	PWR	W	12/74
Ohio						
Oak Harbor	Davis-Besse 1	856	Cleveland Elec. Illum.	PWR	B&W	8/77
North Perry	Perry 1	1,185	Ohio Edison	BWR	GE	11/86
Wisconsin						
Carlton	Kewaunee	530	Wisconsin Public Service	PWR	W	4/74
Two Creeks	Point Beach 1	485	Wisconsin Electric Power	PWR	W	11/70
Two Creeks	Point Beach 2	485	Wisconsin Electric Power	PWR	W	8/72
Total Region V		21,679				
Region VI - Southwest						
Arkansas						
Russellville	Arkansas Nuclear 1	836	Arkansas P&L	PWR	B&W	7/74
Russellville	Arkansas Nuclear 2	858	Arkansas P&L	PWR	C-E	12/78

[Continued]

★ 640 ★

Nuclear Energy Generating Units in the U.S.

[Continued]

Site	Unit Name	Capacity[1] (Net MWe)	Utility[2]	Reactor[3] Type	Reactor[3] Supplier	Date Operable
Louisiana St. Francisville	River Bend 1	936	Gulf State Utilities	BWR	GE	11/85
Taft	Waterford 3	1,075	Louisiana P&L	PWR	C-E	3/85
Texas Bay City	South Texas 1	1,251	Houston L&P	PWR	W	3/88
Bay City	South Texas 2	1,250	Houston L&P	PWR	W	3/89
Total Region VI		6,206				
Region VII - Central						
Iowa Palo	Duane Arnold	500	Iowa Electric	BWR	GE	5/74
Kansas Burlington	Wolf Creek	1,128	Kansas City P&L and Kansas City Gas & Electric	PWR	W	6/85
Missouri Fulton	Callaway 1	1,118	Union Electric	PWR	W	10/84
Nebraska Brownville	Cooper	778	Nebraska Public Power District	BWR	GE	5/74
Fort Calhoun	Fort Calhoun 1	476	Omaha Public Power District	PWR	C-E	8/73
Total Region VII		4,000				
Region IX - West **Arizona** Wintersburg	Palo Verde 1	1,221	Arizona Public Service	PWR	C-E	6/85
Wintersburg	Palo Verde 2	1,221	Arizona Public Service	PWR	C-E	4/86
Wintersburg	Palo Verde 3	1,221	Arizona Public Service	PWR	C-E	11/87
California Avila Beach	Diablo Canyon 1	1,073	Pacific Gas and Electric	PWR	W	11/84
Avila Beach	Diablo Canyon 2	1,079	Pacific Gas and Electric	PWR	W	8/85
Clay Station	Rancho Seco	873	Sacramento	PWR	B&W	10/74

[Continued]

★ 640 ★

Nuclear Energy Generating Units in the U.S.
[Continued]

Site	Unit Name	Capacity[1] (Net MWe)	Utility[2]	Reactor[3]		Date Operable
				Type	Supplier	
San Clemente	San Onofre 1	436	Municipal Utility District Southern California Edison	PWR	W	7/67
San Clemente	San Onofre 2	1,070	Southern California Edison	PWR	C-E	9/82
San Clemente	San Onofre 3	1,080	Southern California Edison	PWR	C-E	9/83
Total Region IX		9,274				
Region X - Northwest **Oregon** Prescott	Trojan	1,104	Portland General Electric	PWR	W	12/75
Washington Richland	WNP 2	1,100	Washington Public Power Supply System	BWR	GE	4/84
Total Region X		2,204				
Total United States (110 Units)		97,869				

Source: Commercial Nuclear Power 1990: Prospects for the United States and the World, U.S. Department of Energy, DOE/EIA-0348(89), Washington, D.C., January 1991, p. 89, from the Energy Information Administration (EIA) in the January 1989 Form EIA-860 survey. Capacity shown is net summer capacity, as reported to the Energy Information Administration. Totals may not equal sum of components due to independent rounding. *Notes:* 1. Net summer capability 2. Principal owner 3. Reactor types: BWR, boiling-water reactor; HTGR, high-temperature gas-cooled reactor; LGR, light-water-cooled, graphite-moderated reactor; PWR, pressurized-water reactor. Reactor suppliers: B&W, Babcock & Wilcox Co.; C-E, Combustion Engineering, Inc.; GE, General Electric; W, Westinghouse Electric Corporation.

★ 641 ★

Nuclear Energy Generation

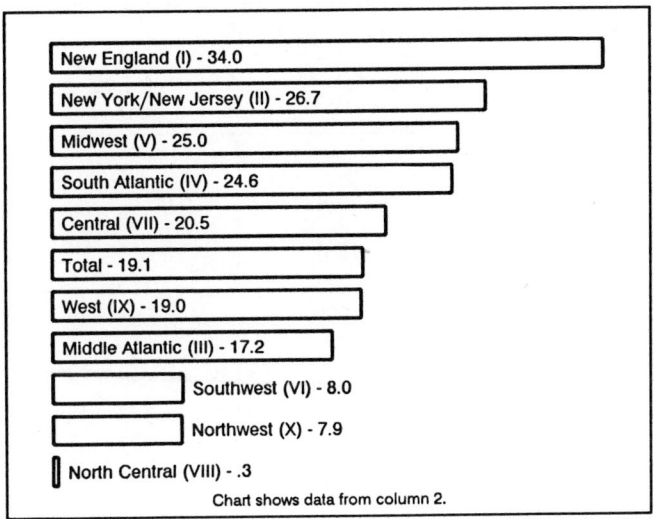

New England (I) - 34.0
New York/New Jersey (II) - 26.7
Midwest (V) - 25.0
South Atlantic (IV) - 24.6
Central (VII) - 20.5
Total - 19.1
West (IX) - 19.0
Middle Atlantic (III) - 17.2
Southwest (VI) - 8.0
Northwest (X) - 7.9
North Central (VIII) - .3

Chart shows data from column 2.

Federal Region	Actual 1989		No New Orders Case (Net TWh)[1]	
	Net TWh[1]	Percent share[2]	2000	2010
New England (I)	33.1	34.0	37.6	34.3
New York/New Jersey (II)	45.9	26.7	44.0	36.9
Middle Atlantic (III)	56.1	17.2	77.1	81.6
South Atlantic (IV)	150.8	24.6	162.0	184.8
Midwest (V)	130.6	25.0	119.4	120.2
Southwest (VI)	31.2	8.0	50.5	53.5
Central (VII)	29.3	20.5	21.6	22.9
North Central (VIII)	.5	.3	0	0
West (IX)	40.4	19.0	48.4	49.2
Northwest (X)	11.4	7.9	11.1	11.8
Total	529.4	19.1	571.7	595.1

Source: Commercial Nuclear Power 1990: Prospects for the United States and the World, U.S. Department of Energy, DOE/EIA-0348(89), Washington, D.C., January 1991, p. 7, from 1989 Data—Energy Information Administration, Form EIA-759, "Monthly Power Plan Report" (preliminary data). Projections—Energy Information Administration, *Annual Outlook for U.S. Electric Power 1990*, DOE/EIA-0474(90), (Washington DC, June 1990). Totals may not equal sum of components due to independent rounding. *Notes:* 1. TWh stands for Terawatthours. One TWh is equivalent to one billion kilowatts. 2. Nuclear generated electricity as a percentage of electricity generated from all sources.

★ 642 ★

Nuclear Power Generating Capacity Worldwide

The data represent projected values in thousands of megawatts for 1980, 1990, and 2000 made in the year shown in the left column.

Source and year of projection	Projection For		
	1980	1990	2000
International Atomic Energy Agency			
1972	315	1,300	3,500
1974	235	1,600	4,450
1976	225	1,150	2,300
1978	170	585	1,400
1980	137	458	910
1982	-	386	833
1984	-	382	605
1986	-	372	505
Worldwatch Institute			
1988	-	320	360

Source: World Watch, July/August 1988, p. 33, from International Atomic Energy Agency, *Annual Reports* (Vienna: 1972-80); IAEA, *Reference Data series No. 1*, Vienna, September 1982; IAEA, *Nuclear Power: Status and Trends* (Vienna: 1984-86); Worldwatch Institute.

★ 643 ★

Nuclear Power Plants Construction in the U.S.

The construction is as of December 31, 1989. Capability shown in megawatts.

Site	Unit Name	Net Summer Capability (Net MWe)	Utility[1]	Reactor[2]		Status[3]		Estimated Operable Date[4]		
				Type	Supplier	% Complete	License	Utility[4]	EIA[5]	
									LR	UR
Region I--New England										
New Hampshire Seabrook	Seabrook 1	1,150	Public Service Co. of New Hampshire	PWR	W	100	LP[6]	3/90	6/90	6/90
Total Region I		1,150								
Region II-- New York/New Jersey	0[8]									
Region III --Middle Atlantic	0									
Region IV--South Atlantic **Alabama** Scottsboro	Bellefonte 1	1,212	Tennessee Valley Authority	PWR	B&W	85	ID	7	6/2000	6/2000
Scottsboro	Bellefonte 2	1,212	Tennessee Valley Authority	PWR	B&W	56	ID	7	6/2009	6/2009
Mississippi Port Gibson	Grand Gulf 2	1,250	Middle South	BWR	GE	34	ID	7	-	-

[Continued]

★ 643 ★

Nuclear Power Plants Construction in the U.S.
[Continued]

Site	Unit Name	Net Summer Capability (Net MWe)	Utility[1]	Reactor[2]		Status[3]		Estimated Operable Date[4]		
				Type	Supplier	% Complete	License	Utility[4]	EIA[5] LR	UR
			Utilities							
Tennessee **Spring City**	Watts Bar 1	1,170	Tennessee Valley Authority	PWR	W	99	CP	6/91	6/92	6/92
Spring Valley	Watts Bar 2	1,170	Tennessee Valley Authority	PWR	W	84	CP	7	3/95	3/95
Total Region IV		6,014								
Region V--Midwest **Ohio** **North Perry**	Perry 2	1,179	Cleveland Electric Illuminating	BWR	GE	44	ID	7	-	6/2009
Total Region V		1,179								
Region VI--Southwest **Texas** **Glen Rose**	Comanche Peak 1	1,150	Texas Utilities Generating Co.	PWR	W	99	CP[9]	10/89	4/90	4/90
Glen Rose	Comanche Peak 2	1,150	Texas Utilities Generating Co.	PWR	W	87	CP	4/91	3/92	3/92
Total Region VI		2,300								
Region VII-- Central		0								
Region VIII--North Central		0								
Region IX--West		0								
Region X--Northwest **Washington** **Richland**	WNP 1	1,250	Washington Public Power Supply System	PWR	B&W	63	ID	7	6/2001	6/2001
Satsop	WNP 3	1,250	Washington Public Power Supply System	PWR	C-E	75	ID	7	-	6/2006
Total Region X **Total United States (11 Units)**		2,500 13,143[8]								

Source: *Commercial Nuclear Power 1990: Prospects for the United States and the World*, U.S. Department of Energy, DOE/EIA-0348(89), Washington, D.C., January 1991, p. 98, from Nuclear Regulatory Commission, *Licensed Operating Reactors*, NUREG-0020 (December 1983); Nuclear Regulatory Commission, *Regulatory Licensing Status Summary Report*, NUREG-0580 (January 1985); and Energy Information Administration, Form EIA-254, "Semiannual Report on Status of Reactor Construction" (1988). Notes: 1. Principal owner. 2. Reactor types: BWR, boiling-water reactor; PWR, pressurized-water reactor. Reactor Suppliers: B&W, Babcock and Wilcox Co.; C-E, Combustion Engineering, Inc.; GE, General Electric Corporation; W, Westinghouse Corp. 3. License Status: CP, construction permit issued; ID, indefinitely deferred; LP, low power operating license issued. 4. Represents the approximate midpoint between the first fuel load date and the commercial operation date, as reported on Form EIA-254, second half 1989. 5. EIA estimates for the Lower Reference (LR) and Upper Reference (UR) cases. 6. Seabrook received a Full-Power License in March 1990. 7. No commercial operation date has been estimated by the utility. 8. Shoreham received a full power license in April 1989. Since the unit is not currently scheduled to operate, it has not been included in the total for units in the construction pipeline or operable units. 9. Comanche Peak received a Low-Power License in February, and a Full-Power License in April of 1990.

★ 644 ★

Operable Nuclear Energy Capacity by Federal Region

```
Total - 97.9
                    South Atlantic (IV) - 26.7
                  Midwest (V) - 21.7
              Middle Atlantic (III) - 13.8
          West (IX) - 9.3
          New York/New Jersey (II) - 8.6
        Southwest (VI) - 6.2
      New England (I) - 5.4
     Central (VII) - 4.0
   Northwest (X) - 2.2
  North Central (VIII) - 0
                    Chart shows data from column 1.
```

Values are shown in gigawatts.

Federal Region	Capacity (Net GWe)[1]		
	1989	No New Orders Case[2]	
		2000	2010
New England (I)	5.4	6.4	5.2
New York/New Jersey (II)	8.6	8.6	6.9
Middle Atlantic (III)	13.8	13.8	13.8
South Atlantic (IV)	26.7	30.2	30.8
Midwest (V)	21.7	21.7	20.4
Southwest (VI)	6.2	8.5	8.5
Central (VII)	4.0	4.0	4.0
North Central (VIII)	0	0	0
West (IX)	9.3	8.4	8.0
Northwest (X)	2.2	2.2	2.2
Total	97.9	103.8	99.7

Source: Commercial Nuclear Power 1990: Prospects for the United States and the World, U.S. Department of Energy, DOE/EIA-0348(89), Washington, D.C., January 1991, p. 7, from Capacities: Energy Information Administration, Form EIA-860, "Annual Electric Generator Report" (1989). Projections—Energy Information Administration, *Annual Outlook for Electric Power 1990*, DOE/EIA-0474(90) (July 1990). *Notes:* 1. Capacity values are based on net summer capability ratings. 2. Totals may not equal sum of components due to independent rounding.

★ 645 ★

Petroleum- and Gas-Fired Generator Capacity

Number and nameplate capacity of petroleum-and gas-fired steam-electric generators in plants that have environmental equipment. Data are shown by state for 1989.

Census Division and State	Generating Units		Scrubbers		Particulate Collectors		Cooling Towers	
	Number of Generators	Capacity[2] (megawatts)	Number of Generators	Capacity[2] (megawatts)	Number of Generators	Capacity[2] (megawatts)	Number of Generators	Capacity[2] (megawatts)
New England	44	7,459	0	0	43	7,044	1	415
Connecticut	17	2,803	0	0	16	2,389	1	415
Maine	9	993	0	0	9	993	0	0
Massachusetts	8	2,850	0	0	8	2,850	0	0
New Hampshire	4	564	0	0	4	564	0	0
Rhode Island	6	249	0	0	6	249	0	0
Vermont	0	0	0	0	0	0	0	0
Middle Atlantic	57	13,552	0	0	54	11,716	4	2,012
New Jersey	14	2,130	0	0	13	1,995	2	311
New York	31	7,841	0	0	31	7,841	0	0
Pennsylvania	12	3,581	0	0	10	1,880	2	1,701
East North Central	15	2,315	0	0	9	730	3	1,441
Illinois	1	210	0	0	0	0	1	210
Indiana	5	284	0	0	2	140	0	0
Michigan	6	1,743	0	0	4	512	2	1,231
Ohio	0	0	0	0	0	0	0	0
Wisconsin	3	78	0	0	3	78	0	0
West North Central	20	1,690	0	0	6	204	17	1,547
Iowa	1	19	0	0	1	19	0	0
Kansas	15	1,536	0	0	1	50	14	1,486
Minnesota	1	75	0	0	1	75	0	0
Missouri	3	61	0	0	3	61	3	61
Nebraska	0	0	0	0	0	0	0	0
North Dakota	0	0	0	0	0	0	0	0
South Dakota	0	0	0	0	0	0	0	0
South Atlantic	67	16,745	3	65	49	12,843	20	4,946
Delaware	7	662	3	65	4	511	3	151
District of Columbia	2	580	0	0	0	0	2	580
Florida	34	10,552	0	0	23	8,700	11	1,853
Georgia	0	0	0	0	0	0	0	0
Maryland	13	2,594	0	0	11	1,276	3	1,480
North Carolina	7	455	0	0	7	455	0	0
South Carolina	0	0	0	0	0	0	0	0
Virginia	4	1,902	0	0	4	1,902	1	882
West Virginia	0	0	0	0	0	0	0	0
East South Central	10	846	0	0	1	147	9	699
Alabama	0	0	0	0	0	0	0	0
Kentucky	1	147	0	0	1	147	0	0
Mississippi	9	699	0	0	0	0	9	699
Tennessee	0	0	0	0	0	0	0	0
West South Central	105	15,938	0	0	5	2,452	103	14,780
Arkansas	7	580	0	0	0	0	7	580
Louisiana	18	2,728	0	0	2	1,184	17	2,136
Oklahoma	19	4,350	0	0	1	567	18	3,783
Texas	61	8,281	0	0	2	701	61	8,281
Mountain	43	3,120	0	0	2	101	43	3,120
Arizona	20	1,597	0	0	0	0	20	1,597
Colorado	3	111	0	0	2	101	3	111
Idaho	NA	3	3	3	3	3	3	3
Montana	0	0	0	0	0	0	0	0
Nevada	6	433	0	0	0	0	6	433
New Mexico	13	910	0	0	0	0	13	910
Utah	1	69	0	0	0	0	1	69
Wyoming	0	0	0	0	0	0	0	0

[Continued]

★ 645 ★

Petroleum- and Gas-Fired Generator Capacity
[Continued]

Census Division and State	Generating Units		Scrubbers		Particulate Collectors		Cooling Towers	
	Number of Generators	Capacity[2] (megawatts)	Number of Generators	Capacity[2] (megawatts)	Number of Generators	Capacity[2] (megawatts)	Number of Generators	Capacity[2] (megawatts)
Pacific Contiguous	33	3,705	0	0	6	527	31	3,379
California	33	3,705	0	0	6	527	31	3,379
Oregon	0	0	0	0	0	0	0	0
Washington	0	0	0	0	0	0	0	0
Pacific Noncontiguous	0	0	0	0	0	0	0	0
Alaska	0	0	0	0	0	0	0	0
Hawaii	0	0	0	0	0	0	0	0
U.S. Total	394	65,370	3	65	175	35,764	231	32,337

Source: Energy Information Administration, *Electric Power Annual 1989*, January 1991, p. 78, from Energy Information Administration, Form EIA-767, "Steam-Electric Plant Operation and Design Report." Totals may not equal sum of components because of independent rounding. These data are only for plants with a fossil-fueled steam-electric capacity of 100 or more megawatts. Data for 1989 are preliminary. Data include petroleum coke. *Notes:* 1. Components are not additive since some generators are included in more than one category and not all units have environmental equipment. 2. Nameplate capacity 3. Not applicable.

★ 646 ★

Renewable Energy by State and Source
Renewable energy (billion BTUs) replaces oil and avoids millions of tons of carbon dioxide.

State	Biomass Total	Geothermal Electric	Geothermal Heat	Conventional Hydro	Solar Thermal Electric	Photo-voltiacs	Wind	Total^ Renewables	Million Barrels of Oil Equiva-lent	Million Tons CO Avoided
Alabama	225,084.1	0.0	11.8	100,007.8	0.0	2.25	0.2	325,106.1	55.3	26.0
Alaska	4,219.0	0.0	51.1	10,406.8	0.0	0.00	1.1	14,678.0	2.5	1.2
Arizona	5,590.2	0.0	233.4	80,322.0	0.0	6.14	9.7	86,161.5	14.6	6.9
Arkansas	125,929.0	0.0	113.3	30,263.6	0.0	0.00	0.2	156,306.0	26.6	12.5
California	215,521.0	225,525.0	1,170.5	412,006.6	7,843.5	217.98	21,761.9	884,046.4	150.3	70.7
Colorado	27,315.0	0.0	374.3	19,921.6	0.0	0.22	1.8	47,612.9	8.1	3.8
Connecticut	73,826.0	0.0	0.0	4,818.9	0.0	0.03	1.3	78,646.2	13.4	6.3
Delaware	10,144.0	0.0	57.7	0.0	0.0	0.00	0.1	10,201.8	1.7	0.8
District of Columbia	328.5	0.0	0.0	0.0	0.0	6.74	0.0	335.2	0.1	0.0
Florida	152,385.0	0.0	1,265.0	2,829.8	0.0	2.67	0.0	156,482.5	26.6	12.5
Georgia	335,388.0	0.0	37.8	39,135.7	n/a	0.09	0.4	374,562.0	63.7	30.0
Hawaii	18,953.7	0.0	0.0	1,002.7	0.0	2.25	427.6	20,386.2	3.5	1.6
Idaho	25,486.3	0.0	647.1	109,399.5	0.0	0.01	0.3	135,533.2	23.0	10.8
Illinois	73,515.0	0.0	283.9	1,981.9	0.0	0.51	14.1	75,795.5	12.9	6.1
Indiana	44,335.0	0.0	534.7	6,006.2	0.0	0.01	2.6	50,878.6	8.6	4.1
Iowa	19,692.0	0.0	65.9	8,543.8	0.0	0.09	0.8	28,302.7	4.8	2.3
Kansas	2,900.0	0.0	25.7	66.6	0.0	0.00	28.7	3,021.0	0.5	0.2
Kentucky	63,551.0	0.0	248.3	34,337.3	0.0	0.25	0.0	98,136.9	16.7	7.9
Louisiana	185,214.0	0.0	126.6	0.0	0.0	0.00	0.0	185,340.6	31.5	14.8
Maine	66,353.0	0.0	0.0	33,558.1	0.0	0.05	1.1	99,912.2	17.0	8.0
Maryland	32,479.0	0.0	131.8	18,174.5	0.0	0.34	0.1	50,785.7	8.6	4.1
Massachusetts	53,363.0	0.0	1.0	12,067.8	0.0	4.67	2.4	65,438.8	11.1	5.2
Michigan	95,779.0	0.0	570.3	18,445.1	0.0	0.09	0.3	114,794.8	19.5	9.2
Minnesota	97,856.0	0.0	152.0	11,606.4	0.0	0.00	9.8	109,624.2	18.6	8.8
Mississippi	152,519.0	0.0	7.6	0.0	0.0	0.00	n/a	152,526.6	25.9	12.2
Missouri	58,700.0	0.0	76.0	14,077.4	0.0	0.00	0.2	72,853.6	12.4	5.8
Montana	18,104.0	0.0	3,928.6	104,303.8	0.0	0.00	0.1	126,336.5	21.5	10.1
Nebraska	2,603.0	0.0	66.2	13,790.3	0.0	0.00	0.5	16,459.9	2.8	1.3
Nevada	5,008.0	8,876.0	842.6	23,499.9	0.0	0.00	0.2	38,226.7	6.5	3.1

[Continued]

★ 646 ★

Renewable Energy by State and Source
[Continued]

State	Biomass Total	Geothermal Electric	Geothermal Heat	Conventional Hydro	Solar Thermal Electric	Photo-voltiacs	Wind	Total^ Renewables	Million Barrels of Oil Equivalent	Million Tons CO Avoided
New Hampshire	35,295.0	0.0	0.0	15,728.1	0.0	0.06	4.6	51,027.7	8.7	4.1
New Jersey	20,652.0	0.0	65.9	591.1	0.0	0.11	0.0	21,309.1	3.6	1.7
New Mexico	17,040.0	0.0	114.5	2,351.0	0.0	2.99	37.1	19,545.6	3.3	1.6
New York	113,173.0	0.0	62.6	253,706.4	0.0	0.00	0.7	366,942.7	62.4	29.4
North Carolina	189,181.0	0.0	129.3	54,780.8	0.0	0.00	0.4	244,091.4	41.5	19.5
North Dakota	640.0	0.0	602.2	24,289.4	0.0	0.00	2.4	25,553.9	4.3	2.0
Ohio	76,896.0	0.0	364.9	5,546.9	0.0	0.00	0.5	82,808.3	14.1	6.6
Oklahoma	20,104.0	0.0	1.0	21,269.8	0.0	3.03	48.7	41,426.6	7.0	3.3
Oregon	128,178.0	0.0	411.4	294,711.2	0.0	0.26	22.5	423,323.3	72.0	33.9
Pennsylvania	78,517.0	0.0	194.3	23,643.4	0.0	0.02	3.3	102,358.1	17.4	8.2
Rhode Island	6,139.0	0.0	0.0	379.4	0.0	0.34	1.2	6,519.9	1.1	0.5
South Carolina	118,818.0	0.0	86.2	39,311.0	0.0	0.00	0.0	158,215.2	26.9	12.7
South Dakota	1,528.0	0.0	487.3	55,848.1	0.0	00.2	0.0	57,863.4	9.8	4.6
Tennessee	103,597.0	0.0	24.7	97,126.7	0.0	0.74	0.1	200,749.2	34.1	16.1
Texas	22,942.0	n/a	226.8	16,210.0	0.0	8.98	31.5	39,419.3	6.7	3.2
Utah	5,500.0	3,175.7	263.0	11,339.8	0.0	0.25	0.0	19,278.8	3.3	1.5
Vermont	22,084.0	0.0	0.0	11,450.6	0.0	0.00	2.8	33,537.3	5.7	2.7
Virginia	131,677.0	0.0	104.3	12,114.9	0.0	0.18	0.0	143,896.5	24.5	11.5
Washington	106,868.0	0.0	47.4	1,023,858.4	0.0	0.01	2.2	1,130,776.0	192.2	90.5
West Virginia	25,806.0	0.0	0.0	12,662.5	0.0	0.00	0.0	38,468.5	6.5	3.1
Wisconsin	37,787.0	0.0	304.2	22,566.9	0.0	0.13	5.5	60,663.7	10.3	4.9
Wyoming	2,820.0	0.0	4,140.7	9,770.1	0.0	0.00	0.0	16,730.8	2.8	1.3

Source: Energy, Summer Issue 1990, p. 16. *Note:* n/a means not available.

★ 647 ★

Renewable Energy Use Worldwide

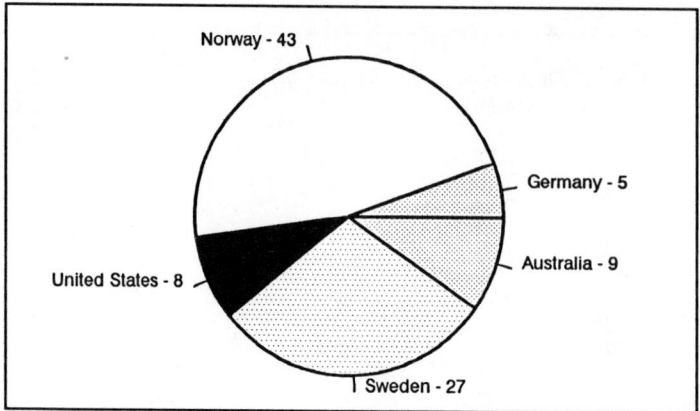

Shares, by nation, of energy derived from renewable sources worldwide. Renewable energy forms include wind power, solar thermal, hydropower, biomass, geothermal, ocean power and photovoltaics. Renewable energy accounts for 17 percent of total energy use worldwide. Shares are shown in percent.

Nation	Shares in Percent
Norway	43
Sweden	27
Australia	9
United States	8[1]
Germany	5

Source: Garbage, January/February 1991, p. 58, from Rocky Mountain Institute, Worldwatch Institute. *Note:* 1. Range is 8 to 9 percent.

★ 648 ★

Wind-Electric Potential as Percent of Electric Generation

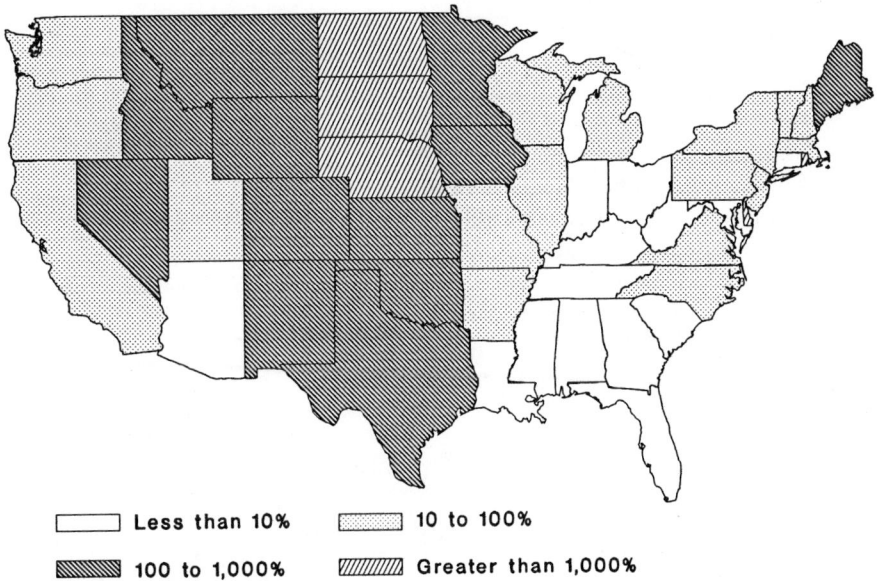

☐ Less than 10% ▦ 10 to 100%

▨ 100 to 1,000% ▥ Greater than 1,000%

Source: Scientific American, September 1990, p. 148. *Notes:* Wind-electric potential is expressed as a percentage of electric generation in the state shown. Areas with percentile rates in excess of 100 percent could be exporters of wind-generated power.

Pulp and Paper

★ 649 ★

EPA Targeted Pulp Mills for High Dioxin Levels

The data show estimates of the risk of cancer during the lifetime of an exposed individual who eats fish downstream of the mill.

Company/ mill site	Cancer risk
International Paper, Georgetown, S.C.	2 in 100
Union Camp, Franklin, Va.	2 in 1,000
Buckeye Cellulose, Perry, Fla.	2 in 1,000
Weyerhaeuser Co., Plymouth, N.C.	2 in 1,000
Westvaco, Covington, Va.	1 in 1,000
Georgia-Pacific, Palatka, Fla.	6 in 10,000
International Paper, Moss Point, Miss.	3 in 10,000
Temple-Eatex, Evadale, Tx.	3 in 10,000
Champion, Canton, N.C.	2 in 10,000
Georgia-Pacific, Crossett, Ark.	2 in 10,000
International Paper, Texarkana, Tx.	2 in 10,000

[Continued]

★ 649 ★

EPA Targeted Pulp Mills for High Dioxin Levels
[Continued]

Company/ mill site	Cancer risk
International Paper, Jay, Me.	1 in 10,000
Boise Cascade, Rumford, Me.	1 in 10,000
St. Joe Paper, Port St. Joe, Fla.	1 in 10,000
Boise Cascade, DeRidder, Rumford, La.	1 in 10,000
Simpson Paper, Anderson, Calif.	1 in 10,000
Simpson Paper, Fairhaven, Calif.	1 in 10,000
Weyerhaeuser Co., Cosmopolis, Wash.	1 in 10,000
Weyerhaeuser Co., Everett, Wash.	1 in 10,000

Source: Pulp & Paper, November, 1990, p. 31, from EPA.

★ 650 ★

Fiber Consumption in the U.S.
Consumption in tons for each ton of paper and board produced.

Year	Total[1]	Woodpulp	Wastepaper	Other[2]
Historical				
1952	1.080	.708	.323	.050
1962	1.029	.762	.242	.026
1970	1.021	.807	.198	.016
1976	1.004	.794	.198	.012
1986	1.025	.810	.209	.005
Projections				
2000	0.998	.785	.210	.002
2010	0.988	.764	.222	.002
2020	0.978	.730	.246	.002
2030	0.976	.709	.267	-[3]
2040	0.977	.697	.280	-[3]

Source: Resource Recycling, November 1989, p. 45, from Ulrich, Alice H. U.S. Department of Agriculture. Forest Service. *U.S. Timber Production, Trade, Consumption, and Price Statistics, 1950-1987*. Misc. Pub. No.1471. Washington, D.C. 1989. Projections: U.S. Department of Agriculture, Forest Service. *Notes:* 1. Data may not add to totals due to rounding. 2. Includes cotton linters, rags, bagasse, straw, kenaf, etc. 3. Less than .001 tons.

★ 651 ★

Fluff Pulp Consumption in the U.S. by End Use

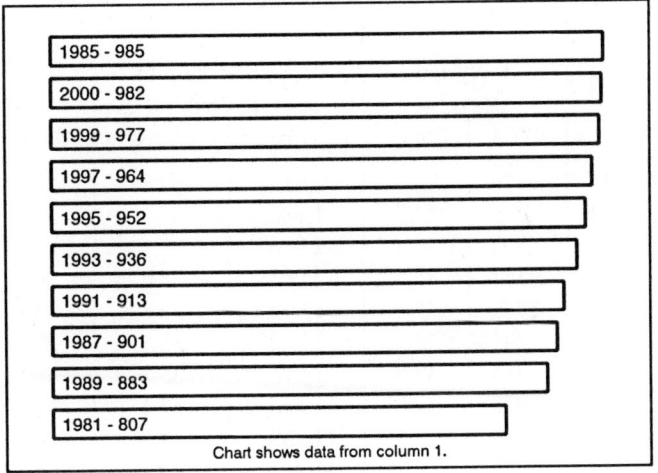

Chart shows data from column 1.

Projected consumption by end use. In thousands of metric tons.

Year	Total[1]	Infant diapers[2]	Adult incontinence products[3]
1981	807	648	89
1985	985	818	103
1987	901	715	121
1989	883	686	138
1991	913	699	158
1993	936	701	182
1995	952	697	204
1997	964	689	223
1999	977	684	243
2000	982	679	252

Source: Pulp & Paper, March 1988, p. 79, from Marketing/Technology Service, Inc. *Notes:* 1. Includes fluff pulp consumed in feminine pads. 2. Based on the forecast that the market share for superabsorbent diapers will steadily increase through the year 2000. 3. Retail and institutional.

★ 652 ★

Folding Boxboard Market by Grade

Folding boxboard shares of the U.S. market, shown in thousands of tons and in percent.

Year	Total	Recycled		Solid Bleached Sulfate (SBS)		Coated Unbleached Kraft	
		Tons	Share	Tons	Share	Tons	Share
1990[1]	5,221	2,443	46.8	1,834	35.1	944	18.1
1989	5,370	2,402	44.7	1,980	36.9	987	18.4
1988	5,292	2,352	44.4	2,016	38.1	924	17.5
1987	5,210	2,342	45.0	2,003	38.4	865	16.6
1986	5,056	2,256	44.6	1,911	37.8	889	17.6
1985	4,805	2,241	46.7	1,742	36.2	822	17.1
1980	4,490	2,234	49.8	1,575	35.1	680	15.1
1975	3,896	1,978	50.8	1,456	37.4	463	11.0
1970	4,080	2,473	60.6	1,263	31.0	343	8.4
1968	4,218	2,730	64.7	1,227	29.1	261	6.2

Source: Resource Recycling, January 1991 from American Paper Institute. Numbers for each year may not add up due to rounding. *Note:* 1. Estimated numbers for 1990.

★ 653 ★

Largest Importers of U.S. Paperstock

Values are shown in thousands of short tons.

Country	1980	1981	1982	1983	1984	1985	1986	1987	1988	1989
Canada	451	357	271	347	326	209	226	287	332	285
Italy	199	114	82	56	-	166	154	140	269	222
Japan	201	84	106	266	309	301	399	660	608	530
Korea	408	518	512	557	773	676	839	939	1,226	1,231
Mexico	588	346	236	427	455	457	580	781	1,133	102
Spain	-	-	-	-	95	104	134	130	170	243
Taiwan	370	386	462	545	726	758	892	895	991	1,169
Venezuela	116	129	129	100	113	-	-	-	67	80
Other	330	279	329	276	439	578	524	591	845	2,119
Total	2,664	2,213	2,127	2,574	3,235	3,286	3,749	4,422	5,640	5,981

Source: Facts 1989 Year Book, Institute of Scrap Recycling Industries, Inc., p. 23, from American Paper Institute. Data may not add to totals due to independent rounding.

★ 654 ★

Paper and Paperboard Production and Consumption

Values are shown in thousands of short tons.

Year	Paper and Paperboard Production	Reported Paperstock Consumption	Paperstock Market Share[1] (percent)
1979	64,345	15,820	25
1980	63,600	15,394	24
1981	64,259	15,518	24
1982	60,958	14,920	25
1983	66,761	16,122	24
1984	70,268	17,183	25
1985	68,833	16,850	25
1986	72,689	18,428	25
1987	74,433	19,201	26
1988[2]	76,662	20,388	27
1989	77,058	21,398	28

Source: Facts 1989 Year Book, Institute of Scrap Recycling Industries, Inc., p. 22, from American Paper Institute. *Notes:* 1. Paper Stock Market Share is calculated from reported paperstock consumption (column 3) divided by paper and paperboard production (column 2). 2. Revised.

★ 655 ★

Paperstock Consumption by Grade

Values are shown in thousands of short tons.

Year	Mixed Grades	Newspapers[1]	Corrugated	Pulp Substitutes	High Grade Deinking	Total All Grades[1]
1979	2,648.0	2,780.0	6,967.0	2,308.0	1,117.0	15,820.0
1980	2,268.0	2,864.0	6,866.0	2,254.0	1,142.0	15,394.0
1981	2,233.0	2,852.0	6,910.0	2,307.0	1,216.0	15,518.0
1982	1,707.0	2,973.0	6,770.0	2,247.0	1,223.0	14,920.0
1983	1,908.0	2,992.0	7,443.0	2,456.0	1,323.0	16,122.0
1984	1,974.5	3,194.8	7,971.7	2,673.4	1,368.6	17,183.0
1985	1,901.5	3,175.0	7,899.5	2,493.7	1,380.4	16,850.1
1986	2,044.5	3,417.8	8,633.6	2,761.5	1,570.3	18,427.7
1987	2,116.2	3,442.5	9,176.7	2,902.8	1,562.9	19,201.1
1988[2]	2,182.3	3,715.4	9,909.4	2,890.3	1,690.2	20,387.6
1989	2,239.7	3,836.8	10,522.0	2,922.6	1,876.4	21,397.5

Source: Facts 1989 Year Book, Institute of Scrap Recycling Industries, Inc., p. 22, from American Paper Institute. *Notes:* 1. Includes estimate for non-paper paperboard uses. 2. Revised.

★ 656 ★

Secondary Fiber Use by Region

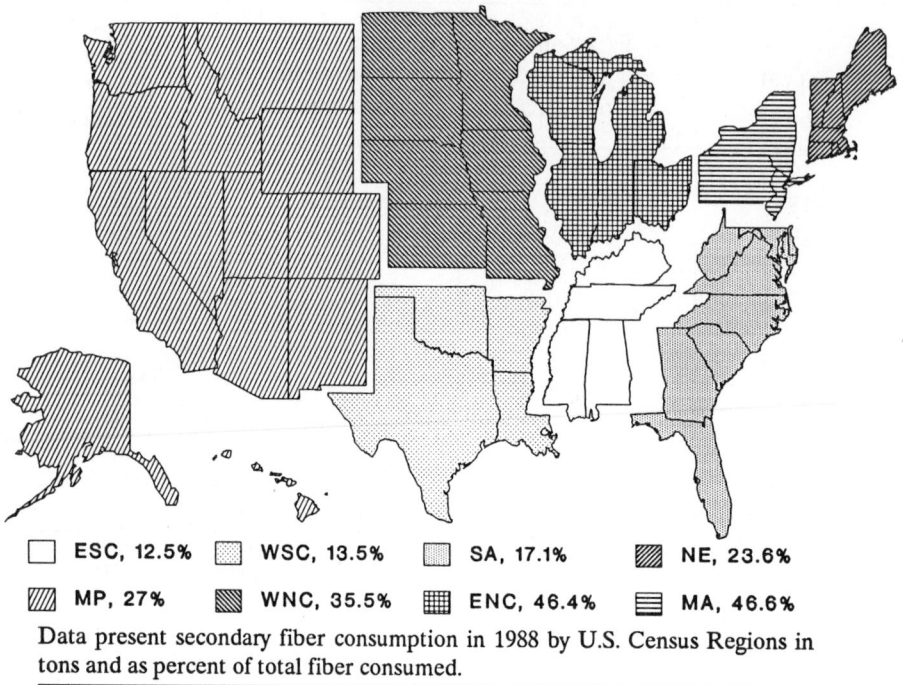

☐ ESC, 12.5%	▦ WSC, 13.5%	▦ SA, 17.1%	▨ NE, 23.6%
▨ MP, 27%	▨ WNC, 35.5%	▦ ENC, 46.4%	☰ MA, 46.6%

Data present secondary fiber consumption in 1988 by U.S. Census Regions in tons and as percent of total fiber consumed.

Region	Tons of Secondary Fiber Consumed	Percent of Total Fiber Consumed
New England (NE)	1,339	23.6
Mid-Atlantic (MA)	2,356	46.6
South Atlantic (SA)	3,420	17.1
East North Central (ENC)	5,612	46.4
East South Central (ESC)	1,349	12.5
West North Central (WNC)	581	35.5
West South Central (WSC)	1,659	13.5
Mountain and Pacific (MP)	3,272	27.0

Source: Pulp & Paper, November 1989, p. 71, from American Paper Institute. Paper, waste.

★ 657 ★

U.S. Paper and Board Annual Capacity

The value is in thousands short tons.

Grades	1989	1990	1991[1]	1992[1]
Total all grades	84,583	87,148	90,340	93,236
Total paper and paperboard	82,444	85,001	88,182	91,077
Total paper	41,326	42,649	44,342	45,600
Newsprint	6,280	6,806	7,123	7,281
Printing/writing	23,811	24,393	25,492	26,460
Uncoated groundwood	1,846	1,808	1,877	1,905
Coated groundwood	4,467	4,607	4,621	4,658
Coated free-sheet	3,675	3,892	4,282	4,735
Uncoated free-sheet	12,149	12,403	13,022	13,463
Cotton fiber	205	210	212	212
Thin paper	287	288	288	289
Solid bleached bristols	1,183	1,185	1,188	1,188
Packaging and industrial converting	5,472	5,475	5,600	5,657
Unbleached Kraft	2,854	2,871	2,889	2,905
Bleached packaging and industrial converting	466	429	442	442
Speciality packaging	657	660	709	722
Special industrial	1,495	1,515	1,559	1,587
Tissue	5,762	5,972	6,127	6,203
Total paperboard	41,119	42,352	43,840	45,476
Unbleached kraft	20,86	21,482	22,409	23,249
Kraft linerboard	19,195	19,781	20,543	21,280
Solid bleached	4,723	4,838	5,051	5,202
Semichemical	5,917	6,003	6,010	6,220
Recycled	9,612	10,029	10,370	10,805
Total construction paper, paperboard, and other	2,139	2,148	2,159	2,180

Source: Pulp & Paper, p. 178, February 1990, from American Paper Institute *Notes:* 1. Capacity additions presented here include only presently known commitments.

★ 658 ★

U.S. Paperstock Exports by Grade

Values are shown in thousands of short tons.

Year	Newspapers	Old Paperboard	Corrugated Paper and Substitutes	High Grade Pulp Paper, n.e.c.[1]	Total
1980	424,864	1,208,690	381,323	649,395	2,664,272
1981	425,060	991,115	322,511	473,863	2,212,549
1982	439,131	886,655	304,139	497,125	2,127,050
1983	461,218	993,436	414,279	704,783	2,573,716
1984	539,431	1,260,845	549,687	885,478	3,235,441
1985	625,631	1,310,876	469,594	879,825	3,285,926
1986	766,087	1,529,722	759,205	693,697	3,748,711
1987	870,240	1,921,679	892,313	738,104	4,422,336
1988	1,008,664	2,277,166	1,469,453	884,835	5,640,118
1989	829,459	2,695,368	1,556,030	899,798	5,980,655

Source: Facts 1989 Year Book, Institute of Scrap Recycling Industries, Inc., p. 23, from American Paper Institute. *Notes:* 1. n.e.c. stands for not elsewhere classified. .

★ 659 ★

Worldwide Paper Consumption

| United States - 639 |
| Sweden - 505 |
| Canada - 465 |
| Japan - 381 |
| Hong Kong - 337 |
| Britain - 315 |
| Taiwan - 289 |
| Italy - 207 |
| USSR - 74 |
| China - 23 |
| Nigeria - 9 |

Consumption is shown in pounds per capita.

Country	Consumption (lbs. per person)
United States	639
Sweden	505
Canada	465
Japan	381
Hong Kong	337
Britain	315
Taiwan	289
Italy	207
USSR	74
China	23
Nigeria	9

Source: U.S. News & World Report, February 29, 1988, p. 75, from *Pulp & Paper.* Figure for USSR is estimated.

Raw Materials

★ 660 ★

Raw Materials Consumption in the U.S.

Estimated daily per capita raw materials consumption in the U.S. in 1989.

Material	Pounds per Capita
Petroleum and coal	40
Other minerals	30
Agricultural products	26
Forest products	19
Total	115

Source: World Watch, November/December 1990, p. 17, from U.S. Government agencies.

Resource Recovery

★ 661 ★

Aluminum Scrap Industry

Values are in thousands of short tons.

Year	Primary Production	Old & New Scrap Consumed	Metal and Scrap		Stocks (Includes Scrap)	Stock Changes	Apparent Aluminum Consumption[1]	Scrap Market Share[2] (percent)
			Imports	Exports				
1979	5,023,000	1,705,031	839,966	773,385	2,555,920	-191,058	6,985,670	24.4
1980	5,130,000	1,693,633	713,040	1,483,211	2,538,002	-17,918	6,071,380	27.8
1981	4,948,000	2,012,423	935,162	867,174	3,303,325	+765,323	6,263,088	32.1
1982	3,609,000	1,978,888	968,056	824,469	3,099,740	-203,585	5,935,060	33.3
1983	3,696,000	2,107,630	1,202,814	855,081	2,504,616	-595,124	6,746,487	31.2
1984	4,518,000	2,092,891	1,628,310	808,882	2,650,000	+145,384	7,284,935	28.8
1985	3,857,000	2,070,719	1,565,204	1,000,752	2,350,000	-300,000	6,792,171	30.5
1986	3,348,000	2,075,140	2,167,857	830,022	2,240,000	-110,000	6,733,055	30.9
1987[3]	3,685,000	2,042,116	2,038,519	1,010,765	2,087,757	-147,243	6,902,113	29.6

[Continued]

★ 661 ★

Aluminum Scrap Industry
[Continued]

Year	Primary Production	Old & New Scrap Consumed	Metal and Scrap		Stocks (Includes Scrap)	Stock Changes	Apparent Aluminum Consumption[1]	Scrap Market Share[2] (percent)
			Imports	Exports				
1988[3]	4,348,000	2,339,102	1,785,942	1,374,581	2,098,779	+11,022	7,087,241	33.0
1989	4,442,000	2,396,411	1,620,396	1,778,026	2,021,637	-77,142	6,757,923	35.5

Source: Facts 1989 Year Book, Institute of Scrap Recycling Industries, Inc., p. 2, from U.S. Bureau of Mines. Bureau of the Census. *Notes:* 1. Apparent Aluminum Consumption is defined as refined production + net trade - stock change. 2. Scrap Market Share is calculated from purchased scrap (column 3) divided by apparent aluminum consumption (column 8). 3. Revised.

★ 662 ★

Aluminum - Used Beverage Can Consumption

Values are shown in thousands of pounds.

	1983	1984	1985	1986	1987	1988	1989
Producers	1,053,000	1,167,700	1,193,775	1,163,931	1,243,000	1,426,000[1]	1,611,000[1]
Secondary smelters, other consumers	24,000	25,000	24,225	14,784	30,700	-	-
Exporters	3,000	3,800	13,814	13,480	60,500	78,600	76,700
Total	1,080,000	1,196,500	1,231,814	1,192,195	1,335,000	1,505,000	1,688,000
Recycling rate (percent)	50.0	51.3	50.5	47.1	50.5	54.6	60.8
Cans per pound	23.0	25.9	26.6	27.0	27.4	28.3	29.3
Cans shipped (Billions of Cans)	56.7	60,452	64,908	68,343	72,458	77,886	81,350

Source: Facts 1989 Year Book, Institute of Scrap Recycling Industries, Inc., p. 2, from ISRI *Note:* 1. Producers, secondary smelters, other consumers combined.

★ 663 ★

Beverage Bottle Recycling by Company

Supplier	Nameplate bottle capacity[1] million lb.	
	Operating as of 7/1/90	Additions through 1/1/92
Wellman, Johnsonville, SC[2]	160	
Du Pont, Wilimington, DE	30 (60)[3]	60 (120)[4]
Day Products, Bridgeport,NJ	40	
Nicon Plastics, Long Is. City, NY[5]	40	
M.A. Polymers, Peachtree City, GA	20	20[6]
St. Jude Polymer, Frackville, PA	20	10[6]
wTe Recycling/ Star, Bedford, MA[7]	20	
Pelo Plastics, Montreal, Quebec	15[8]	
CPR (Rutgers), Piscataway,NJ[9]	5	
Union Carbide PRC, Danbury, CT.[10]		11 (40)[3]
Puretech, Pine Brook, NJ[11]		25
Clean Tech, Dundee, MI[12]		12 (24)[3]
Polymer Resource Group, Baltimore, MD[13]		9 (22)[3]
Johnson Controls, Manchester, MI[14]		20
Agra Industries, Saskatoon, SASK		10
Total	350	177

Source: Modern Plastics, July, 1990, p. 12. *Notes:* 1. Defined as annual volume of PET beverage bottles a plant could reprocess into clean flake when run at full capacity on a continuous basis. Assumes 80% of bottle weight is PET (70:30 ratio of clear and green), 20% is HDPE. 2. Primary captive use. 3. Nameplate capacity for reclaiming plastic bottles of all types is shown in parenthesis. Counted in this table is that nameplate fraction the supplier estimates is specifically for PET beverage bottles. 4. New 30 million lb. plants in Phliladelphia and Chicago are expected to "ream out" at 40 million lb. in 1991. A 40 million lb. West Coast facility is set to open in third quarter 1991. 5. Formerly NyConn Industries 6. Expansion set for summer, 1990. 7. wTe acquired Star Plastics on April 3. 8. Parent company, Robert Peloquin, Inc., expects startup in July; plans to make PET sheet for use in beverage packaging by 1991. 9. Primarily a research facility. 10. New Jersey plant is due onstream in first half 1991. 11. Plant in Pine Brook, NJ, due onstream in mid-1991. 12. Owned by Plastipak 13. Baltimore plant using AKW technology is due onstream in late 1991. 14. Startup of plant in Novi, MI, is set for late 1990; technology is licensed from DSM, a Dutch firm.

★ 664 ★

Iron and Steel Scrap Industry

Values are shown in thousands of short tons.

Year	Receipts From Dealers & Other Sources	Receipts From Other Own Company	Scrap Shipments	Net Domestic Scrap Consumption[1]	Raw Steel Production	Foundry Shipments	Steel Castings Shipments	Apparent Steel Consumption[2]	Scrap Market Share[3] (percent)
1979	43,901	9,290	6,228	46,963	136,341	16,117	2,039	154,497	30.3
1980	39,310	7,527	5,883	40,954	111,835	12,249	1,878	125,962	32.5
1981	40,030	7,359	5,408	41,981	120,828	12,223	1,743	124,794	31.1
1982	27,520	4,195	3,721	27,994	74,577	8,499	916	83,992	33.4
1983	32,808	5,011	3,600	34,219	84,615	9,524	726	94,865	36.0
1984	34,325	5,624	3,889	36,060	92,528	10,900	940	99,274	34.9
1985	37,362	5,983	4,527	38,818	88,259	10,126	889	99,274	39.1
1986	37,123	4,700	3,819	38,004	81,606	8,653	829	91,088	41.8
1987	42,101	5,736	3,029	44,808	89,151	8,924	830	98,905	45.3
1988[4]	47,059	5,505	2,951	49,613	99,924	8,876	1,013	109,813	45.2
1989	43,560	5,510	3,136	45,934	97,943	7,773	1,137	106,853	43.0

Source: Facts 1989 Year Book, Institute of Scrap Recycling Industries, Inc., p. 8, from U.S. Bureau of Mines. American Iron & Steel Institute. *Notes:* 1. Net Domestic Scrap Consumption is defined as receipts from dealers & other sources + other receipts - scrap shipments (excludes home scrap). 2. Apparent Steel Consumption is defined as raw steel production - foundry shipments + steel castings shipments. 3. Scrap Market Share is calculated from net domestic consumption (column 5) divided by apparent steel consumption (column 9). 4. Revised.

★ 665 ★

Lead Scrap Industry

Values are shown in thousands of short tons.

Year	Primary	Lead Recovered From Old and New Scrap	Refined Products Only		Stocks	Stock Changes	Apparent Lead Consumption[1]	Scrap Market Share[2] (percent)
			Imports	Exports				
1979	637,000	883,000	202,000	12,000	219,000	+61,000	1,649,000	54
1980	604,000	745,000	90,000	181,000	200,000	-19,000	1,277,000	58
1981	549,000	707,000	110,000	25,000	224,000	+24,000	1,377,00	51
1982	570,000	630,000	105,000	62,000	188,000	-36,000	1,279,000	49
1983	572,000	550,000	195,000	22,000	170,000	-18,000	1,313,000	42
1984	429,000	698,000	180,000	8,000	157,000	-13,000	1,312,000	53
1985	545,000	679,000	147,000	30,000	196,000	+39,000	1,302,000	52
1986	408,000	689,000	157,000	14,000	115,000	-81,000	1,321,000	52
1987	412,000	783,000	205,000	11,000	121,000	+6,000	1,383,000	57

[Continued]

★ 665 ★

Lead Scrap Industry
[Continued]

| Year | Primary | Lead Recovered From Old and New Scrap | Refined Products Only | | Stocks | Stock Changes | Apparent Lead Consump-tion[1] | Scrap Market Share[2] (percent) |
			Imports	Exports				
1988[3]	432,000	812,000	164,000	15,000	116,000	-5,000	1,398,000	58
1989[4]	437,000	891,000	128,000	37,000	83,000	-33,000	1,452,000	61

Source: Facts 1989 Year Book, Institute of Scrap Recycling Industries, Inc., p. 12, from U.S. Bureau of Mines. *Notes:* 1. Apparent Lead Consumption is defined as a primary production recovered from old scrap and new scrap + net trade + stock changes. 2. Lead market share is calculated from lead recovered from old scrap (column 3) divided by apparent lead consumption (column 8). 3. Revised. 4. Preliminary.

★ 666 ★

Wastepaper Export Value
Value of exports from the U.S. in 1988, shown in millions of dollars.

Grade	Value
Newspaper	87.5
Corrugated	247.8
Mixed	103.8
High grades	249.1
Total	688.2

Source: Resource Recycling, May/June 1989, p. 31, from U.S. Department of Commerce and Resource Recycling.

★ 667 ★

Worldwide Wastepaper Use
Utilization in 1988, shown in millions of tons.

Country	1988 Usage	Change from 1987 %	1988 Recycling Rate %[1]
Algeria	.035	none	31.8
Argentina	.348	-9.4	34.8
Australia	.610	+0.8	32.9
Austria	1.004	+7.6	37.9
Belgium	.262	+0.8	23.1
Brazil	1.500	+0.5	32.3
Bulgaria	.080	none	22.9
Burma	.004	none	14.8

[Continued]

★ 667 ★

Worldwide Wastepaper Use
[Continued]

Country	1988 Usage	Change from 1987 %	1988 Recycling Rate %[1]
Canada	1.811	+6.8	10.9
Chile	.120	+4.3	26.7
China	3.084	+6.5	24.4
Colombia	.261	+9.7	51.8
Costa Rica	.006	+20.0	50.0
Czechoslovakia	.428	unknown	34.0
Denmark	.264	+5.6	76.7
East Germany	.674	-0.1	49.5
Ecuador	.060	+7.1	89.6
El Salvador	0.18	none	62.1
Ethiopia	.001	none	9.1
Finland	.351	+14.7	4.1
France	2.812	+14.3	44.5
Greece	.110	-37.5	29.3
Guatemala	.040	+25.0	87.5
Hong Kong	.017	+70.0	100.0
Hungary	.323	+6.3	60.4
India	1.050	none	54.8
Indonesia	.357	unknown	38.3
Iran	.050	+25.0	35.2
Israel	.110	+10.0	61.5
Italy	2.399	+16.7	44.7
Jamaica	.001	none	7.7
Japan	12.539	+6.7	50.9
Jordan	.012	-25.0	100.0
Kenya	.020	+5.3	18.9
Kuwait	.013	none	56.5
Madagascar	.002	none	25.0
Malaysia	.107	-2.7	52.4
Mexico	1.768	+2.9	68.2
Morocco	.071	-5.3	61.7
Nepal	.004	+33.0	57.1
Netherlands	1.640	+11.0	66.6
New Zealand	.068	none	9.7
Nigeria	.028	none	35.4
Norway	.157	+10.6	9.4
Paraguay	.015	none	100.0
Peru	.100	+44.9	45.9
Poland	.504	+8.9	34.9
Portugal	.305	+16.4	44.8
Rumania	.050	none	6.5
South Africa	.400	none	24.1
South Korea	2.747	+18.9	75.1

[Continued]

★ 667 ★

Worldwide Wastepaper Use
[Continued]

Country	1988 Usage	Change from 1987 %	1988 Recycling Rate %[1]
Spain	2.099	+10.4	61.2
Sweden	.859	+9.8	10.5
Switzerland	.565	+16.3	46.5
Taiwan	2.550	+7.0	86.5
Thailand	.380	none	62.3
Tunisia	.005	none	25.0
Turkey	.324	-4.7	45.3
United Kingdom	2.417	+5.1	56.3
United States	17.745	+4.6	25.5
USSR	2.887	+1.1	26.9
Venezuela	.383	+5.5	54.1
Vietnam	.010	none	16.7
West Germany	4.537	+5.1	42.9
Yugoslavia	.480	-14.3	34.9
Zambia	.005	+25.0	100.0
Zimbabwe	.032	none	39.0

Source: Resource Recycling, October 1989, p. 42, from *Pulp and Paper International*. *Note:* 1. Waste paper consumption as a percent of paper and paperboard production.

Toxic Substances

★ 668 ★

Fifty Facilities With the Largest Toxic Chemical Releases and Transfers

Facility name	City	State	TRI Rank	SIC Code	TRI Total Releases and Transfers (Pounds)
American Cyanamid Co.	Westwego	Louisiana	1	28	176,418,250
Shell Oil Co.-Norco Mfg. Complex	Multorco	Louisiana	2	Mult	158,662,990
Du Pont Beaumont Works	Beaumont	Texas	3	28	111,899,929
Amax Magnesium	Ooele	Utah	4	33	109,750,090
Monsanto Co.	Alvin	Texas	5	28	103,333,180
Vulcan Chemicals	Wichita	Kansas	6	28	92,011,960
BP Chemicals Green Lake	Ort Lavaca	Texas	7	28	78,225,900
Agrico Chemical Co. Div.-Freeport McMoran	Uncle Sam	Louisiana	8	28	63,327,150
Freeport McMoran-Agrico Chemical Co. Div.	Donaldson-	Louisiana	9	28	61,820,000

[Continued]

★ 668 ★

Fifty Facilities With the Largest Toxic Chemical Releases and Transfers
[Continued]

Facility name	City	State	TRI Rank	SIC Code	TRI Total Releases and Transfers (Pounds)
	ville				
Inland Steel Co.	East Chicago	Indiana	10	Mult	61,364,500
BP Chemicals Inc.	Lima	Ohio	11	28	57,746,450
ITT Rayonier Inc.	Fernandina Beach	Florida	12	26	54,369,100
Du Pont Johnsonville Plant	New Johnson- ville	Tennessee	13	28	52,691,910
Columbian Chemicals Co.	Saint Louis	Missouri	14	28	52,477,645
Racon Inc.	Witchita	Kansas	15	28	51,215,854
Occidental Chemical Corp.	White Springs	Florida	16	28	50,342,021
Du Pont Delisle Plant	Pass Christ- ian	Mississippi	17	28	49,061,860
Allied-Signal Inc.	Hopewell	Virginia	18	28	44,758,492
Sterling Chemicals Inc.	Texas City	Texas	19	28	42,999,850
Tennessee Eastman Co.	Kingsport	Tennessee	20	28	42,699,939
Avtex Fibers Front Royal Inc.	Front Royal	Virginia	21	28	37,731,700
BASF Corp.	Geismar	Louisiana	22	28	37,264,998
Monsanto Co.	Cantonment	Florida	23	28	36,249,190
Asarco Inc.	Hayden	Arizona	24	33	35,930,150
Arcadian Corp.	Geismar	Louisiana	25	28	35,655,500
Asarco Inc.	East Helena	Montana	26	33	32,968,162
Du Pont Louisville Works	Louisville	Kentucky	27	28	31,305,496
Nation Steel	Ecorse	Michigan	28	33	29,841,133
Midwest Steel Corp.	Portage	Indiana	29	33	29,404,715
Herculaneum Smelter	Herculaneum	Montana	30	33	28,890,351
Allied-Signal Inc.	Elizabeth	New Jersey	31	28	28,290,620
Wycon Chemical Co.	Cheyenne	Wyoming	32	28	28,135,426
Triad Chemical	Donaldson- ville	Louisiana	33	28	27,666,682
Monsanto Co.	Cahokia	Illinois	34	28	26,346,278
Filtrol Corp.	Vernon	California	35	28	23,533,250
Phelps Dodge Mining Co.	Playas	New Mexico	36	33	22,836,754
Eastman Kodak Co.	Rochester	New York	37	38	22,578,939
Unocal Chemicals Div.	Kenai	Alaska	38	28	20,822,000
Ciba-Geigy Corp.	Queensbury	New York	39	28	20,237,150
Conserv Inc.	Nichols	Florida	40	28	19,913,993
Du Pont Victoria Site	Victoria	Texas	41	28	19,305,153
Upjohn Co.	Kalamazoo	Michigan	42	28	18,302,800
Air Products & Chemicals Inc.	Pasadena	Texas	43	28	17,297,340
BASF Corp.-Fibers Div.	Lowland	Tennessee	44	28	17,215,000
Cyprus Miami Mining Corp.	Claypool	Arizona	45	33	16,938,022
Pfizer Pigments Inc.	East Saint Louis	Illinois	46	28	16,760,052

[Continued]

★ 668 ★

Fifty Facilities With the Largest Toxic Chemical Releases and Transfers
[Continued]

Facility name	City	State	TRI Rank	SIC Code	TRI Total Releases and Transfers (Pounds)
3M Mag Media & Consumer Products	Hutchinson	Minnesota	47	36	16,645,979
Logan Aluminum	Russellville	Kentucky	48	33	16,408,569
Union Camp Corp.	Savannah	Georgia	49	Mult	16,357,150
SCM Chemicals Inc.	Ashtabula	Ohio	50	28	15,889,750
Subtotal					2,261,899,372
Percent of Grand Total					36.24
Total for all others					3,979,131,374
Grand total					6,241,030,746

Source: Toxics in the Community: National and Local Perspectives, U.S. Environmental Protection Agency, EPA 560/4-90-017, September 1990, p. 61.

★ 669 ★

Top Fifty Toxic Air Polluters

Facility	Location	Rank	Pounds emitted
Amax Magnesium	Tooele, UT	1	109,748,910
Tennessee Eastman Co.	Kingsport, TN	2	40,153,450
Avtex Fibers	Front Royal, VA	3	34,410,250
Triad Chemical	Donaldson-ville, LA	4	27,140,610
Eastman Kodak Co.	Rochester, NY	5	21,621,312
Unocal Chemicals Div.	Kenai, AK	6	20,660,250
3M Mag Media & Consumer	Hutchinson, MN	7	16,306,841
Union Camp Corp.	Savannah, GA	8	16,261,250
BASF Corp. Fibers Div.	Lowland, TN	9	15,474,750
Freeport McMoran	Donaldson-ville, LA	10	14,463,500
Mississippi Chemical	Yazoo City, MS	11	14,370,800
Freeport McMoran	Blytheville, AR	12	13,380,750
Westvaco Bleached Board	Covington, VA	13	12,641,000
CF Industries Inc.	Donaldson-ville, LA	14	12,568,000
Hoechst Celanese	Narrows, VA	15	11,791,901
Georgia-Pacific Corp.	Brunswick, GA	16	11,386,820

[Continued]

★ 669 ★

Top Fifty Toxic Air Polluters
[Continued]

Facility	Location	Rank	Pounds emitted
Westinghouse Electric	Hampton, SC	17	8,904,710
Du Pont Johnsonville	New Johnson-ville, TN	18	8,690,340
3M Co. Brownwood	Brownwood, TX	19	8,261,182
GE Plastics	Mount Vernon, IN	20	7,991,771
Texas Eastman Co.	Longview, TX	21	7,796,576
Dow Chemical Co.	Freeport, TX	22	7,725,917
Upjohn Co.	Portage, MI	23	7,427,500
BP Chemicals Inc.	Lima, OH	24	7,286,550
Air Products & Chemicals	Calvert City, KY	25	7,074,850
Reynolds Metals Co.	Sheffield, AL	26	6,529,660
General Electric Co.	Coshocton, OH	27	6,478,058
Westvaco Corp.	Luke, MD	28	6,412,754
Du Pont Delisle Plant	Pass Chris-tian, MS	29	6,361,860
Westvaco Corp. Chem/Div	Covington, VA	30	6,293,647
Conserv Inc.	Nichols, FL	31	6,120,186
Olin Corp.	Lake Charles, LA	32	5,482,625
Uniroyal Plastics Co.	Mishawaka, IN	33	5,461,366
USS Clairton Works	Clairton, PA	34	5,316,551
Gencorp Polymer Prod.	Columbus, MS	35	5,262,476
Union Carbide C&P Co.	Institute, WV	36	5,131,882
American Syn. Rubber	Louisville, KY	37	5,128,352
Bristol-Myers Co.	Syracuse, NY	38	4,998,513
Quantum Chem. Corp. USI	Morris, IL	39	4,867,250
Hoechst Celanese	Rock Hill, SC	40	4,808,418
FMRP Ltd.	Catoosa, OK	41	4,771,908
North American Rayon	Elizabethton, TN	42	4,622,250
Pulp & Paperboard Oper.	Evandale, TX	43	4,520,000
Alcoa	Davenport, IA	44	4,463,500
IBM	Endicott, NY	45	4,456,471
Eli Lilly & Co.	Shadeland, IN	46	4,425,290
Cabot Corp.	Tuscola, IL	47	4,296,400
Maxwell Communication	Broadview, IL	48	4,231,848
Monsanto Co.	Luling, LA	49	4,210,291
Holliston Mills Inc.	Church Hill, TN	50	4,194,222

Source: The Amicus Journal, Summer 1990, p. 20 from the 1988 Toxic Release Inventory.

Transportation

★ 670 ★

Airline Companies Using Stage 2 and Stage 3 Aircraft

Stage 3 aircraft produce less noise. By 2000, federal law mandates that major airlines use only Stage 3 aircraft in the United States.

Airline	Stage 3 Percentage	Total Fleet	Stage 3 Widebody	Stage 3 Narrowbody	Stage 2 Narrowbody
American	58.3	555	131	247	177
United	42.1	473	112	152	209
Delta	38.6	444	79	141	224
Northwest	19.9	331	70	52	209
Continental	42.1	328	43	120	165
USAir	46.8	471	9	216	246
Transworld	22.3	207	59	33	115
Pan American	42.7	152	65	5	82
America West	68.0	107	4	70	33
Southwest	56.6	106	0	60	46

Source: Aviation Week & Space Technology, March 11, 1991, p. 35, from Avmark, Pan American.

★ 671 ★

Energy Intensity of Transport Modes

Automobile, single occupant - 1,860	
Transit bus - 920	
Transit rail - 885	
Walking - 100	
Bicycling - 35	

The data are for 1984.

Mode	Calories/ passenger mile
Bicycling	35
Walking	100
Transit rail	885
Transit bus	920
Automobile, single occupant	1,860

Source: World Watch, July/August 1988, p. 13, from President's Council on Physical Fitness and Sports; *Transportation Energy Data Book*, Edition 9, Oak Ridge National Laboratory, April 1987.

★ 672 ★

Railroad and Road Travel Worldwide

The figures refers to annual railroad and road passenger miles per capita in selected countries during the last half of the 1980's.

Country	Railway passenger miles per capita	Road passenger miles per capita
Ecuador	1	116
Jordan	1	1170
Venezuela	1	-
Colombia	3	421
Kenya	18	-
Cameroon	25	138
Canada	45	3406
Mexico	48	-
United States	49	7753
Chile	56	706
Iraq	58	1061
Tunisia	64	1601
Brazil	69	-

[Continued]

★ 672 ★

Railroad and Road Travel Worldwide
[Continued]

Country	Railway passenger miles per capita	Road passenger miles per capita
Turkey	74	264
Australia	82	-
Thailand	109	367
China	190	-
Hong Kong	216	737
India	235	-
Spain	-	1474
Argentina	249	-
Yugoslavia	313	915
Portugal	357	1664
Britain	361	3557
Luxembourg	362	4953
Egypt	365	-
South Korea	365	378
Belgium	392	2989
Netherlands	396	3688
West Germany	397	4219
South Africa	404	1721
Sweden	444	4334
Italy	448	3008
Bulgaria	538	790
Denmark	581	4194
Austria	602	4039
France	666	4428
Poland	795	901
Czechoslovakia	797	92
Soviet Union	872	109
Romania	908	-
Japan	1702	2775

Source: World Monitor, April 1991, p.p. 4-5, from Europa, 1990 Britannica Book of the Year, The Economist Book of Vital World Statistics, The UN Statistical Yearbook, World Road Statistics.

★ 673 ★

Railroads and Trucks Compared

	Rails	Trucks
Energy Conservation:		
Revenue ton-miles per gallon	288.00	92.00
Safety:		
Accidents per billion ton-miles	4.00	113.00
Fatalities per billion ton-miles	1.35	2.12
Environmental Impact:		
Revenue ton-miles per pound of various pollutants		
Hydrocarbons	15,100.00	1,210.00
Carbon Monoxide	1,510.00	419.00
Nitrogen Oxide	518.00	139.00
Particles	12,600.00	928.00

Source: Traffic Management, July 1990, p. 60, from Association of American Railroads and U.S. Environmental Protection Agency.

Water

★ 674 ★

Facts About Toilets

	Amount	Measure
Gallons flushed in America daily	4.800	billion
Gallons that would be flushed if toilets were replaced by ultra-low flush models	1.536	billion
Water saved	68	percent

Source: Garbage, January/February 1990, p. 12, from U.S. Department of Housing and Urban Development and *Garbage* staff research.

★ 675 ★

Hot Water Use

Amount of hot water expended by various activities.

Activity	Hot Water Use (gal/min)
Bathtub	3.6
Laundry	3.3
Shower	2-5
Kitchen sink	1.6
Dishwasher	1.5
Bathroom sink	0.3

Source: Consumer's Research, August 1989, p. 19.

★ 676 ★

Sales of Water Rights in the Western U.S.

Selected water rights sales in 1988-89.

Buyer/Seller	Amount, acre-feet per year[1]	Cost per acre-foot (dollars)	Purpose
Westminster, CO/Local irrigators	272	6,176	Municipal
Westpac Utilities, Reno, NV/Urban homeowners on formerly irrigated land	2,000	2,000	Municipal
Phoenix, AZ/McMullen Valley Farm[2]	30,000	1,017	Municipal[3]
Albuquerque, NM/Local irrigators	1,360	1,000	Municipal[4]
Nevada Waterfowl Association/Truckee-Carson Irrigation District	35	214	Wetlands/ waterfowl protection
Central Utah Water Conservancy District/Local irrigators	85,000	164	Municipal[5]

Source: World Watch, p. 19, from *Water Market Update* (Santa Fe, NM: Shupe & Associates, vols. 2-3, 1988-1989); Elizabeth Checchio, *Water Farming: The Promise and Problems of Water Transfers in Arizona* (Tucson, AZ: University of Arizona, 1988). *Notes:* 1. One acre-foot equals 325,850 gallons, enough to supply a four-person household for about two years. 2. 1986. 3. Projected needs after the year 2000. 4. Projected needs after the year 2020. 5. In lieu of a previous plan to drain wetlands to increase supplies.

★ 677 ★

Water Consumption Worldwide

Global water consumption is expected to grow in spite of its stabilization in some countries. Irrigation accounts for 70% of total water use. Data are in cubic kilometers per year and in percent.

Water users	1900	1940	1950	1960	1970	1980	1990	%	2000	%
Irrigated area (millions of hectares)	47.3	75.8	101	142	173	217	272		347	
Agriculture										
Total water consumption	525	893	1,130	1,550	1,850	2,290	2,680	(68.9)	3,250	(62.6)
Irretrievable water losses	409	679	859	1,180	1,140	1,730	2,050	(88.7)	2,500	(86.2)
Industry										
Total water consumption	37.2	124.0	178.0	330.0	540.0	710.0	973.0	(21.4)	1,280	(24.7)
Irretrievable water losses	3.5	9.7	14.5	24.9	38.0	61.9	88.5	(3.1)	117	(4.0)
Municipal supply										
Total water consumption	16.1	36.3	52.0	82.0	130.0	200.0	300.0	(6.1)	441.0	(8.5)
Irretrievable water losses	4.0	9.0	14.0	20.3	29.2	41.1	52.4	(2.1)	64.5	(2.2)
Reservoirs										
Total water consumption	0.3	3.7	6.5	23.0	66.0	120	170	(3.6)	220	(4.2)
Irretrievable water losses	0.3	3.7	6.5	23.0	66.0	120	170	(6.1)	220	(7.6)
Total										
Total water consumption	579	1,060	1,360	1,990	2,590	3,320	4,130	(100)	5,190	(100)
Irretrievable water losses	417	701	894	1,250	1,540	1,950	2,360	(100)	2,900	(100)

Source: Nature and Resources, Vol. 26, No. 3, 1990, p. 39. A equals the total water consumption. B equals irretrievable water losses.

Chapter 8
CITIES, STATES, REGIONS, AND NATIONS

Air Pollution

★ 678 ★

Carbon Dioxide Emissions in California and U.S. by Fuel

	Total	Oil	Coal	Gas
California				
Million tons	85	61	1	23
Percent	-	72	1	27
United States				
Million tons	1275	607	430	238
Percent	-	53	26	22

Source: Global Warming and Its Implications for California, Hearings before the Congress, 101st Congress, Santa Monica, CA., May 20, 1989, p. 79, from S. Machado and R. Plitz, 1988. "Reducing the Rate of Global Warming: The States' Role." Renew America, Washington, D.C. Percentages may not add to 100% due to rounding.

★ 679 ★

Carbon Dioxide Emissions in California and U.S. by Sector

	California % of total	US Average % of total
Transport	57.7	31.8
Gasoline	33.7	20.5
Industrial/Commercial	25.1	27.5
Residential	8.5	7.4
Electric Utilities[1]	8.7	33.3

[Continued]

576

★ 679 ★

Carbon Dioxide Emissions in California and U.S. by Sector
[Continued]

	California % of total	US Average % of total
Coal	0[1]	28.2
Oil	0.8	3.0
Gas	7.8	2.2

Source: Global Warming and Its Implications for California, Hearings before the Congress, 101st Congress, Santa Monica, CA., May 20, 1989, p. 78, from S. Machado and R. Plitz, 1988. "Reducing the Rate of Global Warming: The States' Role". Renew America, Washington D.C. *Notes:* 1. Some of California's electricity is produced by coal plants located outside of the State. Thus, slightly more carbon dioxide is actually generated by the energy sector than indicated by the figures above.

★ 680 ★

Carbon Emission From Transportation, Selected Countries
Values are shown in millions of metric tons.

Country	Transport Carbon dioxide	Share of world	Transport share of region's fossil Carbon dioxide
U.S.	413	36%	30%
Canada and Western Europe	266	23	31
Japan, Australia and New Zealand	90	8	30
U.S.S.R. and E. Europe	171	15	12
S. and E. Asia	50	4	19
China	19	2	4
Africa	40	4	26
Latin America	83	7	36
Middle East	21	2	14
World total	1,153	100%	22%[1]

Source: Changing by Degrees: Steps to Reduce Greenhouse Gases, U.S. Congress, Office of Technology Assessment, OTA-O-482, Washington, D.C., February 1991, p. 150, from U.S. Environmental Protection Agency, *Policy Options for Stabilizing Global Climate,* draft report (Washington, DC: 1989). *Note:* 1. Transport share of world's fossil-fuel carbon dioxide emissions.

★ 681 ★

Carbon Emissions From Fossil Fuels Worldwide

Total 1988 emissions were 6 billion metric tons per year.

Country	Percent
United States	24
U.S.S.R/E. Europe	23
China	10
Other Asia	7
Germany	5
Japan	5
Latin America	5
Middle East	3
Africa	3
Other OECD	15

Source: Changing by Degrees: Steps to Reduce Greenhouse Gases, U.S. Congress, Office of Technology Assessment, OTA-O-482, Washington, D.C., February 1991, p. 80, from Office of Technology Assessment, 1991, calculated using data from U.S. Department of Energy, *International Energy Annual* (1988).

★ 682 ★

Carbon Monoxide Pollution in California

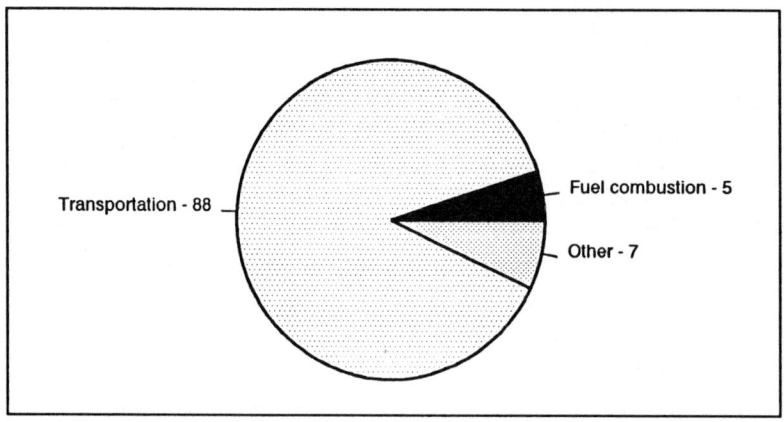

Sources of carbon monoxide	Percent
Transportation	88
Fuel combustion	5
Other	7

Source: Energy, Summer Issue, 1990, p. 22, from California Air Resources Board.

★ 683 ★

Cities With Air Pollution Problems

| Los Angeles metro area - 137.5 |
| Bakersfield, Calif. - 44.2 |
| Fresno, Calif. - 24.3 |
| New York metro area - 17.4 |
| Sacramento, Calif. - 15.8 |
| Chicago metro area - 13.0 |
| San Diego, Calif. - 12.3 |
| Houston metro area - 12.2 |
| Knox County, Maine - 11.1 |
| Baltimore, Maryland - 10.7 |

Number of days per year that cities failed the Clean-Air Standard between 1986 and 1988.

City	Number of Days
Los Angeles metro area	137.5
Bakersfield, Calif.	44.2
Fresno, Calif.	24.3
New York metro area	17.4
Sacramento, Calif.	15.8
Chicago metro area	13.0
San Diego, Calif.	12.3
Houston metro area	12.2
Knox County, Maine	11.1
Baltimore, Maryland	10.7

Source: Garbage, November/December 1990, p. 63, from EPA ozone data, 1986-88.

★ 684 ★

Emissions From Steam-Electric Plants by State

Emissions from fossil-fueled steam-electric plants, shown in thousands of short tons.

Census Division and State	1989[1]			1988[2]		
	Sulfur Dioxide	Nitrogen Oxides	Carbon Dioxide	Sulfur Dioxide	Nitrogen Oxides	Carbon Dioxide
New England	430	156	54,258	427	150	52,592
Connecticut	66	26	13,335	62	25	12,936
Maine	15	5	2,854	15	5	2,756
Massachusetts	267	97	31,332	263	91	29,906
New Hampshire	80	26	6,194	82	27	6,160

[Continued]

★ 684 ★

Emissions from Steam-Electric Plants by State
[Continued]

Census Division and State	1989[1]			1988[2]		
	Sulfur Dioxide	Nitrogen Oxides	Carbon Dioxide	Sulfur Dioxide	Nitrogen Oxides	Carbon Dioxide
Rhode Island	2	2	532	5	2	832
Vermont	0	0	11	0	0	2
Middle Atlantic	1,782	628	209,550	1,793	607	202,675
New Jersey	90	69	17,127	86	63	15,548
New York	426	169	73,864	388	154	68,375
Pennsylvania	1,266	390	118,559	1,319	390	118,752
East North Central	5,517	1,753	399,053	5,414	1,727	391,966
Illinois	889	320	59,487	905	329	61,613
Indiana	1,564	475	104,302	1,499	454	96,169
Michigan	404	278	73,365	422	279	74,672
Ohio	2,370	536	124,813	2,285	518	122,078
Wisconsin	290	144	37,086	303	147	37,434
West North Central	1,633	775	191,585	1,614	762	191,671
Iowa	189	98	28,572	197	93	27,923
Kansas	169	107	29,046	157	108	29,480
Minnesota	152	107	33,547	152	101	31,911
Missouri	886	272	54,191	863	259	53,840
Nebraska	47	70	14,031	50	72	14,770
North Dakota	160	102	28,997	164	110	30,361
South Dakota	30	19	3,201	31	19	3,386
South Atlantic	3,651	1,338	390,220	3,645	1,295	374,487
Delaware	85	31	9,494	118	34	10,476
District of Columbia	4	1	716	3	1	517
Florida	712	322	94,834	718	314	90,481
Georgia	835	216	64,870	896	220	66,825
Maryland	298	102	30,981	277	92	27,546
North Carolina	351	172	51,312	320	159	46,903
South Carolina	170	83	25,190	173	80	24,429
Virginia	189	86	29,095	163	75	24,965
West Virginia	1,007	325	83,728	977	320	82,345
East South Central	2,194	721	185,554	2,305	775	199,096
Alabama	564	193	55,300	502	179	51,072
Kentucky	751	306	70,954	809	346	80,166
Mississippi	117	45	12,449	141	53	15,205
Tennessee	762	177	46,851	853	197	52,653
West South Central	849	937	296,064	815	911	291,096
Arkansas	67	73	23,232	72	76	24,067
Louisiana	91	123	37,234	90	120	36,711
Oklahoma	96	124	37,150	97	127	37,535
Texas	595	617	198,448	556	588	192,783
Mountain	522	668	214,583	521	656	210,096
Arizona	133	123	37,505	117	106	31,958
Colorado	98	111	33,184	112	106	31,688
Idaho	[3]	[3]	[3]	[3]	[3]	[3]

[Continued]

★ 684 ★

Emissions from Steam-Electric Plants by State
[Continued]

Census Division and State	1989[1]			1988[2]		
	Sulfur Dioxide	Nitrogen Oxides	Carbon Dioxide	Sulfur Dioxide	Nitrogen Oxides	Carbon Dioxide
Montana	29	61	19,051	29	62	19,260
Nevada	61	62	20,238	68	65	21,504
New Mexico	72	89	31,853	66	84	30,298
Utah	44	85	30,864	39	86	30,410
Wyoming	85	137	41,888	90	147	44,978
Pacific Contiguous	80	192	48,665	76	193	48,464
California	15	149	38,278	14	151	38,506
Oregon	2	2	539	0	0	0
Washington	63	41	9,848	62	42	9,958
Pacific Noncontiguous	27	15	7,372	26	15	7,129
Alaska	1	1	480	1	1	474
Hawaii	26	14	6,892	25	14	6,655
U.S. Total	16,685	7,183	1,996,904	16,636	7,091	1,969,272

Source: Energy Information Administration, *Electric Power Annual 1989*, January 1991, p. 75, from Energy Information Administration, Form EIA-767, "Steam - Electric Plant Operation and Design Report." Totals may not equal sum of components because of independent rounding. Data include petroleum coke. These data are estimates derived from Form EIA-767, "Steam-Electric Plant Operation and Design Report." *Notes:* 1. Data for 1989 are preliminary. 2. Data for 1988 are revised. 3. Not applicable.

★ 685 ★

Hydrocarbon Pollution in California

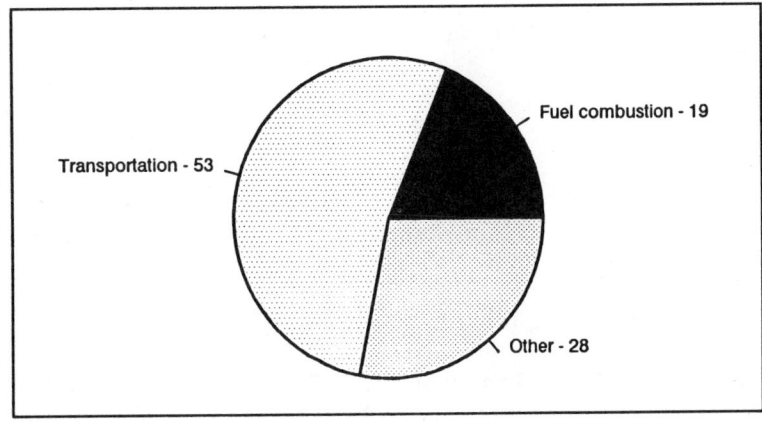

Sources of Hydrocarbons	Percent
Transportation	53
Fuel combustion	19
Other	28

Source: Energy, Summer Issue 1990, p. 22, from California Air Resources Board.

★ 686 ★

Metro Areas Failing to Meet Carbon Monoxide Standards
Number of days exceeding standards in 1987 and 1988.

Metropolitan Area	1987	1988
Albuquerque, NM	14	5
Anchorage, AK	4	10
Baltimore, MD	1	2
Boston-Lawrence-Salem, MA-NH-CMSA	2[1]	-
Chico, CA	-	2
Cleveland-Akron-Lorain, OH CMSA	2[1]	-
Colorado Springs, CO	1	2
Denver-Boulder, CO CMSA	24	10
El Paso, TX	11	3
Fairbanks, AK[2]	18	9
Fort Collins, CO	5	3
Fresno, CA	3	3
Great Falls, MT	3	1
Greeley, CO	3	1
Greensboro-Winston-Salem-High Point, NC	-	2
Hartford-New Britain-Middletown, CT CMSA	7	3
Josephine County, OR[2]	4	2
Klamath County, OR[2]	(NA)	3
Las Vegas, NV	4	26
Los Angeles-Anaheim-Riverside, CA CMSA	48	51
Manchester, NH	4	1
Medford, OR	3	3
Memphis, TN-AR-MS	3	-
Minneapolis-St. Paul, MN-WI	5	8
Missoula County, MT[2]	4	2
Modesto, CA	-	2
New York-Northern NJ-Long Island, NY-NJ-CT CMSA	69	26
Oklahoma City, OK	4	-
Phoenix, AZ	24[1]	11
Portland-Vancouver, OR-WA CMSA	4	3
Provo-Orem, UT	20	5
Raleigh-Durham, NC	2	2
Reno, NV	1	3
Sacramento, CA	12	6
St. Louis, MO-IL	2	-
Salt Lake City-Ogden, UT	2	-
San Diego, CA	-	2
San Francisco-Oakland-San Jose, CA CMSA	1	2
Seattle-Tacoma, WA CMSA	9	3
Spokane, WA	66	37
Steubenville-Weirton, OH-WV	26	31
Washington, DC-MD-VA	2	1

[Continued]

★ 686 ★

Metro Areas Failing to Meet Carbon Monoxide Standards

[Continued]

Metropolitan Area	1987	1988
Winnebago County, WI[2]	(NA)	32
Yakima, WA	4	1

Source: U.S. Department of Commerce, Bureau of the Census, *Statistical Abstract of the United States 1990 (110th ed.)*, Superintendent of Documents, Washington, D.C., p. 204. *Notes:* - Represents zero. NA stands for not available. 1. 1986 data. 2. Not a metropolitan area.

★ 687 ★

Metro Areas Failing to Meet Ozone Standards

Average number of days exceeding standards from 1986 through 1988 and number of days in 1988.

Metropolitan area	1986-1988 avg.	1988
Albany-Schenectady-Troy, NY	4.0	4.0
Allentown-Bethlehem, PA-NJ	3.1	10.1
Altoona, PA	2.0	4.0
Anderson, SC	3.1	3.1
Atlanta, GA	10.2	13.2
Atlantic City, NJ	3.7	6.0
Bakersfield, CA	37.8	54.0
Baltimore, MD	13.3	19.3
Baton Rouge, LA	4.1	6.3
Beaumont-Port Arthur, TX	4.5	6.8
Birmingham, AL	3.7	2.0
Boston-Lawrence-Salem, MA-NH CMSA	10.0	11.4
Buffalo-Niagara Falls, NY CMSA	3.4	8.3
Canton, OH	1.7	5.2
Charleston, WV	2.7	7.0
Charlotte-Gastonia-Rock Hill, NC-SC	5.7	7.1
Chicago-Gary-Lake County, IL-IN-WI CMSA	21.2	16.2
Cincinnati-Hamilton, OH-KY-IN CMSA	5.4	14.1
Cleveland-Akron-Lorain, OH CMSA	5.8	13.3
Columbia, SC	1.6	2.1
Columbus, OH	1.4	4.0
Dallas-Fort Worth, TX CMSA	5.8	4.3
Dayton-Springfield, OH	2.7	6.2
Detroit-Ann Arbor, MI CMSA	3.3	4.1
Edmonson County, KY[1]	2.1	5.2
El Paso, TX	8.1	5.4
Erie, PA	2.4	6.1
Essex County, NY[1]	1.8	5.4
Fayetteville, NC	1.4	3.1
Fresno, CA	31.6	30.3
Grand Rapids, MI	3.1	7.0

[Continued]

★ 687 ★

Metro Areas Failing to Meet Ozone Standards
[Continued]

Metropolitan area	1986-1988 avg.	1988
Greenbrier County, WV[1]	1.4	4.1
Greensboro-Winston-Salem-High Point, NC	7.2	7.2
Greenville-Spartanburg, SC	4.8	4.8
Hancock County, ME[1]	12.0	12.0
Harrisburg-Lebanon-Carlisle, PA	2.2	6.9
Hartford-New Britain-Middletown, CT CMSA	6.9	10.0
Houston-Galveston-Brazoria, TX CMSA	12.6	8.3
Huntington-Ashland, WV-KY-OH	6.2	10.4
Huntsville, AL	1.1	2.1
Indianapolis, IN	1.1	2.1
Jacksonville, FL	1.1	1.1
Jefferson County, NY[1]	5.1	6.1
Johnstown, PA	2.5	7.4
Kansas City, MO-KS	1.7	3.0
Kewaunee County, WI[1]	5.5	10.6
Knox County, ME[1]	8.1	15.6
Knoxville, TN	1.8	5.4
Lafayette, IN	2.1	2.1
Lake Charles, LA	2.0	3.0
Lancaster, PA	1.3	3.0
Lewiston-Auburn, ME	1.5	1.5
Lexington-Fayette, KY	2.7	5.0
Lincoln County, ME[1]	2.4	(NA)
Livingston County, KY[1]	1.8	3.3
Los Angeles-Anaheim-Riverside, CA CMSA	145.4	148.0
Louisville, KY-IN	5.6	4.5
Manchester, NH	2.4	2.0
Memphis, TN-AR-MS	2.7	4.1
Miami-Fort Lauderdale, FL CMSA	2.4	3.0
Milwaukee-Racine, WI CMSA	9.1	14.2
Modesto, CA	6.0	4.0
Montgomery, AL	1.8	1.1
Muskegon, MI	9.0	12.1
Nashville, TN	6.0	11.7
New York-Northern NJ-Long Island, NY-NJ-CT CMSA	18.0	19.4
Norfolk-Virginia Beach-Newport News, VA	3.0	4.0
Owensboro, KY	4.1	10.2
Parkersburg-Marietta, WV-OH	7.2	17.0
Philadelphia-Wilmington-Trenton, PA-NJ-DE-MD CMSA	8.9	18.2
Phoenix, AZ	1.4	1.1
Pittsburgh-Beaver Valley, PA CMSA	6.6	14.8
Portland-Vancouver, OR-WA CMSA	1.8	2.4
Portland, ME	5.4	11.2
Portsmouth-Dover-Rochester, NH-ME	7.8	11.1
Poughkeepsie, NY	1.7	4.0

[Continued]

★ 687 ★

Metro Areas Failing to Meet Ozone Standards
[Continued]

Metropolitan area	1986-1988 avg.	1988
Providence-Pawtucket-Fall River, RI-MA CMSA	6.6	8.5
Raleigh-Durham, NC	4.4	10.2
Reading, PA	3.4	9.2
Richmond-Petersburg, VA	4.4	9.2
Sacramento, CA	8.9	15.5
St. Louis, MO-IL	7.5	7.3
Salt Lake City-Ogden, UT	3.1	2.2
San Diego, CA	11.1	7.1
San Francisco-Oakland-San Jose, CA CMSA	3.4	4.1
Santa Barbara-Santa Maria-Lompoc, CA	1.7	-
Scranton-Wilkes-Barre, PA	3.0	8.1
Sheboygan, WI	9.5	15.5
South Bend-Mishawaka, IN	1.1	3.2
Springfield, MA	7.3	13.4
Stockton, CA	2.3	2.0
Sussex County, DE[1]	3.6	9.9
Tampa-St. Petersburg-Clearwater, FL	1.7	-
Toledo, OH	2.4	6.2
Tulsa, OK	1.1	1.0
Visalia-Tulare-Porterville, CA	8.5	4.0
Washington, DC-MD-VA	8.3	13.8
Waldo County, ME[1]	1.0[2]	(NA)
Worcester, MA	7.3	17.1
York, PA	1.5	4.6
Youngstown-Warren, OH	2.5	5.4

Source: U.S. Department of Commerce, Bureau of the Census, *Statistical Abstract of the United States 1990 (110th ed.)*, Superintendent of Documents, Washington, D.C., p. 204, from U.S. Environmental Protection Agency, press release of July 27, 1989. *Notes:* - Represents zero. NA stands for not available. 1. Not a metropolitan area. 2. Greater than 1.0.

★ 688 ★

Nitrogen Oxide Pollution in California

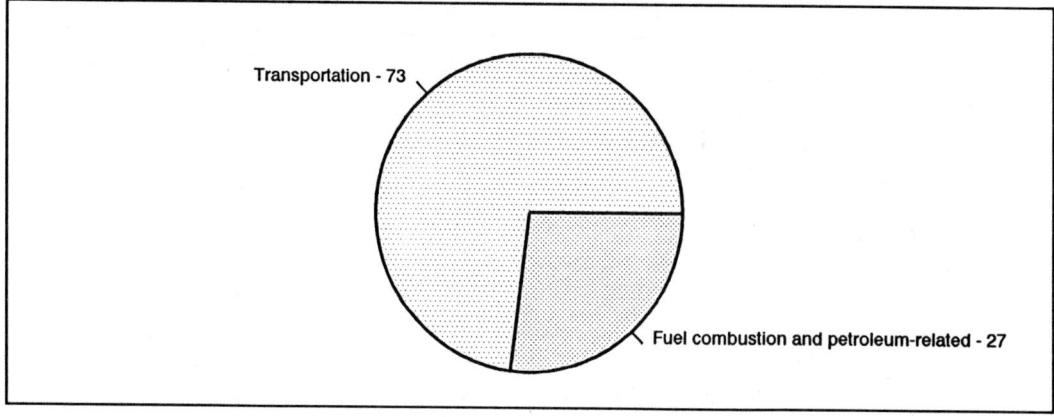

Sources	Percent
Transportation	73
Fuel combustion and petroleum-related	27

Source: Energy, Summer Issue 1990, p. 22, from California Air Resources Board.

★ 689 ★

Sulfur Dioxide Emissions in Europe

1980 sulfur dioxide emissions and projected emissions for the year 2000 based on the assumption that all European countries impose major sulfur dioxide controls. Current policy is a thirty percent reduction—resulting emissions are shown in the second column. Emissions are shown in kilotons of sulfur.

Country	1980	30% Sulfur Dioxide Reduction	Major Sulfur Controls (2000)
Albania	39	27	15
Austria	159	111	89
Belgium	432	303	142
Bulgaria	508	355	363
Czechoslovakia	1832	1282	592
Denmark	226	158	77
Finland	294	206	100
France	1657	1160	448
Germany, East	2415	1691	996
Germany, West	1602	1121	464
Greece	345	242	226
Hungary	813	569	352
Ireland	119	83	71
Italy	1898	1328	640

[Continued]

★ 689 ★

Sulfur Dioxide Emissions in Europe
[Continued]

Country	1980	30% Sulfur Dioxide Reduction	Major Sulfur Controls (2000)
Luxembourg	20	14	12
Netherlands	243	170	155
Norway	72	51	43
Poland	1741	1219	841
Portugal	130	91	91
Romania	757	530	566
Spain	1879	1315	966
Sweden	243	170	100
Switzerland	67	47	38
Turkey	497	348	779
United Kingdom	2342	1639	967
USSR[1]	8588	6012	2878
Yugoslavia	837	586	446
Europe	29752	20826	12455
Percent Reduction		30	58

Source: Environment, March 1988, Vol. 30, No. 2, p. 19, from International Institute for Applied Systems Analysis Acid Rain Project (Laxenburg, Austria). *Note:* 1. European part only.

★ 690 ★

Sulfur & Nitrogen Depositions in Europe

Average nitrogen and sulfur depositions per year, shown in thousands of metric tons, and deposition received from abroad, shown as percent of total. These depositions are significant in that they can impact on water quality, including the acidity of lakes.

Country	Annual Deposition		Deposition Received from Other Countries	
	Nitrogen	Sulfur	Nitrogen	Sulfur
Austria	85	202	97.0	91.0
Belgium	20	100	88.0	55.0
Czechoslovakia	128	692	81.0	46.0
Denmark	19	81	91.0	60.0
East Germany	100	792	82.0	24.0
Finland	49	227	84.0	76.0
France	265	696	68.0	57.0
Greece	27	111	90.0	63.0
Italy	158	565	62.0	36.0
Netherlands	31	112	85.0	75.0
Norway	62	190	90.0	95.0
Poland	203	1,145	73.0	43.0
Spain	133	574	69.0	24.0

[Continued]

★ 690 ★

Sulfur & Nitrogen Depositions in Europe
[Continued]

Country	Annual Deposition		Deposition Received from Other Countries	
	Nitrogen	Sulfur	Nitrogen	Sulfur
Sweden	90	324	88.0	87.0
Switzerland	34	70	92.0	86.0
U.K.	93	609	58.0	21.0
West Germany	240	742	62.0	55.0
Yugoslavia	124	490	94.0	64.0

Source: C&EN, March 27, 1989, p. 13, from United Nations Economic Commission for Europe, European Monitoring & Evaluation Program.

★ 691 ★

Toxic Air Emissions Worldwide

Values shown are for 1988.

Country	Kilotons Sulfur dioxide	Kg per capita	Grams per $ GNP	Kilotons Nitrogen oxides	Kg per capita	Grams per $ GNP
Eastern Germany	5,258	317	31	708	43	4
Czechoslovakia	2,800	179	24	950	61	8
Bulgaria	1,030	114	21	150	17	3
Romania	1,800[1]	78	19	390[2]	17	4
Hungary	1,218	115	17	259	24	4
Poland	4,180	110	20	1,550	41	7
U.S.S.R.[4]	10,124	35	5	4,190	15	2
U.K.	3,664	64	5	2,480	43	3
U.S.[3]	20,700	84	4	19,800	80	4
Sweden	214	25	1	390	46	2
France	1,226	22	1	1,615	29	2
W. Germany	1,300	21	1	2,860	47	3

Source: Chemical Engineering, February 1991, p. 33, from Worldwatch Institute, Report #99 by Hilary French. *Notes:* 1. Romanian SO_2 emissions based on 1980 data. 2. Romanian NO_x emissions based on 1985 data. 3. U.S. data include all sulfur oxides. 4. Data only from European part of U.S.S.R.

★ 692 ★

Trade on U.S. - Canada Border

Exchanges of goods, people, money—and pollutants.

	Units	Denomination
Canadian visitors to the U.S.	13.843	Million[1]
U.S. visitors to Canada	13.341	Million[1]
Canadian immigrants in the U.S.	11,783[2]	
U.S. immigrants in Canada	6,537[2]	
Canadian imports from the U.S.	$72	bil. (US)[3]
U.S. imports from Canada	$182	bil. (US)[3]
Canadian direct investments in the U.S.	$27	bil. (US)[4]
U.S. direct investments in Canada	$61	bil. (US)[4]
Canadian air pollutants in the U.S.	1.5	mil. tons
U.S. air pollutants in Canada	3.2	mil. tons

Source: National Geographic, Volume 177, No. 2, Feb. 1990, p. 106 *Notes:* 1. Tourism. Roughly the same number of visitors-between 13 million and 14 million a year-explore each other's country. Cold weather sports are a Canadian draw. 2. Immigration. Flow depicts citizens of each country who changed sides in 1988. Restrictions lifted by the Free Trade Agreement will increase job-seeking immigrants from Canada to the U.S. 3. Exports/Imports. Goods traded exceed 150 billion dollars (U.S.) a year, more than between any other two nations. About 20 percent of all U.S. merchandise exports go to Canada, which supplies an equal share of U.S. merchandise imports. Cars, trucks, and autoparts make up about a third of the total trade. 4. Direct Investment. Canada's mines, smelters, oil, and chemicals stimulate U.S. investment. Canadian investors look to the U.S. side for oil, manufacturing, and real estate.

Alternative Energy

★ 693 ★

California's Alternative Energy Projects
Values for 1979-1988 are shown in megawatts.

	On-Line[1]	Under Contract
Solar	147	454
Wind	1350	2705
Geothermal	312	594
Cogeneration and Biomass	3816	5584

Source: Global Warming and Its Implications for California, Hearings before the Congress, 101st Congress, Santa Monica, CA., May 20, 1989, p. 82, from IEP(1988). *Notes:* 1. All of these projects are third-party power producers. In addition to these, substantial capacity owned by utilities is already on-line, particularly in the geothermal sector.

Atmosphere

★ 694 ★

Air Emissions in Europe
Emissions of sulfur dioxide and nitrogen oxides in selected countries. Sulfur dioxide plays a role in acid rain and nitrogen oxides contribute to acid rain and smog. Data are preliminary and refer to 1988, except where noted.

Country	Emissions (000 tons)	Emissions per person (kilograms)	Emissions per dollar GNP (grams)
Sulfur Dioxide			
East Germany	5,258	317	31
Czechoslovakia	2,800	179	24
Bulgaria	1,030	114	21
Poland	4,180	110	20
Romania	1,800[1]	78	19
Hungary	1,218	115	17
Soviet Union[2]	18,584	65	10
Britain	3,664	64	5
United States[3]	20,700	84	4
Sweden	214	25	1

[Continued]

★ 694 ★

Air Emissions in Europe
[Continued]

Country	Emissions (000 tons)	Emissions per person (kilograms)	Emissions per dollar GNP (grams)
France	1,226	22	1
West Germany	1,300	21	1
Nitrogen Oxides			
Czechoslovakia	950	61	8
Poland	1,550	41	7
East Germany	708	43	4
Hungary	259	24	4
United States	19,800	80	4
Romania	390[4]	17	4
Bulgaria	150	17	3
Britain	2,480	43	3
West Germany	2,860	47	3
Sweden	390	46	2
France	1,615	29	2
Soviet Union[2]	4,510	16	2

Source: The New York Times, December 9, 1990, p. E3, from Worldwatch Institute. *Notes:* 1. Emissions data from 1980. 2. 1987 data; stationary sources only. 3. Includes sulfur dioxide and other sulfur oxides. 4. Emissions data from 1985.

★ 695 ★

Carbon Dioxide Emissions Worldwide

```
China - 6925
India - 2386
USSR - 1563
          World - 1138
          USA - 1010
          Canada - 875
        W. Europe - 651
      Japan - 564
                    Chart shows data from column 3.
```

Amounts of carbon dioxide emitted from fossil fuels in selected countries and worldwide in 1987.

Source	Carbon Dioxide (mill. tons)	Carbon Dioxide Per Capita (tons)	Carbon Dioxide Per Dollar GNP (grams)
USA	4480	18.37	1010
USSR	3711	13.07	1563
W. Europe	2899	7.61	651
China	2031	1.90	6925
Japan	908	7.43	564
India	549	.70	2386
Canada	388	14.93	875
World	19438	3.88	1138

Source: Sierra, July/August 1989, p. 32, from Oak Ridge National Laboratory/World Watch.

Energy

★ 696 ★

Energy Conservation Technology in D.C. New Building

The values are percent of new commercial buildings using each conservation technology.

Conservation technology	Percentage
Double-entry vestibules	71
Thermal-break windows	68
Variable air-volume systems	68
High-efficiency fluorescent ballasts	62
Air economizers	59
High-efficiency fluorescent fixtures	50
Energy management & control systems	50
High-efficiency motors	47
High-efficiency fluorescent lamps	47
Programmable exterior lighting	44
Increased wall insulation	41
Increased roof insulation	41
Reflective solar glazing	38
Point-of-use water heaters	35
Optimized motor sizing	32
Increased daylighting	32
Strategic task lighting	32
Programmable thermostats	29
Compact fluorescent lamps	29
Lower foot candles	29
Metal halide lamps	29
Low-E glazing	26
High-efficiency water chillers	26
Modular-parallel chillers	21
High-efficiency compressors	21
Curtailable load wiring	18
Water-side economizers	18
Variable-flow fan for cooling tower	18
High-pressure sodium lamps	15
Low-pressure sodium lamps	12
Building orientation	12
Exhaust air heat recovery	12
Operable external shading	12
Integrated refrigeration/HVAC	12

Source: Energy User News, October 1990, p. 4, from American Consulting Engineers Council.

★ 697 ★

Energy Efficiency by Country

```
United States - 29  ████████████████████████
France - 29         ████████████████████████
Japan - 27          ██████████████████████
Australia - 26      █████████████████████
United Kingdom - 23 ███████████████████
Germany - 22        ██████████████████
Italy - 20          ████████████████
Canada - 16         █████████████
Spain - 15          ████████████
Netherlands - 11    █████████
                    Chart shows data from column 1.
```

The values are percent reduction in energy use per unit of Gross Domestic Product.

Country	Percent	
	1988	1980
Australia	26	2
Canada	16	12
France	29	22
Germany	22	15[1]
Italy	20	10[1]
Japan	27	6[1]
Netherlands	11	19[1]
Spain	15	2[1]
United Kingdom	23	16
United States	29	12

Source: Energy User News, November 1990, p. 8, from International Energy Agency *Note:* 1. Total Commercial, Residential and Agricultural.

★ 698 ★

Factors Inhibiting Energy Conservation in D.C. New Building

```
First cost - 46
Aesthetics - 19
            Simple payback - 13
            Occupant comfort - 10
        No experience w/technology - 5
    Maintenance costs - 3
   Poor reliability - 2
  Cash-flow-analysis - 2
 Product availability - 1
```

The values are percentage of times cited in the survey.

Factors	Percentage
First cost	46
Aesthetics	19
Simple payback	13
Occupant comfort	10
No experience w/technology	5
Maintenance costs	3
Poor reliability	2
Cash-flow-analysis	2
Product availability	1

Source: Energy User News, October 1990, p. 4, from American Consulting Engineers Council.

★ 699 ★

Fossil Fuel Use by World Region

Region	Average annual growth in fossil fuel use 1950-95		Energy use by sector late 1980s		
	Total (percent)	Per capita (percent)	Industry (percent)	Buildings (percent)	Transport (percent)
Developed market economies	4.0	1.1	35	32	33
Eastern Europe and U.S.S.R.	5.2	3.4	60	27	13
Centrally planned Asia	9.5	7.8	45	50	5
Developing market economies	6.4	3.7	49	24	27

Source: Changing by Degrees: Steps to Reduce Greenhouse Gases, U.S. Congress, Office of Technology Assessment, OTA-O-482, Washington, D.C., February 1991, p. 274, from Intergovernmental panel on Climate Change, *Energy and Industry Sub Group Report* (Geneva: May 31,1990).

★ 700 ★

Primary Energy Consumption Worldwide

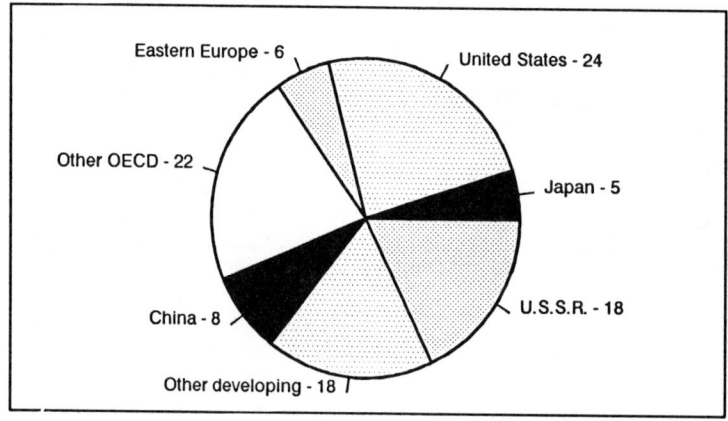

Figures refer to 1988.

Countries	Percent
United States	24
U.S.S.R.	18
China	8
Eastern Europe	6
Japan	5

[Continued]

★ 700 ★

Primary Energy Consumption Worldwide
[Continued]

Countries	Percent
Other OECD	22
Other developing	18

Source: Changing by Degrees: Steps to Reduce Greenhouse Gases, U.S. Congress, Office of Technology Assessment, OTA-O-482, Washington, D.C., February 1991, p. 275, from U.S. Department of Energy, *International Energy Annual*, DOE/EIA-0219(88) (Washington, DC: Energy Information Administration, November 1989). *Note:* OECD stands for Organization for Economic Cooperation and Development.

Forestry

★ 701 ★

Forestry Incentives Program by State

The data is for the fiscal year 1989.

State	Participants (number)	Area served (acres)	Assistance (dollars)		
			Regular	Long term	Total assistance
Alabama	327	12,407	874,705	-	874,705
Alaska	-	-	-	-	-
Arizona	1	56	2,223	-	2,223
Arkansas	345	13,995	692,647	-	692,647
California	22	372	61,267	-	61,267
Colorado	7	149	8,607	-	8,607
Connecticut	-	-	-	-	-
Delaware	14	510	39,902	-	39,902
Florida	281	16,995	1,007,377	-	1,007,377
Georgia	371	14,933	1,335,638	-	1,355,638
Hawaii	-	-	-	-	-
Idaho	9	289	23,675	3,909	27,584
Illinois	65	1,581	21,412	641	22,053
Indiana	76	2,682	65,077	844	65,921
Iowa	17	290	20,977	-	20,977
Kansas	3	46	1,947	-	1,947
Kentucky	68	2,163	91,553	-	91,553
Louisiana	303	14,346	687,409	-	687,409
Maine	24	642	36,242	14,941	51,183
Maryland	44	1,791	125,370	12,438	137,808
Massachusetts	58	1,024	42,276	6,115	48,391
Michigan	73	1,185	61,164	20,009	81,173
Minnesota	17	320	21,922	645	22,567
Mississippi	388	22,047	1,071,518	-	1,071,518

[Continued]

★ 701 ★

Forestry Incentives Program by State
[Continued]

State	Participants (number)	Area served (acres)	Assistance (dollars)		
			Regular	Long term	Total assistance
Missouri	40	1,561	46,053	-	46,053
Montana	-	-	-	-	-
Nebraska	2	21	1,170	-	1,170
Nevada	-	-	-	-	-
New Hampshire	47	687	36,136	815	36,951
New Jersey	2	10	200	-	200
New Mexico	2	21	837	-	837
New York	83	1,246	57,260	10,515	67,775
North Carolina	495	18,489	633,780	-	633,780
North Dakota	-	-	-	-	-
Ohio	43	1,166	36,858		36,858
Oklahoma	25	1,142	57,348	810	58,158
Oregon	102	4,532	452,121	23,118	475,239
Pennsylvania	40	807	36,029	-	36,029
Puerto Rico	6	97	12,794	-	12,794
Rhode Island	5	60	307	1,302	1,609
South Carolina	331	12,290	815,347	-	815,347
South Dakota	13	154	9,822	-	9,822
Tennessee	46	2,438	133,518	-	133,518
Texas	318	12,175	655,653	-	655,653
Utah	-	-	-	-	-
Vermont	36	375	19,454	1,300	20,754
Virginia	563	22,807	813,413	-	813,413
Washington	72	3,866	369,561	-	369,561
West Virginia	90	1,877	59,648	5,604	65,252
Wisconsin	143	2,706	125,959	3,215	129,174
Wyoming	34	1,933	96,432	-	96,432
Total	5,048	198,283	10,762,608	106,221	10,868,829

Source: Agricultural Conservation and Forestry Statistics, 1989, U.S. Government Printing Office, Washington, D.C., 1989, p. 446, from Agricultural Stabilization and Conservation Services.

★ 702 ★

Forestry Practices by State

Data are shown in number of acres.

State	1989				Cumulative 1975-89			
	Planting trees	Improving a stand of forest trees	Site prep for natural regeneration	Special forestry practices	Planting trees	Improving a stand of forest trees	Site prep for natural regeneration	Special forestry practices
Alabama	11,995	338	74	-	260,064	25,023	560	-
Arizona	-	56	-	-	13	1,528	-	-
Arkansas	12,153	737	1,105	-	149,927	101,392	5,891	7,981
California	181	191	-	-	8,276	9,177	-	-
Colorado	26	123	-	-	227	4,418	10	-
Connecticut	-	-	-	-	1,097	7,456	-	2,336
Delaware	176	334	-	-	4,586	1,253	-	-
Florida	15,832	1,123	40	-	211,628	8,347	193	-
Georgia	14,201	550	182	-	227,201	16,612	676	-
Hawaii	-	-	-	-	250	-	-	-
Idaho	75	214	-	-	908	2,521	18	-
Illinois	199	1,232	150	-	2,576	27,363	243	-
Indiana	139	2,338	205	-	3,267	64,736	1,540	-
Iowa	100	190	-	-	2,443	6,208	20	-
Kansas	-	46	-	-	441	4,375	-	-
Kentucky	214	1,508	441	-	3,602	50,624	1,068	2,121
Louisiana	12,779	1,014	553	-	134,132	43,885	1,350	-
Maine	86	372	184	-	6,328	17,486	184	-
Maryland	1,315	476	-	-	20,118	11,307	27	-
Massachusetts	75	919	30	-	300	32,818	30	739
Michigan	1,016	169	-	-	23,763	36,415	-	-
Minnesota	232	59	29	-	14,599	12,425	349	648
Mississippi	21,531	516	-	-	223,156	26,999	1,008	16
Missouri	198	1,363	-	-	11,514	80,027	-	-
Montana	-	-	-	-	116	4,299	107	-
Nebraska	11	10	-	-	553	1,771	-	-
Nevada	-	-	-	-	526	50	-	-
New Hampshire	-	560	127	-	112	25,952	631	-
New Jersey	-	10	-	-	927	12,089	-	-
New Mexico	-	21	-	-	65	6,561	-	-
New York	189	1,057	-	-	3,949	59,332	110	4,323
North Carolina	17,976	513	-	-	243,039	18,215	427	-
North Dakota	-	-	-	-	207	141	-	48
Ohio	90	1,076	-	-	10,707	66,944	566	-
Oklahoma	768	374	-	-	16,814	31,018	-	-
Oregon	2,702	1,830	-	-	37,234	20,304	-	-
Pennsylvania	26	744	37	-	5,133	32,117	195	-
Puerto Rico	97	-	-	-	1,098	10	-	-
Rhode Island	-	60	-	-	132	2,339	-	-
South Carolina	12,072	218	-	-	198,920	9,660	149	-
South Dakota	-	154	-	-	29	3,494	-	-
Tennessee	2,292	-	146	-	23,765	15,210	387	-
Texas	11,079	1,096	-	-	138,683	49,774	-	-

[Continued]

★ 702 ★

Forestry Practices by State
[Continued]

State	1989				Cumulative 1975-89			
	Planting trees	Improving a stand of forest trees	Site prep for natural regeneration	Special forestry practices	Planting trees	Improving a stand of forest trees	Site prep for natural regeneration	Special forestry practices
Utah	-	-	-	-	-	12	-	-
Vermont	20	355	-	-	393	20,388	224	16,368
Virginia	19,223	3,584	-	-	242,549	32,884	29	-
Washington	3,610	256	-	-	28,901	9,647	-	-
West Virginia	272	1,595	10	-	5,765	91,057	73	24,094
Wisconsin	1,183	1,219	304	-	26,958	30,490	1,757	265
Wyoming	-	1,933	-	-	4	9,179	-	-
Total	164,133	30,533	3,617	-	2,296,995	1,145,332	17,822	58,939

Source: *Agricultural Conservation and Forestry Statistics, 1989*, U.S. Government Printing Office, Washington, D.C., 1989, p. 445, from Agricultural Stabilization and Conservation Service. In 1974 the program was part of the Rural Environmental Conservation Program (now called the Agricultural Conservation Program). Data for the program year were published in the 1974 Rural Environmental Conservation Program Summary. In 1975 it became a separately funded program.

★ 703 ★

Payments to States From National Forest Revenues

Values are shown in thousands of dollars, as payments to states and Puerto Rico from receipts from timber sales, grazing fees, and miscellaneous uses, fiscal year[1] 1988-90.[2]

State or other areas	1988	1989	1990
Alabama	1,505	1,396	1,604
Alaska	-	410	5,106
Arizona	6,787	7,718	7,187
Arkansas	5,316	3,888	8,331
California	52,560	63,311	66,992
Colorado	2,528	2,718	3,457
Florida	2,709	1,691	2,326
Georgia	860	797	866
Idaho	9,307	10,344	12,330
Illinois	236	88	38
Indiana	79	69	79
Kentucky	482	449	397
Louisiana	3,423	2,804	2,650
Maine	34	26	37
Michigan	1,339	791	2,057
Minnesota	835	492	724
Mississippi	5,017	5,055	4,466
Missouri	1,569	2,130	2,632
Montana	6,500	8,238	7,582
Nebraska	35	34	41
Nevada	245	345	380

[Continued]

★ 703 ★

Payments to States from National Forest Revenues
[Continued]

State or other areas	1988	1989	1990
New Hampshire	493	375	535
New Mexico	1,927	2,280	2,365
New York	17	6	19
North Carolina	952	613	833
North Dakota	3	3	3
Ohio	176	93	172
Oklahoma	746	516	1,201
Oregon	131,942	144,531	164,155
Pennsylvania	2,665	2,224	3,688
South Carolina	3,071	2,068	2,332
South Dakota	892	1,214	1,697
Tennessee	462	371	437
Texas	3,753	2,745	2,015
Utah	952	1,043	1,323
Vermont	152	130	178
Virginia	432	412	425
Washington	32,490	43,387	47,202
West Virginia	898	594	801
Wisconsin	771	414	767
Wyoming	1,141	1,465	1,491
Puerto Rico	16	15	15

Source: Agricultural Conservation and Forestry Statistics, 1989, U.S. Government Printing Office, Washington, D.C., 1989, p. 464, from Forest Service. *Notes:* 1. Fiscal years Oct. 1-Sept. 30. 2. Payments under the acts of May 23, 1908 (as amended), July 24, 1956, and Oct. 22, 1976, are 25 percent of total receipts remaining after deducting (a) payments to Arizona and New Mexico for school section lands administered by Forest Service, (b) appropriations of receipts under laws authorizing such appropriations for acquisition of lands in specified national forests or portions thereof, and (c) receipts from an area of the Superior National Forest, Minnesota, on account of which the State (for the counties) is paid 0.75 percent of the appraised valuation in lieu of 25 percent of the receipts. Payments made in the following year. 3. Less than $500.

Funding Mechanisms

★ 704 ★

Mechanisms for Funding State Programs

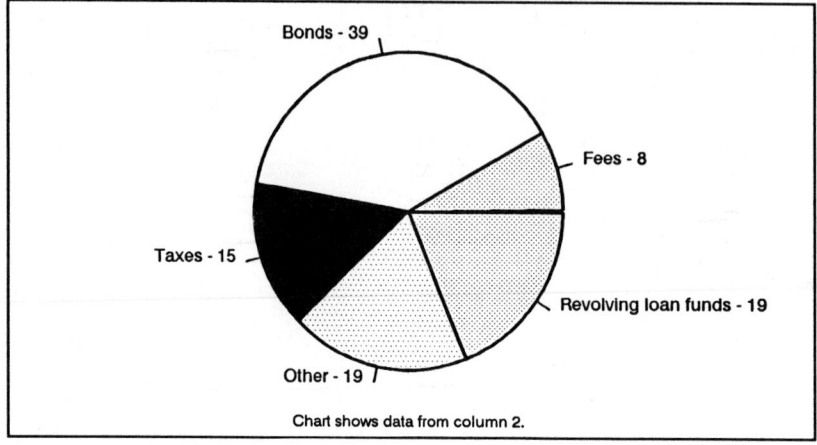

Chart shows data from column 2.

Data show most widely used mechanisms used to fund state programs and percent of total revenues generated by each funding mechanism. Fees, most widely used, generated the least revenue.

Types of funding used	Most widely used (%)	Revenue generated (%)
Fees	63	8
Taxes	9	15
Bonds	7	39
Revolving loan funds	4	19
Other	17	19

Source: C&EN, September 11, 1989, p. 19, from National Governors' Association, "Survey on Alternative Financing Mechanisms for Environmental Programs, 1989".

Hazardous Waste

★ 705 ★

Hazardous Waste Export From California

Five states received the most hazardous waste from California for treatment/disposal. Data represent the amount of waste shipped to each destination in 1989.

States	Thousands of Tons
Utah	58.0
Idaho	37.2
Arizona	32.0
New Jersey	29.9
Kansas	23.2

Source: The Wall Street Journal, July 5, 1991, p. B1, from California Health Department Toxics Program.

★ 706 ★

Hazardous Waste Generation - Anchorage

Data refer to hazardous waste generation by area businesses, as reported by a municipal survey.

Type of waste	Gallons/year
Automotive	25,500
Solvents/cleaners	24,400
Paint waste	7,800
Photo developers	5,800
Corrosives	5,500
Adhesives, Resins, Pigments	3,800
Others	15,300

Source: Disposal Directory for Small Quantities of Hazardous Waste, Municipality of Anchorage, Solid Waste Department, Anchorage, Alaska, January 1989, p. 5.

★ 707 ★

Hazardous Waste Sites by Region

	Sites			State Sites			
	Final	Proposed	Total	Total indentified Hazardous Waste Sites[6]	Sites Needing Attention[6]	Priority List	Inventory or Registry
Region I							
Connecticut	8	6	14	560	560	-	567[1]
Maine	6	2	8	237	117	-	317[1,2]
Massachusetts	22	1	22	1800	1725	1152[3]	1634[2]
New Hampshire	15	0	15	400	400	-	150-175[2]
Rhode Island	8	3	11	280	280	-	-
Vermont	4	4	8	260	241	130[4]	50[2]
Region II							
New Jersey	100	7	107	3225	3000	-	336 (on status report)
New York	73	3	76	1167	1039	1091	615[2]
Region III							
Delaware	12	8	20	200	160	48	200[3]
Maryland	7	3	10	304	254	25[1]	Approx. 300[2]
Pennsylvania	71 (5 delisted)	24	95	1100	1100	-	2295[2]
Virginia	12 (1 delisted)	9	21	450	150	-	-
West Virginia	5	1	6	299	299	-	-
Region IV							
Alabama	10	2	12	500	500	-	500+[2]
Florida	32	15	47	821	821	-	500+[3]
Georgia	7	6	13	753	628	-	-
Kentucky	12	5	17	450	250	-	500[2]
Mississippi	2	1	3	319	300	-	-
North Carolina	15	7	22	799	758	85	781
South Carolina	14	7	21	44	42	42	-
Tennessee	10	3	13	1000	755	281[1]	800-900[2]
Region V							
Illinois	23	16	39	224	224	29	1325[2]
Indiana	30	7	37	1400	1400	-	-
Michigan	65	15	80	1667	1667	2019	-
Minnesota	40	0	40	117	117	157[1]	300[2]
Ohio	29	3	32	1000	700	430[1]	1074[2]
Wisconsin	35	4	39	223	223	60[1]	173[2]

[Continued]

★ 707 ★

Hazardous Waste Site by Region
[Continued]

	Sites			State Sites			
	Final	Proposed	Total	Total identified Hazardous Waste Sites[6]	Sites Needing Attention[6]	Priority List	Inventory or Registry
Region VI							
Arkansas	10	0	10	296	108	7[1]	26[2]
Louisiana	9	2	11	499	257	-	-
New Mexico	6	4	10	510	495	-	-
Oklahoma	8	3	11	30	30	-	-
Texas	24	4	28	88	88	29[1]	over 1000[2]
Region VII							
Iowa	9	15	24	370	164	19(37)[1]	384[2]
Kansas	9	2	11	328	314	-	489[2]
Missouri	14	7	21	1070	446	54	-
Nebraska	3	2	5	40	38	-	-
Region VIII							
Colorado	13	3	16	361	361	-	-
Montana	8	2	10	134	132	159[1]	Approx. 151[2]
North Dakota	2	0	2	47	21	-	-
South Dakota	1	0	1	1	1	-	56 (CERCLIS)
Utah	5	7	12	164	164	-	-
Wyoming	1	2	3	100	86	-	-
Region IX							
Arizona	5	4	9	503	453	23	-
California	52	36	88	25,000	6654	328	Approx. 5000[2]
Hawaii	0	6	6	-	-	-	-
Nevada	0	0	0	0	0	-	-
Region X							
Alaska	1	0	1	-	-	1[1]	277[2]
Idaho	4	0	4	164	164	-	-
Oregon	6	1	7	750[5]	-	-	-
Washington	25	17	42	506	506	-	700[1,2]

Source: An Analysis of State Superfund Programs: 50-State Study, EPA/540/8-89/011, September 1989, p.p. 49-52. NPL stands for National Priority Lists. Notes: 1. Includes some or all NPL sites. 2. Includes unconfirmed sites/potential sites. 3. Investigated/confirmed. 4. Includes all types of hazardous waste sites. 5. ELI information 8/3/89. 6. Source: *Survey of States' Cleanups of Non-NPL Hazardous Waste Sites, 1989*, GAO.

★ 708 ★

Hazardous Waste Sites by State

Hazardous waste sites on the national priority list, by state, for 1989. Includes both proposed and final sites listed on the National Priorities List for the Superfund program as authorized by the Comprehensive Environmental Response, Compensation, and Liability Act of 1980 and the Superfund Amendments and Reauthorization Act of 1986.

State	Total Sites	Non-Federal sites	Federal sites
United States[1]	1,219	1,102	117
Alabama	12	10	2
Alaska	6	2	4
Arizona	11	8	3
Arkansas	11	11	-
California	91	70	21
Colorado	16	13	3
Connecticut	15	14	1
Delaware	20	19	1
District of Columbia	-	-	-
Florida	51	47	4
Georgia	13	11	2
Hawaii	7	6	1
Idaho	9	7	2
Illinois	38	34	4
Indiana	35	35	-
Iowa	21	20	1
Kansas	11	10	1
Kentucky	17	17	-
Louisiana	11	10	1
Maine	9	7	2
Maryland	10	8	2
Massachusetts	25	22	3
Michigan	79	79	-
Minnesota	42	40	2
Mississippi	3	3	-
Missouri	24	21	3
Montana	10	10	-
Nebraska	6	5	1
Nevada	1	1	-
New Hampshire	16	15	1
New Jersey	109	103	6
New Mexico	10	8	2
New York	83	79	4
North Carolina	22	21	1
North Dakota	2	2	-
Ohio	33	30	3
Oklahoma	12	11	1
Oregon	8	7	1
Pennsylvania	97	93	4

[Continued]

★ 708 ★

Hazardous Waste Sites by State

[Continued]

State	Total Sites	Non-Federal sites	Federal sites
Rhode Island	11	9	2
South Carolina	23	22	1
South Dakota	3	2	1
Tennessee	14	12	2
Texas	29	26	3
Utah	12	8	4
Vermont	8	8	-
Virginia	20	19	1
Washington	45	31	14
West Virginia	5	5	-
Wisconsin	40	40	-
Wyoming	3	2	1

Source: U.S. Department of Commerce, Bureau of the Census, *Statistical Abstract of the United States 1990 (110th ed.)*, Superintendent of Documents, Washington, D.C., p. 205, from U.S. Environmental Protection Agency, press release, October 1989. *Notes:* 1. Includes outlying areas, not shown separately. - Represents zero.

★ 709 ★

Household Hazardous Waste Generation - Anchorage

Figures are shown in thousands of gallons per year.

Waste Type	Quantity Range
Automotive (Oil, batteries, antifreeze)	108 - 233
Pesticides	39 - 107
Solvents and other wastes	4 - 131
Total	151 - 471

Source: Disposal Directory for Small Quantities of Hazardous Waste, Municipality of Anchorage, Solid Waste Department, Anchorage, Alaska, January 1989, p. 6.

★ 710 ★

Pesticides in Iowa Public Water Supplies

Pesticides detected in Iowa public water supplies in 1987. Data show percentage of surface water supplies and wells in which pesticides were detected and the percent in which the detected pesticides were present at higher levels than permitted by health standards.

	Detected	Exceeding Standard
Surface water	60.0	4.0
Wells	8.0	0.5

Source: Farm Journal, November 1990, p. 20F, from U.S. Geological Survey.

Hazardous Waste Management

★ 711 ★

Hazardous Waste Disposal Methods - Anchorage

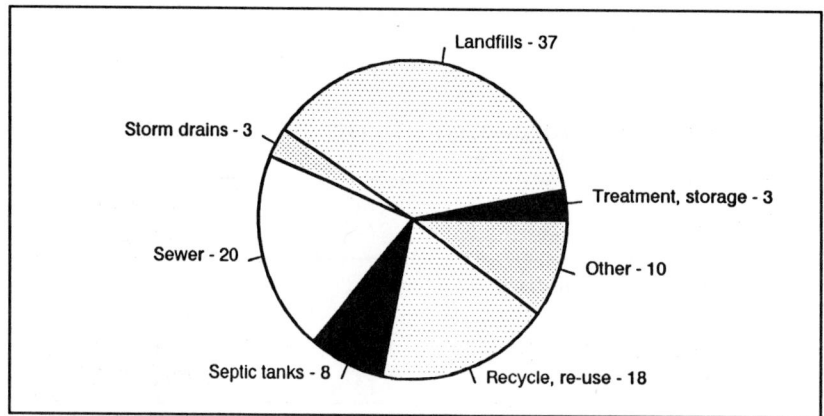

Data shown are the results of a municipal survey of 1,191 business establishments in Anchorage, AK.

Method used	Percentage of Total
Landfills	37
Sewer	20
Recycle, re-use	18
Septic tanks	8
Storm drains	3

[Continued]

★ 711 ★

Hazardous Waste Disposal Methods - Anchorage
[Continued]

Method used	Percentage of Total
Treatment, storage	3
Other	10

Source: Disposal Directory for Small Quantities of Hazardous Waste, Municipality of Anchorage, Solid Waste Department, Anchorage, Alaska, January 1989, p. 7.

★ 712 ★

Hazardous Waste Export Costs - Anchorage

Data show the costs of disposing a single 55-gallon drum of hazardous waste out of state from an origin in Anchorage, AK.

	Range (dollars)
Waste Analysis	100 to 175
Transportation	200 to 300
Disposal Site Profile	50 to 200
Waste Acceptance	0 to 125
Disposal	150 to 700
Total	500 to 1500

Source: Disposal Directory for Small Quantities of Hazardous Waste, Municipality of Anchorage, Solid Waste Department, Anchorage, Alaska, January 1989, p. 24.

★ 713 ★

Underground Injection Release by State

Data refer to 1987 and are drawn from the Environmental Protection Agency's Toxic Release Inventory (TRI) reporting system.

Underground Injection Release State	Rank	TRI Facilities Reporting Underground Injection Releases		TRI Forms Reporting Underground Injection Releases		Amount of TRI Underground Injection Releases	
		Number	Percent	Number	Percent	Pounds	Percent
Alabama	17	3	1.62	13	1.78	1,443,591	0.04
Alaska	-	0	0.00	0	0.00	0	0.00
American Samoa	-	0	0.00	0	0.00	0	0.00
Arizona	-	0	0.00	0	0.00	0	0.00
Arkansas	13	8	4.32	19	2.60	13,016,449	0.40
California	1	11	5.95	26	3.56	1,530,850,645	47.21
Colorado	23	2	1.08	2	0.27	1,117	0.00

[Continued]

★ 713 ★

Underground Injection Release by State
[Continued]

Underground Injection Release State	Rank	TRI Facilities Reporting Underground Injection Releases		TRI Forms Reporting Underground Injection Releases		Amount of TRI Underground Injection Releases	
		Number	Percent	Number	Percent	Pounds	Percent
Connecticut	-	0	0.00	0	0.00	0	0.00
Delaware	32	1	0.54	1	0.14	250	0.00
Florida	10	5	2.70	33	4.52	29,437,389	0.91
Georgia	21	1	0.54	1	0.14	19,500	0.00
Hawaii	19	2	1.08	5	0.68	216,140	0.01
Idaho	-	0	0.00	0	0.00	0	0.00
Illinois	12	8	4.32	19	2.60	14,221,970	0.44
Indiana	7	8	4.32	30	4.11	63,356,466	1.95
Iowa	-	0	0.00	0	0.00	0	0.00
Kansas	5	3	1.62	36	4.93	91,067,410	2.81
Kentucky	11	2	1.08	2	0.27	25,000,250	0.77
Louisiana	3	22	11.89	126	17.26	553,820,180	17.08
Maine	-	0	0.00	0	0.00	0	0.00
Maryland	26	1	0.54	1	0.14	750	0.00
Massachusetts	34	1	0.54	1	0.14	250	0.00
Michigan	15	14	7.57	50	6.85	6,472,752	0.20
Minnesota	33	1	0.54	1	0.14	250	0.00
Mississippi	8	6	3.24	9	1.23	46,433,140	1.43
Missouri	18	3	1.62	3	0.41	1,001,450	0.03
Montana	-	0	0.00	0	0.00	0	0.00
Nebraska	-	0	0.00	0	0.00	0	0.00
Nevada	-	0	0.00	0	0.00	0	0.00
New Hampshire	-	0	0.00	0	0.00	0	0.00
New Jersey	25	4	2.16	4	0.55	780	0.00
New Mexico	-	0	0.00	0	0.00	0	0.00
New York	29	2	1.08	2	0.27	500	0.00
North Carolina	31	1	0.54	1	0.14	250	0.00
North Dakota	-	0	0.00	0	0.00	0	0.00
Ohio	6	7	3.78	30	4.11	71,850,645	2.22
Oklahoma	14	6	3.24	20	2.74	7,171,133	0.22
Oregon	-	0	0.00	0	0.00	0	0.00
Pennsylvania	20	4	2.16	4	0.55	74,000	0.00
Puerto Rico	24	1	0.54	1	0.14	988	0.00
Rhode Island	-	0	0.00	0	0.00	0	0.00
South Carolina	27	1	0.54	1	0.14	750	0.00
South Dakota	-	0	0.00	0	0.00	0	0.00
Tennessee	4	7	3.78	24	3.29	124,406,900	3.84
Texas	2	38	20.54	245	33.56	630,223,666	19.44
Utah	35	1	0.54	1	0.14	3	0.00
Vermont	-	0	0.00	0	0.00	0	0.00
Virgin Islands	-	0	0.00	0	0.00	0	0.00
Virginia	30	1	0.54	1	0.14	250	0.00

[Continued]

★ 713 ★

Underground Injection Release by State
[Continued]

Underground Injection Release State	Rank	TRI Facilities Reporting Underground Injection Releases		TRI Forms Reporting Underground Injection Releases		Amount of TRI Underground Injection Releases	
		Number	Percent	Number	Percent	Pounds	Percent
Washington	28	2	1.08	2	0.27	500	0.00
West Virginia	16	3	1.62	4	0.55	1,719,219	0.05
Wisconsin	22	4	2.16	6	0.82	1,500	0.00
Wyoming	9	1	0.54	6	0.82	30,651,671	0.95
Total		185	100.00	730	100.00	3,242,462,75	7100.00
Percent of all reporting		0.96		0.98		14.40	

Source: *The Toxic Release Inventory, A National Perspective*, U.S. Environmental Protection Agency, Washington, D.C., June 1989, P. 200.

Noise Pollution

★ 714 ★

Noisy Jets at Selected U.S. Airports

Percentage of jets at selected U.S. airports that are Stage 2 and Stage 3 aircraft. Stage 2 jets are older and noisier. In the fall of 1990 legislation was passed requiring the phasing out of Stage 2 jets and the phasing in of Stage 3 jets—which are half as noisy—by the turn of the century. Data are shown in percent.

Airport	Stage 2 Planes	Stage 3 Planes
La Guardia	76.0	24.0
Newark	61.0	39.0
Kennedy	34.0	66.0
Minneapolis	69.0	31.0
Tucson	65.0	35.0
Cleveland	57.0	43.0
Nashville	48.0	52.0
Pittsburgh	40.0	60.0

Source: *The Wall Street Journal*, April 5, 1991, p. B1.

Nuclear Waste

★ 715 ★

Low-Level Waste Disposal by State

Amounts of commercial low-level radioactive waste shipped for disposal by state, as reported by disposal site operators. Prior to 1980 waste brokers did not attribute the waste they shipped for disposal back to the original waste generator.

State	Annual volume in thousands of cubic feet					
	1983	1984	1985	1986	1987	1988
Northeast Compact						
New Jersey[2]	128	116	66	56	50	38
Connecticut[2]	67	58	63	56	40	40
Subtotal	195	174	129	112	90	78
Appalachian Compact						
Pennsylvania[2]	270	219	262	188	145	145
Maryland[1]	47	42	38	19	20	26
Delaware	1	1	1	1	1	1
West Virginia	<1	<1	<1	<1	<1	<1
Subtotal	319	263	302	209	166	172
Southeast Compact						
Tennessee[1]	159	240	237	81	239	161
South Carolina[1]	198	255	136	121	118	96
Virginia	167	98	147	71	68	64
North Carolina[1,2]	166	100	102	82	79	62
Alabama[1]	154	151	102	58	70	51
Georgia[1]	69	87	78	48	30	39
Florida[1]	85	89	59	60	46	31
Mississippi[1]	15	15	22	19	14	18
Subtotal	1,013	1,035	883	540	664	522
Midwest Compact						
Michigan[2]	54	38	55	36	35	25
Ohio	28	19	34	16	19	20
Minnesota	44	70	47	28	20	14
Missouri	8	7	11	24	23	10
Wisconsin	28	29	16	6	9	18
Iowa[1]	26	12	30	10	19	7
Indiana	<1	3	1	0	2	2
Subtotal	189	178	194	120	127	96
Central Midwest Compact						
Illinois[1,2]	219	227	360	227	190	126
Kentucky[1]	3	2	4	4	<1	2
Subtotal	222	229	364	231	191	128
Central States Compact						
Oklahoma	2	5	11	50	83	28
Louisiana[1]	<1	<1	11	23	28	18
Nebraska[1,2]	35	31	37	20	17	13
Arkansas[1]	28	33	25	4	20	7

[Continued]

★ 715 ★

Low-Level Waste Disposal by State
[Continued]

State	Annual volume in thousands of cubic feet					
	1983	1984	1985	1986	1987	1988
Kansas[1]	0	1	2	7	5	5
Subtotal	66	71	86	104	153	71
Rocky Mountain Compact						
Colorado[1,2]	3	9	10	1	4	3
New Mexico[1]	1	1	3	0	1	<1
Nevada[1]	0	0	<1	0	<1	<1
Wyoming	0	0	0	0	0	0
Subtotal	4	10	14	1	6	4
Northwest Compact						
Oregon[1]	49	60	58	109	82	84
Washington[1,2]	45	45	63	53	38	36
Utah[1]	3	5	5	3	3	5
Hawaii	5	3	1.1	2	3	4
Idaho[1]	0	6	1	0	<1	<1
Montana	<1	1	<1	1	<1	0
Alaska	0	0	0	0	<1	0
Subtotal	103	120	139	168	129	129
Southwestern Compact						
California[1,2]	133	159	251	114	99	74
Arizona[1]	0	1	4	5	17	28
North Dakota[1]	0	0	0	0	<1	0
South Dakota	<1	0	<1	<1	0	0
Subtotal	133	160	255	119	116	102
Unaffiliated States						
New York[1,2]	199	147	161	107	70	65
Massachusetts[2]	167	193	106	67	55	47
Texas[1,2]	57	13	11	4	69	9
Vermont	22	13	20	12	8	7
Maine[2]	12	12	13	8	5	6
Rhode Island[1]	2	1	1	1	1	1
New Hampshire[1]	2	2	2	2	<1	<1
District of Columbia	3	2	1	<1	<1	<1
Subtotal	464	383	315	201	208	135
Total	2,709	2,619	2,681	1,805	1,845	1,436

Source: Office of Technological Assessment, *Partnership Under Pressure: Managing Commercial Low-Level Radioactive Waste,* November 1989, pp. 151-152, from *The 1987 State-by-State Assesment of Low-level Radioactive Wastes Received at Commercial Disposal Sites,* National Low-level Radioactive Waste Management Program, December 1985, DOE/LLW-69T, pp. 141. Data for 1988 taken from tables prepared by EG&G Idaho in May 1989 for the U.S. Department of Energy, *Integrated Data Base for 1989: Spent Fuel and Radioactive Waste Inventories, Projections, and Characteristics,* DOE/RW-0006, Rev. 5, 1989. *Notes:* 1. Agreement States. 2. States Planning to host a disposal facility.

Pollution Prevention

★ 716 ★

State Pollution Prevention Programs

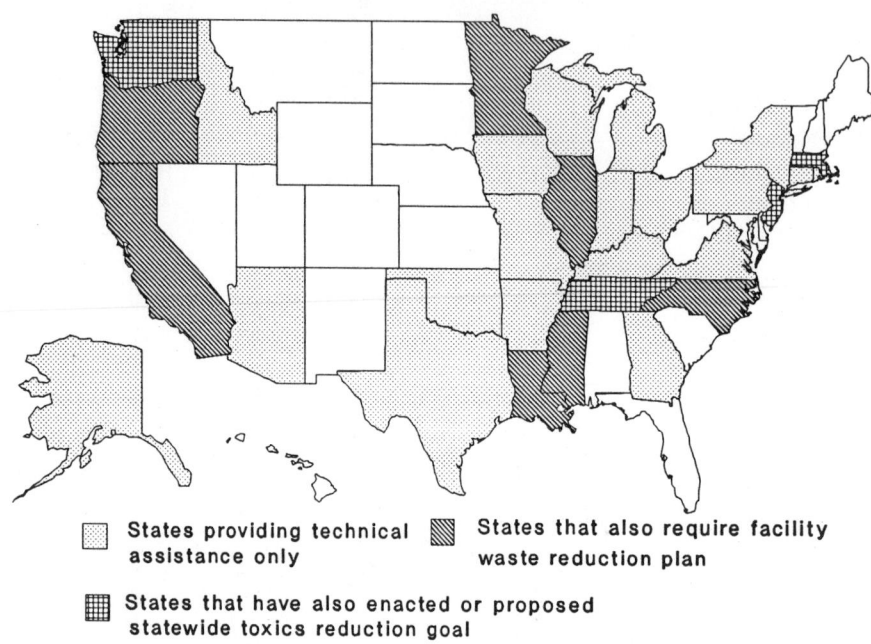

	States providing technical assistance only		States that also require facility waste reduction plan

	States that have also enacted or proposed statewide toxics reduction goal

Source: ENR, July 12, 1990, p. 29, from John M. Scagnelli, Whitman & Ransom; North Carolina Pollution Prevention Program; National Roundtable of State Waste Reduction Programs.

Population

★ 717 ★

Population Growth Trend in the World

Population size is shown in millions.

Rank	1950		1989		2020 (Projected)	
	Countries	Population Size	Countries	Population Size	Countries	Population Size
1	China	563	China	1113	China	1523
2	India	370	India	833	India	1308
3	U.S.S.R.	180	U.S.S.R.	289	U.S.S.R.	355
4	U.S.	152	U.S.	248	U.S.	294

[Continued]

★ 717 ★

Population Growth Trend in the World
[Continued]

Rank	1950		1989		2020 (Projected)	
	Countries	Population Size	Countries	Population Size	Countries	Population Size
5	Japan	84	Indonesia	188	Indonesia	293
6	Indonesia	83	Brazil	151	Nigeria	274
7	Brazil	53	Japan	123	Pakistan	242
8	U.K.	50	Nigeria	115	Brazil	242
9	West Germany	50	Bangladesh	115	Bangladesh	230
10	Italy	47	Pakistan	110	Mexico	152
11	Bangladesh	46	Mexico	86	Philippines	131
12	France	42	Vietnam	67	Japan	131
13	Nigeria	41	Philippines	65	Iran	130
14	Pakistan	39	West Germany	61	Ethiopia	128
15	Mexico	28	Italy	58	Vietnam	121
16	Spain	28	U.K.	57	Egypt	101
17	Vietnam	25	France	56	Turkey	92
18	Poland	25	Turkey	55	Zaire	85
19	Egypt	21	Thailand	54	South Africa	83
20	Philippines	21	Iran	54	Kenya	79
21	Turkey	21	Egypt	53	Thailand	71
22	South Korea	21	Ethiopia	50	Tanzania	69
23	Ethiopia	21	South Korea	43	Myanmar	67
24	Thailand	20	Myanmar	41	South Korea	58
25	Myanmar	19	Spain	39	France	58
26	East Germany	18	Poland	38	Sudan	57
27	Argentina	17	South Africa	39	U.K.	57
28	Iran	16	Zaire	34	Italy	57
29	Yugoslavia	16	Argentina	32	W. Germany[1]	56
30	Romania	16	Colombia	32	Colombia	49

Source: Changing by Degrees: Steps to Reduce Greenhouse Gases, U.S. Congress, Office of Technology Assessment, OTA-O-482, Washington, D.C., February 1991, p. 278, from Office of Technology Assessment, 1991, based on U.S. Department of Commerce, Bureau of the Census, *World Population Profile: 1989*, WP-89 (Washington, DC: U.S. Government Printing Office, September 1989). *Note:* 1. Excluding East Germany.

★ 718 ★

The World's Largest Cities

Cities	Rank in 1970	Rank in 2000
New York	1	4
Tokyo/Yokohama	2	3
Shanghai	3	7
London	4	22
Mexico City	5	1

[Continued]

★ 718 ★

The World's Largest Cities
[Continued]

Cities	Rank in 1970	Rank in 2000
Los Angeles	6	21
Paris	7	27
Buenos Aires	8	10
Beijing	9	18
Sao Paulo	10	2
Osaka/Kobe	11	20
Moscow	12	24
Rio de Janeiro	13	11
Calcutta	14	5
Tianjin	15	25
Bombay	17	6
Cairo	19	15
Seoul	20	12
Jakarta	21	9
Delhi	27	13
Teheran	30	8
Lagos	60	14

Source: Changing by Degrees: Steps to Reduce Greenhouse Gases, U.S. Congress, Office of Technology Assessment, OTA-O-482, Washington, D.C., February 1991, p. 279, from U.N. Department of International Economic and Social Affairs, *Prospects of World Urbanization, 1988*, Population Studies No. 112, ST/ESA/SER.A/112 (New York: 1989).

Radon

★ 719 ★

Houses With Radon by State

State	Houses with Radon (percent)
North Dakota	63
Minnesota	46
Colorado	39
Pennsylvania	37
Wisconsin	27
Wyoming	26
Indiana	26
Massachusetts	24
Kansas	21

[Continued]

★ 719 ★

Houses With Radon by State
[Continued]

State	Houses with Radon (percent)
Rhode Island	19
Connecticut	19
Kentucky	17
Missouri	17
Tennessee	16
Michigan	9
Arizona	7
Alabama	6

Source: Time, September 26, 1988, p. 69.

Resource Recovery

★ 720 ★

Average Weekly Materials for Recycling

Results were obtained from a survey of more than 100 households that volunteered to maintain weekly diaries of the recyclables set out for collection. Data shown are average number of items per week per household.

	Aluminum cans	News-papers	Glass containers	Plastic jugs
Those completing diaries each week	5.7	7.4	2.5	2.8
Those completing diaries 80% of the time	6.6	7.5	2.8	3.1
Those completing diaries less frequently	7.8	8.3	3.4	3.8
Ranges selected	6-7	7-8	3	3-4
28-week average	6.6	7.5	2.6	3.1
Highest week's average	9.7	10.5	3.5	4.8
Lowest week's average	4.6	5.1	1.5	2.1

Source: Resource Recycling, October 1990, p. 86, from City of Lexington, Kentucky.

★ 721 ★

Curbside Polystyrene Collection Program - Fitchburg, WI

Data are based on a nine-month program (April-December 1990) to collect polystyrere at the curbside. Results are for a sample of 3000 homes.

Month	Number of set-outs	Number of bags	Volume (cubic yards)	Weight (pounds)	Weekly set-out rate (percent)	Program participation rate (percent)[1]
April	937	937	50.00	567	8	26
May	1,621	1,656	60.00	1,351	11	59
June	1,298	1,306	49.75	1,592	12	73
July[2]	1,512	1,550	42.50	1,771	11	83
Total	5,368	5,449	202.25	5,281	NA	83

Source: Resource Recycling, October 1990, p. 72. NA stands for applicable. *Notes:* 1. As calculated by using bar codes and a computer scanner, rate is cumulative. 2. July volume is not accurate because a new recycling collector condensed the collected material.

★ 722 ★

Curbside Recycling Programs in Major Cities

Status of curbside recycling programs in the 10 largest cities in the U.S..

Cities	Current number of households[1]	Number of households planned by 1993[1]	Estimated citywide roll-out-date
New York	1,800,000[2]	3,400,000[2]	1993
Los Angeles	100,000	720,000	1992
Chicago	62,000	651,000	1991
Houston	27,000	400,000[3]	1992[3]
Philadelphia	169,000	Undetermined	No set date
San Diego	80,000	Undetermined	No set date
Dallas	14,000	Undetermined	No set date
Phoenix	11,000	At least 21,000[3]	No set date
Detroit	None	None	No plans
San Antonio	16,100	Undetermined	No set date

Source: Resource Recycling, December 1990, p. 27. *Notes:* 1. For standard curbside materials such as paper, and metal, glass and plastic containers. Yard waste collection not included. 2. New York totals include collection from high-rise apartments. 3. Proposed.

★ 723 ★

Estimated Plastic Curbside Collection - Chicago

About 8 million people live in 2.8 million households in the 7 counties in Illinois within 50 miles of Chicago's loop. Plastic is collected from about 150,000 households out of 420,000 served by curbside collection of recyclable materials.

Material	Quantity Pounds per capita per year	Make-up of Mixture %
Total plastics available at curbside	24.7	-
Easily separable items		
HDPE containers	4.3	-
PET containers	2.8	-
Polystyrene items	0.7	-
Remaining Mixture		
LDPE	6.0	35
Polypropylene	3.5	21
HDPE	4.7	28
Polystyrene	1.0	6
PET	0.2	1
Polyvinyl chloride	1.5	9
Total mixture	16.9	100

Source: BioCycle, August 1990, p. 79. *Notes:* HDPE=High Density Polyethylene. PET=Polyethylene terephthalate. LDPE=Low Density Polyethylene.

★ 724 ★

Garbage Recycling in Selected Countries

```
Switzerland - 20
U.S. - 11
Sweden - 10
West Germany - 10
Netherlands - 5
Canada - 4
```

Figures refer to percentage of all garbage recycled in each country.

	Percent of waste recycled
Switzerland	20
U.S.	11
Sweden	10
West Germany	10
Netherlands	5
Canada	4

Source: U.S. News & World Report, April 23, 1990, p. 64, from National Solid Waste Management Association.

★ 725 ★

Glass Recycling in Europe

Country	Rate
Holland	62
Switzerland	47
Austria	44
Belgium	39
Italy	38
West Germany	37
Denmark	32
France	26
Spain	21
United Kingdom	13
Portugal	13

Chart shows data from column 2.

Amount of glass containers collected, shown in metric tons and as a percentage of all glass containers produced in each country in 1987.

Country	Metric tons	Rate (%)
Holland	320,000	62
Switzerland	140,000	47
Austria	85,000	44
Belgium	127,000	39
Italy	580,000	38
West Germany	1,102,000	37
Denmark	35,000	32
France	646,000	26
Spain	261,000	21
United Kingdom	233,000	13
Portugal	29,000	13

Source: Resource Recycling, May/June 1989, p. 45, from glass producers in Western Europe.

★ 726 ★

Household Recycling in Lexington, Kentucky

Average number of waste items placed into recycling carts by a household on a weekly basis. Figures shown are the result of a survey of more than 100 households in Lexington, Kentucky that volunteered to keep weekly diaries of materials they recycled.

Households	Aluminum cans	Newspapers	Glass containers	Plastic jugs
Those completing diaries each week	5.7	7.4	2.5	2.8
Those completing diaries 80 percent of the time	6.6	7.5	2.8	3.1
Those completing diaries less frequently	7.8	8.3	3.4	3.8
Range	6 - 7	7 - 8	3	3 - 4

Source: Resource Recycling, October 1990, p. 96, from the City of Lexington, Kentucky.

★ 727 ★

Oil Recycling Centers by State

Number of oil recycling centers in selected states, as of October 1988.

State	Number
Alabama	300
California	1,000
Connecticut	43
Delaware	27
District of Columbia	35
Florida	300
Georgia	65
Hawaii	20
Kentucky	100
Maine	50
Maryland	200
Michigan	750
Nevada	35
New Jersey	300
Oregon	350
Rhode Island	41
Virginia	527
Wisconsin	150

Source: Resource Recycling, May/June 1989, p. 72.

★ 728 ★

Recycled Materials in Washington State

The values are in short tons (2000 pounds) rounded to the nearest 100 tons. Tonnages are lower than actual, due to underreporting.

Material	1986	1987	1988
Paper			
Newsprint	97,300	166,600	191,100
Corrugated paper	196,500	287,600	302,900
Computer paper	8,000	16,100	15,500
Office and other high grade papers	20,700	32,900	49,800
Mixed waste paper	38,800	34,100	65,600
Metal			
Aluminum cans	8,700	10,800	13,900
Aluminum containers	<100	<100	100
Tinned cans	800	800	1,600
Bimetal cans	<100	0	0
Ferrous metal	NA	423,800	630,900
Nonferrous metal	NA	46,600	54,300
Appliances	NA	24,800	7,700
Glass			
Refillable beer bottles	24,200	19,000	19,100
Container glass	23,800	24,000	26,100
Plastic			
PET containers (polyethylene terephthalate)	0	<100	200
HDPE containers (high density polyethylene)	NA	NA	600
Other recyclable plastic	300	1,700	1,200
Miscellaneous			
Vehicle batteries	NA	22,100	33,100
Tires	NA	10,300	20,000
Used oil	44,300	56,200	57,700

Source: BioCycle, July 1990, p. 49. NA stands for Not available.

★ 729 ★

Recycling in Japan

Table shows estimates for recycling of municipal solid waste (MSW) under assumptions of various metal recovery scenarios.

Scenarios: Estimates of total MSW generation and assumptions of steel recovery	Millions of metric tons			Estimated recycling rate[4] (percent)
	Estimated steel recovery	Total materials recovery[2]	Total post-consumer material[3]	
40 million metric tons				
5% steel, 50% recovery	1.5	20.9	60.9	34.3
10% steel, 100% recovery	6.3	25.7	65.7	39.1
60 million metric tons				
5% steel, 50% recovery	2.1	21.5	81.5	26.4
10% steel, 100% recovery	8.4	27.8	87.8	31.7

Source: Facing America's Trash: What Next for Municipal Solid Waste, U.S. Congress, Office of Technology Assessment, OTA-O-412, Washington, D.C., July 1989., p. 203, from Office of Technology Assessment, 1989. *Notes:* 1. Municipal Solid Waste. 2. Based on adding the estimated amount of steel (column 2) and the amount of other recovered materials (19.4 million metric tons). 3. Total materials recovery, plus MSW generation. 4. Based on (column 3/column 4) x 100.

★ 730 ★

Recycling in U.S. Cities

Percentage of the wastestream that is recycled in selected cities.

City	Percentage of Wastestream
Islip, N. Y.	35.00
Seattle, Wash.	34.00
Montclair, N.J.	30.00
Springfield, Mass.	28.00
Portland, Ore.	26.00

[Continued]

★ 730 ★

Recycling in U.S. Cities
[Continued]

City	Percentage of Wastestream
Minneapolis/St. Paul	12.00
Los Angeles	12.00
New York City	6.00
Tucson, Ariz.	.02
Nationally	13.00

Source: *Garbage*, November/December 1990, p. 63.

★ 731 ★

Recycling Programs in Seattle

Contributions of various Seattle programs to the attainment of a 60 percent waste reduction/recycling goal. Data show percent contribution of each program.

	Percent contribution
City-sponsored recycling	26.4
Curbside	7.8
Self-haul/dump and pick up	4.8
Curbside yard waste	4.8
Self-haul yard waste	3.6
Apartment recycling	2.4
Waste reduction and backyard compost	3.0
Existing private recycling	24.0
New commercial recycling	9.6
Landfilling	40.0

Source: *Resource Recovery*, November 1989, p. 29, from Seattle Solid Waste Utility.

★ 732 ★

Secondary Fiber Recovery Rates Worldwide

Japan - 48.0	
E.F.T.A. - 40.9	
Western Europe - 35.8	
European Community - 35.1	
Rest of Asia - 34.2	
Latin America - 33.6	
World total - 32.7	
United States - 30.2	
Eastern Europe and U.S.S.R. - 29.0	
North America - 29.4	
Oceania - 24.8	
China - 20.4	
Africa - 16.5	

Chart shows data from column 1.

Data are shown in percent of secondary fiber utilized.

Region	1988	2001
North America	29.4	42.9
United States	30.2	44.4
Western Europe	35.8	41.5
E.F.T.A.[1]	40.9	47.8
European Community	35.1	40.7
Eastern Europe and U.S.S.R.	29.0	38.7
Oceania	24.8	31.3
Latin America	33.6	36.8
Japan	48.0	52.0
China	20.4	24.5
Rest of Asia	34.2	40.9
Africa	16.5	19.0
World total	32.7	41.0

Source: Resource Recycling, November 1990, Secondary Fiber Supplement, p. 91, from Jaakko Poyry, 1990. *Note:* 1. E.F.T.A. stands for European Free Trade Association.

★ 733 ★

Solid Waste Recycling Programs by State - 1988

State	Curbside Recycling Programs						Yard Waste Composting Projects (Number)
	Number	Population Served	Multi-Material	Single Item	Mandatory	Voluntary	
Alabama	3	2	2	1	0	3	3
Alaska	0	-	-	-	-	-	0
Arizona	1	2	1	0	0	1	0
Arkansas	2	10,000	2	0	0	2	0
California	62	3,300,000	62	0	0	62	5
Colorado	2	2	2	0	0	2	0
Connecticut	24	2	18	6	12	12	30+
Delaware	0	-	-	-	-	-	1
District of Columbia	0	-	-	-	-	-	1
Florida	8	2	7	1	0	8	-
Georgia	3	2	-	-	-	-	-
Hawaii	0	-	-	-	-	-	0
Idaho	0	-	-	-	-	-	1
Illinois	25+	2	25+	-	0	25+	6
Indiana	9	2	9	0	0	9	0
Iowa	1	15,000	1	0	0	1	1
Kansas	0	-	-	-	-	-	0
Kentucky	0	-	-	-	-	-	0
Louisiana	3	100,000	3	0	0	3	0
Maine	2	25,000	2	0	1	1	0
Maryland	5	2	5	0	0	5	1
Massachusetts	7	2	4	3	2	2	70
Michigan	5+	2	2	2	0	5+	100
Minnesota	93	2	87	6	6	87	78
Mississippi	0	-	-	-	-	-	0
Missouri	8	2	7	1	0	8	10
Montana	0	-	-	-	-	-	0
Nebraska	2	2	2	2	0	2	2
Nevada	0	-	-	-	-	-	0
New Hampshire	2	30,000	2	0	0	2	0
New Jersey	439	2	439	0	439	0	185
New Mexico	0	-	-	-	-	-	1
New York[1]	3	-	-	-	-	-	27
North Carolina	3	15,000	2	1	0	3	1
North Dakota	0	-	-	-	-	-	0
Ohio	13	175,000	11	2	0	13	3
Oklahoma	1	-	1	-	-	1	0
Oregon	106	2,600,000	106	0	0	106	6
Pennsylvania	141	1,300,000	75[1]	2	55	86	63
Rhode Island	8	300,0008	0	8	0	5	
South Carolina	2	2	2	0	0	2	0
South Dakota	0	-	-	-	-	-	0
Tennessee	0	-	-	-	-	-	0

[Continued]

627

★ 733 ★

Solid Waste Recycling Programs by State - 1988
[Continued]

State	Curbside Recycling Programs						Yard Waste Composting Projects (Number)
	Number	Population Served	Multi-Material	Single Item	Mandatory	Voluntary	
Texas	2	100,000+	2	0	0	2	2+
Utah	0	-	-	-	-	-	1
Vermont	1	10,000+	1	0	0	1	2
Virginia	4	2	3	1	1	3	1
Washington	4	500,000+	4	0	0	4	4
West Virginia	2	2	2	0	0	2	1
Wisconsin	50+	2	37	13+	7	43	40
Wyoming	0	-	-	-	-	-	0
Total	1042	8,480,000	932	35	529	504	651

Source: Biocycle, April 1989, p. 38. *Notes:* 1. Programs with three or more materials. 2. Data unavailable. 3. Unknown.

★ 734 ★

Variation in Weekly Material for Recycling

The values are a range of recyclable material prepared weekly for recycling collection by households completing recycling diaries 80 percent of the time.

	Aluminum cans	Newspapers	Glass containers	Plastic jugs
28-week average	6.6	7.5	2.6	3.1
Highest week's average	9.7	10.5	3.5	4.8
Lowest week's average	4.6	5.1	1.5	2.1

Source: Resource Recycling, October 1990, p. 86, from City of Lexington, Kentucky..

★ 735 ★

Voluntary Drop-Off Centers - Characteristics

Data for selected communities.

Location	Population served	Number of	Materials collected						Participation rate (%)
			Newspapers	Glass	Metals	Cardboard	Plastics	Oil	
Champaign Co., IL	171,000	15	x	x	x	x	x	x	18
Columbia Co., PA	50,000	17	x	x	x	x	-	-	25-30
Cook & Lake Co., IL	270,000	18	x	x	x	-	-	-	NA
Delaware Co., PA	500,000	50	-	x	-	-	-	-	25

[Continued]

★ 735 ★

Voluntary Drop-Off Centers - Characteristics
[Continued]

Location	Population served	Number of	Materials collected						Participation rate (%)
			Newspapers	Glass	Metals	Cardboard	Plastics	Oil	
Durham Co., NC	120,000	10	x	x	x	-	-	-	8
Fairfax Co., VA	75,000	8	x	x	x	-	-	-	10
Kent/Ottawa Co., MI	650,000	30	x	x	x	x	x	-	4
Santa Monica, CA	70,000	66	x	x	x	-	-	-	28
Snohomish Co., WA	NA	15	x	x	x	-	-	-	NA
Wayne Co., NY	30,000	4	x	-	x	x	-	-	NA

Source: BioCycle, February 1989, p. 44 NA stands for not applicable.

★ 736 ★

Voluntary Drop-Off Centers - Tonnage Collected

Data for selected communities.

Location	All Materials (Tons)	Annual Tonnage										
		News		Glass		Aluminum		Tin		Others	
		Tons	%	Tons	%	Tons	%	Tons	%	Tons	%
Champaign Co., IL	1000	750	75	160	16.0	5	.5	15	1.5	70[2]	7
Columbia Co., PA	469	271	58	88	19.0	6	1.0	19	4.0	85	18
Cook & Lake Co., IL	7140	5800	81	1200	17.0	75	1.0	65	1.0	-	-
Delaware Co., PA	1800	-	-	1800	100.0	-	-	-	-	-	-
Durham Co., NC	1200	900	75	300	25.0	-	-	-	-	-	-
Fairfax Co., VA	1000	721	72	271	27.0	8[1]	1.0[1]	-	-	-	-
Kent/Ottawa Co., MI	3200	2225	70	669	20.0	1	-	158	5.0	157	5
Santa Monica, CA	1398	1032	74	360	25.5	6[1]	.5[1]	-	-	-	-
Snohomish Co., WA	233	67	29	159	68	7	3	-	-	-	-

Source: BioCycle, February 1989, p. 44. *Notes:* 1. Aluminum and tin combined 2. Old corrugated cardboard.

★ 737 ★

Waste Recovery by Types, Selected Cities

Country	Aluminum	Paper	Glass
Austria	22	44	38
France	25	34	26
West Germany	34	40	39
Italy	36	30	25
Japan	32	51	17
Netherlands	40	46	53

[Continued]

★ 737 ★

Waste Recovery by Types, Selected Cities
[Continued]

Country	Aluminum	Paper	Glass
Sweden	18	42	20
Switzerland	21	43	46
United Kingdom	23	29	12
United States	28	27	10

Source: Resources, Conservation and Recycling, August 1990, p. 10.

★ 738 ★

Waste Stream Recycling Goals - 1991 to 2005

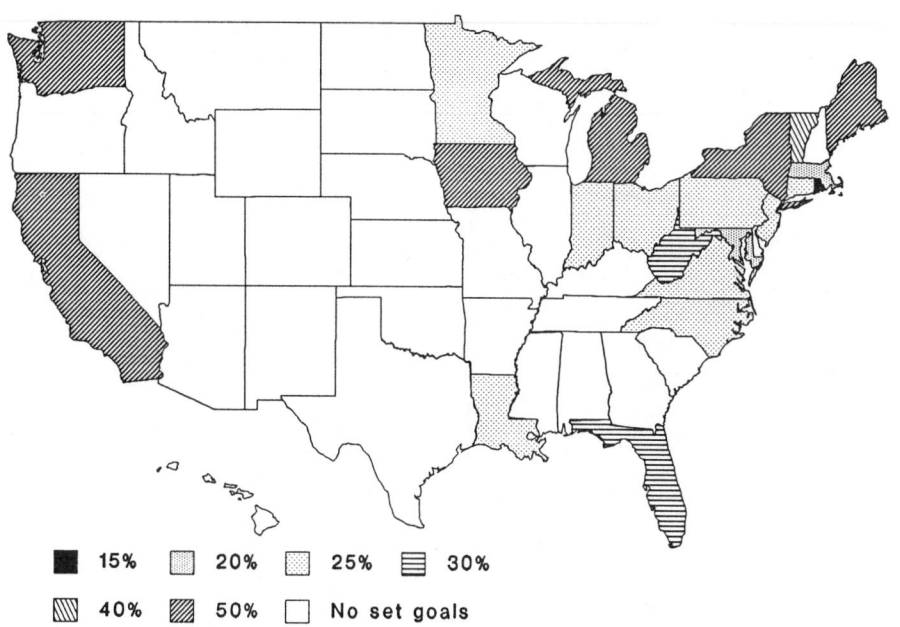

Source: ENR, February 22, 1990, p. 54, from National Solid Waste Management Association. *Note:* Situation depicted is as of October 1, 1989.

★ 739 ★

Wastepaper Curbside Collection Programs

Survey data for household mixed paper curbside collection programs.

Program	Eligible households	Participation rate, percent	Mandatory/ voluntary[1]	Diversion rate, percent[2]	Mixed waste-paper percent[3]	Collection frequency[4]	Collection containers
Seattle (southend), WA	82,000	65	V	22.7	76.7	M	1
Seattle (northend), WA	65,000	88	V	22.7	39.7	W	3
Islip, NY	78,000	90	M	14.0	N.A.	W	1
San Francisco, CA	28,000	75	V	15.0	70.0	W	2
Susquehanna County, PA	27,000	N.A.	V	9.0	65.8	W	2
Ocean City, NJ	20,000	70	M	20.6	62.5	W	1
Redwood, WA	14,600	N.A.	V	N.A.	N.A.	W	3
Groton, CT	14,000	90	M	11.0	55.6	W	2
Bellingham, WA	13,000	65	V	24.7	27.0	W	3
Evesham Township, NJ	9,300	90	M	27.0	66.0	W	2
Renton, WA	9,255	70	V	21.0	15.0	W	3
Bariboo, WI	8,500	60	V	12.0	32.5	M	4
Middle Township, NJ	7,100	93	M	31.8	N.A.	W	2
Longmeadow, MA	5,700	98	M	23.0	100.0	W	1
Kent, WA	5,000	85	V	17.5	N.A.	B	1
Woodbury, NJ	4,100	95	M	24.0	36.0	W	8
San Jose, CA	4,000	81	V	16.0	N.A.	W	4
Wildwood, NJ	3,000	50	M	15.0	N.A.	W	2
Prairie du Sac, WI	2,000	95	M	12.0	32.5	M	4
Potsdam, NY	1,500	68	V	19.1	78.7	W	2

Source: Resource Recycling, January 1991, p. 85, from Sound Resource Management Group, Inc. February 1990. NA stands for not available. *Notes:* 1. M=mandatory collection program; V=voluntary collection program. 2. Diversion rate is calculated for household waste from service population. 3. This number is the percent of the diversion rate attributed to mixed waste paper. Higher percentages of mixed waste paper are generated by programs that collect old newspapers commingled with other mixed scrap paper grades. The Seattle programs illustrate this difference. 4. M = monthly; B = bi-weekly, or every other week; W = weekly.

★ 740 ★

Wastepaper Recovery and Utilization Worldwide

Production and consumption figures are shown in thousands of tons. Utilization rates are shown in percent for each region.

Region	Total paper and board production		Wastepaper consumption		Wastepaper utilization (percent)	
	1988	2001	1988	2001	1988	2001
North America	86,737	115,198	19,778	36,030	22.8	31.3
Western Europe	57,633	78,844	19,811	31,228	34.4	39.6
E.F.T.A. countries	22,350	30,400	2,967	5,198	13.3	17.1
European Community	35,283	48,444	16,844	26,031	47.7	53.7
Eastern Europe	17,988	22,193	4,868	8,746	27.1	39.4
Oceania	2,487	3,864	7023	1,271	28.2	32.9

[Continued]

★ 740 ★

Wastepaper Recovery and Utilization Worldwide
[Continued]

Region	Total paper and board production		Wastepaper consumption		Wastepaper utilization (percent)	
	1988	2001	1988	2001	1988	2001
Latin America	10,506	15,909	4,757	7,801	45.3	49.0
Japan	24,624	34,892	12,538	19,415	50.9	55.6
China	12,645	19,760	3,084	8,305	24.4	42.0
Rest of Asia	12,218	22,431	8,369	15,877	68.5	70.8
Africa	2,524	679	6790	1,092	26.9	30.5
World total	227,362	316,669	74,586	129,766	32.8	41.0

Source: *Pulp & Paper*, September 1990, p. 98.

★ 741 ★

Wastepaper Recovery Rates Worldwide

Recovery rates are shown in percent for each region.

Region	1988	2001
North America	29.4	42.9
U.S.	30.2	44.4
Western Europe	35.8	41.5
E.F.T.A. countries	40.9	47.8
European Community	35.1	40.7
Eastern Europe and U.S.S.R.	29.0	38.7
Oceania	24.8	31.3
Latin America	33.6	36.8
Japan	48.0	52.0
China	20.4	24.5
Rest of Asia	34.2	40.9
Africa	16.5	19.0
World total	32.7	41.0

Source: *Pulp & Paper*, September 1990, p. 98.

★ 742 ★

Worldwide Per Capita Paper Use and Recovery

USA - 699
Sweden - 685
Canada - 543
Japan - 450
Norway - 333
USSR - 78
Latin America - 55
China - 27
Africa - 12
India - 5

Chart shows data from column 1.

Per capita use and amount of wastepaper recycled compared to total consumption. Use data refer to 1988; recycling data refer to 1987.

Country/Region	Pounds per year	Percent recycled
USA	699	29.0
Sweden	685	40.0
Canada	543	20.0
Japan	450	50.0
Norway	333	27.0
USSR	78	19.0
Latin America	55	32.0
China	27	21.0
Africa	12	17.0
India	5	26.0

Source: World Watch, July/August 1990, p. 34, from *The Greenpeace Guide to Paper* (Vancouver: Greenpeace, 1990).

★ 743 ★

Worldwide Recycling Trends

Recycling of waste per year, by type and by country, in the United States, Western Europe, and Japan.

Trends in recycling	Total waste (kg/head/yr)	Recycled[1] (percent)
Paper West Europe Sharply upward in 1970's-1980's, leveling now, falling in Italy and Britain	170-180	40-45 range

[Continued]

★ 743 ★

Worldwide Recycling Trends
[Continued]

Trends in recycling	Total waste (kg/head/yr)	Recycled[1] (percent)
		20-65
Japan 39% in 1975, 49% in 1985, level since	170	50
United States Up from 19% in 1975	270	25
Aluminum West Europe Level since 1984	18-20	30
Japan Level since 1986	22	40
United States Up from 9% in 1975	10	32
Glass West Europe Upward in 1980's, leveling off	25	30 range 8-83
Japan Upward since 1980	7	55
United States Up from 3% in 1975	50	12
Plastic West Europe Consumption and recycling rates rising rapidly	17	5[2]
Japan -	25	0
United States -	55	1

Source: The Economist, April 13,1991, p. 18, from OECD; U.S. Environmental Protection Agency. *Notes:* 1. Does not include incineration. 2. Not post-consumer, mostly collected.

Soil Conservation

★ 744 ★

Agricultural and Emergency Conservation Programs by State

Data are for the fiscal year 1989.

State or Territory	Agriculture conservation program					Emergency conservation program		
	Number of participating farms	Area served 1,000 acres	Assistance (1,000 dollars)			Number of participating farms	Area served 1,000 acres	Assistance 1,000 dollars
			Regular	Long term	Total assistance			
Alabama	3,025	95	3,558	837	4,395	14	2	17
Alaska	19	2	17	44	61	-	-	-
Arizona	452	461	1,154	839	1,993	3	1	14
Arkansas	4,613	183	4,211	620	4,831	34	3	61
California	1,768	269	4,522	1,180	5,702	32	10	129
Colorado	2,653	350	4,032	1,010	5,042	1	1	8
Connecticut	711	22	280	75	355	-	-	-
Delaware	126	6	214	43	257	-	-	-
Florida	2,076	98	2,867	855	3,722	24	1	37
Georgia	3,372	148	4,354	650	5,004	275	8	340
Hawaii	134	6	246	45	291	9	7	77
Idaho	1,689	235	3,121	694	3,815	42	15	76
Illinois	3,434	96	5,071	1,369	6,440	344	12	649
Indiana	2,657	56	2,935	270	3,205	-	-	-
Iowa	4,463	78	5,939	1,075	7,014	530	15	666
Kansas	4,318	176	4,218	841	5,059	-	-	-
Kentucky	4,666	88	3,964	585	4,549	395	19	529
Louisiana	3,369	161	2,828	475	3,303	1	1	2
Maine	1,070	38	1,013	956	1,969	6	1	14
Maryland	497	8	752	201	953	11	1	19
Massachusetts	1,020	32	409	86	495	-	-	-
Michigan	5,947	248	3,887	663	4,550	3	1	5
Minnesota	3,108	112	2,735	361	3,096	-	-	-
Mississippi	3,505	117	3,947	774	4,721	-	-	-
Missouri	4,853	134	6,561	712	7,273	912	60	796
Montana	1,043	466	1,687	538	2,225	334	429	891
Nebraska	3,918	442	4,136	911	5,047	113	34	233
Nevada	268	77	473	391	864	49	183	185
New Hampshire	471	22	487	137	624	-	-	-
New Jersey	684	42	379	23	402	-	-	-
New Mexico	1,165	676	1,762	367	2,129	45	5	28
New York	2,891	76	3,197	1,005	4,202	30	2	31
North Carolina	13,830	283	3,675	400	4,075	47	6	64
North Dakota	4,704	549	3,734	601	4,335	64	14	62
Ohio	530	11	454	130	584	518	12	594
Oklahoma	3,916	187	3,298	613	3,911	-	-	-
Oregon	1,532	219	2,558	1,056	3,614	12	2	25
Pennsylvania	2,385	50	2,165	762	2,927	2	1	10
Rhode Island	120	2	37	17	54	-	-	-
South Carolina	1,954	73	2,031	559	2,590	2	1	2
South Dakota	2,882	380	2,546	194	2,740	218	73	250
Tennessee	4,393	74	3,036	475	3,511	48	1	65
Texas	11,232	1,741	14,733	1,821	16,554	364	1,567	921
Utah	976	150	1,773	1,353	3,126	18	1	80
Vermont	348	7	424	956	1,380	53	3	115
Virginia	4,628	112	3,071	416	3,487	-	-	-
Washington	1,905	262	3,294	677	3,971	28	1	79
West Virginia	2,340	53	1,672	525	2,197	133	5	97

[Continued]

★ 744 ★

Agricultural and Emergency Conservation Programs by State
[Continued]

State or Territory	Agriculture conservation program					Emergency conservation program		
	Number of participating farms	Area served 1,000 acres	Assistance (1,000 dollars)			Number of participating farms	Area served 1,000 acres	Assistance 1,000 dollars
			Regular	Long term	Total assistance			
Wisconsin	3,386	66	2,785	665	3,450	-	-	-
Wyoming	650	271	1,210	975	2,185	12	11	11
United States	135,696[3]	9,510	137,452[2]	30,827	168,279[2]	4,724[3]	2,501	7,180
Guam	1	[1]		-		-	-	-
Puerto Rico	574	42	455	84	539	-	-	-
Virgin Islands	16	[1]	17	-	17	-	-	-
Total	136,287[3]	9,552	137,924	30,911	168,835	4,724[3]	2,501	7,180

Source: Agricultural Conservation and Forestry Statistics, 1989, U.S. Government Printing Office, Washington, D.C., 1989, p. 440, from Agriculture Stabilization and Conservation Service Totals are the sum of rounded data. *Notes:* 1. Less than 500 acres served. 2. Less than $500. 3. Totals are net and may not add.

★ 745 ★

Agricultural Conservation & Pollution Abatement by State - I
The data are for fiscal year 1989.

State or Territory	Diversions (area served) Acres	Conservation tillage Acres	Permanent wildlife habitat (area served) Acres	Sediment retention, erosion, or water control structures) Number	Sod waterways (area served) Acres	Windbreaks (area served) Acres	Irrigation water conservation (area served) Acres
Alabama	598	9,601	63	269	795	-	-
Alaska	320	804	-	-	-	1	-
Arizona	-	-	-	56	-	-	18,510
Arkansas	108	2,266	-	453	50	-	59,434
California	496	2,122	272	136	-	10	97,048
Colorado	2,648	3,093	22	133	70	1,747	88,678
Connecticut	50	369	-	1	23	-	4
Delaware	-	80	21	39	63	-	-
Florida	58	3,757	72	442	181	-	12,572
Georgia	40	6,408	122	8	830	-	-
Hawaii	177	-	-	5	41	292	113
Idaho	170	43,993	4	245	1,253	320	55,038
Illinois	988	4,446	175	1,359	28,825	212	-
Indiana	187	12,454	58	1,372	4,599	15	-
Iowa	165	11,277	238	392	1,359	1,801	-
Kansas	7,193	440	10	57	10,771	702	18,039
Kentucky	2,753	5,368	41	395	5,702	-	-
Louisiana	-	5,454	40	1,757	753	-	22,712
Maine	613	5,014	-	132	964	-	-
Maryland	204	-	4	90	803	-	-

[Continued]

★ 745 ★

Agricultural Conservation & Pollution Abatement by State - I
[Continued]

State or Territory	Diversions (area served) Acres	Conservation tillage Acres	Permanent wildlife habitat (area served) Acres	Sediment retention, erosion, or water control structures) Number	Sod waterways (area served) Acres	Windbreaks (area served) Acres	Irrigation water conservation (area served) Acres
Massachusetts	83	263	-	2	1	-	1,291
Michigan	3,588	78,785	4,871	393	3,941	5,012	-
Minnesota	299	17,675	1,656	236	2,890	38,683	-
Mississippi	860	4,480	47	1,151	69	-	14,531
Missouri	428	1,322	62	353	4,629	- 428	-
Montana	2,050	2,207	192	2	1,330	2,024	23,186
Nebraska	2,820	160	13	107	4,582	8,776	16,707
Nevada	-	-	-	6	-	24	24,532
New Hampshire	56	62	247	17	106	-	-
New Jersey	56	217	-	4	95	-	135
New Mexico	3,602	1,208	2	164	580	44	25,019
New York	2,111	4,656	43	54	1,935	156	4,869
North Carolina	467	31,936	40	194	2,230	-	-
North Dakota	1,992	5,860	8,268	1	9,152	78,513	1,101
Ohio	18	203	10	234	2,323	10	-
Oklahoma	8,818	-	-	318	25,539	121	8,593
Oregon	4,882	9,944	4	243	346	162	29,289
Pennsylvania	2,772	1,907	20	163	7,090	-	-
Rhode Island	5	-	-	1	-	-	-
South Carolina	15	8,763	485	7	423	34	701
South Dakota	502	774	2,350	10	5,373	12,748	1,061
Tennessee	871	10,387	3	561	1,032	-	-
Texas	28,718	57	-	400	24,823	32	170,147
Utah	300	856	2	32	-	-	36,919
Vermont	285	231	511	12	48	-	-
Virginia	145	9,366	30	11	815	-	-
Washington	1,561	15,156	297	113	3,156	68	16,708
West Virginia	20	23	-	-	40	-	-
Wisconsin	574	5,227	624	101	7,005	982	-
Wyoming	40	-	-	49	-	43	26,578
United States	84,706	328,671	20,919	12,280	166,635	152,532	773,515
Guam	-	-	-	-	-	-	-
Puerto Rico	1	1,466	-	1	-	-	233
Virgin Islands	-	-	-	-	-	-	-
Total	84,707	330,137	20,919	12,281	166,635	152,532	773,748

Source: Agricultural Conservation and Forestry Statistics, 1989, U.S. Government Printing Office, Washington, D.C., 1989, p. 441.

★ 746 ★

Agricultural Conservation & Pollution Abatement by State - II

The data are for fiscal year 1989.

State or Territory	Establishing permanent cover Acres	Improving permanent cover Acres	Planting trees Acres	Timber stand improvement Number	Water impoundment reservoirs Acres	Stripcropping Acres	Terrace systems (area served) Acres
Alabama	24,580	759	22,596	2,872	38	108	10,611
Alaska	312	436	-	75	-	-	-
Arizona	-	127,452	-	50	1	-	-
Arkansas	25,348	35,197	972	140	720	-	-
California	1,175	16,139	381	89	11	-	-
Colorado	2,990	15,547	-	-	34	9,604	31,000
Connecticut	870	18	18	153	2	35	5
Delaware	118	42	59	33	7	-	51
Florida	12,357	3,484	16,680	1,856	2	84	946
Georgia	17,382	6,014	34,522	1,510	139	-	73,690
Hawaii	139	577	10	-	1	-	1,685
Idaho	5,281	13,275	95	123	4	3,123	4,445
Illinois	8,110	4,034	270	671	141	2,050	16,429
Indiana	9,720	2,725	529	4,783	179	-	863
Iowa	8,217	1,815	210	392	429	6,621	29,112
Kansas	2,895	2,775	3	52	79	-	102,367
Kentucky	34,995	11,134	138	106	117	442	694
Louisiana	13,952	15,983	787	134	161	-	4,881
Maine	1,536	1,217	831	4,535	-	177	45
Maryland	743	123	1,239	860	24	427	5
Massachusetts	890	135	44	336	-	6	-
Michigan	36,983	5,614	2,712	555	12	828	-
Minnesota	7,943	388	2,507	434	66	5,562	3,190
Mississippi	24,781	1,835	8,389	404	679	136	7,663
MIssouri	33,556	10,155	210	1,303	550	65	44,012
Montana	11,570	30,530	3	115	8	21,959	-
Nebraska	3,155	30,382	-	-	99	2,497	78,087
Nevada	720	19,446	-	-	-	-	-
New Hampshire	607	878	57	383	-	30	2
New Jersey	1,379	-	3	-	-	100	100
New Mexico	426	47,613	-	360	17	-	3,492
New York	20,949	1,539	384	568	3	6,666	207
North Carolina	11,693	39,315	2,738	212	45	1,408	802
North Dakota	17,192	183	291	2	35	1,818	142
Ohio	716	679	31	439	5	183	-
Oklahoma	41,763	1,760	40	-	484	-	57,859
Oregon	6,062	40,299	2,510	3,389	10	-	49,158
Pennsylvania	5,437	3,248	156	605	9	10,666	871
Rhode Island	20	-	7	18	-	-	-
South Carolina	6,852	3,201	16,847	1,459	51	1,143	199
South Dakota	25,558	4,227	-	110	31	4,316	7,300
Tennessee	33,852	3,592	665	40	562	1,593	5,664
Texas	119,240	403,305	403	-	1,319	-	255,275

[Continued]

★ 746 ★

Agricultural Conservation & Pollution Abatement by State - II
[Continued]

State or Territory	Establishing permanent cover Acres	Improving permanent cover Acres	Planting trees Acres	Timber stand improvement Number	Water impoundment reservoirs Acres	Stripcropping Acres	Terrace systems (area served) Acres
Utah	1,619	54,956	-	-	-	-	8,608
Vermont	593	49	9	197	-	97	18
Virginia	13,462	33,525	4,006	1,857	232	744	145
Washington	6,818	38,130	5,219	6,078	9	18,688	36,727
West Virginia	2,384	23,493	50	127	180	-	-
Wisconsin	4,942	879	5,442	1,910	8	21,622	3,985
Wyoming	1,794	75,031	-	275	4	-	285
United States	613,676	1,133,133	132,063	39,610	6,507	122,798	840,620
Guam	-	-	-	-	-	-	-
Puerto Rico	1,129	36,034	55	-	13	-	203
Virgin Islands	-	467	-	-	-	-	-
Total	614,805	1,169,634	132,118	39,610	6,520	122,798	840,825

Source: Agricultural Conservation and Forestry Statistics, 1989, U.S. Government Printing Office, Washington, D.C., 1989, p. 441.

★ 747 ★

Conservation Plans by State

State or Territory	Progress, year ended Sept. 30, 1989		New conservation plans[1] Acres
	New SCD cooperators[3]		
	Number	Acres	
Alabama	1,265	104,675	184,824
Alaska	25	10,809	14,568
Arizona	651	4,315,143	841,792
Arkansas	929	200,388	408,523
California	619	225,590	186,721
Colorado	1,198	1,152,330	1,624,540
Connecticut	30	4,181	8,079
Delaware	99	13,809	30,485
Florida	537	226,692	258,171
Georgia	503,007	116,725	311,379
Hawaii	149	5,477	44,683
Idaho	86	26,313	154,349
Illinois	4,513	692,769	903,647
Indiana	236	26,380	209,573
Iowa	40,577	5,862,368	3,107,616

[Continued]

★ 747 ★

Conservation Plans by State
[Continued]

| State or Territory | Progress, year ended Sept. 30, 1989 | | New conservation plans[1] |
| | New SCD cooperators[3] | | |
	Number	Acres	Acres
Kansas	2,227	1,022,659	1,960,198
Kentucky	5,608	671,948	877,717
Louisiana	1,197	566,876	540,473
Maine	87	35,949	63,649
Maryland	1,131	123,993	249,267
Massachusetts	47	3,708	8,095
Michigan	811	153,036	444,978
Minnesota	3,652	886,360	672,747
Mississippi	1,176	112,551	237,018
Missouri	7,082	1,029,578	1,271,695
Montana	830	1,584,331	6,857,939
Nebraska	2,546	634,620	1,822,099
Nevada	78	176,874	869,151
New Hampshire	57	4,967	9,601
New Jersey	28	2,642	17,634
New Mexico	736	1,474,000	1,634,313
New York	172	26,167	86,215
North Carolina	5,329	451,124	245,026
North Dakota	797	377,705	1,188,413
Ohio	1,071	99,764	144,954
Oklahoma	6,733	2,297,034	4,367,528
Oregon	154	163,270	255,352
Pennsylvania	459	59,084	397,847
Rhode Island	6	85	679
South Carolina	1,761	251,312	193,502
South Dakota	2,813	3,221,634	1,325,025
Tennessee	8,154	639,778	500,569
Texas	13,598	5,097,162	7,055,008
Utah	128	103,630	396,177
Vermont	52	9,417	55,198
Virginia	847	131,009	176,505
Washington	362	375,390	379,355
West Virginia	600	51,083	126,878
Wisconsin	828	227,443	396,306
Wyoming	108	347,215	1,026,329
Caribbean[2]	244	20,202	34,775
Total	625,430	35,417,249	44,177,165

Source: *Agricultural Conservation and Forestry Statistics, 1989*, U.S. Government Printing Office, Washington, D.C., 1989, p. 451, from Soil Conservation Service *Notes:* 1. Includes conservation plans prepared on farms and ranches of SCD cooperators who signed agreements in prior years. 2. Puerto Rico and Virgin Islands. 3. Soil Conservation District.

★ 748 ★

Great Plains Conservation Programs by State

The data is for the year ending September 30, 1989.

State	Designated counties (number)	Active land treatment Contracts in operation 1989	
		(number)	(1,000 acres)
Colorado	38	464	1,493
Kansas	62	783	542
Montana	40	338	2,286
Nebraska	61	519	1,242
New Mexico	19	172	2,113
North Dakota	38	508	1,090
Oklahoma	43	417	567
South Dakota	51	584	2,101
Texas	147	1,158	2,231
Wyoming	19	186	1,952
Total	518	5,129	15,617

Source: Agricultural Conservation and Forestry Statistics, 1989, U.S. Government Printing Office, Washington, D.C., 1989, p. 452, from Soil Conservation Service.

★ 749 ★

Soil Conservation - Land Protected by State

The data show acres of land protected applying soil conservation practices through farmer-district cooperation and cooperation with other agencies, with Soil Conservation Service assistance in the year ending September 30, 1989.

State or Territory	Cropland	Pasture and hayland	Range native pasture	Woodland	Wildlife	Recreation	Other land	Total land protected
Alabama	205,862	121,376	0	116,191	14,147	803	1,030	459,409
Alaska	6,469	3,432	2,075,000	3	26,743	0	300	2,111,947
Arizona	6,448	605	1,171,567	0	276,415	0	0	1,455,035
Arkansas	286,732	205,070	17,978	75,006	23,954	895	3,763	613,398
California	225,019	73,390	134,162	9,399	14,330	727	7,263	464,290
Colorado	548,558	279,968	489,327	8,503	162,368	19	1,675	1,490,418
Connecticut	2,607	0	0	15	0	0	252	2,874
Delaware	46,301	970	0	792	3,128	1	29	51,221
Florida	90,724	113,128	118,566	39,974	35,347	50	134	397,923
Georgia	343,331	121,649	989	653,759	34,905	842	3,925	1,159,400
Hawaii	28,614	15,066	27,256	0	813	0	331	72,080
Idaho	217,137	37,895	115,510	1,699	107	0	4,303	376,651
Illinois	764,392	95,478	129	5,796	54,883	637	1,907	923,222
Indiana	225,390	16,314	0	2,152	7,548	287	873	252,564
Iowa	1,686,988	61,043	11	1,736	266,438	3	3,756	2,019,975
Kansas	1,881,210	30,709	142,211	95	6,594	0	489	2,061,308

[Continued]

★ 749 ★

Soil Conservation - Land Protected by State

[Continued]

State or Territory	Cropland	Pasture and hayland	Range native pasture	Woodland	Wildlife	Recreation	Other land	Total land protected
Kentucky	351,309	120,117	0	11,807	4,755	845	2,674	491,507
Louisiana	359,134	91,563	26,799	177,770	197,474	557	1,677	854,974
Maine	17,805	1,933	0	3,816	5	0	799	24,358
Maryland	98,917	2,894	0	2,439	5,462	7	3,697	113,416
Massachusetts	3,953	362	0	184	0	0	0	4,499
Michigan	280,427	29,508	21	20,342	13,544	994	1,804	346,640
Minnesota	677,658	23,390	279	3,776	16,157	146	9,744	731,150
Mississippi	278,398	440,087	382	113,043	37,136	427	4,216	873,689
Missouri	322,874	143,008	89	8,478	22,122	183	213,052	709,806
Montana	1,143,541	199,705	935,285	1,534	2,454	3	5,041	2,287,563
Nebraska	1,136,409	149,680	780,509	607	57,390	160	53,130	2,177,885
Nevada	7,750	139,308	1,257,239	0	15,712	0	705	1,420,714
New Hampshire	2,760	1,810	0	3,579	213	137	246	8,745
New Jersey	8,062	929	10	16	135	16	9	9,177
New Mexico	209,120	19,988	3,420,221	24,709	13,323	707	1,597	3,689,665
New York	89,774	7,365	56	818	4	108	595	98,720
North Carolina	219,323	14,919	5	5,027	2,462	85	5,634	247,455
North Dakota	1,072,021	114,897	519,605	589	70,965	124	30,751	1,808,952
Ohio	111,643	37,603	22	1,747	720	241	97	152,073
Oklahoma	327,453	272,461	173,771	6,001	6,155	109	21	785,971
Oregon	254,275	29,787	135,884	13,334	7,038	29	6,538	446,885
Pennsylvania	119,447	11,876	2	334	130	40	1,029	132,858
Rhode Island	156	35	0	0	0	0	0	191
South Carolina	96,591	22,079	94	51,636	9,521	220	1,339	181,480
South Dakota	488,946	77,761	558,193	190	17,858	8	9,522	1,152,478
Tennessee	71,311	30,831	0	5,096	825	240	3,625	111,928
Texas	7,012,222	1,925,172	16,063,358	659,116	832,531	32,933	41,542	26,566,874
Utah	52,075	8,797	194,201	3,847	3,537	0	0	262,457
Vermont	2,256	3,643	0	2,028	325	0	18	8,270
Virginia	34,937	51,567	0	2,984	30	3	3,405	92,926
Washington	430,346	43,027	288,563	108,445	10,617	50	136	881,184
West Virginia	13,804	45,166	5	908	1,857	121	321	62,182
Wisconsin	1,014,025	55,689	29	41,120	9,250	6	995	1,121,114
Wyoming	136,939	82,078	583,757	694	24,424	48	22,484	850,424
Caribbean[1]	27,314	26,092	17,949	134	12	0	0	71,501
Total	23,038,757	5,401,220	29,249,034	2,191,268	2,311,863	42,811	456,473	62,691,426

Source: Agricultural Conservation and Forestry Statistics, 1989, U.S. Government Printing Office, Washington, D.C., 1989, p. 450, from Soil Conservation Service. *Note:* 1. Puerto Rico and Virgin Islands.

★ 750 ★

Soil Erosion Reduction in Selected Counties

Amount of potential soil savings resulting from implementation of conservation plans. Values shown are percetages of tons of soil per acre per year.

County and state	Erosion reduction (percent)
Alamance Co., NC	58.0
Dewey Co., OK	85.0
Grundy Co., MO	65.0
Madison Co., TN	58.0
Morgan Co., CO	59.0
E. Pottawatamie Co., IA	66.0
Whitman Co., WA	44.0
Woodford Co., Ill	43.0
York Co., PA	69.0
Average	52.0

Source: Farm Journal, March 1990, p. 28, from the Soil and Water Conservation Society.

Solid Waste Management

★ 751 ★

Composting of Yard Waste by State

The table represents a yard waste composting program study in 1988, sponsored by the EPA, to provide information about the composting options to communities faced with difficult choices in municipal solid waste management.

City or county	State	Public/ private facility	Type of compost technology used	Turning frequency	Grind shred/ screen material	Composting time (months)	Total yard wastes composted (tons/yr)	Tons of finished product (tons/yr)	Yard waste volume reduction (%)
Davis	CA	private	low	1/week	G	3-4[1]	500	250	50-60
East Tawas	MI	public	low	6/year	NA	24-36	138	70-80	65
Mont. Co.	MD	public/ private	intermed	1/month	SH, SC	6-12	15,600	3,500	85
Omaha	NE	public	minimal	2/year	G	18-24	500	350	50-60
Seattle	WA	private	minimal	1/year	G, SH, SC	6-8	3,600	[2]	80
Wellesley[3]	MA-RDF	public	minimal	1/year	SC	24	n/a	1,800	60-65
	MA-DPW	public	low	1/month	SC	12	n/a	800	60-65

[Continued]

★ 751 ★

Yard Waste Composting Facilities by State

[Continued]

City or county	State	Public/ private facility	Type of compost technology used	Turning frequency	Grind shred/ screen material	Composting time (months)	Total yard wastes composted (tons/yr)	Tons of finished product (tons/yr)	Yard waste volume reduction (%)
Westfield[4]	NJ-MCI	private	intermed	>1/week	SH, SC	3-4	1,730	5	80
	NJ-WL	private	intermed	as needed	SH, SC	5	1,400	5	50-70
Woodbury	MN	private	low	1/month	NA	12	~116	6	70

Source: BioCycle, September 1989, p. 38. *Notes:* NA: not applicable; G: grind; SH: shred; SC: screen. 1. The composting process may not be complete in 3-4 months. 2. Pacific Topsoils Inc, composts wastes for Seattle and other cities; hence, it is not possible to separate out data for Seattle alone. 3. MA-RDF - Wellesley's yard waste composting facility located at its Recycling and Disposal Facility for resident drop-off of yard wastes. MA-DPW - Wellesley's yard wastes composting facility located at its DPW yard for landscaper drop-off of leaves. 4. NJ-MCI - Middlebush Compost, Inc., a private facility used by Westfield to compost leaves. NJ-WL - Woodhue Ltd., a private facility used by Westfield to compost grass clippings. 5. Middlebush Compost Inc. and Woodhue Ltd. compost leaves and grass, respectively, from Westfield and primarily leaves from other communities and private clients. It is not possible to separate out data for Westfield alone. 6. Composting Concepts composts yard wastes from Woodbury and other communities; hence, it is not possible to separate out data for Woodbury alone.

★ 752 ★

Discarded Packaging and Food in the U. S. and Mexico City

	Each U.S. Resident (Ounces)	Each Mexico City Resident (Ounces)
Packaging discarded daily	10.8	3.8
Food debris discarded daily (peels, bones, etc.)	4.5	7.0
Wasted food discarded daily (spoiled or uneaten)	2.4	2.4

Source: Garbage, May/June 1990, p. 68, from The Garbage Project, University of Arizona.

★ 753 ★

Disposal of Municipal Solid Waste by State - 1988

Municipal solid waste (MSW) generation and disposal, by method, in 1988. Data shown are in thousands of tons per year and in percent.

State	MSW Annual Tonnage	Percent Recycled/ Composted	Percent Incinerated	Percent Landfilled
Alabama	2,600	10.0	5.0	85.0
Alaska	450	5.0-10.0	5.0	85.0-90.0
Arizona	3,100	-	0	100.0
Arkansas	1,600	1.0	9.0	90.0
California	40,000[2]	11.0-12.0	2.0	86.0-87.0
Colorado	1,700	2.0	<1.0	98.0

[Continued]

★ 753 ★

Disposal of MSW by State - 1988
[Continued]

State	MSW Annual Tonnage	Percent Recycled/ Composted	Percent Incinerated	Percent Landfilled
Connecticut	2,800	<10.0	66.0	24.0
Delaware	750	4.0/12.0	24.0	60.0
District of Columbia	740	2.0	23.0	75.0
Florida	16,400	10.0/1.0	25.0	65.0
Georgia	3,600	-	5.0	95.0
Hawaii	700	3.0	15.0	84.0
Idaho	750	<1.0	<2.0	98.0
Illinois	15,000	2.0	3.0	95.0
Indiana	5,000	-	17.0	83.0
Iowa	2,400	-	3.0	97.0
Kansas	1,800	2.0-3.0/1.0	0	97.0
Kentucky	5,000	-	9.0	91.0
Louisiana	2,600	5.0	0	95.0
Maine	1,000	17.0	37.0	46.0
Maryland	7,000	-	14.0	86.0
Massachusetts	6,100	7.0	31.0	62.0
Michigan	11,800	7.0	3.0	90.0
Minnesota	4,000	12.0/1.0	18.0	69.0
Mississippi	1,800	-	1.0	99.0
Missouri	5,000	7.0	1.0	92.0
Montana	650	-	4.0	96.0
Nebraska	1,000	-	0	100.0
Nevada	900	5.0	0	95.0
New Hampshire	950	<10.0	14.0	76.0
New Jersey	9,000	14.0	2.0	84.0
New Mexico	1,000+	5.0	0	95.0
New York[1]	20,200	-	13.0	87.0[2]
North Carolina	6,000	5.0-10.0	· 1.0	89.0-94.0
North Dakota	450	<5.0	0	95.0
Ohio	11,000[3]	5.0	12.0	83.0
Oklahoma	3,300	-	20.0	80.0
Oregon	2,700	16.0-17.0	2.0	81.0-82.0
Pennsylvania	9,200	-	3.0	97.0
Rhode Island	550	<5.0	0	95.0
South Carolina	2,200	-	4.0	96.0
South Dakota	750	<2.0	0	98.0
Tennessee	4,800	-	11.0	89.0
Texas	17,800	7.0	<1.0	93.0
Utah	1,100	-	15.0	85.0
Vermont	330	15.0	6.0	79.0
Virginia	7,300	-	18.0	82.0
Washington	5,300	22.0	<1.0	77.0
West Virginia	1,200	5.0-7.0	0	93.0-95.0

[Continued]

★ 753 ★

Disposal of MSW by State - 1988
[Continued]

State	MSW Annual Tonnage	Percent Recycled/ Composted	Percent Incinerated	Percent Landfilled
Wisconsin	2,500	1.0	13.0-16.0	84.0-87.0
Wyoming	500	<5.0	0	95.0

Source: Biocycle, April 1989, p. 35. *Notes:* 1. Information provided by the New York State Legislative Commission on Solid Waste Management. 2. Including demolition. 3. Includes some industrial. 4. Includes 5% going out of state - Data unavailable.

★ 754 ★

Incineration in Selected Cities

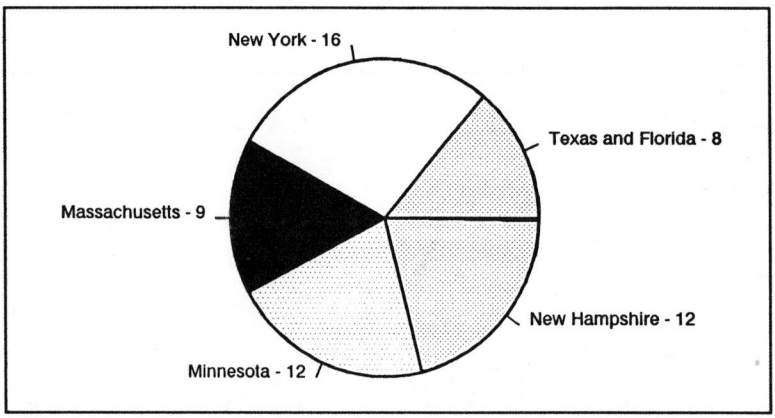

South Dakota, North Dakota, Wyoming, West Virginia and Nebraska have no planned incinerators.

States with Incinerators	Number of Incinerators
New York	16
Minnesota	12
New Hampshire	12
Massachusetts	9
Texas and Florida	8

Source: Garbage, March/April 1991, p. 66, from *Recycling & Incineration,* Island Press.

★ 755 ★

Municipal Solid Waste in Selected Cities and Counties

Data shown are responses by local solid waste management officials in a survey conducted by the Office of Technology Assessment from November 1988 to March 1989. Data may or may not include construction/demolition debris.

City/county	Amount of MSW (x 1,000 tons)	Percentage residential[1]	Per-capita rate (pounds per day)
Albuquerque, NM	310	46	4.3
Austin, TX	178	-[3]	2.1
Bannock County, ID	65	50	5.5
Boston, MA	550	45	5.0
Charlotte, NC	225	-	3.3
Chattanooga, TN	286	58	9.4
Chicago, IL	2,200	50	4.0
Cincinnati, OH	213	-	3.2
Denver, CO	275-500[2]	-	3.1-5.7
Fairfax County, VA	1,039	-	7.5
Gwinnett, GA	386	76	6.7
Hamburg, NY	4	-	2.1
Hillsborough County, FL	535	38	3.7
King County, WA	1,300	-	5.1
Los Angeles, CA	1,432	-	2.4
Marblehead, MA	19	-	4.6
Marion County, OR	216	-	5.7
Minneapolis, MN	160	-	2.5
Newark, NJ	325	-	5.4
New York, NY	7,500	-	5.8
Park County, MT	12	-	7.3
Peterborough, NH	3	-	3.3
Philadelphia, PA	1,700	51	5.8
Phoenix, AZ	1,200	-	7.0
Pinellas County, FL	1,160	-	7.5
Portland, OR	335	-	3.9
Prescott, AZ	52	-	5.7
San Antonio, TX	880	-	4.9
San Francisco, CA	967[2]	-	7.2
San Jose, CA	635	-	4.8
Seattle, WA	687	36	7.7
Shreveport, LA	307	26	7.8
Somerville, MA	36	-	2.2
Springfield, MO	200	-	7.8
Tulsa, OK	240	-	3.6

[Continued]

★ 755 ★

Municipal Solid Waste in Selected Cities and Counties
[Continued]

City/county	Amount of MSW (x 1,000 tons)	Percentage residential[1]	Per-capita rate (pounds per day)
Waukesha County, WI	296	45	5.5
Yakima, WA	17	-	1.9

Source: Facing America's Trash: What Next for Municipal Solid Waste, U.S. Congress, Office of Technology Assessment, OTA-O-412, Washington, D.C., July 1989., p. 77, from Office of Technology Assessment, 1989, after K. Cox, *Background Data on Municipal Solid Waste: Generation, Composition, Costs, Management Facilities, State Activities* (Takoma Park, MD: 1989) *Notes:* 1. For localities collecting all types of MSW and differentiating among residential, commercial, and institutional MSW. 2. Includes both city and county. 3. Includes residential, commercial, and institutional.

★ 756 ★

Solid Waste Composition in Europe

Composition of solid waste in nine countries in the European Economic Community (EEC). Data in percent of total weight unless otherwise noted.

Component	United Kingdom	Federal Republic of Germany	France	Denmark	Italy	Ireland	Belgium	Luxembourg	Netherlands	Average EEC
Putrescibles[1]	21	16.0	20	15	39.0	28	43	56.0	48.0	25.4
Paper and board	30	27.5	35	35	24.0	33	30	25.0	23.0	28.7
Textiles	3	3.0	4	2	3.5	3	2	1.5	1.8	3.1
Plastics	3	4.0	5	4	6.5	4	4	4.6	6.0	4.6
Glass	9	9.0	8	8	5.5	8	10	5.2	13.0	8.3
Metals	9	6.5	5	4	3.5	4	5	3.6	2.9	6.0
Ashes, dust and other	25	34.0	23	32	18.0	20	6	4.1	5.3	23.9
Total	100	100	100	100	100	100	100	100	100	100
Mean calorific value										
(kJ/kg)[2]	9400	7500	8400	8400	6700	9400	7300	7500	7500	7500
(kcal/kg)[3]	2250	1800	2000	2000	1300	2250	1750	1800	1800	1800

Source: Resources, Conservation and Recycling, August 1990, p. 79. *Notes:* 1. Vegetable matter. 2. Kilojoules per kilogram. 3. Kilocalories per kilogram.

★ 757 ★

Solid Waste Disposal Capacity by State - 1988

Data showing solid waste landfill and incineration capacity, by state, for 1988.

State	Landfills			Incinerators		
	Number	Cost/Ton ($)	Remaining Capacity (yrs)	Number	Cost/Ton ($)	Daily Capacity (tons/day)
Alabama	175	9	5-10	2	-	375
Alaska	700+	0-39	15+	3	80	75
Arizona	70	9-12	5	4	-	165
Arkansas	93	-	-	0	-	-
California	620+	26	11	3	16-20	2,100
Colorado	150	6-18	10-15	1	-	-
Connecticut	90	60-110	4-5	5	35-83	5,000
Delaware	3	24-39	20+	1	-	500
District of Columbia	1	10	2	1	22.25	500
Florida	170	15-30	5	9	50-70	9,000
Georgia	195	5-25	5	1	-	500
Hawaii	20	20	5	1	-	200
Idaho	130	8	10+	1	-	50
Illinois	133	10-20	5	1	-	1,250
Indiana	82	15-25	5	1	-	2,360
Iowa	82	10	12	1	-	180
Kansas	130	9	10	0	-	-
Kentucky	88	6-12	4+	1	-	700
Louisiana	42	15-20	10-12	0	-	-
Maine	<200	20-40	-	5	10-40	1,400
Maryland	41	0-46	-	4	22-60	4,700
Massachusetts	194	53-60	-	8	40-75	5,100
Michigan	66	15-19	-	1	-	1,000
Minnesota	91	29	-	11	28-58	2,000
Mississippi	114	4-8	6	1	-	-
Missouri	84	12-15	9	3	-	50
Montana	140	8-10	-	1	-	70
Nebraska	38[1]	8	10	0	-	-
Nevada	150	5-10	5-7	0	-	-
New Hampshire	58	35-45	-	18	35-61	830
New Jersey	70	48	-	1	98	400
New Mexico	41[1]	-	20	0	-	-
New York[1]	241	-	8	7[2]	-	7,000[3]
North Carolina	120	6-12	-	1	23	200
North Dakota	90	9	20	0	-	-
Ohio	103	15-20	10-12	7	15-20	3,750
Oklahoma	200	5-15	20+	3	Up to 30	1,200
Oregon	100	20	20+	1	26	550
Pennsylvania	75	8.25-63	<4.5	2	Up to 52	700
Rhode Island	9	30	1	0	-	-
South Carolina	70	-	-	1	-	240
South Dakota	23	<5	5	0	-	-
Tennessee	120	-	-	5	-	1,450

[Continued]

★ 757 ★

Solid Waste Disposal Capacity by State - 1988

[Continued]

State	Landfills			Incinerators		
	Number	Cost/Ton ($)	Remaining Capacity (yrs)	Number	Cost/Ton ($)	Daily Capacity (tons/day)
Texas	934	7-13.50	12	4	-	125
Utah	17[1]	0-6	-	1	25	450
Vermont	72	40	8	0	-	-
Virginia	307	20	-	7	-	3,700
Washington	100+	15-68	-	1	-	100
West Virginia	58	-	2	0	-	-
Wisconsin	820	15-20	5	7	30-50	885
Wyoming	204	10-12	-	0	-	-
Totals	7,924			136		58,855

Source: Biocycle, April 1989, p. 37. *Notes:* 1. Does not include open dumps. 2. Includes only New York State W-2-E facilities. 3. Includes apartment house incinerators. - Data unavailable.

★ 758 ★

Solid Waste in Kokomo

Data developed March 1, 1989 through May 15, 1989.

Type of Waste	Percent
Landfill	17.6
Glass	7.2
Steel-bimetallic wastes	2.5
Cardboard	2.5
Magazine	2.5
Aluminum	0.7
High-density polyethylene	0.4
PET[1]	0.4
Yard waste	23.6
Household organics	23.3
Newspaper	19.3

Source: BioCycle, January 1991, p. 51. *Note:* 1. Polyethylene terephthalate.

★ 759 ★

State Landfill Capacity

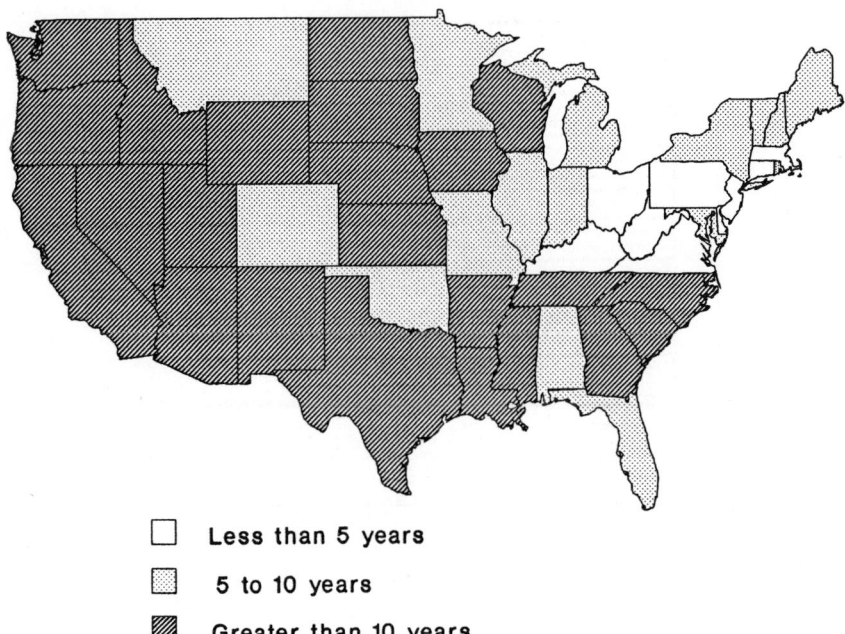

☐ Less than 5 years

▦ 5 to 10 years

▨ Greater than 10 years

Source: Recycling Today, May 1989, p. 78, from National Solid Waste Management Association, 1988.

★ 760 ★

States With Most Beach Waste

| Texas - 1,926.0 |
| Louisiana - 1,641.8 |
| Maryland - 1,636.4 |
| Hawaii - 1,192.3 |
| New York - 1,187.3 |
| North Carolina - 740.9 |
| Mississippi - 620.0 |
| California - 578.4 |
| New Hampshire - 577.1 |
| Florida - 439.1 |

State	Amount of Waste (lbs / mile)
Texas	1,926.0
Louisiana	1,641.8
Maryland	1,636.4
Hawaii	1,192.3
New York	1,187.3
North Carolina	740.9
Mississippi	620.0
California	578.4
New Hampshire	577.1
Florida	439.1

Source: Garbage, September/October 1990, p. 26, from the Center for Marine Conservation.

★ 761 ★

Waste Disposal Trend in New York City

Each New Yorker generated 1,825 pounds of solid waste in 1989 versus 1,188 pounds in 1900—of which ash represented 83 percent.

| Dumping | 1887 | 1989 | |
		Volume %	Tons per day
Dumped at sea	73	-	-
Shoreline filling	18	-	-
Landfilling (inland)	6	-	-
Dumped in river	3	-	-
Landfilled	-	81.0	18,271

[Continued]

★ 761 ★

Waste Disposal Trend in New York City
[Continued]

Dumping	1887	1989	
		Volume %	Tons per day
Incinerated	-	12.5	845
Recycled	-	6.5	1,089

Source: Garbage, September/October 1990, p. 26, from *Garbage in the Cities*, Texas A&M University Press; *New York Environment Book*, Island Press; the New York Historical Society; and the NYC Department of Sanitation.

★ 762 ★

Waste Generation in Selected Countries

Chart shows data from column 2.

Estimated municipal solid waste generation per capita in selected countries shown in pounds per person per day.

Country	Gross discards	Net discards	Year
United States	3.6	3.2	1986
West Germany	-	2.6	1984/85
Sweden	-	2.4	early to mid-1980's
Switzerland	-	2.2	-
Japan	-	3.0	1987

Source: Facing America's Trash: What Next for Municipal Solid Waste, U.S. Congress, Office of Technology Assessment, OTA-O-412, Washington, D.C., July 1989., p. 79, from Franklin Associates, Ltd., *Characterization of Municipal Solid Waste in the United States, 1960 to 2000 (Update 1988)*, report prepared for U.S. EPA, Office of Solid Waste and Emergency Response (Prarie Village, KS: 1988); G. Grossmann, "Municipal Solid Waste Management in the Federal Republic of Germany," pp. 118-126 in *A Selection of Recent Publications (Vol. 2)*, Federal Environmental Agency, Federal Republic of Germany (Berlin: 1988); A.J. Hershkowitz, *International Experiences in Solid Waste Management*, contract prepared for U.S. Congress, Office of Technological Assessment (Elmsford, NY: Municipal Recycling Associates, Inc., 1988); Clean Japan Center, "Waste Volume on the Rise and Measures Against It," *Clean Japan* 14:6-10, February 1988. Gross discards refer to total municipal waste generation, net discards refer to municipal waste remaining after recycling but before energy recovery.

★ 763 ★

Waste Management in Hong Kong

Waste composition and export recycling, shown in metric tons per day. Recycling rate is shown in percent. Data refer to 1987.

Materials	Landfill	Recycling	Recycling rate (percent)
Paper	1,450	1,595	52
Putrescibles	2,090	-	-
Textiles	290	80	22
Leather/wood/rubber	295	1	Neg.
Plastics	990	65	6
Metals	220	1,050	83
Glass bottles	180	2	1
Other	785	-	-
Total	6,300	2,793	31

Source: Resource Recycling, July 1989, p. 27, from Environmental Protection Department, Hong Kong Government. *Note:* Neg. = Negligible.

★ 764 ★

Waste-to-Energy Project in Detroit, Michigan

The project generated $56.04 million for the year ending June 30, 1990 but had a net loss of $2.26 million. Amounts are in millions of dollars.

	Amount
Income	
City of Detroit tipping fee	32.90
Selling steam to Detroit Edison	10.90
Earning of investments	8.80
Selling electricity to Detroit Edison	2.10
Gain on sale of investments	0.88
Miscellaneous	0.46
Total	56.04
Expenses	
Operating expenses	31.20
Interest expenses	24.10
Depreciation & amortization	1.20
General and administrative costs	1.80
Total	58.30

Source: Detroit Free Press, May 20, 1991, p. 8A, from Greater Detroit Resources Recovery Authority audits and city financial documents.

Toxic Accidents

★ 765 ★

Large Toxic Rail Accidents by State

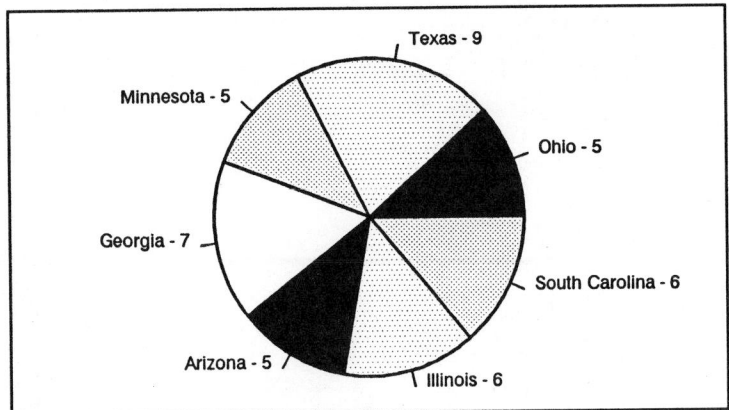

Toxic rail accidents in 1988 involving five or more cars.

State	Cars Releasing Hazardous Materials
Texas	9
Georgia	7
Illinois	6
South Carolina	6
Arizona	5
Minnesota	5
Ohio	5

Source: Transportation of Hazardous Materials by Rail: Hearings Before the Government Activities and the Transportation Subcommittee of the Committee on Government Operations, House of Representatives, 101st Congress, and Session, February 28, 1990, p. 91, from the Federal Railroad Administration.

★ 766 ★

Leading States With Toxic Rail Accidents

Illinois - 78	
Texas - 63	
Louisiana - 28	
California - 22	
Missouri - 19	
Alabama - 16	
Wisconsin - 16	
Georgia - 14	
Ohio - 14	
Virginia - 13	
Arizona - 12	
Indiana - 12	
Oklahoma - 11	
Pennsylvania - 11	
Iowa - 10	

Chart shows data from column 1.

States with ten or more toxic rail accidents in 1988. Rates are shown as number of accidents per thousand miles of track.

State	Number of Incidents	Track miles	Rate	Number of incidents in 1987
Illinois	78	8,380	9.3	49
Texas	63	12,853	4.9	46
Louisiana	28	3,050	9.2	15
California	22	6,438	3.4	12
Missouri	19	5,741	3.3	7
Alabama	16	3,832	4.1	8
Wisconsin	16	3,752	4.3	8
Georgia	14	5,119	2.7	9
Ohio	14	6,238	2.2	11
Virginia	13	3,766	3.4	9
Arizona	12	1,757	6.8	10
Indiana	12	5,069	204	11
Oklahoma	11	3,289	3.3	4
Pennsylvania	11	5,232	2.1	13
Iowa	10	3,646	2.7	7

Source: Transportation of Hazardous Materials by Rail: Hearings Before the Government Activities and the Transportation Subcommittee of the Committee on Government Operations, House of Representatives, 101st Congress, and Session, February 28, 1990, P. 88, from the Federal Railroad Administration.

Toxic Substances

★767★

States With Toxic Chemical Releases and Transfers by Industry - I

The 20 states with the largest Toxic Release Inventory (TRI) total release and transfers, by industry sector. Data show rankings for 1988.

SIC code	SIC	LA	TX	OH	IN	IL	FL	TN	MI	CA	PA	Other states among top 5 for industry
Food and Kindred	20	19	6	7	9	3	17	2	20	1	11	IA(4), WI(5)
Tobacco	21	-	-	-	12	-	-	4	-	-	6	WV(2)
Textiles	22	5	16	11	29	21	33	20	22	14	13	SC(3)
Apparel	23	-	-	1	16	4	-	2	7	9	6	-
Lumber	24	24	4	10	1	18	33	20	12	7	5	MN(2), OR(3)
Furniture	25	36	16	12	5	11	15	4	3	8	6	-
Paper	26	5	13	6	31	26	1	20	16	9	11	WA(3), WI(4)
Printing and Publishing	27	37	22	12	2	1	23	4	25	21	5	-
Chemicals	28	2	1	6	17	8	5	4	15	13	19	-
Petroleum	29	2	1	5	9	7	42	30	22	3	4	-
Plastics	30	47	16	3	1	4	28	7	8	6	13	SC(2)
Leather	31	-	6	18	14	8	27	17	3	20	5	ME(2), WI(4)
Stone/Clay/Glass	32	32	6	4	1	7	22	2	13	12	5	-
Primary Metals	33	23	8	2	4	9	30	16	5	14	3	-
Fabricated Metals	34	32	5	1	10	3	15	21	2	4	7	WI (5)
Machinery Nonelectrical	35	39	5	1	8	3	28	10	17	6	12	WI (2)
Electrical Machinery	36	40	11	5	3	8	17	24	26	4	7	MN(1), MA(2)
Transportation Equipment	37	25	8	3	5	9	7	10	1	2	14	-
Measuring Instruments	38	-	18	15	22	11	8	23	40	3	7	MA(2),OK(4)
Miscellaneous Manufacturing	39	39	20	6	3	8	2	17	19	13	1	AZ(4), IA(5)
Multiple Codes 20-39		1	7	3	2	18	35	4	9	13	10	-
No Codes 20-39		17	3	7	4	12	10	22	19	6	20	AL(2)
TRI Total Rank		1	2	3	4	5	6	7	8	9	10	-

Source: Toxics in the Community: National and Local Perspectives, U.S. Environmental Protection Agency, EPA 560/4-90-017, September 1990, p. 163 *Notes:* No rank is given if there were no reported releases or transfers in a state for a given industry. .

★ 768 ★

States With Toxic Chemical Releases and Transfers by Industry - II

The 20 states with the largest Toxic Release Inventory (TRI) total release and transfers, by industry sector. Data show rankings for 1988.

SIC code	SIC	VA	MO	KS	NY	NJ	UT	NC	GA	KY	MS	Other states among top 5 for industry
Food and Kindred	20	23	21	33	12	22	34	25	26	28	29	IA(4), WI(5)
Tobacco	21	3	-	-	8	-	-	5	1	-	-	WV(2)
Textiles	22	7	8	-	6	12	-	1	2	28	4	SC(3)
Apparel	23	-	-	15	5	-	-	11	3	18	12	-
Lumber	24	6	41	27	34	36	23	13	21	40	14	MN(2), OR(3)
Furniture	25	2	21	-	10	29	33	1	18	28	14	-
Paper	26	12	37	41	19	23	43	8	2	29	32	WA(3), WI(4)
Printing and Publishing	27	3	16	19	8	17	-	9	15	14	7	-
Chemicals	28	7	10	3	14	9	41	16	21	12	11	-
Petroleum	29	18	33	6	21	12	19	38	35	16	14	-
Plastics	30	9	12	27	18	20	42	5	19	23	147	SC(2)
Leather	31	-	1	-	15	7	30	11	-	22	-	ME(2), WI(4)
Stone/Clay/Glass	32	14	26	18	11	19	34	23	9	17	3	-
Primary Metals	33	34	7	39	21	17	1	33	20	10	38	-
Fabricated Metals	34	16	13	34	11	8	38	14	18	26	19	WI (5)
Machinery Nonelectrical	35	38	26	30	4	18	43	13	15	16	27	WI (2)
Electrical Machinery	36	20	10	29	6	25	27	14	22	13	31	MN(1), MA(2)
Transportation Equipment	37	21	4	30	13	24	16	20	12	18	23	-
Measuring Instruments	38	30	24	36	1	5	10	17	19	-	31	MA(2),OK(4)
Miscellaneous Manufacturing	39	23	25	28	9	22	31	15	24	18	29	AZ(4), IA(5)
Multiple Codes 20-39		8	21	24	5	29	43	14	6	22	12	-
No Codes 20-39		34	5	8	1	15	40	21	14	23	38	AL(2)
TRI Total Rank		11	12	13	14	15	16	17	18	19	20	-

Source: Toxics in the Community: National and Local Perspectives, U.S. Environmental Protection Agency, EPA 560/4-90-017, September 1990, p. 163
No rank is given if there were no reported releases or transfers in a state for a given industry.

★ 769 ★

The 25 Counties With the Largest TRI Facilities

County	State	Total No. of TRI[1] Facilities	Percent of Total TRI[1] Facilities
Los Angeles	CA	676	40.67
Cook	IL	543	45.82
Harris	TX	207	20.72
Orange	CA	187	11.25

[Continued]

★ 769 ★

25 Counties With the Largest TRI Facilities
[Continued]

County	State	Total No. of TRI[1] Facilities	Percent of Total TRI[1] Facilities
Dallas	TX	157	15.72
Cuyahoga	OH	155	12.29
Wayne	MI	151	19.92
Santa Clara	CA	142	8.54
Middlesex	NJ	139	15.89
Middlesex	MA	136	24.29
Milwaukee	WI	134	20.78
Providence	RI	118	71.08
New Haven	CT	115	30.03
King	WA	114	37.25
Hamilton	OH	114	9.04
Alameda	CA	113	6.80
Maricopa	AZ	107	68.59
Bergen	NJ	104	11.89
Essex	NJ	101	11.54
Marion	IN	91	12.64
Hennepin	MN	91	30.23
Tarrant	TX	87	8.71
Hartford	CT	87	22.72
Worcester	MA	86	15.36
Bristol	MA	85	15.18
Subtotal		4,040	
% of Grand Total		20.96	
Total for all others		15,238	
Grand Total		19,278	

Source: The Toxic Release Inventory, A National Perspective, U.S. Environmental Protection Agency, Washington, D.C., June 1989, p. 41. *Note:* 1. Toxic release inventory.

★ 770 ★

The Ten Cities With the Largest TRI Off-Site Transfers

City	State	Amount transferred to the City	Percent of total off-site transfers
Ecorse	MI	396,580,500	15.15
Deer Park	TX	111,802,869	4.27
Baton rouge	LA	87,247,936	3.33
Belleville	MI	44,514,531	1.70
Leighton	Al	42,129,100	1.61
Detroit	MI	39,342,280	1.50
Glens Falls	NY	33,792,500	1.29
Cleveland	OH	33,702,290	1.29
Wichita	KS	31,691,406	1.21
Emelle	Al	26,440,690	1.01
Subtotal		847,244,102	32.36
Total for all others		1,770,713,263	67.64
Grand total of Tri Off-site Transfers		2,617,957,365	100.00

Source: The Toxic Release Inventory, A National Perspective, U.S. Environmental Protection Agency, Washington, D.C., June 1989, p. 224. *Notes:* TRI stands for Toxic Release Inventory. .

★ 771 ★

Toxic Chemical Releases - Top Ten States

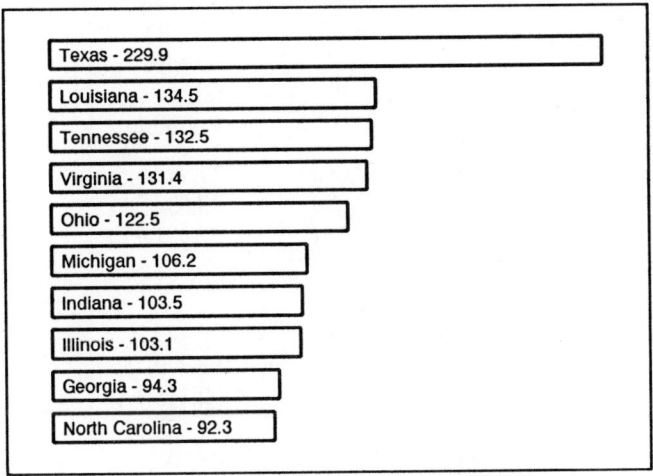

In 1987, 2.4 billion pounds of toxic materials were released into the atmosphere. More than half of this total occurred in ten states.

State	Millions of pounds
Texas	229.9
Louisiana	134.5
Tennessee	132.5
Virginia	131.4
Ohio	122.5
Michigan	106.2
Indiana	103.5
Illinois	103.1
Georgia	94.3
North Carolina	92.3

Source: Newsweek, April 3, 1989, p. 25, from EPA.

★ 772 ★

Toxic Chemical Releases, Transfer and Population by State

Data are shown for 1988.

State	Land area[1] (Sq. miles)	Population[1] (Thousands)	Direct releases[2] (Pounds)	Population density[3]	Release density[4]
Alabama	51,705	4,083	67,365,412	79	1,303
Alaska	591,004	525	26,273,155	1	44
American Samoa	77	-	29,500	-	383
Arizona	114,000	3,386	68,554,330	30	601
Arkansas	53,187	2,388	63,222,530	45	1,189

[Continued]

★ 772 ★

Toxic Chemical Releases, Transfer and Population by State
[Continued]

State	Land area[1] (Sq. miles)	Population[1] (Thousands)	Direct releases[2] (Pounds)	Population density[3]	Release density[4]
California	158,706	27,663	111,722,390	174	704
Colorado	104,091	3,296	13,838,744	32	133
Connecticut	5,018	3,211	32,931,952	640	6,563
Delaware	2,044	644	5,698,813	315	2,788
District of Columbia	68	626	500	9,206	7
Florida	58,664	12,023	226,110,107	205	3,854
Georgia	58,910	6,222	98,279,750	106	1,668
Hawaii	6,471	1,083	2,115,399	167	327
Idaho	83,564	998	14,453,504	12	173
Illinois	56,345	11,582	136,706,167	206	2,426
Indiana	36,185	5,531	212,813,094	153	5,881
Iowa	56,275	2,834	44,938,969	50	799
Kansas	82,277	2,476	116,681,878	30	1,418
Kentucky	40,409	3,727	81,174,022	92	2,009
Louisiana	47,751	4,461	715,743,928	93	14,989
Maine	33,265	1,187	17,949,031	36	540
Maryland	10,460	4,535	23,806,487	434	2,276
Massachusetts	8,284	5,855	28,103,992	707	3,393
Michigan	58,527	9,200	119,999,498	157	2,050
Minnesota	84,402	4,246	53,035,977	50	628
Mississippi	47,689	2,625	111,760,882	55	2,344
Missouri	69,697	5,103	92,908,174	73	1,333
Montana	147,046	809	35,419,648	6	241
Nebraska	77,355	1,594	17,931,771	21	232
Nevada	110,561	1,007	4,215,391	9	38
New Hampshire	9,279	1,057	12,568,509	114	1,355
New Jersey	7,787	7,672	40,403,511	985	5,189
New Mexico	121,593	1,500	24,151,925	12	199
New York	49,108	17,825	96,032,605	363	1,956
North Carolina	52,669	6,413	108,638,688	122	2,063
North Dakota	70,703	672	1,240,612	10	18
Ohio	41,330	10,784	229,473,876	261	5,552
Oklahoma	69,956	3,272	39,605,430	47	566
Oregon	97,073	2,724	21,222,827	28	219
Pennsylvania	45,308	11,936	101,866,198	263	2,248
Puerto Rico	3,515	3,274	15,795,208	931	4,494
Rhode Island	1,212	986	6,317,637	814	5,213
South Carolina	31,113	3,425	65,518,755	110	2,106
South Dakota	77,116	709	2,481,361	9	32
Tennessee	42,144	4,855	203,212,545	115	4,822
Texas	266,807	16,789	595,907,459	63	2,233
Utah	84,899	1,680	135,025,920	20	1,590
Vermont	9,614	548	1,656,692	57	172
Virgin Islands	132	-	1,633,634	-	12,376

[Continued]

★ 772 ★

Toxic Chemical Releases, Transfer and Population by State
[Continued]

State	Land area[1] (Sq. miles)	Population[1] (Thousands)	Direct releases[2] (Pounds)	Population density[3]	Release density[4]
Virginia	40,767	5,904	144,434,862	145	3,543
Washington	68,138	4,538	42,029,962	67	617
West Virginia	24,231	1,897	35,815,259	78	1,478
Wisconsin	56,153	4,807	51,893,559	86	924
Wyoming	97,809	490	45,353,102	5	464
Total	3,622,425	246,051	4,566,065,131	68	1,260

Source: *Toxics in the Community: National and Local Perspectives*, U.S. Environmental Protection Agency, EPA 560/4-90-017, September 1990, p. 138 *Notes:* 1. Land area and population statistics are from Tables 331 and 22 of *Statistical Abstract of the United States*, (Washington, DC: U.S. Department of Commerce, Bureau of the Census, 1989). 2. Direct releases include air emissions, surface water discharges, land disposal, and underground injection. 3. People per square mile. 4. Pounds per square mile.

★ 773 ★

Toxic Chemicals Releases and Transfer by State
State rankings for types of releases and transfers as reported in the Toxic Release Inventory for 1988.

State	Air	Surface water	Land	Underground	Public sewage	Off-site	TRI Total	Carcinogens
Alabama	16	9	23	15	35	20	22	16
Alaska	32	16	50	25	51	46	38	44
American Samoa	53	54	54	54	54	54	53	53
Arizona	38	47	3	45	22	39	24	34
Arkansas	21	7	29	12	36	26	25	29
California	13	6	10	17	4	11	9	7
Colorado	40	44	27	41	33	32	42	32
Connecticut	31	8	31	44	27	19	30	13
Delaware	42	31	42	42	31	37	46	40
District of Columbia	54	53	53	34	52	52	54	54
Florida	18	2	1	8	15	21	6	21
Georgia	12	10	18	20	16	14	18	12
Hawaii	51	46	44	16	40	51	49	48
Idaho	43	39	17	23	41	47	44	41
Illinois	8	4	16	11	2	6	5	9
Indiana	7	13	2	7	14	8	4	5
Iowa	24	25	43	40	21	28	28	26
Kansas	30	28	40	3	25	7	13	39
Kentucky	23	23	21	9	30	10	19	18
Louisiana	4	1	28	1	24	15	1	3
Maine	36	34	35	52	28	41	41	37
Maryland	35	18	26	31	23	31	36	36
Massachusetts	29	29	37	21	11	13	26	14
Michigan	9	26	11	14	12	2	8	8

[Continued]

663

★ 773 ★

Toxic Chemicals Releases and Transfer by State
[Continued]

State	Air	Surface water	Land	Underground	Public sewage	Off-site	TRI Total	Carcinogens
Minnesota	19	20	38	50	20	30	27	30
Mississippi	17	22	19	6	34	27	20	25
Missouri	20	17	4	27	1	22	12	22
Montana	46	41	5	46	50	50	34	45
Nebraska	34	37	48	19	39	36	40	38
Nevada	52	52	24	49	48	43	47	52
New Hampshire	39	33	41	48	42	38	43	35
New Jersey	25	27	25	22	3	5	15	15
New Mexico	47	51	8	47	47	45	39	51
New York	10	21	33	28	7	9	14	4
North Carolina	11	30	9	30	18	17	17	11
North Dakota	50	48	51	33	46	49	52	46
Ohio	2	12	7	4	10	1	3	2
Oklahoma	27	36	30	13	43	25	31	27
Oregon	33	38	34	32	19	33	35	33
Pennsylvania	14	14	12	26	13	4	10	6
Puerto Rico	37	42	47	39	17	34	37	19
Rhode Island	41	35	45	37	32	35	45	42
South Carolina	15	24	32	51	29	23	23	24
South Dakota	45	50	52	35	44	44	48	49
Tennessee	3	11	15	5	8	16	7	10
Texas	1	15	6	2	5	3	2	1
Utah	6	40	13	43	38	40	16	31
Vermont	48	43	49	38	45	42	50	47
Virgin Islands	49	49	46	36	53	53	51	43
Virginia	5	3	22	24	6	24	11	23
Washington	28	5	36	53	37	29	32	28
West Virginia	26	19	39	18	26	18	29	17
Wisconsin	22	32	20	29	9	12	21	20
Wyoming	44	45	14	10	49	48	33	50

Source: Toxics in the Community: National and Local Perspectives, U.S. Environmental Protection Agency, EPA 560/4-90-017, September 1990, p. 130.

Wastewater Treatment

★ 774 ★

Sewage Sludge Production in Europe

Amount of sludge produced in selected European countries and percentages used in agriculture in the 1970s and 1980s.

State	Population (million)	Sludge Production (1,000 dry metric tons per year)	Portion used in Agriculture (%)
Belgium	9.8	30-70	0-45
Denmark	5.1	89-130	45
Finland	1.8	117	40
France	53.4	800	23-30
W. Germany	61.3	1300-2200	32-39
Italy	56.7	1200-1500	20
Netherlands	13.9	200	52
Sweden	8.3	200	60
Switzerland	6.3	122	70
U.K	55.9	1240-1500	41-45

Source: BioCycle, June 1990, p. 36, modified from Genevini, P.L., R. Vismara, V. Mezzanotte. "Utilizzo Agricolo dei fanghi di depurazione. Quaderni, Ingegneria Ambientale, Inquinamento e depurazione," n. 5, Dec. 1986—Lester, J.N. (ed.). *Heavy Metals in Wastewater and Sludge Treatment Processes*. CRC Press, Boca Raton, FL, 1987.

★ 775 ★

States With Greatest Sewage Needs

The table shows current needs for publicly-owned wastewater treatment works eligible for federal financial assistance under the Clean Water Act. Totals include secondary and advanced treatment plants, collector and interceptor sewers, combined sewer overflow facilities and sewer rehabilitation. The values are in millions of dollars.

State	Amount (millions of dollars)
New York	11,683
Massachusetts	5,445
California	5,257
Florida	3,984
New Jersey	3,351
Texas	3,306

[Continued]

★ 775 ★

States With Greatest Sewage Needs
[Continued]

State	Amount (millions of dollars)
Ohio	3,141
Michigan	3,125
Illinois	2,764
Washington	2,143
Indiana	1,582
Pennsylvania	1,439
Connecticut	1,267
North Carolina	1,212
Wisconsin	1,204
Kentucky	1,108
Oregon	982
Missouri	955
Minnesota	902
Tennessee	898
Maryland	866
Louisiana	854
West Virginia	852
Virginia	755
New Hampshire	709
Total U.S.	66,428

Source: ENR, June 29, 1989, p. 59, from Environmental Protection Agency.

Water

★ 776 ★

Polluted Surface Waters by State - I
Size of surface waters across the U.S. that have been affected by toxic substances.

State	Rivers (miles)			Lakes (acres)		
	Total Waters	Monitored for Toxics	Elevated Toxics	Total Waters	Monitored for Toxics	Elevated Toxics
Alabama	40,600	619	110	504,336	202,680	86,080
Arizona	6,671	1,451	906	-	-	-
Arkansas	11,508	2,873	74	-	-	-
Colorado	14,100	4,600	1,294	265,982	10,093	0
Delaware River Basin	291[1]	155	45	-	-	-
District of Columbia	36	26	26	377	136	136
Florida	12,659	2,695	510	2,085,120	546,560	50,560

[Continued]

★ 776 ★

Polluted Surface Waters by State
[Continued]

State	Rivers (miles)			Lakes (acres)		
	Total Waters	Monitored for Toxics	Elevated Toxics	Total Waters	Monitored for Toxics	Elevated Toxics
Georgia	20,000	1,119	10	417,730	39,878	0
Hawaii	349	-	-	-	-	-
Idaho	16,146	-	1,468	727,202	-	32,000
Illinois	14,080	5,425	1,834	305,847	-	13,381
Indiana	90,000	2,306	922	104,540	54,686	1,106
Iowa	18,300	2,624	2,097	81,400	20,700	0
Kansas	19,791	2,697	556	175,189	92,098	0
Kentucky	18,465	-	1,084	228,385	-	-
Louisiana	14,180	-	116	713,719	-	1,170
Maine	31,672	865	435	994,560	38,106	400
Massachusetts	10,704	999	264	-	-	-
Minnesota	91,944	1,855	1,599	3,411,200	1,367,131	1,245,929
Mississippi	15,623	1,075	271	500,000	45,578	0
Missouri	19,630	3,650	458	288,012	-	561
Montana	20,532	-	890	756,450	-	9,100
New York	70,000	3,400	345	750,000	668,000	130,946
North Carolina	37,378	-	382	305,367	282,909	9,688
North Dakota	11,284	6,829	560	625,503	399,381	0
Ohio	43,917	-	1,637	117,323	91,226	29,729
Oklahoma	19,791	4,997	4,608	-	-	-
Pennsylvania	50,000	-	1,508	-	-	-
Puerto Rico	5,373	1,710	1,505	11,146	2,982	981
Rhode Island	724	80	59	16,520	4,968	0
South Carolina	9,900	2,518	180	525,000	354,114	8,560
South Dakota	9,937	3,080	163	1,598,285	548,000	0
Virginia	27,240	3,535	296	161,562	57,992	0
Washington	40,492	1,189	846	613,582	134,834	134,822
West Virginia	28,361	4,574	3,795	19,171	13,465	4,655
Wyoming	19,437	544	7	427,219	6,098	0
Totals	861,115	67,490	30,860	16,730,727	4,981,615	1,759,804

Source: National Water Quality Inventory, 1988, Report to Congress, U.S. Environmental Protection Agency, Washington, D.C., April 1990, p. 104, from 1988 State Section 305(b) reports. - stands for not reported. *Note:* 1. Includes 85 miles of Delaware estuary.

★ 777 ★

Polluted Surface Waters by State - II

Size of surface waters across the U.S. that have been affected by toxic substances.

State	Estuaries (sq. miles)			Oceans (coastal miles)			Great Lakes (Shore miles)		
	Total Waters	Monitored for Toxics	Elevated Toxics	Total Waters	Monitored for Toxics	Elevated Toxics	Total Waters	Monitored for Toxics	Elevated Toxics
Alabama	625	35	0	-	-	-	-	-	-
Arizona	-	-	-	-	-	-	-	-	-
Arkansas	-	-	-	-	-	-	-	-	-
Colorado	-	-	-	-	-	-	-	-	-
Delaware River Basin	782	-	-	-	-	-	-	-	-
District of Columbia	6	6	6	-	-	-	-	-	-
Florida	4,298	1,648	938	8,460	262	85	-	-	-
Georgia	594	44	0	-	-	-	-	-	-
Hawaii	134	34	0	-	-	-	-	-	-
Idaho	-	-	-	-	-	-	-	-	-
Illinois	-	-	-	-	-	-	63	63	63
Indiana	-	-	-	-	-	-	43	43	43
Iowa	-	-	-	-	-	-	-	-	-
Kansas	-	-	-	-	-	-	-	-	-
Kentucky	-	-	-	-	-	-	-	-	-
Louisiana	7,656	-	-	-	-	-	-	-	-
Maine	1,633	10	10	-	-	-	-	-	-
Massachusetts	171	39	16	-	-	-	-	-	-
Minnesota	-	-	-	-	-	-	272	272	272
Mississippi	133	7	0	81	40	0	-	-	-
Missouri	-	-	-	-	-	-	-	-	-
Montana	-	-	-	-	-	-	-	-	-
New York	1,564	1,564	154	130	130	70	577	577	492
North Carolina	3,200	-	-	-	-	-	-	-	-
North Dakota	-	-	-	-	-	-	-	-	-
Ohio	-	-	-	-	-	-	236	-	199
Oklahoma	-	-	-	-	-	-	-	-	-
Pennsylvania	-	-	-	-	-	-	-	-	-
Puerto Rico	-	-	-	434	127	35	-	-	-
Rhode Island	192	100	17	-	-	-	-	-	-
South Carolina	2,155	319	2	-	-	-	-	-	-
South Dakota	-	-	-	-	-	-	-	-	-
Virginia	2,382	1,800	18	-	-	-	-	-	-
Washington	2,943	370	214	-	-	-	-	-	-
West Virginia	-	-	-	-	-	-	-	-	-
Wyoming	-	-	-	-	-	-	-	-	-
Totals	28,468	5,976	1,375	9,105	559	190	1,191	955	1,069

Source: National Water Quality Inventory, 1988, Report to Congress, U.S. Environmental Protection Agency, Washington, D.C., April 1990, p. 104, from 1988 State Section 305(b) reports. - stands for not reported. *Note:* 1. Includes 85 miles of Delaware estuary.

★ 778 ★

Safe Drinking Water in Selected Countries

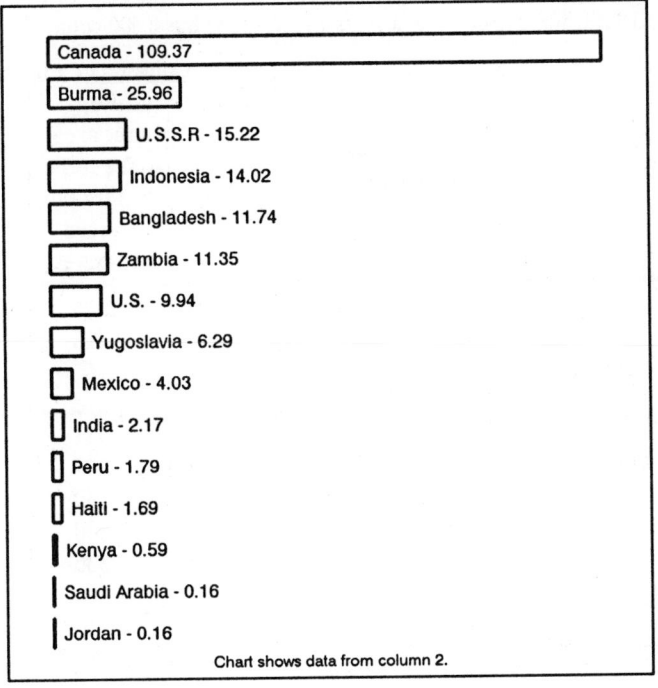

Canada - 109.37
Burma - 25.96
U.S.S.R - 15.22
Indonesia - 14.02
Bangladesh - 11.74
Zambia - 11.35
U.S. - 9.94
Yugoslavia - 6.29
Mexico - 4.03
India - 2.17
Peru - 1.79
Haiti - 1.69
Kenya - 0.59
Saudi Arabia - 0.16
Jordan - 0.16

Chart shows data from column 2.

Country	% of popula- tion that can get safe drinking water	Per capita availability of water annually, in thousands of cubic meters
Canada	100	109.37
Burma	31	25.96
U.S.S.R	100	15.22
Indonesia	47	14.02
Bangladesh	78	11.74
Zambia	56	11.35
U.S.	100	9.94
Yugoslavia	75	6.29
Mexico	69	4.03
India	75	2.17
Peru	58	1.79
Haiti	42	1.69
Kenya	28	0.59
Saudi Arabia	95	0.16
Jordan	99	0.16

Source: Time, August 20, 1990, p. 59.

★ 779 ★

Water Availability in Selected Countries

The decrease of per capita water availability is proportional to the increase of the world's population. In 1850, per capita availability was 33,300 cubic meters a year; today it is 8,500 cubic meters a year.

Country	Area (000 square kilo-meters)	Population[1] (millions)	Long-term annual streamflow			
			(cubic kilo-meters)	Per unit area (000 cubic meters per square kilometer)	Per capita (000 cubic meters)	Percentage of world stream flow
Brazil	8,512	130	9,230	1,084	71.0	20.7
USSR	22,274	275	4,740	213	17.0	11.0
People's Republic of China	9,561	1,024	2,550	267	2.5	5.7
Canada	9,976	25	2,470	248	99.0	5.6
India	3,288	718	1,680	511	2.3	3.8
United States of America	9,363	234	1,940	207	8.3	4.4
Norway	324	4	405	1,250	99.0	0.9
Yugoslavia	256	23	256	1,000	11.0	0.6
France	544	55	183	336	3.4	0.4
Finland	337	5	110	326	22.0	0.2
World land area[2]	134,800	4,665	44,500	330	9.5	-

Source: Nature & Resources, vol. 26, No. 3, 1990, p. 37. *Notes:* 1. For 1983. 2. Without Antarctica.

Wetlands

★ 780 ★

Water Bank Programs by State

Status of agreements carried out, 1980 through September 30, 1989, by states.

State	Number of agreements	Designated acres			Annual payment Dollars
		Total	Wetlands	Adjacent	
Arkansas	310	46,698	30,051	16,647	328,191
California	95	25,065	6,713	18,352	382,178
Louisiana	274	40,618	19,754	20,864	480,664
Maine	36	1,396	467	929	12,975
Michigan	37	1,721	517	1,204	33,093
Minnesota	1,214	60,576	17,835	42,741	1,622,641
Missouri	459	65,045	25,410	39,635	552,790
Montana	107	13,178	2,750	10,428	208,250

[Continued]

★ 780 ★

Water Bank Programs by State
[Continued]

State	Number of agreements	Designated acres			Annual payment Dollars
		Total	Wetlands	Adjacent	
Nebraska	78	5,339	1,107	4,232	130,896
North Dakota	1,133	160,292	51,944	108,348	2,591,907
South Dakota	630	69,665	19,964	49,701	1,022,582
Wisconsin	383	19,444	7,598	11,846	497,324
Total	4,756	509,037	184,110	324,927	7,863,491

Source: Agricultural Conservation and Forestry Statistics, 1989, U.S. Government Printing Office, Washington, D.C., 1989, p. 444, from Agricultural Stabilization and Conservation Service.

★ 781 ★

Wetland Area by State

State	Acres (in thousands)	Percent of Total State Land Area
Alabama	3,069	9
Alaska	-	-
Arizona	-	-
Arkansas	2,764	8
California	389	1
Colorado	675	1
Connecticut	261	8
Delaware	223	18
Florida	11,333	33
Georgia	5,298	14
Hawaii	110	-
Idaho	-	-
Illinois	712	2
Indiana	285	1
Iowa	-	-
Kansas	435	1
Kentucky	205	1
Louisiana	8,674	30
Maine	1,731	9
Maryland	438	7
Massachusetts	542	11
Michigan	5,583	15
Minnesota	7,540	15
Mississippi	4,067	13
Missouri	836	2

[Continued]

★ 781 ★

Wetland Area by State
[Continued]

State	Acres (in thousands)	Percent of Total State Land Area
Montana	-	-
Nebraska	1,906	4
Nevada	-	-
New Hampshire	190	3
New Jersey	916	19
New Mexico	482	1
New York	1,184	4
North Carolina	5,690	18
North Dakota	2,868	7
Ohio	-	-
Oklahoma	1,270	3
Oregon	-	-
Pennsylvania	498	2
Rhode Island	84	13
South Carolina	4,659	24
South Dakota	1,548	3
Tennessee	787	3
Texas	3,957	2
Utah	584	1
Vermont	-	-
Virginia	1,045	4
Washington	748	2
West virginia	102	>1
Wisconsin	4,410	13
Wyoming	-	-

Source: National Water Quality Inventory, 1988, Report to Congress, U.S. Environmental Protection Agency, Washington, D.C., April 1990, p. 97, from U.S. Fish and Wildlife Service, *National Wetlands Inventory*, June 1988. *Note:* - Reliable wetland area data not available.

Chapter 9
LAWS AND REGULATIONS

Compliance

★ 782 ★

Pollution Decreases Since Enactment of the Clean Air Act

Pollutant	Percent Decrease or Increase (+)
Nitrogen oxide[1]	+7.0
Volatile organic compounds[2]	26.0
Sulfur oxides[1]	27.0
Carbon monoxide[3]	40.0
Particulates[4]	63.0
Lead[3]	96.0

Source: Garbage, July/August 1990, p. 26, from the EPA. *Notes:* 1. From burning fossil fuels. 2. From cars, paint, and petroleum volatilization. 3. From car, truck, bus emissions. 4. From crushed-stone and grain industries.

★ 783 ★

Power Plants Facing Emission Reductions
Power plants across the U.S. affected by acid rain provisions.

State	Power plants Affected
Alabama	2
Florida	2
Georgia	5
Illinois	8
Indiana	15
Iowa	6

[Continued]

★ 783 ★

Power Plants Facing Emission Reductions
[Continued]

State	Power plants Affected
Kansas	1
Kentucky	10
Maryland	3
Michigan	1
Minnesota	1
Mississippi	1
Missouri	8
New Hampshire	1
New Jersey	1
New York	5
Ohio	15
Pennsylvania	9
Tennessee	4
West Virginia	6
Wisconsin	6

Source: Electrical World, December 1990, p. 9.

Enforcement

★ 784 ★

Actions Against Environmental Crimes
Enforcement actions taken by the U.S. Department of Justice from 1983 through 1989.

Fiscal Year	Indictments	Pleas/ Convictions	Fines Imposed in dollars	Jail Terms yr/mo/day	Actual Confinement yr/mo/day
1983	40	40	341,100	11/0/0	5/0/0
1984	43	32	384,290	5/3/0	1/7/0
1985	40	37	565,850	5/5/0	2/11/0
1986	94[1]	67[1]	1,917,602	124/2/2	31/4/12
1987	127	86	3,046,060	32/4/7	14/9/22
1988	124	63	7,091,876	39/3/1	8/3/7
1989	101	107	12,750,330	53/1/0	37/2/0
Total	569	432	26,097,108	268/8/10	98/11/11

Source: Council on Environmental Quality, *20th Annual Report 1990*, Washington, D.C., p. 174, from U.S. Department of Justice, Environmental Crimes Section, Information Sheet (1989). *Note:* 1. Pesticide investigation in Texas and Louisiana not included in total.

★ 785 ★

Air Pollution Standards Violations - Selected Cities

City	Number of days above WHO standard	
	Sulfur Dioxide	Particu- lates
New Delhi	6	294
Xian	71	273
Beijing	68	272
Shenyang	146	219
Tehran	104	174
Bangkok	0	97
Madrid	35	60
Kuala Lampur	0	37
Zagreb	30	34
Sao Paulo	12	31
Paris	46	3
New York	8	0
Milan	66	n.a
Seoul	87	n.a

Source: World Watch, May/June, 1990, p. 31, from United Nations Environment Program and World Health Organization, *Assessment of Urban Air Quality* (Nairobi: Global Environment Monitoring System, 1988). *Notes:* For Madrid, San Paulo, and Paris, the reading is of smoke rather than particulates. na - Not available. WHO - World Health Organization.

★ 786 ★

Asbestos Enforcement

Increased enforcement activity by the U.S. Environmental Protection Agency is shown by contractors' reports and inspection actions for the 1985 to 1989 period.

Fiscal year	Job notices to EPA	EPA, state inspections
1985	21,000	8,600
1988	55,000	20,000
1989	65,000	23,000

Source: ENR, August 31,1989, p. 10, from U.S. Environmental Protection Agency.

★ 787 ★

Enforcement of the Hazardous Materials Transportation Act

Civil enforcement actions taken by the U.S. Department of Transportation in 1987 and 1988.

Agency and year	Actions Initiated	Actions Completed	Letters of Warning	Penalties Total in dollars	Penalties Average in dollars
Federal Aviation Administration					
1987	112	45	-	357,600	7,964
1988	112	37	-	279,500	7,554
Federal Highway Administration					
1987	N/A	65	-	290,300	4,466
1988	N/A	18	-	103,300	5,722
Federal Railroad Administration					
1987	43	43	-	565,800	13,158
1988	34	38	-	379,125	9,793
Research and Special Programs Administration					
1987	81	36	170	142,125	3,948
1988	120	98	161	392,900	4,009
U.S. Coast Guard					
1987	1,083	272	64	111,118	884
1988	1,131	321	120	119,687	823

Source: Council on Environmental Quality, *20th Annual Report 1990*, Washington, D.C., p. 171, from U.S. Department of Transportation, *Annual Report on Hazardous Materials Transportation - Calendar Year 1988*, DOT, Washington, D.C. (1989). *Note:* - Not available.

★ 788 ★

EPA Clean Air Enforcement Actions

Enforcement actions initiated from 1989, by act and fiscal year.

	Fiscal Year									
	1980	1981	1982	1983	1984	1985	1986	1987	1988	1989
Clean Air Act	86	112	21	41	141	122	143	191	224	336
Clean Water Act	569	562	329	781	1,644	1,031	990	1,214	1,345	2,146
Safe Drinking Water Act	569	562	329	781	1,644	1,031	990	1,214	1,345	2,146
Resource Conservation & Recovery Act	0	159	237	436	554	327	235	243	309	453
Comprehensive Environmental Response, Compensation & Liability Act	0	0	0	0	137	160	139	135	224	220
Federal Insecticide, Fungicide, Rodenticide Act	176	154	176	296	272	236	338	360	376	443
Toxic Substance Control Act	70	120	101	294	376	733	781	1,051	607	538
Total	901	1,107	864	1,848	3,124	2,609	2,626	3,194	3,085	4,136

Source: Council on Environmental Quality, *20th Annual Report 1990*, Washington, D.C., p. 155, from U.S. Environmental Protection Agency, Fiscal Year 1989 Enforcement Accomplishments Report, EPA, Washington, D.C. (1990).

★ 789 ★

Safe Drinking Water Act Violations

Data shown are violations in 1988, by state.

State	Number of Violations
Highest	
New Jersey	20,350
Pennsylvania	7,405
Washington[2]	7,094
Puerto Rico[2]	5,459
Alaska[2]	5,359
Lowest	
Michigan[1]	0
Rhode Island	46
Maine	61
Connecticut	95
Hawaii	118

Source: Garbage, November/December 1990, p. 63, from *Danger on Tap*, National Wildlife Federation, 1988. *Notes:* 1. 1987 data. 2. Federal Data Incomplete.

★ 790 ★

Transportation Department Hazardous Materials Penalties

Total HAZMAT (hazardous materials) civil penalties collected by Department of Transportation Administrations.

Administrations	Fiscal Year penalties in dollars			
	1985	1986	1987	1988
Federal Air Administration	291,100	383,250	305,900	154,100
Federal Highway Administration	437,225	366,500	292,300	218,650
Federal Railroad Administration	655,050	621,575	646,750	396,425
Research & Special Programs Administration	127,925	79,163	126,625	335,900
U.S. Coast Guard	104,100	23,645	83,150	87,900
Total	1,615,400	1,474,133	1,454,725	1,192,975

Source: Transportation of Hazardous Materials by Rail: Hearings Before the Government Activities and the Transportation Subcommittee of the Committee on Government Operations, House of Representatives, 101st Congress, and Session, February 28, 1990, p. 58, from the Department of Transportation.

★ 791 ★

Underground Storage Tank Inspection Deadlines

Environmental Protection Agency estimates that half a million tanks are leaking; to protect groundwater from leaking underground storage tanks, all must be equipped with leak-detection devices by 1993.

Tank age in years	Deadline
25+ (or age unknown)	Dec. 1989
20-25	Dec. 1990
15-19	Dec. 1991
10-14	Dec. 1992
0-9	Dec. 1993

Source: Chemical Engineering, January 1991, p. 31.

★ 792 ★

Water Quality in Rivers & Streams - Violation Rate

In percent. Violation level based on U.S. Environmental Protection Agency water quality criteria (shown in footnotes). Violation rate represents the proportion of all measurements of a specific water quality pollutant which exceeds the "violation level" for that pollutant. "Violation" does not necessarily imply a legal violation. Data based on U.S. Geological Survey's National Stream Quality Accounting Network (NASQAN) data system; for details, see source. Years refer to water years. A water year begins in October and ends in September.

Pollutant	1975	1980	1981	1982	1983	1984	1985	1986	1987	1988
Fecal coliform bacteria[1]	36	31	30	33	34	30	28	24	23	22
Dissolved oxygen[2]	5	5	4	5	4	3	3	3	2	2
Phosphorus, total, as phosporus[3]	5	4	4	3	3	4	3	3	3	4
Lead, dissolved[4]	[6]	5	3	2	5	[7]	[7]	[7]	[7]	[7]
Cadmium, dissolved[5]	[6]	1	1	1	1	[7]	[7]	[7]	[7]	[7]

Source: U.S. Department of Commerce, Bureau of the Census, *Statistical Abstract of the United States 1990 (110th ed.)*, Superintendent of Documents, Washington, D.C., p. 202., from U.S. Geological Survey, national-level data, unpublished; State-level data, *Water-Data Report*, annual series prepared in cooperation with the State governments. Mg = miligrams. *Notes:* 1. Above 200 cells per ml. 2. Below 5 mg per liter. 3. Above 1.0 mg per liter. 4. Above 50 micrograms per liter. 5. Above 10 micrograms per liter. 6. Base figure too small to meet statistical standards for reliability of derived figures. 7. Less than 1.

Environmental Impact Statements

★ 793 ★

Impact Reports Filed by Federal Agencies

Federal Agencies	1987	1988	1989
Agriculture	75	68	101
Commerce	9	3	5
Defense	2	4	1
Air Force	9	3	12
Army	10	3	11
COE	76	69	47
Navy	9	6	4
Energy	11	16	12
EPA	19	23	24
GSA	1	3	0
HUD	6	0	2
ICC	2	0	0
Interior	110	120	65
NRC	3	2	3
Transportation	101	91	77
TVA	0	0	0
Other	12	17	28
Total	455	428	392

Source: Council on Environmental Quality, *20th Annual Report 1990*, Washington, D.C., p. 439, from U.S. Environmental Protection Agency, Office of Federal Activities, Unpublished data. Washington, D.C. Years refer to calendar years. Number of Environmental Impact Statements (EISs) includes draft EISs, EIS supplements, and Final EISs filed during the specified year. Some proposed projects may have several draft and final EISs filed over a period of years.

Goals

★ 794 ★

Clean Water Act Goals in Estuaries

State	Fishable Goal (square miles)				Swimmable Goal (square miles)			
	Assessed	Meeting	Not Meeting	Not Attainable	Assessed	Meeting	Not Meeting	Not Attainable
Alabama	53	50	3	-	53	50	3	-
Connecticut	600	598	2	0	600	570	30	0
Delaware River Basin	866	845	21	-	866	855	11	-
District of Columbia	6	0	6	0	6	0	6	0
Florida	2,655	2,364	291	0	2,655	2,364	291	0
Georgia	594	584	10	-	-	-	-	-
Hawaii	40	40	0	0	40	40	0	0
Louisiana	4,928	4,926	2	-	4,928	4,928	0	-
Maine	1,633	1,595	38	0	1,633	1,623	10	0
Maryland	1,981	0	1,981	-	1,981	1,974	7	-
Massachusetts	171	116	55	-	171	79	92	-
Mississippi	133	132	1	0	133	132	1	0
New Hampshire	17	17	0	0	17	17	0	0
New Jersey	259	117	124	18	189	117	54	18
New York	1,564	1,234	283	47	1,564	1,487	30	47
Rhode Island	191	178	6	7	191	178	6	7
South Carolina	663	640	23	-	663	636	27	-
Texas	1,990	1,990	0	-	1,990	0	-	
Virginia	1,800	1,604	196	-	1,800	1,604	196	-
Washington	2,114	2,008	106	0	2,114	1,963	151	0
Totals	22,258	19,038	3,148	72	21,594	20,607	915	72

Source: National Water Quality Inventory, 1988, Report to Congress, U.S. Environmental Protection Agency, Washington, D.C., April 1990, p. 58, from 1988 State Section 305(b) reports. *Note:* - Not reported.

★ 795 ★

Clean Water Act Goals in Great Lakes

State	Fishable Goal (shoreline miles)				Swimmable Goal (shoreline miles)			
	Assessed	Meeting	Not Meeting	Not Attainable	Assessed	Meeting	Not Meeting	Not Attainable
Illinois	63	0	63	0	63	63	0	0
Indiana	43	0	43	0	43	43	0	0
Minnesota	272	272	0	-	-	-	-	-
New York	577	114	463	0	577	563	14	0
Ohio	236	0	236	-	236	231	5	-
Totals	1,191	386	805	0	919	900	19	0

Source: National Water Quality Inventory, 1988, Report to Congress, U.S. Environmental Protection Agency, Washington, D.C., April 1990, p. 37, from 1988 State Section 305(b) reports. *Note:* - Not reported.

★ 796 ★

Clean Water Act Goals in Lakes and Reservoirs

State	Fishable Goal (miles)				Swimmable Goal (miles)			
	Assessed	Meeting	Not Meeting	Not Attainable	Assessed	Meeting	Not Meeting	Not Attainable
Alabama	491,566	405,486	86,080	-	491,566	405,486	86,080	-
Colorado	124,973	123,111	1,862	0	124,973	124,973	0	0
Connecticut	21,701	18,826	2,875	0	21,701	21,701	0	0
District of Columbia	136	0	136	0	136	0	136	0
Florida	947,200	846,080	101,120	0	947,200	846,080	101,120	0
Georgia	417,730	412,357	5,373	-	417,730	412,357	5,373	-
Illinois	183,572	166,248	17,324	0	183,572	77,176	106,396	0
Indiana	104,540	104,424	116	0	104,540	104,361	179	0
Iowa	80,249	79,534	712	3	80,249	77,350	686	2,213
Kansas	173,884	173,809	75	-	173,884	173,809	75	-
Kentucky	214,483	214,483	0	0	214,483	214,483	0	0
Louisiana	517,476	517,390	86	-	517,476	517,390	86	-
Maine	994,560	979,558	15,002	0	994,560	958,080	36,480	0
Maryland	17,448	17,442	6	-	17,448	17,446	2	-
Mississippi	500,000	500,000	0	0	500,000	500,000	0	0
Missouri	288,012	285,701	2,311	0	288,012	288,012	0	0
Montana	663,363	650,763	12,600	0	663,363	663,363	0	0
New Hampshire	149,854	149,854	0	0	149,854	149,854	0	0
New Mexico	47,308	47,308	0	0	47,308	47,308	0	0
New York	750,000	537,000	213,000	0	750,000	670,000	80,000	0
North Carolina	305,367	295,687	9,680	-	305,367	303,180	2,187	-
North Dakota	619,334	608,657	9,792	885	619,334	614,067	5,267	0

[Continued]

★ 796 ★

Clean Water Act Goals in Lakes and Reservoirs
[Continued]

State	Fishable Goal (miles)				Swimmable Goal (miles)			
	Assessed	Meeting	Not Meeting	Not Attainable	Assessed	Meeting	Not Meeting	Not Attainable
Ohio	-	-	-	-	100,259	21,799	78,460	-
Oregon	504,928	504,928	0	-	504,928	504,928	0	-
Puerto Rico	11,146	6,395	2,581	2,170	11,146	6,395	3,915	836
Rhode Island	16,089	14,443	1,122	524	16,089	14,443	1,122	524
South Carolina	410,407	410,107	300	-	410,407	408,742	1,665	-
South Dakota	662,532	662,532	0	0	662,532	662,532	0	0
Tennessee	538,657	496,337	42,320	-	538,657	521,235	17,422	-
Texas	1,410,240	1,410,240	0	-	1,410,240	1,408,585	1,655	-
Vermont	225,350	222,772	2,274	304	203,647	202,808	838	1
Virginia	160,985	147,248	13,737	0	121,777	121,648	0	129
Washington	156,518	122,834	33,684	0	156,518	155,938	580	0
West Virginia	19,171	17,441	1,730	0	19,171	19,171	0	0
Wyoming	427,219	427,219	0	0	245,311	245,311	0	0
Totals	12,155,998	11,576,214	575,898	3,886	12,013,438	11,480,011	529,724	3,703

Source: National Water Quality Inventory, 1988, Report to Congress, U.S. Environmental Protection Agency, Washington, D.C., April 1990, p. 27, from 1988 State Section 305(b) reports *Note:* - Not reported.

★ 797 ★

Clean Water Act Goals in Oceans

State	Fishable Goal (coastal miles)				Swimmable Goal (coastal miles)			
	Assessed	Meeting	Not Meeting	Not Attainable	Assessed	Meeting	Not Meeting	Not Attainable
Alabama	50	50	0	0	50	50	0	0
Florida	835	835	0	0	835	835	0	0
Hawaii	824	824	0	0	824	824	0	0
Maryland	32	32	0	-	32	32	0	-
Mississippi	81	81	0	0	81	81	0	0
New Hampshire	18	18	0	0	18	18	0	0
New York	130	60	70	0	130	129	1	0
Puerto Rico	434	415	19	0	434	219	24	191
Virginia	112	112	0	0	112	112	0	0
Washington	163	163	0	0	163	163	0	0
Totals	2,679	2,590	89	0	2,679	2,463	25	191

Source: National Water Quality Inventory, 1988, Report to Congress, U.S. Environmental Protection Agency, Washington, D.C., April 1990, p. 73, from 1988 State Section 305(b) reports. *Note:* - Not reported.

★ 798 ★

Clean Water Act Goals in Rivers and Steams

State	Fishable Goal (miles)				Swimmable Goal (miles)			
	Assessed	Meeting	Not Meeting	Not Attainable	Assessed	Meeting	Not Meeting	Not Attainable
Alabama	11,174	9,925	801	448	11,174	9,925	801	448
Arkansas	10,820	10,581	239	-	10,099	8,107	1,992	-
Colorado	10,823	8,960	1,040	823	10,000	9,474	526	0
Connecticut	880	738	140	2	880	682	196	2
Delaware	467	349	118	-	467	309	158	-
Delaware River Basin	206	206	0	0	206	194	12	-
District of Columbia	26	0	26	0	26	0	26	0
Florida	7,943	7,308	600	35	7,943	7,308	600	35
Georgia	20,000	19,443	557	-	-	-	-	-
Hawaii	349	349	0	0	349	349	0	0
Illinois	12,970	12,488	482	0	2,994	730	2,189	75
Indiana	5,181	4,089	1,015	77	5,181	4,269	835	77
Iowa	8,235	6,714	1,497	24	8,235	1,638	580	6,017
Kansas	6,910	6,590	320	-	5,079	4,027	1,052	-
Kentucky	8,633	7,841	792	-	2,406	1,308	1,098	-
Louisiana	8,483	8,458	25	-	8,483	8,390	93	-
Maine	31,672	31,377	295	0	31,672	31,377	295	0
Maryland	9,300	8,660	640	-	9,300	9,286	14	-
Massachusetts	1,646	1,498	148	-	1,646	760	886	-
Mississippi	15,622	15,200	422	0	15,622	14,785	837	0
Missouri	19,630	10,147	1,037	8,446	19,630	10,147	1,037	8,446
Montana	19,505	18,891	614	0	19,505	19,505	0	0
Nebraska	5,690	4,476	1,214	-	2,264	810	1,454	-
New Hampshire	1,331	1,160	171	0	1,331	950	334	47
New Jersey	1,867	1,463	404	-	592	91	501	-
New Mexico	576	554	22	0	576	576	0	0
New York	70,000	53,700	15,000	1,300	70,000	69,200	800	0
North Carolina	33,275	22,375	10,900	-	33,275	22,375	10,900	-
North Dakota	9,851	9,389	462	0	9,851	9,287	564	0
Ohio River Valley	981	941	40	0	981	819	162	0
Oklahoma	19,791	18,834	436	521	19,791	17,663	2,128	0
Oregon	27,738	26,197	1,541	-	27,738	26,772	966	-
Pennsylvania	13,242	9,642	3,600	-	13,242	9,642	3,600	-
Puerto Rico	5,373	3,587	1,359	327	5,373	3,650	1,151	572
Rhode Island	581	465	27	89	581	465	27	89
South Carolina	3,795	3,477	318	-	3,795	2,199	1,596	-
South Dakota	3,750	2,840	910	0	939	659	280	0
Tennessee	11,081	10,857	224	-	11,081	10,420	661	-
Texas	13,998	13,843	155	-	13,998	12,616	1,382	-
Vermont	5,162	4,990	172	0	5,162	4,787	132	243
Virginia	3,532	1,210	2,322	-	3,532	1,210	2,322	-
Washington	4,637	3,168	1,469	0	4,637	2,898	1,739	0
West Virginia	14,340	13,005	1,335	0	14,340	13,005	1,335	0

[Continued]

★ 798 ★

Clean Water Act Goals in Rivers and Steams
[Continued]

State	Fishable Goal (miles)				Swimmable Goal (miles)			
	Assessed	Meeting	Not Meeting	Not Attainable	Assessed	Meeting	Not Meeting	Not Attainable
Wyoming	19,437	19,430	7	0	947	947	0	0
Totals	480,503	415,515	52,896	12,092	414,923	353,611	45,261	16,051

Source: National Water Quality Inventory, 1988, Report to Congress, U.S. Environmental Protection Agency, Washington, D.C., April 1990, p. 12, from 1988 State Section 305(b) reports *Note:* - Not reported.

★ 799 ★

Power Plants to Meet Clean Air Act

```
Indiana - 15
Ohio - 15
Kentucky - 10
Pennsylvania - 9
Illinois - 8
Missouri - 8
Wisconsin - 6
Iowa - 6
West Virginia - 6
Georgia - 5
New York - 5
Tennessee - 4
Maryland - 3
Florida - 2
Alabama - 2
Michigan - 1
Minnesota - 1
New Hampshire - 1
New Jersey - 1
Kansas - 1
Mississippi - 1
```
Chart shows data from column 1.

The 110 plants named in the legislation representing 89,545 MW of power production capacity must comply with restriction in Title IV by January 1, 1995 unless they qualify for extension.

State	Number of Targeted Plants	Generation Capacity (Megawatts)
Alabama	2	3,363
Florida	2	2,771
Georgia	5	8,444
Iowa	6	977
Illinois	8	6,002
Indiana	15	11,275
Kansas	1	158
Kentucky	10	4,649
Maryland	3	2,390
Michigan	1	650
Minnesota	1	163
Missouri	8	6,547

[Continued]

★ 799 ★

Power Plants to Meet Clean Air Act

[Continued]

State	Number of Targeted Plants	Generation Capacity (Megawatts)
Mississippi	1	750
New Hampshire	1	459
New Jersey	1	299
New York	5	2,408
Ohio	15	14,131
Pennsylvania	9	7,675
Tennessee	4	6,331
Wisconsin	6	2,740
West Virginia	6	7,363
Total Targeted Capacity		89,545

Source: Electric Light and Power, March 1991, p. 4, from Arthur Andersen, Cambridge Energy Research Associates.

★ 800 ★

Statewide Solid Waste Management Goals

Percentiles related to goal to be achieved. Thus 10% under Source Reduction indicates a goal of 10% waste reduction by the deadline year.

State	Source Reduction	Recycling	Composting	Source Red. Recycling & Composting	Source Red. & Recycling	Recycling & Composting	Other	Mandated	Deadline
California				50%[2]				Yes	2000
Connecticut	[3]	25%						Yes	1991
Delaware		10%	20%				60%[4]	No	1994
District of Columbia		35%					50%[4]	Yes	1994
Florida					30%			Yes	1995
Illinois		25%						Yes	2000
Indiana		25%						No	1992[5]
Iowa					50%			No	2000
Louisiana				25%				Yes	1992
Maine						50%		No	1994
Massachusetts	10%	38%	3%				49%[4]	No	2000
Michigan	8-12%	20-30%	8-12%				35-45%[4,6]	No	2005
Minnesota		25%						Yes	1993
Missouri				35%				No	2000
New Jersey		25%[7]						Yes	N/A
New York	10%					40%	33%[4]	No	2000
North Carolina				25%				Yes	1993
Ohio					25%			Yes	1994
Pennsylvania	[8]	25%						Yes	1997
Rhode Island		15%						Yes	1993
Vermont		40%						Yes	2000
Virginia		25%						Yes	1995

[Continued]

★ 800 ★

Statewide Solid Waste Management Goals
[Continued]

State	Source Reduction	Recycling	Composting	Source Red. Recycling & Composting	Source Red. & Recycling	Recycling & Composting	Other	Mandated	Deadline
Washington				50%				Yes	1995
Wisconsin	2%	10%	10%				45%[4,6]	No	2000

Source: BioCycle, April 1990, p. 35. *Notes:* 1. Includes leaf or yard waste composting. 2. May include 10 percent waste transformation. 3. Goal is no change in waste generation rate. 4. Incineration. 5. Or within five years of solid waste plan adoption. 6. Reuse goal of 4-6 percent for Michigan and 2 percent for Wisconsin. 7. Does not include leaf composting as part of the goal. 8. Goal is to reduce the amount of waste generated.

Guidelines

★ 801 ★

Agriculture - Manure Application Guidelines

Data were developed by the University of Minnesota for the Soil Conservation Service. The technical guide recommends that all livestock producers observe setback distances, shown in feet, when placing organic wastes next to surface waters, ditches, and other water conduits or water bodies.

Time of year	Slope (percent)	Soil texture	Separation distances (feet)
May-October	0.0-6.0	Coarse	100
November-April	0.0-6.0	Coarse	200
May-October	0.0-6.0	Med./fine	200
November-April	0.0-6.0	Med./fine	300
May-October	>6.0	Coarse	200
May-October	>6.0	Med./fine	300
November-April	>6.0	All soil	[1]

Source: Farm Journal February 1990, p. 24, from Minnesota Pollution Control Agency. *Note:* 1. Not recommended.

★ 802 ★

EEC Limits for Heavy Metals in Soils and Sludges

Element	Soils[1] (mg/kg)	Sludges (mg/kg)	Max Addition to Soils[2] (kg/ha yr)[1]
Cd	1-3.0	20-40	0.5
Cu	50-140.0	1000-1750	12.0
Ni	30-75.0	300-400	3.0
Pb	50-300.0	750-1200	15.0
Zn	150-300.0	2500-4000	30.0
Hg	1-1.5	16-25	0.1
Cr[3]	-	-	-

Source: BioCycle, June 1990, p. 37 *Notes:* 1. Limits valid for soil at pH values between 6 and 7. 2. On a 10-year average. 3. The Council of the European Communities will fix values for Cr later on the basis of new proposals.

★ 803 ★

EPA Recommendation for Minimum Recycled Paper Percent

EPA recommends that minium content percentages should be the highest possible but no lower than the recommended levels.

	Minimum percentage of recovered materials	Minimum percentage of postconsumer recovered materials	Minimum percentage of recycling wastepaper[1]
Newsprint	-[2]	40	-
High-grade bleached printing and writing paper:			
Offset printing	-	-	50
Mimeo and duplicator paper	-	-	50
Writing (stationery)	-	-	50
Office paper (e.g. notepads)	-	-	50
Paper for high-speed copiers	-	-	-
Envelopes	-	-	50
Forms bond, including computer paper and carbonless	-	-	-
Book paper	-	-	50
Bond paper	-	-	50
Ledger	-	-	50
Cover stock	-	-	50
Cotton fiber paper	25	-	-
Tissue products:			
Toilet tissue	-	20	-
Paper towels	-	40	-
Paper napkins	-	30	-

[Continued]

★ 803 ★

EPA Recommendation for Minimum Recycled Paper Percent
[Continued]

	Minimum percentage of recovered materials	Minimum percentage of postconsumer recovered materials	Minimum percentage of recycling wastepaper[1]
Facial tissue	-	5	-
Doilies	-	40	-
Industrial wipers	-	0	-
Unbleached packaging:			
Corrugated boxes	-	35	-
Fiber boxes	-	35	-
Brown paper (e.g. bags)	-	5	-
Recycled paperboard:			
Recycled paperboard products, including folding cartons	-	80	-
Pad backing	-	90	-

Source: Pulp & Paper, September 1989, p. 49. *Notes:* 1. Wastepaper refers to specified postconsumer and other recovered materials. 2. The Environmental Protection Agency found sufficient production of these papers with recycled content to assure adequate competition.

★ 804 ★

Maximum Heavy Metals for Agricultural Land

Element	CEC[1] Limit in soil (mg/kg)	Max. Increase (CEC) Concentration in soil/yr at 25 cm depth (mg/kg soil)	Max. Increase (EPA) Concentration in soil/yr at 25 cm depth (mg/kg soil)
Cd	1-3.0	0.05	5.5
Cu	50-140.0	3.7	14.1
Ni	30-75.0	0.9	24.0
Pb	50-300.0	4.6	38.5
Zn	150-300.0	9.2	52.3
Hg	1-1.5	0.03	4.6

Source: BioCycle, June 1990, p. 38 *Note:* 1. Council of the European Communities.

★ 805 ★

Recommended Minimum Standards - Insulation Products

EPA recommended minimum content standards for recovered materials in building insulation products.

Material type	Percent by Weight	Source
Cellulose loose-fill and spray-on	75	postconsumer recovered paper
Perlite composite board	23	postconsumer recovered paper
Plastic rigid foams Polyisocyanurate/polyurethane rigid foam	9	recovered material
foam-in-place	5	recovered material
glass fiber reinforced	6	recovered material
Phenolic rigid foam	5	recovered material
Rock wool	50	recovered material

Source: BioCycle, May 1989, p. 61.

Legislation

★ 806 ★

CFC Law Provisions, 1989-1990

Chlorofluorocarbon legislative provisions proposed at the state and local level in the 1989-1990 time frame. Data show the provisions and frequency of introduction.

	Frequency (in percent)
Recover and Recycle	18.0
Foam and Insulation Products	14.3
Container-Size Sales	13.3
Certification and/or Permits	10.5
Disposal	6.7
Use in Manufacture, Production, etc.	5.7
Study Evaluate and/or Recommend	5.7
Non-Essential Product Bans	4.8
Intentional Venting	3.8
HCFCs	2.9
Labelling Requirements	2.9
Other	11.4

Source: ASHRAE Journal, January 1991, p. 10, from Alliance for Responsible CFC Policy.

★ 807 ★

Disposal Bans by State

State	Act	Year	Effective Date
Connecticut			
Designated recyclables[1]	87-544	1987	1/91
Nickel/Cadmium batteries	89-385	1989	1993
Florida			
Auto batteries, tires	SB 1192	1988	1/89
Yard waste[2]			1/92
Batteries, Tires			7/89
White goods			1/90
Demolition debris[2]			7/89
Used oil			10/88
Hawaii			

[Continued]

★ 807 ★

Disposal Bans by State
[Continued]

State	Act	Year	Effective Date
Auto batteries	HB 1445	1989	1/90
Illinois			
Auto batteries	PA-86-723	1989	9/90
Tires	PA-86-452	1989	7/95
Yard waste	PA-86-1430	1989	7/90
Iowa			
Beverage containers	HF 753	1989	7/90
Auto batteries			7/90
Used oil			7/90
Tires[4]			7/91
Yard waste			1/91
Non-degradable grocery bags			7/92
Minnesota			
Auto batteries	115A.915	1987	1/88
Tires	115A.904	1984	7/85
White goods	115A.9561	1989	7/90
Yard waste (Metro Area)	115A.931	1988	1/90
Yard waste (Statewide)	115A.931	1988	1/92
Used oil	115A.916	1987	1/88
New Jersey			
Leaves	PL 1987,C.102	1987	9/88
North Carolina			
Auto batteries	SB 111	1989	1/91
Tires[4]			3/90
Used oil			10/90
White goods			1/91
Yard waste[2]			1/93
Ohio			
Yard waste	HB 592	1988	12/93
Oregon			
Auto batteries	HB 3305	1989	1/90
Pennsylvania			
Auto batteries	101	1988	9/88
Leaves			9/26/90
Washington			
Auto batteries	ESHB 1671	1989	8/89

[Continued]

★ 807 ★

Disposal Bans by State
[Continued]

State	Act	Year	Effective Date
Wisconsin Yard waste	296	1987	1/93
Wyoming Auto	W.S. 35-11	1989	6/89

Source: BioCycle, April 1990, p. 37 *Notes:* 1. Leaves, lead acid batteries, used oil, scrap metal, corrugated cardboard, newspaper, glass food containers, metal food containers, white office paper (for commercial establishments only). 2. Cannot be placed in landfills. 3. Only pertains to beverage containers returned to wholesalers through Iowa's mandatory deposit law. 4. Only pertains to unshredded tires.

★ 808 ★

Mandatory Deposit Laws by State

State	Beverage Containers	Auto Batteries	Act	Year	Effective Date
Connecticut	x		CGS SEC 22A-243-246	1978	1980
Delaware	x[1]		Title 7, Del. Code, Chap 60	1979	1982
Florida		x[2]	SB 1192	1988	1/89
Illinois		x[2]	PA86-723	1989	9/90
Iowa	x		Chap. 445C	1978	1979
Maine	x		PL 1975,C.739 (As Amended)	1975	1978
Massachusetts	x		301 CMR 4.00	1981	1983
Michigan	x		MCL 445.571-.576 (As Amended)	1976	1978
Minnesota		x[3]	115A.9561	1989	10/89
New York	x		Title 10, C. 200	1982	1983

[Continued]

★ 808 ★

Mandatory Deposit Laws by State

[Continued]

State	Beverage Containers	Auto Batteries	Act	Year	Effective Date
Oregon	x		ORS 459.810-.890	1971	1972
		x^2	HB 3305	1989	1/90
Pennsylvania		x^2	101	1988	9/26/88
Rhode Island		x^3	23-60-1	1987	7/89
Vermont	x		Title 10, C. 53	1972	1973
Washington		x^3	ESHB 1671	1989	8/89
Wyoming		x^2	WS 35-11-509-513	1989	6/89

Source: BioCycle, April 1990, p. 38 *Notes:* 1. Any containers that holds a carbonated beverage, except aluminum. 2. Retailers are required to accept old lead acid batteries when a person purchases a new battery. 3. $5.00 deposit charged if an old battery is not returned when a new one is purchased.

★ 809 ★

Plastics Legislation in 1990

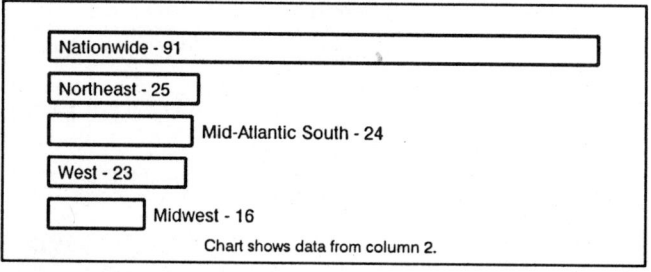

Number of proposed and enacted state bills in 1990 that would affect plastics and solid waste management.

Region	Proposed	Enacted
Northeast	201	25
Mid-Atlantic South	133	24
Midwest	98	16
West	75	23
Nationwide	508	91

Source: Recycling Today, January 1991, p. 36, from the Council for Solid Waste Solutions.

★ 810 ★

Recycled Newsprint Legislation in the U.S.

Fees or credits	Consumption[2]		Status
	Goal (percent)	Timetable	
State laws:			
California			
Penalties not to exceed $1,000/violation	25	1/1/91	Passed
	20	1993	Passed
Connecticut			
Florida			
10c/ton tax until 10/92; 50c/ton if goal not reached	50	1992	Passed
Illinois			
10c/ton tax; penalties not to exceed $5,000/violation	10	1992	Pending
	50	1998	
Louisana			
10c/ton tax			Failed
Maryland			
$30/ton credit on recycled newsprint consumed over goal	20	1992[3]	Pre-filed
	40	1994	
Massachusetts			
$56/ton credit on recycled newsprint			Pending
Missouri			
H.B 949 10% of the cost/ton of virgin newsprint consumed	10	1992	Pending
	50	1996	
S.B.513	10	1993	Filed
	50	1997	
Nebraska			
$1/ton tax			Failed
New Jersey			
A.B 4809	45	1990[4]	Pending
	90	1992	
A.B. 4703	45	1989	Pending
	90	1991	
New York			
Paper not meeting requirement not to be sold in state		1991[4]	Failed
North Carolina			
10c/ton tax			Failed
Oregon			
$1/ton tax			Failed
Rhode Island			
$11/ton tax by 1991; $56/ton by 1994			Pending
South Dakota			
10%/ton cost of virgin newsprint used short of goal	10	1992	Drafted
	50	1996	
Vermont	25	1991	Pre-filed
Virginia			
10c/ton tax			Failed

[Continued]

★ 810 ★

Recycled Newsprint Legislation in the U.S.
[Continued]

Fees or credits	Consumption[2] Goal (percent)	Consumption[2] Timetable	Status
Wisconsin			
$500 maximum penalty for not reporting	5	1991[5]	Pending
	20	2003	
Federal laws:			
S.B. 1763 Credits for excess recycled newsprint made is transferable	10	1990	Pending
	30	2000	
S.B. 1764 Credits for excess recycled newsprint used is transferable	15	1992	Pending
	40	2000	

Source: Pulp & Paper, March 1990, p. 31, from American Newspaper Publishers Association. *Notes:* 1. Fees are generally taxes or penalties on virgin-fiber newsprint consumed. Credits generally apply to recycled-fiber newsprint used, and are usually used to offset taxes/penalties. 2. Applies to amount of total consumption that must be recycled-fiber based, unless otherwise noted. Ranges imply goals to be phased-in between these dates. 3. Goals are aggregate of recycled fiber consumed in proportion to total newsprint consumed by individual publisher. 4. State task force has proposed voluntary guidelines. (New York's proposal is to increase recycled newsprint consumption gradually from 7% in 1990 to 40% by 2000.) 5. Goals are aggregate of statewide recycled fiber consumed in proportion to total newsprint consumed. Compromise reached late in 1989 proposes to make all consumption goals voluntary and only applicable when recycled-fiber newsprint is available in the quantity, at the quality, and of competitive price to virgin-fiber newsprint.

★ 811 ★

Recycling Legislation

State	General Solid Waste Management	Purchasing Preferences for Recyclables	Recycling: Program Requirements	Recycling: Planning and Goals	Recycling: Study	Recycling: Mandatory Source Separation	Nondegradables: Bans/ Restrictions	Nondegradables Taxes	Nondegradables: Incentives to Recycle	Labeling: Recyclable or Degradable	Waste-To-Energy Requirements
Arizona	-	-	-	-	S 1412	-	-	-	-	-	-
California	-	-	A 2831	-	-	-	A 2766	-	-	A 3299	A 2831
			A 612			-		-	-		
Connecticut	-	H 5885	-	-	-	-	-	-	-	-	-
Florida	S 1192	S 1192	S 1192	S 1192	-	S 1192	S 1192	S 1192	S 1192	S 1192	-
Hawaii	-	-	S 2882	-	-	-	-	-	-	-	-
Illinois	-	H 3389	H 4033	S 1616	-	-	-	-	-	-	-
Iowa	-	S 2086	-	-	-	-	-	-	H 2453	-	-
Louisiana	-	-	-	-	-	-	-	-	-	-	-
Maryland	H 714	-	H 714	H 714	-	H 714	-	-	-	-	-
Massachusetts	-	S 1176	-	-	-	-	-	-	-	-	-
Maine	-	-	-	-	-	-	H 1592	-	-	-	-
							H 1797				
Michigan	-	-	-	H 4174	-	-	H 4881	-	-	H 1806	S 907
Minnesota	H 2031	-	-	-	-	-	H 2031	-	-	H 2031	H 2031
New Hampshire	-	HR 53	-	-	-	-	-	-	-	-	-
New York	S 8107	S 8107	S 8107	S 8107	-	-	-	-	-	-	-
Ohio	H 592	-	-	H 592	-	-	-	-	H 1634	-	-
Oklahoma	S 435	S 435	S 435	S 435	-	-	-	-	-	-	-
Pennsylvania	S 528	S 528	S 528	S 528	-	S 528	S 528	-	-	-	H 1387
Rhode Island	-	-	S 2245	-	-	-	S 3050	-	-	-	-
Tennessee	-	-	-	-	HJR 627	-	-	-	-	-	-
Virginia	-	-	H 572	-	HJR 80	-	-	-	-	-	-
Washington	-	S 6446	H 1340	-	-	-	-	-	-	-	-
Wisconsin	-	A 648	-	-	-	-	-	-	-	A 650	-

Source: BioCycle, February 1989, p. 69 Letters and numbers refer to State Senate, Assembly and House bills.

★ 812 ★

State Mandated Recycling

States requiring local governmental units to include recycling as an element in solid waste management.

State	Type Government Required to Plan	Deadline For Plan	Act	Year Enacted
California	Cities and Counties	1/91[1]	AB 939	1989
Florida	Counties	7/89	SB 1192	1988
Illinois	Counties	[2]	PA 85-1198-& PA 86-228	
Iowa	Cities & Counties	N/A	HF 753	1989
Maryland	Counties[3]	7/90	HB 714	1988
Michigan	Counties	1990	PA 641 & PA 6	1979 1988
Minnesota	Counties	10/4/90	HF 1, S.S.89	
New Jersey	Counties	10/87	PL 1987,C.102	
North Carolina	Counties	10/90	SB 111	1989
Vermont	Waste Districts	7/90	78	1987
Virginia	Municipal- ities	7/90	HB 1743	1989

Source: BioCycle, April 1990, p. 36 N/A stands for not applicable. *Notes:* 1. Cities must adopt and submit plans to counties by 7/91. 2. 9/91 for counties over 100,000 population and cities over 1,000,000. 3/95 for counties with less than 100,000 population. 3. Baltimore City is also required to plan.

★ 813 ★

States Requiring Local Recycling Programs

State	Local Government Unit Involved	Deadline	Act
Connecticut	Cities	1/91	87-544
Maryland	Counties	1/94	HB 714 - 1988
Minnesota	Counties	10/90	HF 1; S.S. 89
North Carolina	[1]	7/91	SB 111 - 1989

[Continued]

★ 813 ★

States Requiring Local Recycling Programs
[Continued]

State	Local Government Unit Involved	Deadline	Act
Oregon Washington	[2] Counties and Cities	7/86 [3]	SB 405 - 1983 ESHB 1671-1989

Source: BioCycle, April 1990, p. 36 *Notes:* 1. Designated local government, which could be either a county or municipality. 2. The legislation did not place responsibility on any particular level of government or on the private sector. In practice, municipalities have assumed the responsibility. The legislation called for municipalities with a population of 4,000 or greater to have curbside recycling service. Programs must be fully implemented two years after plan adoption. 3. 7/91 for Spokane, Snohomish, King, Pierce and Kipsap Counties; 7/92 for all other counties west of the Cascade Mountains; 7/94 for all counties east of the Cascade Mountains.

★ 814 ★

States Requiring Local Units to Reach Waste Reduction Goals

State	Goal	Deadline	Type of Govt. Unit	Act	Year Enacted
California	50%[1]	1/2000	County/City	AB 939	1989
Florida	30%	12/31/94	County	SB 1192	1988
Louisiana	25%	12/31/92	Parish[2]	185	1989
Maryland	20%[3]	1994	County	HB 714	1988
Minnesota	35%[4]	12/31/93	County	HF 1; S.S.89	
New Jersey	25%	[5]	Municipality	PL 1987,C.107	
North Carolina	25%	1/93	County/ Municipality	SB 111	1989
Ohio	25%	6/24/94	SW Planning Dist.	HB 592	1988
Rhode Island	15%	[6]	Municipality	23-18, 23-19 & 37-15	1986
Vermont	40%	1/1/2000	SW Mgmt. Dist.	78	1987
Virginia	25%	12/31/95	Municipality	HB 1743	1989

Source: BioCycle, April 1990, p. 36 *Notes:* 1. May include 10 percent waste transformation. 2. Also targets major municipalities. 3. 20% recycling rate for counties with populations of more than 100,000. 15% recycling rate for counties with populations of less than 100,000. 4. 35% recycling rate for the seven counties in the Twin Cities metro area. 25% recycling rate for the remainder of Minnesota's counties. 5. Within two years after the implementation of the county recycling plan. 6. Within three years of a programs implementation.

★ 815 ★

States Requiring Mandatory Recycling Ordinances

The following states have passed legislation that requires municipalities to develop recycling programs and pass ordinances requiring participation of both residential and commercial waste generators.

State	Municipalities Involved	Deadline	Act
District of Columbia	N/A	N/A	7-226-1989
New Jersey	All	8/88	PL 1987, C107
New York	All	9/92	Chap 70-1988
Pennsylvania	[1]	9/26/91	101 - 1988
Rhode Island	All	[2]	23-18 - 1986

Source: BioCycle, April 1990, p. 35 N/A stands for not applicable. *Notes:* 1. All municipalities with 10,000 and above must pass mandatory ordinances. For municipalities with populations between 5,000 and 10,000, only those that have a population density of 300 people per square mile must pass ordinances. 2. Deadline is based on the implementation schedule of each municipality. All municipalities should have ordinances by 12/31/90.

★ 816 ★

States With Packaging/Product Taxes or Fees

State	Type of Product/Package	Type of Fee/Tax		Act	Effective Year	Date
		Amount	Per			
California	Tires	$.25	New Tire	AB 1843	1989	7/90
Florida	Tires	$1.00	New Tire	SB 1192	1988	1/90
	Newsprint	$.10	Ton[1]			1/89
	Containers	$.01	Container[2]			10/92
Illinois	Tires	$.50	Title	PA 86-452	1989	1/90
Louisiana	Tires	Not Set Yet		Act 185	1989	N/A
Maine	Tires	$1.00	New Tire	Chap. 585	1989	7/90
	White Goods	$15.00	Each			7/90
	Brown Goods	$15.00	Each			7/90
	Auto	$1.00	Battery			7/90
North Carolina	Tires	1% Sales Tax		SB 111	1989	1/90
Oklahoma	Tires	$1.00	New Tire	HB 1533	1989	7/89
Oregon	Tires	$1.00	New Tire	HB 2022	1987	1/88

[Continued]

★ 816 ★

States With Packaging/Product Taxes or Fees

[Continued]

State	Type of Product/ Package	Type of Fee/Tax		Act	Effective Year	Date
		Amount	Per			
Rhode Island	Tires	$.50	New Tire	H 5504 (C)	1989	1/90
	Used Oil	$.05	Quart			1/90
	Antifreeze	$.10	Gallon			1/90
	Org. Solvents	$.0025	Gallon			1/90
Virginia	Tires	$.50	New Tire	HB 1745	1989	1/90
Washington	Tires	$1.00	New Tire	ESHB 1671	1989	10/89
Wisconsin	Tires	$2.00	New Tire[4]	WA 110	1987	5/88

Source: BioCycle, April 1990, p. 39 N/A means not available. *Notes:* 1. Increases to $.50/ton in 1992 if at least newsprint is not made with at least 50% recycled fiber. 2. If a 50% recycling rate is not achieved for these containers by 1992, the fee will increase to $.02/container. 3. $3.00/each new vehicle purchased to cover costs of disposing of materials which are difficult to manage in disposal. 4. On new vehicles.

Permits

★817★

Stormwater Permitting Authority by State

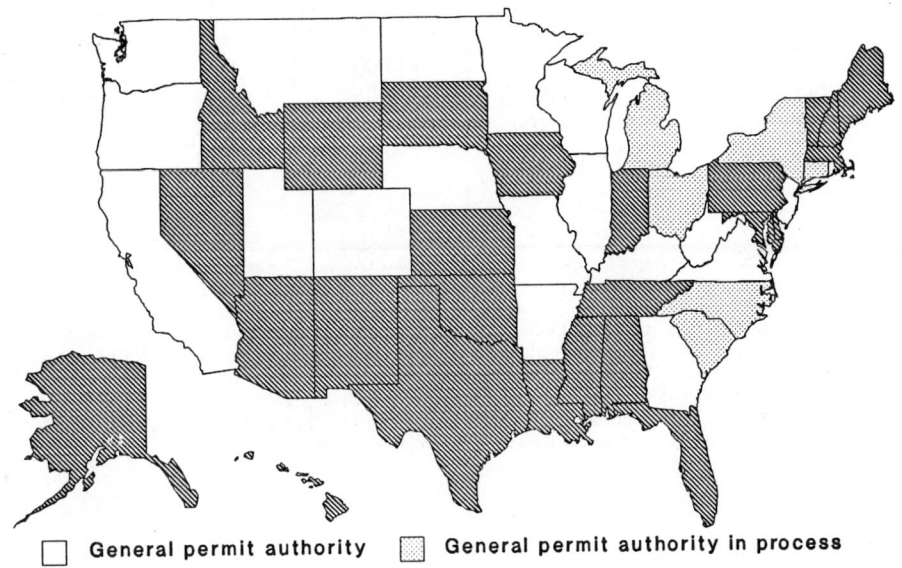

☐ General permit authority   ▦ General permit authority in process

▨ No general permit authority; EPA-managed

Source: ENR, June 17, 1991, p. 8, from U.S. Environmental Protection agency; Water Pollution Control Federation.

Policy

★818★

Greenhouse Gas Emission Policies of OECD Countries

Jurisdiction	Base level year	Stabilization year	Percent reduction target	Target year
Australia	1988	2000	20%[3]	2005
Austria	1987	[5]	20%[4]	2005
Canada[2]	1988	2005	[5]	[5]
Denmark	1988	2005	20%[4]	2000
France	1989/90	2000	[5]	[5]

[Continued]

★ 818 ★

Greenhouse Gas Emission Policies of OECD Countries
[Continued]

Jurisdiction	Base level year	Stabilization year	Percent reduction target	Target year
Germany[1]	1987	-	25%[4]	2005
Italy	1990	2000	20%[4]	2005
Japan	1990	2000	[5]	[5]
Netherlands	1989/90	1995	5%[4]	2000
New Zealand	1990	[5]	20%[4]	2005
Norway	1989	2000	[5]	[5]
Sweden[2]	1988	[5]	[5]	[5]
United Kingdom	1990	2005	[5]	[5]

Source: Changing by Degrees: Steps to Reduce Greenhouse Gases, U.S. Congress, Office of Technology Assessment, OTA-O-482, Washington, D.C., February 1991, p. 304, from OTA Survey of Embassies; Organization for Economic Cooperation and Development and International Energy Agency, "Summary of Actions in Member Countries to Deal With the Problem of Climate Change (Note by the Secretariat)," IEA/SLT(90)51(1st Revision), draft (Paris: Standing Group on Long-Term Cooperation, Committee for Energy Research and Development, Oct. 24, 1990). OECD stands for Organization for Economic Cooperation and Development. *Notes:* 1. Excluding eastern Germany. The German Bundestag's Enquete Commission has proposed a new target of 30 percent CO_2 reduction by 2005 for the entire country. 2. Tentative. 3. All gases. 4. Carbon dioxide. 5. Not declared.

★ 819 ★

State Procurement of Recycled Products

State	Paper Only	Recycled Products	Act	Year
California		x	AB 4	1989
Colorado		x	Ex. Order DO 11789	1989
Connecticut		x	88-231	1988
District of Columbia	x		7-226	1989
Florida		x	SB 1192	1988
Hawaii		x	HR 66	1989
Illinois	x		HB 3389	1988
Iowa	x		HF 753	1989
Louisiana		x	185	1989
Maine	x		PL 1989, C.585	1989
Maryland		x	HB 714	1988
Massachusetts		x	Exec Order 287	1987
Michigan	x		PA 412	1988
		x	PA 413	1988
Minnesota		x	HF 1, SS 89	1989
Missouri		x	HB 438	1989
New Hampshire		x	Exec Order	1988

[Continued]

★ 819 ★

State Procurement of Recycled Products
[Continued]

State	Paper Only	Recycled Products	Act	Year
New Jersey		x	89-3 PL 1987, C. 102	1987
New York	x		SFL C.849 Sec. 177 (As Amended)	1987
North Carolina		x	SB 111	1989
Ohio	x		HB 592	1988
Oklahoma	x		Title 74, Sec. 85.50-.57	1988
Oregon		x	ORS 279.371-.379	1975
Pennsylvania		x	101	1988
Rhode Island		x	23-18	1986
Vermont		x	78	1987
Virginia	x		HB 1747	1989
Washington		x	SSB 6446	1988

Source: BioCycle, April 1990, p.40.

Regulations

★ 820 ★

Fishing Restriction Reported by State

	No. of restrictions		Area affected			
	Advisories	Bans	River miles	Lake acres	Estuary Sq. miles	Great Lakes Shore miles
Arizona	2	0	-	-	-	-
Arkansas	0	1	-	-	-	-
California	8	12	92	292,867	3	-
Colorado	5	0	-	-	-	-
Connecticut	3	0	65	-	225	-
Delaware	2	0	-	-	-	-
Delaware River Basin	4	0	-	-	-	-
District of Columbia	0	0	-	-	-	-
Florida	0	0	-	-	-	-
Hawaii	2	0	-	-	-	-
Illinois	8	4	534	990,021	-	-

[Continued]

★ 820 ★

Fishing Restriction Reported by State

[Continued]

	No. of restrictions		Area affected			
	Advisories	Bans	River miles	Lake acres	Estuary Sq. miles	Great Lakes Shore miles
Indiana	10	12	585	-	-	43
Iowa	1	0	-	-	-	-
Kansas	3	1	44	-	-	-
Kentucky	1	1	112	-	-	-
Louisiana	6	0	25	1,066	-	-
Maine	1	4	128	1,976	-	-
Maryland	3	1	-	-	-	-
Massachusetts	7	1	-	-	-	-
Michigan	38	3	383	24,128	-	3,288
Minnesota	235	50	1,599	1,245,929	-	272
Mississippi	0	1	12	-	-	-
Missouri	15	0	833	700	-	-
Montana	1	0	-	-	-	-
Nevada	1	0	-	-	-	-
New Hampshire	0	0	-	-	-	-
New Jersey	6	7	-	-	72	-
New Mexico	0	0	-	-	-	-
New York	16	24	-	-	-	-
North carolina	1	0	-	1,900	-	-
North Dakota	0	0	-	-	-	-
Ohio	5	6	160	-	-	-
Ohio River Valley	1	0	40	-	-	-
Oklahoma	2	0	-	-	-	-
Oregon	1	0	-	1,139	-	-
Pennsylvania	6	2	-	-	-	-
Rhode Island	1	1	-	-	-	-
South Carolina	2	0	-	-	-	-
South Dakota	0	0	-	-	-	-
Tennessee	13	0	204	-	-	-
Vermont	1	1	0	174,175	-	-
Virgin Islands	0	0	-	-	-	-
Virginia	2	1	296	-	-	-
Washington	12	0	19	-	34	-
West Virginia	1	0	48	-	-	-
Wisconsin	160	1	304	102,083	-	495
Wyoming	0	1	4	0	-	-
Totals	586	135	5,487	2,835,984	334	4,098

Source: National Water Quality Inventory, 1988, Report to Congress, U.S. Environmental Protection Agency, Washington, D.C., April 1990, p. 107, from 1988 State Section 305(b) reports. - Not reported.

★ 821 ★

Fishing Restrictions Nationwide

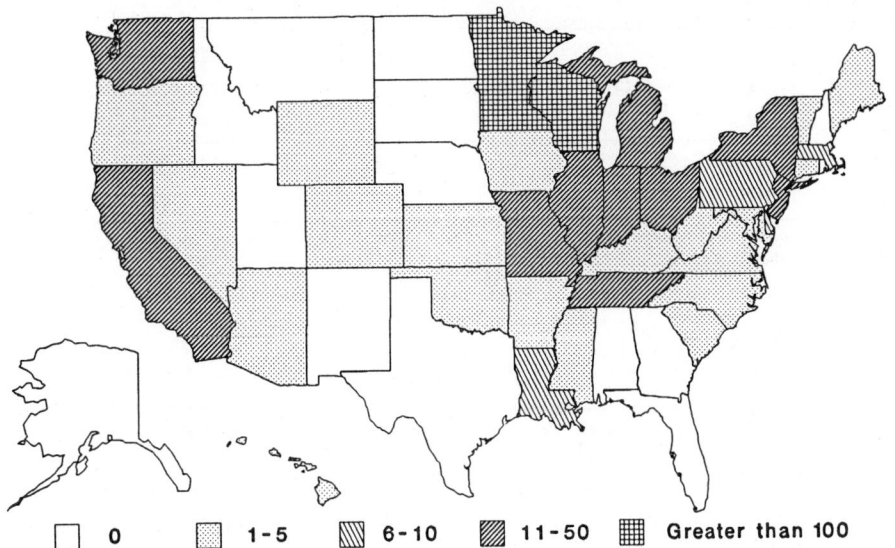

| | 0 | | 1-5 | | 6-10 | | 11-50 | | Greater than 100 |

Source: The Quality of Our Nation's Water: A Summary of the 1988 National Water Quality Inventory, U.S. Environmental Protection Agency, EPA 440/4-90-005, May 1990, p. 21, from 1988 State Section 305(b) Reports.

Standards

★ 822 ★

Drinking Water Standards

New drinking water standards announced by the U.S. Environmental Protection Agency with effect in July 1992.

Currently used pesticides and nitrates	Maximum Containment Level (mg/l)
Alachlor	0.002
Aldicarb	0.003
Aldicarb sulfone[1]	0.003
Aldicarb sulfoxide[1]	0.003
Atrazine	0.003
Carbofuran	0.040
2,4-D	0.070
Methoxychlor	0.040

[Continued]

★ 822 ★

Drinking Water Standards
[Continued]

Currently used pesticides and nitrates	Maximum Containment Level (mg/l)
Nitrate	10.000
Nitrite	1.000

Source: Farm Journal, February 1991, p. 24H. *Note:* 1. These chemicals are degraded from aldicarb by plants.

★ 823 ★

Drinking Water Standards for Livestock

Substance/comments	Recommended maximum safe levels (ppm)[1]
Nitrates:	
NO$_3$	450
NO$_3$-N	100[2]
Sulfate	1000-1500[3]
Total dissolved solids (TDS)	3000[4]
Total coliform bacteria	N/A[5]
Fluoride	1.50
Calcium	500.00
Magnesium	125.00
Copper	0.60
Arsenic	0.20
Cadmium	0.05
Lead	0.10
Barium	10.00
Iron	3.00[6]

Source: Farm Journal, March 1991, p. AC-4, from Karen Mancl/Ohio State University. N/A stands for not available. *Notes:* 1. Parts per million (ppm). 2. Higher levels may harm livestock, depending on amounts in feed. 3. May cause severe diarrhea 4. Most livestock can tolerate levels up to 10,000 ppm, but production would be affected. 5. Low bacteria counts are desirable. 6. An amount this small may cause animals to stop drinking.

Chapter 10
POLITICS AND OPINION

Environmental Groups

★ 824 ★

Environmental Groups' Operating Budgets
The values are in millions of dollars.

Environmental Groups	1989 Operating Budget
National Wildlife Federation (NWF)	85.0
National Audubon Society (NAS)	35.0
Sierra Club (SC)	32.0
The Wilderness Society (WS)	20.0
National Resources Defense Council (NRDC)	16.0
Environmental Defense Fund (EDF)	15.0
Izaak Walton League of America (IWL)	1.7

Source: Farm Journal, Mid-February 1991, p. 8, from Mongoven, Bisco, Duchin and Individual AG Groups.

★ 825 ★

Green Parties in Western Europe
The data represent the percentage of votes in elections.

	Belgium	W. Germ.	France	Britain	Switz.	Sweden
National Parliamentary Elections						
1978	0.8		2.1			
1979				0.1	0.8	
1980		1.5				
1981	4.5		1.1			
1982						1.6
1983		5.6		0.2	6.4[2]	
1985	6.2					1.5

[Continued]

★ 825 ★

Green Parties in Western Europe
[Continued]

	Belgium	W. Germ.	France	Britain	Switz.	Sweden
1986			1.2			
1987	7.1	8.3		1.3	8.3[2]	
1988						5.5
European Parliamentary Elections[1]						
1979	3.4	3.2	4.4	0.1	n/a	n/a
1984	8.2	8.2	6.7[2]	0.5	n/a	n/a
1989	13.9	8.4	10.6	14.5	n/a	n/a

Source: World Watch, January/February 1990, p. 25, from Ferdinand Muller-Rommel (ed.), *Politics in Western Europe. The Rise and Success of Green Parties and Alternative Lists* (Boulder, CO: Westview Press, 1989); Washington Office of the European Community. *Notes:* 1. Sweden and Switzerland are not members of the European Community and therefore do not take part in the elections to the European Parliament. 2. Combined results of two green parties.

★ 826 ★

ISRI Membership
Membership of the Institute of Scrap Recycling Industries (ISRI) by category as of 1989.

Category	Number	Percent
Scrap metals recycling		
brokers and processors	1,759	
metal consumers and producers	110	
	1,869	81.9
Waste paper recycling		
brokers and processors	100	
waste paper consumers	4	
	104	4.6
Equipment manufacturers and dealers	217	9.5
Service organizations[2]	38	1.7
Glass recycling	1	.1
Plastics recycling	4	.2
Waste haulers	5	.2
Buy-back center operators	5	.2
Miscellaneous/unknown	40	1.8
	2,283	100.2

Source: Resource Recycling, October 1989, p. 56, from membership rolls. *Notes:* 1. Determination of the type of operation for each member location listed in the 1989 ISRI directory for which data were presented. 2. Such as laboratories, insurance companies, truckers, etc.

★ 827 ★

National Recycling Coalition Membership

Membership by category as of Spring 1989.

Category	Number	Percent
Academic	30	1.8
Association and trade groups[1]	54	3.3
Beverage industry[2]	21	1.3
Consultants[3]	141	8.6
End users		
Glass	8	
Metal	15	
Paper	8	
Other[4]	3	
	34	2.1
Environmental and community groups	67	4.1
Equipment manufacturers and dealers	36	2.2
Government agencies:		
Local and regional	469	
State	63	
Federal	8	
	540	33.0
Individuals	230	14.1
Others/unknown[5]	85	5.2
Processors:		
Glass	5	
Metal	46	
Paper	50	
Other	12	
	113	6.9
Plastic producers and reclaimers	33	2.0
Recycling center operators[6]	137	8.4
Waste management firms:		
Haulers	91	
Waste incineration	20	
Other	3	
	114	7.0
	1,635	100.00

Source: Resource Recycling, October 1989, p. 56, from membership rolls. *Notes:* 1. Such as national associations and state glass, plastic and litter prevention groups. 2. Such as beverage producers and local beer and soft drink wholesalers. 3. Includes engineering, law, public relations and research firms, and laboratories. 4. Such as scrap rubber and used oil consumers. 5. Such as large industrial corporations, unions, packaging companies, banks, etc. 6. Drop-off and buy-back center operations.

★ 828 ★

Recycling Organization Membership

Estimated membership of the National Recycling Coalition and the Institute of Scrap Recycling Industries.

State	NRC		ISRI	
	Number	Percent	Number	Percent
Alabama	7	0.4	48	2.0
Alaska	2	0.1	-	-
Arizona	12	0.6	20	0.8
Arkansas	4	0.2	18	0.7
California	310	16.3	194	7.9
Colorado	15	0.8	27	1.1
Connecticut	22	1.2	44	1.8
Delaware	4	0.1	7	0.2
District of Columbia	26	1.4	6	0.2
Florida	25	1.3	69	2.8
Georgia	14	0.7	53	2.2
Hawaii	-	-	1	0.1
Idaho	2	0.1	-	-
Illinois	210	11.1	148	6.0
Indiana	16	0.8	71	2.9
Iowa	20	1.1	38	1.5
Kansas	5	0.3	15	0.6
Kentucky	3	0.2	20	0.8
Louisiana	8	0.4	17	0.6
Maine	3	0.2	8	0.3
Maryland	18	0.9	35	1.4
Massachusetts	23	1.2	64	2.6
Michigan	141	7.4	122	5.0
Minnesota	154	8.1	38	1.5
Mississippi	-	-	12	0.5
Missouri	28	1.5	49	2.0
Montana	1	0.1	5	0.2
Nebraska	133	7.0	8	0.3
Nevada	1	0.1	5	0.2
New Hampshire	22	1.2	7	0.2
New Jersey	135	7.1	92	3.8
New Mexico	4	0.1	4	0.2
New York	45	2.4	196	8.0
North Carolina	48	2.5	53	2.2
North Dakota	1	0.1	5	0.2
Ohio	42	2.2	184	7.5
Oklahoma	2	0.1	18	0.7
Oregon	6	0.3	14	0.6
Pennsylvania	33	1.7	206	8.4
Rhode Island	10	0.5	9	0.4
South Carolina	2	0.1	34	1.4
South Dakota	-	-	4	0.2
Tennessee	7	0.4	40	1.6
Texas	78	4.1	139	5.7

[Continued]

★ 828 ★

Recycling Organization Membership
[Continued]

State	NRC		ISRI	
	Number	Percent	Number	Percent
Utah	-	-	16	0.7
Vermont	36	1.9	1	0.1
Virginia	38	2.0	39	1.6
Washington	36	1.9	22	0.9
West Virginia	-	-	6	0.2
Wisconsin	133	7.0	53	2.2
Wyoming	1	0.1	4	0.2
Puerto Rico	1	0.1	3	0.1
Canada	7	0.1	88	3.6
Other foreign[2]	4	0.1	73	3.0
Total	1,898	101.6	2,452	100.9

Source: Resource Recycling, October 1989, p. 38, from membership rolls. *Notes:* 1. In terms of ISRI, this list shows the location of member plants and offices. The data for NRC are from the mid-1989 membership rolls. 2. NRC has members in four foreign countries other than Canada, and ISRI has members in 29 foreign countries other than Canada.

★ 829 ★

U.S. Environmental Groups

Organization	Date Founded	Members (thousands)	Budget ($m)
National Wildlife Federation	1936	5,800	85.3
National Audubon Society	1905	550	35.0
Sierra Club	1892	500	32.0
World Wildlife Fund	1961	312	1.4
Wilderness Society	1935	300	20.0
Natural Resources Defense Council	1970	125	16.0
Natural Resources Defense Fund	1967	100	15.0
National Parks and Conservation Association	1919	95	3.8
Izaak Walton League	1922	50	1.6
Friends of the Earth	1969	30	2.5

Source: The Economist, October 20, 1990, p. 93, from Burson-Marsteller.

Opinion

★ 830 ★

American People's Contributions to Earth

Recycle bottles or cans - 46
Recycle paper - 26
Use biodegradable detergents - 24
Avoid sprays with fluorocarbons - 23
Buy recycled products - 14
Donate to Green groups - 8
Cut down on driving - 8

1,413 Americans were surveyed of which 501 do nothing to save the Earth.

	Percentage of Households
Recycle bottles or cans	46
Recycle paper	26
Use biodegradable detergents	24
Avoid sprays with fluorocarbons	23
Buy recycled products	14
Donate to Green groups	8
Cut down on driving	8

Source: U.S. News & World Report, February 4, 1991, p. 71, from USN&WR-Basic data: S.C. Johnson & Son Inc.

★ 831 ★

Building Nuclear Plants

Percentage of survey respondents who considered each issue to be "very serious".

Issue	Percent
Disposal of radioactive waste	89
Plant workers' safety	77
The possibility of an accident	75
The plant's cost	56

Source: Time, April 29, 1991, p. 60, from a telephone poll of 1,000 American adults taken for Time/CNN on April 10-11 by Yankelovich Clancy Shulman.

★ 832 ★

Energy Source Preferences

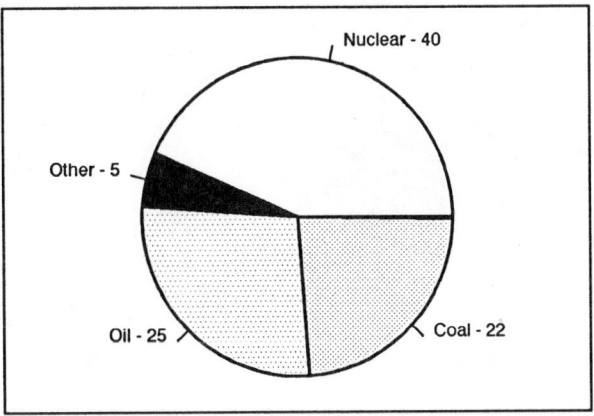

The percentages refer to the survey questions, "Which energy source should the U.S. rely on for most of its increased energy needs in the next ten years?"

Source	Percent
Nuclear	40
Oil	25
Coal	22
Other	5

Source: Time, April 29, 1991, p. 55, from a telephone poll of 1,000 American adults taken for Time/CNN on April 10-11 by Yankelovich Clancy Schulman. *Note:* Sampling error is plus or minus 3%. "Not sures" omitted.

★ 833 ★

Facilities That Most Need Repairing

Responses to the *American City & Country 1988 Annual Survey of Issues and Trends.*

Facilities	1986 (percent)	1987 (percent)	1988 (percent)
Streets/Bridges	64.7	62.1	63.2
Wastewater Systems	50.6	42.7	44.8
Water Supply Systems	29.1	26.5	25.7
Public Buildings	16.5	11.4	14.5
Refuse Disposal	6.9	8.5	11.5
Parks/Recreation	7.3	8.1	8.6

Source: American City & Country, November 1988, p. 33.

★ 834 ★

For or Against Nuclear Power

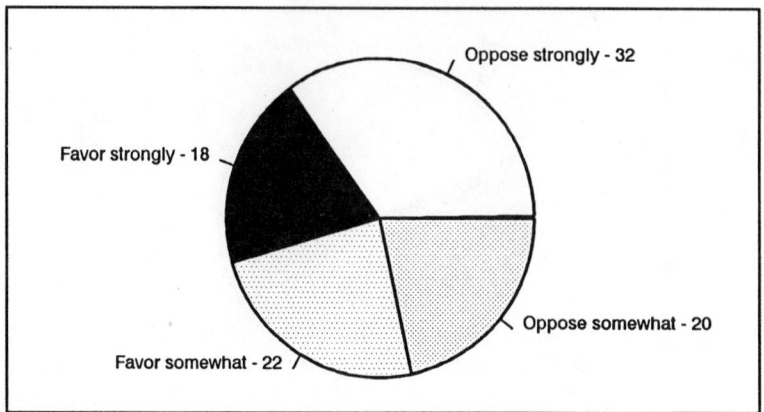

The percentages refer to the survey question, "Do you favor or oppose building more nuclear power plants in this country?"

Source	Percent
Oppose strongly	32
Oppose somewhat	20
Favor somewhat	22
Favor strongly	18

Source: Time, April 29, 1991, p. 55, from a telephone poll of 1,000 American adults taken for Time/CNN on April 10-11 by Yankelovich Clancy Schulman. *Note:* Sampling error is plus or minus 3%. "Not sures" omitted.

★ 835 ★

Future Trash Disposal Needs

Survey data on future methods of waste handling as reported by cities.

	1987 (percent)	1988 (percent)	1989 (percent)
Public landfill	32.2	34.2	37.7
Private landfill	17.5	21.2	15.1
Resource recovery	27	28.3	43.3
Other	9	9.1	9.9

Source: American City & County, December 1989, p. 12, from 1989 AC&C Issues Survey.

★ 836 ★

Industry's Environmental Effects

The figures refer to opinion leaders' ratings.[1]

Industry	Best (in percent)	Worst (in percent)
Electric Utility	41	4
Nuclear Power	33	6
Automobile	8	21
Chemical	5	27
Oil	2	35
Don't know	11	7

Source: Electric Light and Power, July 1990, p. 1. *Notes*: 1. *Cambridge Reports* survey 2/21/90-3/21/90, reported by U.S. Committee for Energy Awareness. Included: Federal officials, legislators; state officials, legislators; business; financial institutions; public interests groups; academia; national and local news media.

★ 837 ★

Likelihood of a Major Nuclear Accident

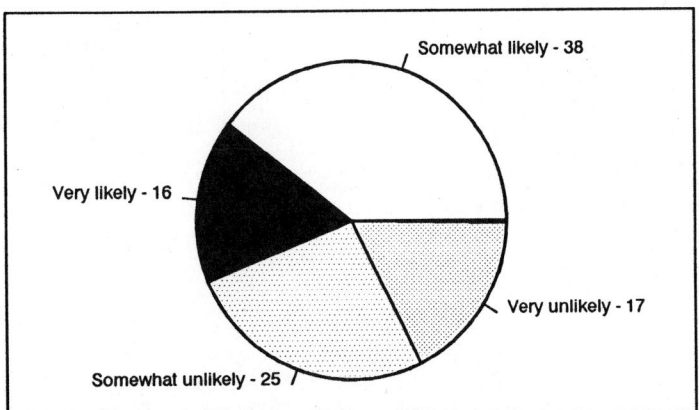

Survey response to a question about the likelihood that an accident like Chernobyl could happen in the United States.

Opinion	Percent
Very likely	16
Somewhat likely	38
Somewhat unlikely	25
Very unlikely	17

Source: Time, April 29, 1991, p. 64, from a telephone poll of 1,000 American adults taken for *Time/CNN* on April 10-11 by Yankelovich Clancy Shulman.

★ 838 ★

Nationwide Support for National Deposit Law

Opinion	Percent
Strongly support	44.2
Somewhat support	26.2
Strongly oppose	10.9
Neither oppose nor support	10.6
Somewhat oppose	7.1
Missing	0.9

Source: American City & County, April 1991, p. 14 Percentages do not equal 100 due to rounding.

★ 839 ★

Need for Legal Restraints

Values are the results of a public opinion poll. Data reflect what percentage of those polled felt more legal restrictions were needed for each issue shown.

	Percent
Recycling	47
Separating garbage from trash	33
Showing X-rated movies	32
Dogs	27
Water use	14
Where cars may be used	7

Source: Adweek, April 22, 1991, p. 10, from The Roper Organization.

★ 840 ★

Need for New Facilities

Responses to the *American City & Country 1988 Annual Survey of Issues and Trends*.

Facilities	1986 (percent)	1987 (percent)	1988 (percent)
Streets/Bridges	38.7	40.3	41.6
Wastewater Systems	37.9	33.2	33.6
Water Supply Systems	22.6	24.1	25.4
Public Buildings	13.8	12.3	17.41

[Continued]

★ 840 ★

Need for New Facilities
[Continued]

Facilities	1986 (percent)	1987 (percent)	1988 (percent)
Refuse Disposal	7.3	6.2	12.7
Parks/Recreation	4.6	9.0	7.4

Source: American City & Country, November 1988, p. 33.

★ 841 ★

Opinions on Tax Hikes for the Environment

Responses to the question, "Would you be willing to raise your taxes in order to control pollution/improve the environment?"

	1970 (percent)	1990 (percent)
Willing	54	69
Unwilling	34	29
Not sure	12	2

Source: U.S. News & World Report, April 23, 1990, p. 61, from Associated Press; Louis Harris & Associates; Marist Institute.

★ 842 ★

Periodicals Using Nonrecycled Paper

More than 50% people subscribing to magazines and newspapers will still do so if they know that the magazine or newspaper does not use recycled paper.

	Percentage
Magazine	
Very likely to cancel	14
Somewhat likely to cancel	32
Not likely to cancel	52
Don't know	2
Newspaper	
Very likely to cancel	16
Somewhat likely	25

[Continued]

★ 842 ★

Periodicals Using Nonrecycled Paper
[Continued]

	Percentage
Not likely	56
Don't know	3

Source: Advertising Age, January 29, 1991, p. 10.

★ 843 ★

Potential Threats to U.S. Security

The data represent top-priority threats to U.S. security in the opinion of 900 Americans surveyed.

Top-priority threats	Percentage
Global environmental problems	47.0
Spread of nuclear and chemical weapons	46.0
Domestic social concerns	35.0
Third world poverty	32.0
Economic competitiveness with Europe and Japan	28.0
Drugs	28.0
Spread of Communism	15.0
Persian gulf conflict	15.0
Defense Department waste and corruption	14.0
Terrorist attacks	13.0
Nuclear war with the U.S.S.R	10.0
Soviet agression in Europe	5.0
Soviet or Chinese aggression in Asia	1.0

Source: U.S. News & World Report, June 12, 1989, p. 69, from Roosevelt Center for American Policy Studies.

★ 844 ★

Public Concerns About Environment Awareness

Results of a household survey of 1,514 consumers, asking whether they thought the public, the government, and industry were concerned enough about the environment.

	Too worried (percent)	Not worried enough (percent)
American public	7	68
Government	3	73
Business/Industry	2	76

Source: Advertising Age, January 29, 1991, p. 10.

★ 845 ★

Public Opposition to Nuclear Power Plants

Changes in public opposition in selected countries to nuclear power plant construction.

Country	Percent opposed	
	Before Chernobyl	After Chernobyl
United Kingdom	65	83
West Germany	46	83
Italy	-	79
United States	67	78
Yugoslavia	40	74
Canada	60	70
Finland	33	64
France	-	52

Source: World Watch, July/August 1988, p. 29, from Worldwatch Institute, based on Gallup and other polls. Wording and polling techniques varied, but data are broadly comparable. Pre-Chernobyl figures are from polls taken between 1982 and 1986.

★ 846 ★

Public's Top Environmental Concerns

The 29 top environmental concerns of the public and the percentage of surveyed respondents who rated each problem "very serious".

Problem	Percent
Active hazardous waste sites	67
Abandoned hazardous waste sites	65
Water pollution from industrial wastes	63
Occupational exposure to toxic chemicals[1]	63
Oil spills	60
Destruction of the ozone layer[1]	60
Nuclear power plant accidents	60
Industrial accidents releasing pollutants	58
Radiation from radioactive wastes	58
Air pollution from factories[1]	56
Leaking underground storage tanks	55
Coastal water contamination	54
Solid waste and litter	53
Pesticide risk to farm workers[1]	52
Water pollution from agricultural runoff	51
Water pollution from sewage plants	50
Air pollution from vehicles[1]	50
Pesticide residues in foods	49
Greenhouse effect[1]	48
Drinking water contamination[1]	46
Destruction of wetlands	42
Acid rain	40
Water pollution from city runoff	35
Nonhazardous waste sites	31
Biotechnology	30
Indoor air pollution	22
Radiation from x-rays	21
Radon in homes[1]	17
Radiation from microwave ovens	13

Source: Science, August 10, 1990, p. 616, from a March 1990 Roper Poll. *Note:* 1. Item also appears on the EPA list of worst environmental problems.

★ 847 ★

Threats to U.S. Economy

Quality of Public Education - 24	
Size of the Federal Deficit - 23	
The Drug Problem - 15	
Growing Health Care Costs - 9	
Environmental Pollution - 8	
Don't Know / No Answer - 5	
Providing Care for the Elderly - 3	
Shortage of People to Fill Entry-Level Positions - 3	
Lack of Technically Skilled Employees - 3	
Growing Number of People on Welfare - 2	
The Spread of AIDS - 2	
Adult Illiteracy - 2	
Lack of Adequate Public Transportation - 1	

Results of a survey of 251 executives of Fortune 1000 companies when asked to identify the most serious threat to the U.S. economy.

Issue	Percentage of Responses
Quality of Public Education	24
Size of the Federal Deficit	23
The Drug Problem	15
Growing Health Care Costs	9
Environmental Pollution	8
Providing Care for the Elderly	3
Shortage of People to Fill Entry-Level Positions	3
Lack of Technically Skilled Employees	3
Adult Illiteracy	2
Growing Number of People on Welfare	2
The Spread of AIDS	2
Lack of Adequate Public Transportation	1
Don't Know / No Answer	5

Source: USA Today, December 1990, p. 1, from *The Chivas Regal Report on American Business Leaders: Executive Attitudes in a Time of Upheaval.*

★ 848 ★

U.S. & Soviet Teenagers' Major Concerns

Type of worry	U.S students degree of concern	Soviet students degree of concern
Your mother or father dying	3.20	3.75
Nuclear war	3.11	3.89
Poor grades	2.83	3.24
Your own death	2.71	3.07
Illness, disability or accident	2.71	3.28
Not finding a satisfying job	2.71	-
World hunger	2.70	3.64
Being a victim of violent crime	2.65	3.11
Nuclear - power - plant accident	2.54	3.62
Getting cancer	2.46	-
Parents might divorce	-	2.98
Environmental pollution	-	3.44

Source: U.S. News & World Report, October 17, 1988, p. 82, from *New England Journal of MediciNote: 1 means "not at all worried" and 4 means "very worried".*

Protests

★ 849 ★

Environmental Protests in the Soviet Union

Place	Date	Number of Participants	Reason
Yerevan, Armenia	Oct. 1987	2,000-4,000	Industrial pollution
Ufa, Ural Mountain Region	Nov. 1987	2,000	Chemical plant
Yerevan, Armenia	Feb. 1988	5,000	Planned chemical plant
Kirishi, near Leningrad	March 1988	12,000	Hazards at a chemical plant
Nizhni Tagil, Ural Mountain Region	April 6, 1988	10,000	Air pollution
Baltic Coast	Sept. 3, 1988	50,000 -	Pollution in

[Continued]

★ 849 ★

Environmental Protests in the Soviet Union
[Continued]

Place	Date	Number of Participants	Reason
Ignalina, Lithuania	Sept. 17,1988	100,000 6,000 - 15,000	Baltic Sea Nuclear power plant
Lithuania	Oct. 1988	600,000	Ignalina nuclear power plant
Pacific Coast	March 1989	[1]	Nuclear powered ship

Source: World Watch, May/June 1989, p. 27, from Watchworld Institute, based on various reports. *Note:* 1. Number of participants not given.

Television Coverage

★ 850 ★

Sources Cited and Shown on the Air in Environmental Risks Stories

Source	Number of Stories that Cite the Source Type...[1]	...As a Percent of All Stories Aired[2]	Number of Sources Shown on the Air...	...As a Percent of All Sources Shown on the Air[3]	Ratio of III to I
Federal government	193	34	134	15	0.69
State government	55	10	48	6	0.87
County government	5	1	5	1	1.00
Local government	29	5	31	4	1.07
Foreign government	45	8	24	3	0.53
Industry	139	25	114	13	0.82
Worker	46	8	64	7	1.39
Environmental advocate	65	12	59	7	0.91
Citizen	130	23	219	25	1.68
Expert	87	15	122	14	1.40
Other	31	6	33	4	1.06
Can't tell	8	1	10	1	1.25

Source: Environment, March 1989, p. 20. *Notes:* 1. The first column counts stories that either mention sources or show them on the air. 2. Based on 564 stories. This column sums to more than 100 percent because some stories cited more than one source. 3. Based on 863 on-air sources.

★ 851 ★

Sources Cited by Type of Story

Number of times source types were cited in environmental risk stories with 1, 2, and 3 or more source types.

Source	Single-Source-Type Stories	Percent	Two-Source-Type Stories	Percent	Three-Or-More-Source-Type Stories	Percent	Total	Percent
Federal government	89	54	42	20	62	13	193	23
State government	9	5	16	8	30	6	55	7
County government	1	1	1	<1	3	1	5	<1
Local government	9	5	4	2	16	3	29	3
Foreign government	11	7	13	6	21	5	45	5
Industry	21	13	43	20	75	16	139	17
Worker	1	1	13	6	32	7	46	6
Environmental advocate	4	2	20	10	41	9	65	8
Citizen	11	7	29	14	90	20	130	16
Expert	5	3	20	10	62	14	87	10
Other	2	1	6	3	23	5	31	4
Can't tell	1	1	3	1	4	1	8	1
All sources	164	100	210	100	459	100	833	100
Number of stories[1]	164		105		126		395	

Source: Environment, March 1989, p. 40 *Notes:* 1. 833 source types were cited in 395 of the 564 stories; no sources were cited in 169 (30 percent) of the 564 stories.

Appendix I

REPORT LITERATURE SOURCES

PRIMARY SOURCES

U.S. FEDERAL AGENCIES

This section lists reports used directly as primary sources. With one exception, all the reports are from Federal agencies; they are arranged by agency name in alphabetical order; if more than one report from the same agency was used, the reports are listed in alphabetical order by title. The last report in this section is headlined Other Government. Each listing of a report is followed by one or more references to tables in the book; the references are arranged in their order of appearance.

Executive Office of the President, Council on Environmental Quality

— *20th Annual Report 1990*, Council on Environmental Quality, Washington, D.C. *Tables*: 38, 81, 122, 149, 154, 214, 215, 222, 224, 235, 252, 297, 299, 300, 305, 306, 307, 308, 311, 312, 314, 318, 319, 320, 321, 322, 390, 412, 539, 784, 787, 788, 793

Executive Office of the President, Office of Management and Budget

— *Budget of the United States Government*, Fiscal Year 1991, Office of Management and Budget, Washington, D.C. *Tables*: 304, 349

U.S. Congress

— *Climate Surprises*, Hearing before the Congress, 101st Congress, May 8, 1989. *Table*: 88

— *Beneath the Bottom Line: Agricultural Approaches to Reduce Agricultural Contamination of Groundwater*, U.S. Congress, Office of Technology Assessment, OTA-F-418, Washington, D.C., November 1990. *Tables*: 46, 58, 61, 62, 63

— *Catching Our Breath: Next Steps for Reducing Urban Ozone*, U.S. Congress, Office of Technology Assessment, OTA-F-412, Washington, D.C., July 1989. *Tables*: 99, 275, 359, 360, 362, 363

— *Changing by Degrees: Steps to Reduce Greenhouse Gases*, U.S. Congress, Office of Technology Assessment, OTA-O-482, Washington, D.C., February 1991. *Tables*: 70, 72, 73, 74, 75, 76, 77, 78, 79, 80, 272, 326, 354, 364, 534, 542, 550, 551, 552, 568, 569, 589, 592, 631, 680, 681, 699, 700, 717, 71⸍ 8

— *Complex Cleanup: The Environmental Legacy of Nuclear Weapons Production*, U.S. Congress, Office of Technology Assessment, OTA-O-484, Washington, D.C., February 1991. *Tables*: 117, 118, 119, 293, 574

— *Coping With An Oiled Sea: An Analysis of Oil Spill Response Technologies*, U.S. Congress, Office of Technology Assessment, Washington, D.C., March 1990. *Table*: 248

— *Facing America's Trash: What Next for Municipal Solid Waste*, U.S. Congress, Office of Technology Assessment, OTA-O-412, Washington, D.C., July 1989. *Tables*: 153, 183, 193, 458, 461, 462, 464, 469, 575, 576, 577, 578, 579, 602, 729, 755, 762

— *Global Warming and Its Implications for California*, Hearings before the Congress, 101st Congress, Santa Monica, CA., May 20, 1989. *Tables*: 678, 679, 693

— *Orbiting Space Debris: A Space Environmental Problem* - Background Paper, U.S. Congress, Office of Technology Assessment, OTA-BP-ISC-72, Washington, D.C., September 1990. *Tables*: 36, 37

— *Partnership Under Pressure: Managing Commercial Low-level Radioactive Waste*, U.S. Congress, Office of Technology Assessment, Washington, D.C., November 1989. *Tables*: 120, 121, 123, 287, 290, 291, 391, 392, 393, 394, 715

— *Technologies for Reducing Dioxin in the Manufacture of Bleached Wood Pulp*, U.S. Congress, Office of Technology Assessment, OTA-BP-054, May 1989. *Table*: 246

— *Transportation of Hazardous Materials by Rail: Hearings Before the Government Activities and the Transportation Subcommittee of the Committee on Government Operations*, House of Representatives, 101st Congress, and Session, February 28, 1990. *Tables*: 253, 254, 255, 256, 257, 765, 766, 790

U.S. Department of Agriculture

— *Agricultural Conservation and Forestry Statistics, 1989*, U.S. Government Printing Office, Washington, D.C., 1989. *Tables*: 340, 341, 368, 369, 453, 484, 555, 557, 558, 561, 563, 564, 565, 566, 567, 570, 571, 701, 702, 703, 744, 745, 746, 747, 780

U.S. Department of Commerce, Bureau of the Census

— *Statistical Abstract of the United States 1990 (110th ed.)*, Superintendent of Documents, Washington, D.C. *Tables*: 39, 49, 50, 65, 66, 68, 227, 249, 251, 296, 303, 313, 315, 316, 344, 425, 449, 470, 477, 527, 528, 535, 540, 583, 686, 687, 708, 792

U.S. Department of Energy

— *1991 Gas Mileage Guide*, U.S. Department of Energy, Washington, D.C., October 1990. *Table*: 268

— *Annual Energy Review 1989*, U.S. Department of Energy, Washington, D.C., DOE/EIA-0384 (89), May 24, 1990. *Table*: 366

— *Commercial Nuclear Power 1990: Prospects for the United States and the World*, U.S. Department of Energy, DOE/EIA-0348(89), Washington, D.C., January 1991. *Tables*: 288, 289, 294, 295, 639, 640, 641, 643, 644

— *Electric Power Annual 1989*, January 1991. *Tables*: 83, 84, 361, 585, 626, 629, 630, 632, 633, 645, 684

— *Financial Statistics of Selected Investor-Owned Electric Utilities 1989*, January 1991. *Tables*: 262, 267, 298, 323, 324

U.S. Department of Health and Human Services

— *Evaluating Hazardous Waste Education & Training*, U.S. Department of Health and Human Services, Washington, D.C., U.S. Government Printing Office: 1991-281-821:44112, 1991. *Tables*: 492, 493, 494, 495, 496

U.S. Department of Transportation

— *Highway Statistics 1989*, U.S. Department of Transportation, Federal Highway Administration, Washington, D.C., 1989. *Tables*: 586, 587, 588

U.S. Environmental Protection Agency

— *An Analysis of State Superfund Programs: 50-State Study*, EPA/540/8-89/011, U.S. Environmental Protection Agency, Washington, D.C., September 1989. *Table*: 707

— *Characterization of Municipal Solid Waste in the United States: 1990 Update*, U.S. Environmental Protection Agency, EPA/530-SW-90-042, Washington, D.C., June 1990. *Tables*: 124, 129, 131, 132, 133, 135, 136, 137, 138, 139, 142, 143, 144, 145, 146, 147, 148, 151, 155, 157, 158, 160, 162, 164, 165, 166,

171, 172, 173, 174, 175, 176, 177, 180, 185, 388, 411, 413, 423, 424, 431, 434, 435, 456, 459, 467, 472

— *Managing Asbestos in Place : A Building Owner's Guide to Operations and Maintenance Programs for Asbestos Containing Materials*, U.S. Environmental Protection Agency, 20T-2003, Washington, D.C., July 1990. *Table*: 194

— *National Air Quality and Emissions Trends Report, 1988*. EPA-450/4-90-002, U.S. Environmental Protection Agency, Research Triangle Park, NC. *Tables*: 40, 41, 42, 43, 51, 54, 56, 80, 86, 90, 94, 97, 98, 100

— *National Water Quality Inventory*, 1988 Report to Congress, U.S. Environmental Protection Agency, Washington, D.C., April 1990. *Tables*: 216, 217, 218, 231, 233, 476, 478, 776, 777, 781, 794, 795, 796, 797, 798, 820

— *The Potential Effects of Global Climate Change on the United States*, Draft Report to Congress, U.S. Environmental Protection Agency, October 1988. *Tables*: 225, 226

— *The Quality of Our Nation's Water: A Summary of the 1988 National Water Quality Inventory*, U.S. Environmental Protection Agency, EPA 440/4-90-005, May 1990. *Tables*: 47, 55, 230, 821

— *Risk Assessment, Management and Communication of Drinking Water Contamination*, U.S. Environmental Protection Agency, EPA/625/4-89/024, Washington, D.C., 1989. *Table*: 345

— *Third International Conference on New Frontiers for Hazardous Waste Management Proceedings*, Sept. 10-13, EPA/600/9-89/072, August 1989. *Table*: 114

— *Toxics in the Community: National and Local Perspectives*, U.S. Environmental Protection Agency, EPA 560/4-90-017, Washington, D.C., September 1990. *Tables*: 238, 243, 668, 767, 768, 772, 773

— *The Toxic Release Inventory, A National Perspective*, U.S. Environmental Protection Agency, Washington, D.C., June 1989. *Tables*: 93, 186, 187, 189,

190, 191, 195, 196, 198, 199, 200, 201, 204, 205, 206, 382, 386, 387, 465, 466, 473, 481, 713, 769, 770

— *Preliminary Data Summary for the Hazardous Waste Industry* (PB 90-126517), U.S. Environmental Protection Agency, Washington, D.C., September 1989. *Tables*: 274, 285, 378, 501

OTHER GOVERNMENT

Municipality of Anchorage

— *Disposal Directory for Small Quantities of Hazardous Waste*, Municipality of Anchorage, Solid Waste Department, Anchorage, Alaska, January 1989. *Tables*: 706, 709, 711, 712

REPORTS CITED BY PRIMARY SOURCES

This section lists reports cited by others as the original source of their data. The reports may have been cited in periodicals or other reports. They are arranged under three headings: U.S. Federal Agencies, Other Government Bodies, and Private Institutions and Companies. Within each section, institutions are listed in alphabetical order, each followed by one or more reports, in alphabetical order by title. Each listing of a report is then followed by one or more references to tables in the book; the references are arranged in the order of their appearance in the book.

U.S. FEDERAL AGENCIES

Federal Energy Regulatory Commission

— *Annual Report of Major Electric Utilities, Licensees and Others*, FERC Form 1, Federal Energy Regulatory Commission, Washington, D.C. *Tables*: 262, 267, 298, 323, 324

Nuclear Regulatory Commission

— *Licensed Operating Reactors*, NUREG-0020, Nuclear Regulatory Commission, Washington, D.C., November 1986. *Tables*: 639, 643

U.S. Congress

— *Composting Technologies, Costs, Programs, and Markets*, Cal Recovery Systems, Inc., contract report prepared for U.S. Congress, Office of Technology Assessment, Richmond, CA, January 1989. *Table*: 458

— *Composting Technologies, Costs, Programs and Markets*, Ron Albrecht Associates, Inc., contract report prepared for U.S. Congress, Office of Technology Assessment, Annapolis, MD: December 1988. *Table*: 458

— *International Experiences in Solid Waste Management*, A. Herschkowitz, Municipal Recycling Associates, contract prepared for U.S. Congress, Office of Technology Assessment, Elmsford, NY, October 1988. *Tables*: 461, 469

U.S. Department of Agriculture

— *Agricultural Resources: Inputs, Situation and Outlook*, AR- 15, U.S. Department of Agriculture, Washington, D.C., August 1989. *Table*: 58

— *Agricultural Resources: Situation and Outlook Report*, U.S. Department of Agriculture, Economic Research Service, Washington, D.C., February 1988. *Tables*: 535, 539

— *An Analysis of the Land Situation in the United States: 1989-2040, A Technical Document Supporting the 1989 RPA Assessment*, General Technical Report RM-181, U.S. Department of Agriculture, U.S. Forest Service, Fort Collins, CO, 1989. *Table*: 568

— *An Analysis of the Timber Situation in the United States: 1989-2040, Part I: The Current Resource and Use Situation, Draft*, U.S. Department of Agriculture, U.S. Forest Service, Washington, D.C., 1989. *Table*: 568

— *National Resources Inventory: 1977, 1982, and 1987*, U.S. Department of Agriculture, Soil Conservation Service, Washington, D.C. *Table*: 224

— *Report of the Forest Service, Fiscal Year 1989* , U.S. Department of Agriculture, U.S. Forest Service, Washington, D.C., February 1990. *Table*: 569

— *The Status of Land Disturbed by Mining in the United States: Basic Statistics by State and County as of July, 1977*, U.S. Department of Agriculture, Washington, D.C., 1979. *Table*: 390

— *U.S. Forest Planting Report*, U.S. Department of Agriculture, Forest Service, Washington, D.C., 1989. *Table*: 222

U.S. Department of Commerce

— *Pollution Abatement Costs and Expenditures*, U.S. Department of Commerce, Bureau of the Census, Current industrial reports, MA-200. Washington, D.C. *Tables*: 297, 299, 300, 305, 306, 306, 308, 311, 312, 313, 314, 318, 319, 319, 321, 322

— *World Population Profile: 1989*, WP-89, U.S. Department of Commerce, Bureau of the Census, Washington, D.C., September 1989. *Table*: 717

U.S. Department of Energy

— *1987 Annual Report on Low-Level Radioactive Waste Management Program*, U.S. Department of Energy, Washington, D.C., August 1988. *Table*: 291

— *The 1987 State-by-State Assesment of Low-level Radioactive Wastes Received at Commercial Disposal Sites*, National Low-level Radioactive Waste Management Program, DOE/LLW-69T, U.S. Department of Energy, Washington, D.C., December 1988. *Table*: 715

— *Alternate Fuels*, U.S. Department of Energy, DOE/EIA-0348(89), Washington, D.C., January 1991. *Tables*: 585, 632, 633

— *Annual Electric Generator Report*, Form EIA-860, U.S. Department of Energy, Energy Information Administration, Washington, D.C., 1989. *Tables*: 632, 633, 644

— *Annual Outlook for U.S. Electric Power 1990*, DOE/EIA-0474(90), U.S. Deparment of Energy, Energy Information Administration, Washington D.C., June 1990. *Tables*: 641, 644

— *Conceptual Design Report: Alternative Concepts for Low-Level Radioactive Waste Disposal*, prepared by Rogers & Associates Engineering Corp. for the National Low-Level Waste Management Program, DOE/LLW-60T, June 1987. *Tables*: 287, 291

— *Draft Strategy Document*, DOE/Iffice of Health and Environmental Research, Subsurface Science Program, Co-Contaminant Chemistry Subprogram, Washington, D.C., March 1990. *Table*: 119

— *Energy and Materials Use in the Production and Recycling of Consumer-Goods Packaging*, ANL/CNSV-TM-58, Argonne National Laboratory, prepared for U.S. Department of Energy, Argonne, IL, February 1981. *Table*: 602

— *Facility Life Cycle Cost and Average User Fee Projections for Small-Volume Low-Level Radioactive Waste Disposal Facilities*, EG&G Idaho, DOE Contract No. DE-ACO7-76IDO1570, February 1989. *Table*: 291

— *Household Energy Consumption and Expenditure*, U.S. Department of Energy, Energy Information Administration, Washington, D.C., 1989. *Tables*: 272, 550

— *Integrated Data Base for 1989: Spent Fuel and Radioactive Waste Inventories, Projections, and Characterstics (DRAFT)*, DOE/RW-0006, Rev. 5, U.S. Department of Energy, Washington, D.C., August 1988. *Tables*: 117, 120, 198, 290, 391, 392

— *Integrated Data Base for 1990: Spent Fuel and Radioactive Waste Inventories, Projections, and Characteristics*, U.S. Department of Energy, Washington, D.C., 1989. *Table*: 122

— *International Energy Annual, 1988*, DOE/EIA-0219(88), U.S. Department of Energy, Energy Information Administration, Washington, D.C., November 1989. *Tables*: 542, 589, 592, 681, 700

— *Life Cycle Costs and Average User Fee Projections for Small-Volume Low-Level Radioactive Waste Disposal Facilities*, EG&G Idaho, DOE Contract No. DE-ACO7- 76IDO157, February 1989. *Table*: 287

— *Manufacturing Energy Consumption Survey: Changes in Energy Efficiency 1980- 1985*, DOE/EIA-0516(85), U.S. Department of Energy, Energy Information Agency, Washington, D.C., January 1990. *Table*: 551

— *Monthly Power Plant Report*, Form EIA-759, U.S. Department of Energy, Energy Information Administration, Washington, D.C. *Tables*: 629, 630, 641

— *Nuclear Plant Cancellations: Causes, Costs, and Consequences*, DOE/EIA-0392, U.S. Department of Energy, Energy Information Administration, Washington, D.C., April 1983. *Table*: 639

— *Semiannual Report on Status of Reactor Construction*, Form EIA-254, U.S. Department of Energy, Energy Information Administration, Washington, D.C., 1988. *Tables*: 639, 643

— *Steam-Electric Plant Operation and Design Report*, Form EIA-767, Energy Information Administration, Washington, D.C. *Tables*: 84, 361, 626, 645

— *U.S. Commercial Nuclear Power*. DOE/EIA-0315, U.S. Department of Energy, Energy Information Administration, Washington, D.C., November 1984. *Table*: 639

U.S. Department of the Interior

— *The Abandoned Mine Program: 1977-1987*, U.S. Department of the Interior, Washington, D.C., 1987. *Table*: 390

— *Mineral Commodity Summaries*, U.S. Department of the Interior, U.S. Bureau of Mines, Washington, D.C., 1989. *Tables*: 527, 528

— *Mineral Facts and Problems, 1985*, Bulletin 675, U.S. Department of the Interior, U.S. Bureau of Mines, Washington, D.C., 1985. *Tables*: 575, 577

— *Minerals Yearbook*, U.S. Department of the Interior, U.S. Bureau of Mines, Washington D.C. *Tables*: 149, 575, 577

— *Surface Coal Mining Reclamation: 10 Years of Progress, 1977-1987*, U.S. Department of the Interior, Washington, D.C., 1987. *Table*: 390

U.S. Department of Transportation

— *Annual Report on Hazardous Materials Transportation - Calendar Year 1988*, U.S. Department of Transportation, Washington, D.C., 1989. *Table*: 787

— *Highway Statistics*, annual, U.S. Department of Transportation, U.S. Federal Highway Administration, Washington, D.C. *Table*: 583

— *Highway Statistics Summary to 1985*, U.S. Department of Transportation, U.S. Federal Highway Administration, Washington, D.C. *Table*: 583

— *Transportation Safety Information Report*, U.S. Department of Transportation Systems Center, Cambridge, MA. *Table*: 251

U.S. Environmental Protection Agency

— *Current Knowledge of Fertilizer-Derived Nitrous Oxide Emissions*, Eichner, M.J., 1988, paper prepared for U.S. Environmental Protection Agency, Washington, D.C. *Tables*: 60, 65

— *National Pollutant Emission Estimates 1940-1987*, U.S. Environmental Protection Agency, Washington, D.C. *Table*: 66

— *Policy Options for Stabilizing Global Climate*, draft report, U.S. Environmental Protection Agency, Washington, D.C., 1989. *Table*: 680

— *Report to Congress: Solid Waste Disposal in the United States, Vol. II*, EPA/530-SW-88-011B, U.S. Environmental Protection Agency, Washington, D.C., October 1988. *Tables*: 193, 462

— *Survey of State and Territorial Subtitle D Municipal Landfill Facilities*, draft final report prepared by Westat, Inc. for U.S. Environmental Protection Agency, Wshington, D.C., October 13, 1987. *Table*: 464

— *U.S. Progress in Implementing the Great Lakes Water Quality Agreement*, U.S. Environmental Protection Agency, Chicago, 1989. *Table*: 215

U.S. International Trade Commission

— *Synthetic Organic Chemicals*, annual, U.S. International Trade Commission, Washington, D.C. *Table*: 540

OTHER GOVERNMENT BODIES

Commonwealth of Pennsylvania

— *Proposal for Development and Operation of the Appalachian States Low-Level Radioactive Waste Compact Regional Disposal Facility*, US Ecology, Inc., prepared for the Commonwealth of Pennsylvania, October 1988. *Table*: 291

Federal Republic of Germany

— *Municipal Solid Waste Management in the Federal Republic of Germany*, G. Grossmann, in *A Selection of Recent Publications (Vol. 2)*, Federal Environmental Agency, Federal Republic of Germany, Berlin, 1988. *Table*: 762

Organization for Economic Cooperation and Development (OECD)

— *France Environmental Data Compendium*, Organization for Economic Cooperation and Development (OECD), Paris, 1989. *Table*: 477

— *Summary of Actions in Member Countries to Deal With the Problem of Climate Change (Note by the Secretariat)*, IEA/SLT(90)51 (1st Revision), draft, Organization for Economic Cooperation and Development and International Energy Agency, Paris, October 1990. *Table:* 818

United Nations

— Affairs, *Prospects of World Urbanization, 1988*, Population Studies No. 112, ST/ESA/SER.A/112, United Nations, Department of International Economic and Social Affairs, New York, 1989. *Table:* 718

PRIVATE INSTITUTIONS AND COMPANIES

American Paper Institute, Inc.

— *Statistics of Paper, Paperboard and Woodpulp*, annual, American Paper Institute, Inc., New York, N.Y. *Table:* 449

American Public Transit Association

— *Mass Transit: The Clean Air Alternative*, American Public Transit Association, Washington, D.C., 1989. *Table:* 95

British Petroleum Company

— *BP Statistical Review of World Energy*, British Petroleum Company, London, UK, June 1990. *Tables:* 542, 589, 592

Chemical Manufacturers Association

— *Production, sales, and calculated release of CFC-11 and CFC-12 through 1988*, Chemical Manufacturers Association, Washington, D.C., 1989. *Table:* 81

Electric Power Research Institute

— *Updated Costs for Decommissioning Nuclear Power Facilities*, EPRI NP-4012, Palo Alto, CA, May 1985. *Tables:* 288, 289, 294, 295

Gas Research Institute

— *Baseline Projection Data Book, 1988 GRI Baseline Projection of U.S. Energy Supply and Demand to 2010*, Gas Research Institute, Washington, D.C., 1988. *Tables*: 68, 326

— *Industrial Natural Gas Markets: Facts, Fallacies, and Forecasts*, Gas Research Institute, Washington, D.C., 1989. *Table*: 552

Great Lakes Water Quality Board

— *1986 Report on Water Quality: Report to the IJC*, Great Lakes Water Quality Board, International Joint Commission. *Table*: 214

Institute for Local Self-Reliance

— *Garbage in Europe: Technologies, Economics, and Trends*, Institute for Local Self-Reliance, Washington, D.C., 1988. *Tables*: 461, 469

Institute of Scrap Recycling Industries, Inc.

— *Facts 1989 Year Book*, Institute of Scrap Recycling Industries, Inc., Washington D.C., 1990. *Tables*: 653, 654, 655, 658, 661, 662, 664, 665

Motor Vehicle Manufacturer's Association

— *Facts and Figures '89*, Motor Vehicle Manufacturer's Association, Detroit, MI, 1990. *Table*: 534

Renew America

— *Reducing the Rate of Global Warming: The States' Role*, Renew America, Washington, D.C. *Tables*: 678, 679

Swedish Association of Public Cleansing and Solid Waste Management

— *Solid Waste Management in Sweden*, Swedish Association of Public Cleansing and Solid Waste Management, Malmo, Sweden, February 1988. *Tables*: 461, 469

World Resources Institute

— *Breathing Easier: Taking Action on Climate Change, Air Pollution, and Energy Insecurity,* James J. MacKenzie, World Resources Institute. *Tables*: 89, 92, 96

Worldwatch Institute

— *Mining Urban Wastes: The Potential for Recycling,* C. Pollock, Worldwatch Paper 76, Worldwatch Institute, Washington, D.C., April 1987. *Tables*: 461, 469

Appendix II

PERIODICALS SOURCES

PRIMARY SOURCES

This section lists periodicals cited in sources to tables and maps throughout the book. The following listing shows primary sources; these, in turn, may have drawn their data from the report literature (see previous section), from organizations (see next section), or from other periodicals (see this section, next subdivision). Each periodical listing is followed by one or more references to tables in the book; the references are arranged in order of appearance.

Advertising Age, published by Crain Communications Inc., 740 Rush Street, Chicago, Ill 60611-2590. *Tables*: 842, 844

Adweek, published by A/S/M Communications, Inc., 49 E. 21st St., New York, NY 10010. *Table*: 839

American City & County, published by Communication Channels, Inc., 6255 Barfield Road, Atlanta, GA 30328. *Tables*: 263, 342, 421, 515, 573, 833, 835, 838, 840

Amicus Journal, published by the Natural Resources Defense Council, 40 West 20th Street, New York, NY 10011. *Table*: 669

ASHRAE Journal, published by The American Society of Heating, Refrigeration and Air-Conditioning Engineers Inc., 1791 Tullie Circle NE, Atlanta, GA 30329. *Tables*: 351, 352, 353, 355, 356, 538, 806

Aviation Week & Space Technology, published by McGraw-Hill, Inc., 1221 Avenue of the Americas, New York, NY 10020. *Table*: 670

BioCycle, published by The JG Press, Inc., 419 State Avenue, Second Floor, Emmaus, PA 18049. *Tables*: 279, 280, 281, 282, 328, 329, 337, 347, 348, 406, 409, 432, 454, 457, 479, 510, 519, 520, 521, 523, 600, 618, 623, 723, 728, 733, 735, 736, 751, 753

Bulletin of the Atomic Scientists, published by the Educational Foundation for Nuclear Science, 6042 S. Kimbark Avenue, Chicago, IL 60637. *Tables*: 580, 581

Business Week, published by McGraw-Hill, Inc., 1221 Avenue of the Americas, New York, NY 10020. *Tables*: 365, 590, 591

C&EN, published by the American Chemical Society, 1155 Sixteenth St., N.W., Washington, DC 20036. *Tables*: 317, 334, 335, 339, 375, 377, 379, 380, 381, 384, 497, 498, 500, 704

Chemical Engineering, published by McGraw-Hill, Inc., 1221 Avenue of the Americas, New York, NY 10020. *Tables*: 437, 543, 691, 791

Chemical Week, published by McGraw-Hill, Inc., 1221 Ave. of Americas, New York, NY 10020. *Tables*: 278, 346, 372, 546

Chemicalweek, published by the Chemical Week Association, P.O. Box 1074, Southeastern, PA 19398. *Tables*: 374, 428, 499, 524, 525, 526

Christian Science Monitor, published by The Christian Science Publishing Society, One Norway St., Boston, MA 02115. *Tables*: 530, 562

Consumer's Research, published by Consumers' Research Inc., 800 Maryland Ave., N.E., Washington, DC 20002. *Tables*: 250, 271, 302, 532, 675

Detroit Free Press, published by Knight Ridder Newspaper, Inc., 301 Lafayette, Detroit, MI 48231. *Table*: 764

Economist, published by The Economist Newspaper, NA, Incorporated, 111 West 57th Street, New York, NY 10019-2211. *Tables*: 367, 559, 609, 610, 611, 743, 829

Editorial Research Reports, published by Congressional Quarterly, Inc., 1414 22nd St., N.W., Washington, DC 20037. *Table*: 376

Electric Light and Power, published by the PennWell Publishing Company, 1421 S. Sheridan Road, Tulsa, OK 74112. *Tables*: 260, 350, 358, 371, 485, 553, 637, 799, 836

Electrical World, published by McGraw-Hill Inc., 11 West 19th St., New York, NY 10011. *Tables*: 258, 783

Energy, published by Business Communication Co., Inc., 25 Van Zant Street, Norwalk, CT 06855. *Tables*: 333, 635, 646, 682, 685, 688

Energy User News, published by The Chilton Company, One Chilton Way, Radnor, PA 19089. *Tables*: 696, 697, 698

ENR, published by McGraw-Hill Inc., 1221 Ave, of the Americas, New York, NY 10020. *Tables*: 264, 266, 283, 286, 292, 383, 486, 487, 490, 491, 504, 505, 507, 508, 544, 545, 716, 738, 775, 786, 817

Environment, published by Heldref Publications, 4000 Albemarle Street. N.W., Washington, DC 20016. *Tables*: 689, 850, 851

Environment Today, published by Enterprise Communications, Inc., 1905 Powers Ferry Road, Ste. 120, Marietta, GA 30067. *Tables*: 385, 489

Environmental Action, published by Environmental Action Inc., 1525 New Hampshire Ave., N.W. Washington, D.C. 20036. *Tables*: 549, 596

Farm Journal, published by Farm Journal, Inc., 230 W. Washington Square, Philadelphia, PA19105. *Tables*: 452, 584, 710, 750, 801, 822, 823, 824

Financial World, published by Financial World Partners, 1450 Broadway, New York, NY 10018. *Table*: 310

Fortune, published by The Time Inc. Magazine Company, Time & Life Building, Rockefeller Center, New York, NY 10020-1393. *Table*: 514

Garbage, published by Old House Journal Corp., 435 Ninth St., Brooklyn, NY 11215. *Tables*: 270, 273, 373, 433, 460, 468, 480, 506, 522, 529, 547, 554, 597, 612, 647, 674, 683, 730, 752, 754, 760, 761, 782, 789

Hazmat World, published by Tower-Borner Publishing, Inc., Building C, Suite 206, 800 Roosevelt Road, Glen Ellyn, IL 60137-5851. *Table*: 488

Independent Energy, published by Alternative Sources of Energy, 107 So. Central Ave., Milaca, MN 56353. *Table*: 636

Journal of Environmental Health, published by the National Environmental Health Association, 720 S. Colorado Blvd., Suite 970 South Tower, Denver, CO 80222. *Table*: 247

Modern Plastics, published by McGraw-Hill, Inc., 1221 Ave. of Americas, New York, NY 10020. *Tables*: 357, 389, 436, 463, 601, 663

Money, published by The Time Inc. Magazine Company, Time & Life Building, Rockefeller Center, New York, NY 10020-1393. *Table*: 395

National Geographic, published by the National Geographic Society, 17th & M St., N.W., Washington, DC 20036. *Table*: 692

Nature and Resources. *Tables*: 677, 779

New England Journal of Medicine, 1172 Commonwealth Ave., Boston, MA 02134. *Table*: 848

New York Times, published by the New York Times Co., 229 W. 43rd St., New York, NY 10036. *Tables*: 370, 694

Newsweek, published by Newsweek, Inc., 444 Madison Avenue, New York, NY 1002. *Table*: 771

OECD Observer, published by the Organization for Economic Co-operation and Development, Chateau de la Muette 2, rue Andre- Pascal F 75775 Paris Cedix 16. *Table*: 638

Packaging, Cahners Plaza 1350 E. Touhy Ave., Des Plaines, IL 60017-5080. *Table*: 327

Plastics World, published by the Cahners Publishing Company, 275 Washington St., Newton, MA 02158. *Tables*: 598, 604, 605

Pollution Engineering, published by the Cahners Publishing Company, 275 Washington St., Newton, MA 02158-1630. *Tables*: 259, 284, 407, 599

Power, published by McGraw-Hill, Inc., 11 West 19th Street, New York, NY 10011. *Tables*: 455, 536

Pulp & Paper, published by Miller Freeman Publications, 600 Harrison St., San Francisco, CA 94107. *Tables*: 309, 419, 439, 445, 447, 448, 450, 451, 513, 548, 649, 651, 656, 657, 740, 741, 803, 810

Recycling Today, published by GIE Inc., 4012 Bridge Ave., Cleveland, OH 44113-3320. *Tables*: 269, 759, 809

Resource Recovery, 1707 H St., N.W., Washington, D.C. 20006. *Tables*: 441, 442, 731

Resource Recycling, published by Resource Recycling, Inc., 1206 N.W. 21st, Portland, OR 97209. *Tables*: 325, 330, 338, 343, 396, 397, 398, 401, 404, 405, 408, 415, 416, 417, 418, 427, 429, 430, 438, 440, 443, 444, 446, 509, 512, 593, 594, 595, 650, 652, 666, 667, 720, 721, 722, 725, 726, 727, 732, 734, 739, 763, 826, 827, 828

Resources, Conservation and Recycling, published by Pergamon Press PLC. *Tables*: 420, 471, 737, 756

Science, published by the American Association for the Advancement of Science, 1333 H Street, N.W., Washington, DC 20005. *Tables*: 301, 332, 336, 537, 846

Scientific American, published by Scientific American, Inc., 415 Madison Avenue, New York, NY 10017. *Table*: 648

Sierra, published by the Sierra Club, 730 Polk St., San Francisco, CA 94109. *Table*: 695

Technology Review, published by the Association of Alumnae of the Massachusetts Institute of Technology, MIT, Building W59, Cambridge, MA 02139. *Table*: 483

Time, published by The Time Inc. Magazine Company, Time & Life Building, Rockefeller Center, New York, NY 10020-1393. *Tables*: 628, 719, 778, 831, 832, 834, 837

Traffic Management, published by Cahners Publishing Co., 221 Columbus Ave., Boston, MA 02116. *Table*: 673

USA Today, published by Society for the Advancement of Education, 99 W. Hawthorn Ave., Valley Stream, NY 11580. *Tables*: 634, 847

U.S. News & World Report, published by U.S. News & World Report Inc., 2400 N Street, N.W., Washington, DC 20037-1196. *Tables*: 261, 560, 659, 724, 830, 841, 843, 848

Wall Street Journal, published by Dow Jones, 420 Lexington Ave., New York, NY 10170. *Tables*: 276, 502, 503, 531, 705, 714

Waste Age, published by the National Waste Management Association, Suite 1000, 1730 Rhode Island Ave., N.W., Washington, DC 20036. *Table*: 511

Water Environment & Technology, published by the Water Pollution Control Federation, 601 Wythe St., Alexandria, VA 22314-1994. *Table*: 422

World Monitor, published by The Christian Science Publishing Society, One Norway Street, Boston, MA 02115. *Table*: 672

World Wastes, published by Communications Channels, Inc., 6255 Barfield Road, Atlanta, GA 30328. *Tables*: 265, 331, 516, 517, 518

WorldWatch, published by Worldwatch Institute, 1776 Massachusetts Ave., N.W., Washington, DC 20036. *Tables*: 277, 482, 533, 556, 627, 642, 660, 671, 742, 785, 825, 845, 849

PERIODICALS CITED BY PRIMARY SOURCES

The following periodicals were cited as original sources in the report literature (see Appendix I) or in periodicals (see above). Following each periodical listed will be one or more references to tables, arranged in the order of their appearance. Periodicals listed below may also be included in the listing, above, of primary sources.

American Metal Market, published by American Metal Market Co., 7 E. 1th St., New York, NY 10003. *Table*: 330

Beverage Industry, Beverage Marketing Corp., 2670 Commercial Avenue, Mingo Junction, OH 43938. *Table*: 595

Business Communications, British Telecom, Intel House/Room 107, 24 Sthwrk Brd., London SE1 9HJ, England. *Table*: 357

Europa, Interuniversity Centre for European Studies, P.O. Box 8892, Montreal, PQ Canada. *Table*: 672

Modern Plastics, published by McGraw-Hill, Inc., 1221 Ave. of Americas, New York, NY 10020. *Tables*: 600, 618, 623

Oil Spill Intelligence Report, Cutter Information Corporation, 1100 Massachusetts Ave., Arlington, MA 02174-4328. *Table*: 250

Packaging, Cahners Plaza 1350 E. Touhy Ave., Des Plaines,. *Table*: 598

Plastics News, published by Crain Communications, Inc., 1725 Merriman Rd., Akron, OH 44313. *Table*: 328

Pulp & Paper and *Pulp & Paper International*, published by Miller Freeman Publications, 600 Harrison St., San Francisco, CA 94107. *Tables*: 447, 509, 659

Resource Recycling, published by Resource Recycling, Inc., 1206 N.W. 21st, Portland, OR 97209. *Tables*: 325, 405, 666

Appendix III

ORGANIZATIONAL SOURCES

The following listing shows organizations—from the public and the private sectors—that were cited as sources of information in primary sources. The organizations are listed below in alphabetical order. After each organization will be found one or more references to tables; these references are arranged in the order of their appearance.

Alex Brown & Sons Inc. *Table*: 507

Alliance for Responsible CFC Policy. *Tables*: 541, 806

Aluminum Association. *Tables*: 325, 396, 397

American Coalition for Ethanol. *Table*: 584

American Consulting Engineers Council. *Tables*: 696, 698

American Council for an Energy-Efficient Economy. *Table*: 277

American Forest Council. *Table*: 560

American Iron & Steel Institute. *Table*: 664

American Metal Market. *Table*: 531

American National Can. *Table*: 330

American Newspaper Publishers Association. *Table*: 810

American Paper Institute. *Tables*: 419, 421, 422, 443, 444, 445, 446, 447, 652, 653, 654, 655, 656, 657, 658

American Petroleum Institute. *Tables*: 590, 591

American Recycling Market Inc. *Table*: 330

Andover International Associates. *Tables*: 338, 418

Arthur Andersen. *Table*: 799

Associated Press. *Table*: 841

Association of American Railroads. *Table*: 673

Association of State and Territorial Solid Waste Management Officials. *Table*: 376

Avmark. *Table*: 670

Booz-Allen & Hamilton Inc. *Tables*: 499, 508

British Plastics Federation. *Table*: 611

British Plastics Waste Management Institute. *Table*: 609

Burson-Marsteller. *Table*: 829

Cahners Economics. *Table*: 259

California Air Resources Board. *Tables*: 682, 685, 688

California Department of Conservation. *Table*: 594

California Health Department Toxics Program. *Table*: 705

California/Nevada Soft Drink Association. *Table*: 594

Cambridge Energy Research Associates. *Table*: 799

Can Manufacturers Institute. *Tables*: 325, 397, 593

Canadian Pulp & Paper Association. *Table*: 447

Center for Marine Conservation. *Table*: 760

Chemical Manufacturers Association. *Tables*: 372, 375, 381

Chemical Manufactures Association. *Table*: 374

Chemical Specialties Manufacturers' Association. *Table*: 546

Chemical Waste Management Company. *Table*: 373

City of Lexington, Kentucky. *Tables*: 720, 726, 734

Council for Solid Waste Solutions. *Table*: 809

E.H. Pechan and Associates. *Table*: 91

Edison Electric Institute. *Tables*: 260, 271

Environmental Action Coalition. *Table*: 612

European Community. *Table*: 825

European Confederation of Pulp, Paper & Board Industries. *Table*: 447

Executive Office of the President, Office of Management and Budget. *Tables*: 334, 544

F.W. Dodge Co. *Tables*: 264, 266, 283

FAO. *Table*: 556

Franklin Associates, Ltd. *Tables*: 130, 131, 132, 133, 134, 135, 136, 137, 138, 139, 143, 144, 145, 146, 147, 148, 155, 156, 157, 158, 160, 162, 164, 166, 167, 169, 170, 171, 172, 173, 175, 177, 180, 276, 388, 399, 400, 402, 403, 410, 411, 412, 413, 414, 421, 422, 423

Freedonia Group. *Tables*: 437, 500

Fund Management. *Table*: 278

GSX Chemical Services, Inc. *Table*: 373

General Services Administration. *Table*: 544

Gildea Resource Center. *Table*: 401

Government Advisory Associates. *Table*: 518

Greater Detroit Resources Recovery Authority. *Table*: 764

Greenpeace. *Tables*: 580, 581, 742

Harris Upham & Co. *Table*: 286

Harvey J. Stengel and Associates. *Table*: 273

Hong Kong Environmental Protection Department. *Table*: 763

IAEA. *Table*: 642

Industrial Fabrics Association. *Table*: 463

Institute of Scrap Recycling Industries, Inc. *Tables*: 405, 417

International Atomic Energy Agency. *Tables*: 628, 642

International Energy Agency. *Table*: 697

International Institute for Applied Systems Analysis. *Table*: 689

International Institute of Synthetic Rubber Producers. *Table*: 620

Jaakko Poyry, 1990. *Tables*: 430, 732

Karen Mancl/Ohio State University. *Table*: 823

Kline & Co. *Table*: 525

Lipper Analytical Services, Inc. *Table*: 506

Louis Harris & Associates. *Table*: 841

Marist Institute. *Table*: 841

Marketing Intelligence Service. *Table*: 549

Marketing/Technology Service, Inc. *Tables*: 548, 651

Mercer Meidinger Hansen Inc. *Table*: 486

Merrill Lynch. *Table*: 506

Mongoven, Bisco, Duchin. *Table*: 824

Motor Vehicle Manufacturers Association. *Table*: 533

National Association of Recycling Industries, Inc. *Table*: 448

National Governors' Association. *Tables*: 331, 704

National Roundtable of State Waste Reduction Programs. *Table*: 716

National Society of Professional Engineers. *Table*: 487

National Solid Waste Management Association, 1988. *Table*: 759

National Solid Waste Management Association. *Tables*: 389, 724, 738

National Solid Wastes Management Assoc. *Table*: 460

National Tire Dealers and Retreaders Association. *Table*: 343

National Wildlife Federation. *Table*: 789

New York City Department of Sanitation. *Table*: 761

New York Historical Society. *Table*: 761

North Carolina Pollution Prevention Program. *Table*: 716

Oak Ridge National Laboratory. *Tables*: 671, 695

Organization for Economic Cooperation and Development (OECD). *Tables*: 529, 743

Organization for Economic Development and Cooperation (OECD). *Table*: 638

Pan American. *Table*: 670

Plastics Waste Management Institute. *Table*: 611

President's Council on Physical Fitness and Sports. *Table*: 671

Recoupe Recycling Technologies. *Table*: 339

Recycling Processor Survey. *Table*: 330

Rocky Mountain Institute. *Table*: 647

Roosevelt Center for American Policy Studies. *Table*: 843

Roper Organization. *Tables*: 839, 846

S.C. Johnson & Son Inc. *Table*: 830

SRI International. *Tables*: 524, 526, 606, 607

Salomon Brothers Inc. *Table*: 286

Seattle Solid Waste Utility. *Table*: 731

Shell Briefing Service. *Table*: 562

Shupe & Associates. *Table*: 676

Smith Barney. *Table*: 286

Society of the Plastics Industry. *Tables*: 603, 606, 607, 608, 614, 615, 616, 617, 621, 622, 624, 625

Soil and Water Conservation Society. *Table*: 750

Sound Resource Management Group, Inc. *Tables*: 408, 739

State of Minnesota Pollution Control Agency. *Table*: 801

Strategic Analysis. *Table*: 428

Teledyne Brown Engineering. *Table*: 36

Union Carbide Corp. *Tables*: 606, 607

United Nations Environment Program. *Table*: 785

United Nations, Food & Agricultural Organization. *Table*: 447

United Nations. *Table*: 690

University of Arizona. *Tables*: 676, 752

U.S. Bureau of Mines. *Tables*: 396, 661, 664, 665

U.S. Bureau of the Census. *Tables*: 661, 661

U.S. Council for Energy Awareness. *Table*: 628

U.S. Department of Agriculture. *Tables*: 273, 554, 650

U.S. Department of Commerce. *Tables*: 259, 396, 405, 415, 416, 429, 438, 480, 547, 666

U.S. Department of Energy. *Tables*: 292, 334, 485

U.S. Department of Housing and Urban Development. *Table*: 674

U.S. Department of Transportation. *Table*: 532

U.S. Department of Treasury. *Table*: 302

U.S. Environmental Protection Agency. *Tables*: 38, 46, 259, 261, 317, 335, 370, 383, 385, 398, 468, 522, 530, 649, 669, 673, 683, 743, 771, 775, 782, 786, 817

U.S. Forest Service. *Table*: 559

U.S. Geological Survey. *Tables*: 39, 47, 49, 710

U.S. International Trade Commission. *Tables*: 622, 625

Volkswagen Corp. *Table*: 367

Warren Brookes. *Table*: 271

Water Pollution Control Federation. *Table*: 817

Wertheim Schroder & Co. *Table*: 286

William T. Lorenz & Co. *Table*: 346

World Health Organization. *Table*: 785

Appendix IV

ABBREVIATIONS AND ACRONYMS

The following listing shows the abbreviations used in *Statistical Record of the Environment* with some exceptions. The listing of very well known corporations were omitted (IBM); and the abbreviated names of companies that could not be determined from the source were also left unexplained.

#	Number	A-SP	Aerated static pile
%	Percent	AVG	Average
<	Less than	A-W	Aerated windrow
>	Greater than	B	Biweekly
A	Architect	B&W	Babcock and Wilcox Co.
A	Assembly bill	BB	Bedminster bioconversion
A-B	Agitated bin	BHE	Benzene hexachloride
A-BT	American Bio-tech	BILL	Billion
A-C	Allis-Chalmers	BLK	Bleached kraft paper
ADAPTS	Air Deliverable Anti-Pollution Transfer Systems	BMW	Bayerische Motoren Werke, German automobile manufacturer
AE	Architect-Engineer		
AEC	Atomic Energy Commission	BOC	US Bureau of the Census
AIChE	American Institute of Chemical Engineers	BOD	Biological oxygen demand
		BOM	Bureau of Mines
AIDS	Acquired Immune Deficiency Syndrome	BTU	British thermal unit
		BWR	Boiling water reactor
AMOCO	American Oil Company	BXB	Boxboard cuttings
API	Amer Petroleum Inst	C	Cent
AQTX	Aquatic toxicity	C	Construction
A-S-H	Ashbrook, Simon, Hartley	CBS	Coated book stock

CE	Consulting Engineer	DER	Department of Environ-mental Research
C-E	Combustion Engineering		
CEC	Council of the European Communities	DO	Dissolved oxygen
		DOA	Department of Agriculture
C&EN	Chemical and Engineering News	DOC	Department of Commerce
		DOE	Department of Energy
CEQ	U.S. Council on Environ mental Quality	DOI	Department of Interior
		DOT	Department of Trans-portation
CFC	Chlorofluorocarbon		
CLP	Consideration low priority	D/Y	Days per year
CM	Claims-made	EA	Engineer-Architect
CMA	Chemical Manufacturers Association	EC	Engineer-Contractor
		EDB	Ethylene dibromide
CNG	Compressed natural gas	EDF	Environmental Defense Fund
CNN	Cable News Network		
CO	Carbon monoxide	EEC	European Economic Community
CO	Company		
CO2	Carbon dioxide	EFTA	European Free Trade Association
COD	Chemical oxygen demand		
COE	Corps of Engineers	EIA	Energy Information Administration
CORP	Corporation		
CP	Construction permit	EIS	Environmental Impact Statements
CSMA	Chemical Specialities Manufactures Association		
		ENR	Engineering News Record
CTG	Control technique guide-lines	ENV	Environmental Engineer
		EPA	Environmental Protection Agency
CU YD	Cubic yard		
CU METER	Cubic meter	ERIC	Environmental Risk Insurance Co.
CWIP	Construction work in progress		
		ETA	Employment and Training Administration
CY	Cubic yard		
CYD	Cubic yard per day	F	Fahrenheit
CYM	Cubic yard per month	FAA	Federal Aviation Admin-istration
CYY	Cubic yard per year		
D	Degree	FAO	Food and Agriculture Organization
D	Design		
DBA	Dihydro-dimethyl benzopyranbutyric acid	FBC	Fluidized-bed combustion
		FDA	Food and Drug Admin-istration
DC	Darling's Compost		
DDT	Dichlorodiphenyltri-chloroethane	FERC	Federal Energy Regulatory Commission
DEPT	Department	FGIC	Financial Guaranty Insur-ance Corporation

FHWA	Federal Highway Admin-istration		HUD	Department of Housing and Development
F.O.B.	Free on board		HVAC	Heating, ventilating and air conditioning
FOE	Friends of the Earth			
FRA	Federal Railway Admin-istration		HWDMS	Hazardous Waste Disposal Management System
FS	Feasibility study		I	Involuntary
FSI	Furnace sorbent injection		ICC	Interstate Commerce Commission
FT	Foot or feet			
FT3	Cubic feet		ICPP	Idaho Chemical Processing Plant
FY	Fiscal year			
G	Gallon		ID	Indefinitely deferred
G	Graduate		IGCC	Integrated gas combined cycle
G	Grind			
GA	General Atomic Company		IISRP	International Institute of Synthetic Rubber Producers
GAL	Gallon			
GDR	German Democratic Republic		IJC	International Joint Com-mission
GDS	Gallons per day septage			
GE	General Electric		I/M	Inspection and Mainte-nance
GE	Soil or Geotechnical Engineer			
GM	Gram		IN	Inches
GNP	Gross National Product		INC	Incorporated
GPD	Gallons per day		INCL	Including
GPO	US Government Printing Office		IPS	International Process System
GRI	Gas Research Institute		IRRI	International Rice Research Institute
GSA	Geological Society of America		ISRI	Institute of Scrap Re-cycling Industries
GWE	Gigawatt Electrical			
H	House bill		I-V	In-vessel
HAZMAT	Hazardous material		IWK	Izaak Walton league of America
H-B	Horizontal bin			
HC	Hydrocarbon			
HCFC	Hydrochlorofluoro carbon		K	Kilo
HDPE	High density polyethylene		K	Potash
HFC	Hydrofluorocarbon		K	Thousand
HHS	Department of Health and Human Services		KCAL	Kilocalories
			KG	Kilogram
HHV	Higher heating value		KJ	Kilojoules
HMIS	Hazardous Material Information System		L	Linier board
			L	Liter
HTGR	High temperature gas-cooled reactor		LB	Pound
			LBS	Pounds

LDA	Lime dual alkali	MSW	Municipal Solid Waste
LDG	Ledger and computer printout	MT	Metric ton
		MT/Y	Metric tons per year
LDPE	Low density polyethylene	MW	Megawatt
LGR	Light water-cooled reactor	MWP	Mixed waste paper
		M3	Cubic meter
LLNL	Lawrence Livermore National Laboratory	N	Non-credit
		NA	Not applicable
LLW	Low level radioactive waste	NA	Not available
		NAS	National Audoban Society
LNG	Liquified Natural Gas	NASA	National Aeronautics and Space Administration
LP	Low power		
LPG	Liquidfied Petroleum Gas	NASQAN	National Stream Quality Accounting Network
LPW	Lumens per watt		
LR	Lower reference	NC	No change
LS	Lime stone	NEPA	Natl Environmental Policy Act of 1969
LSD	Line spray dryer		
LSFO	Limestone/forced oxidation	NIOSH	National Institute for Occupational Safety and Health
M	Mandatory		
M	Medium		
M	Meter	NO2	Nitrogen oxide
MAGLIME	Magnesium enhanced lime	NOAA	US National Oceanic and Atmospheric Admin
MAX	Maximum		
MED	Medium	NPL	National Priorities List
MET	Metric	NR	Non-returnable
METR	Metric	NRC	National Recycling Council
MG	Magnesium	NRC	National Research Council
MG	Milligram	NRDC	National Research Defense Council
MGD	Million gallons per day		
MI	Mile	NSF	US Natl Science Foundation
MIL	Million	NSWMA	National Solid Waste Management Association
MIL DOL	Million dollars		
MIL LB	Million pounds	NTIS	US Natl Technical Information Service (DOC)
MILL	Million		
MIN	Minimum	NWC	Northwest Cascade
MIN	Minor	NWF	National Wildlife Federation
MIN	Minute		
MISC	Miscellaneous	NYC	New York City
MM	Millimeter	NEG	Negligible
MO	Month	NO	Number
MOD	Moderate	O	Occurence
MOD W	Modified windrow	O	Operational
MPG	Miles per gallon	O	Oxygen

OCC	Old corrugated cardboard		works
ODP	Ozone depletion potential	PP	Polypropylene
OE	Office of Education	PPM	Parts per million
OECD	Organization of Economic	PREL	Preliminary
	Cooperation and Develop-	PROD	Product
	ment	P.S.U.	Pennsylvania State Uni-
O&M	Operating and Mainte-		versity
	nance	PVC	Polyvinyl chloride
ONP	Old newspaper	PWR	Pressurized water
OPEC	Organization of Petroleum		reactor
	Exporting Countries	RACT	Reasonably available
ORNL	Oak Ridge National		control technology
	Laboratories (DOE)	RCRA	Resource Conservation
OS	Occurance with a sunset		and Recovery Act
OSHA	Occupational Safety and	R&D	Research and development
	Health Administration	RDF	Refuse-derived fuel
OSW	Office of Saline Water	RFDI	Inhalation reference doses
OSW	Office of Solid Waste	RGS	Rags
OSWER	Office of Solid Waste and	RI	Recyc. Incorporation
	Energy Response	RI	Remedial investigation
OTA	Office of Technology	RO	Reported occurrence
	Assessment	RPA	Rubber peptizing agent
OTH	Speciality paper grades	RQ	Reportable quantities
P	Phosphate	RQCH	Reportable quantities for
P	Planner		chronic
P	Procurement	RSPA	Research and Special
PAC	Pacific Telesis Group		Program Administration
PAC	Pollution Abatement and	S	Senate bill
	Control	SAT	Satellite
PAGs	Polyalkylene glycols	SB	Senate bill
PB	Plumblum (lead)	SBS	Solid bleached sulfate
PCB	Polychlorinated biphenyl	SC	Screen
PCT	Polychlorinated Terphenyl	SC	Sierra Club
PET	Polyethylene terephthalate	SCD	Soil conservation district
pH	Pouvoir hydrogene	SCR	Selection catalytic reduction
	(negative logarithm of	SH	Shred
	effective hydrogen in	SIC	Standard industrial code
	concentration)	SJC	San Joaquin Composting
PLP	Wood pulp	SO	Sulfur oxide
PM	Particulate matter	SO_2	Sulfur dioxide
PM	Project manager	SP	Static pile
PO	Polystyrene	SQ KM	Square kilometer
POTW	Publicly-owned treatment	SQ MI	Square mile

TCDD	Tetrachloro-p-dibenzo-dioxin	USDOE	United States Department of Energy
TDS	Total dissolved solids	USFS	US Forest Service
TLC	Twin Landfill Corporation	USGS	US Geological Survey)
TPD	Tons per day	USN&WR	US News & World Report
TPY	Tons per year	U.S.S.R.	Union of Soviet Republics
TRI	Toxic Release Inventory	UV	Ultraviolet
TSDFS	Treatment, Storage, and Disposal facilities	V	Voluntary
TSDR	Transportation, Storage, Disposal or Recycling	VOC	Volatile organic compound
		W	Weekly
TV	Television	W	Westinghouse Electric Corporation
TVI	Temporary variance authority	W	With
TWH	Tetrewatt hour	WHO	World Health Organization
U	Undergraduate	WK	Week
UNEP	United Nations Environment Program	WMO	World Metreological Organization
UR	Upper reference	WQC	Waste quality criteria
USBM	US Bureau of Mines)	WS	the Wilderness Society
USCG	United States Coast Guard	WSA	Water soluble adjuvant
USDA	United States Department of Agriculture	WTD	Wet tons per day
		WVDP	West Valley Demonstration Project
USDI	US Department of the Interior	YD	Yard
		YR	Year

KEYWORD INDEX

The *Keyword Index* is an alphabetical arrangement of the topics covered in the book as well as "line items" within tables. The primary reference numbers that follow subject index terms are page numbers; reference numbers in brackets are entry numbers. Page references to line item citations are to the page on which the item appears rather than to the first page of the table. Organization names are reproduced as they appear in the tables. Thus variant renditions of the same organization will appear in sequence, e.g., *American Cyanamid* and *American Cyanamid Co.* Some names are names of ships; they are, however, not identified as such.

Africa continued:
— carbon emissions, transportation 577 [680]
— paper use 633 [742]
— river runoff 45 [48]
— wastepaper recovery 632 [741]
— wastepaper utilization 632 [740]
Aggregate 364 [455]
Agra Industries
— Saskatoon, SK 562 [663]
Agrichemicals 54, 55, 56, 57, 58, 437, 441 [57], [58], [59], [60], [61], [62], [63], [64], [535], [539]
See also: Fertilizers; Herbicides; Pesticides
— hazardous waste generation 90 [110]
Agrico Chemical Co. Div.-Freeport McMoran
— toxic releases, transfers 566 [668]
Agricultural conservation 274, 299, 635 [340], [368], [744]
Agricultural land 688, 689 [802], [804]
Agricultural pesticides 441 [539]
Agricultural products consumption 560 [660]
Agricultural waste 171, 453 [210], [553]
Agriculture 15, 17, 54, 55, 57, 86, 93, 274, 427, 498, 575, 636, 638, 679 [16], [20], [58], [59], [63], [104], [113], [340], [523], [609], [677], [745], [746], [793]
— causing fishing restrictions 177 [218]
— irrigated areas 21 [23]
— use of plastics 499 [610]
Agriculture and fish kills 189 [233]
Air
— asbestos fibers 152 [188]
— lead exposure 196 [244]
— radiation levels 35 [38]
— rail, marine transportation 291, 292 [359], [360]
Air conditioning 70, 288, 438, 450 [82], [355], [536], [550]
— auto 61, 286 [69], [352]
— energy consumed 450 [550]
— energy costs 220 [272]
— room, global warming 83 [101]
Air cycle machines 439 [538]
Air economizers 593 [696]
Air emissions 159, 371 [197], [466]
Air Force 679 [793]
Air pollution 59, 60, 61, 62, 63, 64, 65, 66, 67, 68, 69, 70, 71, 73, 74, 75, 76, 77, 78, 79, 80, 81, 82, 156, 163, 169, 222, 251, 300, 335, 438, 568, 576, 577, 578, 579, 581, 582, 583, 586, 587, 588, 589, 722 [65], [66], [67], [68], [69], [70], [71], [72], [73], [74], [75], [76], [77], [78], [79], [80], [81], [82], [83], [84], [85], [86], [87], [88], [89], [90], [91], [92], [93], [94], [95], [96], [97], [98], [99], [100], [193], [202], [207], [276], [314], [370], [420], [536], [669], [678], [679], [680], [681], [682], [683], [684], [685], [686], [687], [688], [689], [690], [691], [692], [849]
— abatement costs 235 [296]
— indoor 180 [221]
— toxic chemicals 150, 157, 160, 161, 162, 166 [186], [195],

Air pollution continued:
[198], [199], [200], [205]
Air pollution control 209, 210, 211, 212, 285, 286, 287, 288, 289, 290, 291, 292, 293, 294 [258], [259], [260], [261], [262], [351], [352], [353], [354], [355], [356], [357], [358], [359], [360], [361], [362], [363]
— market size 408 [508]
— utilities 257 [323]
Air pollution control expenditures
— utilities 212 [262]
Air pollution from factories 720 [846]
Air pollution from vehicles 720 [846]
Air pollution prevention 217 [269]
Air pollution standards 675 [785]
Air Products & Chemicals Inc. 569 [669]
— toxic releases, transfers 567 [668]
Air Products & Chemicals Inc./Dakota Gasification Co. 386 [485]
Air quality spending 247 [309]
Air quality standards 582, 583 [686], [687]
Air transportation 67 [79]
Air, EPA research 271 [335]
Aircraft
— carbon dioxide emissions 63, 65 [73], [77]
— noise control 570 [670]
— noise pollution 611 [714]
Aircraft bombs 475 [581]
Aircraft carriers 474, 476 [580], [582]
Aircraft emissions 82 [99]
Airplane noise 611 [714]
AirPol Inc. 386 [485]
Airport buildings
— construction 213 [264]
Airport paving 213 [264]
Airports 213 [263]
Akron, OH 265, 381, 415, 427 [329], [479], [510], [523]
Alabama 7, 8, 16, 17, 18, 19, 37, 38, 39, 40, 46, 48, 166, 167, 187, 219, 236, 257, 278, 369, 426, 537, 606, 609, 680, 682, 683 [7], [8], [18], [19], [20], [21], [22], [40], [41], [42], [43], [49], [50], [205], [206], [231], [271], [298], [323], [344], [465], [522], [640], [708], [713], [794], [797], [798]
— acid rain impacts 673 [783]
— chemicals releases and transfers 663 [773]
— conservation plans 639 [747]
— conservation programs 635 [744]
— conservation, agriculture 636, 638 [745], [746]
— curbside recycling 627 [733]
— erosion control 641 [749]
— forest revenues 600 [703]
— forestry incentive programs 597 [701]
— forestry practices 599 [702]
— forests 8 [9]
— gasohol use 478 [586]
— gasoline use 479 [587]

Commercial offices
— construction 213 [264]
Commercial printing 125, 126, 127, 128, 129, 131, 331, 332, 342 [155], [156], [157], [158], [160], [161], [164], [413], [414], [431]
Commercial stores 289 [355]
Commonwealth Edison Co. 237, 258 [298], [323]
Commonwealth Edison Co. of IN, Inc. 237, 258 [298], [323]
Commonwealth Electric Co. 238, 258 [298], [323]
Commonwealth of Massachusetts 411 [510]
Communication equipment 67 [79]
Communication paper 197 [246]
Communications
— construction 213 [264]
Compact fluorescent lamps 593 [696]
Compaction 228 [284]
Compacts 316 [391]
Compensation 387, 388 [486], [487], [488]
CompGro 427 [523]
Compliance 673 [782], [783]
Compliance managers
— salaries 388 [488]
Compliance reporting 679 [793]
Composition of solid waste 147 [183]
Compost markets 427 [523]
Compost price 265 [329]
Compost recovery 111, 112, 117, 118, 125, 126, 134, 135 [135], [136], [145], [146], [155], [156], [166], [167]
Composted/shredded refuse
— nutrient concentrations 56 [61]
Composting 116, 117, 118, 131, 329, 330, 337, 342, 350, 351, 363, 365, 372, 373, 375, 643, 644, 649, 686 [143], [145], [146], [164], [410], [411], [423], [424], [431], [434], [435], [454], [457], [458], [467], [468], [471], [751], [753], [757], [800]
See also: Sludge
— facilities 343, 643 [432], [751]
— sludge 265, 381, 427 [329], [479], [523]
— yard waste 627 [733]
Comprehensive Environmental Response
— Compensation & Liability Act 676 [788]
Compressed natural gas 163, 221 [202], [275]
Compressors 593 [696]
Computer paper 623 [728]
— recycled, Washington 623 [728]
Computer print 170 [209]
Computer use in environmental management 467 [573]
Concrete bunkers 232 [291]
Concrete containers and concrete vaults
— radioactive disposal 232 [291]
Concrete products 364 [455]
Conduits 492 [603]
Confined-zone dispersion flue-gas desulfurization 386 [485]
Confinement 674 [784]

Congo
— elephant population 185 [229]
Connecticut 7, 8, 16, 19, 37, 38, 39, 40, 46, 48, 166, 167, 187, 237, 257, 278, 369, 409, 535, 606, 610, 680, 683 [7], [8], [18], [19], [22], [40], [41], [42], [43], [49], [50], [205], [206], [231], [298], [323], [344], [465], [510], [640], [708], [713], [794], [798]
— chemicals releases and transfers 663 [773]
— conservation plans 639 [747]
— conservation programs 635 [744]
— conservation, agriculture 636, 638 [745], [746]
— construction, waste recovery 227 [283]
— curbside recycling 627 [733]
— disposal bans 691 [807]
— drinking water 677 [789]
— erosion control 641 [749]
— fishing 703 [820]
— forestry incentive programs 597 [701]
— forestry practices 599 [702]
— forests 8 [9]
— gasoline use 479 [587]
— gasoline use on highways 481 [588]
— hazardous waste disposal 305 [376]
— hazardous waste sites 604 [707]
— houses with radon 617 [719]
— land use 22 [25]
— local recycling mandates 697 [813]
— mandatory deposits 693 [808]
— membership organizations 710 [828]
— MSW disposal 645 [753]
— nuclear power 520 [635]
— procurement program 702 [819]
— radioactive disposal 612 [715]
— recycling 622 [727]
— recycling legislation 696 [811]
— recycling program funding 225 [281]
— renewable energy 548 [646]
— sewage treatment 666 [775]
— shore debris 42 [45]
— sludge composting 344 [432]
— soil conservation 28, 30, 275 [30], [31], [341]
— soil conservation districts 26 [28]
— solid waste disposal 649 [757]
— solid waste legislation 686 [800]
— steam-electric plants 71, 511, 547, 579 [84], [626], [645], [684]
— toxic chemicals 662 [772]
— toxic rail accidents 206 [256]
— toxic waste transport 164 [203]
— tree planting 10 [10]
— water pollution 681 [796]
— wetlands 671 [781]
Connecticut Light & Power Co. 237, 257 [298], [323]
Connecticut Resource Recovery Authority 409 [510]

Corpus Christi State University
— education in hazardous waste management 394 [494]
Corrosion inhibitors 428, 430 [524], [526]
Corrosives 603 [706]
Corrugated 326, 336, 338, 359, 555 [404], [421], [422], [426], [448], [655]
— potential for recovery 336 [421]
Corrugated and kraft
— exports of 340 [429]
Corrugated board 273 [339]
— in solid waste 147 [183]
Corrugated boxes 105, 106, 107, 108, 109, 128, 129, 131, 137, 144, 321, 323, 342, 689 [129], [130], [131], [132], [133], [160], [161], [164], [171], [179], [399], [400], [431], [803]
— in landfills 124 [152]
Corrugated paper 353, 354, 355, 356, 357, 359, 558, 564, 623 [438], [439], [443], [444], [446], [448], [658], [666], [728]
— recycled, Washington 623 [728]
Corrugated Services Inc. 419 [513]
Cosmetics 158 [196]
Cosmic radiation 191 [236]
Cost/benefit 221, 222 [274], [275], [276], [277]
Cost/value engineers
— salaries 387 [487]
Costa Rica
— wastepaper 565 [667]
Cote D'Ivoire
— elephant population 185 [229]
Cotton 54, 57 [58], [63]
— cloth 490 [599]
— diapers 217 [269]
— linters 552 [650]
Cotton fiber paper 688 [803]
Cottonwood and aspen 460, 461 [564], [565]
Council of the European Communities 689 [804]
Cover stock 688 [803]
Cowdung
— Hawaiian 60 [67]
Cowens Ford Dam 538 [640]
Cowlitz County 155 [191]
CP-SS Capital Inc./TECO Power Services Corp. 386 [485]
CPR (Rutgers), Piscataway, NJ 562 [663]
CQ Inc./Combustion Engineering Co. 385 [485]
CR&R 409 [510]
Crater Lake
— pollution levels 25 [27]
Creek water
— Castro Valley, California, asbestos fibers 152 [188]
Cretan Star 200 [248]
Crop residues 54, 362 [57], [452]
Cropland 22, 299, 362, 641 [25], [368], [369], [453], [749]
— nitrogen source 54 [57]
Cropland erosion 182 [224]
Cropland protective cover 299 [368]

Crops 22, 57 [25], [63]
Crowley, LA, wetlands 280, 281 [347], [348]
Crude oil 485 [592]
— carbon content 62 [70]
Cruise missile submarines 474, 476 [580], [582]
Cruise missiles 475 [581]
Cruisers 475, 476 [580], [582]
Crustaceans 184, 190 [227], [235]
CSX
— toxic rail accidents 204 [254]
Cull trees 459 [563]
Cumberland College
— education in hazardous waste management 394 [494]
Cumberland County Improvement Authority 412 [510]
Cumru Township, Berks Co 415 [510]
Cups
— paper 126, 127, 128, 141, 331, 332 [157], [158], [160], [175], [413], [414]
— plastic 126, 127, 141, 331, 332 [157], [158], [175], [413], [414]
— polystyrene 144 [179]
Cups/containers 491 [601]
Curbside collection 617, 618, 628, 631 [720], [721], [734], [739]
— Chicago, IL 619 [723]
Curbside recycling 328, 618, 627, 686 [408], [722], [733], [800]
— Seattle 625 [731]
Curbside yard waste 625 [731]
Curtailable load wiring 593 [696]
Cut plate/structural exports 341 [429]
Cutlery
— plastic 144 [179]
Cuyahoga County 154, 659 [190], [769]
CWA 676 [788]
Cyanide 98 [119]
Cyanizine in groundwater 56 [62]
Cyclic crudes/intermediates
— hazardous waste generation 90 [110]
Cyclohexanone 98 [119]
Cypress 460 [564]
Cyprus Miami Mining Corp.
— toxic releases, transfers 567 [668]
Czechoslovakia 586, 587, 588 [689], [690], [691]
— air pollution 590 [694]
— coal facts 443 [542]
— lignite production 444 [543]
— natural gas 483 [589]
— surface transportation 572 [672]
— wastepaper 565 [667]
D-103 Libya 199 [248]
Dade County 410 [510]
Dairy cattle 363 [454]
Dairy products 58 [64]

El Paso Electric Co. 240, 260 [298], [323]
El Paso, TX 582, 583 [686], [687]
El Salvador
—wastepaper 565 [667]
Elections 707 [825]
Electric and electronic equipment 150, 151, 241, 312 [186], [187], [299], [386]
Electric costs 219 [271]
Electric dryers 222 [277]
Electric Energy Inc. 237, 258 [298], [323]
Electric Energy Systems and Storage 269 [333]
Electric generation 484 [590]
—wind potential 551 [648]
Electric lighting 64 [74]
—carbon gas emissions 66 [78]
Electric power plants 173 [212]
Electric preheaters 296 [365]
Electric utilities 67, 212, 215, 236, 257, 261, 291, 292, 296, 673 [79], [262], [267], [298], [323], [324], [359], [360], [366], [783]
Electric utility boiler 291, 292 [359], [360]
Electric utility industry 715 [836]
Electric utility supply-side measures 288 [354]
Electric vehicles
—solar 163 [202]
Electric water heater 222 [277]
Electrical and electronic equipment
—energy consumption 451 [551]
Electrical and electronic equipment industry
—toxic emissions 160 [197]
Electrical devices
—use of plastics in 499 [610]
Electrical engineers
—salaries 388 [487]
Electrical equipment
—consumption of thermoplastics 508 [621]
—consumption of thermoset plastics 510 [624]
Electrical machinery 211, 251, 252 [259], [313], [316]
—toxic chemicals 657, 658 [767], [768]
Electrical products
—mercury used in 474 [579]
Electricals 498 [609]
Electricity 262, 294, 491, 514, 516, 519 [326], [364], [602], [628], [631], [634]
—coal-fired plants 294 [364]
—construction 213 [264]
Electrification 439 [538]
Electrolytes 329, 330 [410], [411]
Electronics
—cadmium content 471 [576]
—lead content 473 [578]
—resin consumption 505 [618]
—use of thermoplastics 509 [623]
Elephants 185 [229]

Elgin
—Joliet & EIL, toxic rail accidents 205 [254]
Eli Lilly & Co. 569 [669]
Emcoal Corp. 386 [485]
EMCON Associates 391 [490]
Emelle 660 [770]
Emergency cleanup 310 [384]
Emergency conservation 274, 635 [340], [744]
Emergency preparedness 244 [303]
Emergency tillage 362 [452]
Emissions
—sulfur dioxide 212 [261]
Emissions reductions 291, 292, 294 [359], [360], [363]
Emory University
—education in hazardous waste management 395 [494]
Empire District Electric Co. 238, 259 [298], [323]
Enclosed static pile composting 381 [479]
End users 709 [827]
Endangered species 184, 185, 189, 190 [228], [229], [232], [234], [235]
Energy 222, 230, 231, 234, 243, 450, 451, 452, 453, 521, 593, 594, 595, 596, 679, 714 [276], [288], [289], [294], [295], [303], [550], [551], [552], [553], [637], [696], [697], [698], [699], [700], [793], [834]
See also: Fuels; Power and utilities; Utilities
—conservation 300, 301, 573, 593, 595 [370], [371], [673], [696], [698]
—consumption 452, 491, 596 [552], [602], [700]
—costs 222 [277]
—cycle research 272 [336]
—demand 73 [85]
—efficiency 269, 594 [333], [697]
—management 593 [696]
—management & control systems 593 [696]
—nuclear 520, 535, 543, 544, 546 [635], [640], [641], [643], [644]
—production 169 [207]
—R&D 270 [334]
—recovery 125, 302, 314, 350, 351, 364, 372 [154], [372], [388], [434], [435], [456], [467]
—renewable 296, 550 [366], [647]
—sources, preferences 712, 713, 714 [831], [832], [834]
—supply 243 [303]
—use 86, 335, 571, 594 [104], [420], [671], [697]
Energy & Environmental Research Corp. 385, 387 [485]
Energy/acid rain, EPA research 271 [335]
Enforcement 310, 674, 675, 676, 677, 678 [384], [784], [785], [786], [787], [788], [789], [790], [791], [792]
Engelmann and other spruces 461 [565]
Engineered soil 369 [464]
Engineering 498 [609]
—use of plastics in 499 [610]
Engineering design
—environmental 389 [489]

Georgia-Pacific Corp. 248, 417, 568 [310], [511], [669]
— Crossett, Ark. 551 [649]
— Palatka, Fla. 551 [649]
Georgia Power Co. 237, 258 [298], [323]
Georgia State University
— education in hazardous waste management 395 [494]
Geothermal electric energy 548 [646]
Geothermal energy 296, 550, 590 [366], [647], [693]
Geothermal heat 548 [646]
Geothermal power generating projects 520 [636]
Geraghty & Miller Inc. 390, 391, 406 [489], [491], [507]
Germany 513 [627]
   See also: East Germany; West Germany
— carbon emissions 578 [681]
— East 586 [689]
— East, auto registration 436 [534]
— energy efficiency 594 [697]
— greenhouse gas policies 702 [818]
— nuclear power 514, 522 [628], [638]
— recycling 367, 373 [461], [469]
— renewable energy 550 [647]
— West 586 [689]
— West, auto registration 436 [534]
Ghana
— autos 435 [533]
— elephant population 185 [229]
Gila County 155 [191]
Gilton Solid Waste Management 409 [510]
Giuseppi Guilietti 200 [248]
Glaciers 49 [51], [52]
Glass 102, 104, 114, 115, 116, 117, 118, 119, 123, 139, 140,
  142, 146, 147, 149, 326, 328, 329, 330, 335, 338, 366, 373,
  374, 488, 629, 648, 709 [124], [128], [140], [142], [143],
  [144], [145], [146], [147], [151], [173], [174], [176], [181],
  [182], [185], [404], [407], [410], [411], [412], [420], [425],
  [426], [459], [469], [470], [596], [737], [756], [827]
   See also: Stone, clay and glass
— automotive 434 [531]
— containers 113, 338, 342, 487, 617, 622, 628, 699 [139],
  [426], [431], [594], [720], [726], [734], [816]
— crushers 214 [265]
— beach waste 103 [125]
— bottles 106, 107, 327, 342, 654 [130], [131], [406], [431],
  [763]
— in solid waste 148 [183]
— in landfills 124 [152]
— jars 106, 107 [130], [131]
— Kokomo, IN 650 [758]
— lead content 473 [578]
— liquor bottles 105, 108, 109, 321 [129], [132], [133], [399]
— packaging 105, 106, 107, 108, 109, 131, 137, 321, 322 [129],
  [130], [131], [132], [133], [164], [171], [399], [400]
— processing 327 [406]
— products 113 [139]

Glass continued:
— recovery 352 [436]
— recycled 263 [327]
— recycled, Washington 623 [728]
— recycling 267, 633, 708 [331], [743], [826]
— soft drink bottles 105, 108, 109, 321 [129], [132], [133],
  [399]
Glass/ceramics 103 [126]
Glass fiber reinforced insulation standards 690 [805]
Glen Ridge Radium Site 93 [114]
Glens Falls 660 [770]
Glenville State College
— education in hazardous waste management 395 [494]
Global change research 272 [336]
— budget 244 [304]
Global climate 272 [336]
Global conditions 12, 13 [11], [12], [13]
Global warming 64, 70, 83, 84, 85, 86, 87, 88, 183, 577 [75],
  [82], [101], [102], [103], [104], [105], [106], [107], [225],
  [226], [680]
   See also: Greenhouse effect
— sea level rise 183 [225], [226]
Glycol ethers 153 [189]
— effects 196 [243]
Goals 680, 681, 682, 683, 685, 686 [794], [795], [796], [797],
  [798], [799], [800]
— recycling 630 [738]
Goats 455 [557]
Golden Drake 199 [248]
Golden State (Corp.) 417 [511]
Golder Associates Corp. 391 [490]
Goshen 413 [510]
Government 467, 468, 719 [573], [574], [844]
   See also: Federal government; State government
— waste 338 [426]
Government agencies 709 [827]
Government facility radioactive wastes 96 [116]
Government Institutes, Inc. 399 [496]
Government service
— construction 213 [264]
Graduate education 393 [493]
Graham Recycling 418 [512]
Grain 57 [63]
Grain products 58 [64]
Grand Canyon (rim)
— pollution levels 25 [27]
Grand Central Recycling 415 [510]
Grand Rapids, MI 583 [687]
Grand Trunk
— toxic rail accidents 205 [254]
Grand Valley State University
— education in hazardous waste management 395 [494]
Grand Zenith 200 [248]

Milwaukee 409, 416 [510]
Milwaukee County 659 [769]
Milwaukee-Racine, WI CMSA 584 [687]
Mimeo and duplicator paper 688 [803]
Mine ore 121 [149]
Mine waste management 315 [390]
Mineral 537 [640]
— national forests 457 [559]
Minerals consumption 560 [660]
Mining 6, 93, 169, 173 [6], [113], [207], [212]
— asbestos 431 [527]
— landfill liners 368 [463]
— surface 315 [390]
— reclamation 315 [390]
— waste 335 [420]
Minneapolis, MN 647 [755]
— aircraft noise 611 [714]
Minneapolis-St. Paul, MN-WI 582 [686]
— recycling 625 [730]
Minnesota 16, 17, 19, 37, 38, 46, 48, 166, 167, 184, 187, 238, 259, 278, 370, 412, 540, 606, 610, 681 [18], [19], [22], [40], [41], [49], [50], [205], [206], [228], [231], [298], [323], [344], [465], [510], [640], [708], [713], [795]
— acid rain impacts 674 [783]
— chemicals releases and transfers 664 [773]
— conservation plans 640 [747]
— conservation programs 635 [744]
— conservation, agriculture 637, 638 [745], [746]
— construction, waste recovery 227 [283]
— curbside recycling 627 [733]
— disposal bans 692 [807]
— erosion control 642 [749]
— fishing 704 [820]
— forest revenues 600 [703]
— forestry incentive programs 597 [701]
— forestry practices 599 [702]
— forests 9 [9]
— gasohol use 478 [586]
— gasoline use 479 [587]
— gasoline use on highways 482 [588]
— hazardous waste disposal 305 [376]
— hazardous waste sites 604 [707]
— houses with radon 616 [719]
— incinerators 646 [754]
— land use 23 [25]
— local recycling mandates 697 [813]
— mandated recycling 697 [812]
— mandatory deposits 693 [808]
— membership organizations 710 [828]
— MSW disposal 645 [753]
— national forest visitors 465 [570]
— power plants 685 [799]
— procurement program 702 [819]
— radioactive disposal 612 [715]

Minnesota continued:
— recycling grants 223 [279]
— recycling incentives 226 [282]
— recycling legislation 696 [811]
— recycling loans 224 [280]
— recycling program funding 225 [281]
— renewable energy 548 [646]
— sewage treatment 666 [775]
— sludge composting 346 [432]
— soil conservation 29, 31, 275 [30], [31], [341]
— soil conservation districts 26 [28]
— solid waste disposal 649 [757]
— solid waste legislation 686 [800]
— steam-electric plants 72, 512, 547, 580 [84], [626], [645], [684]
— toxic chemicals 662 [772]
— toxic rail accidents 207, 655 [256], [765]
— toxic waste transport 164 [203]
— tree planting 11 [10]
— waste reduction 698 [814]
— water bank programs 670 [780]
— water pollution 667, 668 [776], [777]
— wetlands 671 [781]
Minnesota Power & Light Co. 238, 259 [298], [323]
Minot, ND, wetlands 281 [348]
Miscellaneous manufacturing 150, 151, 312 [186], [187], [386]
— toxic chemicals 657, 658 [767], [768]
— toxic emissions 160 [197]
Miscellaneous plastics
— exports of 340 [429]
Miscellaneous supplies 230, 231, 234 [288], [289], [294], [295]
Missiles
— nuclear 475 [581]
Mississippi 7, 8, 16, 17, 18, 19, 32, 33, 37, 38, 39, 40, 46, 48, 166, 167, 187, 238, 259, 278, 370, 538, 606, 610, 658, 680, 682, 683 [7], [8], [18], [19], [20], [21], [22], [32], [33], [34], [35], [40], [41], [42], [43], [49], [50], [205], [206], [231], [298], [323], [344], [465], [640], [708], [713], [768], [794], [797], [798]
— acid rain impacts 674 [783]
— beach waste 652 [760]
— chemicals releases and transfers 664 [773]
— conservation plans 640 [747]
— conservation programs 635 [744]
— conservation, agriculture 637, 638 [745], [746]
— curbside recycling 627 [733]
— erosion control 642 [749]
— fishing 704 [820]
— forest revenues 600 [703]
— forestry incentive programs 597 [701]
— forestry practices 599 [702]
— forests 9 [9]

Nutrient status
— lakes 19 [22]
Nutrients 7, 13, 16, 32, 37, 56 [7], [14], [18], [32], [40], [61]
O&M
— retrofits 287 [354]
Oak 461 [565]
Oak Harbor 540 [640]
Oak Ridge DOE field office 233 [292]
Oak Ridge Reservation 468 [574]
Oakland County 412 [510]
Oakland Scavenger/WMI 409 [510]
Occidental Chemical Corp.
— toxic releases, transfers 567 [668]
Occupation
— cancer cause 192 [237]
Occupational exposure to toxic chemicals 720 [846]
Ocean City, NJ, curbside collection, paper 631 [739]
Ocean County 412 [510]
Ocean dumping 373 [468]
Ocean power 550 [647]
Oceania 341, 626 [430], [732]
— river runoff 45 [48]
— wastepaper recovery 632 [741]
— wastepaper utilization 631 [740]
Oceans 32, 33, 47, 49, 75, 668, 682 [32], [33], [34], [35], [50], [51], [88], [777], [797]
— carbon uptake 3 [3]
— radon source 156 [192]
OECD 4 [4]
  See also: Organization for Economic Cooperation and Development
— carbon emissions 578 [681]
— energy demand 73 [85]
— nuclear power 521 [638]
OECD countries 701 [818]
Off-highway oil
— carbon dioxide emissions 63 [72]
Off-site disposal
— toxics 663 [773]
Off-site incineration 310, 311 [383], [385]
Off-site releases 154, 660 [190], [770]
Office and other high grade papers
— recycled, Washington 623 [728]
Office equipment 287 [354]
Office of Solid Waste 307 [378]
Office paper 125, 126, 127, 128, 129, 131, 141, 144, 331, 332, 342, 688 [155], [156], [157], [158], [160], [161], [164], [175], [179], [413], [414], [431], [803]
Offices
— construction 213 [264]
— waste 338 [426]
Offset printing 688 [803]
Offshore leaks 199 [248]
Ogden 403 [502]

Ogden Allied Abatement and Decontamination Service Inc. 404 [504]
Ogden Martin 421, 422, 423 [516], [517], [518]
Ogden Projects 420 [514]
Ohio 13, 14, 39, 40, 46, 48, 166, 167, 184, 188, 219, 239, 259, 278, 370, 415, 426, 493, 494, 540, 606, 610, 657, 661, 681 [14], [15], [42], [43], [49], [50], [205], [206], [228], [231], [271], [298], [323], [344], [465], [510], [522], [604], [605], [640], [708], [713], [767], [771], [795]
— acid rain impacts 674 [783]
— chemicals releases and transfers 664 [773]
— conservation plans 640 [747]
— conservation programs 635 [744]
— conservation, agriculture 637, 638 [745], [746]
— construction, waste recovery 227 [283]
— curbside recycling 627 [733]
— disposal bans 692 [807]
— erosion control 642 [749]
— fishing 704 [820]
— forest revenues 601 [703]
— forestry incentive programs 598 [701]
— forestry practices 599 [702]
— forests 9 [9]
— gasohol use 478 [586]
— gasoline use 480 [587]
— gasoline use on highways 482 [588]
— hazardous waste disposal 305 [376]
— hazardous waste sites 604 [707]
— land use 23 [25]
— membership organizations 710 [828]
— MSW disposal 645 [753]
— national forest visitors 465 [570]
— power plants 686 [799]
— procurement program 703 [819]
— radioactive disposal 612 [715]
— recycling legislation 696 [811]
— recycling program funding 225 [281]
— renewable energy 549 [646]
— sewage treatment 666 [775]
— sludge composting 348 [432]
— soil conservation 29, 31, 275 [30], [31], [341]
— soil conservation districts 26 [28]
— solid waste disposal 649 [757]
— solid waste legislation 686 [800]
— steam-electric plants 72, 512, 547, 580 [84], [626], [645], [684]
— toxic chemicals 662 [772]
— toxic rail accidents 207, 655, 656 [256], [765], [766]
— toxic waste transport 164 [203]
— tree planting 11 [10]
— waste reduction 698 [814]
— waste removal 214 [266]
— water pollution 667, 668, 682 [776], [777], [796]
— wetlands 672 [781]